Linux Filesystems

William von Hagen

D1711766

SAMS

201 West 103rd St., Indianapolis, Indiana, 46290 USA

Linux Filesystems

Copyright © 2002 by Sams Publishing

International Standard Book Number: 0-672-32272-2

Library of Congress Catalog Card Number: 2001093563

Printed in the United States of America

First Printing: December 2001

04   03   02   01   4   3   2   1

Trademarks

Warning and Disclaimer

ASSOCIATE PUBLISHER
Jeff Koch

ACQUISITIONS EDITOR
Katie Purdum

DEVELOPMENT EDITOR
Mark Cierzniak

MANAGING EDITOR
Matt Purcell

PROJECT EDITOR
Andrew Beaster

COPY EDITOR
Geneil Breeze

INDEXER
Sandy Henselmeier

PROOFREADER
Melissa Lynch

TECHNICAL EDITOR
Jason Byars

TEAM COORDINATOR
Denni Bannister

MEDIA DEVELOPER
Dan Scherf

INTERIOR DESIGNER
Anne Jones

COVER DESIGNER
Aren Howell

PAGE LAYOUT
Octal Publishing, Inc.

Contents at a Glance

Table of Contents

About the Author

William von Hagen has been a Unix system administrator and fanatic since 1982 and an avid user of distributed filesystems since the mid-1980's at Carnegie-Mellon University. He has worked as a system administrator, writer, computing facilities operations manager, developer, development manager, documentation manager, and drummer. An avid computer collector specializing in workstations, he owns more than 200 computer systems (which the city of Pittsburgh requests that he never turn on at the same time).

Dedication

*To my wife, Dorothy Fisher, for her love and support; to
Morgan Gable, in a feeble attempt to make up for an endless stream of
excuses as to why I couldn't go out for dinner or movies; and
to friends like Kevin Brunelle, Gregg Kostelich, Joe O'Lear (What's Up, Doc?),
Jim Morgan, Kim Walter, and Joe Wargo, without whom my life could never
have been as much fun as it has been so far.*

Acknowledgments

Thanks to Katie Purdum and Sams for the opportunity to write a book on some of my favorite topics, and thanks especially to Andy Beaster, Geneil Breeze, Jason Byars, Mark Cierzniak, and Dan Scherf for making this a much better book than it otherwise would have been. All errors are mine, but many improvements are theirs. Thanks to Marta Justak for her patience, sense of humor, and support, as well as for making this book possible in the first place.

About the Technical Reviewer

Jason Byars (darth@purdue.edu) is a graduate student at Purdue University. He has a Bachelor of Science degree in Computer Engineering and enjoys both the hardware and software aspects of the field. His interests draw him to robotics, 3D graphics, software development, and IT work. He has been a fan of Linux since going to Purdue in the fall of 1996.

Tell Us What You Think!

As the reader of this book, *you* are our most important critic and commentator. We value your opinion and want to know what we're doing right, what we could do better, what areas you'd like to see us publish in, and any other words of wisdom you're willing to pass our way.

As an Associate Publisher for Sams, I welcome your comments. You can fax, e-mail, or write me directly to let me know what you did or didn't like about this book—as well as what we can do to make our books stronger.

Please note that I cannot help you with technical problems related to the topic of this book, and that due to the high volume of mail I receive, I might not be able to reply to every message.

When you write, please be sure to include this book's title and author as well as your name and phone or fax number. I will carefully review your comments and share them with the author and editors who worked on the book.

Fax: 317-581-4770

E-mail: feedback@samspublishing.com_

Mail: Jeff Koch, Associate Publisher
          Sams Publishing
          201 West 103rd Street
          Indianapolis, IN 46290 USA

Introduction

I can see several possible responses to a book on Linux filesystems. The first might be "Who cares?" The second, slightly more enlightened, response would be "Well, that sounds boring but potentially useful—maybe I should get it in case I ever need a reference or need to press some flowers." The third response (the one that I'm hoping for) is "Finally!" Although there have been many articles on journaling and networked/distributed filesystems, and all operating system and kernel texts devote some token space to discussing how and where data is stored, this book is a first as far as I know. Until now, there really hasn't been a single, readable, comprehensive source that explores the different types of local and networked filesystems available for Linux, compares them, and provides hands-on guidance for installing, administering, and testing them.

As the mechanism for organizing, storing, and retrieving data on the various storage devices available on computer systems, filesystems exist in a sort of purgatory of interest and awareness. At the one end of the spectrum, filesystems are a tip of the operating system iceberg, a piece of the low-level functionality of your computer system that most users never think of or care about. On the other hand, as the piece of system software that users may interact with most frequently, studying how different types of filesystems work and what different filesystems can buy you in terms of usability and productivity can actually be interesting. As a part of the magic that makes computers work, filesystems are more easily grasped and less narcolepsy-inducing than discussing how the operating system manages processes and executes programs.

Most people will also benefit by learning about some of the applications that interact directly with filesystems and that are discussed in this book. All of us have lost data at one time or another, either due to system crashes, overenthusiastic rm commands, or simple carelessness (or so I've heard). All of us have certainly run out of disk space on a computer at one time or another and wondered if there wasn't an easier, better way to manage disks and data storage than spending a few hours looking around for files that you don't "really" need and can therefore delete to free up some space.

The primary goal of this book is to educate people about many of the new types of filesystems available for Linux. Using these new filesystems can increase the availability of your computer systems, minimize downtime, reduce problems and related costs, simplify administration, and increase productivity. I hope that this book also demonstrates that computer books don't have to be dull dust magnets and that complex topics can be discussed without requiring electric shocks to keep readers awake. I was playing drums in a punk rock band when I had my computer epiphany after seeing my first video game. Maybe things won't get that weird for you.

> **NOTE**
>
> Disclaimer: Many companies donated or contributed to the Linux filesystems discussed in this book. I don't have a financial interest in any of the companies who contributed this software to Linux or in any Linux hardware or software company. To be honest, I worked for IBM for a few years and once owned stock in the company, but I sold it years ago. Similarly, I once owned SGI stock, but I sold it before the bottom dropped out, so I'm not upset. I'm a Linux lover with an interest in filesystems and networking, just like any other person with a network of 10–20 machines in his house and a basement full of old Unix machines.

Who Is This Book's Intended Audience?

This book has a wide range of potential readers, ranging from masochists to people who are generally interested in computer topics for a variety of reasons. The following groups of people should find this book interesting and potentially useful:

- System administrators interested in getting the most from their Linux systems, in terms of increased performance, interoperability, and faster restart times, for the benefit of the users of their systems. Many system administrators get too caught up in fighting fires to find the time to scour newsgroups and SlashDot to keep up with the latest developments in filesystems. This book provides that information without sounding like a thesis.

- MIS/IT managers who are studying Linux for use in their businesses and want to know what their options are. These readers will specifically be interested in things like interoperability and compatibility with Windows, Novell, and Macintosh systems that they probably already use in their businesses. They will also be interested in advanced network filesystems such as OpenAFS, comparing this to NFS, which they probably already use. OpenAFS essentially circumvents interoperability concerns by instituting a higher-level disk storage model on all systems on which it runs (which is essentially "all systems").

- Linux programmers who want to use distributed filesystems to improve the availability of the applications that they are writing and the data used and created by those applications.

- Linux system operators who want to learn how using journaling filesystems can decrease the amount of data lost in a system crash. (Linux is, of course, very stable; someone can always cut the power to it or kick the cord out of a wall.)

- Users of Linux systems interested in getting the most from the Linux systems that they use.

- Academicians and students interested in knowing what high-performance and distributed file systems exist for Linux.

- Curious randoms like myself who run and manage their own Linux systems and want to experiment with options for better performance and interoperability through networking.

Downloading, uncompressing, and reading the source code for every available Linux filesystem is a cheap and authoritative alternative to reading this book, but I wouldn't recommend that to anyone who doesn't have a serious sleeping disorder.

What Can This Book Offer?

This book provides a solid foundation in filesystem concepts, the filesystems currently available for Linux, the advantages and disadvantages (where appropriate) of each, and some comparative data and benchmarks to help you evaluate your options and make some intelligent choices. Linux is an ideal platform for research and experimentation because it is a true multi-tasking, multiuser computer operating system. Besides which, almost everyone can dig up an old PC or two that isn't sexy enough to run the latest version of Windows but that can still be a powerful computing resource when coupled with an inexpensive, robust operating system such as Linux.

Beyond simply presenting filesystem theory, this book provides genuine HOWTO information that can help you install and experiment with different filesystems. Knowledge is a good thing, and more is always better. Whether you're a home user, manager, or techno-weenie, this book can help you make decisions about how to improve the computing environment you're involved with, increasing your users' productivity, your value in the eyes of your superiors, and the value of your computer systems (and Linux) to your corporate or academic environment.

How This Book Is Organized

This book is organized into sequential sheets of paper that are numbered for easy reassembly in case the binding ever dissolves. In terms of the information that these pages contain, the organization of the book is the following:

- Chapter 1, "Introduction to Filesystems," introduces you to the terminology used to describe data storage and different types of filesystems. It also explains the fundamental concepts behind filesystems, explores the different types of filesystems available today for Linux, and introduces you to some of the fundamental problems and issues encountered when using and administering different types of filesystems.

- Chapter 2, "Filesystems and Interoperability," discusses how using the networked filesystems covered in this book makes it easier for people to access their data from different computers. This increases user productivity by letting people use the software that best suits their requirements regardless of the system it runs on. It also increases administrative efficiency and reduces administrative and operational costs by centralizing the administration of data resources used throughout a networked environment.

- Chapter 3, "Overview of Journaling Filesystems," provides a detailed overview of journaling filesystems and journaling filesystem concepts. It also introduces each of the journaling filesystems discussed in Chapter 4, "The ext3 Journaling Filesystem," examining their goals and capabilities in detail.

- Chapter 4, "The ext3 Journaling Filesystem," provides detailed how-to information for obtaining, installing, using, and administering the ext3 journaling filesystem. The ext3 filesystem adds journaling capabilities to the standard Linux ext2 filesystem while maintaining compatibility with its utilities, data structures, and so on.

- Chapter 5, "IBM's JFS Journaling Filesystem," provides detailed how-to information for obtaining, installing, using, and administering the JFS journaling filesystem. This filesystem was originally developed at IBM but has since been released to the Open Source community and is being actively developed and supported by people at IBM.

- Chapter 6, "The ReiserFS Journaling Filesystem," provides detailed how-to information for obtaining, installing, using, and administering the ReiserFS journaling filesystem. The ReiserFS filesystem was the first journaling filesystem added to the Linux kernel code and offers many advanced design features.

- Chapter 7, "The XFS Journaling Filesystem," provides detailed how-to information for obtaining, installing, using, and administering the XFS filesystem. This filesystem was developed by Silicon Graphics, Inc. (SGI), and has been in production use on its IRIX workstations for years. SGI recently released the source code for XFS to the Open Source community and is actively involved in supporting and enhancing XFS for Linux.

- Chapter 8, "Third-Party Journaling Filesystems," provides an overview of commercial journaling filesystems.

- Chapter 9, "Logical Volume Management," discusses logical volume management, which supports creating filesystems that are not bound by the physical limitations of a single device or partition. This chapter also discusses associated techniques for flexible and secure data storage, such as the popular Redundant Array of Inexpensive Disks (RAID).

- Chapter 10, "Comparing Journaling Filesystem Performance," provides a statistical comparison of the performance of the journaling filesystems discussed in this book. This chapter is designed to help you select which journaling filesystem might be best suited to your needs.

- Chapter 11, "Overview of Distributed Filesystems," provides a detailed overview of networked (distributed) filesystems and distributed filesystem concepts. It also introduces each of the distributed filesystems discussed in subsequent chapters, examining their goals and capabilities in detail.

- Chapter 12, "The NFS Distributed Filesystem," provides detailed how-to information for obtaining, installing, using, and administering the NFS distributed filesystem, the most popular networked filesystems available for Linux.

- Chapter 13, "The OpenAFS Distributed Filesystem," provides detailed how-to information for obtaining, installing, using, and administering the OpenAFS distributed filesystem. The OpenAFS filesystem is a powerful distributed computing environment that includes its own volume management, authentication, and administration utilities.

- Chapter 14, "Comparing Distributed Filesystem Performance," provides a statistical comparison of the performance of the NFS and OpenAFS filesystem. This chapter is designed to help you select which distributed filesystem might be best suited to your needs.

- Chapter 15, "Backing Up, Restoring, and Managing Linux Filesystems," discusses issues involved in backing up and managing computing environments that use journaling, distributed, and interoperability filesystems. This chapter also provides a detailed discussion of installing, configuring, and using Amanda, a client/server backup system originally developed at the University of Maryland and widely used in networked computing environments.

- Chapter 16 "Compatibility Filesystems, Interoperability, and Filesystem Adapters," provides a detailed overview of compatibility filesystems, concepts, and the system-specific file-sharing protocols that different compatibility filesystems support. It also introduces each of the compatibility filesystems discussed in subsequent chapters, examining their goals and capabilities in detail.

- Chapter 17, "Using Netatalk for Macintosh and AppleTalk Connectivity," provides detailed how-to information for obtaining, installing, using, and administering the Netatalk interoperablity filesystem, used to connect Linux and Macintosh file servers and printers.

- Chapter 18, "Using Samba for Windows Interoperability," provides detailed how-to information for obtaining, installing, using, and administering the Samba interoperablity filesystem, used to connect Linux and Microsoft Windows systems, file servers, and printers.

- Chapter 19, "NetWare Filesystem Support in Linux," provides detailed how-to information for obtaining, installing, using, and administering the Novell Core Protocol (NCP) tools provided with Linux. These tools enable you to connect Linux and Novell NetWare file servers and printers. This chapter also discusses how to use mars_new, a Novell NetWare server emulator that runs under Linux, to export Linux files and directories to Novell NetWare users.

- Appendix A, "Using the CD-ROM: Installing, Updating, and Compiling Kernels," provides general information about configuring, compiling, and installing Linux kernels. The information in the appendix is used throughout this book in the how-to information that explains building kernels that incorporate the advanced filesystems discussed throughout this book.

Conventions Used in This Book

Linux is a free implementation of Unix. Throughout this book, I'll be discussing filesystems using terminology that primarily originated with Unix filesystems and was therefore carried forward into Linux. Whenever possible, I'll introduce this terminology in terms of both Unix and Linux, but subsequently refer to it only in terms of Linux. After all, this is a Linux book!

> **NOTE**
>
> If you're still wed to a version of Unix other than Linux, this book provides a wealth of relevant conceptual and empirical information about different filesystems and filesystem options for any version of Unix. Also, because most of the filesystems and associated software discussed in this book are GPL, you can easily obtain the source code for these filesystems and tools and compile them for your version of Unix, a SMOP (small matter of programming) indeed. However, if you'd prefer to be a part of the future of workstation computing immediately rather than approaching it obliquely, why not just run Linux. An alternative is to set up a few Linux servers running the software discussed in this book, integrate them into your current computing environment as shared, centralized resources, and see what happens. . .

The following typographic conventions are used in this book:

- Lines of code, commands, statements, variables, and any text you type or see onscreen appear in a computer typeface.
- Placeholders in command and syntax descriptions appear in an italic computer typeface. Replace the placeholder with the actual filename, parameter, or whatever element it represents.
- Italics highlight technical terms when they first appear in the text and are being defined.
- A code continuation character ➧ is used at the end of a command or line of code that continues onto the next line. Sometimes a command or line of code is too long to fit on a single line in the book, given the book's limited width. If you see a backslash at the end of a line containing a command or line of code, remember that you should interpret the next line as part of the current command or line of code.

Introduction to Filesystems

IN THIS CHAPTER

The computer industry is caught up in a never-ending quest for faster hardware, more memory, and bigger disks. Regardless of this hardware glut, the pure speed and capacity of your hardware often has little to do with what you can actually accomplish with your computer. For most applications other than games and intense audio/video/multimedia processing, the performance and capabilities of the operating system, application software, and storage systems in your machine have a much bigger impact than whether you're using a one or two zillion gigahertz processor. Having a gigabyte or two of memory doesn't matter much at all when most of what you're doing is writing vast amounts of data to relatively slow disk drives. Unfortunately, features such as data transfer rates, cache sizes, and reliability just aren't the things that sexy computer ads are made of.

The bottom line of any computer system is storing, retrieving, manipulating, and saving information. As a writer and computer systems administrator, I'm always amazed when friends who are equally computer savvy say to me "Your laptop is so slow. Why don't you upgrade?" Frankly, if I could type faster than my primary laptop's 233 Mhz Pentium processor could handle, I'd be posing for Ripley's Believe It or Not ads or touring with the circus rather than writing books. On the other hand, if it took five minutes for me to save a chapter of whatever I'm working on, or if I could never find the space to save a modified file without deleting something else, I'd drop-kick my laptop into the river in a heartbeat and buy the brightest, shiniest Linux-capable laptop available today.

Filesystems, the topic of this book, are a big part of the key to building a community of happy users and satisfied systems administrators. *Filesystem* is the generic term used to describe any kind of structured data storage used by a computer system. Most users don't even have to know what type(s) of filesystem(s) their system uses or how they work. The basic issue is that they do work and that users can get their work done. Filesystems aren't popular except to the most elite and detail-oriented PhDs, hackers, and computer geeks, but they are critical to everyone. The speed with which you can save information, whether you can always reliably retrieve the information you've saved, how easy it is to get at that data from different locations and computer systems, the ease with which you can expand the amount of storage available to you—all these are critical to making computers help people be as productive as possible.

This book divides filesystems into three general classes:

- **Local filesystems**—Filesystems that exist on disk drives attached to your computer and can only be used by your system. Every computer comes with at least one built-in filesystem, or you'd never be able to save a file.
- **Local filesystems shared over a network**—Filesystems on one machine's local disk that are made available to other systems via the network, using protocols such as SMB, CIFS, AppleTalk, or NFS.

- **Networked filesystems**—Filesystems that exist on file servers and other systems and can only be accessed over a network. I'll also refer to these as *distributed filesystems* because they enable you to access storage and other resources distributed across other hosts on your network.

- **Compatibility filesystems**—Primarily software packages that enable you to access personal computer files and directories from different types of computer systems. I'll also refer to these as *filesystem adapters* because these software packages implement the network file sharing protocols used by different types of personal computers instead of physically implementing local instances of personal computer filesystems. The most common examples of these are packages that enable you to access files stored on a Linux system or file server from a Microsoft Windows or Apple Macintosh desktop (or vice versa), files located on a Novell server from a Linux system (or vice versa), and so on.

Another critical aspect of providing a robust, cost-effective computing environment for your company, your college or university, or just your home, is the capability to use a powerful but free operating system such as Linux. Not only does Linux consistently receive awards for continuous uptime and reliability, but its open source nature means that thousands, perhaps millions, of skilled programmers are working to improve and enhance Linux. Every Linux user is the direct beneficiary of their efforts. Also, because the source code for Linux is freely available, Linux is a natural choice for an environment in which to research, develop, and release new products and (especially) system-level services such as filesystems.

As you'll see in this book, the growing popularity of the Open Source movement and growing recognition of Linux as a powerful operating system that has a definite place in enterprise computing has led many commercial entities, such as IBM and SGI, to release the source code for some of their development and research efforts under the GNU Public License (GPL). The idea of IBM opening up its source code and donating it so that the whole world can see and work on it would be scary if it weren't the absolute right thing to do. (The public relations benefits that companies like IBM and SGI reap from announcing that they are releasing projects under the GPL for Linux is a separate issue.)

Advantages of Networked and Journaling Filesystems

Today's powerful computer systems, huge inexpensive disk drives, and ubiquitous networking provide a seemingly infinite number of possibilities regarding where and how your data can be stored and retrieved. As companies attempt to save time and money while keeping their computer systems and data available 24 hours a day, 7 days a week, the reliability, speed, and availability of the filesystem in which that data is stored is critical, but many other factors have a big influence. The next few sections provide an overview of some of the most important reasons for using networked and journaling filesystems. I'll explain journaling filesystems in greater detail later in this chapter, but for now just think of them as filesystems that keep a record of the changes you make to them to guarantee that the filesystem is correct.

Centralizing and Simplifying Administration

Most users have their own personal computer or workstation nowadays, joined together by a corporate, academic, or home network. After keeping computer systems running, the fundamental task of any MIS or IT shop is backing up user data so that it can be restored in the event of a natural calamity (act of God) or system crash (often an act of Redmond). Backing up data stored on the local disks of thousands of individual computers is a nightmare at best, and an impossibility in reality. Modern computer operations therefore usually look for ways of centralizing user data while decentralizing processing power. In other words, you have the power to do whatever you want with your data on your desktop, but your computer operations staff has the ability to back up a centralized store of data.

Enter networked/distributed filesystems for everyday use, pioneered by geniuses such as the folks at Apollo Computer and Novell. These early systems introduced the concepts of file servers—centralized data repositories that can be administered as single entities—and clients—the computer systems used by people like you and me. Centralized data storage on file servers has wider implications than simply making it convenient to back up the data for an entire company from one place. If the data used by different computers is stored in a centralized location, accessed remotely, and therefore independent of the computer system on which it was created, why limit users to always working from the same machine?

Easy Access to Centralized Data

Many of the distributed filesystems discussed in this book originated in academic environments, where students often did their work from groups of publicly available computers situated around campus in places with historical names such as RJE (Remote Job Entry) sites. The idea that a student would have to always work at the same computer system at one of these is laughable. An alternative to this would be to force every student to carry her work around on a floppy, Zip disk, tape, or removable hard drive. That's about as practical as using square wheels on a bicycle to solve parking problems. After all, how many "I lost my floppy disk" excuses do you expect a professor to hear?

Before personal computers came along, people used mainframes from terminals scattered all over the known universe. All the data was stored on the mainframe, simplifying operations, and all user authentication (logins, passwords, and so on) was similarly centralized on the mainframe. Extending this single-point-of-authentication model to distributed filesystems was a logical improvement. Users can log in on any publicly available computer system that can access the file servers and access their data in exactly the same way as if it was available locally. The cool way of saying this is "Wherever you go, there you are," a phrase taken from the *Buckaroo Banzai* movie of the late 1980s, popularized as a filesystems mantra by Transarc Corporation (where I worked for most of the 1990s), and subsequently used by many people (including myself) as the title for articles and presentations).

Today, the notion of a mobile user community is more critical than ever, as people attempt to access their e-mail, files, and other data from a variety of remote locations and devices ranging from wristwatches to PDAs (Personal Digital Assistants) to more standard devices such as laptops. Any MIS department or IT group trying to devise a mechanism for backing up 10,000 Palm Pilots and Handsprings will need Prozac more than oxygen unless they implement distributed file and mail systems.

Improving System Restart Times

Aside from the problem of providing a central way for users to access their data and prove their identities, a related problem is the amount of time required for computer systems to make that data available on the rare occasions when the computers crash or have to be restarted for some specific reason. Some amount of data has to be stored locally on mobile computer systems, whether that information is just a PROM's (Programmable Read-Only Memory chip) worth of data that tells the machine how to boot over the network or is a local complete operating system. Relatively inexpensive devices such as PDAs (Personal Digital Assistants) and diskless workstations aside, most of the computers you and I use store an operating system in a filesystem on a local disk and boot from the local disk (that is, one physically connected to that computer), turning on network access as a part of the boot process. When accessing local disk drives, the design of the filesystem in which the operating system is stored is a critical part of the boot process.

When booting, one of the first things that any computer system does is perform a consistency check on itself, making sure that the hardware into which an operating system is to be loaded is working correctly, and that the operating system that it is about to load can be successfully and correctly read from the disk. If a computer's local filesystem is slow or prone to damage when that computer is turned off, dropped, or shot in a drive-by, restart times will be slow, users will be cranky, time will be wasted, and companies will lose virtual money (that is, they won't be making money that they might be making if people were actually working). Enter journaling filesystems, which automatically keep a record of changes made to your filesystem and let you focus on that information when restarting a computer system.

The easiest way to verify the correctness and accuracy of a filesystem is to examine each bit of data on each disk drive, making sure that it is correct. Regardless of whether the data on those drives is statistical research, marketing projections, or accurate information, files have to contain the same data that they did when the computer system became unavailable, and the system must be able to read that data correctly. The process of checking all the information on the drives that make up a computer's filesystems can be fast if your filesystem is only a few megabytes in size. Unfortunately, it's been years since operating systems fit in a few megabytes. With today's multimegabyte files and multigigabyte disks, checking entire devices can take a while.

As I'll discuss later in Chapter 3, "Filesystem Consistency and Journaling Filesystems," journaling filesystems eliminate the need to check entire filesystems by requiring that only recent changes to existing filesystems be checked when a computer system is restarted. Computer systems that use journaling filesystems can restart in a trivial amount of time compared to those that have to examine entire disks. This reduces coffee-break time when your system is restarting but is a good thing if your business depends on making data available to customers and employees, or if you have a term paper or thesis due in a half an hour.

Making It Easy to Expand Storage

The multimegabyte files mentioned in the previous section introduce another interesting problem. If users routinely require huge amounts of disk space, even the largest disk drives can fill up pretty quickly. Continually feeding new disk drives to a rapacious user community isn't a good solution to this problem because there still has to be an easy way of invisibly adding this storage to existing computer systems. Few users would be amused if their account were unavailable each time they ran out of disk space while an operator frantically moved their data from one disk to a larger one. New disk drives also could be added as new directories available to users, but this would quickly become an administrative nightmare.

The solution to this sort of problem is *logical volumes* in which filesystems and data storage are not limited to the confines of a single disk drive but can invisibly span multiple drives. I'll discuss logical volume management later in Chapter 9, "Logical Volume Management," and will explore using the logical volume manager available for current versions of Linux. Logical volume management is a logical extension (pardon the expression) of making data and the space in which to store more available to users quickly, reliably, and invisibly.

Basic Storage Device Terminology

To discuss filesystems in more detail throughout the rest of this book, the next few sections provide a basic dictionary of the terms used to describe data storage, starting at the device level and working up to the logical terminology used to describe filesystems. Different types of filesystems differ in terms of where and how your data is stored, but the terminology used to describe that data storage itself is the same. Defining this terminology up front will make it easier to read the rest of this book.

Random access storage devices, such as hard drives, CD-Rs, DVD-Rs, floppy disks, Zip disks, Jazz disks, Super disks, and so on, consist of rotating platters on which the data is stored and accessed by read/write heads. These heads move along the radius of the platters and retrieve or record information in specific locations as it passes underneath the head. Data on the platters is organized in concentric circles, known as *cylinders* or *tracks*. The cylinders are divided into *sectors*, also known as *physical blocks*, in which discrete units of data are stored. Sectors are the smallest portions of the data on a drive (see Figure 1.1) that can be written or read at one time on these kinds of devices.

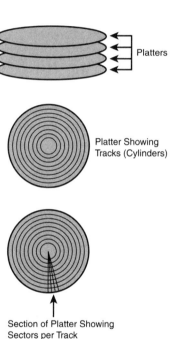

Platters

Platter Showing
Tracks (Cylinders)

Section of Platter Showing
Sectors per Track

FIGURE 1.1
Anatomy of a disk drive.

CD, DVD, floppy, Jaz, Zip, Super drives, and similar devices are removable media designed to be readable in any compatible device and are usually described in terms of their capacity or physical size. Because hard drives have different capacities, they are usually simply described in terms of their capacity. The nerdier among us describe them in terms of their geometry (the number of cylinders, heads, and sectors that they contain) and the speed at which the platters rotate. Another term you may hear to describe hard drives is their *form factor*, which is simply their physical size, including the case in which the platters, heads, and so on, are enclosed.

The classic way to define the location of a specific sector of data on a hard drive is to identify the sector number, the track in which it is located, and the disk head that can read the data. Accessing today's large hard drives in terms of individual sectors would require long instructions and huge data references. In fact, today's hard drives are so large that a technique known as *Logical Block Addressing (LBA)* is used to simplify locating data. LBA works by assigning numeric values sequentially to each sector on the disk, beginning with zero. A specific sector then can be found without having to refer to specific head, cylinder, and sector values. A single numeric logical block address also requires less space than storing and manipulating three values. Logical block addressing is more space-efficient than head/cylinder/sector addressing and can be much faster when both the disk hardware and software drivers use this scheme.

Hard drives are usually divided into physical partitions. Physical partitions each can hold a single filesystem, be redefined into a single logical partition that can hold multiple filesystems, or be combined together by software to form a pool of storage on which one or more logical filesystems can be created. Drives are partitioned to reduce the amount of time required to locate a specific piece of data on the drive. More about this in the next section.

Basic Filesystem Concepts

More interesting than the nitty-gritty details of how bits are arranged on spinning pieces of metal and plastic is the terminology used to describe filesystems. Most people could care less about the realities of plugging a hard drive into a system and making that data accessible. However, when that physical storage is available to the operating system, it becomes much more interesting because it can actually be used to read, manipulate, and write data, which is the primary reason that computers exist.

The terms *sector* and *block* are used interchangeably when discussing hardware, but block has a different meaning in "filesystem-speak," where it is used as a logical unit rather than a physical one. In filesystems, a block is the fundamental allocation unit from which the filesystem is constructed. A filesystem therefore consists of a specific number of logical blocks. Block size differs between filesystems but is always an even multiple of the physical sector size. Block size is either predefined for a specific type of filesystem or set when a specific filesystem of a specific type is created.

There are two main goals of selecting an appropriate logical block size for use in a filesystem: minimizing the number of filesystem Input/Output (I/O) operations necessary to read and write files, and minimizing the amount of space wasted when files in the filesystem turn out to be smaller than the block size. In real life, files vary widely in size. Selecting the "right" block size for a filesystem is therefore a compromise between wasting as little space as possible and minimizing the number of blocks that have to be allocated to store a file.

Selecting an optimal block size with an eye towards minimizing I/O is straightforward: if a filesystem is primarily going to store large files that are read and written in big pieces, selecting a large block size for that filesystem is a good idea. Fewer blocks are required to hold the contents of a large file, and large blocks can be read at once. Similarly, if a filesystem is primarily used to store small text files, selecting a smaller block size is a good idea because it's difficult to predict the size of a text file, but most tend to be relatively small. Minimizing I/O leads to fast and efficient data transfers.

Selecting an optimal block size with respect to minimizing the amount of space wasted when writing files is trickier. For example, assume that I create a file that's 11 bytes long on a filesystem whose block size is 2K (2048 bytes). That's 2037 bytes wasted, which could add up quickly if every user made a habit of creating 11-byte files. If an entire filesystem was filled up with files of this size, 99 percent of the disk partition containing that filesystem would actually be wasted. Minimizing wasted space leads to efficient data storage.

To reduce this kind of wasted space, most modern filesystems also have the notion of *fragments*. Fragments are allocation units in the filesystem that are multiples of the sector size but are less than or equal to the size of a block. When file data doesn't fit neatly into a specific number of blocks, the excess is stored in a fragment. As more fragments are associated with a specific file, the data that they contain is combined into blocks and the fragments are released.

NOTE

Fragments in this sense are unrelated to *physical fragmentation*, which is the tendency of the blocks of a file to become discontiguous. Filesystems initially try to allocate the blocks associated with a specific file together, so that they can be read or written as a unit. Unfortunately, over time, the blocks associated with a file tend to end up being in different parts of a disk as new blocks are allocated to the file and old blocks are released when a file is edited. See "Filesystem Issues and Concerns" later in this chapter for more information.

Design of Unix/Linux Filesystems

Filesystems are created using low-level software that partitions disks and creates filesystems on specific partitions. Without imposing some organization on a disk drive, operating system software wouldn't know where to look to find files and the information that the filesystem uses to organize them. One of my favorite bits of technical writing ever is the following quote from a Hewlett-Packard manual shipped with one of its Unix (HP-UX) workstations in the mid 1980s:

> On a clear disk, you can seek forever.

In geek-speak, this means that without imposing some organization on the devices used to store your data, your operating system would have no idea where to look for specific information.

After identifying the drive on which data is physically located, partitioning a disk provides the highest level of "physical" organization of your data. Partitioning a disk slices it up into one or more sections (called *partitions*) that each can be accessed by an operating system. Partitions can hold a single filesystem, can hold multiple logical filesystems (such as DOS's quaint notion of an "extended" partition), or can be combined together by software to form a pool of storage that can be allocated to create one or more logical filesystems (using Logical volume management, discussed in more detail in Chapter 9). Drives are partitioned for many reasons, the most important of which are

- To reduce the amount of time required to locate a specific piece of data on the drive. It simply takes less time (and less location information) to find a specific piece of data in a smaller pool of information.

- To limit the amount of data that can be lost or damaged if a specific filesystem becomes corrupted.

- To speed up administrative operations such as defragmentation, consistency checking, and filesystem repair.

- To simplify administrative operations, such as backups. It's simpler to back up partitions that will fit on a single tape or other backup media because no operator intervention is required (such as switching tapes). Multiple partitions also enable you to install system files and applications programs on different partitions than user accounts. You then can back up the partition containing user accounts without accidentally backing up vast amounts of relatively unchanging executables, system files, and so on.

Actually, depending on your application, there are times when partitioning might actually hurt performance. A good example of this would be a large database application, which scatters the databases, tables, and indices that it uses across multiple partitions on the same drive. Opening all these at once and accessing them simultaneously would cause truly excessive movement of the disk heads as they seek different blocks on different filesystems on the same drive at approximately the same time.

TIP

Database applications that simultaneously access multiple databases, tables, and index files often benefit from storing those items on different drives so that seeking for data can be done in parallel by multiple drives, rather than serially, as would be the case if they were on the same drive and/or partition. Actually, many enterprise database systems dispense with the additional overhead of going through a filesystem at all, by directly accessing raw (unformatted) partitions on which they organize and manipulate data using their own routines.

The term *volume* is used as a handy catch-phrase to refer to any collection of physical and logical partitions that contains a single filesystem. In the rest of this book, I'll use the term volume as often as possible, except where it's necessary to reinforce that a specific filesystem can be stored on a combination of physical and logical partitions.

Modern filesystems on physical or logical partitions consist of hierarchically organized files and directories. Just as files are containers for data, directories are containers for files and/or other directories. The classic analogy for hierarchical filesystems is a filing cabinet with multiple drawers containing files stored in folders. Folders can contain either files or other folders. It's therefore easy to find a specific file or folder by describing it in terms of the drawer and folders in which it is contained. Locating a file in a directory in a specific filesystem is exactly like saying "open drawer W, find folder X, look in there for folder Y, and pull out file Z."

Each filesystem has a root directory, which is its top-level directory. When you make a filesystem available to a computer system, you map the root directory of that filesystem onto a directory, known as a mount point, in another filesystem. The top-level directory of a Unix or Linux filesystem is the directory simply known as '/' (slash), which is actually the top level of a specific filesystem on your machine. Other filesystems are then mounted as directories on your machine. On Linux systems, the most common filesystem mountpoints are the directories /boot, /usr, /usr/local, /home, /opt, /var, and /tmp.

Blocks, Inodes, Indirect Blocks

At a conceptual level, filesystems contain two fundamental types of data structures: ones that provide information about the filesystem itself, and ones that organize and contain the information that users hope to find there. Information about the filesystem itself is called *metadata* because it is data about data and is used by the operating system to access the information in the filesystem. From the filesystem point of view, directories themselves are an example of metadata because they provide information about where to find the inodes that correspond to different files. Directories are the only type of filesystem metadata visible to both the filesystem and to users.

Most Linux and Unix filesystems are physically organized using data structures that largely mirror the concept of files and directories. The primary data structure in a Unix filesystem is the *index node*, or *inode*. One inode is associated with each file and directory in a filesystem, and provides important information about that file or directory, such as when it was created and last accessed, and (most importantly) where the blocks containing the data for that file or directory actually are located on the disk. Inodes are numbered sequentially in a filesystem when they are allocated. To see the number of the inode associated with a file, you can use the `ls -i` command, as in the following example:

```
[wvh@distfs bin]$ ls -i
1294351 agenda  1294346 cleanup_mp3s  1294350 myhash  1294344 tilde
```

Because one inode is associated with each file and directory in a filesystem, you can use the `df -i` command (show free disk space in terms of inodes) to get a rough idea of how many files and directories exist in a given filesystem:

```
[wvh@distfs bin]$ df -i
Filesystem         Inodes    IUsed    IFree IUse% Mounted on
/dev/hda5         2562240    19220  2543020   1% /
/dev/hda1            6024       33     5991   1% /boot
/dev/hdb5         1507328     8515  1498813   1% /home
/dev/hdb1         1507328    40513  1466815   3% /opt
/dev/hda8           64256      176    64080   1% /tmp
/dev/hda9         1553440   149066  1404374  10% /usr
/dev/hda6         1281696     3166  1278530   1% /var
```

In this example, the third column (`IUsed`) shows the number of inodes used on each filesystem. From this column, for example, you can tell that 19220 files and directories exist on my / partition, and only 33 files and directories exist on my /boot partition. From the fifth column (`IUse%`), which tells the percentage of available inodes in each filesystem that actually have been used, you also can infer that I'm either working with a small number of huge files or I'm not doing a lot of work on my computer system. I assure you that it's the former.

The data structure for a Linux inode in a stock Linux 2.4.4 kernel is defined in the file /usr/src/{kernel-version}/include/linux/fs.h, and is shown in Listing 1.1.

LISTING 1.1   The Data Structure for a Standard Linux Inode

```
struct inode {
        struct list_head        i_hash;
        struct list_head        i_list;
        struct list_head        i_dentry;

        struct list_head        i_dirty_buffers;

        unsigned long           i_ino;
        atomic_t                i_count;
        kdev_t                  i_dev;
        umode_t                 i_mode;
        nlink_t                 i_nlink;
```

LISTING 1.1   Continued

```
uid_t                     i_uid;
gid_t                     i_gid;
kdev_t                    i_rdev;
loff_t                    i_size;
time_t                    i_atime;
time_t                    i_mtime;
time_t                    i_ctime;
unsigned long             i_blksize;
unsigned long             i_blocks;
unsigned long             i_version;
unsigned short            i_bytes;
struct semaphore          i_sem;
struct semaphore          i_zombie;
struct inode_operations   *i_op;
struct file_operations    *i_fop; /* former ->i_op->default_file_ops */
struct super_block        *i_sb;
wait_queue_head_t         i_wait;
struct file_lock          *i_flock;
struct address_space      *i_mapping;
struct address_space      i_data;
struct dquot              *i_dquot[MAXQUOTAS];
struct pipe_inode_info    *i_pipe;
struct block_device       *i_bdev;

unsigned long             i_dnotify_mask; /* Directory notify events */
struct dnotify_struct     *i_dnotify; /* for directory notifications */

unsigned long             i_state;

unsigned int              i_flags;
unsigned char             i_sock;

atomic_t                  i_writecount;
unsigned int              i_attr_flags;
__u32                     i_generation;
union {
        struct minix_inode_info        minix_i;
        struct ext2_inode_info         ext2_i;
        struct hpfs_inode_info         hpfs_i;
        struct ntfs_inode_info         ntfs_i;
        struct msdos_inode_info        msdos_i;
        struct umsdos_inode_info       umsdos_i;
        struct iso_inode_info          isofs_i;
        struct nfs_inode_info          nfs_i;
```

LISTING 1.1 Continued

```
                struct sysv_inode_info          sysv_i;
                struct affs_inode_info          affs_i;
                struct ufs_inode_info           ufs_i;
                struct efs_inode_info           efs_i;
                struct romfs_inode_info         romfs_i;
                struct shmem_inode_info         shmem_i;
                struct coda_inode_info          coda_i;
                struct smb_inode_info           smbfs_i;
                struct hfs_inode_info           hfs_i;
                struct adfs_inode_info          adfs_i;
                struct qnx4_inode_info          qnx4_i;
                struct reiserfs_inode_info      reiserfs_i;
                struct bfs_inode_info           bfs_i;
                struct udf_inode_info           udf_i;
                struct ncp_inode_info           ncpfs_i;
                struct proc_inode_info          proc_i;
                struct socket                   socket_i;
                struct usbdev_inode_info        usbdev_i;
                void                            *generic_ip;
        } u;
};
```

Although that data structure is fascinating, the logical information that it contains is more relevant to most people. Perhaps the most interesting field in the data structure itself is the u entry at the end, which is the union of the structures that provide information about all the filesystem-specific types of inodes. Each time a new filesystem type is added to the kernel, the inode_info structure for that type of filesystem should be added to the primary inode definition. Actually, as long as a new inode_info structure is the same size as previous ones, you can get away with not adding it, but this book is about interesting filesystems and good administrative practices, not poor programming techniques.

Logically, an inode contains the following significant information (and more, of course):

- File type and access mode
- File/directory ownership
- File/directory group ownership
- The time that the file/directory was created (ctime), most recently read (atime), and most recently modified (mtime).
- File/directory size
- The number of storage blocks associated with the file (including single, double, and triple indirect blocks)

- The number of references (links) to the file
- Flags that define the characteristics of the file

Of these, the idea of indirect blocks is probably the most interesting. Requiring an inode to contain an explicit list of the blocks containing data for the file or directory it is associated with would place an artificial limitation on the maximum size of a file or the maximum number of files that a directory can reference. To liberate files and directories from such limitations, Linux uses indirect blocks, which are other blocks that contain the addresses of other blocks associated with a file or additional entries in a directory. Single indirect blocks simply contain the addresses of other blocks of data; double indirect blocks contain the addresses of single indirect blocks associated with the file, and triple indirect blocks contain the addresses of double indirect blocks associated with the file. Simple, no? Figure 1.2 provides an illustration of the relationships between these standard filesystem constructs.

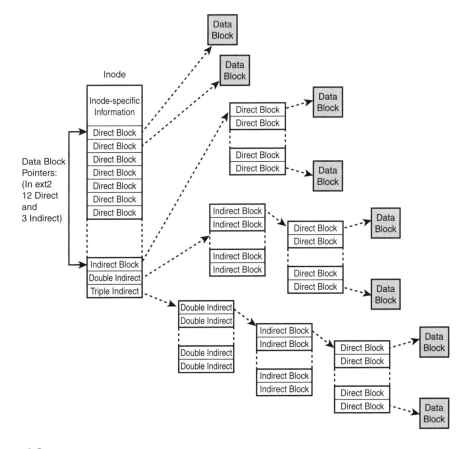

FIGURE 1.2

Identifying the storage associated with a large file using indirect blocks.

Although inodes are the primary data structure used in all Linux filesystems, different Linux filesystems create them at different times. Many filesystems, like the standard Linux ext2 filesystem, preallocate inodes when you create a filesystem on a volume. This is convenient but limits the number of files and directories that you can create on that volume. You can control the number of inodes created in a filesystem by using command-line options when running the commands used to create filesystems, but the default values are chosen so that they are high enough to be sufficient 99 percent of the time.

It's been years since I saw a system log that reported that a filesystem had run out of inodes. However, because this is possible, many modern filesystems (such as the journaling filesystems JFS, ReiserFS, and XFS, which are discussed later in this book in Chapter 5, "IBM's JFS Journaling Filesystem"; Chapter 6, "The ReiserFS Journaling Filesystem"; and Chapter 7, "SGI's XFS Journaling Filesystem") allocate inodes as new files and directories are created rather than when the filesystem is created. Using this model, you can still run out of disk space in a filesystem, but you can never run out of inodes. Applications such as ext2resize, resize2fs, and parted enable you to resize existing ext2 partitions, and therefore enable you to create additional inodes in that type of partition, but this is a manual operation rather than an automatic one like allocating inodes as needed.

All filesystems initially allocate some data structures regardless of whether they preallocate inodes. The most critical data structure for any filesystem is its superblock, which is the data structure used to find all the metadata for that filesystem, such as the inode list, list of free blocks, filesystem state information, and so on. The superblock is the starting point for any program (such as fsck) that checks and helps maintain the consistency of the filesystem.

In this sense, "consistency" means whether the snapshot of the filesystem represented by its metadata actually matches the state of the filesystem on disk. This includes things such as whether all the blocks that the filesystem believes should be associated with files are actually associated with files, that none of the blocks that the filesystem believes are available are actually associated with files, and so on. The superblock is so critical that all filesystems maintain multiple copies of the superblock. Information about the location of these copies is displayed when a filesystem is created using the /sbin/mkfs program, which is actually just a wrapper program for filesystem-specific creation applications such as /sbin/mkfs.ext2 (/sbin/mke2fs), /sbin/mkfs.reiserfs (/sbin/mkreiserfs), and so on.

The primary determinants of the performance of different types of filesystems are how long it takes to locate files by name within each type of filesystem, and how quickly specific data in the files in that type of filesystem can be located. Different filesystems offer different solutions for each of these. In most standard Unix filesystems, files in a directory are located by doing a linear search of the filenames listed in the directory itself and those listed in any indirect blocks, secondary indirect blocks, or triple indirect blocks.

As any self-respecting Computer Science 101 class teaches you, a linear search is the slowest possible type of search because no shortcuts are available to let you avoid having to examine each item until you find the one that you're looking for. This problem is the reason that old-time Unix users will tell you to avoid creating directories with huge numbers of entries. Large numbers of files and directories in a single directory can cause the worst possible performance scenarios during filesystem lookups.

Luckily, newer filesystems such as the ReiserFS, XFS, and JFS journaling filesystems have a solution to this problem. They all store directory entries using types of balanced tree data structures (B+Tree and B*Tree), indexed by name, which minimize search time for any entry. Filesystems that impose some sort of order on directory entries eliminate the need to minimize the number of files and directories in a directory because looking up the filename is a function rather than a sequential comparison.

B-Trees are a type of binary tree optimized to minimize the number of accesses required to locate an item by maintaining a relatively shallow tree. This is especially important for lookups that require disk access, which is relatively slow compared to in-memory lookups. In a classic binary tree, each node contains a value and a pointer to nodes containing lower and higher values based on an index value, as shown in Figure 1.3. Binary trees are usually relatively deep because of the limitations of the contents of each node but provide fast lookups.
B-Trees are balanced trees that minimize the depth of the tree, and in which each node can have a variable number of keys. Because each node can contain multiple values, insert operations into nodes with free key values can be instantaneous, without requiring that the tree be traversed or transformed (rebalanced). B+Trees and B*Trees are optimized versions of B-Trees with different constraints on whether each node contains index entries or data.

As mentioned earlier, another metric that influences the performance of specific types of filesystems is the speed at which data can be allocated when creating a file and later located when reading that file. The speed at which data can be accessed is generally a combination of the size of the blocks that make up the filesystem, the time required to move the disk heads to the cylinder where each data block is located, and the time it takes for the sector containing that data to pass underneath the disk head. Using larger block sizes when creating a filesystem increases the chances that you'll find a specific piece of data after a relatively smaller number of disk reads but is more wasteful of space in the filesystem. Using 4 KB or 8 KB blocks is a time-saver when searching for information but wastes a lot of space if you're storing 500-byte files. The amount of time it takes for disk sectors containing the data you're looking for to pass under the disk head is known as *rotational delay* and is why disk drives with higher speeds generally provide faster data access.

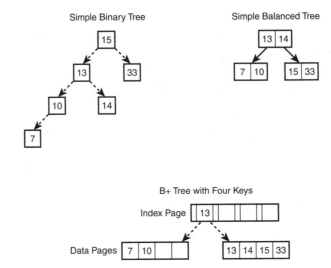

FIGURE 1.3

Binary and balanced trees.

If you can come up with a model for the average size of most of the files in a specific filesystem, you can usually find a fairly optimal block size. However, this still leaves the problem of the time it takes to physically move the disk heads from block to block within a file. Of course, this problem only becomes worse as filesystems age and begin to suffer from physical fragmentation, as discussed later in this chapter in the section "Filesystem Issues and Concerns." (In a nutshell, physical fragmentation means that in existing filesystems, new blocks allocated for existing files are less likely to be allocated near the previous block. This is because the space near the previous end of any existing file is likely to be occupied by another file because the filesystem is filling up.)

Early attempts at reducing data access time, such as the concept of cylinder groups introduced by the Fast File System (FFS) in BSD Unix, minimized head movement by trying to allocate data blocks across all the cylinders over which the disk heads were positioned at any given time. Although this was a significant improvement over previous allocation schemes, this type of allocation is still constrained by the size of the blocks in the filesystem.

One timesaving mechanism available in many newer filesystems is the idea of allocating extents of blocks whenever disk space is allocated. *Extents* are a physically linear series of blocks that can therefore be read one after the other, without requiring that disk heads be repositioned. The Linux ext2 filesystem allocates extents whenever physically sequential blocks are available, trying to anticipate the growth of files as they are created, as do the journaling filesystems discussed in this book. Once again, as filesystems age and the blocks of storage associated with files become physically fragmented, allocating extents becomes possible less of the time, which is a good argument for defragmenting filesystems as often as possible.

VFS: The Key to Supporting Multiple Filesystems

The authors and contributors to Unix and Linux are no dummies. Over the years (and as this book demonstrates), one of the greatest features of Unix and Linux systems is the continuous development of enhancements and extensions to the basic system. This book focuses on new filesystems that have been added to Linux and are now actively supported and used.

If you've ever done any programming, construction, or writing, you know how irritating it is when something has been created without any regard for future enhancement and expansion. Programs that weren't designed in a modular fashion or use hardwired constants, houses in which every slot in the breaker box is full, and plumbing without any intermediate shut-off valves all demonstrate short-sightedness rather than precision. Operating systems such as Linux that are actively under development by thousands of hackers in random locations all over the known universe can't afford to contain these sorts of built-in limitations, and luckily they don't. Each successive release of Linux provides more generalized interfaces, a greater number of plug-in interfaces, and consequently is easier for people to work with.

Years ago, adding support for new devices to a Unix kernel meant a substantial amount of driver hacking and a significant number of kernel recompiles until you got everything just right. Today, a new device driver can be added relatively easily by taking advantage of the loadable kernel module (LKM) support in Linux (modulo the effort to write the driver in the first place, which I'm not overlooking).

Some of the flexibility and generalization provided by Linux and other modern versions of Unix is a side effect of the fact that today's system have significantly more memory than older Unix systems because increased memory requirements are usually a side effect of generalization, but so what? Unless you're working in an embedded architecture or other situation where your primary goal is shoehorning Linux into a limited amount of space, memory is relatively cheap nowadays.

Part of the beauty of Linux is the fact that it can be customized to fit individual requirements. People who are working with limited memory and disk/flash space requirements can throw away whatever they want to produce a custom Linux installation that is as streamlined as possible. The rest of us can just shell out another $50 to $100 and add another 256 MB to our systems. Everybody's happy.

An open filesystem interface was one of the first generic interfaces present in Unix, dating back to BSD days courtesy of Sun Microsystems (that is, back when Sun ran a reasonable version of Unix). As discussed in the previous section, the inode is the fundamental construct of

Linux and Unix filesystem data structures. Sun opened up the architecture of the Unix filesystem for all time by introducing the concept of virtual inodes (vnodes) in its Virtual File System (VFS) interface. Vnodes in local filesystems refer to inodes in an instance of a specific filesystem implementation. Vnodes in networked filesystems refer to information that enables the operating system to locate and access a remote file or directory. Concepts such as vnodes are elegant in their simplicity, though still not for the weak-of-heart in terms of implementation. The Linux Virtual Filesystem implementation is done through a kernel interface known as the *Virtual Filesystem Switch*.

Because the object of this book is to introduce you to filesystem concepts and different filesystem implementations rather than to help you implement one, I'll skip over providing 100 pages of source code to explain the VFS implementation and needlessly fatten this book. After all, you can get the Linux source code as easily as I can. On the other hand, a high-level description of how Linux uses its VFS implementation to access filesystem-specific information should help clarify just how elegant, flexible, and extensible the VFS implementation is.

In general, each type of filesystem that the current Linux system knows about is registered with the kernel using the register_filesystem() call, which passes a pointer to the superblock data structure for that type of filesystem as one of its arguments. When a specific filesystem is mounted, its type is identified by the mount operation (ext2 is the default, of course), and the kernel allocates a vfsmount data structure for that specific filesystem. This structure records the filesystem's mountpoint and contains a pointer to its superblock, plus other information needed to interact with that filesystem (such as whether the filesystem supports quotas and is usingthem). The kernel always maintains a linked list of currently mounted filesystems, each represented by a vfsmount structure.

Each superblock contains a pointer to a superblock_operations data structure that contains pointers to the procedures/methods used to perform various filesystem metadata operations, such as allocating, accessing, deallocating, and getting status information for inodes in that filesystem, and so on. When opening a file, the kernel uses pathname information to check mountpoints and determine the filesystem and type of filesystem on which that file is located. The kernel then uses a pointer in the file data structure to access the specific procedures/methods to use to read and write the file, seek to a specific point within it, get status information, flush pending file operations, and so on.

Physical and Logical Storage

The previous sections of this chapter all discussed the storage requirements of filesystems and volumes in terms of physical disks. At the moment, there are relatively few exceptions to disk storage:

- The bubble memory craze of a decade or so ago never really panned out

- RAM disks are relatively uncommon because they are still confined by relatively small amounts of memory (compared to the size of physical disks nowadays) and also have to be backed by disk storage if they are to survive reboots and power outages.

- Holographic storage seems like a promising possibility, but hasn't escaped from research labs yet (at least not in my price range).

Disk storage as we know it today really isn't a bad thing because today's drives have larger capacity and are faster than ever before. Both of these trends are likely to continue. However, the problem with physical storage is that any filesystem that you create on a physical disk partition can grow no larger than the physical partition. Although needing a partition greater than 10 gigabytes or so might be difficult to conceive of for the casual home user, placing constraints on volume size can be a serious problem for the business and scientific communities. Identifying the largest volume that you can create at the moment is as easy as reading the label on a hard drive; identifying the largest volume you'll ever need is a philosophical problem that has no answer. Filesystems such as ext2 and many of the journaling filesystems available today provide administrative utilities that enable you to resize partitions of those types, but these still are constrained by the size of the physical device on which those filesystems are located.

Of course, Linux and Unix have an answer to the problem of physical devices whose size is finite—logical volumes. A logical volume is a pool of storage space composed of free partitions from any number of different hard drives. You can create filesystems on logical volumes just as you would on a physical volume, except that you easily can add more space to a logical volume by adding new disks or partitions to the pool of storage space from which the logical volume was created. You then can use the administrative utilities for the appropriate type of filesystem to increase the size of that volume. The pool of storage space composed of physical partitions and from which logical volumes are created is known as a *volume group*.

Another term specific to logical volumes is *physical volumes*, which refers to the physical disks and partitions allocated to a volume group. When a volume group is created and new physical volumes are associated with it, *physical extents* are preallocated on the physical volumes. These physical extents are conceptually similar to the blocks in a standard filesystem, although they are typcally much larger. After physical extents have been created on a physical volume, the extents are added to a volume group and are then assigned to specific logical volumes within that volume group. You then create a filesystem on the logical volume, and voila! Figure 1.4 shows the relationships between the components at various levels of a logical volume.

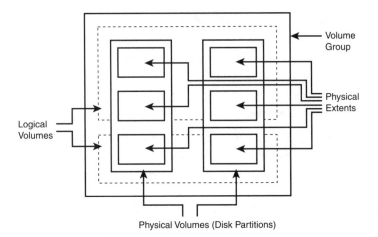

FIGURE 1.4
Construction of a logical volume.

Volume groups and logical volumes provide a great, open-ended solution to the problem of physical storage devices of finite size. The size of each of these is still constrained by the size of the data structures used to define volume group, logical volume, and physical extent size, but at least this is a problem that can be easily fixed. Current physical extent sizes range from 4 MB to 512 MB, and the current Linux kernel limits a logical volume to 65536 physical extents. Doing the math shows that the maximum size of a logical volume at the moment is 32 terabytes, though the current Linux kernel limits the size of a block device to a mere 2 terabytes. Oh well, at least we all have something to look forward to!

Local and Networked Filesystems

Local filesystems are located on storage devices physically connected to your computer. Access to data on local filesystems is therefore fast because they are directly connected to your machine. On the other hand, local filesystems are useful only if you and any other users who need access to the data that they contain can connect to the machine on which they are located. When necessary, connecting to the machine on which specific data is physically located generally isn't a problem in today's networked environment, especially on true multiuser systems such as Linux, where you can always open an SSH (Secure Shell) or telnet connection to the machine, as long as the machine is up and working correctly.

Networked filesystems are filesystems where your data is actually stored on file servers and other systems, and can therefore only be accessed over a network. These are also often known as distributed filesystems, because they enable you to access storage and other resources distributed across other hosts on your network. Networked filesystems provide users with the freedom to access their information from any system on which they can log in and have access to those networked resources.

Networked filesystems offer many advantages over local filesystems. Networked/distributed filesystems

- Reduce the chance that the failure of a single workstation will prevent you from accessing your data. Most networked filesystems enable you to log in on any machine on which they are available and access your data in exactly the same way.

- Can eliminate the chance that a single hardware failure will prevent you from accessing your data by providing copies of a single network filesystem on multiple file servers. (Unless it's a network failure!)

- Provide central locations for data that must or should be shared among all users.

- Simplify accessing existing data from faster systems. Suppose that you have written an application to test CPU and memory performance, or that your work or research depends on CPU and memory-intensive calculations. Running your application on a faster, more powerful machine is as simple as logging in on that machine and running the application from the networked filesystem (as long as the executable application runs on both platforms).

- Provide the opportunity to centralize administrative operations such as backups.

- Promote interoperability and flexibility. As discussed extensively in the next chapter, networked filesystems make it easy for people to use the software and hardware that is best suited to their requirements.

The appropriate combination of fast local filesystems, journaling filesystems, and networked filesystems available today provide users and administrators with the capability to maximize computer uptime, performance, and the availability of user data while expediting common operational tasks (such as backups) and minimizing the impact of individual hardware failures. I also suspect that this will only get better. Although it's true that more advanced local and networked filesystems often require additional administrative overhead and time during installation, the payback is quick and well worth it.

Filesystem Issues and Concerns

This section discusses the things that administrators and system architects are most concerned about when selecting, integrating, and using a filesystem. As mentioned earlier, most "normal" users could care less how or where their data is stored as long as it's always available to them and they can access it quickly and easily. This section goes into more detail about some of the concerns of system administrators, analysts, operators, and programmers in terms of selecting any filesystem for storing and retrieving data. Together with filesystem-specific installation, administrative, and implementation issues, these general filesystem concerns are the basis of the analysis and comparisons of the filesystems throughout the rest of this book.

Performance

The performance of anything is critical to whether it will be used (unless there is no alternative), how happy people are with it, and how quickly people will try to replace it. As mentioned earlier, the performance of a filesystem is the bottom line for its acceptance. Users could care less about the elegance of a filesystem implementation or its ease of administration if it is slow, unreliable, or (worst case) both.

With the exception of filesystems developed purely as research animals, every filesystem that has made the transition from R&D into commercial life makes substantial claims about its performance and other advantages. I didn't realize how much junk mail William Shakespeare had received from the computer industry until I read this sarcastic quote of his from *Troilus and Cressida*:

> "All lovers swear more performance than they are able ... ; vowing more than the perfection of ten, and discharging less than the tenth part of one."

Filesystem performance impacts MIS/IT personnel at a number of different stages of system operation:

- When booting the system, minimizing restart times effectively improves the general performance of a system by reducing the amount of time that it is unavailable. Journaling filesystems reduce startup time by minimizing the time it takes to verify the consistency of a filesystem.

- During day-to-day operations, increasing the speed at which the system makes data available to users is the most obvious measure of performance in users' eyes. This can be done by fine-tuning specific filesystems based on the way they are being used, the type of data that they contain, and so on.

- During day-to-day operations, the extensive use of intelligent caching by some networked filesystems improves response time. Caches that survive across system restarts, known as *persistent caches*, also protect users from losing modified data if the server on which the data is actually stored goes down.

- During day-to-day operations, logical volumes reduce downtime and enhance filesystem availability by enabling administrators to allocate additional space to existing filesystems without taking down the system or making filesystems unavailable for noticeable periods of time. Filesystems that allocate internal data structures, such as inodes, dynamically reduce the amount of time it takes to check an entire filesystem (whenever necessary). They also remove limitations on the number of files and directories that a filesystem can contain and enable dynamic filesystem administration.

- During day-to-day operations, the capability of some networked filesystems to provide copies of filesystems increases the availability of critical software by reducing downtime due to remote server problems.

- During day-to-day operations, the distributed authentication mechanisms associated with networked filesystems free users from having to use any specific workstation.

Operating system, filesystem, and other low-level software are the primary channels for interaction between application software and your computer's hardware, and are therefore in a critical, interesting, and vulnerable position. Using sophisticated filesystems can both improve the actual performance of your system and increase your users' perceptions of how useful and available a computer system is.

Efficient Data Storage

Earlier in this chapter, I went into detail regarding how to select optimal block sizes for filesystems to strike the right balance between increasing access speed and minimizing wasted space. I won't duplicate that here but will provide a relevant bit of advice from the man page for tunefs, a filesystem tuning and optimization utility for SunOS and Solaris:

> "You can tune a filesystem, but you can't tune a fish."

With that concept (and the previous discussion of this topic) firmly in hand, this section focuses on an even more common problem that gradually degrades the performance of many filesystems—physical fragmentation.

Physical fragmentation is the tendency of the blocks allocated of a file to become discontiguous. Filesystems initially try to allocate the blocks associated with a specific file together so that they can be either read or written as a unit or at least read relatively quickly. Unfortunately, over time the blocks associated with a file tend to end up being in different parts of a disk as new blocks are allocated to the file and old blocks are released when a file is edited, appended to, or so on. Figure 1.5 provides a simple illustration of fragmentation.

In step 1 of this example, all is well when files are created and initial disk storage is assigned to them. Unfortunately, steps 2 and 3 show that discontiguous blocks usually begin to be allocated as soon as files are edited and require additional data storage. This situation can get even worse as existing files are deleted and the storage associated with them is returned to the system's list of free storage, as shown in Figure 1.6, which continues from Figure 1.5.

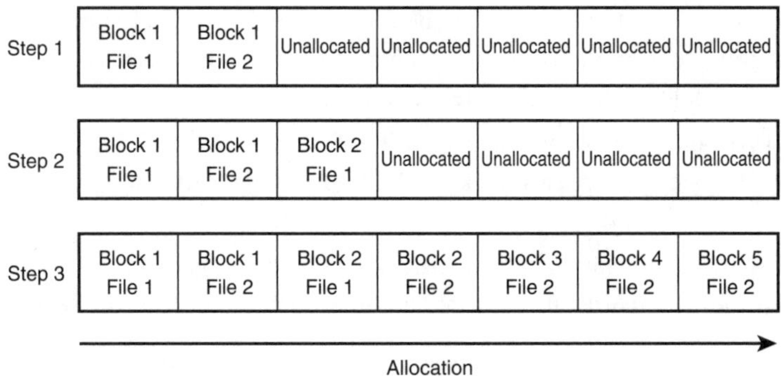

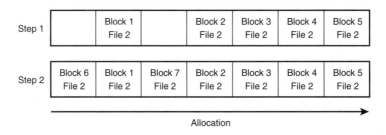

Figure 1.5

A simple example of fragmentation.

Figure 1.6

An example of continuing fragmentation in existing files.

In step 1 of this figure, the first file has been deleted, returning the blocks that it formerly allocated to the system's list of available blocks. In step 2, what was originally the second file has grown again and claimed the space formerly associated with file 1 in as inefficient a manner as possible.

Most multiuser filesystems take great pains to avoid fragmentation when creating files. Because Linux systems usually support multiple users who often create new files at the same time, the Linux ext2 filesystem preallocate eight blocks whenever a file is created in an attempt to initially keep the file together as much as possible.

The different ways of freeing and reusing filesystem space used today are the product of years of learning. However, the mechanisms for undoing fragmentation (known as *defragmentation*) are similar across systems. For example, one of the funniest disk allocation schemes I ever saw was in the disk operating system used by early versions of Ohio Scientific microcomputers in the late 1970s. These systems (single-user, thank goodness) had to save files in contiguous extents on the disk. That's not so bad, except that they also had no way of reclaiming space after it was freed. When you increased the size of a file, the DOS saved the new file to the end of the filesystem and left the space it had previously occupied marked as used. You had to run a special administrative utility to copy the data to another disk and repack so that you could reuse the freed space.

As silly as the previous paragraph sounds, the fastest and easiest way to defragment any filesystem isn't all that different. Even today, doing a complete backup of a filesystem at the file level (not an image dump!), verifying the integrity of that backup, erasing the storage space formerly associated with that filesystem, and then restoring the filesystem is the most common mechanism for defragmenting a filesystem. Because the backup is restored by file, the space for each file will be allocated contiguously. When the filesystem is remounted, it will not contain any physical fragmentation—for a little while, at least.

Extended Metadata Support

As users and applications become more sophisticated, their requirements and wish lists increase in parallel. As filesystem research and therefore filesystems proceed, many filesystems are beginning to provide capabilities beyond those originally envisioned by Linux and Unix. Operating system standards such as VFS enable new filesystems to be quickly and easily integrated into existing operating systems, whereas programmatic standards such as POSIX interfaces ensure that new filesystems can easily work with existing applications. By supporting these standards but also providing their own enhancements and related tools, new filesystems can enhance the functionality of an operating system due to extended capabilities that they provide.

One of the more exciting features to appear in some of the enhanced filesystems for Linux discussed in this book are improved mechanisms for limiting and enabling access to files based on file protection beyond the scope of that provided by the operating system itself. Filesystems such as AFS, XFS, and NFS (to some extent) provide Access Control Lists (ACLs), which support file protections that can be as granular as granting or denying access to files and directories to specific users. The groups on which ACLs are based can be existing system groups (from /etc/group) or user-defined collections of existing users and groups. Support for access control lists, originally introduced in systems such as Honeywell's MULTICS and Apollo's AEGIS and DOMAIN/OS, provides exciting opportunities for expanding the file access permissions provided natively by Linux.

Opportunities for storing additional information in filesystem metadata also provide exciting possibilities for future filesystem development. For example, locating files by name is the most obvious way of finding them, but isn't necessary the only way of doing so. Some sophisticated filesystems are moving towards enabling users to locate, identify, and view files through other means. Rooted in database technologies, the most obvious of these is assigning logical attributes to files and indexing filesystems according to those attributes. This enables users and administrators to query the filesystem to find types and classes of files, and provides the opportunity for presenting different views of the filesystem. The only filesystem that I'm aware of that does this at the moment is BFS, the Be File System, which is only (currently) available for the Be operating system. This filesystem therefore doesn't get much press outside the few hundred people who actively use the BeOS (myself included, although using the word actively is pushing it).

Introducing the Benchmarks

Even though I am totally objective and without prejudice in my observations, many people are more comfortable with comparisons that use actual empirical data. To simplify comparisons between the different filesystems discussed in this book, I'll provide output from the following standard industry benchmarks. The source code for these benchmarks is provided on the CD-ROM that accompanies this book and compiles on a variety of systems:

- Bonnie—A filesystem benchmark that performs a series of I/O tests on a specified file. Using a single file for benchmarking purposes provides a focused set of interesting data points for pure file I/O without the overhead of filesystem calls such as directory lookups and similar operations.

- IOzone—A filesystem benchmark that tests file I/O performance for read, write, reread, and rewrite operations through file descriptors, FILE I/O, memory-mapped I/O, random I/O, and so on. The variety of I/O operations tested by IOzone helps level the playing field across filesystems optimized for specific, but different, types of I/O operations.

- Postmark—A filesystem and file operation benchmark that tests filesystem performance by simulating file creation, extension, deletion, and renaming operations that would take place when a filesystem was used to support a small mail server. The transactional nature of many of these operations provides a good mechanism for examining how caching benefits a distributed filesystem and how specific filesystems actually perform.

These benchmarks frequently are used to assess the performance of different filesystems and provide data that looks great on overheads.

Filesystems and Interoperability

IN THIS CHAPTER

Chapter 1, "Introduction to Filesystems," discussed the essentials of data storage, all the way down to the sectors used to hold the smallest units of information that can be addressed by a disk drive. Sectors are essentially the lowest common denominator of physical storage devices. From the human perspective of the information stored on a computer, files are their equivalent. If I want to exchange some logical unit of information with you, such as a document or spreadsheet, I do so by giving you either a physical copy of the file containing that information or access to that file using some single computer system that we both have access to. In the simplest sense, interoperability is just the capability for both of us to share access to data. It sounds so simple.

Interoperability is the computer equivalent of the age-old cry "can't we all just get along?" I don't know anyone who uses computers with any regularity who hasn't at some point been frustrated by trying to exchange data with a friend or coworker who used a different computer system. Unfortunately, ever since the creation of the second computer system, exchanging data between computer systems has been a problem.

This chapter begins by providing a history of hardware and software compatibility and interoperability to put these concepts in perspective within the computer industry. This chapter also explores some of the most common mechanisms used to share data and interoperate between computer systems and introduces the notion of a distributed filesystem that enables different types of computer systems to share data in real-time rather than exchange it. The chapter concludes by exploring different ways of implementing and organizing a filesystem that enables an entire enterprise to quickly and invisibly get the most out of its information and computing resources.

Standardization and the Birth of Information Sharing

In the earliest days of computing, computers were pure hardware—the first computers were even hardwired to execute specific programs. The stored program concept, where a single computer could load and execute different programs, was a revolutionary notion when it was invented by Presper Eckert (or John von Neuman, if you choose to ignore facts and instead subscribe to popular computer mythology). Implementing the stored program concept brought with it some equally novel creations, such as a way of storing programs and (even more importantly) a way of reading them back into a computer and executing these imported bits of executable code.

The cleverest early computers could therefore load and run different programs, essentially booting an application and running it until it had accomplished its purpose or everyone got bored and went home. Not all that much later, clever computer scientists invented the idea of a software monitor, an application that existed only to load and run other programs. These monitor applications were the predecessors of operating systems, much like an inch-long mammal is the ancestor of humanity—it's somewhat hard to spot an immediate resemblance, but many things are conceptually similar if you really look closely.

Early computer manufacturers were therefore focused on selling or leasing their own incredibly expensive hardware to their customers. Being able to exchange data with other manufacturers' computer systems wasn't an important concept—such a thing actually could be detrimental because it would enable customers to switch to other manufacturers' computer systems, which was not "a good thing."

Although holding onto your customers is a powerful motivator for differentiating and distancing yourself from your competitors, this really isn't the primary reason that early computer systems were different from each other. A more important reason for the differences between early computer systems was the fact that the birth and subsequent development of the computer was a time of exciting, revolutionary innovation. People were inventing things that we take for granted today, such as stored programs, different mediums for long-term program storage, associated devices for reading and writing such media, and so on.

The inventor of hard disk storage didn't have to worry about interoperating with anything else because there wasn't anything else. (The fact that early hard drive platters were five feet across and weighed a few hundred pounds was also a deterrent for sharing them between disk drives.) Who was to know which computer system, storage medium, way of writing and organizing stored data, and so on, would catch on? Everybody hoped it was theirs, and why not?

As the product lines of different computer manufacturers stabilized, their data formats and storage media became more standardized. An existing customer of Joe Random's computer company isn't going to be especially motivated to switch to its newer systems unless he can move to those computer systems with his existing programs and data intact. Moving data, which is just raw information organized in a deterministic way, wasn't conceptually difficult, but moving programs to new systems required a way of divorcing programs from the specific hardware that they originally ran on. This, coupled with the fact that it's easier to debug, maintain, and enhance computer programs that contain instructions such as "MOVE AGE to TEMP-AGE" as opposed to "01110000011101," was a big factor in the development of high-level languages for programming computers.

The cost of early computer systems and the fact that some companies refused to sell them created a whole new industry, manufacturing and selling compatible devices that worked with existing computer systems. If the manufacturer of your computer equipment charged a large rental fee for something that you could buy outright from someone else and use forever, you could save money by stamping its rented equivalent "Return to Sender" and doing so. These third-party devices had to be 100 percent compatible with the devices that they replaced to improve productivity rather than hamper it, but could do more than just cut costs. They also provided opportunities for improving your system piecemeal by replacing existing devices with faster, higher-capacity, or simply more usable versions of the same thing. Compatible devices from third-party manufacturers could also simply be added to existing systems, not replacing any existing device but instead augmenting an existing system.

Good examples of compatible devices produced by third parties are things such as line printers, display and print terminals, tape drives, disk drives, and so on. In some cases, compatible devices could introduce improvements independent of a specific computer manufacturer, such as faster or higher density storage devices, as long as they could send and receive data from the computer that they were attached to in the same way.

Enterprising individuals such as Gene Amdahl eventually realized that limiting the development of compatible devices to peripherals was simply a conceptual limitation and began producing computer systems, such as Amdahl's IBM mainframe clones, that were 100 percent compatible with the programs, data, and peripherals of existing systems but faster, better, or maybe even just cheaper. Gene doesn't get the popular credit for inventing the clone industry that he deserves because so few of us actually have mainframes in our homes.

The point of this hardware history lesson is that the idea of compatible hardware and data formats is a notion that developed slowly but has since caught on for a variety of practical and financial reasons. "Compatibility is the ancestor of interoperability" may sound like something you'd find in a fortune cookie at the IBM cafeteria, but it's still an important point to remember.

Compatible Devices and Compatible Media

The compatible device industry has a fraternal twin, the third-party manufacturers of supplies for those devices. After all, if you no longer had to rent your line printer or tape drive from IBM, you certainly didn't have to buy your line printer paper or magnetic tapes from IBM either.

Although there were probably plenty of hard feelings in the early days of compatible device and computer supplies manufacturers, most computer manufacturers eventually began to see that the existence of companies that wanted to specialize in manufacturing add-ons or day-to-day computer consumables could be liberating. This freed the computer companies from having to worry about inventing, designing, and manufacturing everything themselves, enabling them to focus on improving the computers and sponsoring research and development efforts that would develop new technologies that they could at least sell for a while before someone produced a compatible version. Even the greediest megalomaniacal computer company had to grudgingly admit that not having to finance, budget for, and manage related industries such as paper mills and magnetic tape manufacturing plants was probably a good thing.

The supplies that keep a computer system running are a significant part of the cost of owner-ship for that computer system in the long term. When I worked on larger computer systems in the 1980s, every computer room had rack after rack of the magnetic tapes used for backups, carefully labeled, organized, and cross-indexed. Backups aren't really all that useful if you can't find them. Some of these tapes were used for daily backups and were thus overwritten daily, but the majority were longer-term backups—weekly backups that we saved for a few weeks, monthly backups that we saved for up to a year, and archives that were backups of all the user data on the computer, and which we saved forever. The cost of all these tapes added up over time!

The growth of compatible equipment manufacturers and associated media suppliers (tapes, removable disks, paper), as well as the wide variety of computer manufacturers to choose from, eventually helped narrow the field of storage devices that were used in computer operations. Early Univac computer systems used wide reels of thin metal tape to store their data. Even though punch cards had largely been standardized in size and shape from the beginning (because they were originally used for tabulating and counting machines), computer companies such as Univac and later Remington-Rand punched circular holes rather than standard rectangular ones. As time passed, these sorts of unique approaches to data storage disappeared, because either the computer manufacturer itself went away or the computer manufacturers wanted to buy standard peripherals from peripheral manufacturers and adapt them to their systems.

Over the years, some of the standard data storage media that have come and gone are the following:

- 80-column punch cards (ancient history)
- 8-inch floppy disks (now a historical item)
- 5.25-inch floppy disks (also over)
- 3.5-inch floppies (now largely an artifact due to their limited capacity but still occasion-ally used for booting some computer systems)
- Removable 14-inch hard drive platters (single and stacked)
- Bernoulli Cartridges (8-inch and 5.25-inch)
- QIC cartridge backup tapes
- DC-300, DC-600, and so on cartridge backup tapes
- Syquest Cartridges (5.25-inch and 3.5-inch)
- Zip and Jazz disks
- LS120 Super Disks
- 1/2-inch magnetic tape (largely an artifact but still found in some mainframe shops for compatibility with old backups)

- 4mm tapes
- 8mm tapes
- DAT tapes
- DLT tapes
- CD-ROM disks

This list may awaken fond memories for some and bouts of laughter for others. Like any other aspect of technology, the evolution of removable storage media is a road paved with both success and failure.

Sneakernet—First Generation File Sharing

The first mechanism for sharing data files and programs between computer systems was through writing them to some removable medium on one computer system, removing the media from that computer, carrying it to another computer, and then reading the information back into the new computer system. In a humorous bit of revisionism, the introduction of networking as a file sharing technique has given this method for file sharing the name *sneakernet*, because rather than using a network to carry the information from one system to another, a human being literally carried the information from one system to another. Hence the "sneakers" (tennis shoes) that such a person might have worn.

Using sneakernet as a file sharing mechanism required that the two computer systems both had removable media drives of the same type, so that computer system B could read the data written on computer system A. Aside from having the same type of devices, the way in which the data was written to the media and the format of the data written on that media had be understandable by both computer systems.

This wasn't always as feasible as it seems. For example, most of the personal computer systems in the 1980s used 5.25-inch floppy disks, but some systems used hard-sectored disks, whereas the majority used soft-sectored disks. Hard-sectored disks were preformatted disks that had multiple holes in the floppy used to make sure that the disk head was properly aligned with the floppy disk before reading data. Because hard-sectored disks imply physical formatting holes, they can't be reformatted (unless you're amazingly good with glue and an exacto knife). Soft-sectored disks are the ones still in use today, with a single alignment hole and where the information about the layout of the data on the disk is read from the disk and formatting is therefore done under software control. Although soft-sectored disks usually come preformatted, they can be reformatted easily whenever necessary.

This problem even persisted with 3.5-inch disks when used by different computer systems. For example, early 3.5-inch floppy disks used by the Macintosh computer system used a format called GCR (Group Coded Recording), which provided additional information about each disk sector. 400K and 800K 3.5-inch floppies written on a Macintosh, therefore, featured a different sector size than that used on PC systems of the time, making it impossible to exchange data between the two without using a software utility that could read the raw information off the disks byte-by-byte and reconstruct it appropriately. Although this was interesting and amusing, it was also time-consuming.

Even after you managed to physically transport information from one computer system to another, you could still run into problems. For example, many mainframes encoded characters using a format known as EBCDIC (Extended Binary Coded Decimal Interchange Code), which was totally different from the ASCII (American Standard Code for Information Interchange) notation that most of us are familiar with. Supposing that both computers used ASCII codes, many earlier computers stored information in fundamentally different ways depending on which byte of a computer word was read first. The two options are *big-endian*, where information in a word was stored low byte, high byte, and *little-endian*, where the information was stored high byte, low byte.

Even assuming that computers had the same endian orientation, computer systems such as Suns and DEC Vaxen used different internal formats for things such as the representation of floating-point data. This sort of thing is the reason why the cost of aspirin was a significant operational expense for many early computer installations, and there are mental health care provisions in the benefits package of almost any computer-related company.

To get some idea of the number of different ways of storing data on removable media, check out the options available in the Linux dd (dump data) program, the Linux version of the ancient Unix program by the same name. On the surface, this program is simple: it enables you to read data from one device (or, therefore, file on Unix systems) and write it to another. This placid application is actually more like Loch Ness than a swimming pool. Under the surface of the dd application lurk convoluted, mind-numbing options such as `conv=swab` (swap bytes during conversion), `ibs` (input block size), `obs` (output block size), `cbs` (conversion buffer size), `conv=ascii` (convert from EBCDIC to ASCII), `conv=ebcdic` (convert from ASCII to EBCDIC), and `conv=ibm` (convert from ASCII to alternated EBCDIC), and dandies like `conv=block` (pad newline-terminated records with spaces to cbs size). Anyone for a hemlock cocktail?

Utility programs such as dd are one-size-fits-all utilities in the finest Unix tradition. Aside from writing data in one format at one end and then hoping that the intended recipient could actually read that data, alternatives such as ANSI (American National Standards Institute) tape record formats were provided. The computer equivalent of Esperanto, the goal of using a standard format was that everyone could write tapes in a single, well-known format, which everyone else could therefore read. One of my first jobs out of college involved figuring out how to migrate computer accounts (and all the user data) from a DEC TOPS-20 mainframe to a standalone 4.2 BSD system. My eventual solution was to write ANSI-standard tapes on the TOPS-20 system

2

FILESYSTEMS AND
INTEROPERABILITY

using its DUMPER utility and then read them back in on the BSD system using shell scripts that first extracted a catalog of the files on the tape and then used that catalog to supply the names of files read back in from the tape via a public-domain ANSI tape reading application called ansir. Those were the good old days, and I will always remember them as fondly as any visit to the dentist's office.

The Introduction of Networked File Sharing

As networks were invented and began their slow rise to ubiquity in business and academic computer installations, using the network to transfer files from one computer system to another was a natural innovation. The smallest bit of discrete, formatted information that can be read from or written to a network in any protocol is generically referred to as a *packet*, which is the conceptual equivalent of the sector on a hard drive.

However, even this type of data exchange was prone to conceptual problems. Just as removable storage media often used different formats, early networks used different protocols (the "language" and format in which discrete units of information were exchanged between computer systems over the network). Protocols such as XNS (Xerox Network System protocol), IDP (Internetwork Datagram Protocol), SPP (Sequenced Packet Protocol), IPX (Internetwork Packet Exchange), and SPX (Sequenced Packet Exchange) are all now largely extinct but were important (if not the only) protocols in their day. Today, most information is exchanged across networks using the UDP (Universal Datagram Protocol) and TCP/IP (Transmission Control Protocol/Internet Protocol) protocols. Older network protocols often still can be used today because they are supported by encapsulating packets in older formats within new-style packet formats, such as TCP/IP.

Even assuming that two different computer systems supported the same network protocol and could therefore exchange information with each other, other problems in networked data exchange also had to be solved. Exchanging binary programs between different types of computer systems was almost always useless because different computer systems used different processors with different instruction sets and different ways of organizing programs to load and run them. A less obvious problem was the endian problem discussed in the previous section, where the bytes within a computer word were read and written in a different sequence. Early file transfer applications such as FTP (still in use today) therefore featured many bizarre options such as ITS to take into account the difference in word sizes and data organization between the types of computers available at the time.

Supposing that you've finally hashed out all the options you need for physically transferring files between two different computer systems and can successfully do it, a final, insurmountable problem presents itself. What if you need to share data between two computer systems and that data is constantly changing? Until the invention of networks, this was essentially impossible, even given an army of operator drones who could continuously read and write tapes and shuffle them between computer systems.

The need for multiple users to access a shared pool of continuously changing data is fundamental to computers. The early solution for this problem was attaching zillions of terminals to a single computer system and sharing access to the data. Regardless of whether those terminals are attached to the central computer using serial or network connections, this is only a solution if everybody is using the same type of computer system, but that's needlessly restrictive in today's day and age. The real solutions to providing users with shared access to data are the compatibility and distributed filesystems discussed in the latter two thirds of this book.

What Is Interoperability?

Interoperability is the capability of multiple users at different computer systems to share access to data at the same time. Whether these users are using the same type of computer system should not matter as long as the applications running on that computer system can read and write the same data formats. Interoperability would be impossible without today's ubiquitous networks. Sharing files over a network by transferring them from one computer system to another is like handing out ice cubes, whereas sharing access to data is like enabling multiple users to drink from the same faucet. When you share access to a file over a network, you automatically see any changes made to the data that it contains, regardless of where those changes were made from, assuming that the software you're using is smart enough to notice that the data has changed.

Most modern computer systems have visions of interoperability—though often only with other computers of exactly the same kind. For example, many businesses today depend on the network support built into Microsoft Windows. Windows systems can share disks and directories with each other over a network and provide reasonably fine-grained permissions and locking. Nice, but only useful if you have a Windows system. Third-party software is available to enable Windows systems to share files and directories to Macintosh systems running versions of the MacOS prior to Mac OS X, but what if you add a Linux or Unix system into the mix?

Truly modern and open computer systems such as Linux support real solutions to the interoperability problem. This is one of the cases in which the Open Source philosophy pays off big time in terms of better living through open-source software. This book explains how to use all the most popular interoperability filesystems for which the source code and binaries are freely available on the Internet.

Two basic types of interoperability filesystems are available:

- Distributed filesystems that run on all platforms and are therefore virtually platform-independent. These filesystems unify all the computers in one or more locations into a logical whole because each computer can access the same centralized data. Examples of these types of filesystems are AFS, Coda, NFS, and InterMezzo. At one time, Novell's NetWare software fell into this category, but support from Novell for non-PC platforms has been on the wane over the past few years (as has the general use of NetWare, another Microsoft casualty).

- Filesystems that run on a variety of systems to provide compatibility with a specific network resource sharing protocol. These are software-only "adapters" between filesystem protocols used on a network. Running the software on a specific type of system enables other systems that speak the supported protocol to access shared resources. Examples of these types of software filesystem adapters are Samba, Netatalk, and the NetWare Core Protocol (NCP) software suite available on Linux systems.

If interoperability is your goal, the type of interoperability filesystem you use depends on your computing environment. For example, if your computer environment is composed of Windows systems into which you are introducing Linux or other Unix systems as servers because of their power, reliability, and cost savings, running Samba on the Linux and Unix systems may satisfy all your requirements. This enables all your Windows systems to seamlessly mount exported Linux and Unix directories. You also can use Samba to access printers attached to Linux and Unix systems, just as you would share a printer in a "pure" Windows environment. As I'll discuss in Chapter 20, "Using Samba," you can even configure a Linux system to use the authentication information provided by a Windows authentication server.

Similar to the previous example, computing environments that are composed of Macintosh computers but that want to introduce Linux or other Unix systems can provide interoperability by running a filesystem adapter such as Netatalk. Netatalk adds support for the AppleTalk protocol to Linux and other Unix systems, enabling your Macs to see folders and partitions exported by Linux or Unix systems. Netatalk also enables Linux and Unix systems to print to AppleTalk printers. Unfortunately, the life span of the AppleTalk protocol is limited. Software such as Netatalk primarily is useful in environments running versions of the Macintosh operating system (MacOS) prior to Mac OS X. Mac OS X is based on Unix and can therefore use the Unix-oriented distributed filesystems (and run Samba, as well).

The previous two examples highlight the fact that microcomputer environments into which you're introducing Linux or Unix systems may not require a full-blown distributed filesystem to guarantee interoperability. However, Unix computing environments where the infrastructure must support a number of different Unix systems as well as Macintosh systems and the occasional PC are a totally different story. In these types of environments, a true, platform-independent distributed filesystem is really the only interoperability solution. I personally prefer running distributed filesystems whenever possible, simply because this provides an open-ended solution into which any type of new system easily can be added. As discussed later in this chapter, introducing a true distributed filesystem into an existing computing environment has some operational costs, but no software cost. Thanks, open source movement!

Why Interoperate?

So far, this chapter has focused on easily sharing access to data as the primary motivation for interoperability. Although this has direct and obvious benefits, other motivations for interoperability are just as important.

A fundamental benefit of interoperability that is often overlooked is the fact that interoperability lets different groups within your computing environment use different types of computer systems and therefore different software packages. This lets people get their jobs done using the systems and software best suited to the task at hand.

One of the classic complaints about Linux is that there just isn't much high-quality, user-oriented software available for it. Although many excellent software packages are already available for Linux, and software such as the GIMP (GNU Image Manipulation Program) is narrowing the graphics gap, you may need to use packages such as Quark Express or Adobe Illustrator for business reasons. By using a combination of a distributed filesystem and the Netatalk filesystem adapter, your layout and art groups can use Macs, the platform of choice for these tasks and applications, without having to worry about how they're going to back up their data or share it with the folks in prepress.

A nice side benefit of using distributed filesystems and selected filesystem adapters to let different people within your organization use different computer systems but share access to data is that this provides your organization with greater flexibility when hiring new employees. Because your networked computing environment doesn't require any specific arcane expertise, you can hire people with the artistic and business skills that you want and rely on your MIS/IT department to tie them into your distributed computing environment.

Designing an Enterprise Filesystem

Like any other project that affects your entire computing environment, putting together a distributed filesystem that ties together all the computer systems in an enterprise requires careful planning. As highlighted in the previous section, different computing environments have different requirements. Some may not even "need" a full-blown distributed filesystem. However, by discussing all your distributed filesystem choices and comparing them in terms of features, scope, performance, and ease of administration, this book is designed to give you the information you need to select the distributed filesystem that best suits your needs.

NOTE

In this section, I'll use the term *enterprise filesystem* to mean the combination of distributed filesystems and filesystem adapters that best suits the needs of your computing environment, regardless of whether it is located in a business, academic, or truly sophisticated home setting.

This section highlights the major questions that MIS/IT managers need to ask themselves to select the software to provide interoperability within any computing environment. Convincing your bosses that you should use journaled local filesystems rather than generic local Linux filesystems is usually a no-brainer, but selecting and implementing a distributed filesystem for interoperability purposes is a whole different beast. This is not just a matter of selecting the best software but also requires a careful examination of any additional requirements that a distributed computing environment may introduce—for example, personnel and capital costs associated with installing a new filesystem and migrating to it, selling your management on the benefits of changing the way your computing environment is organized, and so on.

Your mission, should you choose to accept it. . .

Selecting a Distributed Filesystem

Selecting the right distributed filesystem for your computing environment is the most important aspect of designing an enterprise filesystem. The following items provide a checklist of the major points to consider when selecting the ultimate filesystem for your computing environment:

- What computer systems are used in your computing environment? Making a careful list of these can help you identify whether you need a full-blown distributed filesystem or whether you just need to add one or more filesystem adapters to some of the systems you are already using. Having an explicit list of the computer systems used in your computing environment also can make it easy for you to verify that the distributed filesystem you select runs on all those types of systems.

- What protocols are used by the systems in your computing environment? Knowing the primary protocols used for data exchange on all your systems is straightforward, but having such a list can be handy when deciding between simply adding filesystem adapters and implementing a full-blown distributed filesystem.

- Do all these systems already come with a single networked filesystem sufficient for your needs? If all the systems in your computing environment are Unix boxes that come with NFS, that may be all you need to provide an interoperable computing environment. On the other hand, NFS may not provide the security and consistency guarantees that you need, or may not have sufficient performance to make it preferable to other distributed filesystems just because it is free on your Unix systems. Similarly, if you are trying to link Unix boxes, PCs, and Macs, you may want to evaluate using NFS plus the Samba and Netatalk filesystem adapters against the cost of purchasing NFS clients for all your PCs and Macs.

- Which distributed filesystems are available for all the types of systems in your computing environment? Are they all actively used and supported? If a specific distributed filesystem isn't available for some of the systems that you need to support, can you make do with filesystem adapters to provide interoperability for those types of systems?

- Is training available for system administrators if it should prove to be necessary? Is it only available from the distributed filesystem vendor or through third parties? Is on-site training available?

- Will you be adding new types of systems to your computing environment? If you can anticipate this sort of growth, which distributed filesystems are supported on those types of systems?

- What is the approximate size of your user community? In what ways do your users need to share access to data and storage? How well do the different distributed filesystems scale in terms of number of users, number of attached systems, and capacity for shared data and devices?

- Is there a single sign-on mechanism available for the selected filesystem and any other systems that you must use? The fewer passwords anyone has to remember, the better, as long as your computing environment is secure. Can you integrate the security mechanism used by different distributed filesystems with any networkwide security scheme that you currently are using? Distributed filesystems such as AFS and Coda come with their own authentication/login mechanisms that are supersets of those provided with most Unix systems. Can these be integrated with anything that you are currently using and must still continue to use?

Operational Issues for a Distributed Filesystem

Like anything new, adding distributed filesystems and filesystem adapters to an existing computing environment requires that MIS/IT support and operations staff learn the ins and outs of the new software. A thorough understanding of the new systems is especially important in the period immediately after the adoption of a new system because this will probably be the time during which MIS/IT staff receive the greatest number of questions and/or problem reports.

This section summarizes the most important items that MIS/IT managers must consider in terms of the impact of a distributed filesystem and filesystem adapters on their staff:

- What administrative utilities are available for various distributed filesystems and filesystem adapters? Are they compatible with your existing administrative procedures?

- What types of training on the new filesystem are available and necessary for new and existing MIS/IT staff members?

- Will you to add personnel to maintain the new distributed filesystem environment? For example, will you have to add different shifts to start doing backups at night for bandwidth reasons?

- How will the new filesystem be integrated with and affect current network dependencies in client/server applications such as databases, Lotus Notes, and so on?

- What extra security concerns does a networked filesystem introduce?

Cost/Benefit Analysis for a Distributed Filesystem

As mentioned earlier, convincing your boss that you should use journaled local filesystems rather than generic local Linux filesystems is usually a no-brainer. After you've completed any testing that you want or need to do and are ready to make the switch, converting existing local filesystems to journaled equivalents essentially costs nothing more than the time spent doing it. You can use the same hardware and software, and won't need any significant software training other than learning to use a few filesystem-specific utilities and understanding how to answer questions in yet another version of the standard system administration utilities.

For an MIS/IT organization that is used to managing local data, a few client/server applications, and perhaps even some small existing distributed filesystems, switching to an enterprise filesystem is a different matter. Even if your boss has an unlimited budget, is a techno-weenie, and immediately sees the benefits of true interoperability and centralized administration, there is bound to be a bean counter somewhere in your organization who will need to make sure that you have balanced the value of switching to a distributed system against its costs. This section identifies the most common points to consider when presenting the savings and costs associated with moving to a distributed filesystem:

- After the capital and personnel costs of implementing a distributed filesystem, your group is likely to see cost savings due to increased scalability, centralizing operations, reduced downtime due to limiting the impact of the failure of any one computer system or filesystem, ease of expansion (adding new disks to file servers, moving user directories when volumes run out of space), and so on.

- Moving to a distributed filesystem may change your requirements for future employees. Is it easy to find people who already know how to use and administer a specific distributed filesystem, or will you have to train all new MIS/IT personnel? Will you require a larger staff to manage the new distributed filesystem? Distributed filesystems often reduce the number of help desk requests that you receive, but may increase the number of people you need to prepare, deploy, and integrate computer systems. For example, the networked authentication mechanisms used by most distributed filesystems make it easy for people to reset passwords over the network, and the easy availability of backup filesystems provided by distributed filesystems such as AFS and Coda reduces the number of file/directory restores that have to be done by operations staff.

- If you are moving to a distributed filesystem, you will need to dedicate specific machines as file servers. Will you need to purchase additional hardware to do this or can you simply convert existing systems into servers without reducing the number of computer systems available to your users?

- What other new costs may be incurred by going to a distributed filesystem? Can your current network handle the additional bandwidth introduced by increasing your dependency on the network? Is it fast enough for the new user and administrative load that will be introduced? Will it be fast enough next year?

- Do you have specific applications that can benefit from the introduction of a networked filesystem? Are there any current problems or hacks that introducing a distributed filesystem may eliminate or resolve?

2

FILESYSTEMS AND INTEROPERABILITY

Overview of Journaling Filesystems

IN THIS CHAPTER

Chapter 1, "Introduction to Filesystems," introduced "journaling filesystem" as the general term for a specific type of local filesystem that helps reduce system restart times. They do this by reducing the amount of information that a system has to examine to verify the integrity of a filesystem.

This chapter begins by providing a detailed overview of how Linux identifies filesystems, verifies that they are usable, and makes them available to users. This discussion builds on the basics of standard Linux/Unix filesystem organization explained in Chapter 1. Understanding how Linux makes filesystems available to users and what's involved in verifying the structure of a "standard" Linux filesystem (ext2fs) provides a firm foundation for discussing journaling filesystems. The remainder of the chapter explains the differences between journaling and non-journaling local filesystems, shows how journaling filesystems track filesystem changes, and highlights the major reasons why these types of filesystems are becoming more common on today's computer systems.

Finding, Checking, and Mounting Filesystems

To explain many of the performance and design advantages of different types of filesystems, it's useful to first understand how a Linux system identifies the filesystems available to it; determines their types; and mounts, supports, and uses them. This section provides a general overview of these topics, which are relevant to any type of filesystem regardless of whether they are local or available over a network.

Filesystem Consistency

As discussed in Chapter 1, filesystems are the mechanism for successfully storing and retrieving data on a computer system. The data structures that define the organization of a filesystem must be correct when a filesystem is being used. To users, filesystems are hierarchical collections of files and directories. To Linux and other Unix systems, filesystems consist of many *inodes* that contain information about files and directories (known as filesystem *metadata*, data about data) and the data blocks that actually contain the directory entries and file data. It's easy to see the confusion that could arise if multiple inodes in a filesystem thought that some specific data block was a part of the file that they represented.

Suppose that you were editing a status report for your manager and I was working on a file containing my collection of ribald drinking songs. If the inode that identified the blocks in your presentation and the one that pointed to the blocks in my drinking song archive each claimed that a specific data block belonged to its file, one of us is going to be surprised when we actually look at our file.

Filesystems whose internal data structures are correct are referred to as being *consistent*. It is always the responsibility of the system that hosts a filesystem (that is, on which the filesystem is physically stored) to verify the consistency of that filesystem before making it available to the operating system and to users. This is true regardless of whether the filesystem is a standard local filesystem, a journaling filesystem, or a networked filesystem. In the case of networked filesystems, the server that exports the networked filesystem and manages the physical media on which it is stored must verify its consistency before making it available over the network.

The primary characteristics of consistent filesystems are the following:

- A bit in the filesystem's superblock is set to indicate that the filesystem was successfully unmounted when the system was last shut down.
- All the filesystem metadata is correct.

Verifying the consistency of a filesystem would be fast if those two points could be verified quickly. Unfortunately, verifying that filesystem metadata is correct actually involves checking a number of different points:

- Each allocation unit (whether it is a block or an extent) belongs only to a single file or directory, or is marked as being unused. The list of which blocks are allocated and unused (free) in a filesystem is usually stored in a bitmap for that filesystem, where each bit represents a specific data block. Filesystems that allocate and manage extents rather than just blocks also maintain information about free extents and their size and range.
- No file or directory contains a data block marked as being unused in the filesystem bitmap.
- Each file or directory in the filesystem is referenced in some other directory in that filesystem. From a user's point of view, this means that there is a directory path to each file or directory in the filesystem.
- Each file has only as many parent directories as the reference count in its inode indicates. Although each file exists only in a single physical location on the disk, multiple directories can contain references to the inode that holds information about this file. These references are known as *hard links*. The file can therefore be accessed through any of these directories, and deleting it from any of these directories decrements the link count. A file is actually deleted only when its link count is 0—in other words, when it is no longer referenced by any directory.

Verifying all these relationships may take a while if it's necessary to manually check each of them. Whether this consistency check is necessary is the fundamental difference between journaling and non-journaling filesystems.

Locating and Identifying Filesystems

When your system boots, the boot block on your primary disk identifies the root filesystem and the location of the kernel to boot. As discussed in the previous section, when your system boots, it needs to verify the consistency of each of its local filesystems. The root filesystem initially is mounted read-only for standard processes so that its consistency can be verified. After this is done, it is remounted in read-write mode, and your system verifies the existence and consistency of any other filesystems that it will be using. The list of filesystems available to your system is contained in the file /etc/fstab.

Each line in /etc/fstab provides information about one of the filesystems that should be available to your system. A sample section of an /etc/fstab file looks like the following (it will be different on each computer system):

```
LABEL=/           /             ext2      defaults                      1 1
LABEL=/boot       /boot         ext2      defaults                      1 2
LABEL=/home       /home         ext2      exec,dev,suid,rw,usrquota     1 2
/dev/cdrom        /mnt/cdrom    iso9660   noauto,owner,ro               0 0
/dev/fd0          /mnt/floppy   auto      noauto,owner                  0 0
/dev/hdb1         /opt          xfs       defaults                      1 2
/dev/hdb6         /opt2         reiserfs  exec,dev,suid,rw,notail       1 2
LABEL=/tmp        /tmp          ext2      defaults                      1 2
LABEL=/usr        /usr          ext2      defaults                      1 2
LABEL=/var        /var          ext2      defaults                      1 2
none              /proc         proc      defaults                      0 0
none              /dev/pts      devpts    gid=5,mode=620                0 0
/dev/hda7         swap          swap      defaults                      0 0
/dev/cdrom1       /mnt/cdrom1   iso9660   noauto,owner,kudzu,ro         0 0
/dev/cdrom2       /mnt/cdrom2   iso9660   noauto,owner,kudzu,ro         0 0
/dev/lvm/vol1     /books        reiserfs  exec,dev,suid,rw,notail       1 2
/dev/lvm/vol2     /proj         xfs       defaults                      1 2
```

The fields in each /etc/fstab entry (that is, each line) are the following:

- The first field is the device or remote filesystem to be mounted. This is usually the Linux device file for the partition to be mounted but also can be an entry of the form hostname:directory for networked filesystems such as NFS. Ext2 filesystems also can be identified by the name that they were assigned in the filesystem volume label when the filesystem was created. For example, the entry LABEL=/ in the example /etc/fstab file could be replaced with /dev/hda5 because that is the disk partition where my root filesystem actually lives. However, using labels is more flexible than using specific partition device files because the device file associated with a specific partition may change if the disk containing that partition is moved to another system or if other disks are added to an existing system.

- The second field is the directory on which the specified filesystem should be mounted. For special types of filesystems that should not be mounted, such as the Linux /proc filesystem, this field should contain the entry none. Dist partitions that are formatted as swap space contain the entry swap in this field.

- The third field identifies the type of filesystem. Common entries in this field are ext2 (the standard Linux local filesystem type), vfat (a Microsoft Windows partition), iso9660 (the standard CD-ROM filesystem), nfs (networked filesystems using Sun's NFS protocol), and swap (swap space). After reading this book, you will also want to use entries such as ext3 (the journaling equivalent of the ext2 filesystem), jfs (a journaling filesystem originally from IBM), reiserfs (the journaling filesystem built into the 2.4 or better Linux kernels shipped with most Linux distributions), and xfs (a journaling filesystem originally from Silicon Graphics). If a filesystem is not currently used but you want to keep an entry for it in /etc/fstab, you can put the word "ignore" in this field, and that filesystem will not be mounted, checked for consistency, and so on.

The types of filesystems that are compiled into your kernel are listed in the file /proc/filesystems, but this can be misleading. Your kernel usually also supports other types of filesystems, but as loadable modules rather than being hard wired into the kernel. For example, the /proc/filesystems file on my system contains the following entries:

```
nodev    sockfs
nodev    tmpfs
nodev    pipefs
nodev    binfmt_misc
nodev    proc
         ext2
nodev    coda
         reiserfs
         xfs
nodev    devpts
```

Filesystems whose types are prefaced by a nodev entry are not associated with physical devices but are used internally by applications and the operating system.

NOTE

Several fairly fundamental types of filesystems, such as iso9660 (CD-ROM) filesystems aren't listed. It would be highly unlikely that I wouldn't want support for CD-ROM filesystems, but because I use CDs with filesystems on them infrequently, I specified that they be supported as a loadable module when I configured and built the kernel for this system. This helps keep the kernel as small as possible without sacrificing performance. Devices supported through loadable modules work slightly slower than devices directly supported in the kernel, largely because of the overhead of locating, loading, and placing external calls to the module.

- The fourth field contains a comma-separated list of any options to the `mount` command that should be used when the filesystem is mounted. Many mount options are filesystem-specific, but some common generic ones are the following:

  - `async`—Writes to the filesystem should be done asynchronously.

  - `auto`—The filesystem should be automatically mounted when detected or when a command such as `mount -a` is executed.

  - `defaults`—Use the default options: `async`, `auto`, `dev`, `exec`, `nouser`, `rw`, `suid`.

  - `dev`—The character or block device containing the filesystem is local to the system.

  - `exec`—You can execute programs, scripts, or anything else whose permissions indicate that it is executable from that filesystem.

  - `gid=value`—Set the group ID of the mounted filesystem to the specified numeric group ID when the filesystem is mounted.

  - `noauto`—Don't automatically mount when a filesystem is detected or when the command `mount -a` is issued. Usually used with removable media such as floppies and CD-ROMs.

  - `nouser`—You must be root to mount the filesystem; the filesystem can't be mounted by any nonroot user.

  - `owner`—The ownership of the filesystem is set to the user who mounted it—usually root if the filesystem is automatically mounted by the system.

  - `ro`—Mount the filesystem read-only.

  - `rw`—Mount the filesystem read-write.

  - `suid`—Allow programs on the filesystem to change the user's user or group ID when it is executed if the user's permission bits indicate that they should do this. Be careful when using this option with imported filesystems that you don't actually administer, because running a program that sets the UID to root is a common way of hacking into a system.

  - `uid=value`—Set the user ID of the mounted filesystem to the specified numeric user ID when the filesystem is mounted.

For more information on generic options available to the `mount` command, see the man page for the `mount` command in section 8 of the online Linux manual. When discussing each of the filesystems covered in this book, I'll also explain any filesystem-specific mount options associated with that filesystem.

> **NOTE**
>
> Like the `fsck` command discussed in the next section, the `mount` command executes filesystem-specific versions of `mount` whenever necessary. For example, when filesystems of types smb, smbfs, ncp, or ncpfs are mounted (which use filesystem adapters to access DOS Server Message Block and NetWare Core Protocol filesystems), the `mount` command attempts to execute files in `/sbin` with the names `/sbin/mount.smb`, `/sbin/mount.smbfs`, `/sbin/mount.ncp`, and `/sbin/mount.ncpfs`, respectively.

- The fifth field is used by the `dump` command, a standard Linux/Unix filesystem backup command, to identify filesystems that should be backed up when the `dump` command is executed. If the fifth field contains a `0` (or is missing), the `dump` command assumes that the filesystem associated with that `/etc/fstab` entry does not need to be backed up.

- The sixth field is used by the Linux/Unix filesystem consistency checker (discussed in the next section) to identify filesystems whose consistency should be verified when the system is rebooted, and the order in which the consistency of those filesystems should be checked. If the sixth field contains a `0` (or is missing), the `fsck` program assumes that the filesystem associated with that `/etc/fstab` entry does not need to be checked.

Verifying Filesystem Consistency

Verifying that a standard filesystem is consistent requires a special utility that checks each filesystem to guarantee that all the items listed in the previous section are true. This is known as the `fsck` (filesystem consistency check) utility. (Truly ancient Unix folks like myself will fondly remember its conceptual parents, `dcheck`, `icheck`, and `ncheck`.) Each type of filesystem has its own version of `fsck` that understands the organization of a specific type of filesystem. On Linux systems, all these versions of `fsck` live in the directory `/sbin`, and typically have names of the form `fsck.filesystem-type`. For example, listing this directory on one of my Linux systems shows versions of `fsck` for ext2, ext3, minix, msdos, and ReiserFS filesystems:

```
[wvh@distfs /sbin]$ ls -al *fsck*
-rwxr-xr-x    2 root      root      40316 Jul 12   2000 dosfsck
-rwxr-xr-x    3 root      root     451240 Jun 24 04:54 e2fsck
-rwxr-xr-x    1 root      root      16572 Jun 24 04:54 fsck
lrwxrwxrwx    3 root      root     451240 Jul  1 19:48 fsck.ext2
lrwxrwxrwx    3 root      root     451240 Jul  1 19:48 fsck.ext3
-rwxr-xr-x    1 root      root      16380 Apr  8 10:12 fsck.minix
-rwxr-xr-x    2 root      root      40316 Jul 12   2000 fsck.msdos
lrwxrwxrwx    1 root      root         10 Jun 30 13:55 fsck.reiserfs -> reiserfsck
-rwxr-xr-x    1 root      root       2408 Jun  1 21:47 fsck.xfs
-rwxr-xr-x    1 root      root     221820 Mar  5 13:19 reiserfsck
```

When you restart a computer system, the fsck utility reads the list of filesystems that should be mounted and the type of each filesystem from the text file /etc/fstab, as explained in the previous section.

As mentioned in the previous section, the last field in each line of /etc/fstab indicates whether a filesystem should be checked for consistency and the order in which that consistency check should be done. A value of 0 in this field indicates that the consistency of that filesystem should not be checked. Other numeric values indicate which fsck "pass" the filesystems should be checked in. Because fsck can take a while on large or complex filesystems, multiple copies of fsck can run at the same time and can therefore check different filesystems in parallel. In the example /etc/fstab shown in the previous section, the root filesystem / would be checked first, and then the other filesystems on different disks would be checked in parallel. Filesystems on a single disk are checked sequentially—checking them in parallel would be slow and a waste of perfectly good disk head movement.

The fsck program then checks whether the filesystem's clean bit is set. If this bit is set, fsck does no further checking and proceeds to the next filesystem. If this bit is not set, fsck begins the potentially laborious process of verifying (and correcting) that filesystem by executing the specific version of fsck associated with that type of filesystem.

Verifying the Consistency of a Non-Journaling (ext2) Filesystem

On non-journaling filesystems, the fsck program has to actually check the integrity of and relationships between all the inodes and data blocks in the filesystem. This can take a substantial amount of time, especially for larger non-journaling filesystems. Eliminating this sort of delay when restarting a system is one of the primary motivations for adopting journaling filesystems. However, even more important than eliminating the time required to do this sort of exhaustive checking of a filesystem is eliminating the need for this sort of consistency checking. If you eliminate the need for this sort of checking, you get reduced startup time for free. More about this later.

This section discusses the version of fsck used to check and repair the consistency of ext2 filesystems. This is the program /sbin/e2fsck, usually executed by the /sbin/fsck wrapper program as fsck.ext2.

All versions of fsck work by making a number of different passes over the filesystem they are checking. Checking the consistency of a filesystem in multiple steps has some distinct advantages:

- Enabling a single pass to focus on verifying or collecting a specific aspect of filesystem consistency. This simplifies the operation of the program (as well as simplifying debugging and development!).

- Minimizing the resources necessary to perform any single consistency check. Memory allocation by `fsck` tends to grow during the first few passes, as additive information about the filesystem is collected.

- Simplifying collecting the information necessary for full consistency checking. Each subsequent pass can capitalize on the information collected in the previous one.

The ext2 version of `fsck` is designed to minimize both head movement during disk reads and the number of times that data has to be read from the disk. The five passes of the ext2 version of `fsck` are the following:

- Pass 1 verifies the consistency of all the inodes in the specified filesystem. This pass checks whether the mode of the file or directory associated with that inode is valid, all block references contain valid block numbers, the size and block count fields of the inode are correct, and no data block is associated with multiple inodes. During this pass, `fsck` gathers three types of information about the filesystem:

  - It builds bitmaps that identify the inodes in the filesystem that are in use, are directories, are regular files, and so on.

  - It builds bitmaps that identify the blocks in the filesystem that are in use and any that are claimed by multiple inodes.

  - It identifies the data blocks associated with each inode that represents a directory.

  The easiest way to think of the bitmaps that `fsck` constructs is as arrays in which each bit is a boolean value associated with the inode whose number corresponds to that bit's offset into the bitmap.

  If the bitmap that identifies blocks claimed by multiple inodes is not empty, `fsck` invokes three "sub-steps" of pass 1, known as passes 1B, 1C, and 1D. Pass 1B rescans the data blocks associated with each inode in the filesystem and builds a complete list of the blocks that are claimed by multiple inodes and the inodes that claim each of them. Pass 1C traverses the entire filesystem hierarchy to identify the path to each file or directory associated with an inode that claims a disk block also claimed by another. Pass 1D prompts the user as to how each duplication should be resolved: either by copying the duplicated block and giving each file or directory a copy, or by simply deleting the affected file or directory.

- Pass 2 checks each directory in the filesystem, identifying them using the directory bitmap constructed in pass 1 (rather than having to reread the disk). For each directory, pass 2 verifies that

  - The length of the directory entry and file/directory name are both valid.

  - The inode number is greater than 1 and less than the total number of inodes in the filesystem.

- The inode number refers to an inode actually in use (as determined by checking the bitmap of used inodes constructed in pass 1).
- The first entry in the directory is ., and the inode associated with that entry is the inode of that directory.
- The second entry in the directory is ...

Note that all the information verified in pass 2 can be checked by examining either the information collected in pass 1 or an inode. Pass 2 therefore does not require any disk I/O other than reading the directory inodes in the filesystem. Pass 2 itself collects the inode number of the parent inode for each directory inode in the filesystem (the inode referenced by the .. entry) but does not do any verification of those values.

- Pass 3 verifies the directory structure within the filesystem by marking the root inode for the filesystem as done, and then examining every other directory inode in the filesystem, using the information about its parent inode that was collected in pass 2 to walk up the filesystem from that inode until it reaches a directory inode that is marked done. If this is unsuccessful or a directory inode is visited twice when tracing up the filesystem, the fsck application disconnects the inode from the filesystem and connects it to the lost+found directory located at the top of each filesystem for this purpose.
- Pass 4 checks the reference counts for all inodes in the filesystem, comparing the link counts calculated in pass 1 to values computed during passes 2 and 3. Any files that have a link count of zero are connected to the lost+found directory.
- Pass 5 verifies the summary information about the filesystem contained in the superblock against information calculated during the previous passes and compares the block and inode bitmaps constructed in previous passes against those located in the filesystem header. If these differ, pass 5 overwrites the on-disk bitmaps with those constructed during this run of fsck.

Depending on the option with which you've called fsck, it either corrects problems automatically, prompts whether it should correct problems that it has detected, or simply reports problems without doing anything about them. One of the more interesting aspects of fsck is how it handles files and directories that are detected but that are either not linked into the filesystem anywhere or located in a directory whose inode or indirect blocks were damaged so severely that they could not be corrected. Files and directories of this sort are moved to that filesystem's lost+found directory, which is a subdirectory of the root of all ufs, ext2, and standard Unix-like filesystems.

The lost+found directory is created by the mkfs command when you create these types of filesystems (it usually gets inode 11, though this isn't mandatory) and initially consists of an empty directory that has a relatively large number of preallocated directory entries (16384 for ext2 filesystems, by default). These directory slots are preallocated because of the chance that it may be necessary to link many files and subdirectories into this directory in the event of a major filesystem problem. It certainly would be "disappointing" to be running fsck, have it detect major filesystem corruption, find many disconnected files and directories, and have no free directory entries to which to link them. Directory entries are preallocated in lost+found directories because, in terms of anti-Darwinian survival traits, allocating additional indirect blocks to an existing directory when trying to resolve massive filesystem problems is right up there with adjusting the trigger mechanism on a shotgun while staring down the barrel.

If changes have been made to the root filesystem when it is checked by fsck, the system is automatically rebooted at this point. If changes were made to any other filesystem, the filesystem is simply marked as clean and can thus be mounted after the consistency of all filesystems has been checked and repaired.

Getting Information About Filesystems

If you're interested enough about filesystems to read this book, you're probably already familiar with the Linux and Unix commands used to retrieve information about the size and contents of a filesystem. However, just in case, this section provides a quick overview of the commands commonly used to retrieve this information and their most popular options.

Using the df Command

The df (disk free) command provides information about one or more mounted filesystems. By default, without any arguments, it displays the following information about all mounted filesystems:

- The device associated with the filesystem
- The total size of the filesystem in 1 KB blocks
- The amount of space used on the filesystem
- The amount of space on the filesystem still available to users
- The percentage of the filesystem currently used
- The directory on which the filesystem is mounted

NOTE

When administering a Linux system, you may occasionally see the df command report that 100 percent of a filesystem is in use even though you can still read and write files on that filesystem. This is due to the fact that most filesystems reserve a certain amount of space for use during crises such as when a filesystem fills up. Otherwise,

continues

any user who was editing a file when someone else accidentally filled up the filesystem could easily lose his work. The amount of space reserved for such unhappy occasions is set by the command used to create the filesystem. For example, ext2 filesystems reserve 5 percent of the space on an ext2 filesystem when it is created. (You can change this percentage using the `mke2fs` program's `-m` option.) For information about the amount of space reserved by other types of filesystems, see the man page for the application used to create filesystems of that type.

The following is sample output from running the `df` command on one of my systems:

```
[wvh@journal wvh]$ df
Filesystem           1k-blocks      Used Available Use% Mounted on
/dev/hda5            12389324   2373784   9386196  21% /
/dev/hda1               54416      4357     47250   9% /boot
/dev/hdc1             5119940     32840   5087100   1% /reiser_test
/dev/hdc2             5115336       144   5115192   1% /xfs_test
/dev/test/vol1        3145628     32840   3112788   2% /lvm_reiser_test
/dev/test/vol2        5238080       144   5237936   1% /lvm_xfs_test
```

When used on other types of Unix systems, the df command may report filesystem sizes in terms of different-sized blocks. For this reason, it's a good idea to get into the habit of executing the df command on any Unix system as "df -k", which forces the output to be given in terms of 1K blocks (even though this is the default on Linux systems). You don't want to find yourself accidentally miscalculating the amount of space remaining on a filesystem just because the df command for that version of Unix uses a different default block size.

Some other options often used with the `df` command are shown in Table 3.1.

TABLE 3.1 Options used with the `df` command

df Option	Meaning
-h	Displays size information in human-readable form, such as 1.2G, 53M, 348K, and so on
-I	Displays size and usage information in terms of inodes rather than data blocks
-l	Limits the `df` command to only displaying information about local filesystems
-m	Displays size information in megabytes

These are my favorite `df` options or the ones that I've seen people using with some frequency. For complete information about all the options available to the df command, see the online manual page.

You can follow the df command and its options with the mountpoint of a specific filesystem if you want information only about that filesystem. You also can provide the name of the device on which a specific filesystem is located to get information about that filesystem regardless of whether it is mounted.

Using the du command

The df command is primarily used by system administrators to verify that the amount of space remaining on various partitions is sufficient for the needs of their users. Both users and system administrators often use the related du (disk usage) command to find out the amount of space used by specific files and directories. Although you can obtain this information about files by simply using ls, the du command provides some convenient options for summarizing the disk usage associated with all the files and subdirectories of a specific directory. These options make it easy to identify users (or system directories) using an inappropriately large amount of disk space. You can largely eliminate the ability of users to use more disk space than they "should" by using quotas on the filesystems where users can create files and directories, but that's another topic that I will discuss later in this section.

Popular options for the du command are shown in Table 3.2.

TABLE 3.2   Options used with the du command

du Option	Meaning
-c	Lists the disk usage of the specified files and directories and then displays a total of those values.
-h	Displays size in human-readable form such as 1.2G, 53M, 348K, and so on.
-k	Displays size information in terms of 1K blocks.
-l	Counts the size of each hard link to another file. For example, if a certain directory contains six hard links to a specific file, using the -l option counts the size of the file each time a link is encountered and adds that to the total disk space associated with a directory. By default, multiple hard links to a file are ignored in a disk usage summary, and the size of that file is only added to the disk usage total once.
-L	Follows symbolic links when calculating sizes. By default, the size of a symbolic link is the size of the link itself, which is essentially the length of the name of the file or directory to which the link points.
-S	Does not include the size of subdirectories. This option is useful to determine the amount of disk space consumed by all the files in the current directory only.

TABLE 3.2 Continued

du Option	Meaning
-s	Only prints a summary of the disk usage for files and directories specified as arguments to the du command. By default—with no arguments—the du -s command summarizes disk usage in the current directory.

For a complete list of all the options available for use with the du command (including some truly arcane ones!), see the online manual page.

Introduction to Journaling Filesystems

Some of the more inspired among us may have kept (or still keep) a journal to record the changes in our lives. Journals and diaries help us keep track of exactly what's happening to us, and also often come in handy when we need to look back and see what was happening at a specific point in time. Though not nearly so melodramatic as personal journals, this is almost exactly the same model used by journaling filesystems, which keep a record of the changes made to the filesystem in a special part of the disk called a journal or log. My analogy between filesystems and life breaks down at this point, because journaling filesystems record prospective changes to that filesystem in the log before they actually perform those operations on the filesystem. If the computer system crashes while actually making those changes to the filesystem, the operating system can use the information in the log to bring the filesystem up-to-date by replaying the log, which is usually done when it remounts the journaling filesystem or verifies its consistency.

After a computer crashes, as discussed earlier in this chapter, the integrity of standard local filesystems must be verified by performing an exhaustive examination of all the data and data structures that they contain. Changes to the filesystem may only have been partially written to disk, and the operating system has no way to determine whether all writes to a filesystem completed successfully other than by completely checking the integrity of the filesystem. This sort of check is usually unnecessary after an orderly shutdown or restart of a computer system because shutdown and restart procedures always flush all pending writes to disk and mark a filesystem as clean before unmounting it. Filesystems marked as clean do not have to be checked when a computer restarts.

Unlike standard filesystems, journaling filesystems can be made consistent by replaying any actions in the log that are not marked as having been written to disk. As discussed later, these actions range from a record of any changes to file and directory metadata (for example, files and directories that were created, deleted, moved, or whose size changed) to a complete record of the changes to the data in any file. It is not always possible to restore every change made to a journaling filesystem, because information about some of them may be incompletely written to the log. However, you can almost always safely assume that the journaling filesystem is consistent and can be brought up to date by re-executing the pending changes that were recorded in a few log records, rather than having to examine the whole filesystem. As filesystems and disks grow larger and larger, the time it would take to verify the integrity of a filesystem grows, as do the potential time savings gained by using a journaling filesystem.

> **NOTE**
>
> The terms "logging" and "journaling" are usually used interchangeably when referring to filesystems that record changes to filesystem structures and data to minimize restart time and maximize consistency. I tend to use the term "journaling," because this makes it hard to confuse journaling filesystems with log-based filesystems, which are a completely different animal. Log-based filesystems use a log-oriented representation for the filesystem itself and also usually require a garbage collection process to reclaim space internally. Journaling filesystems use a log, which is simply a distinct portion of the filesystem and disk, and can even be a file within the filesystem. Where and how logs are stored and used are explained later in this section. Journaling filesystems themselves usually follow the more classic filesystem organization explained in Chapter 1, though they often use faster algorithms and heuristics for sorting and locating files, directories, and data.

Logs are the key feature of journaling filesystems. As mentioned earlier, information about filesystem changes is written to the log (logged) before those changes actually are made to a filesystem. Traditional filesystems with fixed disk structures but no journaling capability, such as ext2, have to do synchronous writes to the filesystem to guarantee the integrity of the changes that they are making. The ext2 filesystem, in particular, uses some clever mechanisms for bunching related writes together to minimize head movement on the disk and also to minimize the amount of time that access to the filesystem is literally paused while those writes are taking place.

Because the filesystem must always be consistent when it is being used, there are almost always some number of pending writes held in buffers by the operating system. Though modern Linux and Unix systems automatically flush all pending writes to all filesystems when the system is being shut down or rebooted, older Unix systems (and early versions of Linux with more primitive types of filesystems) didn't always do such a good job. This is why you'll often see older Unix sysadmins religious type the sync command (which flushes all pending writes to disk) a few times before shutting down or rebooting a system—it's essentially the Unix version of saying a few "Hail Marys."

The ext2 filesystem is a remarkably high-performance local filesystem. One indication of this is the fact that the filesystem itself has been ported to various microkernel environments such as GNU Hurd and Mach. Although simplifying porting code to new environments is part of the goal of Open Source software, people don't bother unless the code in question is well-written, powerful, and useful. When writing files, the ext2 filesystem preallocates a few extra contiguous blocks whenever possible to minimize fragmentation as files that are being edited continue to grow.

Whenever possible, the ext2 filesystem also minimizes the distance between the inode for a file and the data blocks that contain the file data to minimize head movement as much as possible when accessing files. The ext2 filesystem also uses the idea of block groups, logical subsets of the data storage available on a disk, to provide performance optimizations. Block groups are conceptually related to the cylinder groups used in earlier high-performance filesystems such as the Berkeley Fast File System (FFS). Block groups can be viewed logically as filesystems within a filesystem because they contain their own superblocks to help localize information about free and used blocks into smaller units, reduce the size of the bitmaps that reflect free and used blocks, and simplify allocating data blocks as close as possible to the inode identifying the file associated with them.

Regardless of the optimization implemented in the ext2 filesystem, writes to the filesystem still have to be synchronous with other access to the filesystem at some point. Multiple users accessing multiple files created at widely different points in time will still have to write data that is probably located all over the disk, pausing access to the filesystem while widely separated head movement takes place. Although writing pending filesystem changes to a log and then later writing those same changes to the filesystem essentially causes two units of information to be written for each single write destined for the filesystem, only writes to the log have to be synchronous with access to the filesystem.

Migrating logged changes to the actual filesystem can largely be done asynchronously, except when another process requests access to a file or directory for which changes are already pending in the log. In this case, the pending changes in the log must be written to disk before the new process can be granted access to that file or directory. Journaling filesystems also can offset much of the additional time required by "double writes" by clever organization and use of the log itself, as explained later in this chapter.

The next few sections discuss the type of information stored in a log, where logs themselves are stored and how they are written to, and how journaling filesystems use log information during normal operation and when a system is restarted.

Contents of a Journaling Filesystem Log

Two different approaches to journaling are used by different filesystems, each with its own advantages and disadvantages:

- The log contains only a record of the changes made to filesystem metadata associated with each write operation.
- The log contains a record of the changes to both file data and filesystem metadata associated with each write operation.

The common denominator of logging changes to filesystem metadata is what guarantees the integrity of a journaling filesystems. Even after a system crash, the structure of files, directories, and the filesystem can be made consistent by re-executing any pending changes that are completely described in the log. Log entries in the log usually are transactional, meaning that the beginning and end of each single change is recorded because related sets of changes must either be completely performed or must not have been performed at all. For example, assume that I save a new version of a file that I am editing. This causes the following things to happen in the filesystem (though not necessarily in this order):

- New blocks are allocated to hold the new data (this always happens first).
- The newly allocated blocks are marked as being used in the filesystem.
- The new file data is written to the newly allocated blocks on disk.
- The inode or indirect block identifying the chain of data blocks associated with the file is updated to include the new blocks.
- The time stamps for when the file was last accessed and written are updated.

Aside from logging these events, the log would contain information that indicated that all these events were associated with each other. If your computer crashed at this exact moment, you would either want all these things to happen or none of them to occur. Marking blocks as used that were not actually written to disk would waste space and also just be wrong. The actions associated with each filesystem change are therefore referred to as being *atomic*—all of them must occur or none of them can.

Continuing with this example, a journaling filesystem that only logged changes to filesystem metadata would have a record of all these changes except for the actual contents of the new blocks. Replaying only atomic metadata would guarantee the consistency of the filesystem, but the modified file might contain garbage at the end because the new information written to it was not logged. To be completely safe, logs that keep a record of changes to file data must also contain a record of the information present before changes are made to the file. This provides an "undo" record that enables a journaling filesystem to erase changes that it made on the behalf of transactions that did not complete.

The more information you write to the log, the more time required to perform those writes, especially because writes to the log must be done synchronously to guarantee their integrity. The flip side of this coin is that storing both file and directory data and metadata changes increases the extent to which replaying the log gives you an exact picture of all the changes to the filesystem made up to the point at which the system crashed. From a user's point of view, this reduces the chance that changes that the user made to her data will not be visible when the system comes back up and her directory is available again.

The journaling filesystems described in the rest of this book take different approaches to the question of whether to log modified file data, directory data, and metadata, or simply to log metadata changes. Each chapter identifies the approach taken by that specific filesystem.

Where Logs Are Stored

Just as different journaling filesystems store different types of information in their logs, they also store those logs in different places. This section provides an overview of various log storage locations and the advantages and disadvantages of each.

The simplest place to store a log is as an actual file within the filesystem to which you are logging changes. This is the approach taken by the ext3 journaling filesystem, largely because a primary goal of the ext3 filesystem is to add journaling capabilities while otherwise maintaining compatibility with an existing type of filesystem, in this case ext2. Storing the journal as a file within a filesystem has two obvious performance problems. First, at some level, writing to the log has to be done through standard filesystem calls, and second, if the filesystem that contains the log is damaged somehow, you may lose the log. This is especially true for ext3 filesystems because they essentially can be summed up by the following equation:

ext3 = ext2 + journal

A general problem with storing the log within a filesystem that it is keeping track of is that this can be slow due to the fact that writes to the log may compete for disk head movement with writes to the filesystem.

A second place to store the log is in a special portion of the filesystem not accessible to user programs. This enables you to use custom calls to write to the log in an optimized fashion, speeding up performance. This also substantially reduces the chance that the log will be lost if the filesystem is damaged because the log is associated with the filesystem but is stored as a specially formatted section rather than a file. However, this approach still has the problem that that writes to the log may compete for disk head movement with writes to the filesystem. In this case, however, storing the journaling filesystem within a logical volume can eliminate this competition if the log and data portions of the filesystem end up being stored on different physical devices. At the moment, this is almost impossible to guarantee, but it's something to consider for the future.

The final location for storing the log is outside the filesystem in a dedicated portion of some disk drive. This removes both the problems of corruption to the filesystem extending to the log and of log writes competing with filesystem writes for disk head movement (as long as the journaling filesystem and the log are stored on different physical devices).

The journaling filesystems described in the rest of this book store their logs in different locations. Each chapter identifies the approach taken by that specific journaling filesystem and discusses its advantages and disadvantages.

Verifying the Consistency of a Journaling Filesystem

Long-time Unix fans are used to thinking of the filesystem consistency checker as the application that guarantees the integrity of a filesystem during the boot process. This isn't true for journaling filesystems, which need only scan the log and re-execute any transactions that are completely present in the log but not marked as completed. Journaling filesystems are automatically brought up-to-date when they are mounted. The kernel code for each journaling filesystem replays any necessary portions of the log before it attaches them to the Linux filesystem.

The Linux boot process has certain expectations about how filesystems are verified to be consistent. Filesystems are generally marked as dirty when they are mounted, with the expectation that they will be marked as clean (not dirty) when they are unmounted. At boot time, the fsck wrapper executes the appropriate version of fsck for each filesystem that is to be checked. If the filesystem is not dirty, versions of fsck, such as fsck.ext2 (which is a hard link to e2fsck), report general statistics about that filesystem and then exit.

Because checking the consistency of a journaling filesystem is usually unnecessary, the best way of avoiding an unnecessary fsck is to mark journaling filesystems as not needing to have their consistency verified in the /etc/fstab file (by setting the sixth field to a 0). (Some journaling filesystems, such as JFS, replay the log when their fsck program is run rather than when they are mounted.) This is often overlooked, so most journaling filesystems therefore include an fsck utility with a name of the form fsck.filesystem-type so that it can be correctly called by the standard /sbin/fsck wrapper. The journaling filesystems discussed in this book take different approaches to what these "journaling fscks" do if executed because a journaling filesystem is still marked as dirty.

The following list summarizes the behavior of the versions of fsck that accompany the journaling filesystems discussed in this book:

- /sbin/fsck.ext3 is a symbolic link to /sbin/e2fsck, which is the fsck utility for both ext2 and ext3 filesystems (because they're essentially the same thing). If e2fsck is executed as fsck.ext3, it tries to mount and umount the filesystem to cause the kernel code to replay the journal and fix anything that needs to be fixed when attaching the filesystem.

- fsck.jfs is a real program that replays the transaction log and continues to check the filesystem if it is still marked as dirty.

- fsck.reiserfs may not exist depending on the Linux distribution that you are using, but I always create it as a symbolic link to /sbin/reiserfsck just for good form. reiserfsck requires that you type "Yes" to run it, which always fails during the automatic boot process, so it is never really executed.

- fsck.xfs is my absolute favorite. Whoever came up with this approach not only has a lot of faith in his kernel code but also has a great sense of humor. Here's the online manual page for fsck.xfs:

```
fsck.xfs(8)                                              fsck.xfs(8)

NAME
        fsck.xfs - do nothing, successfully

SYNOPSIS
        fsck.xfs [ ...]

DESCRIPTION
        fsck.xfs is called by the generic Linux fsck(8) program at
        startup to check and repair an XFS filesystem.  XFS  is  a
        journaling  filesystem  and  performs recovery at mount(8)
        time if necessary, so fsck.xfs simply exits  with  a  zero
        exit status.

FILES
        /etc/fstab.

SEE ALSO
        fsck(8), fstab(5), xfs(5).
```

That just about says it all.

> **NOTE**
>
> You will only have the fsck.xfs man page after installing the XFS utilities, as explained in Chapter 7, "SGI's XFS Journaling Filesystem."

Advantages of Journaling Filesystems

Although some of the advantages of journaling filesystems have been discussed earlier, this section summarizes the most important performance and reliability improvements provided by journaling filesystems. These are

- Faster system restart time after a crash because the computer does not have to examine each filesystem in its entirety to guarantee its consistency. Journaling filesystems can be made consistent by simply replaying outstanding, complete entries in the log. Incomplete entries in the log are simply discarded when the log is replayed.

- Greater flexibility. Journaling filesystems often create and allocate inodes as they are needed, rather than preallocating a specific number of inodes when the filesystem is created. This removes limitations on the number of files and directories that can be created on that partition. Not having to manage lists of inodes that have not yet been allocated also reduces some of the overhead associated with maintaining filesystem metadata and reduces the overhead involved if you subsequently want to change the size of a journaling filesystem.

- Faster file and directory access. All the journaling filesystems discussed in this book use more sophisticated algorithms for storing and accessing files and directories than do traditional non-journaling filesystems. The JFS, ReiserFS, and XFS journaling filesystems all use advanced data structures such as B-Trees, B+Trees, or B*Trees to speed up looking up and storing inodes.

- Writing to the log can be optimized. Like all filesystem updates made by non-journaling filesystems, writes to the log used by a journaling filesystem must be made synchronously. However, the logs used by journaling filesystems typically can be written to more quickly than a filesystem itself for two main reasons: they can be written to in raw fashion rather than having to go through the filesystem, and log writes almost always consist of appending data rather than inserting it. Most logs are preallocated, fixed-size, circular, and use custom read and write routines.

3

OVERVIEW OF
JOURNALING
FILESYSTEMS

The ext3 Journaling Filesystem

IN THIS CHAPTER

The ext3 journaling filesystem is a natural choice to begin the part of this book that discusses journaling filesystems. The ext3 filesystem is a fascinating and unique example of a journaling filesystem that maintains backward compatibility with a nonjournaling filesystem. The ext3 filesystem was designed to make it as easy as possible to add journaling capabilities to existing ext2 filesystems.

This chapter begins by discussing the origins and structure of the ext3 filesystem and how it differs from the ext2 filesystem. It then discusses the auxiliary software used with ext3 filesystems and how to add support for ext3 filesystems to a Linux system where it is not already present. The chapter concludes by discussing the most common administrative tasks associated with ext3 filesystems and how to install, use, and administer ext3 filesystems.

Overview

Filesystems are the most critical portion of any computer system. As mentioned earlier in this book, it's easier to overlook instability in any other aspect of a computer system than it is to lose faith in the filesystem where you and other users actually store your data. Any filesystem can "lose" data on rare occasions where files are being edited and the computer system crashes, but this obviously must be the exception to the rule. In general, when users store data on a computer system, they expect to be able to find that information the next time they use the system. WORN filesystems (write once, read never) have never been popular with anyone.

The primary concern when adding a new type of filesystem to your computer system and committing actual user data to that filesystem is its reliability. The VFS layer of most modern Linux and Unix systems makes it relatively easy to add a new type of filesystem to existing computer systems by simply plugging it in, but beneath this layer is a huge amount of new code in which potential problems may lurk. The benchmarks used in this book to help evaluate the performance of different types of filesystems barely scratch the surface of the types of testing that precede the adoption of any new type of filesystem to computer systems on which users must actually get work done. At the same time, all progress involves hard work and occasional pain—you can't move forward by standing still.

The ext3 filesystem development team took a unique approach to creating a new type of journaling filesystem. Because the ext2 filesystem is well understood, stable, and thoroughly trusted by anyone who has ever saved data on a Linux system, the developers decided that the easiest way to add a journaling filesystem to Linux was to add journaling capabilities to the ext2 filesystem. This provides some unique advantages for developing and implementing the new journaling filesystem:

- The development team working on the new filesystem can leverage the years of development and testing that went into the development of the ext2 filesystem.

- The new filesystem can continue to use the excellent utilities that have been developed to analyze, repair, and fine-tune ext2 filesystems.

- The new filesystem can instantly take advantage of any improvements, enhancements, and fixes made to the existing ext2 filesystem.

- The process of migrating existing ext2 filesystems to the new filesystem is almost instantaneous, administratively simple, and (if necessary) reversible.

According to Dr. Stephen Tweedie, the leader of the ext3 development team and primary designer of the ext3 filesystem, the first step in the development of the ext3 filesystem was making a copy of the source code for the ext2 filesystem and changing all the references to "ext2" to "ext3."

The ext3 journaling filesystem is structurally identical to the standard Linux ext2 filesystem with the exception of the file necessary to contain the journal itself. Obviously, the internals of every filesystem update operation are different to actually do journaling, but the physical layout of the filesystem on disk is identical between the two. The inode and related filesystem data structures used in the ext3 filesystem are the same as those in the ext2 filesystem. The fact that the ext3 filesystem is 100 percent compatible with the existing ext2 filesystem makes it possible to convert existing ext2 filesystems to ext3 without reformatting the partition or logical volume on which an existing ext2 filesystem is located.

TIP
One of the most time-consuming aspects of adding a journaling filesystem to an existing computer system is migrating data from existing partitions to journaling filesystem partitions. The ext3 journaling filesystem eliminates the need to do this by providing backward compatibility with an existing filesystem. This makes it well worth considering even if just from an operational point of view. Using the procedures described later in this chapter, you can quickly convert an existing ext2 filesystem to ext3 and guarantee that your system recognizes the filesystem as an ext3 filesystem when it is mounted.

4

THE EXT3
JOURNALING
FILESYSTEM

As the standard filesystem for Linux systems everywhere, the ext2 filesystem already supports many special features designed to help provide data security and reliability in the event of a system crash. For example, you can use the `chattr` (change attribute) command's `-S` option to set a bit on specific ext2 directories to guarantee that metadata updates to those directories will be made synchronously, rather than ext2's default behavior of asynchronous updating. (Synchronous updates are written to disk before any other operations on that filesystem are performed. Asynchronous updates are written to disk whenever the computer and filesystem can find the time to do so.) Although this has a slight impact on performance, this is an important feature for directories that are updated frequently and whose consistency is important to many users. Good examples of these sorts of directories are the central directories used by news servers and mail transfer agents.

Aside from the performance impact, features such as these also require that you manually identify these sorts of directories during installation and tweak them accordingly. It's difficult to automate directory-specific optimizations because applications such as different mail and news servers use different directories. Similarly, sophisticated directory-level settings such as these force all operations on these directories to be synchronous, even if only a subset of the operations on those directories actually require this sort of guarantee. For information on related per-file and per-directory journaling modes for the ext3 filesystem, see "Setting Per-File and Directory Journaling Modes" later in this chapter.

The ext3 filesystem removes the need to tweak specific directories and filesystems by globally adding consistency guarantees through its journaling capabilities. To maintain compatibility with ext2 filesystems and to be able to automatically take advantage of enhancements made to the ext2 filesystem itself, the ext3 filesystem is largely implemented through a logging/journaling layer written by the ext3 team and implemented as a standalone subsystem in the Linux kernel. This journaling subsystem is known as JBD, for the *journaling block device* subsystem. (It was originally known as the *journaling file subsystem*, or JFS, which tended to generate more confusion than anything else due to other uses of the acronym.)

> ## NOTE
>
> The most clever aspect of implementing the ext3 JBDjournaling layer as an independent kernel subsystem is that this does not limit its use to the ext3 filesystem. Other filesystems and server applications can easily integrate calls to this subsystem into their code. Not only is this an elegant implementation, but it continues to highlight the benefits of open source operating systems. Everyone can take advantage of new features and subsystems such as JBD because everyone has access to the source code, can see enhancements as they are added, and can easily identify their application programming interface (API).

To use the JBD subsystem with a specific filesystem, you first register a journal that can be identified either by inode number or by name. Being able to register journals by name enables you to store the journal for each filesystem on any device, not necessarily the same device on which the filesystem that is being journaled is located. This provides several potential benefits:

- Improves performance by writing filesystem journaling information to devices that are faster than the disks on which your filesystem is located.

- Reduces disk use by writing the journaling information for multiple filesystems to a single, fast device.

- Improves performance by minimizing disk head movement on a journaling filesystem by decoupling journal updates from updates to the filesystem itself. Because journal updates are sequential and the journal is circular and reused, this also minimizes disk head movement associated with updating the journal.

- Maximizes the usability and stability of the journal itself because this isolates the journal from damage or corruption of the disk or partition on which a journaling filesystem is located.

The flip side of the possible performance improvements provided by using a separate logging device is the short-term catastrophe that arises when journaling filesystems log to a different device, and that device fails. The best preventative medicine for this situation is to always keep a spare disk of exactly the same type handy. You can use the dd program to duplicate the log drive (with all the journaling filesystems cleanly unmounted and the system in single-user mode) to produce a usable clone of the log drive that you can swap in if the original fails. You can also use hardware RAID to maintain a live copy of the log drive, but you should carefully investigate the performance impact of doing so before simply adopting hardware RAID as a solution.

The ext3 JBDsubsystem provides transactional logging similar to that originally developed for use by databases. As used by the ext3 filesystem and explained later in this chapter, you can specify whether you want to log all changes to both file data and metadata or whether you simply want to log metadata changes. Regardless of which of these you select, the ext3 JBD subsystem guarantees the atomicity of the changes associated with a specific filesystem update. It does this by stamping all log records with an identifier for the transaction with which they are associated and by using specific types of log records that indicate that a transaction has been committed.

For performance reasons, the ext3 JBD subsystem uses a write-behind mechanism that caches all the transactions associated with each filesystem update but guarantees that either all of them will be written to the journal or none of them will be. When absolutely necessary, this default write-behind behavior can be overridden by applications that use directories that are marked as requiring synchronous updates or by opening files in synchronous mode (O_SYNC), but the performance implications of forcing synchronous filesystem updates before returning control to an application are straightforward, negative, and often impolite.

4

THE EXT3
JOURNALING
FILESYSTEM

> **NOTE**
>
> There are two basic types of transactional logging: redo and undo. The primary difference between these two is how quickly modified data is available in the journaling database or filesystem. Redo logging means that changes to data are recorded in the log before actually being made on disk. If the system crashes after a transaction was committed to the log but before updates were actually made to the on-disk database or filesystem, replaying the log when the system reboots causes the updates to occur.
>
> Any transactions that did not commit will not have actually made changes to the database or filesystem. Undo logging means that updates to the filesystem essentially occur in parallel with log entries. If the system crashes before a transaction is committed, the log must provide sufficient information to undo any changes associated with uncommitted transactions. When using undo logging, log entries must therefore record the state of data or metadata before changes were made, as well as the changes that are being made. Most journaling filesystems, including ext3, use redo logging.

Selecting between logging all data and metadata changes (the ext3 filesystem's *journaled* mode) or simply logging metadata changes (the ext3 filesystem's *writeback* mode) is done through mount options supplied when an ext3 filesystem is mounted. Logging changes to both data and metadata is both more robust and substantially slower than logging metadata changes only. It is more robust because it includes a complete record of changes to all filesystem data in the log; it is slower because each committed filesystem update actually causes two sets of writes—the first set to the log when all the pending changes are logged, and the second set when those changes are actually made to the filesystem.

The ext3 filesystem's third logging mode, *ordered* logging, provides most of the guarantees of fully journaled data mode without the performance penalties inherent in that mode. It does this by flushing all data associated with a transaction to the disk before the transaction itself commits. This guarantees that file data is always updated before related metadata is updated on disk, so file data is always consistent with any log records that are replayed after a system restart.

The most obvious considerations for synchronizing updates when designing a journaling filesystem or journaling subsystem are related to updating existing files and directories. Deleting files and directories in journaling filesystems presents its own set of concerns. The ext3 JBD subsystem includes many sophisticated features specifically oriented toward guaranteeing consistency throughout delete operations. These include

- Preventing the disk blocks associated with files and directories that have been deleted from being reused before the transactions associated with those delete operations have been committed

- Logging the state of the bitmaps that identify free blocks in a journaling filesystem

- Providing a special pass when replaying log records that identifies files and directories that have been deleted in committed transactions and avoids replaying any log records associated with those files and directories

The ext3 filesystem and the JBD subsystem that it uses are sophisticated, well-designed additions to the core feature set of modern versions of Linux. The ext3 filesystem development team and specifically its leader, Dr. Stephen Tweedie, have written papers and made many presentations at Linux conferences discussing the details of its implementation and the various considerations that went into its design. For detailed information about the design, implementation, and internals of the ext3 filesystem, these provide more information than would be palatable here.

NOTE

My favorite discussion of the ext3 filesystem is a presentation by Stephen Tweedie that can be found online at `http://olstrans.sourceforge.net/release/OLS2000-ext3/OLS2000-ext3.html`, to which this overview of the ext3 filesystem owes a great deal.

TIP

If you use the ext3 filesystem or are simply interested in its current status, the most up-to-date resource on the Web related to the ext3 filesystem is the ext3-users mailing list. The ext3 development team maintains a constant presence on this list, making it a great resource for detailed information about day-to-day enhancements, bug fixes, and problem reports for the ext3 filesystem. To subscribe to the ext3-users mailing list, see the URL `https://listman.redhat.com/mailman/listinfo/ext3-users`.

Support Software for ext3 Filesystems

Support for the ext3 filesystem is built into certain Linux distributions, such as Red Hat 7.2 or better. Whether or not your favorite Linux distribution includes integrated support, the ext3 filesystem depends on the people who packaged your distribution. This section discusses the utilities associated with the ext3 filesystem and the Linux packages in which they are found. If your Linux distribution does not include support for the ext3 filesystem, you can always add it yourself by obtaining the following:

- Source code or binaries for a version of the Linux kernel that includes support for ext3

- Source code and patches to the version of the kernel that you are using to add ext3 support to the version of the kernel that you are currently using
- Source code or binary packages for the utilities used to mount, modify, and use the ext3 filesystem

If the Linux distribution and version of Linux that you are running does not include support for the ext3 filesystem, the CD that accompanies this book includes a sample kernel source code distribution in the CD's kernel subdirectory and associated ext3 patches in the CD's ext3 directory. Information on installing the kernel source code and applying the patches, and ext3-specific information about building and installing a kernel are provided later in this chapter.

If the Linux distribution and version of Linux that you are running do not include support for the ext3 filesystem, you also will need to install several Linux utility packages (and compile them, if installing the source code) to install, use, and administer the ext3 filesystem on your computer. The following is a list of the Linux utility packages that you will need to install and the specific utilities that they provide for use with the ext3 filesystem. These are located in the utils subdirectory of the CD that accompanies this book:

- e2fsprogs 1.22 or better—The e2fsprogs package provides the basic utilities used to manage and administer the ext2 filesystem. Because the ext2 and ext3 filesystems share the same internal structures, the ext2 filesystem utilities are inherently relevant to ext3 filesystems, and some have been enhanced to enable you to manipulate ext3-specific attributes and data. You can always obtain the most recent e2fsprogs package from the URL http://e2fsprogs.sourceforge.net. The e2fsprogs utilities of most interest to ext3 filesystem users are the following:
  - chattr—Change the attributes of files and directories in the filesystem. The j attribute of files and directories is specific to the ext3 filesystem.
  - debugfs—Enables you to open, examine, and modify ext2 and ext3 filesystems. For ext3 filesystem users, the debugfs command is primarily useful to enable you to examine the basic features of a filesystem and clear metadata bits such as has_journal (which indicates that the filesystem is journaled) and needs_recovery (which, if set, indicates that the ext3 filesystem being examined is not consistent and that its journal should therefore be replayed). For more information about using the debugfs command in this fashion, see the section "Converting an ext3 Filesystem to ext2" later in this chapter.
  - e2fsck—The filesystem consistency check utility for ext2 and ext3 filesystems. As discussed earlier in this book, checking the consistency of an ext3 filesystem initially causes the e2fsck program to mount the filesystem, forcing the ext3 JBD subsystem to replay the log. If this does not restore the filesystem to consistency, the e2fsck program proceeds as described in "Checking ext3 Filesystem Consistency" later in this chapter.

- `lsattr`—List the attributes of files and directories in the filesystem. This enables you to see any special journaling modes that have been defined for files, directories, or directory hierarchies in an ext3 filesystem by using the `chattr` command's j attribute.

- `mke2fs`—The filesystem creation utility for ext2 and ext3 filesystems. For ext3 filesystems, the `mke2fs` utility now includes the `-j` (create journal) and `-J` (specify journal parameters) options to automatically create ext3 filesystems. For more information about using the `mke2fs` program to create ext3 filesystems, see the section "Creating an ext3 Filesystem" later in this chapter.

- `resize2fs`—Reduce or increase the size of an ext2 or ext3 filesystem. This command does not require any special options for processing or manipulating an ext3 filesystem, relying on the fact that ext2 and ext3 filesystems are identical at the disk and data structure levels.

- `tune2fs`—This command enables you to modify various parameters of ext2 and ext3 filesystems. This command is much like the `debugfs` command except that it is totally command-line driven and does not provide the interactive examination environment provided by `debugfs`. For ext3 filesystems, the `tune2fs` utility provides a `-j` option that enables you to add journaling capabilities to an existing ext2 filesystem. For more information about using the tune2fs command in this way, see the section "Converting an ext2 Filesystem to ext3" later in this chapter.

- `findsuper`—This command is not automatically compiled or installed when you compile and install the e2fsprogs package. Located in the misc subdirectory of the directory created when you extracted the contents of the archive containing the e2fsprogs package, you can compile this program manually (`gcc -o findsuper findsuper.c`) and use it to help detect spare superblocks in an ext3 or ext2 filesystem. This can be useful in an emergency situation where the primary superblock on an ext2 or ext3 filesystem has been damaged, and you therefore cannot check the consistency of or access the filesystem.

- util-linux-2.11h or better—The util-linux package provides many of the basic system utilities used with Linux. The most important of these to ext3 filesystem users are following:

  - `mount`—The mount utility enables you to mount a filesystem on an existing directory in a Linux filesystem. For ext3 filesystems, the mount command's `-t` (type) option takes the "ext3" type specification as an argument. Filesystems to be automatically mounted are listed in the file `/etc/fstab` as explained in the section "Locating and Identifying Filesystems" in Chapter 3, "Overview of Journaling Filesystems." For more information about using the `mount` command and the various options it provides for ext2 and ext3 filesystems, see "Mounting an ext3 Filesystem" later in this chapter.

4

THE EXT3
JOURNALING
FILESYSTEM

- `rescuept`—This utility attempts to identify the partition table for a damaged disk and is designed for use in emergency situations. The `rescuept` utility recognizes partition tables and ext2, FAT, swap, and extended partitions and can identify superblocks in ext2 filesystems. You then can use the information provided by `rescuept` to reconstruct the partition table for your system by using the standard `fdisk`, `cfdisk`, or `sfdisk` utilities. The `rescuept` utility is not automatically compiled or installed when you build the util-linux package, is not actively maintained, and complains about the large disks that are common in modern systems, but can still be useful. (It is automatically installed with some Linux distributions, such as Red Hat, but its documentation is not installed.) The `rescuept` utility can be useful for ext3 filesystems because they have the same on-disk layout as ext2 partitions.

TIP

A utility that provides similar functions to the `rescuept` utility, is kept relatively up-to-date, but is not part of a standard Linux utility package is Michail Brzitwa's `gpart`. The home page for this utility is located at `http://www.stud.uni-hannover.de/user/76201/gpart/`. For your convenience, a copy of the source code for this utility is located in the utils subdirectory of the CD that accompanies this book. Like the `rescuept` utility, `gpart` can be useful for ext3 filesystems because they have the same on-disk layout as ext2 partitions. The `gpart` utility recognizes many more partition types than `rescuept`, including LVM partitions and journaling filesystem partitions of types such as ReiserFS and XFS.

Other than the e2fsprogs and util-linux packages, the quota package included with most Linux distributions also has had some enhancements related to supporting quotas on ext3 filesystems, but these changes are in most recent versions of the quota package. Just in case, the source code for the 3.01pre8-1 version of the quota package is included in the utils subdirectory of the CD.

Installing the source code or binary versions of these packages and using the ext3-specific utilities that they include are explained later in this chapter. For detailed reference information about any of these commands, consult the online manual pages for the appropriate command by typing **man *<command-name>***.

Adding ext3 Support to Your System

As mentioned earlier, many more modern Linux distributions (such as versions of Red Hat Linux 7.2 and greater) provide built-in support for the ext3 filesystem in the kernel that they provide. The kernel is the bootable core of the Linux operating system and provides the infrastructure required for Linux itself to run. In general, Linux kernel versions 2.4.9-ac3 and better include built-in support for the ext3 filesystem.

This section provides hands-on, how-to information about installing, activating, using, and administering ext3 filesystems.

Building and Installing a Kernel with ext3 Support

In case the Linux kernel used by the Linux distribution that you are running does not include integrated support for the ext3 filesystem (or you simply want to experience the joys of building your own kernel), the CD that accompanies this book includes the source code for version 2.4.9 of the Linux kernel. The CD also includes the patches necessary to add support for the ext3 filesystem to that kernel. This is the latest version of the Linux kernel that is stable at the time of this writing.

> **NOTE**
>
> If you have never built a kernel before, doing so is a great learning experience. Although the whole idea of prepackaged Linux installation is to protect users from the need to "roll their own" kernel and Linux utilities, compiling a kernel is an excellent way to familiarize yourself with the conceptual internals and organization of Linux. The instructions in this book for compiling kernels create kernels that have special names and thus will not overwrite the current version of the Linux kernel that you are using.

Patching the Linux 2.4.9 Kernel for ext3 Support

Appendix A, "Using the Software on the CD-ROM," provides detailed information about installing Linux kernel source and selecting kernel configuration options. This section provides basic information about installing the specific version of the Linux kernel source that we'll be using in the examples throughout the rest of this chapter. The procedures described in this section are generally relevant even if you want to add and activate ext3 support in a different version of the Linux kernel sources, such as newer versions of the kernel or the version of the Linux kernel that was shipped with the Linux distribution that you are using.

> **TIP**
>
> If you are familiar with building Linux kernels and want to install and activate ext3 support in the most up-to-date version of the Linux kernel, you can obtain the latest version of the Linux kernel from the central Web repository for Linux kernel sources, http://www.kernel.org. Then check the Web site of one of the ext3 filesystem developers (such as Andrew Morton's at http://www.uow.edu.au/~andrewm/linux/ext3/) to check for patches for that Linux kernel version to download and install them, if necessary.

4

THE EXT3
JOURNALING
FILESYSTEM

To add support for the ext3 filesystem to the Linux 2.4.9 kernel to guarantee that you can work through the specific examples given in this chapter, you must patch the source for the generic Linux 2.4.9 kernel after installing it. Patches are changes to existing files that are inserted to update those files. General information about patches and their installation also is provided in Appendix A.

The source for the Linux 2.4.9 kernel is located in the kernel subdirectory of the CD that accompanies this book. Install this kernel as described in "Installing the Kernel Source Code" in Appendix A; then use the following steps to add ext3 support to that kernel:

1. Make sure that the X Window System is running and use the su command to become root in an xterm or other terminal window.

2. Change your working directory to the directory created when you installed the Linux kernel source code as described in Appendix A:

   ```
   cd /usr/src/linux-2.4.9
   ```

3. Use the patch command to apply the patch from the patch subdirectory of the CD included with this book:

   ```
   patch -p1 < /mnt/cdrom/patches/ext3-2.4-0.9.6-249.gz
   ```

   The -p1 option tells the patch command how much of the filenames listed in the patch file to preen to correctly locate the files that should be patched.

The output of the patch command lists the name of each file being patched. When the patch program completes, you're ready to configure a kernel with support for the ext3 filesystem.

Activating ext3 Support in the Kernel

This section explains how to activate support for the ext3 filesystem in the source code for the Linux 2.4.9 kernel. For an overview of the conceptual basics behind building a modern Linux kernel and activating support for different features and hardware in the kernel, see "Configuring Your Kernel" in Appendix A.

NOTE

It's generally a good idea to compile in support for any filesystems that your system uses regularly. Filesystems that you only interact with occasionally (such as AppleTalk or various network filesystems) can still be compiled as modules to keep your kernel as small as possible.

> **TIP**
>
> If you have already compiled a kernel for the computer system on which you are building a new kernel, you can use the configuration information from that kernel to save time when configuring the new kernel. Reusing existing configuration data from an existing kernel is explained in Appendix A.

This section explains the options that are specific to activating support for the ext3 filesystem in the kernel we are building. This section describes how to configure ext3 options using the X Window System-based Linux kernel configurator:

1. Log in as root or use the `su` command to become root.

2. In a terminal window running under an X Window System window manager or desktop, change the directory to /usr/src/linux-2.4.9 and execute the `make xconfig` command. The commands related to compiling and loading support for the Linux X Window System kernel configurator display in the window in which you executed the `make xconfig` command. Eventually, the X Window System Linux kernel configurator displays, as shown in Figure 4.1.

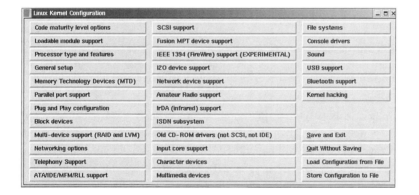

FIGURE 4.1

The X Window System-based Linux kernel configurator.

3. Select the Code Maturity Level Options command or button. A new dialog displays, as shown in Figure 4.2.

4. Click the Y radio button beside the Prompt for Development and/or Incomplete Code/ Drivers option, and click the Main Menu button to return to the primary `make xconfig` dialog.

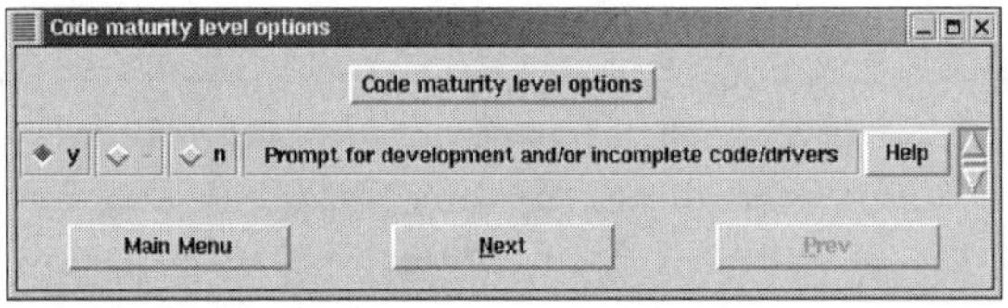

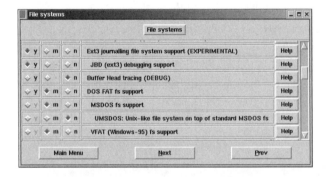

FIGURE 4.2

The Code Maturity Level Options dialog.

5. Click the File Systems button in the X Window System kernel configuration dialog. A new dialog displays, as shown in Figure 4.3.

FIGURE 4.3

The File Systems Configuration dialog.

6. Scroll down until you see the Ext3 Journaling File System Support (EXPERIMENTAL) entry. Click Y beside this entry.

7. Click Y beside the JBD (ext3) Debugging Support entry. This is an optional feature that enables you to collect debugging information if you encounter a problem when using the ext3 filesystem. Selecting this option does not activate debugging output but only gives you the opportunity to activate it later (from any Linux command line) if it should be necessary to submit a problem report to the ext3 development team.

8. Scroll down until you see the Second Extended Filesystem Support entry and make sure that it is selected. If it is not, click Y beside this entry.

9. Click the Main Menu button to return to the primary make xconfig dialog.

10. After selecting any other kernel configuration options relevant to the kernel that you are building (such as those specific to the hardware in your system), save your updated kernel configuration.

    If you reused the configuration data from an existing kernel, use the Store Configuration to File button to display a dialog that enables you to explicitly save your new kernel configuration with the name .config in the main directory of the kernel that you are configuring.

If you configured the current kernel from scratch (that is, without reading in configuration data from another kernel), simply click the Save and Exit button.

11. Click OK to close the final dialog and return to the Linux shell prompt.

You're now ready to compile the kernel.

Compiling and Installing an ext3 Kernel

After applying patches to and configuring the Linux 2.4.9 kernel, you're ready to compile and install your new Linux kernel. All the information that you need to compile and install this kernel is provided in Appendix A. This section just provides a checklist for the steps that you should follow.

After you've installed, patched, and configured the Linux 2.4.9 for ext3 filesystem support and to match your hardware, you must do the following to install and use that kernel:

1. Add a special extension for this kernel to its Makefile, making it easy to identify the special features in the kernel. I typically name kernels that support different filesystems along the lines of `linux-<kernel-version>-<filesystem-type>`.

2. Execute the following `make` commands in this order to correctly initialize dependencies and to build and install the new kernel and any associated loadable modules:

   - `make dep`

   - `make`

   - `make modules`

   - `make install`

   - `make modules_install`

   I suggest doing these steps as discrete commands to make it easy to spot any compilation or installation failures along the way. If you're really cocky, you can reduce these commands to the following single command-line, but you'd still be wise to scroll back to make sure that there were no problems:

   `make dep ; make install ; make modules_install`

3. Modify boot loader configuration files for the boot loader you're using on your system, as described in "Booting a New Kernel" in Appendix A and rerun lilo if necessary.

You're now almost ready to reboot your system and use the ext3 filesystem. Before doing that, however, you must also compile and install the utilities discussed in the next section to ensure that your system can mount and administer ext3 filesystem volumes both correctly and optimally.

Upgrading and Installing Related Utilities

This section explains how to install versions of the utilities necessary to mount, configure, and administer ext3 filesystems. After configuring, compiling, and installing a new kernel, installing utility programs will seem quick and painless.

Before following the instructions in this section, make sure that you actually need to compile and install new versions of these utilities by checking the version of each one installed on your system. You can do this quickly and easily by using the rpm command to query the version of the packages installed on your system. If the rpm command is not supported on your Linux distribution, use the package utility on your system to find out what versions of the e2fsprogs and util-linux packages are installed on your system.

To use the rpm command to determine the version of the e2fsprogs package installed on your system, execute the following command:

```
rpm -qf /sbin/e2fsck
```

As discussed earlier in this chapter, your system must support version 1.22 or better of the e2fsprogs package to successfully work with ext3 filesystems.

To use the rpm command to determine the version of the util-linux package installed on your system, execute the following command:

```
rpm -qf /bin/mount
```

As discussed earlier in this chapter, your system must support version 2.11h or better of the util-linux package to successfully work with ext3 filesystems.

If you already have updated these utilities on your system or are running a Linux distribution that already includes appropriate versions of these, you can skip this section and move directly to the section "Administering ext3 Filesystems."

NOTE

When installing system utilities or other programs that I plan to make publicly available, I typically store the source code or RPMs in the directory /usr/src/utilities. This keeps it in a well-known central location but also makes it clear that these are not utilities that accompanied the distribution of Linux that I am running. This also provides a single directory that is easily backed up and archived if for some reason I need to initialize and re-create my /usr filesystem. We're all doing backups, right?

Upgrading and Installing the util-linux Package

As mentioned earlier, you must be using version 2.11h or better of the Linux util-linux package to ensure that you have the correct version of the mount utility to correctly attach an ext3 filesystem to your existing Linux system. The mount options that you select may be specific to your particular installation, but you need an up-to-date version of mount to successfully use any of them with ext3 filesystems. Remember that the compatibility of the ext2 and ext3 filesystem means that you can always mount an ext3 filesystem as an ext2 filesystem simply to access it, but you will not be able to take advantage of journaling or recover any in-progress transactions from the journal itself. The source code for the latest util-linux package available when this book was written is located in the utils subdirectory of the CD that accompanies this book and has been tested using the procedures described in this section. To download the absolute latest version of the util-linux package, see a standard Linux archive site such as `http://www.rpmfind.net/linux/RPM/`. This site enables you to download binary and source RPMs for any newer versions of the util-linux package that are available.

To install version 2.11h of the util-linux package, included on the CD that accompanies this book, do the following:

1. Mount the CD and extract the util-linux package from the file
   `utils/util-linux-2.11h.tar.gz` to a directory on your system using a
   command such as the following:

   ```
   cd <target-directory>
   tar zxvf <path-to-CD>/utils/util-linux-2.11htar.gz
   ```

2. Change directory to `<target-directory>`/util-linux-2.11h and run the configure
   script to correctly configure the util-linux Makefile for your system and Linux distribution:

   ```
   ./configure
   ```

   This produces verbose output that's not useful to replicate here.

3. After the Makefile is configured correctly, execute the make command to build the new
   versions of the utilities in the util-linux package:

   ```
   make
   ```

   Once again, this produces verbose, system-specific output that's not useful to replicate
   here.

4. After all the utilities are compiled, install them on your system using the following
   command:

   ```
   make install
   ```

Your system now has versions of the util-linux utilities and associated textinfo and reference (man page) documentation installed that are compatible with the ext3 filesystem.

4

THE EXT3
JOURNALING
FILESYSTEM

Upgrading and Installing the e2fsprogs Package

As mentioned earlier, you must be using version 1.22 or better of the Linux e2fsprogs package to ensure that you have all the utilities related to installing, administering, and using the ext3 filesystem. The source code for the latest e2fsprogs package available when this book was written is located in the utils subdirectory of the CD that accompanies this book. To download the absolute latest version of the e2fsprogs package, see the e2fsprogs home page at `http://e2fsprogs.sourceforge.net`.

To install version 1.23 of the e2fsprogs package, included on the CD that accompanies this book, do the following:

1. Mount the CD and extract the e2fsprogs package from the file `utils/e2fsprogs-1.23.tar.gz` to a directory on your system using command such as the following:

   ```
   cd <target-directory>
   tar zxvf <path-to-CD>/utils/e2fsprogs-1.23.tar.gz
   ```

2. Change directory to `<target-directory>/e2fsprogs-1.23` and run the configure script to correctly configure the e2fsprogs Makefile for your system and Linux distribution:

   ```
   ./configure
   ```

   This produces verbose output that's not useful to replicate here.

3. After the Makefile is configured correctly, execute the make command to build the new versions of the utilities in the e2fsprogs package:

   ```
   make
   ```

   Once again, this produces verbose, system-specific output that's not useful to replicate here. The number of compiler defines (-Dfoo) for this package is both interesting and amusing, but not surprising. The e2fsprogs utilities enable you to interact with ext2 and ext3 filesystems at a level only slightly above the kernel level. For this reason, it's not surprising that these have to be closely tied to the specific capabilities of your compiler, kernel, and operating system. Remember that the ext2 filesystem is open source and is therefore not limited to being used on Linux systems!

4. After all the utilities are compiled, install them on your system using the following command:

   ```
   make install
   ```

Your system now has versions of the e2fsprogs utilities and associated texinfo and reference (man page) documentation installed that are compatible with the ext3 filesystem. If you want to read detailed reference information about application development using the libraries required by these utilities, you either can use the texinfo system to read that information (info libext2fs) or change your working directory to the doc subdirectory and execute the make command there to produce a TeX dvi file that you can then print and use for reference.

Administering ext3 Filesystems

This section assumes that you either are using a Linux system on which the ext3 filesystem is already supported or have compiled a kernel and related utilities with ext3 support as explained in the previous sections. The examples in this section were all produced using the mount program from version 2.11h of the util-linux package and the chattr, debugfs, e2fsck, mke2fs, resize2fs, and tune2fs utilities from version 1.23 of the e2fsprogs package. If you are using newer versions of the utilities from these packages, your output may differ slightly, but the procedures described in this section should be the same.

Creating an ext3 Filesystem

Creating filesystems under Linux is ordinarily done using the /sbin/mkfs command. The mkfs command's -t option enables you to specify the type of filesystem that you want to create. The mkfs command actually invokes different filesystem-specific programs based on the type of filesystem that you are creating. For example, executing the /sbin/mkfs -t ext2 /dev/<whatever> command actually invokes the /sbin/mkfs.ext2 command to create the specified filesystem. The mkfs command passes any extra arguments to the appropriate filesystem-specific program.

The program that actually creates ext2 and ext3 filesystems is the program mke2fs. The mkfs command invokes programs named by appending the filesystem type to the basename mkfs, separating the two by a period. When the e2fsprogs package is installed, a hard link is created from /sbin/mke2fs to /sbin/mkfs.ext2, which makes the mkfs wrapper program work correctly when invoked with the ext2 argument. (It also works correctly when no type argument is supplied to mkfs because the ext2 filesystem is the default filesystem type for Linux.) Unfortunately, at this time, no hard or symbolic link from /sbin/mke2fs to /sbin/mkfs.ext3 is automatically created. You can create this link yourself by executing the following command:

```
cd /sbin; ln -s mke2fs mkfs.ext3
```

However, at this time, you will still have to pass the -j argument to the mkfs command to tell mke2fs to create an ext3 filesystem.

Until the ext3 filesystem is fully integrated with the mke2fs/mkfs program nomenclature, the best way to create an ext3 filesystem is to explicitly create it using the mke2fs command, as in the following example:

```
mke2fs -j /dev/<whatever>
```

This creates an ext2 filesystem on the device /dev/*<whatever>*, and also creates the journal necessary to use this as ext3 filesystem. ext3 filesystems must be greater than 2 megabytes in size, or the mke2fs program will complain and exit without creating a filesystem.

4

THE EXT3
JOURNALING
FILESYSTEM

The following example shows the output from creating an ext3 filesystem on the partition
/dev/hdc3:

```
[root@journal]# mke2fs -j /dev/hdc3
mke2fs 1.23, 15-Aug-2001 for EXT2 FS 0.5b, 95/08/09
warning: 124 blocks unused.
Filesystem label=
OS type: Linux
Block size=4096 (log=2)
Fragment size=4096 (log=2)
262656 inodes, 524288 blocks
26220 blocks (5.00%) reserved for the super user
First data block=0
16 block groups
32768 blocks per group, 32768 fragments per group
16416 inodes per group
Superblock backups stored on blocks:
        32768, 98304, 163840, 229376, 294912
Writing inode tables: done
Creating journal (8192 blocks): done
Writing superblocks and filesystem accounting information: done
This filesystem will be automatically checked every 21 mounts or
180 days, whichever comes first.  Use tune2fs -c or -i to override.
```

The Creating journal line in this output example shows that an ext3 filesystem was created
with the default size of 8192 blocks. The mke2fs program currently uses the following default
journal sizes:

- 1024 blocks if the filesystem is smaller than 32,768 blocks
- 4096 blocks if the filesystem is smaller than 262,144 blocks but greater than or equal to
  32,768 blocks
- 8192 blocks if the filesystem is greater than or equal to 262,144 blocks

By default, filesystem block size is selected based on the size of the filesystem that you are
creating. In the previous example, the filesystem block size is 4096 bytes because the size of
the partition is approximately 2 GB. Therefore, a 32 MB journal was created by default.

NOTE

The frequency with which a filesystem is automatically checked for consistency is
either after a randomly calculated number of times that the filesystem was mounts or
180 days, whichever is less. The random mount count is calculated using the filesystem UUID as a seed value, helping guarantee that all filesystems will not be checked
after the same number of mounts.

Specifying an Alternate Journal Size for an ext3 Filesystem

The mke2fs program provides the -J option that enables you to control certain aspects of the journal being created. You can use the -J size=<journal-size> option to provide a specific size for the journal in megabytes, overriding the default size. The following is an example of using the -J option to specify the size of a journal:

```
[root@journal]# mke2fs -j -J size=128 /dev/hdc3
mke2fs 1.23, 15-Aug-2001 for EXT2 FS 0.5b, 95/08/09
warning: 124 blocks unused.
Filesystem label=
OS type: Linux
Block size=4096 (log=2)
Fragment size=4096 (log=2)
262656 inodes, 524288 blocks
26220 blocks (5.00%) reserved for the super user
First data block=0
16 block groups
32768 blocks per group, 32768 fragments per group
16416 inodes per group
Superblock backups stored on blocks:
        32768, 98304, 163840, 229376, 294912
Writing inode tables: done
Creating journal (32768 blocks): done
Writing superblocks and filesystem accounting information: done
This filesystem will be automatically checked every 30 mounts or
180 days, whichever comes first.  Use tune2fs -c or -i to override.
```

> **NOTE**
>
> If you specify the -J option, the -j option is implied and therefore unnecessary. This command could therefore have been issued as mke2fs -J size=128 /dev/hdc3, but is shown with all related options for the sake of clarity.

The mke2fs program lets you create a journal of any size between 1024 and 102400 filesystem blocks, but the default values are usually sufficient. In the previous example, a journal of 128 MB was requested. Because the default block size for a filesystem of that size is 4096 bytes, 32768 blocks were allocated to the journal.

Specifying a journal size other than the default values is usually unnecessary. The space in the journal that is used to record filesystem transactions is released for reuse after those transactions are committed. If the journal happens to fill during normal operations, direct filesystem access will pause while the JBD layer attempts to commit and free any transactions in the journal that can be committed. A larger journal may be useful if you are journaling both data and metadata changes and these transactions involve relatively large amounts of data. However, because a journal must be read into memory during recovery after a filesystem restart, larger journals can result in slower restart times. Similarly, a smaller journal may guarantee faster system restart but may fill up more frequently, potentially reducing filesystem performance.

> **NOTE**
>
> Though highly unlikely, make sure that you never create a journal larger than the amount of available memory on your system. In the absolute worst case (when the entire journal was filled with uncommitted transactions), this could prevent the system from reading the journal into memory after a restart, preventing automatic recovery and restart.

Specifying an Alternate Journal Location for an ext3 Filesystem

The mke2fs program's -J option also enables you to identify a separate device as the location of the journal. As mentioned earlier in this chapter in the "Overview" section, this can provide both performance and reliability improvements. An external journaling device is a specially formatted device that can serve as the location of the journal for multiple filesystems. You can use the -J journal=<device> option to identify the device to which journaling should be done.

Before specifying an alternate device as the location of the journal for an ext3 filesystem, you must format that device as a journal_dev using the mke2fs command, as in the following example:

```
[root@journal]# mke2fs -O journal_dev /dev/hdb2
mke2fs 1.23, 15-Aug-2001 for EXT2 FS 0.5b, 95/08/09
Filesystem label=
OS type: Linux
Block size=4096 (log=2)
Fragment size=4096 (log=2)
0 inodes, 524412 blocks
0 blocks (0.00%) reserved for the super user
First data block=0
0 block group
32768 blocks per group, 32768 fragments per group
0 inodes per group
Superblock backups stored on blocks:
Zeroing journal device: done
```

After the journal device has been formatted, you then can use it with any new ext3 filesystems that you create, as in the following example:

```
[root@journal e2fsprogs-1.23]# mke2fs -j -J device=/dev/hdb2 /dev/hdc3
mke2fs 1.23, 15-Aug-2001 for EXT2 FS 0.5b, 95/08/09
Filesystem label=
OS type: Linux
Block size=1024 (log=0)
Fragment size=1024 (log=0)
263168 inodes, 2097648 blocks
104882 blocks (5.00%) reserved for the super user
First data block=1
257 block groups
8192 blocks per group, 8192 fragments per group
1024 inodes per group
Superblock backups stored on blocks:
        8193, 24577, 40961, 57345, 73729, 204801, 221185, 401409, 663553,
        1024001, 1990657
Writing inode tables: done
Adding journal to device /dev/hdb2: done
Writing superblocks and filesystem accounting information: done
This filesystem will be automatically checked every 39 mounts or
180 days, whichever comes first.  Use tune2fs -c or -i to override.
```

> **NOTE**
>
> You can supply multiple arguments to the -J option by separating them with a comma. This would look something like the following:
>
> ```
> mke2fs -j -J size=128,device=/dev/hdb2 /dev/hdc3
> ```

Verifying Filesystem Type Information

After creating an ext3 filesystem, you can verify that the filesystem is an ext3 journaling filesystem by using the debugfs command's request option (-R) to request information about the feature bits set for the filesystem, as in the following example:

```
[root@journal]# debugfs -R features /dev/hdc3
debugfs 1.23, 15-Aug-2001 for EXT2 FS 0.5b, 95/08/09
Filesystem features: has_journal filetype sparse_super
```

The has_journal option identifies this filesystem as an ext3 filesystem. You then can use the mount command to mount this filesystem on any directory of your Linux system and begin using it, as explained in the next section.

Mounting an ext3 Filesystem

Simply creating an ext3 filesystem is no more useful than simply buying a new car—you have to use it to impress anyone or get any real value out of it. The key to using any filesystem is mounting it so that it is available to your computer system and its users. The section "Locating and Identifying Filesystems" in Chapter 3 explained how Linux systems use the entries in an /etc/fstab file to locate devices containing filesystems, identify the directory on which those filesystems should be mounted, find out the type of each filesystem, and determine the options to be used when mounting those filesystems. All this information then is passed to the mount command when you restart your computer. You can obviously also mount any filesystem from a command line, but that filesystem will not be automatically mounted the next time you restart your computer system.

Many of the most common filesystem mount options were discussed in Chapter 3. This section explains the mount options specific to the ext3 filesystem. Because the ext3 filesystem is 100 percent compatible with the ext2 filesystem, both the generic options for the mount command and the mount options for the ext2 filesystem also can be used with ext3 filesystems. For more information about generic and ext2-specific mount options, see the online reference information for the mount command ("man mount").

> **NOTE**
>
> One generic mount option that you should avoid using with an ext3 filesystem is the sync option, which forces all I/O to the filesystem to be done synchronously. Using this option would invalidate the primary reason for using an ext3 filesystem and would actually cause the filesystem to be slower than a default ext2 filesystem that (by default) uses lazy writes to write data to the filesystem to maximize performance. If synchronous writes are necessary for specific critical files and directories in an ext3 filesystem, you can use the chattr command to set synchronous writes on a per-file and directory basis as explained in the section "Setting Per-File and Directory Journaling Modes" later in this chapter.

The mount options specifically provided to tailor aspects of the behavior of ext3 filesystems are the following:

* journal=inum—Specifies the number of an inode on the ext3 filesystem that will be assigned to the filesystem journal if a journal file does not already exist. Any data previously associated with that inode is discarded. This option has no effect if a journal file already exists on the ext3 filesystem.

* journal=update—Update the ext3 filesystem's journal to the current format. Versions of the ext3 filesystem prior to 0.0.3 used a different journal format.

- noload—Do not load the ext3 filesystem's journal. This option causes the mount to behave as if the journal was empty and the filesystem was clean.

- data={journal,ordered,writeback}—Specifies the journaling mode to be used for file data (filesystem metadata is always journaled):

  - The "journal" journaling mode means that all data updates are committed to the filesystem journal before any associated changes are actually made to the filesystem data. This is the safest data journaling mode, guaranteeing that no updates are made to the filesystem before they are completely recorded in the log and can therefore be replayed after a filesystem restart. This guarantees that filesystem data and metadata are always consistent up through the last committed transaction. This journaling mode is the only mode supported in versions of the ext3 filesystem prior to 0.0.3.

  - The "ordered" journaling mode means that data updates are forced to the filesystem before associated metadata updates are committed to the journal. If a computer crashes after data updates have been made but before metadata changes are made to the log, data updates made to existing blocks owned by files may survive the restart, but newly allocated blocks will be reclaimed by fsck. (This is the default journaling mode for data if no other option is specified.)

  - The "writeback" journaling mode means that filesystem data updates can be made lazily (that is, when convenient for the filesystem and disk drive), even after related metadata changes have been committed to the log. By enabling lazy data writes, this is the highest performance journaling mode but can cause old data to appear in files that were being updated at the time of a system crash. Although all file metadata changes were committed to the log, there is no guarantee that all the associated data changes were actually made. In other words, newly allocated blocks may have been marked as being associated with updated files, but there is no guarantee that all the updated data was actually written to those blocks at the moment that the system went down.

Converting an ext2 Filesystem to ext3

Because of the compatibility maintained between ext2 and ext3 filesystems, existing ext2 filesystems can be converted quickly to ext3 filesystem, even if they currently are mounted. (It's still suggested that you do this in single-user mode for safety and performance sake.)

To convert an existing ext2 filesystem to ext3, execute the following command:

```
# tune2fs -j /dev/<whatever>
```

Sample output from executing this command on the filesystem /dev/hda5 on one of my systems is the following:

```
[root@journal]# tune2fs -j /dev/hda5
tune2fs 1.23, 15-Aug-2001 for EXT2 FS 0.5b, 95/08/09
```

```
Creating journal inode: done
This filesystem will be automatically checked every 36 mounts or
180 days, whichever comes first. Use tune2fs -c or -i to override.
```

> **NOTE**
>
> If the filesystem you are converting to ext3 is mounted when you execute the tune2fs
> command, the journal will be created as a file named .journal that is visible in the
> top-level directory of the filesystem on the specified partition. If the filesystem is not
> mounted when you execute the tune2fs command, the journal file that is created
> will not be visible to the user.

Setting Per-File and Directory Journaling Modes

As mentioned in the "Overview" section of this chapter, the ext2 filesystem supports features, such as the -S file attribute, designed to help provide data security and reliability in the event of a system crash without the benefit of using a journaling filesystem. This option forces meta-data updates for specific files and directories to be done synchronously while permitting the remainder of the filesystem to use the default lazy-write characteristics of the ext2 filesystem. This combination maximizes performance while still providing robust guarantees for specific files and directories that may need them.

The designers of the ext3 filesystem recognized that analogous situations may occur in ext3 filesystems, and therefore provided the option for the chattr command to set the journaling mode for specific files, directories, and directory hierarchies. This enables an ext3 filesystem to use the highest performance journaling mode (writeback), while enabling specific files, directories, and directory hierarchies in that filesystem to use the slower but more robust data journaling mode.

To set a specific file, such as a critical log file, to use full data journaling, use the chattr command's -j option, as in the following example:

```
chattr +j <filename>
```

For example, I could set full data journaling mode on the file /ext3_test/banking.log using this command:

```
chattr +j /ext3_test/banking.log
```

After you've set this mode on a file, you can verify that the mode is set using the lsattr command, as in the following example and sample output:

```
[root@journal]# lsattr /ext3_test/banking.log
------------j /ext3_test/banking.log
```

If you want to associate full data journaling with a directory, so that any new or existing files in that directory have this mode set, you can use the chattr command -R (recursive) option, as in the following example:

```
[root@journal]# chattr -R +j /ext3_test/news/outgoing
[root@journal]#
[root@journal]# lsattr /ext3_test/news/outgoing
------------j /ext3_test/news/outgoing/785875
```

To verify that this command has not only set full-data journaling on the current contents of that directory but also that new files created in that directory will also have this attribute set, you can create a file and check its attributes, as in the following example:

```
[root@journal]# touch /ext3_test/news/outgoing/6764389
[root@journal]#
[root@journal]# lsattr /ext3_test/news/outgoing/6764389
------------j /ext3_test/news/outgoing/6764389
```

Checking ext3 Filesystem Consistency

The standard Linux filesystem consistency checker is the fsck program, just as it is on Unix systems. On Linux systems, fsck is located in /sbin. Like the mkfs program, the /sbin/fsck program is actually a wrapper program that calls a filesystem-specific version of fsck that is named /sbin/fsck.<filesystem-type>. For example, the name of the program executed by the /sbin/fsck program to check the consistency of an ext3 filesystem is named /sbin/fsck.ext3. The /sbin/fsck program determines the system-specific version of fsck to call based on either information it extracts from the /etc/fstab file or by examining the filesystem itself. Examining the filesystem is necessary, for example, when the /etc/fstab file gives the filesystem type as "auto," which essentially means "figure it out yourself" to both the mount and fsck utilities.

As discussed in Chapter 3, the ext3 filesystem takes a unique approach to verifying consistency, largely due to its relationship with the ext2 filesystem. The program /sbin/fsck.ext3 is actually just a hard link to the program /sbin/fsck.ext2. When called as /sbin/fsck.ext3 or /sbin/fsck.ext2, and the program can determine that the filesystem it is checking is an ext3 filesystem, the program first checks whether the filesystem header is marked as needing recovery (through the flag named needs_recovery). If so, the fsck utility attempts to mount the filesystem on a temporary directory because mounting an ext3 filesystem forces the journal to be replayed and therefore clears the needs_recovery bit. If this is successful and the filesystem is otherwise marked as clean, the fsck program exits. If the filesystem is still marked as dirty (that is, not clean), the fsck program runs the standard ext2 fsck code to check the internal consistency of the ext2 portions of the filesystem.

> **NOTE**
>
> For a detailed explanation of the steps involved in checking the consistency of the ext2 filesystem, see "Checking the Consistency of a Non-Journaled Filesystem" in Chapter 3.

General Issues in Resolving Problems with ext3 Filesystems

Let's face it, software usually contains bugs. I certainly have friends in the industry who point with pride to the fact that their 24x7 IBM mainframes can run programs on PL/1 card images from 1964 with no problems until the cows come home, but that's such a pitiful spectacle in itself that it's only worth mentioning for humor value. Most of the time—probably 99.9 percent of the time—any ext3 filesystem problems are automatically resolved by rebooting and replaying the journal. However, the ext3 filesystem is still actively under development. Its origins in the ext2 code base give it a greater measure of initial stability than most other filesystems. Although many sites are actively using it, you still may encounter problems with ext3 filesystems, especially under high-load conditions or when using newer features, such as journaling to a separate device. Here, too, the origins of the ext3 filesystem in the ext2 filesystem give you some unique opportunities for problem resolution.

This section provides some tips for recovering from the .1 percent of the problems that you can't automatically recover from. You may never need to use the procedures described in this section. In fact, I hope you won't, but just in case. . .

The primary problem that you may encounter with an ext3 filesystem is where the journal or the underlying ext2 filesystem experiences corruption that can't be automatically repaired. Although the chances of these problems occurring are remote, the ext2 underpinnings of the ext3 filesystem increase the chances that you will be able to repair and continue to use the filesystem in question. For example

- If an ext3 filesystem won't pass the fsck and you know that the filesystem contains data that you must absolutely recover, you can try one of the following to let you attempt to retrieve critical data from the filesystem before actually repairing the consistency problems:
  - Mounting the filesystem as a read-only ext3 filesystem, preventing the filesystem from loading (replaying) the contents of the journal
  - Mounting the filesystem as a read-only ext2 filesystem before attempting any further recovery

Because the filesystem is guaranteed to be inconsistent with respect to the journal and may also have ext2-specific consistency problems, attempting to access data in the filesystem may crash your system, but you may already be hosed, so? This approach at least gives you the opportunity to copy critical data off the filesystem. There are no guarantees about the consistency of any data that you retrieve from the filesystem (because pending updates may be present in the journal and related metadata and data updates may been "half done"), but it's worth a try in critical situations.

- If the journal on an ext3 filesystem is so corrupted that you can't get through the stage of the fsck process where it mounts an ext3 filesystem to replay the journal, you can unset the bits that identify the filesystem as ext3 and then check the consistency of the filesystem as an ext2 filesystem. Although this loses any update information present in the journal and may expose ext2 filesystem inconsistencies depending on the journaling mode that you were using on that filesystem, this should still enable you to repair the filesystem. You then can turn the filesystem back into an ext3 filesystem, associate the journal with the same inode that it was previously associated with (typically inode 11 for ext3 filesystems created from scratch) if possible, and put the filesystem back into production.

- If the ext3 filesystem can't be accessed at all due to underlying ext2 filesystem problems (such as a bad superblock), you can use standard, time-tested mechanisms for repairing ext2 filesystems, such as checking the consistency of the filesystem using an alternate superblock. Depending on the number of problems discovered by an ext2 fsck using an alternate superblock, applying pending updates from the journal may be a bad idea, in which case you may want to re-create the journal rather than replay it.

The next sections explain the ext3-related procedures used in these emergency recovery situations.

NOTE

After using any of the procedures in this or subsequent sections that convert an ext3 filesystem to ext2 by auditing filesystem attributes, make sure that you modify the /etc/fstab file appropriately. If you do not, mounting the filesystem automatically may fail the next time you restart your system.

Mounting an ext3 Filesystem Without Reloading the Journal

You usually only want to mount an ext3 filesystem without reloading the journal if journal consistency problems are preventing the filesystem from being verified by the fsck program or mounted, but the underlying ext2 filesystem is clean. You can determine the state of the filesystem by using the debugfs command's stats query, as in the following example:

```
[root@journal]# debugfs /dev/hdc3
debugfs 1.23, 15-Aug-2001 for EXT2 FS 0.5b, 95/08/09
debugfs:  stats
Filesystem volume name:    <none>
Last mounted on:           <not available>
Filesystem UUID:           ee62e35b-fdfb-4784-a597-4e496594ee18
Filesystem magic number:   0xEF53
Filesystem revision #:     1 (dynamic)
Filesystem features:       has_journal filetype needs_recovery sparse_super
Filesystem state:          clean
[subsequent output deleted]
```

Even if the journal needs recovery and the underlying filesystem is dirty (that is, not clean), mounting the filesystem without requiring that it be verified by the fsck program may enable you to access data in case of an emergency.

> **NOTE**
>
> Future releases of the mount command will support a "noload" option that enables you to mount an ext3 filesystem without replaying the journal. For the time being, you can mount an ext3 filesystem without replaying the journal by mounting it read-only. This is the equivalent of a noload mount as far as replaying the journal is concerned, but the filesystem will not be writable as it would be if it were simply mounted without loading/replaying the journal.

To mount an ext3 filesystem read-only, preventing the filesystem from replaying the journal, execute a command such as the following:

```
mount -o ro -t ext3 /dev/<whatever> <mount-point>
```

You can then copy data off this filesystem. If this succeeds, you can then remove the journal and re-create it, as in the following examples:

```
[root@journal mount]# tune2fs -O '^has_journal' /dev/hdc3
tune2fs 1.23, 15-Aug-2001 for EXT2 FS 0.5b, 95/08/09
Journal removed
[root@journal mount]# tune2fs -j /dev/hdc3
tune2fs 1.23, 15-Aug-2001 for EXT2 FS 0.5b, 95/08/09
Creating journal inode: done
This filesystem will be automatically checked every 39 mounts or
180 days, whichever comes first.  Use tune2fs -c or -i to override.
```

Mounting an ext3 Filesystem as ext2

If unrecoverable filesystem corruption that prevents the use of the fsck program on an ext3 filesystem from completing is present in the journal, mounting an ext3 filesystem as an ext2 filesystem gives you the opportunity to extract information from the filesystem before proceeding with further recovery efforts. This also gives you a highly unstable filesystem, especially if ext2 filesystem corruption is also present. You should usually only attempt this in single-user mode to minimize anyone else trying to access the filesystem and should also mount the filesystem read-only so that no process attempts to update the filesystem.

To do this, use the following `mount` command:

```
mount -o ro -t ext2 /dev/<whatever> <mount-point>
```

For example, to mount the ext3 filesystem /dev/hdc3 as a read-only ext2 filesystem on the directory or problem, you would execute the following command:

```
[root@journal] mount -o ro -t ext2 /dev/hdc3 /problem
```

Converting an ext3 Filesystem to ext2

If you are experiencing problems with the journal of an ext3 filesystem and the underlying ext2 filesystem is not clean, you can remove the journal, which effectively turns the filesystem into a standard ext2 filesystem. You can then use the `fsck` program to check the consistency of the filesystem.

You can remove the journal of an ext3 filesystem in two different ways, by using either the `debugfs` or `tune2fs` commands. The `tune2fs` command is less useful in this situation, however, because you cannot remove the journal of an ext3 filesystem that is marked as needing recovery. You must first clear the `needs_recovery` flag.

The following is an example of using the `debugfs` command to remove a journal:

```
[root@journal] debugfs -w /dev/hdc3
debugfs 1.23, 15-Aug-2001 for EXT2 FS 0.5b, 95/08/09
debugfs:  features
Filesystem features: has_journal filetype needs_recovery sparse_super
debugfs:  features -needs_recovery -has_journal
Filesystem features: filetype sparse_super
debugfs:  quit
```

For future reference, the following is an example of using the `tune2fs` command to remove a journal:

```
[root@journal]# tune2fs -O '^has_journal' /dev/hdc3
tune2fs 1.23, 15-Aug-2001 for EXT2 FS 0.5b, 95/08/09
Journal removed
```

4

THE EXT3
JOURNALING
FILESYSTEM

IBM's JFS Journaling Filesystem

IN THIS CHAPTER

Say what you want about IBM and its traditional taste in clothing, but IBM has come out of the Linux closet in a big way. IBM is one of the staunchest supporters of Linux and one of its heaviest promoters as an enterprise business solution. (Though I'm as sick as anyone of those stupid ads in which two spacesuited zeros curiously examine various technologies.) IBM shocked everybody when it invested heavily in the Apache Web server project in 1998—some of the most surprised people being IBM employees who were working on other Web servers and barely heard the huge flushing noise before they had to scramble to find other projects.

Having worked for IBM for a while after it acquired a startup that I was working for, I must confess that most of what I wanted to believe about IBM was wrong. Although IBM is deeper in "administrivia" than any company I've ever seen and it has a drowning man's death grip on turkeys like Lotus SmartSuite, it's an amazing company to work for if you're actually into hardware and software. IBM is not just about computing from the Bizarro planet (also known as mainframes)—it has a tremendous history of innovation in both hardware (little things like Winchester disks, the ancestor of all modern hard drives, being one of my personal favorites) and software (such as SGML, which begat both HTML and XML). Since its conversion to Linux, IBM has begun porting most of its software to Linux, offers Linux as a supported operating system on almost all its hardware, and has some truly amazing projects going where you can install Linux into LPARs (mainframese for logical partitions) and run as many copies of Linux as you want as virtual machines on a single mainframe.

To the benefit of the entire Linux community (especially those of us without mainframes), IBM has also released some of its most interesting and innovative software projects to the Open Source community. Two of these are discussed in this book—OpenAFS, the open-source version of IBM's AFS distributed filesystem product, and JFS, its Journal File System, which is the subject of this chapter.

Overview

JFS is IBM's full journaling filesystem, originally developed for use on its AIX and OS/2 systems but now released to the Open Source community via the Gnu Public License (GPL). JFS has a unique history, having originally been developed for AIX but subsequently rewritten from the ground up for IBM's ill-fated OS/2 operating system. When sales of OS/2 slowed from the original 15 or 20 copies per month to the occasional yearly sale, JFS was ported back to AIX. The new AIX code base was then used as the core (pardon the expression, Unix fans) of the development of the Linux port. This history gives JFS some advantages over newer journaling filesystems such as the ReiserFS, because the code base has undergone extensive testing under other operating systems.

JFS is a full 64-bit filesystem, giving it a potential capacity of between 512 terabytes and 32 petabytes per filesystem, depending on the block size used when a filesystem is created. In theory, JFS supports block sizes of 512, 1024, 2048, and 4096 bytes, but only the block size of

4096 bytes is currently supported on Linux. Like other 64-bit filesystems under Linux at the moment, the true capacity of JFS is limited by constraints within the Linux VFS layer, so the actual maximum capacity of a JFS filesystem at the time of this writing is 16 terabytes based on VFS limitations. This is further reduced by restrictions on the maximum size of a block device (2 terabytes) in versions of the Linux kernel up to and including 2.4. As with all the other journaling filesystems discussed in this book, it's comforting to know that JFS has storage and reference capabilities beyond those currently supported by the operating system. You can safely adopt JFS today and be confident that your JFS storage can grow as soon as the addressing capabilities of the operating system are improved. Two terabytes should keep most of us bust for a little while, at any rate.

At the other end of the spectrum, the minimum size of a JFS filesystem is 16 MB, which means that you cannot create a JFS filesystem on removable media such as floppy disks. This isn't much of a disappointment because creating a journaling filesystem on a floppy disk would be the filesystem designer's equivalent of making a ship in a bottle—conceptually interesting but not useful for any reason other than making someone else wonder how you did it (followed quickly by wondering why you bothered).

Certain aspects of JFS use their own terminology, which shouldn't surprise anyone accustomed to using to products from IBM. IBM uses the term "aggregate" to refer to a pool of available storage such as a formatted disk partition, formatted disk, or logical volume. One or more *filesets* (what we would typically think of as filesystems) can then be created and managed within an aggregate using the mkfs.jfs utility. Both aggregates and filesets therefore contain superblock and related information about the storage that they represent.

> **NOTE**
>
> The current release of JFS for Linux only supports one fileset per aggregate, but the aggregate/fileset terminology has been preserved until this limitation is removed in subsequent releases of JFS. The use of terms such as aggregate and fileset are consistent with their use in distributed filesystems such as DCE DFS (Distributed Computing Environment Distributed File System), an overview of which was provided in Chapter 8, "Third-Party Journaling Filesystems." Preserving this terminology is not just nostalgia for the DCE DFS but shows that the data structures used in JFS aggregate metadata are designed for future expansion.
>
> Once again, you can use JFS today and be confident that you won't run up against some conceptual limitation in the relatively near future. JFS is a robust, usable filesystem that satisfies current requirements while still keeping an eye on the future. Throughout the rest of this chapter, I'll use the more common term, filesystem, to refer to general aspects of JFS filesets and journaling filesystems in general, and I'll use fileset whenever information is specific to JFS filesets.

JFS logs information about changes to filesystem metadata as atomic transactions. If the system is restarted without cleanly unmounting a JFS fileset, any transactions in the log that are not marked as having been completed on disk are replayed when the filesystem is checked for consistency before it is mounted, restoring the consistency of the filesystem metadata. Because the log contains metadata only rather than actual user data, this guarantees the structural consistency of the filesystem but not the contents of the files in the filesystem. Files being edited when the system went down will not reflect any updates not successfully written to disk.

JFS keeps track of filesystem metadata changes in its log to ensure the consistency of the filesystem so that it can be made available as quickly as possible after a system is restarted for any reason. Logging user data, which is possible in other journaling filesystems such as the ext3 filesystem, is much slower than simply logging metadata. This is largely due to the amount of information that the system has to write twice—once to the log, as a record of pending changes, and then once again to the filesystem itself. Logging changes to actual file data further decreases the possible performance of a filesystem by adding the overhead required to maintain the log. Logging changes to file data also substantially increases disk space requirements because the log for an active filesystem can be large.

> **TIP**
>
> If you need to guarantee the consistency of writes to specific files in a journaling filesystem, such as JFS, that does not support file logging, open those files using the open() command's O_SYNC or O_DSYNC options. This forces any updates to these files to be made synchronously, meaning that the writes must complete before any other filesystem activity can take place. This also means that developers must identify files for which consistency is critical but improves overall filesystem performance compared to the overhead of logging all file data changes.

The actual log for a JFS fileset is maintained in the JFS aggregate where that fileset is located. A single log can be used by multiple filesets at the same time (after JFS on Linux supports multiple filesets within an aggregate). At the moment, each aggregate contains both a single fileset and a single log.

Like the Linux ext2 and XFS journaling filesystems, JFS divides the space available for use (in the case of JFS, within each aggregate) into allocation groups. The size of an allocation group is defined when a fileset is created and is stored in the superblock for the aggregate. Each allocation group maintains its own data structures to manage free and allocated space within itself. This provides several advantages, such as

- Allocation groups can therefore use relative block, extent, and inode pointers for data structures specific to a given allocation group, saving space in its internal data structures.

- Space allocation within an allocation group provides another level of indirection for filesystem allocation and block references, increasing the potential size of a JFS filesystem as compared to a filesystem that had to provide explicit block references global to the filesystem.

- Maintaining data structures, such as superblocks, that are specific to each allocation group helps increase performance by reducing locking delays and generally supporting parallel allocation and access across different allocation groups.

- Dividing a filesystem into some number of allocation groups, each of which maintains its own data structures, makes it easier to subsequently increase the size of the filesystem by simply adding new allocation groups to an existing filesystem. As discussed later in this section, other advanced features of JFS (such as dynamic inode allocation) also help simplify the process of increasing the size of XFS filesystems both internally and administratively.

During allocation, JFS attempts to cluster file and directory inodes and disk blocks together to maximize disk locality, reducing the amount of head movement required when searching for related disk blocks. The size of the allocation groups used in JFS reduces the possibility of physically locating the disk space associated with specific files close to each other but instead provides "logical locality," where all the disk storage associated with a file is optimally located in the same allocation group.

It's rare to create a fileset whose size is an even multiple of the allocation group size and is actually unnecessary unless you're obsessive. In JFS, the last allocation group is handled as a complete allocation group even though it rarely has as much available storage as the other, full-sized allocation groups. To resolve this inequity, the bitmap representing block allocation within the partial allocation group is constructed such that nonexistent blocks in the allocation group simply appear to have already been allocated. Truly clever.

When a JFS fileset is created on a Linux system, it not only reserves space for the log in the aggregate in which it is created but also reserves a certain amount of working space for use by its fileset consistency checking application, `fsck.jfs`. The information in this section can be extracted and examined for debugging purposes using various utilities discussed later in the section "Support Software for JFS Filesystems." Using the `fsck.jfs` utility is explained later in this chapter, in the section "Checking JFS Filesystem Consistency."

JFS is designed to maximize performance and minimize inherent limitations as much as possible. Like XFS, JFS does not preallocate inodes but allocates them as needed when files and directories are created. As with other filesystems that dynamically allocate inodes, this helps remove potential limitations in the number of files and directories that can be created in a JFS fileset. JFS provides two different forms of directory organization, optimized for both ends of the spectrum of directory sizes. Small directories containing up to eight entries are stored within the directory inode, reducing disk consumption and the need to allocate separate inodes for each of these entries. This limit of eight entries does not include the generic references to the directory itself ('.') and its parent directory ('..'), which are stored elsewhere in the directory inode. Larger directories follow a more standard inode allocation mechanism, where the inodes are organized as B+Trees indexed by name, making it easy to find a specific directory entry as quickly as possible.

JFS uses extents for both inode and data allocation. As explained in Chapter 1, "Introduction to Filesystems," extents are ranges of adjacent, free disk blocks allocated together. In JFS, extents can range in size from 1 to 16777215 (2**24 - 1) blocks. Extent-based allocation helps minimize internal fragmentation (whether or not the data associated with a specific file is as contiguous as possible). Like any filesystem, creating, deleting, and moving files and directories in the course of normal operations tends to create some fragmentation within the filesystem itself. Known as *external fragmentation*, this simply means that the extents used by files and directories that currently exist in the filesystem may be separated from each other by extents that were formerly associated with files and directories that have since been deleted.

> **NOTE**
>
> The JFS development team is working on a defragmentation utility called `defragfs` that system administrators can run to pack unused extents together by moving used extents on the fileset. The defragmentation process will also combine multiple extents allocated to a single file, maximizing contiguous allocation for existing files. The in-progress source code for this utility is included in the `jfsutils` package, but the `defragfs` utility contained in the JFS utilities included with this book should not be considered safe to use on any production fileset at this time.

As with XFS, JFS provides direct support for *sparse files*, which are logically large files that contain relatively little data. Data can be written to any location in a sparse file without allocating space for any intervening portions of the file that do not yet contain user data. Although a sparse file reports its size as its maximum size, data blocks are only allocated when data is actually written to the file—reading information from any location in a sparse file that has not previously been written returns zero-filled data. Sparse files are typically used by applications, such as databases, whose large, record-oriented files need to provide random access to a large address space without simultaneously wasting disk space that has not yet been written with user data.

JFS currently lacks support for many of the advanced features of XFS, such as quota support, ACLs, extended file attributes, and so on, and therefore does not come with an extensive collection of utilities such as those provided with XFS. Sophisticated utilities for defragmenting and increasing the size of existing JFS filesets are actively under development but not ready for production use at the time of this writing. However, having been developed and used for years on both OS/2 and AIX machines, it has a performance pedigree that still makes it well worth considering for use in production Linux environments.

Support Software for JFS Filesystems

Built-in support for the JFS filesystem is not yet present in any commercial Linux distribution that I have used. Whether or not your favorite Linux distribution includes integrated support for the JFS filesystem depends on the people who packaged your distribution. This section discusses the utilities associated with the JFS filesystem and the features that they provide.

If your Linux distribution does not include support for the JFS filesystem, you can always add it yourself by obtaining the following:

- Source code or binaries for a version of the Linux kernel that includes support for JFS
- Source code and patches to the version of the kernel that you are using to add JFS support to that kernel
- Source code or binary packages for the utilities used to mount, modify, use, and administer JFS filesets and aggregates

Unlike journaling filesystems such as ext3, adding JFS support to your system does not require that you install and update any standard Linux packages (other than the kernel itself).

If the Linux distribution and version of Linux that you are running does not include support for the JFS filesystem, the CD that accompanies this book includes a sample kernel source code distribution in the CD's `kernels` subdirectory and associated JFS patches in the CD's `JFS` directory. Information about installing the kernel source code and applying the patches, and JFS-specific information about building and installing a kernel is provided later in this chapter.

If the Linux distribution and version of Linux that you are running does not include support for the JFS filesystem, you will also need to compile and install the `jfsutils` package, version 1.0.4, which is also included in the `JFS` subdirectory of the CD. This package contains the following JFS-related utilities:

- `fsck.jfs`—The utility for checking the consistency of a JFS fileset and correcting it whenever necessary.
- `logdump`—Writes the contents of the log for a specific JFS fileset into a text file.
- `logredo`—Applies all committed transactions in the log for a specified JFS fileset, restoring the consistency of that filesystem.
- `mkfs.jfs`—Creates a JFS fileset. This is the program invoked when you execute the command `mkfs -t jfs...` Program options enable you to specify various parameters

for JFS fileset creation. See the section "Creating a JFS Filesystem" later in this chapter for a complete discussion of using this utility.

- xchkdmp—Formats the contents of a JFS fsck dump file produced by the xchklog utility.

- xchklog—Dumps information about the last filesystem consistency check performed on a specified fileset.

- xpeek—Examines or modifies a JFS fileset. This is similar to the debugfs command provided for use with ext2 and ext3 filesystems, or the xfs_admin command provided with the XFS journaling filesystem.

> **NOTE**
>
> As you may notice, the JFS utilities included with this book also include two in-progress utilities: defragfs, a JFS fileset defragmentation utility, and extendfs, a utility for increasing the size of an existing JFS fileset. These utilities are actively under development, but the versions included in the JFS utilities that accompany this book should not be used on a production fileset. You can check the JFS Web site (http://oss.software.ibm.com/developerworks/opensource/jfs/) for newer versions of these utilities that may be safe to use.

JFS does not require changes to basic Linux system packages other than the kernel itself. This is largely because it does not currently support extended filesystem features such as ACLs, extended file attributes, and so on. Using JFS does not require many specialized utilities because it is essentially just a journaling filesystem without many bells and whistles at this point.

Adding JFS Support to Your System

As mentioned earlier, JFS support is not yet provided in any Linux distribution that I've had the opportunity to use. Luckily, being able to add new system services and applications to your system is one of the most exciting and empowering aspects of open-source operating systems such as Linux.

This section provides hands-on, how-to information about building and installing a kernel that provides support for JFS filesystems, and about installing, activating, using, and administering JFS filesets.

Building a Kernel with JFS Support

The CD that accompanies this book includes the source code for version 2.4.7 of the Linux kernel, which is the most advanced version of the Linux kernel for which patches are readily available, and against which substantial testing has been done. The 2.4.7 kernel is therefore the kernel version that I have chosen to use to show how easy it is to add JFS support to your Linux system. The CD also includes the patches necessary to add support for the JFS filesystem to that kernel.

> **NOTE**
>
> As mentioned in each chapter that involves compiling applications, if you have never built a kernel before, doing so is a great learning experience. Although the whole idea of prepackaged Linux installation is to protect users from the need to "roll their own" kernel and Linux utilities, compiling a kernel is an excellent way to familiarize yourself with the conceptual internals and organization of Linux. The instructions in this book for compiling kernels create kernels that have special names and will thus not overwrite the current version of the Linux kernel that you are using.

Patching the Linux 2.4.7 Kernel for JFS Support

Appendix A, "Using the CD-ROM: Installing, Updating, and Compiling Kernels," provides detailed information about installing Linux kernel source and selecting kernel configuration options. This section provides basic information about installing the specific version of the Linux kernel source that we'll be using in the examples throughout the rest of this chapter. The procedures described in this section are generally relevant even if you want to add and activate JFS support in a different version of the Linux kernel sources, such as newer versions of the kernel or the version of the Linux kernel that was shipped with the Linux distribution that you are using.

> **TIP**
>
> If you are familiar with building Linux kernels and want to install and activate JFS support in the most up-to-date version of the Linux kernel, you can obtain the latest version of the Linux kernel from the central Web repository for Linux kernel sources, `http://www.kernel.org`. Then check the Web site for JFS (`http://oss.software.ibm.com/developerworks/opensource/jfs/`) to check for patches for that Linux kernel version to download and install them, if JFS support is still not present in that version of the Linux kernel. One of these days. . .

Adding support for the JFS filesystem to the default Linux 2.4.7 kernel sources works slightly differently than simply patching the existing kernel code. To provide a single set of source files that can be used to update multiple versions of the Linux kernel, IBM packages the updated files to add support for JFS for multiple versions of the Linux kernel together. To add support for the JFS filesystem to the Linux 2.4.7 kernel, you simply install the kernel source and then unpack the files associated with JFS in the kernel source directory. Unpacking the JFS source creates a jfs directory and installs enhanced versions of some of the files required to build the Linux kernel. You then replace the existing files with the versions into which JFS support has been integrated and then configure and install the new kernel. To simplify things even further, I've provided a small shell script that does this for you based on the version of the Linux kernel that you're updating.

The source for the Linux 2.4.7 kernel is located in the kernels subdirectory of the CD that accompanies this book. Install this kernel as described in "Installing the Kernel Source Code" in Appendix A; then use the following steps to add JFS support to that kernel:

1. Make sure that the X Window System is running and use the su command to become root in an xterm or other terminal window.

2. Change your working directory to the directory created when you installed the Linux source code as explained in Appendix A:

   ```
   cd /usr/src/linux-2.4.7
   ```

3. Extract the contents of the JFS files for the Linux kernel into that directory:

   ```
   tar zxvf <Path-to-CD>/jfs/jfs-1.0.4.tar.gz
   ```

4. Use the install_jfs shell script provided in the jfs subdirectory of the CD to replace the default kernel files with the versions of the JFS files for the Linux 2.4.7 kernel:

   ```
   sh <Path-to-CD>/jfs/install_jfs 2.4.7
   ```

   This shell script lists each of the files that it is updating and saves the original versions of those files with the extension .old in case you want to compare them to the new files to see what has changed. After this shell script completes, you're ready to configure a kernel with support for the JFS filesystem.

Activating JFS Support in the Kernel

This section explains how to activate support for the JFS filesystem in the source code for the Linux 2.4.7 kernel. For an overview of the conceptual basics behind building a modern Linux kernel and activating support for different features and hardware in the kernel, see "Configuring Your Kernel" in Appendix A.

NOTE

It's generally a good idea to compile in support for any filesystems that your system uses regularly. You must install any type of filesystem that you use for your system's root partition as part of the kernel, not as a module. Filesystems that you only inter-act with occasionally (such as AppleTalk or various network filesystems) can still be compiled as modules to keep your kernel as small as possible.

If you have already compiled a kernel for the computer system on which you are building a new kernel, you can use the configuration information from that kernel to save time when configuring the new kernel. Reusing existing configuration data from an existing kernel is explained in Appendix A.

This section explains the options specific to activating support for the JFS filesystem in the kernel we are building. This section describes how to configure JFS options using the X Window System-based Linux kernel configurator:

1. Log in as root or use the su command to become root.

2. In a terminal window running under an X Window System window manager or desktop, change the directory to /usr/src/linux-2.4.7 and execute the make xconfig command. The commands related to compiling and loading support for the Linux X Window System kernel configurator display in the window in which you executed the make xconfig command. Eventually, the X Window System Linux kernel configurator displays, as shown in Figure 5.1.

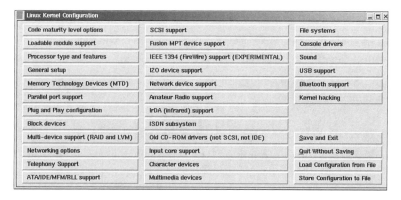

FIGURE 5.1

The X Window System-based Linux kernel configurator.

3. Click the File Systems button in the X Window System kernel configuration dialog. A new dialog displays, as shown in Figure 5.2.

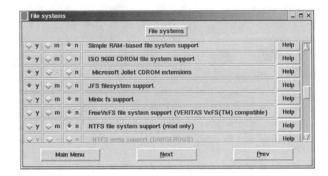

FIGURE 5.2

The X kernel configurator's File Systems Configuration dialog.

4. Scroll down until you see the JFS Filesystem Support entry. Click Y beside this entry.

5. Click the Main Menu button to return to the primary `make xconfig` dialog.

6. After selecting any other kernel configuration options relevant to the kernel that you are building (such as those specific to the hardware in your system), save your updated kernel configuration.

   If you reused the configuration data from an existing kernel, use the Store Configuration to File button to display a dialog that enables you to explicitly save your new kernel configuration with the name `.config` in the main directory of the kernel that you are configuring.

   If you configured the current kernel from scratch (that is, without reading in configuration data from another kernel), simply click the Save and Exit button.

7. Click OK to close the final dialog and return to the Linux shell prompt. You're now ready to compile the kernel!

Compiling and Installing a JFS Kernel

After updating and configuring the Linux 2.4.7 kernel, you're ready to compile and install your new Linux kernel. All the information that you need to compile and install this kernel is provided in Appendix A. This section just provides a checklist for the steps that you should follow.

After you install, patch, and configure the Linux 2.4.7 kernel for JFS filesystem support and to match your hardware, you must do the following to install and use that kernel:

1. Add a special extension for this kernel to its Makefile, making it easy to identify the special features in the kernel. I typically name kernels that support different filesystems along the lines of `linux-<kernel-version>-<filesystem-type>`.

2. Execute the following `make` commands in this order to correctly initialize dependencies and to build and install the new kernel and any associated loadable modules:

```
make dep
make
make modules
make install
make modules_install
```

I suggest doing these steps as discrete commands to make it easy to spot any compilation or installation failures along the way. If you're really cocky, you can reduce these commands to the following single command line, but you'd still be wise to scroll back to make sure that there were no problems:

```
make dep ; make install ; make modules ; make modules_install
```

3. Modify the boot loader configuration file for the boot loader you're using on your system, as described in "Booting a New Kernel" in Appendix A and rerun `lilo` if necessary.

You're now almost ready to reboot your system and use the JFS filesystem. Before doing that, however, you must also compile and install the utilities discussed in the next section to ensure that your system can create, mount, and use JFS filesets.

Installing the JFS Utilities

This section explains how to configure, compile, and install the various utilities that enable you to administer and use JFS filesystems on your Linux system. These utilities support all the basic features of any filesystem, such as creating, repairing, and producing diagnostic data for JFS filesets.

To install version 1.0.4 of the `jfsutils` package, included on the CD that accompanies this book, do the following:

1. Mount the CD and extract the `jfsutils` package from the file `jfs/jfsutils-1.0.4.tar.gz` to a directory on your system using a command like the following:

```
cd <target-directory>
tar zxvf <path-to-CD>/jfs/jfsutils-1.0.4.tar.gz
```

2. Change directory to `<target-directory>/jfsutils` and execute the `make` command to build the new versions of the utilities in the *jfsutils* package:

```
make
```

This produces verbose, system-specific output that's not useful to replicate here.

3. After all the utilities are compiled, install them on your system using the following commands:

```
make install
```

Your system now has version 1.0.4 of the jfsutils utilities and associated reference (man page) documentation installed.

Administering JFS Filesystems

This section explains how to create and use JFS filesets on your Linux systems. It begins by explaining how to create a JFS fileset using default values and then explores the various options provided to enable you to customize JFS filesets when creating them. Subsequent sections of this chapter explain how to mount a JFS fileset, exactly what occurs when checking the consistency of a JFS filesystem, and the syntax of the xpeek filesystem debugger provided with the JFS filesystem.

This section is somewhat smaller than equivalent sections for other journaling filesystems discussed in this book, such as XFS. This is because, depending on your perspective, JFS support on Linux is either simpler or not as sophisticated as the support for filesystems such as XFS. Few JFS-specific utilities are provided as part of the jfsutils package, and of those that are provided, few are designed for purposes other than debugging. As JFS becomes more widely used on Linux, utilities currently under development will achieve the level of functionality and testing that would enable me to recommend them. Utilities that will be available for JFS in upcoming releases are the defragfs utility, which will enable system administrators to defragment JFS partitions, and the extendfs utility, which will simplify expanding the size of an existing JFS fileset. Similarly, when quota, ACL, and extended attribute support are available for JFS, related utilities will be available to help you manage those aspects of a JFS filesystem.

One set of utilities for JFS that is particularly conspicuous by its absence is a set of backup and restore utilities that understand JFS filesystem data structures. These utilities are not necessary for journaling filesystems such as ext3 because it uses the standard ext2 data structures, which the dump and restore programs understand. The XFS filesystem provides its own xfsdump and xfsrestore utilities to support the extra data that XFS files, directories, and filesystems contain. At the time of this writing, the standard Linux dump utility cannot read JFS fileset headers and will therefore exit immediately after complaining about a bad magic number in the JFS superblock. (The magic number is used to identify the filesystem type.)

Without valid backups in dump format, the Linux restore program is therefore irrelevant for JFS filesystems. At this time, JFS filesets can only be backed up using utilities such as tar or cpio that back up a filesystem by walking through its directory structure rather than directly accessing filesystem data structures. You can use a utility such as dd to copy an entire aggregate to a backup device, but this makes it impossible to selectively restore individual files and directories. You can also use a centralized backup utility such as Amanda (discussed in the "Centralizing Backups" section of Chapter 15, "Backing Up, Restoring, and Managing Linux Filesystems") with JFS filesystems because this utility invokes filesystem-level backup utilities such as tar.

Creating a JFS Filesystem

Like most other modern Linux filesystems, JFS filesystems are created by using the /sbin/mkfs wrapper program and specifying the -t jfs option. This causes the /sbin/mkfs wrapper program to pass all the other command-line arguments to the /sbin/mkfs.jfs program, which is the JFS-specific filesystem creation utility.

> **NOTE**
>
> The examples used in this section execute the mkfs.jfs command directly, to emphasize the name of the command actually doing real work. (And the name of the command that you will want to supply to the man command if you want to see the detailed online reference information available for the mkfs.jfs command.)

The mkfs.jfs utility can take a number of command-line arguments that enable you to fine-tune different aspects of the fileset that you are creating, but the following is an example of using it in its simplest form and the resulting output:

```
# mkfs.jfs /dev/hdc2
mkfs.jfs development version: $Name: v1_0_4 $
Warning!  All data on device /dev/hdc2 will be lost!
Continue? (Y/N) y
Format completed successfully.
2097648 kilobytes total disk space.
```

> **NOTE**
>
> By default, the mkfs.jfs application is interactive, requiring that you confirm that you want to create a fileset on the specified partition. This is because, as with any filesystem creation utility, creating a JFS partition on a partition erases any other filesystems and data that may have previously been located on that partition. You can skip the interactive mode when executing the mkfs.jfs utility by specifying the -f option to force the mkfs.jfs utility to create the partition without requiring confirmation.

The output from the `mkfs.jfs` command lists the total capacity of the fileset that you have just created. Like the `mkfs.xfs` utility used to create XFS filesystems, the `mkfs.jfs` utility is exceptionally fast because it does not have to do many of the time-consuming tasks required by filesystems such as ext2 and ReiserFS, which preallocate filesystem structures such as inodes.

After mounting an empty JFS fileset (as explained later in this chapter, in the section "Mounting a JFS Filesystem"), displaying the list of mounted volumes shows that very little of the available space in a JFS filesystem is used by the JFS fileset itself, as in the following example:

```
# df /dev/hdc2
Filesystem          1k-blocks     Used Available Use% Mounted on
/dev/hdc2            2088164       388   2087776  1% /jfs_test
```

Compare this to the output of the `df` command after formatting and mounting the same partition as a standard ext2 partition:

```
# df /dev/hdc2
Filesystem          1k-blocks     Used Available Use% Mounted on
/dev/hdc2            2064144        20   1959244  1% /ext2_test
```

The amount of available space on the partition is substantially different, even though the ext2 filesystem claims to be using many fewer disk blocks initially. Note that the basic size of the filesystem itself is also reported as being different, even though exactly the same partition was used. The difference in these initial size and availability values is due to two reasons:

- ext2 filesystems use a significant amount of space when preallocating inodes and other internal filesystem structures, which is not done when creating JFS filesystems.

- JFS filesets do not pre-reserve "slop space" (as opposed to swap space) that is set aside for use by the superuser as the fileset fills up. The default amount of space reserved for the use of the superuser in an ext2 filesystem is 5 percent and can be overridden by using the `-m` option when creating an ext2 filesystem.

The default values used when creating a JFS fileset are suitable for creating JFS filesets for most purposes. The next two sections explain using a specific `mkfs.jfs` option to create a JFS filesystem with a different journal size and the reasons why you might want to do this, and then provide an overview of all the options available to the `mkfs.jfs` command.

Specifying an Alternate Journal Size for JFS Filesystems

By default, 4 percent of the size of the aggregate (disk or partition) on which a JFS fileset is created is reserved for the log for that aggregate. As mentioned earlier in this chapter, JFS is designed to eventually support creating multiple filesets on a single aggregate, all of which can share the same log. Creating multiple filesets per aggregate is not currently supported under Linux, but when it is, specifying a particular log size for a fileset will be useful, especially in the case where multiple filesets share that log.

Even now, there are cases in which you might want to specify a log size greater than the default value. You may want to increase the size of the log if, for example:

- You know that the applications using a specific filesystem frequently perform many filesystem operations under the control of a single process, and may therefore have long-running filesystem metadata transactions.
- The filesystem is heavily used by many simultaneous users.

The `mkfs.jfs` command provides the `-ls` (log size) option to enable you to specify a log size other than the default value of 4 percent. Log size is always specified in megabytes, and therefore does not require that you provide the units. The size of the log that you want to create is separated from the `-ls` option by a colon, rather than a space as is commonly done with more traditional Linux and Unix commands.

NOTE

You can also use the `-ls` option to specify a log size smaller than the default size if you absolutely must maximize the amount of disk space in a fileset that is available for use by programs. Like the logs used by the other journaling filesystems discussed in this book, the space available in the JFS log is recycled after metadata transactions are actually committed to the filesystem. Using a smaller log size may be suitable on JFS filesets where you know that most of the filesystem activity will be done by short-lived processes that modify relatively small amounts of filesystem metadata.

A good example of this may be a partition used to hold Internet news or to store the e-mail for your system. Such filesystems would also be candidates for using a smaller block size because the files that they create and use are typically also very small, but block sizes other than 4 KB are not currently supported in JFS.

For example, to create a fileset with a 10 MB log, you would use a command like the following:

```
# mkfs.jfs -ls:10 -f /dev/hdc2
mkfs.jfs development version: $Name: v1_0_4 $
Format completed successfully.
2097648 kilobytes total disk space
```

Note that the amount of total disk space reported is the same in this and the previous example—this is because that figure reflects the size of the aggregate, not the fileset. After mounting the fileset, using the df command shows that the fileset is indeed larger due to the reduced size of the log:

```
# df /dev/hdc2
Filesystem              1k-blocks       Used Available Use% Mounted on
/dev/hdc2                 2087140        388   2086752   1% /jfs_test
```

> **NOTE**
>
> At the moment, the maximum size of the log for a JFS fileset is 10 percent of the fileset size. This constraint is hardwired into the mkfs.jfs source code but really shouldn't be a problem given the size of today's filesystems.

Summary of JFS Filesystem Creation Options

The mkfs.jfs command has the following options:

- -f—Do not ask for confirmation before creating the file system.
- -1—Causes exhaustive block verification to be done and lists bad blocks encountered when creating the fileset. Using this option takes virtually forever and causes performance of your system to nose-dive during the JFS fileset creation process.
- -ls:log_size—Enables you to specify the size of the log in megabytes. If this option is not used, the default size of the log is 4 percent of the size of the aggregate.
- -os2:1—Sets bits in the filesystem header that provide support that is not case sensitive for compatibility with OS/2. This option is rarely used, except perhaps by the 11 people who use OS/2. However, it is comforting to know that the option is available if you really need to implement this sort of totally misleading and often incomprehensible behavior in a filesystem.
- -v:volume_label—Enables you to specify a label for the volume. The volume labels used by JFS cannot currently be used with the standard volume label syntax in the /etc/fstab file because the mount program doesn't understand where to find them in the JFS fileset header.

In addition to the options supported in the version of the jfsutils package provided with this book, other options that will eventually be supported by the mkfs.jfs command are the following:

- -bs:block_size—Will enable you to specify the block size (512, 1024, 2048, or 4096) used when creating a JFS fileset
- -ld:log_device—Will enable you to specify the name of a log device to use with the JFS filesystem that you are creating

These options are not currently supported but are already present in the source code for the mkfs.jfs utility, so one of these days they (and other options, in the standard Linux/Unix tradition) will be available.

Mounting a JFS Filesystem

Mounting a JFS fileset enables you to actually access it through the filesystem of your Linux machine. Mounting JFS filesets is easier than mounting any other type of journaling filesystem under Linux because the Linux mount command does not currently provide any special options for use with JFS filesets. Mounting a jfs filesystem is therefore as simple as executing a command like the following:

```
# mount -t jfs /dev/hdc2 /jfs_test
```

To add JFS filesets to the standard file system mount table found in the file /etc/fstab, you simply add standard entries like the following:

```
/dev/hdc2      /jfs_test      jfs      defaults           0 1
```

Because no JFS-specific mount options are currently supported by the mount command, the standard defaults entry in the mount options section is fine, although you can also use any of the generic options that the mount command provides for all filesystems, as explained in Chapter 3, "Overview of Journaling Filesystems."

When adding entries for JFS filesets to the /etc/fstab file, the contents of the last two fields in the /etc/fstab entry are important:

- It is important that the next-to-last column in the /etc/fstab file contains a 0 if you are using the standard Linux dump utility to do backups. A 0 in this column tells the dump utility that it should not attempt to back up this filesystem. At the time of this writing, the standard Linux dump utility cannot read JFS fileset headers and will therefore exit immediately after complaining about a bad magic number in the JFS superblock. This may cause your backup script to fail and will certainly not give you any backups of your JFS filesystems.

- It is important that the last column contains a 1, rather than a 0, as is normally used with the ext3 and XFS journaling filesystems. The value in this column indicates whether the filesystem-specific consistency checking utility should be run before mounting the filesystem. JFS is not integrated into the mount command and Linux kernel to the same extent as the ext3 and XFS journaling filesystems are, and therefore mounting a fileset does not force the log to be replayed and the fileset to be brought up-to-date whenever necessary. Instead, any log replay or other cleanup necessary to restore the consistency of a JFS fileset is done by the fsck.jfs program, as explained in the next section.

As mentioned in the previous section "Creating a JFS Filesystem," at the time of this writing, the `mount` command does not understand how to read a JFS volume label. When JFS volume labels are actually supported by the `mount` command, the following two `/etc/fstab` entries would be equivalent if you had formatted a JFS partition with a command like `mkfs.jfs -v:/jfs_test /dev/hdc2`:

```
/dev/hdc2              /jfs_test      jfs       defaults       0 1
LABEL=/jfs_test        /jfs_test      jfs       defaults       0 1
```

Hopefully, direct support for JFS filesystems will be added to the `mount` command, at which point this syntax will be valid, as it is with other filesystems.

Checking JFS Filesystem Consistency

The standard Linux filesystem consistency checker is the `fsck` program, just as it is on Unix systems. On Linux systems, `fsck` is located in `/sbin`. Like the `mkfs` program, the `/sbin/fsck` program is actually a wrapper program that calls a filesystem-specific version of `fsck` that is named `/sbin/fsck.<filesystem-type>`. For example, the name of the program executed by the `/sbin/fsck` program to check the consistency of a JFS fileset is named `/etc/fsck.jfs`. The `/sbin/fsck` program determines the system-specific version of `fsck` to call based on either information it extracts from the `/etc/fstab` file or by examining the filesystem itself. Examining the filesystem is necessary, for example, when the `/etc/fstab` file gives the filesystem type as `auto`, which essentially means "figure it out yourself" to both the `mount` and `fsck` utilities.

> **NOTE**
>
> The examples used in this section execute the `fsck.jfs` command directly, to emphasize the name of the command actually doing real work. (And the name of the command that you will want to supply to the `man` command if you want to see the detailed online reference information available for the `fsck.jfs` command.)

The primary advantages of journaling filesystems are that they provide faster system restart times and help minimize the amount of filesystem changes that you can lose after a system crash. Unlike the ext3 and XFS filesystems, which are more closely integrated into the kernel and the Linux `mount` command, the JFS filesystem does not automatically replay its journal when it is mounted, but rather when its consistency is verified using the `fsck.jfs` command. Normally, replaying the journal for any journaling filesystem restores it to a consistent state as far as filesystem metadata is concerned, and all is well.

However, as with any random problems that may cause computer systems to reboot, there are cases in which the JFS filesystem is actually damaged or inconsistent beyond the type of information recorded in the journal. In general, the most common instance of this situation is problems with the disk subsystem(s) on which JFS filesets are stored. These can be either hard disk or controller problems and "normally" reveal themselves when you begin to see error messages on the console that report problems reading from or writing a specific disk.

JFS provides the fsck.jfs utility to check and correct problems in JFS filesets, as well as to replay the log before the fileset is mounted. Normally, the fsck.jfs command either doesn't have to do anything (as when the fileset was cleanly unmounted before the system was restarted), or has to perform minimal replay of committed log entries to restore the consistency of the fileset.

The fsck.jfs utility can take a number of command-line arguments that enable you to control the degree to which it examines a JFS fileset, but the following is an example of using it in its simplest form and the resulting output:

```
# fsck.jfs /dev/hdc2
Block size in bytes:  4096
File system size in blocks:  524412
Phase 1 - Check Blocks, Files/Directories, and Directory Entries.
Phase 2 - Count Links.
Phase 3 - Rescan for Duplicate Blocks and Verify Directory Tree.
Phase 4 - Report Problems.
Phase 5 - Check Connectivity.
Phase 6 - Perform Approved Corrections.
Phase 7 - Verify File/Directory Allocation Maps.
Phase 8 - Verify Disk Allocation Maps.
File system checked READ ONLY.
File system is clean.
```

Note that manually executing the fsck.jfs command from a command line executes the fsck.jfs command on the specified fileset in read-only mode, causing it to only report errors that it encounters rather than actually repair them. You must use one or more of the options provided by the fsck.jfs command to actually update and repair a JFS fileset, if necessary.

The options available for use with the fsck.jfs command are the following:

- -a—Known as autocheck mode, using this option causes the fsck.jfs command to replay the transaction log, repair all problems automatically, and continue checking the fileset only if the aggregate state is dirty. This mode is typically the default mode used when the fsck.jfs program is called before mounting a JFS fileset after a computer system is restarted.

- -c—Tells the fsck.jfs program to continue checking the fileset only after successfully replaying the transaction log if the state of the aggregate is marked as dirty in its header.

- -d—Displays additional status, diagnostic, and debugging messages displayed when the fsck.jfs command is executed. This information provides details about the number of files, directories, and free blocks available in the fileset, and also provides summary information about the amount of space within the fileset used by JFS itself.

- -f:*fix-level*—Using this option enables you to specify the type of filesystem repairs that the fsck.jfs command will perform. Valid fix levels are the following:

  - 0—Reports any errors encountered when replaying the transaction log, but does not attempt to repair them.

  - 1—Reports any errors encountered when replaying the transaction log and interactively prompts you for permission to repair them.

  - 2—Automatically repairs any errors encountered when replaying the transaction log.

  If the -f option is not specified on the mkfs.jfs command line, the default behavior of the fsck.jfs program is the same as if the -f:0 option has been used. If the -f option is specified, but no fix level is provided, fix level 2 is assumed.

- -o—Omits replaying the transaction log. This option is rarely used and is intended to help you work around situations in which the transaction log is corrupted and replaying it could therefore corrupt, rather than repair, the fileset.

- -r—Runs the fsck.jfs command in interactive autocheck mode, which replays the transaction log automatically but subsequently prompts you for confirmation if any other problems are encountered. This option is commonly used when verifying the consistency of a fileset prior to mounting it after a computer system has been restarted.

As shown in the output from the fsck.jfs command shown earlier in this section, the fsck.jfs command performs eight discrete steps when simply examining the consistency of a fileset. When invoked with an option such as -f:2 that will actually modify and repair the fileset if necessary, the fsck.jfs command does the following:

1. Opens the fileset and examines the primary superblock to find the beginning of the fileset and fileset parameters such as the block size used in the filesystem and the total size of the fileset.

2. Replays the transaction log, if any outstanding but complete transactions are found in the log.

3. (fsck.jfs phase 1) Checks all the blocks currently allocated to files in directories in the filesystem and verifies that all file and directory entries actually point to valid extents in the filesystem.

4. (fsck.jfs phase 2) Counts the links to each file and directory in the filesystem to verify that the link count for each file and directory in the fileset actually matches the number of times that file or directory is referred to.

5. (fsck.jfs phase 3) Scans the filesystem for any blocks that more than one file or directory claims to own and verifies the structure of the B+Tree used to hold directory information.

6. (fsck.jfs phase 4) Displays a list of any problems that were encountered in the filesystem. The filesystem is not modified during this phase.

7. (fsck.jfs phase 5) Checks that every file and directory found in the filesystem is actually linked into the filesystem B+Tree at some point.

8. (fsck.jfs phase 6) Performs any corrections necessary to resolve the problems identified in phase 4.

9. (fsck.jfs phase 7) Using the lists of all blocks and extents currently allocated to files and directories, verifies the summary bitmaps for the blocks allocated to files and directories stored in the fileset header.

10. (fsck.jfs phase 8) Verifies the summary bitmaps for all disk blocks in the filesystem, including disk blocks allocated to JFS filesystem structures themselves, and recalculates all information about disk usage within the filesystem.

11. If any necessary repairs have been completed correctly, or if none were necessary, the fsck.jfs program marks the fileset as "clean" and exits.

The steps performed by the fsck.jfs are essentially the same as those done when manually verifying the consistency of any filesystem. Some steps are specific to the disk structures and extent-based allocation used in JFS aggregates and filesets, but the conceptual process is the same across almost all filesystems.

Using the xpeek Utility

The xpeek program is a powerful, low-level filesystem editing and debugging utility program that is conceptually similar to the debugfs command provided for use with ext2 and ext3 filesystems or the xfs_db command provided for use with XFS filesystems. The name of the xpeek program is doubtless inspired by the classic peek and poke commands provided in the BASIC programming language to enable you to directly read and write memory and program locations.

The cases in which you need to use the xpeek program are specific to a particular problem that you are trying to resolve. The xpeek program is also actively under development—some of the options listed in its help output are not yet completely implemented. This section provides a summary of the commands provided by the xpeek program, noting those which are unimplemented at the time of this writing.

NOTE

Using the xpeek program incorrectly can damage a JFS fileset beyond repair. Use the xpeek program only to make changes to a JFS fileset when absolutely necessary, and, if possible, always back up the JFS fileset before trying to repair problems using xpeek.

TIP

If, for some reason, you are using the xpeek utility on a valid JFS fileset, always unmount the fileset before running xpeek. Experimenting with xpeek on a mounted fileset that others might be using is the conceptual equivalent of learning to juggle by using loaded revolvers. You'll be lucky to only shoot yourself in the foot.

The xpeek program provides an interactive environment in which you can examine and modify various aspects of a JFS fileset. At the time of this writing, the commands available inside the xpeek program are the following:

- alter *<block>* *<offset>* *<hex-string>*—Enables you to replace the data located at a specified offset from a given block with a given hexadecimal string. The block number is specified as a decimal value, whereas the offset and replacement string must both be supplied as hexadecimal values.

- btree *<block>* *<offset>*—Displays a node of the B+Tree located at a hexadecimal offset from the specified block. This command is not currently implemented, but will eventually make it possible for you to walk the JFS B+Tree within xpeek and examine the attributes of various nodes.

- cbblfsck —Displays the portion of a JFS fileset in which bad block information is stored. Only IBM would feel that cbblfsck was a reasonable command.

- directory *<inode_number>* *<fileset>*—Displays the directory entry associated with the specified inode. The fileset value must always be zero but is provided for the future, when multiple filesets can be created and housed on a single aggregate. This command will eventually have a subcommand mode in which you can modify directory entries, but this mode is not currently implemented.

- display *<block>* *<offset>* *<format>* *<count>*—Displays *<count>* objects located at the specified *<offset>* from *<block>*, using the specified *<format>*. The *<block>* and *<count>* are specified as decimal values, whereas the *<offset>* is a hexadecimal value.

The `<format>` must be one of a (ASCII), b (block allocation map), d (decimal), i (inode), I (inode allocation map), s (superblock), x (hexadecimal), or X (extent allocation descriptor).

- dmap—Displays the header for the block allocation map in the current aggregate. Executing this command enters an interactive mode in which you can modify specific entries, walk through the entire map in hexadecimal or using the B+Tree in which it is stored, or return to the xpeek program's top command level.

- dtree `<inode_number>` `<fileset>`—Enables you to examine the B+Tree starting at a given decimal inode number. The fileset value must always be zero but is provided for the future, when multiple filesets can be created and housed on a single aggregate. Executing this command enters an interactive mode in which you can examine or modify specific entries, walk through the directory B+Tree, or return to the xpeek program's top command level.

- fsckwsphdr—Displays the header of the fileset workspace reserved for use by the fsck.jfs program. This is another easy-to-remember command.

- help—Displays a summary of the syntax for using both implemented and currently unimplemented xpeek commands.

- iag `<IAG_number>` <a | s> `<fileset>`—Displays information about the primary (a) or secondary (s) inode table used for the allocation group specified by `<IAG_number>`. The fileset value must always be zero but is provided for the future, when multiple filesets can be created and housed on a single aggregate. Executing this command enters an interactive mode in which you can display or modify the maps used to store inode extent information within that allocation group, or simply return to the xpeek command's top command level.

- inode `<inode_number>` <a | s> `<fileset>`—Displays information about the specified inode and enters an interactive mode in which you can query different inode tables.

- logsuper—Displays the superblock for the current aggregate's log and enters an interactive mode in which you can modify entries or return to the xpeek command's top command level.

- quit—Exits xpeek. This is certainly its most popular command.

- set `<variable>` `<value>`—Enables you to set the value of a user-defined variable within the xpeek program, presumably to use it for something. This command is not currently implemented.

- superblock <p | s>—Displays the primary (p) or secondary (s) superblock for the current aggregate and enters an interactive mode in which you can modify existing entries or return to the xpeek command's top command level.

- `s2perblock <p | s>`—Displays the primary (p) or secondary (s) superblock for the alternate superblock for the current aggregate and enters an interactive mode in which you can modify existing entries or return to the `xpeek` command's top command level. This is one of my favorite `xpeek` commands because I can pronounce it as "stupor block."

- `unset <variable>`—Deletes a variable that you previously set within the `xpeek` program. This command is not currently implemented, but that's okay because you can't currently set user-defined variables anyway.

- `xtree <inode_number> <fileset>`—Displays the allocation B+Tree associated with a file inode. Executing this command with a valid file inode enters an interactive mode in which you can examine and modify entries, as well as walking the B+Tree.

It's easy to poke fun at some of the current limitations of the subcommands provided by the `xpeek` command when listing them, but I'd be singing a different tune if a JFS fileset or aggregate was damaged, and the `xpeek` utility was my only hope to recover data that I depended on. The immaturity of some subcommands in the `xpeek` utility is a reflection of how new JFS is to Linux, not of a bad implementation. Community contributions to and enhancements of the commands currently supported in the `xpeek` command is only a matter of time, as more installations adopt JFS as their journaling filesystem of choice.

The ReiserFS Journaling Filesystem

IN THIS CHAPTER

The ReiserFS journaling filesystem is unique in many respects. Not only was it the first journaling filesystem to be publicly available for Linux, but it was also the first journaling filesystem to be accepted and integrated into the Linux kernel source code. Partially because of this, but also due to its excellent overall performance, the ReiserFS journaling filesystem is the filesystem of choice for the SuSE Linux distribution, is an installation option for the Mandrake Linux distribution, and is bundled with most other Linux distributions.

This chapter provides an overview of ReiserFS, discussing its approach to journaling and filesystem development, as well as many of its futuristic and intriguing characteristics. Because ReiserFS is already integrated into current versions of the Linux kernel code, chances are that your Linux system already has the capability to create and use ReiserFS filesystems. ReiserFS development is active and aggressive, so the CD that accompanies this book explains how to build and patch the latest version of the Linux kernel at the time of this writing so that you can take advantage of the latest and greatest improvements to ReiserFS. The chapter concludes by discussing how to use and administer ReiserFS filesystems, including information on manually verifying the consistency of ReiserFS filesystems and resolving problems if they appear.

Overview

ReiserFS began life as a personal project of Hans Reiser, a colorful and opinionated German PhD who still directs its development. As you all know from reading this book, a stable and high-performance journaling filesystem is almost essential for adopting Linux as the operating system for serious enterprise computing. ReiserFS is well worth considering because it's already used in this way by many businesses with serious storage commitments, such as mp3.com.

The development of ReiserFS has been helped along by significant investments from Linux software and hardware vendors. The staunchest supporter of ReiserFS (outside its core development team) has always been SuSE, the German Linux distribution, which was the first Linux vendor to bundle and ship a Linux distribution that contained and actively promoted ReiserFS. It's easy to see why a Linux vendor like SuSE (`http://www.suse.com`) would invest in the ReiserFS project because having a high-performance journaling filesystem in its Linux distribution makes it easier to sell Linux as an enterprise computing solution.

Other current backers at the time of this writing (at least, those listed on the main ReiserFS Web page at `http://www.namesys.com`) are BigStorage and ApplianceWare. Vendors of storage products such as ApplianceWare and BigStorage can increase the value, reliability, and performance of their storage products (and also one-up their competitors) by using a journaling filesystem. ApplianceWare (`http://www.applianceware.com`) makes high-performance Network Attached Storage (NAS) devices. BigStorage (`http://www.bigstorage.com`) sells

The ReiserFS Journaling Filesystem

CHAPTER 6

133

6

THE REISERFS
JOURNALING
FILESYSTEM

high-performance, high-capacity storage devices and NAS devices, and resells associated backup and Hierarchical Storage Management (HSM) software.

> **NOTE**
>
> Reading the ReiserFS Web site is intense. Not only does it feature a revolving door of financial backers, but the focus of the site is always on the future. For example, at the moment, most of its focus is on Reiser4, the next generation of ReiserFS, coming to a Linux system near you in late 2002. The constant focus on the future can be somewhat disconcerting to those who want to get work done now, but I try to think of it as being exciting and inspirational. The downside of trying to make sense of the Web site is that it's difficult to tell what's there now and what will be available "real soon now."
>
> Reiser4 will feature some truly advanced features, most notably arbitrary metadata along the lines of the extended attributes provided by the XFS filesystem, and filesystem plug-ins to simplify customizing the capabilities and security of the filesystem. At the moment, adding plug-ins is planned to require recompiling the filesystem, which isn't exactly a plug-in as far as I'm concerned, but I'm sure that will change by the time Reiser4 hits the streets. Reiser4 received funding from DARPA, the Defense Advanced Research Projects Agency folks who brought you the ARPAnet, forerunner of the Internet. It's nice to know that my tax dollars are actually doing something useful for a change.

The ReiserFS was merged into the basic Linux kernel distribution with kernel revision 2.4.1, although sets of patches are available to integrate it into later 2.2.X kernels. ReiserFS provides the following basic features that differentiate it from other journaling filesystems for Linux:

- Efficient storage—ReiserFS uses a mechanism called *tail-packing*, which enables it to combine small files and file fragments (portions of a file that are less than a full block in size) and store them directly in the B+Tree nodes. This decreases "wasted space" in the filesystem due to filesystem blocks that contain substantially less than 4 KB of data (the ReiserFS block size).

- Sophisticated B*Trees—ReiserFS uses B* balanced trees to organize directories, files, and data. This provides fast directory lookups, intrinsic support for large directories, and blazingly fast delete operations.

- Availability—ReiserFS comes with any Linux system that uses a 2.4.1 or greater kernel. No fuss, no muss—you've got a journaling filesystem out of the box.

ReiserFS is designed to support block sizes from 512 to 64 KB bytes, but currently only supports 4 KB blocks. Its efficiency in packing fragments into other blocks helps overcome this limitation. In fact, migrating an existing ext2 filesystem to ReiserFS produces some impressive results—it's great to copy an existing filesystem onto a new ReiserFS filesystem and find that your files take up less space than they used to. Tail-packing provides much of the storage efficiency of filesystems that offer smaller block sizes without incurring the additional overhead of the need to allocate greater numbers of blocks for each file.

Speaking of small files, ReiserFS has gotten something of a bad reputation for its performance when writing huge numbers of small files under a heavy load. Older versions of ReiserFS specifically had problems interacting with other in-kernel services, such as the Kernel NFS daemon, knfsd. NFS is a distributed filesystem that comes with all current Linux systems, and is therefore frequently used to share filesystems and directories in networked environments. Like ReiserFS, NFS is often the distributed filesystem of choice for many Linux and Unix system administrators because "it's already there" and is easy to configure. As a distributed filesystem, NFS is often used to share centralized directories to which many users require access, such as mail directories and news servers.

Because both of these tend to write large numbers of small files quickly, they place heavy demands on underlying local filesystems, such as ReiserFS. This is compounded by the fact that the NFS daemon can run inside the kernel and can therefore write files even more quickly than a standard, user-space NFS daemon. Happily, these problems have been eliminated in the versions of ReiserFS in newer Linux kernels, such as the 2.4.9 kernel used for the examples in this chapter. However, many Linux sysadmins seem to retain an almost superstitious fear of this combination.

As an additional storage efficiency, ReiserFS supports *sparse files*, which are files with a large address space that contain relatively little data. Data can be written to any location in a sparse file without allocating more disk space than the data actually requires (modulo some small amount of filesystem metadata). Although a sparse file reports its size as its maximum size, data blocks are only allocated when data is actually written to the file—reading information from any location in a sparse file that has not previously been written returns zero-filled data. Sparse files are also supported in journaling filesystems such as JFS and XFS. Figure 7.3, in the chapter on the XFS filesystem, illustrates the difference in storage requirements between standard and spare files.

Like other modern filesystems such as XFS and JFS, ReiserFS does dynamic inode allocation, which minimizes the amount of filesystem storage preallocated to filesystem data structures. Minimizing the amount of filesystem information preallocated also has two other benefits:

- Removes artificial limitations on the number of files and directories that can be created in the filesystem. The number of files and directories you can create is limited by the amount of space on this filesystem, not the number of preallocated inodes available.

The ReiserFS Journaling Filesystem

CHAPTER 6

135

6

THE REISERFS
JOURNALING
FILESYSTEM

- Simplifies expanding the size of an existing ReiserFS filesystem by reducing the number of data structures in the filesystem that have to be updated. To expand an existing ReiserFS filesystem (or any other filesystem that does not preallocate inodes), you essentially only have to format the new space and update a few filesystem data structures such as the size of the bitmaps used to track allocated blocks, internal references to the number of blocks available in the filesystem, and so on.

ReiserFS uses block-based allocation, instead of using extents like JFS and XFS, and therefore tracks allocated blocks in a filesystem using bitmaps, like traditional Unix filesystems. Unlike XFS and JFS, ReiserFS is still a 32-bit filesystem, and ReiserFS filesystems can therefore be up to 16 terabytes in size. Current Linux limitations in block structured devices and the VFS layer mean that this isn't much of a problem at the moment. By the time these restrictions are removed, hopefully Reiser4, a fully 64-bit filesystem, will be available.

NOTE

As a cutting-edge filesystem actively under development, ReiserFS is always undergoing enhancements, not all of which are backward compatible with earlier versions of the ReiserFS. For example, the on-disk organization of the current version of the ReiserFS, version 3.6, is incompatible with the on-disk layout of version 3.5 of the ReiserFS. As explained in the section, "Mounting ReiserFS Filesystems," later in this chapter, you can automatically migrate an existing ReiserFS 3.5 filesystem to 3.6 by supplying special options when mounting the filesystem.

ReiserFS journals filesystem metadata updates rather than both data changes and metadata updates. This helps guarantee the consistency of the filesystem itself after a system restart, although the data that files contain may be out-of-date or partially updated, depending on whether the data writes to the file completed before the system went down. The journaling support in ReiserFS uses some clever strategies to maximize metadata consistency even in the event of a sudden system failure. For example, when updating filesystem metadata, ReiserFS does not overwrite the existing metadata but instead writes it to a new location as close as possible to the existing metadata. If a system goes down while a metadata update is taking place, this guarantees the consistency of the filesystem's existing metadata because it is not freed until the update transaction is completed.

To summarize, ReiserFS is a high-power journaling filesystem built into every version of Linux running a 2.4.1 or greater kernel. It is already extensively used on Linux systems and therefore has some substantial history in Linux terms. ReiserFS isn't perfect—for example, its use of balanced trees causes performance problems when creating new files on filesystems that are more than 90 percent full, due to the overhead of shifting a huge number of nodes when balancing the trees.

Support Software for ReiserFS Filesystems

This section discusses the utilities associated with the ReiserFS filesystem and the Linux packages in which they are found. Although all Linux distributions that use kernels newer than 2.4.1 support ReiserFS, the CD that accompanies this book provides the 2.4.9 Linux kernel and associated patches for the ReiserFS to enable you to run the latest and greatest version. This also enables you to run a version of the ReiserFS in which many of its "well-known" problems (perhaps "much talked about" would be a better term), such as the knfsd interaction issues discussed in the previous section, have been fixed. Information about installing the kernel source code, applying the patches, and ReiserFS-specific information about building and installing a kernel is provided later in this chapter.

The CD that accompanies this book also includes the latest and greatest version of the utilities associated with ReiserFS. Unlike the utility packages associated with many of the other filesystems discussed in this book, all the ReiserFS utilities are centralized into a single package, reiserfsprogs. The latest version of this package at the time of this writing, reiserfsprogs-3.x.0j, is provided in the reiserfs directory on the CD that accompanies this book. This package contains the following utilities:

- debugreiserfs —A noninteractive filesystem debugging utility for ReiserFS filesystems, this utility enables you to print the contents of different aspects of a ReiserFS filesystem, such as the journal, the block allocation bitmap, specific blocks, and so on. If you encounter problems when using ReiserFS, this utility will also extract filesystem metadata in compact form, enabling you to send it to the ReiserFS folks for debugging or analysis purposes.
- mkreiserfs—The utility used to create ReiserFS filesystems.
- reiserfsck—The utility used to verify the consistency of a ReiserFS filesystem and repair it if necessary.
- resize_reiserfs—A utility that enables you to expand the size of an existing ReiserFS filesystem.

Adding ReiserFS Support to Your System

As mentioned earlier in this chapter, the ReiserFS filesystem is intrinsically available in any Linux distribution that uses the Linux 2.4.1 or better kernel. However, like any kernel subsystem, it may or may not be enabled in your particular Linux distribution. Also, more than almost any other Linux project that I've ever seen, the ReiserFS filesystem is constantly being updated and improved. Enhancements and optimizations are always being made, and any bugs found are quickly fixed. Making sure that you have a kernel in which ReiserFS support is active and that provides the latest and greatest version of ReiserFS makes it possible for you to use and accurately assess the benefits and performance of the ReiserFS.

The CD that accompanies this book provides the source code for the Linux 2.4.9 kernel, which includes many enhancements and fixes to earlier versions of the ReiserFS filesystem. This section provides hands-on, how-to information about installing the Linux 2.4.9 kernel, applying mandatory patches, and activating ReiserFS support in that kernel. It also provides detailed information about installing the latest versions of the utilities that make it possible to create, administer, use, and repair possible problems in ReiserFS filesystems.

Building a 2.4.9 Kernel with ReiserFS Support

Linux kernel 2.4.9 is the mostadvanced version available at the time of this writing, and the one that I've therefore chose to use to show how easy it is to activate ReiserFS support on your Linux system. The CD also includes the patches necessary to correct problems in the ReiserFS that were found and fixed after the 2.4.9 kernel was released.

> **NOTE**
>
> As mentioned in each chapter, if you have never built a kernel before, doing so is a great learning experience. Although the whole idea of prepackaged Linux installation is to protect users from the need to "roll their own" kernel and Linux utilities, compiling a kernel is an excellent way to familiarize yourself with the conceptual internals and organization of Linux. The instructions in this book for compiling kernels create kernels that have special names and will thus not overwrite the current version of the Linux kernel that you are using.

Patching the Linux 2.4.9 Kernel for ReiserFS Support

Appendix A, "Using the CD-ROM: Installing, Updating, and Compiling Kernels," provides detailed information about installing Linux kernel source and selecting kernel configuration options. This section provides basic information about installing the specific version of the Linux kernel source that we'll be using in the examples throughout the rest of this chapter. The procedures described in this section are relevant even if you want to add and activate ReiserFS support in a different version of the Linux kernel sources, such as newer versions of the kernel or the version of the Linux kernel that was shipped with the Linux distribution that you are using.

To use the best possible version of the ReiserFS and to guarantee that your results match the output examples given in this chapter, you must patch the source for the generic Linux 2.4.9 kernel after installing it. *Patches* are changes to existing files that are inserted to update those files. General information about patches and their installation is also provided in Appendix A.

The source for the Linux 2.4.9 kernel is located in the kernel subdirectory of the CD that accompanies this book. Install this kernel as described in "Installing the Kernel Source Code" in Appendix A; then use the following steps to add ReiserFS support to that kernel:

1. Make sure that the X Window System is running and use the su command to become root in an xterm or other terminal window.

2. Change your working directory to the directory created when you installed the Linux kernel source code, as explained in Appendix A:

   ```
   cd /usr/src/linux-2.4.9
   ```

3. Use the patch command to apply the ReiserFS patches from the patch subdirectory of the CD included with this book:

   ```
   patch -p1 < <path-to-cdrom>/patches/A-panic-in-reiserfs_read_super.patch
   patch -p1 < <path-to-cdrom>/patches/B-journal-replay.patch
   patch -p1 < <path-to-cdrom>/patches/C-old-format.patch
   patch -p1 < <path-to-cdrom>/patches/D-clear-i_blocks.patch
   patch -p1 < <path-to-cdrom>/patches/E-pathrelse.patch
   patch -p1 < <path-to-cdrom>/patches/F-reiserfs_get_block-cleanup.patch
   patch -p1 < <path-to-cdrom>/patches/G-blockalloc-for-disk-90_25full.patch
   ```

   The -p1 option tells the patch command how much of the filenames listed in the patch file to preen to correctly locate the files that should be patched.

The output of the patch command lists the name of each file that is being patched. After the patch program completes, you're ready to configure the 2.4.9 kernel with support for the latest and greatest ReiserFS filesystem.

Activating ReiserFS Support in the Kernel

This section explains how to activate support for the ReiserFS filesystem in the source code for the Linux 2.4.9 kernel. For an overview of the conceptual basics behind building a modern Linux kernel and activating support for different features and hardware in the kernel, see "Configuring Your Kernel" in Appendix A.

> **NOTE**
>
> It's generally a good idea to compile support for any filesystems that your system uses regularly into the kernel. Filesystems that you only interact with occasionally (such as AppleTalk or some network filesystems) can still be compiled as modules to keep your kernel as small as possible. These modules are automatically loaded whenever necessary, but aren't a part of the kernel executable per se.

> **TIP**
>
> If you have already compiled a kernel for the computer system on which you are building a new kernel, you can use the configuration information from that kernel to save time when configuring the new kernel. Reusing existing configuration data from an existing kernel is explained in Appendix A.

This section explains the options specific to activating support for the ReiserFS filesystem in the kernel we are building. This section describes how to configure ReiserFS options using the X Window System-based Linux kernel configurator:

1. Log in as root or use the su command to become root.
2. In a terminal window running under an X Window System window manager or desktop, change directory to the directory /usr/src/linux-2.4.9 and execute the make xconfig command. The commands related to compiling and loading support for the Linux X Window System kernel configurator display in the window in which you executed the make xconfig command. Eventually, the X Window System Linux kernel configurator displays, as shown in Figure 6.1.
3. Select the Code Maturity Level Options command or button. A new dialog displays, as shown in Figure 6.2.

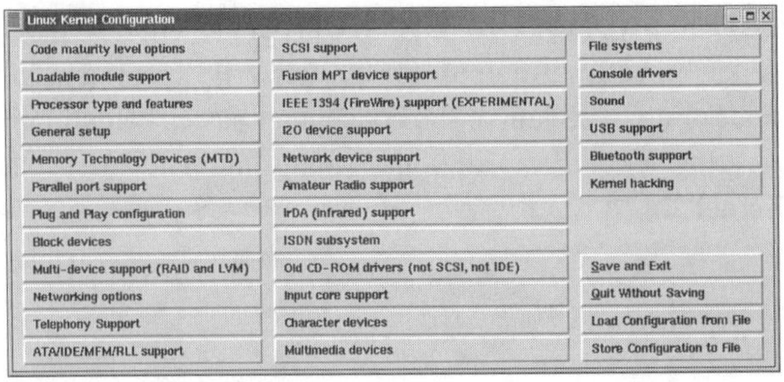

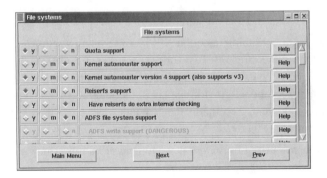

FIGURE 6.1

The X Window System-based Linux kernel configurator.

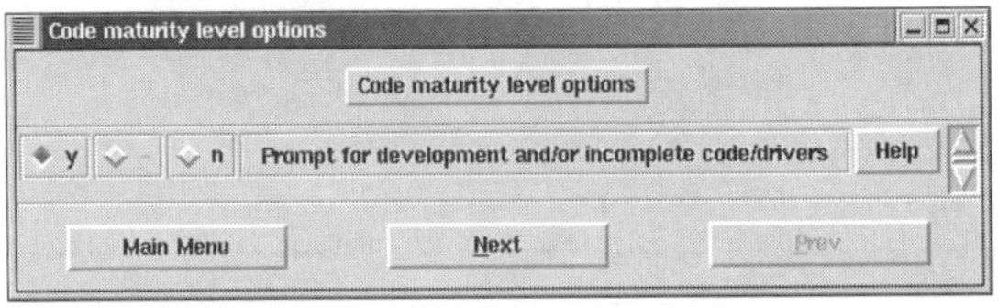

FIGURE 6.2

The Code Maturity Level Options dialog.

4. Click the Y radio button beside the Prompt for Development and/or Incomplete Code/Drivers option, and click the Main Menu button to return to the primary make xconfig dialog.

5. Click the File Systems button in the X Window System Kernel Configuration dialog. A new dialog displays, as shown in Figure 6.3.

FIGURE 6.3

The File Systems Configuration dialog.

6. Scroll down until you see the ReiserFS Support entry. Click Y beside this entry.

7. Click N beside the Have ReiserFS Do Extra Internal Checking entry unless you are having a problem with an existing ReiserFS filesystem. Enabling this option causes the ReiserFS kernel routines to do extra internal checking and potentially display useful error or warning messages. Performing these additional internal checks makes the ReiserFS kernel code run much more slowly than usual but may help you by providing error messages or other information that you can send to the ReiserFS folks to get their assistance in resolving the problem you're having.

8. Click the Main Menu button to return to the primary `make xconfig` dialog.

9. After selecting any other kernel configuration options relevant to the kernel that you are building (such as those specific to the hardware in your system), save your updated kernel configuration.

10. If you reused the configuration data from an existing kernel, use the Store Configuration to File button to display a dialog that enables you to explicitly save your new kernel configuration with the name `.config` in the main directory of the kernel that you are configuring.

11. If you configured the current kernel from scratch (that is, without reading in configuration data from another kernel), simply click the Save and Exit button.

12. Click OK to close the final dialog and return to the Linux shell prompt. You're now ready to compile the kernel!

Compiling and Installing a ReiserFS Kernel

After applying patches to and configuring the Linux 2.4.9 kernel, you're ready to compile and install your new Linux kernel. All the information that you need to compile and install this kernel is provided in Appendix A. This section just provides a checklist for the steps that you should follow.

After you've installed, patched, and configured the Linux 2.4.9 kernel for ReiserFS filesystem support and to match your hardware, you must do the following to install and use that kernel:

1. Add a special extension for this kernel to its Makefile, making it easy to identify the special features in the kernel. I typically name kernels that support different filesystem along the lines of `linux-<kernel-version>-<filesystem-type>`.

2. Execute the following `make` commands in this order to correctly initialize dependencies and to build and install the new kernel and any associated loadable modules:

```
make dep
make
make modules
make install
make modules_install
```

I suggest doing these steps as discrete commands to make it easy to spot any compilation or installation failures along the way. If you're really cocky, you can reduce these commands to the following single command-line, but you'd still be wise to scroll back to make sure that there were no problems:

```
make dep ; make install ; make modules ; make modules_install
```

3. Modify boot loader configuration files for the boot loader you're using on your system, as described in "Booting a New Kernel" in Appendix A and rerun LILO if necessary.

You're now almost ready to reboot your system and use the ReiserFS filesystem. Before doing that, however, you must also compile and install the utilities discussed in the next section to ensure that your system can mount and administer ReiserFS filesystem volumes both correctly and optimally.

Building and Installing the `reiserfsprogs` Package

To install version 3.x.0j-pre10 of the `reiserfsprogs` package, included on the CD that accompanies this book, do the following:

1. Mount the CD and extract the `reiserfsprogs` package from the file `reiserfs/reiserf-sprogs-3.x.0j-pre10.tar.gz` to a directory on your system using a command like the following:

```
cd <target-directory>
tar zxvf <path-to-CD>/reiserfs/reiserfsprogs-3.x.0j.tar.gz
```

2. Change directory to `<target-directory>/reiserfsprogrs-3.x.0j` and run the configure script to correctly configure the `reiserfsprogs` Makefile for your system and Linux distribution:

```
./configure --mandir=/usr/man
```

This produces verbose output that's not useful to replicate here. The `--mandir` option is necessary to correctly set the name of the directory in which the man pages for the `reiserfsprogs` utilities are installed.

3. After the Makefile is correctly configured, execute the `make` command to build the new versions of the utilities in the `reiserfsprogs` package:

```
make
```

Once again, this produces verbose, system-specific output that's not useful to replicate here.

4. After all the utilities are compiled, install them on your system using the following command:

```
make install
```

Your system now has version 3.x.0j of the `reiserfsprogs` utilities and associated reference (man page) documentation installed.

Administering ReiserFS Filesystems

This section explains how to create and use ReiserFS filesystems on your Linux systems. It begins by explaining how to create a ReiserFS filesystem using default values and then explores the various options provided to enable you to customize ReiserFS filesystems when creating them. Subsequent sections of this chapter explain how to mount a ReiserFS filesystem, what the various mount options that are available do, and which ones to use in most cases. It concludes by discussing how to manually check the consistency of a ReiserFS filesystem and how to increase the size of an existing ReiserFS filesystem.

> **NOTE**
>
> As with many of the filesystems discussed in this book, one set of ReiserFS utilities that is particularly conspicuous by its absence is a set of backup and restore utilities that understand ReiserFS filesystem data structures. These utilities are not necessary for the ext3 journaling filesystem because it uses the standard ext2 data structures, which the standard Linux `dump` and `restore` programs understand. The XFS filesystem provides its own `xfsdump` and `xfsrestore` utilities to support the extra data that XFS files, directories, and filesystems contain.
>
> At the time of this writing, the standard Linux `dump` utility cannot read ReiserFS filesystem headers or data structures, and will therefore exit immediately after complaining about a bad magic number in the ReiserFS superblock. (The magic number is used to identify the filesystem type.) Without valid backups in dump format, the Linux restore program is therefore irrelevant for ReiserFS filesystems.
>
> At this time, ReiserFS filesystems can only be backed up using utilities such as `tar` or `cpio` that back up a filesystem by walking through its directory structure rather than directly accessing filesystem data structures. You can also use a utility such as `dd` to copy an entire ReiserFS filesystem to a backup device, but this makes it impossible to selectively restore individual files and directories. A final alternative is to use a centralized backup application such as Amanda (discussed in the "Centralizing Backups" section of Chapter 15, "Backing Up, Restoring, and Managing Linux Filesystems") with ReiserFS filesystems because this application invokes filesystem-level backup utilities such as `tar`.

Creating a ReiserFS Filesystem

Like most other modern Linux filesystems, ReiserFS filesystems are created by using the /sbin/mkfs wrapper program and specifying the -t reiserfs option. This causes the /sbin/mkfs wrapper program to pass all the other command-line arguments to the /sbin/mkfs.reiserfs program, which would ordinarily be the ReiserFS-specific filesystem creation utility. In the case of ReiserFS, the utility used to create ReiserFS filesystems is actually named /sbin/mkreiserfs, so the "file" /sbin/mkfs.reiserfs is actually a symbolic link to /sbin/mkreiserfs. If executing the command mkfs -t reiserfs /dev/*whatever* produces an error message rather than a ReiserFS filesystem on the target partition, you can make things work normally by creating a symbolic link from /sbin/mkfs.reiserfs to /sbin/mkreiserfs using the following command:

```
ln -s /sbin/mkreiserfs /sbin/mkfs.reiserfs
```

The example used in this section executes the mkreiserfs command directly, to emphasize the name of the command actually doing real work. (And the name of the command that you will want to supply to the man command if you want to see the detailed online reference information available for the mkreiserfs command.) The mkreiserfs utility can take a number of command-line arguments that enable you to fine-tune different aspects of the filesystem that you are creating, but the following is an example of using it in its simplest form and the resulting output:

```
# mkreiserfs /dev/hdc2
<------------mkreiserfs, 2001------------->
reiserfsprogs 3.x.0j
=================================================================
LEAF NODE (8211) contains level=1, nr_items=2, free_space=3932 rdkey
-----------------------------------------------------------------
|###|type|ilen|f/sp| loc|fmt|fsck|                    key          |
|   |    |    |e/cn|    |   |need|                                 |
-----------------------------------------------------------------
| 0|1 2 0x0 SD, len 44, entry count 0, fsck need 0, format new|
(NEW SD), mode drwxr-xr-x, size 48, nlink 2, mtime 09/20/2001 19:09:57 blocks 8
-----------------------------------------------------------------
| 1|1 2 0x1 DIR, len 48, entry count 2, fsck need 0, format old|
###: Name          length    Object key          Hash    Gen number
  0: ".            "( 1)      1 2          0    1, loc 40, state 4 ??
  1: "..           "( 2)      0 1          0    2, loc 32, state 4 ??
=================================================================
Creating reiserfs of 3.6 format
Block size 4096 bytes
Block count 524412
Used blocks 8228
```

The ReiserFS Journaling Filesystem

CHAPTER 6

145

6

THE REISERFS
JOURNALING
FILESYSTEM

```
Free blocks count 516184
First 16 blocks skipped
Super block is in 16
Bitmap blocks (17) are :
        17, 32768, 65536, 98304, 131072, 163840, 196608, 229376, 262144,
        294912, 327680, 360448, 393216,
 425984, 458752, 491520, 524288
Journal size 8192 (blocks 18-8210 of file /dev/hdc2)
Root block 8211
Hash function "r5"
ATTENTION: YOU SHOULD REBOOT AFTER FDISK!
(y/n)        ALL DATA WILL BE LOST ON '/dev/hdc2'! y
Initializing journal - 0%....20%....40%....60%....80%....100%
Syncing..
ReiserFS core development sponsored by SuSE Labs (suse.com)
Journaling sponsored by MP3.com.
To learn about the programmers and ReiserFS, please go to
http://www.devlinux.com/namesys
Have fun.
```

Well, that's a tad verbose, but it's certainly friendly enough. Because we've installed and are using a prerelease version of the mkreiserfs application, the amount of extraneous debugging output provided by mkreiserfs isn't surprising, just irritating. (I've even taken the liberty of removing some blank lines from the example output.) It seems that it would be friendlier to turn on all this by using a special command-line option, but nobody asked me.

Summary of ReiserFS Filesystem Creation Options

The mkreiserfs application provides several command-line options to enable you to customize its behavior. These are the following:

- -h *<name>*—Enables you to specify the name of the hash function used to sort directory names in a directory. Valid names are r5 (the default hashing function), tea, and rupasov. These hashing functions are explained in the section "Mounting ReiserFS Filesystems" later in the chapter because they are also available as options when you mount a ReiserFS filesystem.

- -v *<version>*—Enables you to specify the ReiserFS format used when creating the filesystem. Valid options are 1 (create a filesystem compatible with ReiserFS 3.5 and earlier) and 2 (create a ReiserFS 3.6 filesystem).

- -q—Produces less verbose output. Ironically, it doesn't change the number of output lines produced but just removes one of the whizzy output functions that would otherwise frequently redraw the line that displays the percentage of the filesystem that has been formatted. You might appreciate this if you are logged in at 300 baud or if you are using a printing console like the old DEC LA120 on your Linux system. I would guess that the number of people who do either of those things is more Boolean than it is an integer, but I suppose that I could be wrong.

Mounting ReiserFS Filesystems

Like all other journaling filesystems, the journal for a ReiserFS filesystem is automatically read when a ReiserFS filesystem is mounted to guarantee the consistency of the filesystem.

The standard Linux mount program has many ReiserFS-specific options, some of which are used to override existing filesystem parameters, primarily for performance reasons under certain circumstances. All the mount options specific to ReiserFS are explained in the section "Mounting ReiserFS Filesystems." You can also combine these with the standard options to the mount command, which were explained in Chapter 3, "Overview of Journaling Filesystems."

Options to the mount command can either be specified using the mount command's -o option when manually executing the mount command from a command line, or (more commonly) are specified in the entry for a specific filesystem in the filesystem table definition file, /etc/fstab.

- conv—Tells version 3.6 reiserfs software that you are mounting a ReiserFS version 3.5 filesystem. Using this mount option causes the ReiserFS code to use ReiserFS 3.6 format for any new files, directories, nodes, or journal entries created. After you mount a ReiserFS filesystem using this option, you can no longer mount it on a system that runs ReiserFS 3.5, because the format of the new objects is incompatible with the old filesystem. If you are mounting a ReiserFS 3.5 filesystem on a system running ReiserFS 3.6, you should also use the hash=detect mount option, explained later in this section.

> **NOTE**
>
> The conv mount option is primarily useful in emergencies, when you need to quickly mount and use a disk from another computer system that contains ReiserFS 3.5 partitions. In general, if you can afford the time, backing up Reiser 3.5 partitions using tar and restoring them to a new ReiserFS 3.6 partition is a better idea because ReiserFS 3.6 filesystems provide better performance than Reiser 3.5 filesystems. Backing up and restoring the filesystem also eliminates fragmentation internal to files on the filesystem when the tar command writes them sequentially to disk from your backup media.

- hash={rupasov,tea,r5,detect}—Specifies the hashing algorithm used to locate and write files within directories. The different hashing algorithms provided in ReiserFS filesystems are the following:

- The `rupasov` hashing function is a fast hashing function that places lexically similar filenames close to each other, but therefore increases the probability of collisions during hashing.

- The `tea` hashing function is a Davis-Meyer function (implemented by Jeremy Fitzhardinge) that creates hash keys by permuting bits in the filename. This produces distinct keys with a low probability of collisions but requires more computation than the other hashing functions. This hashing function is a good choice for ReiserFS filesystems that have large directories causing `EHASHCOLLISION` errors when you use them with the standard `r5` hashing algorithm.

- The `r5` hashing function is a modified version of the `rupasov` hash with a significantly reduced probability of hashing collisions. This is the default hash function used when no hash function is specified.

- The `detect` argument to the hash option is not a hashing algorithm but causes the `mount` command to examine the filesystem before mounting it to detect the hashing function used when the filesystem was created. You therefore do not have to specify the hash type, because the `mount` command then writes this information to the ReiserFS filesystem's superblock. This option is only useful the first time that you mount a ReiserFS 3.5 (or earlier) filesystem on a ReiserFS 3.6 system. It's safe to continue to use this option thereafter, but it will only be wasting time because the superblock already contains the appropriate information.

- `hashed_relocation`—Tunes the block allocator, providing performance improvements on ReiserFS filesystems that primarily contain larger files.

- `noborder`—Disables the border allocator algorithm invented by Yury Rupasov. This `mount` option is designed for use during testing and benchmarking, and should not be used in a production environment.

- `nolog`—Disables journaling. This disables writing to the journal but nothing else. All internal journaling-related calculations are still done. Disabling the journal provides performance improvements at the expense of fast crash recovery because you will have to run the `reiserfsck` command if the system crashes while a ReiserFS filesystem is being used in nonjournaling mode.

- `notail`—Disables tail-packing, where small files and fragments are stored directly in the nodes of the B+Tree instead of requiring separately allocated blocks.

- `no_unhashed_relocation`—Tunes the block allocator, providing performance improvements on ReiserFS filesystems that primarily contain smaller files by relocating them using a hashing scheme.

- `replayonly`—Replays the transactions in the journal, but does not actually mount the filesystem. This is used by `reiserfsck` when checking a potentially corrupted ReiserFS filesystem and should not be used as a standard mount option.

- resize=nblocks—Tells the ReiserFS code that the device is actually *<blocks>* in size instead of using the size information contained in the ReiserFS superblock. This option is used internally when you use the resize_reiserfs program to increase or decrease the size of a ReiserFS partition. See the section "Changing the Size of ReiserFS Filesystems" later in the chapter for more information about expanding or shrinking the size of existing ReiserFS filesystems.

At this point, the generic format of an entry in the /etc/fstab file for a ReiserFS filesystem shouldn't be much of a surprise to anyone:

```
/dev/hdc2              /music       reiserfs      defaults       0 0
```

Remember that ReiserFS filesystems are incompatible with the standard Linux dump program, so you will want to have a 0 in the next-to-last column of the /etc/fstab entry for all ReiserFS filesystems to ensure that any automated filesystem backups done using dump don't fail when they encounter a ReiserFS entry in the /etc/fstab file. You should also put a 0 in the last column to ensure that the reiserfsck program doesn't attempt to check the consistency of a ReiserFS filesystem at boot time. The reiserfsck program requests confirmation from the command line each time it runs, which makes it fairly unusable in noninteractive situations. The only time you should need to run the reiserfsck program is if mounting a ReiserFS filesystem fails.

ReiserFS can be a fast filesystem, but there are always ways to improve its performance. In general, I tend to use /etc/fstab entries like the following for ReiserFS partitions containing user data to maximize overall performance:

```
/dev/hdc2   /music   reiserfs   defaults,noatime,nodiratime,notail   0 0
```

These options do the following:

- defaults—A standard mount option gives me the standard set of async, exec, dev, nouser, suid, rw mount options.
- noatime—Doesn't update the access time for files. Because few humans use the last file access time for anything, not updating it is a natural performance improvement. This is especially useful for filesystems that hold transient data, such as mail queues, where files are short-lived and the last access time is irrelevant. This also prevents the annoying situation where your system automatically runs the sync command every 5 seconds (and therefore updates the atime for the sync program every 5 seconds). If your sync binary is located on a ReiserFS filesystem, this may prevent your system from ever spinning down the disks and entering sleep mode if automatic power management (APM) is active.
- nodiratime—Doesn't update the access time for directories. I tend to disable this for the same reasons that I disable file access time updates.

The ReiserFS Journaling Filesystem

CHAPTER 6

149

6

**THE REISERFS
JOURNALING
FILESYSTEM**

- `notail`—This provides performance improvements at the expense of losing some of the space-saving features of ReiserFS. You should probably not use this option on ReiserFS partitions if you absolutely can't afford to buy additional disks because you'll want to use your available disk space as efficiently as possible, which ReiserFS excels at. However, ReiserFS performance is poor if your disks are consistently more than 90 percent full. If this is the case, consider using one of the other journaling filesystems discussed in this book rather than ReiserFS.

Designating certain options as more useful than others is based entirely on my experience using the ReiserFS filesystem in a variety of circumstances, and on the fact that `mtime` is more important to me than `atime`. Your mileage may vary.

Checking ReiserFS Filesystem Consistency

Unless this is the first sentence that you've read in this book, you probably know that the primary advantages of journaling filesystems are that they provide faster system restart times and help minimize the amount of filesystem changes that you can lose after a system crash. For this reason (as noted in the previous section), the last column in an entry in the `/etc/fstab` file for a ReiserFS filesystem should always be 0 because there is no need to check the consistency of a ReiserFS filesystem each time you restart your system, regardless of why you're restarting it. ReiserFS partitions automatically replay the journal and perform any outstanding metadata updates when they are mounted.

Unfortunately, this is not a perfect world. Hardware failure, emerging hardware problems on your disks or controller subsystems, or even (gasp) bugs in Linux or the ReiserFS code may corrupt a ReiserFS filesystem. Occasionally, problems occur that are more serious than those that can be corrected by automatically replaying the journal, and manual intervention is therefore necessary to restore its consistency.

ReiserFS provides the `reiserfsck` utility to manually check for consistency problems in ReiserFS filesystems and repair them. By default, the `reiserfsck` utility is an interactive application that requires the name of the filesystem that you want to check as an argument and provides the following command-line options:

- `-a`—Causes `reiserfsck` to assume that it was invoked by someone running `fsck -A`, which is deemed so irritating that `reiserfsck` returns immediately even if the filesystem was not cleanly unmounted.
- `--check`—Checks filesystem consistency, which is the default action of `reiserfsck`. Using this option enables you to check a ReiserFS filesystem currently mounted read-only.
- `--create-leaf-bitmap <filename>`—Creates an output file containing a bitmap that represents the leaf structure of the B+Tree (the actual files in the filesystem). This option can also be abbreviated as `-c`.

- --fix-fixable—Causes reiserfsck to automatically any repair any directory problems that it encounters that don't require rebuilding the entire filesystem B+Tree. Problems that using this option will automatically repair are pointers to nonexistent data blocks, incorrect directory size and allocated block information, directory entries that refer to nonexistent files or directories, and so on. This option can also be abbreviated as -x.

- --fix-non-critical—Causes reiserfsck to automatically repair problems such as incorrect file size, invalid file modes, and duplicate object IDs (which are supposed to be unique). This option can also be abbreviated as -o.

- --interactive—Causes the reiserfsck program to stop after each step in the fsck process. This has no effect if the filesystem is marked as being clean because reiserfsck exits automatically in that case. This option can also be abbreviated as -i.

- --logfile <filename>—Causes reiserfsck write its output to the specified file rather than to standard error, which is its default behavior. This option can also be abbreviated as -l.

- --nolog—Further reduces the amount of output produced while running reiserfsck. This option can also be abbreviated as -n.

- -p—Does nothing except prevent error messages about unknown options as a result of people running the fsck -a -p command to preen every filesystem in the /etc/fstab file.

- --quiet—Causes the reiserfsck program to produce less output. This option can also be abbreviated as -q.

- -r—Does absolutely nothing.

- --rebuild-sb—Rebuilds and repairs the superblock if necessary.

- --rebuild-tree—Rebuilds the filesystem tree using leaf nodes found by literally searching through the entire device on which the filesystem is located. This is rarely necessary, but may be your last resort if the filesystem B+Tree itself is corrupted. As you might expect, this takes an incredibly long time. To be on the safe side, back up any data that you can from the partition before rebuilding the filesystem tree—because reiserfsck operations aren't journaled, a system restart while rebuilding your filesystem could be even more fatal than whatever corruption you started with. Unless the filesystem is huge, I tend to use dd to save an actual image of the filesystem before rebuilding the B*Tree—this at least gives you the option of restoring the filesystem in its corrupted state and trying again if the rebuild operation fails due to a power outage or system crash.

- --scan-in-bitmap <filename>—Reads the specified file, which must contain a ReiserFS leaf bitmap (produced using the --create-leaf-bitmap option) and only scans the blocks marked as used.

- -V—Prints the reiserfsck version string and exits immediately thereafter.

Changing the Size of ReiserFS Filesystems

Every good filesystem inevitably fills up—nature abhors free disk space. When a filesystem located on a physical device such as a hard drive fills up, you traditionally have two alternatives:

- You can copy the contents of that filesystem onto another, larger, disk partition, unmount the original filesystem, mount the new partition on the existing mountpoint, and recycle the original partition.

- You can try kludges like moving part of the directory structure from the existing filesystem onto another one and then creating appropriate symlinks.

The first of these is time consuming, and the second quickly gets confusing, especially if you're a new system administrator who has inherited a heavily symlinked tower of Babel from someone else. Both of these are frustrating if there happen to be other filesystems on the disk that's full and you realize that you could easily have created a single larger partition if you'd just had the foresight to do so.

Logical volume management (LVM), discussed in Chapter 9, "Logical Volume Management," was originally developed to provide a way of making it easy to liberate filesystems from the size constraints of physical storage devices. LVM combines multiple physical devices into a single logical pool of storage from which filesystems can be created that may be larger than any single physical device that is part of the pool. The Linux LVM implementation provides the lvextend command that enables you to increase the size of an existing logical volume, which is almost a good thing. Unfortunately, this doesn't do you much good if you can't increase the size of the filesystem that it contains to take advantage of the additional space. You can't make your clothes larger by increasing the size of your closet.

To resolve problems such as these, the ReiserFS provides the resize_reiserfs command that increases the size of an existing ReiserFS filesystem. The filesystem that you are resizing must be unmounted to guarantee that no one is accessing it while you're changing things and that the journal is inactive as well. Combining the power of the lvextend and resize_reiserfs commands does exactly what you want. Assuming that there is free space in the volume group where the logical volume is located, you can increase the size of both the logical volume and the filesystem that it contains, as in the following example:

```
# df /src
/dev/vg1/volume2        1048540     32840     1015700    4% /src
#
# unmount /src
#
# lvextend -L +500M /dev/vg1/volume2
lvextend -- extending logical volume "/dev/vg1/volume2" to 1.49 GB
lvextend -- doing automatic backup of volume group "vg1"
lvextend -- logical volume "/dev/vg1/volume2" successfully extended
```

```
#
# mount /dev/vg1/volume2 /src
# df /src
/dev/vg1/volume2        1048540      32840    1015700    4% /src
```

At this point, you've resized the logical volume, but not the filesystem that it contains, so you see exactly the same disk usage statistics. Now to increase the size of the filesystem itself:

```
# unmount /src
#
# resize_reiserfs -v /dev/vg1/volume2
<-------------resize_reiserfs, 2001------------->
reiserfsprogs 3.x.0j
Fetching on-disk bitmap..done
ReiserFS report:
blocksize              4096
block count            390144 (262144)
free blocks            370976 (242980)
bitmap block count     12 (8)
Syncing..done

# mount /dev/vg1/volume2 /src
#
# df /src
/dev/vg1/volume2        1560524      76620    1483904    5% /src
```

Logical volumes were designed to facilitate operations such as this, assuming that filesystems provide utilities like resize_reiserfs, which is true for most filesystems. The extend2fs utility enables you to resize ext2 partitions, the xfs_growfs enables you to resize XFS partitions, and distributed filesystems such as AFS provide their own sets of utilities to manage the volumes that they use.

You might think that filesystem resizing tools such as these are primarily useful on logical volumes, but that's not the case. You can do exactly the same thing with filesystems located on physical storage devices as long as there are free partitions on the disk that are adjacent to the partition that you want to resize. Typically, one doesn't have spare partitions sitting around unused on production hardware, but maybe your budget or planning skills are better than mine. If you don't currently have adjacent free partitions on a disk containing the filesystem that you want to resize, you can often free up partitions by moving their contents to other disks and recycling the original partition.

The process for resizing a filesystem located on a physical device is the following:

1. Do backups of every partition on the disk.
2. Free one or more partitions located immediately after the one that you want to resize by moving the data that they contain to another partition.

3. Use the Linux `fdisk`, `cfdisk`, `sfdisk`, or `parted` commands to delete the freed partitions.

4. Delete the partition that you want to resize.

5. Create a new partition with exactly the same starting point as the partition that you want to resize. The new partition should span all the disk space consumed by the original partition and the one(s) that you freed.

6. Execute the `resize_reiserfs` command with no arguments other than the name of the new partition that you created. This should be the same name that it had before—only its size is different.

7. Mount the newly resized partition. Voila! The filesystem is larger, its original contents are still present, and you're a hero.

WARNING

When resizing physical partitions, the starting block of the filesystem has to be the same as it was originally. In other words, you can add space only to the end of an existing filesystem. You can't free up a partition before the one that you want to resize and combine the two. Filesystem superblocks are typically located at specific offsets from the beginning of a filesystem, based on the block size. If you delete an existing partition located before the partition that you want to resize, repartition the disk so that a single partition now spans the two, and then increase the size of the filesystem in that partition, the wrong thing will happen. You will be resizing the filesystem in the first partition, not the second one. This will make you extremely unpopular if you don't have backups.

With no arguments, the `resize_reiserfs` command increases the size of a ReiserFS filesystem to fill the block device on which it is located, whether that is a physical device or a logical volume. The `resize_reiserfs` command also provides the following command-line options to give you more control over resizing ReiserFS filesystems:

- `-s [+|-]size`—Specifies the amount by which you want to increase (or decrease the size of the filesystem. Available units are K (kilobytes), M (megabytes), and G (gigabytes). For example, to increase the size of a specified ReiserFS filesystem by one gigabyte, you would use a command like the following:

```
resize_reiserfs -s +1G /dev/whatever
```

To decrease the size of the filesystem by 500 megabytes, you would use a command like the following:

```
resize_reiserfs -s -500M /dev/whatever
```

The only case in which I can see wanting to reduce the size of an existing filesystem is if it is located on a logical volume and you need to increase the size of another logical volume in the same volume group but don't currently have any free disk space in the volume group.

- -f—Forces the resize to occur without performing any consistency or capacity requirements on the filesystem.

- -q—Produces no output other than any error messages that may occur.

- -v—Displays verbose output, telling you each change that the resize_reiserfs command is making to the filesystem. This option is on by default. (Which makes you wonder why it's an option, but nobody asked me.)

The resize_reiserfs command is an impressive utility that has always worked flawlessly for me. Resizing partitions on a physical disk takes some getting used to. The first time I did this, I was pretty paranoid when I deleted the partition containing my data and re-created it with a new size. Did I mention that you should do backups? A typo in the starting block field can be disastrous.

Modifying Other Aspects of Existing ReiserFS Filesystems

One of the aspects of a ReiserFS filesystem that you may want to customize is the size of the journal used to record filesystem metadata changes. By default, the size of the journal for a ReiserFS filesystem is always 8192 filesystem blocks (4 KB blocks). This cannot be changed when you create a ReiserFS filesystem because it is a constant that appears in the code for the current version of mkreiserfs. However, you may want to increase the size of the log if, for example, you know that an application using a specific filesystem frequently performs many filesystem operations under the control of a single process, if the filesystem is heavily used by many simultaneous and active users, or if the filesystem is huge and you anticipate that it will eventually support many simultaneous processes doing I/O of one sort or another.

Unfortunately, you can't always get what you want. ReiserFS has announced the reiserfstune utility to enable you to change the size of the journal on an existing ReiserFS filesystem. Unfortunately, this application is currently under development and has not yet been released by the ReiserFS folks. However, if you are actively using the ReiserFS filesystem on large or heavily used partitions, you may want to check the reiserfsprogs download site (ftp://www.namesys.com/pub/reiserfsprogs) for newer versions of the reiserfsprogs utilities that include the reiserfstune utility.

The reiserfstune utility will also enable you to relocate the journal for a ReiserFS filesystem to a separate device. Locating the journal for a journaling filesystem to another device can provide substantial performance improvements by enabling the filesystem and its journal to be written in parallel, instead of filesystem updates having to contend with journal updates on the same disk. Locating the journal on a faster drive than the filesystem itself can further improve performance (or can at least give you something to do with old disk drives that no longer have enough storage capacity to be used for filesystems).

As mentioned in the introductory section of this chapter, the ReiserFS filesystem is an active, aggressive project. At the moment, the associated `reiserfsprogs` utilities package contains a relatively small number of critical utilities. However, as you can see from upcoming utilities such as `reiserfstune`, the ReiserFS folks understand the need for additional utilities to enable system administrators to make optimum use of the ReiserFS filesystem in a wide variety of circumstances. Given the design and basic orientation of Linux, you can even contribute your own. As things stand now, the ReiserFS filesystem is already widely used in production environments. Its future will probably only be brighter. And then there's Reiser4. . .

The XFS Journaling Filesystem

IN THIS CHAPTER

This chapter discusses the XFS journaling filesystem, originally developed by Silicon Graphics, Inc., (SGI) for use with its IRIX operating system and subsequently released to the Linux community and the rest of the world as open-source in the year 2000. The chapter begins with an overview of XFS, discussing the aspects of its design and implementation that make it a high-performance journaling filesystem, and then explains how to add support for the XFS filesystem to your Linux system. The chapter concludes by discussing how to use and administer XFS filesystems, including information on manually verifying the consistency of XFS filesystems and resolving problems if they appear.

Overview

The XFS filesystem is a high-performance journaling filesystem that has some substantial advantages over the other journaling filesystems discussed in this book. Some of the primary reasons for considering XFS are

- It has been in use for a long time and is thus very robust.
- It provides special support for high-performance, real-time files in a dedicated portion of the filesystem.
- It already provides support for enhanced access control for files and directories. Advanced access control features, such as access control lists to augment standard Linux security, are planned for other Linux filesystems and already exist in advanced distributed filesystems for Linux such as AFS.
- It uses sophisticated algorithms for file and directory lookup and disk space allocation.

Initially, the most interesting of these is the fact that it has been in production use since 1994, running on every SGI workstation at thousands of customer sites. Because this gives it more history than even Linux's standard ext2 filesystem, adopting XFS for personal and even production use is a relatively safe bet as far as the base filesystem code goes. The stability and history of a filesystem is an important factor when considering for use in any environment but is especially so in a production business or academic environment. There's no question that moving XFS to Linux has the potential to expose problems because the underlying operating system and volume management code are completely different. However, with thousands of satisfied users and administrators, it's easy to feel confident about the XFS code base and its potential for high performance and quick recovery/restart times.

For anyone who isn't familiar with Silicon Graphics workstations, SGI began life in the early 1980s as a manufacturer of washing machine-sized workstations whose focus was on providing high-resolution, high-performance pipelined graphics. Given SGI's graphical focus, a high-performance filesystem was necessary to store all those bits, so its first customized filesystem was known as EFS, which was essentially an extent-based version of the Berkeley Unix Fast File System (FFS), which was mentioned in Chapter 1, "Introduction to Filesystems." As disk capacities and performance increased over the years, SGI decided to implement a new filesystem, XFS, to add journaling capabilities and remove many of the limitations of FFS and EFS, such as preallocated filesystem inodes. SGI first released XFS with IRIX 5.3 in 1994 and has been continually refining and enhancing it ever since.

As the premier graphics and multimedia workstation in the Unix market for years, some special concerns for SGI when developing the XFS filesystem were the following:

- High throughput for streaming video and audio
- Support for huge files required by video and high-resolution graphics packages
- The capability to store huge amounts of data
- Support for many files (and therefore large directories)

NOTE

As an interesting side note, in the formative years of the World Wide Web, SGI workstations were well-known as premier machines for use as Web servers and at Internet Service Providers (ISPs) who supported many customers. The primary reasons for the popularity of SGI systems as Web servers and at ISPs were fast I/O, support for many files and directories, and easy expansion of existing filesystems to support more users/directories/files. Does anything there ring a bell? Of course—these are all features provided by XFS.

Data Storage in XFS Filesystems

XFS filesystems are full 64-bit filesystems composed of up to three general areas:

- The data section, where actual filesystem data and metadata are located.
- The log, where filesystem metadata changes are recorded transactionally. The log is typically written sequentially during normal filesystem operation and is only read when an XFS filesystem is mounted.
- An optional real-time section, used to store the data of files that require constant, high-speed I/O. (Real-time subvolumes are actively under development for XFS under Linux and should not be used at the present time.)

The data section of an XFS filesystem is divided into allocation groups, as shown in Figure 7.1. Allocation groups are distinct subsets of the storage available in the data section of an XFS filesystem and are not visible to users. They are the conceptual equivalents of the cylinder groups used in the Berkeley FFS, dividing an XFS filesystem into discrete pools of storage space that typically range in size from .5 to 4 GB.

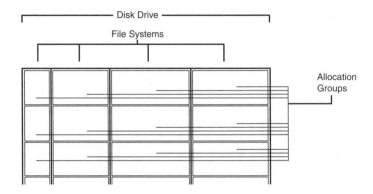

FIGURE 7.1

How XFS filesystems are organized on disk.

Each allocation group maintains its own data structures to manage free space, inodes, and allocated space within itself. This provides several advantages, such as

- Allocation groups can therefore use relative block and inode pointers for data structures specific to a given allocation group, saving space in its internal data structures.

- Space allocation within an allocation group provides another level of indirection for filesystem allocation and block references, increasing the potential size of an XFS filesystem as compared to a filesystem that had to provide explicit block references that were global to the filesystem.

- Maintaining data structures, such as superblocks, specific to each allocation group helps increase performance by reducing locking delays and generally supporting parallel allocation and access across different allocation groups.

- Dividing a filesystem into some number of allocation groups, each of which maintains its own data structures, makes it easier to subsequently increase the size of the filesystem by simply adding new allocation groups to an existing filesystem. As discussed later in this section, other advanced features of XFS (such as dynamic inode allocation) also help simplify the process of increasing the size of XFS filesystems both internally and administratively.

One of the goals of the cylinder groups introduced in FFS was to promote *disk locality*, which means that the disk blocks allocated to files and directories could be located within the same cylinder group, reducing head movement when subsequently accessing those blocks. The size of the allocation groups used in XFS reduces the possibility of physically locating the disk space associated with specific files close to each other but instead provides *logical locality*, where all the disk storage associated with a file is optimally located in the same allocation group.

To improve performance when allocating disk space to files, XFS uses extent-based allocation rather than specifically allocating individual blocks to a file. As explained in Chapter 1, extents are ranges of adjacent, free disk blocks allocated together. Rather than containing an entire chain of block and indirect block references, the data structures that identify the on-disk location of files and directories in allocation-based filesystems contain the initial location of the first block in the extent and its length. Figure 7.2 shows the difference between allocation and storage references in block and extent-based filesystems.

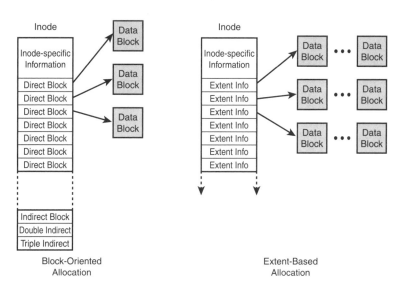

FIGURE 7.2
Storage allocation in block-oriented and extent-based filesystems.

The use of extent-based allocation helps preserve the goal of disk locality and also

- Provides higher performance during allocation than individually allocating multiple blocks for a file.

- Provides higher performance when reading file data because blocks can initially be read sequentially instead of reading multiple blocks in scattered disk locations. Per-read improvements in file read operations then generally help increase parallelism between access requests for multiple files in the allocation group or filesystem.

- Reduces the size of the chains of data structures necessary to track the disk space allocated to a file, improving performance and reducing the size of filesystem metadata.

- Reduces the number of lookups necessary when reading an existing file. Reading one extent record is faster than reading many individual block references.

- Reduces file fragmentation because it increases the chance that all the data associated with a specific file will be contiguous.

The XFS filesystem also uses a sophisticated delayed allocation mechanism when writing files to disk. This algorithm enables XFS to do a better job of extent allocation for new and updated files, and generally improves performance by reducing the number of distinct writes that XFS has to make to the filesystem.

In addition to using extents for locality and performance reasons, XFS applies some heuristics during directory creation that are designed to improve performance. Whenever a new directory is created in an XFS filesystem, it is located in a different allocation group than its parent, and a certain amount of contiguous space is preallocated for items in that directory. XFS also tries to allocate file inodes and extents as near as possible to the on-disk location of the directory in which they are located.

Like any other Unix or Linux filesystem, XFS uses inodes for each file and directory to track related file/directory/allocation metadata. However, XFS allocates inodes as needed instead of preallocating them when an XFS filesystem is created. This reduces wasted space in the filesystem by not requiring that these structures be preallocated and therefore consume disk space. More importantly, it maximizes the flexibility of an XFS filesystem by not "locking" the filesystem into containing a specific number of files and directories. Any XFS filesystem can contain any number of files and directories up to the limit imposed by its 64-bit data structures. This also makes it easy to increase the size of an existing XFS filesystem without requiring tedious exercises such as copying data out, resizing the filesystem, and then copying data back in.

New allocation groups can easily be added with a small number of changes to filesystem metadata because no new inodes need to be preallocated within the filesystem and the majority of the data structures specific to the any new allocation groups are internal to those allocation groups. The only real limitation in increasing the size of an existing XFS filesystem is that the new allocation groups must be the same size as the allocation groups created when the filesystem itself was created.

Like other modern filesystems, the size of the logical blocks used in an XFS filesystem is flexible. XFS block sizes range from 512 bytes to 64 KB. Combined with the 64-bit data structures used throughout XFS, this makes 18,000 petabytes (18 million gigabytes) the maximum theoretical size of an XFS filesystem, with a maximum file size of 9,000 petabytes. Unfortunately, Linux still imposes lower limitations on the size of a block device, but as the Linux kernel removes these limitations, the XFS filesystem will be ready to take advantage of these new capabilities.

7

Special Features of XFS

XFS intrinsically supports *sparse files*, which are logically large files that contain relatively little data. Data can be written to any location in a sparse file without allocating more disk space than the data actually requires (modulo some small amount of filesystem metadata). Though a sparse file reports its size as its maximum size, data blocks are only allocated when data is actually written to the file—reading information from any location in a sparse file that has not previously been written returns zero-filled data. Sparse files are perfect for some databases and other large, record and data-oriented files that need to provide random access to a large address space without simultaneously wasting disk space that is not yet required. See Figure 7.3 for an illustration of the logical size and allocation requirements of a sparse file before and after writing to it.

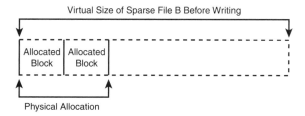

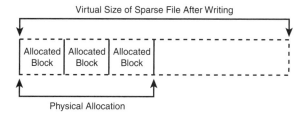

FIGURE 7.3

Block allocation for sparse files.

In addition to using allocation groups and extent-based allocation to improve performance, XFS also provides improved performance over many other filesystems by using balanced binary trees (B+Trees) to support most filesystem metadata. B+Trees were introduced in the "Design of Unix/Linux Filesystems" section of Chapter 1. XFS uses B+Trees to

- Manage dynamically allocated inodes. Inodes are allocated within each allocation group in sets of 64 inodes, and a B+Tree tracks both their location and which inodes within that set are used.

- Track the location of free extents rather than the bitmaps used by traditional filesystems. XFS uses a pair of B+Trees to track extent allocation within each allocation group, one of which is indexed by the starting block of each extent (for use in minimizing fragmentation during allocation) and the other of which is indexed by the length of each free extent (for use in quickly allocating extents of optimal size).

- Index directory entries by name rather than using the traditional linear directory scan to find a specific entry. Because filenames are variable length records ranging from 1 to 256 characters, the B+Tree that stores directory entries uses 4-byte hashes derived from the filenames as its index keys. Using fixed-size keys offsets the additional lookups required by duplicate keys that can exist in the hash tables.

- Track per-file extent allocation that overflows the number of direct extent entries that can be kept in an inode.

Given the fact that SGI workstations are the premier multimedia workstations in the Unix world, the performance requirements for XFS aren't exactly a surprise. However, in addition to performance-oriented features that XFS shares with other modern filesystems, such as extent-based allocation, dynamic inode creation, and the extensive use of B+Trees, XFS provides some incredibly clever features designed to satisfy the requirements of demanding multimedia applications.

The most interesting of these, a feature unique to XFS, is its capability to create real-time subvolumes in XFS filesystems to provide Guaranteed Ratio I/O (GRIO). These are designed for use by high-performance files that require deterministic throughput. An XFS real-time subvolume is a portion of an XFS filesystem that only holds data for high-performance (real-time) files. All metadata associated with real-time files is stored in the primary data portion of the filesystem. Identifying new files for which real-time performance is necessary is done through an `ioctl` when the file is created. Existing files can be copied to the real-time section of an XFS filesystem using the `xfs_rtcp` command, which automatically makes them as real-time files. XFS real-time subvolumes also use a different block allocation strategy that is optimized for fast allocation that minimizes fragmentation. This allocator isn't as efficient as the one used in the standard data portion of an XFS filesystem but guarantees high-speed allocation with minimal head movement.

> **WARNING**
>
> The real-time subvolume support in XFS under Linux is not complete. It should not be used as of this writing. Something to look forward to!

XFS is a modern high-performance filesystem that uses sophisticated algorithms, data structures, and advanced heuristics. The extensive testing and use that it has gotten as the primary filesystem used in SGI workstations for years makes it a proven performer that is well worth considering for use in production Linux environments.

Support Software for XFS Filesystems

Built-in support for the XFS filesystem is not yet present in any commercial Linux distribution that I have used. Whether your favorite Linux distribution includes integrated support for the XFS filesystem depends on the people who packaged your distribution. This section discusses the utilities associated with the XFS filesystem and the Linux packages in which they are found. If your Linux distribution does not include support for the XFS filesystem, you can always add it yourself by obtaining the following:

- Source code or binaries for a version of the Linux kernel that includes support for XFS
- Source code and patches to the version of the kernel that you are using to add XFS support to that kernel
- Source code or binary packages for the utilities used to mount, modify, and use XFS filesystems

If the Linux distribution and version of Linux that you are running does not include support for the XFS filesystem, the CD that accompanies this book includes a sample kernel source code distribution in the CD's kernels subdirectory and associated XFS patches in the CD's XFS directory. Installing the kernel source code, applying the patches, and XFS-specific information about building and installing a kernel are provided later in this chapter.

If the Linux distribution and version of Linux that you are running does not include support for the XFS filesystem, you will also need to install and compile several XFS-related utility packages to install, use, and administer XFS filesystems on your computer. The following is a list of these and the specific utilities that they provide for use with the XFS filesystem. These are also located in the XFS subdirectory of the CD that accompanies this book:

- `acl-1.1.2` or better—Provides support for Access Control Lists on files and directories in an XFS filesystem. Access Control Lists provide an open, configurable set of privileges that you can assign to specific users and groups of users on a per-file and directory basis. XFS ACLs conform to the proposed POSIX 1003.1e standard (since withdrawn, but at least SGI didn't just randomly implement whatever ACLs seemed handy).
- `chacl`—Lets you change, examine, or remove user, group, mask, or other ACLs on files or directories.
- `getfacl`—Lets you examine file Access Control Lists for files and directories.

- `setfacl`—Lets you set file and directory Access Control Lists.

- `attr-1.1.3` or better—Provides support for extended attributes on files and directories in an XFS filesystem. Extended attributes are name/value pairs that you can associate with different filesystems objects and which can then be used by attribute-aware applications to pass hints such as character sets, preview graphics, and so on.

- `attr`—Add, create, and remove extended attributes from files.

- `dmapi-0.2.2` or better—Libraries to support the Data Management API for XFS filesystems. DMAPI is a standard API for hierarchical storage management as defined in the X/Open document: "Systems Management: Data Storage Management (XDSM) API" (February 1997).

- `xfsdump-1.1.3` or better—Utilities for backing up and restoring XFS filesystems in a fashion similar to the class Unix `dump`/`restore` programs.

- `xfs_copy`—Copy an XFS filesystem to one or more target devices, files, and so on. The source filesystem must be unmounted to ensure that it does not change (and therefore no data is being written to its journal) during the copy process.

- `xfsdq`—Dump summary quota information for an XFS filesystem.

- `xfsrq`—Restore summary quota information for an XFS filesystem.

- `xfsdump`—An incremental `dump` utility for XFS filesystems, analogous to the standard Unix `dump` program but with provisions to handle XFS-specific metadata such as ACLs, attributes, unique identifiers, and so on.

- `xfs_estimate`—Estimate the space that an exiting directory would take in an XFS filesystem. Useful when moving existing filesystems or directory hierarchies to XFS filesystems. Program options enable you to experiment with estimating space consumption on XFS filesystems using different block sizes, log sizes, log locations, and so on.

- `xfs_fsr`—Reorganize an existing XFS filesystem for optimal disk space layout and use. This program operates on a mounted filesystem, defragmenting the filesystem on a file-by-file basis to make the best possible use of extents.

- `xfsinvutil`—Checks the inventory database written by the `xfsdump` utility, verifies its consistency, and optionally prunes old `dump` records that are no longer relevant.

- `xfsrestore`—Restores an XFS filesystem that was archived using the `xfsdump` program. The `xfsrestore` program can either restore a single `xfsdump` set (known as *simple mode*), or can incrementally restore a hierarchical collection of dump sets to completely re-create an XFS filesystem (known as *cumulative mode*).

- `xfsprogs-1.3.5` or better—The essential set of utilities for creating, expanding, repairing, verifying the consistency of, and examining XFS filesystems.

- `fsck.xfs`—One of my favorite XFS programs, this is a short C program that simply returns `True` however it is called and is used to provide a version of `fsck` that uses the standard naming conventions for filesystem-specific consistency checkers. All the standard consistency guarantees for XFS filesystems are, of course, enforced when the journal is replayed as the filesystem is mounted.

- `mkfs.xfs`—Create an XFS filesystem. This is the program invoked when you execute the command `mkfs -t xfs`. Program options enable you to specify various parameters for XFS filesystem creation. See the section "Creating an XFS Filesystem" later in this chapter for a complete discussion of using this utility.

- `xfs_admin`—Uses the `xfs_db` command to examine or modify the parameters of an unmounted XFS filesystem.

- `xfs_bmap`—Print the list of disk blocks used by any file in an XFS filesystem.

- `xfs_check`—Check the consistency of an unmounted or read-only XFS filesystem. If errors are detected, the filesystem can be repaired using the `xfs_repair` utility. If the errors are potentially fatal, the `xfsdump` utility can be used to try to preserve information from the filesystem, but may fail depending on the type of inconsistencies that are detected.

- `xfs_db`—Examine or modify an XFS filesystem. The `xfs_db` program is rarely used to modify an XFS filesystem interactively but is often executed by administrative scripts.

- `xfs_freeze`—Suspend or resume access to a mounted filesystem. Suspending access to an XFS filesystem flushes all pending and journaled updates to disk and provides a consistent XFS filesystem from which a snapshot or live dump can be taken.

- `xfs_growfs`—Expand the size of an existing, mounted XFS filesystem.

- `xfs_info`—Display information about a mounted XFS filesystem and verify sets of arguments that you could subsequently pass to `xfs_growfs` to expand the filesystem.

- `xfs_logprint`—Print the log of an XFS filesystem. This command is typically used for debugging problems in an XFS filesystem.

- `xfs_mkfile`—Create one or more XFS files of a specified size.

- `xfs_ncheck`—Print a list of inodes and the filesystem-relative pathnames of the files that they correspond to. This program is the XFS analogue of the classic Unix `ncheck` program.

- `xfs_repair`—Repair a corrupted, inconsistent, or damaged XFS filesystem, as reported by the `xfs_check` utility.

- `xfs_rtcp`—Copy one or more files to the real-time section of an XFS filesystem.

Adding XFS Support to Your System

As mentioned earlier, XFS support is not yet provided in any off-the-shelf Linux distribution that I've had the opportunity to use. Luckily, being able to add new system services and applications to your system is one of the most exciting and empowering aspects of open-source operating systems such as Linux.

This section provides hands-on, how-to information about building and installing a kernel that provides support for XFS filesystems, and about installing, activating, using, and administering XFS filesystems themselves.

Building a Kernel with XFS Support

The CD that accompanies this book includes the source code for version 2.4.9 of the Linux kernel, the most advanced version of Linux available at the time of this writing. This is therefore the version of the kernel that I've chosen to use to show how easy it is to add XFS support to your Linux system. The CD also includes the patches necessary to add support for the XFS filesystem to that kernel.

> **NOTE**
>
> As mentioned in each chapter, if you have never built a kernel before, doing so is a great learning experience. Although the whole idea of prepackaged Linux installation is to protect users from the need to "roll their own" kernel and Linux utilities, compiling a kernel is an excellent way to familiarize yourself with the conceptual internals and organization of Linux. The instructions in this book for compiling kernels create kernels that have special names and will thus not overwrite the current version of the Linux kernel that you are using.

Patching the Linux 2.4.9 Kernel for XFS Support

Appendix A, "Using the the CD-ROM: Installing, Updating, and Compiling Kernels," provides detailed information about installing Linux kernel source and selecting kernel configuration options. This section provides basic information about installing the specific version of the Linux kernel source that we'll use in the examples throughout the rest of this chapter. The procedures described in this section are generally relevant even if you want to add and activate XFS support in a different version of the Linux kernel sources, such as newer versions of the kernel or the version of the Linux kernel shipped with the Linux distribution that you are using.

> **TIP**
>
> If you are familiar with building Linux kernels and want to install and activate XFS support in the most up-to-date version of the Linux kernel, you can obtain the latest version of the Linux kernel from the central Web repository for Linux kernel sources, http://www.kernel.org. Then check the Web site for XFS (ftp://oss.sgi.com/ projects/xfs/download) to check for patches for that Linux kernel version to download and install them, if XFS support is still not present in that version of the Linux kernel. One of these days, XFS will just be in the default kernel (please), and that will be that.

To add support for the XFS filesystem to the Linux 2.4.9 kernel to guarantee that you can work through the specific examples given in this chapter, you must patch the source for the generic Linux 2.4.9 kernel after installing it. Patches are changes to existing files inserted to update those files. General information about patches and their installation is also provided in Appendix A.

The source for the Linux 2.4.9 kernel is located in the kernels subdirectory of the CD that accompanies this book. Install this kernel as described in "Installing the Kernel Source Code" in Appendix A; then use the following steps to add XFS support to that kernel:

1. Make sure that the X Window System is running, and use the su command to become root in an xterm or other terminal window.

2. Change your working directory to the directory created when you installed the Linux source code in the previous section:

   ```
   cd /usr/src/linux-2.4.9
   ```

3. Use the patch command to apply the patch from the patch subdirectory of the CD included with this book:

   ```
   patch -p1 < /mnt/cdrom/patches/patch-2.4.9-xfs-2001-08-19
   ```

4. The -p1 option tells the patch command how much of the filenames listed in the patch file to preen to correctly locate the files that should be patched.

The output of the patch command lists the name of each file being patched. After the patch program completes, you're ready to configure a kernel with support for the XFS filesystem.

Activating XFS Support in the Kernel

This section explains how to activate support for the XFS filesystem in the source code for the Linux 2.4.9 kernel. For an overview of the conceptual basics behind building a modern Linux kernel and activating support for different features and hardware in the kernel, see "Configuring Your Kernel" in Appendix A.

> **NOTE**
>
> It's generally a good idea to compile in support for any filesystems that your system uses regularly. Filesystems that you only interact with occasionally (such as AppleTalk or various network filesystems) can still be compiled as modules to keep your kernel as small as possible.

> **TIP**
>
> If you have already compiled a kernel for the computer system on which you are building a new kernel, you can use the configuration information from that kernel to save time when configuring the new kernel. Reusing existing configuration data from an existing kernel is explained in Appendix A.

This section explains the options specific to activating support for the XFS filesystem in the kernel we are building. This section describes how to configure XFS options using the X Window System-based Linux kernel configurator:

1. Log in as root or use the su command to become root.

2. In a terminal window running under an X Window System window manager or desktop, change directory to the directory /usr/src/linux-2.4.9 and execute the make xconfig command. The commands related to compiling and loading support for the Linux X Window System kernel configurator display in the window in which you executed the make xconfig command. Eventually, the X Window System Linux kernel configurator displays, as shown in Figure 7.4.

3. Select the Code Maturity Level Options command or button. A new dialog displays, as shown in Figure 7.5.

4. Click the Y radio button beside the Prompt for Development and/or Incomplete Code/Drivers option and click the Main Menu button to return to the primary make xconfig dialog.

5. Click the File Systems button in the X Window System kernel configuration dialog. A new dialog displays, as shown in Figure 7.6.

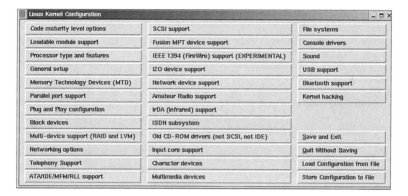

FIGURE 7.4

The X Window System-based Linux kernel configurator.

FIGURE 7.5

The Code Maturity Level Options dialog.

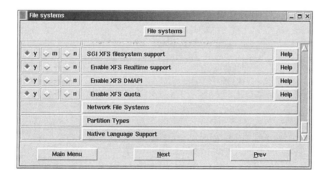

FIGURE 7.6

The File Systems Configuration dialog.

6. Scroll down until you see the Page Buffer support entry and click Y to enable the buffer cache used by the XFS filesystem on top of the standard Linux page cache. The buffer cache provides better performance in XFS by aggregating writes.

7. Click Y beside the SGI XFS Filesystem Support entry.

8. Click Y beside the Enable XFS Realtime Support entry. This is an optional feature that enables you to reserve a section of any XFS filesystem as a subvolume for use with real-time files—files to which updates can't be delayed, such as streaming media files. This is not currently implemented under Linux, but will soon be. You should get in the habit of selecting this option for XFS.

9. Click N beside the Enable XFS DMAPI entry unless you are going to be using hierarchical storage management devices to back up your data.

10. Click Y beside the Enable XFS Quota entry. This enables you to use per-user quotas in an XFS filesystem. XFS stores quota information as recoverable filesystem metadata.

11. Click the Main Menu button to return to the primary `make xconfig` dialog.

12. After selecting any other kernel configuration options relevant to the kernel that you are building (such as those specific to the hardware in your system), save your updated kernel configuration.

13. If you reused the configuration data from an existing kernel, use the Store Configuration to File button to display a dialog that enables you to explicitly save your new kernel configuration with the name `.config` in the main directory of the kernel that you are configuring.

14. If you configured the current kernel from scratch (that is, without reading in configuration data from another kernel), simply click the Save and Exit button.

15. Click OK to close the final dialog and return to the Linux shell prompt. You're now ready to compile the kernel!

Compiling and Installing an XFS Kernel

After applying patches to and configuring the Linux 2.4.9 kernel, you're ready to compile and install your new Linux kernel. All the information that you need to compile and install this kernel is provided in Appendix A. This section just provides a checklist for the steps that you should follow.

After you've installed, patched, and configured the Linux 2.4.9 kernel for XFS filesystem support and to match your hardware, you must do the following to install and use that kernel:

1. Verify that the XFS patch added a special extension for this kernel to its Makefile, making it easy to identify the special features in the kernel. I typically name kernels that support different filesystems along the lines of `linux-<kernel-version>-<filesystem-type>`. In this case, the XFS patch set does this automatically.

2. Execute the following make commands in this order to correctly initialize dependencies and to build and install the new kernel and any associated loadable modules:

```
make dep
make
make modules
make install
make modules_install
```

3. I suggest doing these steps as discrete commands to make it easy to spot any compilation or installation failures along the way. If you're really cocky, you can reduce these commands to the following single command line, but you'd still be wise to scroll back to make sure that there were no problems:

```
make dep ; make install ; make modules ; make modules_install
```

4. Modify the boot loader configuration files for the boot loader you're using on your system, as described in "Booting a New Kernel" in Appendix A and rerun LILO if necessary.

You're now almost ready to reboot your system and use the XFS filesystem. Before doing that, however, you must also compile and install the utilities discussed in the next section to ensure that your system can mount and administer XFS filesystem volumes both correctly and optimally.

Installing Related Utilities

This section explains how to configure, compile, and install the various utilities that enable you to administer and use XFS filesystems on your Linux system. These utilities support all the basic features of any filesystem, such as creating, resizing, repairing, and removing XFS filesystems, and also enable you to take advantage of advanced capabilities such as Access Control Lists and setting per-directory and per-file attributes.

> **NOTE**
>
> Unlike the utilities provided with many of the other distributed filesystems discussed in this book, some of the XFS-related utilities are dependent on include files and libraries that are part of other XFS-related utility packages. Be sure to make and install the XFS utilities in the order specified in this section. If the configure script or make process fails when configuring and compiling any of the utilities in this chapter, double-check that you've built them in the correct order and that you've execute the `make install-dev` installation command to install public versions of the include files and libraries associated with the XFS utilities that you have already compiled and installed.

Building and Installing the `xfsprogs` Package

To install version 1.3.5 of the `xfsprogs` package, included on the CD that accompanies this book, do the following:

1. Mount the CD and extract the `xfsprogs` package from the file `xfs/xfsprogs-1.3.5.src.tar.gz` to a directory on your system using a command like the following:

   ```
   cd <target-directory>
   tar zxvf <path-to-CD>/xfs/xfsprogs-1.3.5.src.tar.gz
   ```

2. Change directory to `<target-directory>`/`xfsprogs-1.3.5` and run the configure script to correctly configure the `xfsprogs` Makefile for your system and Linux distribution:

   ```
   ./configure
   ```

   This produces verbose output that's not useful to replicate here.

3. After the Makefile is correctly configured, execute the `make` command to build the new versions of the utilities in the `xfsprogs` package:

   ```
   make
   ```

   Once again, this produces verbose, system-specific output that's not useful to replicate here.

4. After all the utilities are compiled, install them on your system using the following commands:

   ```
   make install
   make install-dev
   ```

Your system now has a version of the `xfsprogs` utilities and associated reference (man page) documentation installed.

Building and Installing the XFS DMAPI Library

To install version 0.2.2 of the XFS DMAPI library, included on the CD that accompanies this book, do the following:

1. Mount the CD and extract the `dmapi` package from the file `xfs/dmapi-0.2.2.src.tar.gz` to a directory on your system using a command like the following:

   ```
   cd <target-directory>
   tar zxvf <path-to-CD>/xfs/dmapi-0.2.2.src.tar.gz
   ```

2. Change directory to `<target-directory>`/`dmapi-0.2.2` and run the configure script to correctly configure the XFS `dmapi` Makefile for your system and Linux distribution:

   ```
   ./configure
   ```

   This produces verbose output that's not useful to replicate here.

3. After the Makefile is correctly configured, execute the `make` command to build the new version of the XFS DMAPI library:

```
make
```

Once again, this produces verbose, system-specific output that's not useful to replicate here.

4. Once the XFS DMAPI library is compiled, install it on your system using the following commands:

```
make install
make install-dev
```

Your system now has a version of the XFS DMAPI library and associated reference (man page) documentation installed.

Building and Installing the `acl` Package

To install version 1.1.2 of the `acl` package, included on the CD that accompanies this book, do the following:

1. Mount the CD and extract the `acl` package from the file `xfs/acl-1.1.2.src.tar.gz` to a directory on your system using a command like the following:

```
cd <target-directory>
tar zxvf <path-to-CD>/xfs/acl-1.1.2.src.tar.gz
```

2. Change directory to *<target-directory>*/acl-1.1.2 and run the configure script to correctly configure the `acl` Makefile for your system and Linux distribution:

```
./configure
```

This produces verbose output that's not useful to replicate here.

3. After the Makefile is correctly configured, execute the `make` command to build the new versions of the utilities in the `acl` package:

```
make
```

Once again, this produces verbose, system-specific output that's not useful to replicate here.

4. After all the utilities are compiled, install them on your system using the following commands:

```
make install
make install-dev
```

Your system now has a version of the `acl` utilities and associated reference (man page) documentation installed.

Building and Installing the `attr` Package

To install version 1.1.3 of the `attr` package, included on the CD that accompanies this book, do the following:

1. Mount the CD and extract the `attr` package from the file `xfs/attr-1.1.3.src.tar.gz` to a directory on your system using a command like the following:

   ```
   cd <target-directory>
   tar zxvf <path-to-CD>/xfs/attr-1.1.3.src.tar.gz
   ```

2. Change directory to *<target-directory>*/attr-1.1.3 and run the configure script to correctly configure the `attr` Makefile for your system and Linux distribution:

   ```
   ./configure
   ```

   This produces verbose output that's not useful to replicate here.

3. After the Makefile is correctly configured, execute the `make` command to build the new versions of the `attr` utility and related libraries:

   ```
   make
   ```

   Once again, this produces verbose, system-specific output that's not useful to replicate here.

4. After the `attr` utility and related libraries are compiled, install them on your system using the following commands:

   ```
   make install
   make install-dev
   ```

Your system now has the new version of the `attr` utility and its associated reference (man page) documentation installed.

Building and Installing the `xfsdump` Package

To install version 1.1.3 of the `xfsdump` package, included on the CD that accompanies this book, do the following:

1. Mount the CD and extract the `xfsdump` package from the file `xfs/xfs dump-1.1.3.src.tar.gz` to a directory on your system using a command like the following:

   ```
   cd <target-directory>
   tar zxvf <path-to-CD>/xfs/xfsdump-1.1.3.src.tar.gz
   ```

2. Change directory to *<target-directory>*/xfsdump-1.1.3 and run the configure script to correctly configure the `xfsdump` Makefile for your system and Linux distribution:

   ```
   ./configure
   ```

   This produces verbose output that's not useful to replicate here.

3. After the Makefile is correctly configured, execute the `make` command to build the new versions of the utilities in the `xfsdump` package:

```
make
```

Once again, this produces verbose, system-specific output that's not useful to replicate here.

4. After all the utilities are compiled, install them on your system using the following command:

```
make install
```

Your system now has the new version of the `xfsdump` program, related utilities, and associated reference (man page) documentation installed. Now reboot your system and make sure that you select the XFS-enabled kernel before proceeding to experiment with XFS.

Administering XFS Filesystems

It's clearly important to understand the design issues addressed by different types of filesystems and the different features that they provide. This type of knowledge is critical to make appropriate choices to satisfy your home, academic, or business requirements and also makes for great small talk at cocktail parties. However, the real test of a great filesystem, and certainly the most fun, comes from actually using it.

More than any other journaling filesystem discussed in this book, SGI's XFS filesystem comes with an amazingly rich assortment of associated tools that make it feasible to do just about anything with or to an XFS filesystem. This is partially the result of the fact that it already has a long pedigree, having been the one true filesystem on SGI systems for years. Over the years, SGI's developers and customers have continually refined and enhanced XFS-related utilities—in many cases, adding the zillions of command-line options that any good Unix program should have, and in others, simply implementing the tools that they needed to get their work done, resolve problems, and use and administer XFS on a daily basis.

No one understands how quickly robust utilities can appear to fill a perceived need better than a Linux user—after all, that's essentially how Linux itself came to be. Thanks to SGI's release of XFS to the open-source community, we can all instantly take advantage of the fruits of SGI's labor. This isn't to say that nothing remains to be done or that nothing can be improved; further development, enhancement, and refinement of XFS are in progress right now. For example, actual support for the real-time subvolumes found and used in XFS under IRIX would be nice. However, as you'll see in this section, XFS has a significant head start, utility-wise, over the other journaling filesystems discussed in this book.

Creating an XFS Filesystem

Like most other modern Linux filesystems, XFS filesystems are created by using the /sbin/mkfs wrapper program and specifying the -t xfs option. This causes the /sbin/mkfs wrapper program to pass all the other command-line arguments to the /sbin/mkfs.xfs program, which is the XFS-specific filesystem creation utility.

The example used in this section executes the mkfs.xfs command directly, to emphasize the name of the command that is actually doing real work. (And the name of the command that you will want to supply to the man command if you want to see the detailed online reference information available for the mkfs.xfs command.) The mkfs.xfs utility can take a number of command-line arguments that enable you to fine-tune different aspects of the filesystem that you are creating, but the following is an example of using it in its simplest form and the resulting output:

```
# mkfs.xfs /dev/hdc2
meta-data=/dev/hdc2          isize=256     agcount=8, agsize=65552 blks
data     =                   bsize=4096    blocks=524412, imaxpct=25
         =                   sunit=0       swidth=0 blks, unwritten=0
naming   =version 2          bsize=4096
log      =internal log       bsize=4096    blocks=1200
realtime =none               extsz=65536   blocks=0, rtextents=0
```

> **NOTE**
>
> If you are creating an XFS filesystem on a partition of device on which another type of filesystem already exists, you will have to use the -f option to force the mkfs.xfs utility to overwrite the existing filesystem.

The mkfs.xfs utility is exceptionally fast because it does not have to do many of the time-consuming tasks required by filesystems such as ext2, which preallocate filesystem structures such as inodes. The output from this command shows the values for different portions of the XFS filesystem that was just created.

General Filesystem Metadata Information:

- isize (inode size)—256 bytes (default value).
- agcount (number of allocation groups)—8 (default value for filesystems between 128 MB and 8 GB).
- agsize (allocation group size)—Calculated based on the number of allocation groups being created and the size of the disk or partition on which the filesystem is being created. Allocation groups range in size from 16 MB to slightly less than 4 GB.

Data Section Information:

- `bsize` (block size)—4096 bytes (default value on systems with a 4 KB page size, such as Linux).

- `blocks` (total number of blocks)—Calculated based on the blocks size and the size of the disk or partition on which the filesystem is being created, minus the disk space consumed by the log, the optional real-time section, and the overhead for allocation groups, the filesystem itself, and so on.

- `imaxpct` (maximum percentage of the filesystem that can consist of inodes)—25 percent (default value).

- `sunit` (stripe unit, the size of the units in which data is striped on the disk or partition)— 0 (the default is not to use striping).

- `swidth` (stripe width, the width of the stripes on the disk or partition)—0 blocks (the default is not to use striping).

- `unwritten` (a boolean indicating whether unwritten extents are flagged as such)—0 (default value—this feature is not yet used on Linux).

Naming (Directory) Information:

- XFS filesystems support two types of directories, version 1 and version 2. Version 2 directories are the default and are recommended on Linux systems because of the way that the `glibc` get directory entries (`getdents`) function interacts with the kernel.

- `bsize` (directory block size)—4096 bytes (default value).

Log Information:

- XFS filesystems can store the log internally (within the filesystem with which the log is associated) or externally.

- `bsize` (log block size)—4096 bytes (default value).

- `blocks` (total number of blocks in the log)—Calculated based on the size of the filesystem being created.

Real-time Information:

XFS filesystems can contain an optional real-time section, where the data associated with files that need high-speed, consistent I/O can be located. The real-time portion of an XFS filesystem is divided into a number of fixed-size extents.

> **NOTE**
>
> As mentioned earlier in this chapter, real-time subvolumes are not yet supported on Linux and should not be used.

- `extsz` (extent size)—65536 bytes (default value).
- `blocks` (total number of blocks in the real-time subvolume)—0 (the surprising default value when a real time subvolume is not used).
- `rtextents` (number of real-time extents)—0 (the default number when a real-time subvolume is not used).

> **NOTE**
>
> When migrating existing systems to XFS, the `xfs_estimate` utility can be valuable and is an excellent example of the impressive collection of utilities that exist for use with the XFS filesystem. This utility examines an existing filesystem (without crossing mountpoints) and estimates the amount of size that the filesystem would take if it were moved to an XFS filesystem. You can use its `-b` (block size) parameter to determine the results of converting an existing filesystem to XFS using different block sizes, using internal and external logs of different sizes, and so on.
>
> Experimenting with different block sizes can be tedious, but using `xfs_estimate` to help select an optimal block size can result in significant space savings and a filesystem that is "tuned" to the types and sizes of files that you will be storing on it. Excellent examples of this are filesystems used to store mail queues, Internet news, and so on.

The XFS `mkfs.xfs` command has many options that provide fine control over the way in which an XFS filesystem is created. The next three sections discuss some of the more common ways in which you might want to customize XFS filesystems when creating them.

Specifying an Alternate Journal Size

One aspect of an XFS filesystem that you might want to customize is the size of the journal, or log in SGI-speak, used to record filesystem metadata changes. By default, the size of the log is calculated when the filesystem is created and is a function of the size of the filesystem. However, you might want to increase the size of the log if, for example, you know that the applications using a specific filesystem frequently perform many filesystem operations under the control of a single process or if the filesystem is heavily used by many simultaneous users.

To specify the size of the journal used by an XFS filesystem, you would use the -l size=*number* option, where *number* is the size of the journal. This size can be specified in the following ways:

- In bytes by simply specifying a number with no alphabetic suffix
- In blocks (based on the filesystem block size) by following the number with the letter b
- In kilobytes by following the number with the letter k
- In megabytes by following the number with the letter m
- In gigabytes by following the number with the letter g

If you happen to think in hexadecimal or octal, you can specify numeric values in those bases by prefixing the numbers with 0X (zero x) for hexadecimal values and 0 (capital letter O) for octal.

For example, to create an XFS filesystem on the device /dev/hdc2 and create a 10 MB log, the octal and hexadecimally challenged would use a command like the following:

```
# mkfs.xfs -f -l size=10m /dev/hdc2
```

This would produce output like the following:

```
meta-data=/dev/hdc2              isize=256    agcount=8, agsize=65552 blks
data     =                       bsize=4096   blocks=524412, imaxpct=25
         =                       sunit=0      swidth=0 blks, unwritten=0
naming   =version 2              bsize=4096
log      =internal log           bsize=4096   blocks=2560
realtime =none                   extsz=65536  blocks=0, rtextents=0
```

Note that the log is still internal but consists of 2,560 blocks, each of which are 4 KB in size, totaling 10 MB.

Specifying an Alternate Journal Location

Another aspect of an XFS filesystem that you may want to customize is the location of the journal. By default, the log for an XFS filesystem is internal to that filesystem and occupies a distinct section of the filesystem. You may want to locate the log for a given XFS filesystem on another filesystem for a variety of performance reasons, thereby increasing parallelism between appending to the log and writing to the filesystem itself. Relocating the log for an XFS filesystem to another partition on the same disk would be a waste of time because the same disk heads would still be contending for read/write access to the same physical disk, but locating the journal for one or more XFS filesystems or disks on the partitions of a separate disk may well increase performance by enabling the system to log metadata updates and actually update filesystems essentially in parallel. This can be even more of a performance advantage on heavily used systems.

To specify the location of the journal used by an XFS filesystem, you would use the -l
logdev=*device* option, where *device* is the name of the disk partition where you want to put
the log for the filesystem you are creating.

For example, to create an XFS filesystem on the device /dev/hdc2 and use the 10 MB partition /dev/hdb1 as its log, you would use a command like the following:

```
# mkfs.xfs -f -l logdev=/dev/hdb1 /dev/hdc2
```

This would produce output like the following:

```
meta-data=/dev/hdc2              isize=256    agcount=8, agsize=65552 blks
data     =                       bsize=4096   blocks=524412, imaxpct=25
         =                       sunit=0      swidth=0 blks, unwritten=0
naming   =version 2              bsize=4096
log      =/dev/hdb1              bsize=4096   blocks=2560
realtime =none                   extsz=65536  blocks=0, rtextents=0
```

Note that the log information shows the log device to be /dev/hdb1, on which 2,560 blocks
that are each 4 KB in size have been allocated.

> **NOTE**
>
> When creating a log on another disk or partition, you either have to specify a valid
> size for the log or specify a partition that is already a valid size for the log. The maxi-
> mum size of the log for an XFS filesystem is 65536 blocks. If you specify a target parti-
> tion that is larger than 65536 blocks and do not specify a valid size, the mkfs.xfs
> command exits without creating the filesystem and displays a message like the fol-
> lowing, followed by a usage message for the mkfs.xfs command:
>
> ```
> log size XXXXXX blocks too large, maximum size is 65536 blocks
> ```

Specifying an Alternate Block Size

Creating filesystems with smaller or larger block sizes is a standard form of filesystem optimization. If a filesystem is dedicated to a specific type of task, such as serving as a repository
for electronic mail or Internet news, you can often predict the average size of the files that will
be created on that filesystem and use a smaller (or larger) block size to minimize the amount of
space wasted by files when they are smaller than the block size. For example, the text files
used to store Internet news postings tend to be small—using the default block size of 4 KB on
a filesystem that primarily stores news posts would waste a substantial amount of space.

Some other journaling filesystems, most notably the ReiserFS, use sophisticated algorithms
such as tail-packing to group leftover block fragments into single blocks, minimizing this type
of wasted space. The extent-based allocation used by XFS does not lend itself well to algo-

rithms such as these because its focus is more toward efficient, high-speed allocation of sets of contiguous blocks (extents) than toward squeezing the most storage out of a given partition. For XFS filesystems, selecting an appropriate block size and using the xfs_fsr (XFS Filesystem Reorganize) utility to optimize disk layout and allocation is your best bet for maximizing the storage capabilities of a filesystem.

To specify the block size that you want to use on an XFS filesystem, you would use the -b log=*number* or -b size=*number* options, where *number* is the block size in bytes. If you use the log=*number* form, you must specify the number as a base 2 logarithm value—that is, the power of two that you want to use as the block size. If you use the size=*number* form, you must specify the block size in bytes.

For example, to create an XFS filesystem on the device /dev/hdc2 with a block size of 1 KB, you could use either of the following two commands:

```
# mkfs.xfs -f -b log=10 /dev/hdc2
```

or

```
# mkfs.xfs -f -b size=1024 /dev/hdc2
```

In both cases, you would see output like the following:

```
meta-data=/dev/hdc2        isize=256   agcount=8, agsize=262206 blks
data      =                bsize=1024  blocks=2097648, imaxpct=25
          =                sunit=0     swidth=0 blks, unwritten=0
naming    =version 2       bsize=4096
log       =internal log    bsize=1024  blocks=3072
realtime  =none            extsz=65536 blocks=0, rtextents=0
```

Mounting an XFS Filesystem

Like all other journaling filesystems, the journal for an XFS filesystem is automatically read when an XFS filesystem is mounted to guarantee the consistency of the filesystem.

The mount program has many XFS-specific options, some of which are used to override existing filesystem parameters, such as the log location and various disk stripe settings, and others that are designed to let you fine-tune performance and activate specific features. For the most part, you should rarely need to tweak the default mount settings for XFS filesystem, but just in case, some of the more common mount settings that you may want to specify for XFS filesystems are the following:

- biosize=*size* —Sets the amount of buffered filesystem I/O to the specified size, which must be given as a base 2 logarithm value. Valid values are 13 (8 KB bytes—only valid on systems, such as Linux, with a 4 KB page size), 14 (16 KB), 15 (32 KB), and 16 (64 KB).

You might want to change this value, for example, on critical filesystems to guarantee that as little I/O as possible is buffered, but reducing the buffered I/O size results in an obvious performance penalty because data must be written to disk more frequently.

- `dmapi` or `xdsm`—Enables the DMAPI (Data Management API or data Migration API, depending on whom you ask) event callouts, enabling the filesystem to be stored on a hierarchical storage management device. This is also known as the XDSM (eXtended Data Storage Management) API, hence the alternate option.

- `logbufs=value`—Sets the number of log buffers that are held in memory. Valid values are from 2-8, inclusive. The default value is 8 buffers for filesystems with a 64 KB block size, 4 buffers for filesystems with a 32 KB block size, 3 buffers for filesystems with a 16 KB block size, and 2 buffers for all other filesystem block sizes.

  Increasing the number of buffers may increase performance by reducing the frequency with which log buffers must be flushed to the log but requires additional memory and increases the amount of data that may not be written to the log in the event of a crash.

- `logbsize=value`—Sets the size of the log buffers held in memory. Valid values are 16 KB or 32 KB. The default size of a log buffer for machines with less than 32 MB of memory is 16 KB—machines with more memory use 32 KB log buffers.

- `logdev=device`—Lets you specify an external device as the location for the XFS filesystem's metadata journal.

- `noatime`—Prevents last access time values form being updated when a file is read. This can save a substantial amount of time if you're not concerned about preserving this information because this substantially reduces the amount of filesystem metadata changes that would otherwise have to be logged.

- `norecovery`—Enables you to mount a filesystem without replaying the log. This is discussed later in this chapter in the section "Mounting an XFS Filesystem Without Replaying the Journal."

- `osyncisdsync`—Makes writes to files opened with the O_SYNC flag (synchronous mode for both file data and file metadata) behave as if they had been opened with the O_DSYNC flag set (synchronous mode for file data only). These affect whether the `fsync()` or `fdatasync()` calls are used to flush file buffers to the disk after any write to the file is done. Unfortunately, these two calls are currently identical in Linux. When `fdatasync()` is independently implemented, using this mount flag improves performance but increases the chance that filesystem metadata (such as time stamp updates) may be lost if the system crashes.

- `quota`, `usrquota`, or `uqnoenforce`—Activates user disk quotas.

- `grpquota` or `gqnoenforce`—Activates group disk quotas.

- `sunit=value` and `swidth=value`—Enables you to override the stripe unit and stripe width used when an XFS filesystem was created. These mount options are only useful for XFS filesystems directly located on hardware RAID devices. In all other cases, the stripe unit and stripe width defined when the filesystem was created are read from the superblock.

XFS filesystems are typically automatically mounted at boot time when the `/etc/fstab` file is read. XFS filesystems are identified in this file as being of type `xfs`, but the partition or disk on which the filesystems themselves are located can be identified in the `/etc/fstab` file in one of three ways:

- By explicitly referencing to the partition containing the filesystem and identifying it as an XFS filesystem. This can be either done in the `/etc/fstab` file or by invoking the `mount` command from the command line, using the `-t xfs` option.
- By referring to the filesystem label. XFS filesystems can be labeled when they are created by using the `-L label` option to the `mkfs.xfs` program, or by using the `xfs_admin` command's `-L label` option after the filesystem has already been created. You can clear a filesystem label by specifying `--` (two dashes) as the value of the filesystem label using the `xfs_admin` command.
- By referring to the filesystem's Universal Unique IDentifier (UUID). UUIDs are of the form `c1b9d5a2-f162-11cf-9ece-0020afc76f16` and are automatically generated for XFS filesystems when they are created using the `mkfs.xfs` program. You can also set the UUID for an XFS filesystem after it already exists by using the `xfs_admin` command's `-U UUID` option or the `xfs_db` command after the filesystem has already been created.

Mounting a filesystem using the name of the partition on which the filesystem is located is the classic way of mounting a filesystem. For example, to mount the XFS filesystem located on the partition `/dev/hdc2` on the directory `/xfs_test` using the default `mount` options, you would issue the following command:

```
mount -t xfs /dev/hdc2 /xfs_test
```

Mounting filesystems using labels is gaining in popularity because labels provide a way of referring to a specific filesystem without associating it with a specific device. This is especially handy for filesystems located on external drives because it makes it easy to move these drives to other systems and mount them without worrying about the order in which they appear on the bus or hub. This can also be useful on internal IDE drives—for example, if you identify filesystems by partition name, have filesystems on the slave device of your second IDE controller, and add a drive as the master on that controller, you would have to edit your `/etc/fstab` file to correctly rename the partitions on which those filesystems are located. If those filesystems were identified by label, you wouldn't have to change anything.

The `mkfs.xfs` program does not automatically label filesystems when they are created. Before querying an XFS filesystem label or manually labeling the filesystem, you must unmount it. The following is an example of the command used to determine the label of an unmounted XFS partition:

```
# xfs_db -c 'label' /dev/hdc2
label = ""
```

The following is an example of setting the label of this same disk to the string `"xfs_test"`:

```
# xfs_admin -L /xfs_test /dev/hdc2
writing all SBs
new label = "/xfs_test"
```

Given the label `"/xfs_test"` for the filesystem located on the partition `/dev/hdc2`, the following two `/etc/fstab` entries are equivalent:

```
/dev/hdc2          /xfs_test      xfs      defaults      1 0
LABEL=/xfs_test    /xfs_test      xfs      defaults      1 0
```

The third way of mounting a filesystem is by referring to its UUID. Identifying a filesystem by its UUID to mount it provides the same sort of device independence as referring to a filesystem by label but provides a way of referring to a filesystem that is, well, unique. After all, they don't call them universal unique identifiers for nothing. As you can see from the labeling example earlier in this section, people (myself included) tend to label disks using the name of their mountpoint as the label. (This is the default action when Linux distributions such as Red Hat format disks during the installation process.) Although this certainly embeds some useful information in the filesystem label (helping you answer questions like "Where was this filesystem intended to be mounted anyway?" when you examine a partition on an external disk), every Linux system has a partition that is to be mounted at /, which doesn't exactly make this label unique across computer systems.

Universal unique identifiers were created to associate unique but identifiable sequences of characters with computer systems and devices, especially in networked environments. For filesystems, they help prevent you from accidentally mounting the same filesystem twice when you are using hardware that provides different access paths to the same devices and partitions. Unlike XFS filesystem labels, UUIDs for XFS filesystems are automatically generated and assigned when an XFS filesystem is created. The following is an example of the command used to determine the UUID of an unmounted XFS partition:

```
# xfs_db -c 'uuid' /dev/hdc2
uuid = 8180d55b-4ed4-4966-8ff1-91eb099d1cf0
```

Given that `8180d55b-4ed4-4966-8ff1-91eb099d1cf0` is the UUID of the filesystem `/dev/hdc2`, the following two `/etc/fstab` entries are equivalent:

```
/dev/hdc2               /xfs_test       xfs       defaults       1 0
UUID=8180d55b-4ed4-4966-8ff1-91eb099d1cf0   /xfs_test  xfs   defaults      1 0
```

You can set the UUID of an XFS filesystem in different ways. Why set a UUID when it's almost guaranteed to be unique in the first place? The most common case in which you would want to do this is if you are attempting to mount a clone of an existing XFS filesystem. This is usually a snapshot of an XFS filesystem that lives on a logical volume but can also be the case if you have use a command such as dd to do a block-by-block copy of one filesystem to another. The most common ways of setting the UUID of an XFS filesystem are the following:

- Automatically, using the xfs_db command in expert mode to generate a new random UUID, as in the following example command and output:

  ```
  # xfs_db -x -c 'uuid generate' /dev/hdc2
  clearing log and setting uuid
  writing all SBs
  new uuid = ace30ae3-d2e2-459f-b2fd-a7db090b257e
  ```

- Automatically, using the xfs_admin command's -U option as in the following sample command and output:

  ```
  # xfs_admin -U `uuidgen` /dev/hdc2
  clearing log and setting uuid
  writing all SBs
  new uuid = c6ff0c75-0795-4c6f-bd91-1238fd5c2686
  ```

  This example used back quotes around the `uuidgen` command on the xfs_admin command line to execute that command and then uses its output (a random UUID) as the argument to the xfs_admin command's -U option.

- Manually, by supplying a specific UUID as an argument to the xfs_admin command's -U option, as in the following sample command and output:

  ```
  # xfs_admin -U bc4eeccf-9638-4f75-a80a-3ba92ba499af /dev/hdc2
  clearing log and setting uuid
  writing all SBs
  new uuid = bc4eeccf-9638-4f75-a80a-3ba92ba499af
  ```

NOTE

Before changing entries for critical partitions in /etc/fstab to take advantage of features like XFS filesystem UUIDs and labels, experiment with changing a noncritical /etc/fstab entry. Try mounting and unmounting the specified filesystem to make sure that the syntax of your new /etc/fstab entries is correct.

7

THE XFS
JOURNALING
FILESYSTEM

Configuring File and Directory Access Control in XFS Filesystems

Unlike all other journaling filesystems discussed in this book, XFS intrinsically provides support for Access Control Lists, which are an open, configurable set of privileges that you can assign to specific users and groups of users on a per-file and directory basis. XFS ACLs conform to the proposed POSIX ACL standard, last seen in the hands of Amelia Earhart. Regardless of when the rest of the universe implements ACLs, users of the XFS journaling filesystem (and the AFS distributed filesystem, discussed in Chapter 13, "The OpenAFS Distributed Filesystem") can use ACLs today to provide infinitely finer control than standard Linux/Unix protections regarding who can access which files and directories, and what they can do to them. XFS ACLs are limited to more precisely defining the privileges of standard Linux users and groups. The ACLs used by OpenAFS are much more powerful because they enable you to create your own virtual groups and associate them with specific files and directories.

Simply put, an ACL is a list of Linux users and/or groups and the access rights that they have to a specific file or directory. ACLs enable you to define totally granular permissions such as "only the users wvh, kwalter, and jeffpk can write this file, but the users darth and davep can at least read it" without requiring that you create hundreds of special-purpose Linux groups.

NOTE

The primary shortcomings of standard Unix file protections are that they are fairly limited in scope and that some of the things that would make them more flexible are things that only the superuser can do. For example, without using ACLs, there is no way to enable more than one user to write to a specific file without resorting to using Unix groups, which can only be created by root.

If your local sysadmin is a friend of yours (or if you're the sysadmin in the first place), the classic Unix protection solution for situations like these is to create a new group containing you and everyone that you want to be able to write to a certain file, change the group ownership of any files and directories that you all want to be able to write to that group, and then force everyone to use the Linux/Unix newgrp command to change his group membership to that group before attempting to update those files and directories. As much as I love Unix, that's about as clear as mud and as intuitive and easy-to-remember as an IP address.

Two basic types of ACLs are available on XFS filesystems:

- ACLs used to control access to specific files and directories
- Per-directory ACLs known as "mask" ACLs that define the default access control ACLs that will be assigned to any files created within that directory

Conversationally and in print, ACLs are represented in a standard format consisting of three colon-separated fields:

- The first field of an ACL entry is the entry type, which can be one of the following: user (u), group (g), other (o), and mask (m).

- The second field of an ACL entry is a username, numeric UID, group name, or numeric GID, depending on the value of the first field. If this field is empty, the ACL refers to the user or group that owns the file or directory. Mask and other ACLs must have an empty second field.

- The third field is the access permissions for this ACL. These are represented in two forms:

  - A standard Unix-like permissions string rwx (Read, Write, and eXecuTe permissions, where eXecute permissions on directories indicate the capability to search that directory. Each letter may be replaced by a - (dash), indicating that no access of that is permitted). These three permissions must appear in this order.

  - A relative symbolic form that is preceded by a + (plus) sign or a ^ (caret) symbol, much like the symbolic permissions designed for use with the chmod command by people who are octally challenged. In this ACL representation, the + or ^ symbols are followed by single r, w, or x permission characters, indicating that these permissions should be added to the current set for a file or directory (the plus symbol) or that these permissions should be removed from the current set (the caret) for a given file or directory.

When listed or stored in files, different ACL entries are separated by whitespace or new lines. Everything after a # character to the end of a line is a comment and is ignored.

As mentioned in the section "Support Software for XFS Filesystems" earlier in the chapter, the XFS acl package provides the following three utilities for ACL creation, modification, and examination:

- chacl—Lets you change, examine, or remove user, group, mask, or other ACLs on files or directories

- getfacl—Lets you examine file Access Control Lists for files and directories

- setfacl—Lets you set file and directory Access Control Lists

As an example of using ACLs, let's use a directory with the following contents and permissions:

```
$ ls -al
drwxr-xr-x    2 wvh      wvh            23 Aug 31 00:19 .
drwxr-xr-x    3 wvh      wvh            47 Aug 31 00:19 ..
-rw-r-----    1 wvh      wvh         31372 Aug 31 00:19 resume.xml
```

The default ACL for this directory is the following:

```
$ getfacl .
# file: .
# owner: wvh
# group: wvh
user::rwx
group::r-x
other::r-x
```

The default ACL for the file `resume.xml` is the following:

```
$ getfacl resume.xml
# file: resume.xml
# owner: wvh
# group: wvh
user::rw-
group::r--
other::---
```

The default ACL for a file in a directory for which a default ACL has not been set reflects the default Unix permissions associated with the user that created the file. The default Unix permissions for a file are based on the setting of the umask environment variable.

> **NOTE**
>
> The umask is the classic Unix mechanism for setting the default protections of file and directories that you create. By default, the umask is a three-digit octal number applied against standard file protections of octal 666 (ironically) when you create a file or octal 777 when you create a directory. The default umask value on most Linux distributions is 002, meaning that any file you create is created with the octal protection mode 664—both the owner and group can read and write any file that you create, but randoms (others) can only read the file. Similarly, any directory that you create is created with the octal protection mode 775—both the owner and group can create files in that directory, and anyone can list the contents of the directory and search for files in it.
>
> Most people set this umask to 022 to change this so that files can only be written by their owners (that is, are created with an octal protection of 644), and directories can only be written to by their owners (that is, are created with an octal protection of 755). The capability to define a umask is built into all Unix shells; for more information about setting or using the umask, see the online documentation for the shell that you are using.

There are three common ways to change the ACL of a file or directory:

- By setting it explicitly using the `setfacl` command
- By using the `chacl` command to modify an existing ACL
- By using the `setfacl` command's `-m` option to modify an existing ACL

For the examples in this chapter, I'll use the `chacl` command to change ACLs because this doesn't overwrite the existing ACL (as using the `setfacl` command to explicitly set it would do) but provides more information about how ACLs really work than using the shorthand version of the `setfacl` command.

ACLs provide fine-grained control over the permissions on files and directories far above and beyond standard Unix protections. For example, to add the user `kwalter` as someone who could read the file `resume.xml`, I would use a `chacl` (change ACL) command such as the following:

```
$ chacl u::rw-,g::r--,o::---,u:kwalter:r--,m::rw- resume.xml
```

No, that isn't static from a bad modem or Internet connection (though it probably is a command in the old TECO editor)—that's the way that ACLs look in real life. As mentioned previously, ACLs consist of three colon-separated fields that represent the permission of the user (owner of the file), group (the group ownership to the file), and others. When changing an ACL with the `chacl` command, you need to first specify the ACL of the file and then append the changes that you want to make to that ACL. The `u::rwx,g::r--,o::---` portion of the ACL in this example is the existing ACL of the file; the `u:kwalter:r--,m::rw-` portion specifies the new user that I wanted to add to the ACL for that file and the effective rights mask to be used when adding that user's ACL. The effective rights mask is the union of all the existing user, group, and other permissions for a file or directory. You must specify a mask when adding a random user to the ACL for a file.

Using the `getfacl` command to retrieve the ACL for my resume shows that the user `kwalter` has indeed been added to the list of people who have access to the file:

```
$ getfacl resume.xml
# file: resume.xml
# owner: wvh
# group: wvh
user::rwx
group::r--
other::---
user:kwalter:rw-
mask::rw-
```

Using the `ls -al` command shows that the visible, standard Unix file and directory permissions haven't changed:

```
$ ls -al
drwxr-xr-x    2 wvh       wvh              23 Aug 31 00:19 .
drwxr-xr-x    3 wvh       wvh              47 Aug 31 00:19 ..
-rw-r-----    1 wvh       wvh           31372 Aug 31 00:19 resume.xml
```

You can verify that the user `kwalter` now has access to the file by asking the user to attempt to read the file, which will succeed. (If you know the user's password, you can check this yourself by telneting to your machine, logging in as that user, and examining the file using a text editor or a command such as `more` or `cat`.)

Even more interesting and useful than just giving specific individuals read access to files is the capability for specific users to write specific files. For example, to add the user `kwalter` as someone who could both read and write the file `resume.xml`, I would use a `chacl` (change ACL) command such as the following:

```
$ chacl u::rw-,g::r--,o::---,u:kwalter:rw-,m::rw- resume.xml
```

Using the `getfacl` command shows that the user `kwalter` now has both read and write access to the file:

```
$ getfacl resume.xml
# file: resume.xml
# owner: wvh
# group: wvh
user::rw-
group::rw-
other::---
user:kwalter:rw-
mask::rw-
```

As before, you can verify that the user `kwalter` now has both read and write access to the file by asking the user to attempt to read and write the file, which will succeed. (If you know the user's password, you can check this yourself by telneting to your machine, logging in as that user, and editing and saving the file using a text editor.)

I'm a big fan of ACLs because they give knowledgeable users total control over who can access their files and directories. ACLs are already supported in XFS but eventually will be supported in all Linux filesystems, removing one of the main administrative complaints about Unix systems (and silencing one more argument for using odious systems such as Windows NT/2000/XP). I can't lie and say that ACLs are easy to use at the moment, but like the rest of Linux and other fine wines, things will only improve with time. See Chapter 13 for more information about using ACLs, specifically the incredibly rich (and easier to use) set provided by OpenAFS and its commercial brother, IBM AFS.

Checking XFS Filesystem Consistency

As you know by now, the primary advantages of journaling filesystems is that they provide faster system restart times and help minimize the amount of filesystem changes that you can lose after a system crash. When executed, the `fsck.xfs` program simply returns success because XFS filesystems re-execute any pending journal entries when an XFS filesystem is mounted during a system reboot. Normally, this restores filesystem consistency, and all is well. However, as with any random problems that may cause computer systems to reboot, there are cases in which you may suspect that an XFS filesystem may not be consistent. The most common instance of this situation is problems with the disk subsystem(s) on which XFS filesystems are stored. These can be either hard disk or controller problems, and "normally" reveal themselves when you begin to see error messages on the console that report problems reading from or writing a specific disk.

XFS provides two separate utilities that help you manually check XFS filesystems for consistency problems: `xfs_check` (discussed in this section), which identifies XFS filesystem consistency problems if they are present, and `xfs_repair` (discussed later in this chapter in the section "Using the `xfs_repair` Utility"), which helps you repair XFS filesystem consistency problems. Checking for and repairing XFS consistency problems are divided into two separate utilities for two primary reasons:

- The `xfs_check` utility is a shell script that uses the `xfs_db` program in noninteractive mode to examine the specified filesystem. It is therefore much faster than `xfs_repair` because it only has to scan the filesystem instead of allocating data structures and tracking information that would be required when actually repairing an inconsistent XFS filesystem.

- For a number of years, there was no specific `xfs_repair` utility because of the stability and robustness of XFS. Journal replay at mount time restores the consistency of an XFS in almost all cases, and the emergence of hardware problems on a disk or controller are usually most easily and permanently resolved by replacing the ailing hardware and restoring the XFS filesystem from backups.

You should unmount an XFS filesystem before running the `xfs_check` utility. Running `xfs_check` on a mounted filesystem often generates errors because the journal is active and the filesystem may be in active use. For safety's sake, always unmount an XFS filesystem before running `xfs_check`.

In most cases, the XFS filesystem you are checking will not actually have consistency problems, and the `xfs_check` utility will therefore exit silently, without displaying any messages, as in the following example:

```
# xfs_check /dev/hdc2
#
```

If you're not quite so lucky and the filesystem that you are checking is actually inconsistent, you may see any number of error messages, such as the following:

```
# xfs_check /dev/hdc2
xfs_check: unexpected XFS SB magic number 0xa7b9acbd
bad superblock magic number a7b9acbd, giving up
#
```

If you see a message like this one, or any similarly serious message, use the `xfs_repair` utility, as described later in this chapter.

Backing Up and Restoring XFS Filesystems

Regardless of how robust a filesystem is, backups are a necessary part of any serious computer installation that actually depends on the data stored on its computer systems. The data that a computer installation depends on can range from your personal collection of family recipes to the US government's Internal Revenue Service tax records for every US citizen for the last 10 years. You might argue that the world would be a better place without your grandmother's recipe for Jello salad or the IRS in general, but that's not going to help you when everyone starts waxing nostalgic for Jello salad or a legion of IRS auditors are taking numbers at your door.

Backups provide the opportunity to restore files that have been accidentally deleted, but more importantly protect against problems such as hardware failures ranging from the failure of a disk drive to the destruction of all or part of a data center due to fire, explosion, earthquake, or a comet striking the earth. Backups take a lot of time and have no immediate benefit, just like sleep. However, you can only go without either of these for a relatively short amount of time until you're endangering yourself and others. (As an aside, the other important task related to actually doing backups is verifying that they can be read and that the tapes or CDs actually contain data. I was burned by this once and will never be burnt again.)

The standard Linux/Unix `dump` (back up a filesystem) and `restore` utilities are powerful, time-tested utilities that work well and have saved more butts than Preparation H. Unfortunately, the standard Linux `dump`/`restore` utilities are not currently equipped to deal with filesystems, such as XFS, that do not use standard inodes and filesystem headers, or that contain extended filesystem data such as ACLs, extended file and directory attributes, and so on. Also, being designed to back up any type of filesystem, the standard `dump`/`restore` utilities can't easily take advantage of possible optimizations available for different types of filesystems.

> **WARNING**
>
> You cannot use the standard Linux dump/restore utilities to back up XFS filesystems. If you absolutely do not want to use the xfsdump utility, your only options are writing your own backup system (yikes!), using a third-party backup solution that supports XFS filesystems, or using truly minimal but classic utilities such as dd to archive XFS filesystem data.

To resolve these problems, the XFS filesystem provides its own dump and restore utilities, cleverly named xfsdump and xfsrestore. Each of these has many options, as you might guess. This section discusses the most commonly used options for each. For complete information, see the online reference information for both utilities.

Using the xfsdump Utility

Like its Linux/Unix ancestor, the xfsdump utility provides the capability to do full or incremental backups. Full backups (often referred to as *epochs*, or *level 0 dumps*) are complete backups of all files and directories located on one or more filesystems. Incremental backups are backups of all files and directories that have changed since a previous, lower-numbered backup. The *xfsdump* utility keeps track of which backups have been done in binary files located in the directory /var/xfsdumps/Inventory rather than in the /etc/dumpdates file used by the Linux/Unix dump program. This enables the xfsdump utility to keep track of much more information than can be provided in the relatively simple entries used by the standard dump program. You can check the contents of this file at any time by using the xfsdump utility's -I option, which produces output like the following:

```
# xfsdump -I
file system 0:
      fs id:        c1fba169-94be-45e0-bade-d80dab54d93e
      session 0:
        mount point:  journal.vonhagen.org:/home/wvh/writing
        device:       journal.vonhagen.org:/dev/vg1/xfs_vol
        time:         Sun Sep  2 16:40:23 2001
        session label:  "Std_Sunday"
        session id:   2a773dcd-51c6-4d7e-bfbf-d53f62078c95
        level:        0
        resumed:      NO
        subtree:      NO
        streams:      1
```

```
stream 0:
        pathname:       /dev/st0
        start:          ino 132 offset 0
        end:    ino 2097287 offset 0
        interrupted:    NO
        media files:    1
        media file 0:
                mfile index:    0
                mfile type:     data
                mfile size:     105805312
                mfile start:    ino 132 offset 0
                mfile end:      ino 2097287 offset 0
                media label:    "Yellow"
                media id: 7d3cc222-7ad8-4548-b282-59017752c18d
```

Tracking all this type of information simplifies restoring filesystems because the xfsrestore utility can identify the sequence backup media that you must use to restore a specified filesystem. The xfsdump program's -I option also accepts a number of subcommands that enable you to limit the dump sets about which information is displayed based on criteria such as the dump level, the filesystem mountpoint, the device on which the filesystem is located, the filesystem ID, the media label, and so on.

A standard xfsdump command line looks like the following and produces the following output:

```
[wvh]# xfsdump -l 0 -o -L Std_Sunday -M Yellow -f /dev/st0  /dev/vg1/xfs_vol
xfsdump: version 3.0 - Running single-threaded
xfsdump: level 0 dump of journal.vonhagen.org:/home/wvh/writing
xfsdump: dump date: Sun Sep  2 16:40:23 2001
xfsdump: session id: 2a773dcd-51c6-4d7e-bfbf-d53f62078c95
xfsdump: session label: "Std_Sunday"
xfsdump: ino map phase 1: skipping (no subtrees specified)
xfsdump: ino map phase 2: constructing initial dump list
xfsdump: ino map phase 3: skipping (no pruning necessary)
xfsdump: ino map phase 4: skipping (size estimated in phase 2)
xfsdump: ino map phase 5: skipping (only one dump stream)
xfsdump: ino map construction complete
xfsdump: estimated dump size: 105794176 bytes
xfsdump: creating dump session media file 0 (media 0, file 0)
xfsdump: dumping ino map
xfsdump: dumping directories
xfsdump: dumping non-directory files
xfsdump: ending media file
xfsdump: media file size 105805312 bytes
xfsdump: dump size (non-dir files) : 105772248 bytes
xfsdump: dump complete: 348 seconds elapsed
```

The options on this command line, any associated options, and the meaning of each are the following:

- -l 0—The -l option enables you to specify the level of the dump that you want to do. In this case, I did a level 0 (epoch) dump of the filesystem, meaning that all files and directories were backed up.

- -o—The -o option enables you to overwrite anything that may already be present on the backup media. By default, the xfsdump utility will not overwrite any backup media on which existing XFS filesystem dumps (created with the xfsdump program) are present.

- -L Std_Sunday—The -L option specifies a label for the backup session. The label should be something meaningful to you and your backup sequence—most sites typically use labels that reflect the day of the week on which the backups were done, the dump level, or something along those lines. You can subsequently use this label to identify the information related to a specific backup's session in the output produced by the xfsdump -I command.

- -M Yellow—The -M option specifies a label to be written to the backup media to which you are writing backups. Once again, this label should be something that is meaningful to your backup strategy, such as the tape set on which the backup was done (I color-code mine, as you might guess), or something else along those lines. You can subsequently use this with the xfsdump -I mobjlabel=<label> command to inventory only the dump sets that have been written to backup media and assigned that specific label.

- -f /dev/st0—The -f option specifies the file or device to which you want to write the current dump set.

- /dev/vg1/xfs_vol—The name of the device on which the filesystem that you want to back up is stored or the name of the mountpoint on which that filesystem is mounted.

In addition to the features mentioned previously, the xfsdump program provides some sophisticated capabilities for doing things like only backing up specific files or subdirectories, interrupting and resuming dumps, and so on. If you are a system administrator and use XFS filesystems at your installation, you'll be pleasantly surprised by its extensive and eminently usable capabilities.

Using the xfsrestore Utility

The xfsrestore utility is the companion utility to xfsdump, enabling you to read backup tapes and restore their contents. The xfsrestore utility provides many options to give you fine-grained control over restoring specific files or files matching specific criteria.

The most common way of invoking the xfsrestore command is simply to specify the backup device on which the backup media for the specified filesystem is present and then to identify the mountpoint for the filesystem that you want to restore, as in the following sample command line and output:

```
# xfsrestore -f /dev/st0 /home/wvh/writing
xfsrestore: version 3.0 - Running single-threaded
xfsrestore: searching media for dump
xfsrestore: examining media file 0
xfsrestore: dump description:
xfsrestore: hostname: journal.vonhagen.org
xfsrestore: mount point: /home/wvh/writing
xfsrestore: volume: /dev/vg1/xfs_vol
xfsrestore: session time: Sun Sep  2 17:55:21 2001
xfsrestore: level: 0
xfsrestore: session label: "Std_Sunday"
xfsrestore: media label: "Yellow"
xfsrestore: file system id: c1fba169-94be-45e0-bade-d80dab54d93e
xfsrestore: session id: 0dcd2372-67b1-4411-b085-35386f25b90e
xfsrestore: media id: aa9aec93-9ea4-459a-b1b9-2c6736a83454
xfsrestore: using online session inventory
xfsrestore: searching media for directory dump
xfsrestore: reading directories
xfsrestore: directory post-processing
xfsrestore: restoring non-directory files
xfsrestore: restore complete: 114 seconds elapsed
```

If you are unsure of whether the file that you want is present on a backup tape, the xfsrestore command's -i (interactive) option can be useful, just as the equivalent option for the standard Linux/Unix restore command. After executing xfsrestore with this option, the xfsrestore program builds a miniature filesystem in memory and puts you at a command prompt internal to the xfsrestore program. You can then change virtual directories in the restore image, verifying that the files you want to restore are present and marking them for subsequent restoral.

For complete information about the xfsrestore command, see the online reference page for that command, available by typing the man xfsrestore or info xfsrestore commands.

Resolving Problems with XFS Filesystems

As discussed earlier in "Checking XFS Filesystem Consistency," the XFS filesystem did not have a filesystem repair utility for much of its history, primarily because one was rarely necessary. Regardless of how uncommon it is to find an XFS filesystem in an inconsistent state that can't be repaired simply by replaying the journal, it may happen. As noted earlier, the most common cause of this is imminent hardware failure or other hardware-related problems, but it's still important to be aware of your alternatives if you ever encounter this sort of problem.

If an XFS filesystem is in an inconsistent state that can't be resolved by replaying the journal when the filesystem is mounted, your system's automatic reboot will fail because the filesystem could not automatically be mounted while the filesystem is marked as dirty (that is, is inconsistent). In this case, first check the system boot log to see why the filesystem mount failed, making sure that the device on which the XFS filesystem is located was detected during system reboot. If the device could not be found, is internal, and other devices attached to the same controller could be found, it is likely that the drive on which the filesystem is located has failed. If no drive on that controller could be found, the controller itself may have failed.

If your problem is indeed a hardware failure, explaining how to deal with hardware failures is straightforward and is also outside the scope of this book. It basically boils down to this: if there is a hardware problem that requires that you replace a disk, grab your backup tapes and start restoring files using xfsrestore after fixing the hardware. If you have no backup tapes and your resume is on a partition other than the one on the defunct drive, I'd suggest that you start printing it out because you will probably need it soon.

If your problem is not a permanent hardware failure, you're essentially in luck because you have options that are much faster than replacing disks and restoring data. The final two sections of this chapter discuss your options. Which of these applies to you depends on the part of the problematic XFS filesystem in which the inconsistency lies. The final two sections of this chapter discuss how to deal with XFS filesystem inconsistencies in the log and in other portions of the filesystem.

Mounting an XFS Filesystem Without Replaying the Journal

In some cases, the log associated with an XFS filesystem can get corrupted. This can be due to problems in the kernel, problems in the XFS filesystem journaling code, or even a hardware glitch of some sort. The xfs_repair utility, discussed in the next section, is designed to resolve log corruption problems as well as all other XFS filesystem inconsistencies.

If an XFS filesystem cannot be mounted because the log cannot be replayed, but you want to try to recover data from the filesystem before using xfs_repair, you can use the following command to try to mount the filesystem without replaying the log:

```
mount -t xfs -o ro,norecovery filesystem mountpoint
```

This command mounts an XFS filesystem in read-only mode without replaying or recovering the log. Because you did not replay the log, the filesystem will almost certainly be inconsistent because any metadata changes in the log will not have been replayed, but this can give you access to files in the partition. You should immediately copy them out of the filesystem; then unmount it and use the xfs_repair utility to try to fix the partition itself.

Using the `xfs_repair` Utility

The `xfs_repair` utility resolves inconsistencies in an XFS filesystem. Like any filesystem consistency checker, it may make changes to your filesystem, such as move files to the filesystem's `lost+found` directory to resolve directory inconsistencies, zero or remove inodes, update file/block mappings to resolve problems where multiple files claim the same block, rewrite the filesystem superblock from a copy if the primary superblock is bad, and many similar changes.

> **NOTE**
>
> In XFS filesystems, the `lost+found` directory is automatically created when the `xfs_repair` utility is executed. If a `lost+found` directory already exists in an XFS filesystem on which you are running the `xfs_repair` utility, that directory is deleted and then created again to ensure that no name conflicts can occur.

> **NOTE**
>
> The `xfs_repair` utility itself fails if it cannot find a valid superblock anywhere on the filesystem and may also fail if can't read blocks due to hardware problems. In the latter case, you may be able to recover the filesystem by using the `dd` utility to copy the filesystem to another partition of identical size, unmounting the first filesystem, and then running `xfs_repair` to attempt to repair the copy. Any data residing in blocks that could not be read will still be lost, but you may be able to recover the filesystem itself.

The `xfs_repair` utility tries to repair a damaged XFS filesystem by performing seven general recovery steps:

1. Find and verify a superblock. If `xfs_repair` cannot read the filesystem's primary superblock, it searches the filesystem for blocks that conform to the superblock data structure and attempts to use the first one of these that it finds as the superblock. After it has found a valid superblock, it rewrites the primary superblock from the one that it has found.

2. Check the consistency of the internal log and zero out its contents. It then scans the data portion of the filesystem to verify the consistency of any filesystem data structures, detect misaligned or damaged inodes, and so on.

3. Scan each allocation group to verify its internal consistency, detect inodes that are not in the list of allocated inodes, delete inodes that are not actually associated with file data, and so on.

4. Check the block lists associated with all files in all allocation groups, resolve problems such as blocks claimed by multiple files, and so on.

5. Verify all allocation group data structures, allocated inode lists, and other internal data structures.

6. Check and correct any unlinked or crosslinked files and directories in the filesystem by walking the entire inode and directory tree, linking any unreferenced files and inodes into the filesystem's lost+found directory if possible.

7. Verify and correct all file hard link counts.

The xfs_repair utility has relatively few options. The most useful of these are the following:

- -l log-device —Enables you to specify the external log device associated with a damaged XFS filesystem.

- -n—Report problems and exist without making any changes. Using this option may cause the xfs-repair utility to exit long before it would if it were actually repairing a filesystem because there are many cases in which subsequent analysis and repair may be dependent on first correcting earlier errors.

The following is sample output from running xfs_repair on a heavily damaged filesystem:

```
# xfs_repair /dev/hdc2
Phase 1 - find and verify superblock...
bad primary superblock - bad magic number !!!
attempting to find secondary superblock...
...............................................................
........................................................found
candidate secondary superblock...
verified secondary superblock...
writing modified primary superblock
sb root inode value 18446744073709551615 inconsistent with calculated value
        13835049877664432192
resetting superblock root inode pointer to 18446744069414584384
sb realtime bitmap inode 18446744073709551615 inconsistent with calculated
value
        13835049877664432193
resetting superblock realtime bitmap ino pointer to 18446744069414584385
sb realtime summary inode 18446744073709551615 inconsistent with calculated
value
        13835049877664432194
resetting superblock realtime summary ino pointer to 18446744069414584386
Phase 2 - using internal log
        - zero log...
        - scan filesystem freespace and inode maps...
zeroing unused portion of secondary superblock 0 sector
```

```
bad length 65552 for agf 0, should be 262206
flfirst -1 in agf 0 too large (max = 128)
fllast -4 in agf 0 too large (max = 128)
bad length # 65552 for agi 0, should be 262206
reset bad agf for ag 0
reset bad agi for ag 0
freeblk count 1 != flcount -5 in ag 0
bad magic # 0x58414749 in btbno block 0/1
expected level -3 got 0 in btbno block 0/1
bno freespace btree block claimed (state 4), agno 0, bno 1, suspect 0
bad agbno 16318461 for btbcnt root, agno 0
bad magic # 0xbebdabbc in inobt block 0/3
expected level 0 got 65535 in inobt block 0/3
dubious inode btree block header 0/3
badly aligned inode rec (starting inode = 4294967286)
bad starting inode # (4294967286 (0x0 0xfffffff6)) in ino rec, skipping rec
badly aligned inode rec (starting inode = 252)
ir_freecount/free mismatch, inode chunk 0/252, freecount 251658240 nfree 0
badly aligned inode rec (starting inode = 0)
bad starting inode # (0 (0x0 0x0)) in ino rec, skipping rec
badly aligned inode rec (starting inode = 4294967295)
bad starting inode # (4294967295 (0x0 0xffffffff)) in ino rec, skipping rec
zeroing unused portion of secondary superblock 1 sector
bad magic # 0xa7b9acbd in btbno block 1/2
expected level 0 got 65535 in btbno block 1/2
block (1,1) multiply claimed by bno space tree, state - 4
block (1,2) multiply claimed by bno space tree, state - 7
block (1,7129) multiply claimed by bno space tree, state - 1
...
bad starting inode # (4194304 (0x2 0x0)) in ino rec, skipping rec
badly aligned inode rec (starting inode = 4194304)
bad starting inode # (4194304 (0x2 0x0)) in ino rec, skipping rec
ir_freecount/free mismatch, inode chunk 2/224, freecount -1 nfree 64
badly aligned inode rec (starting inode = 4294967295)
bad starting inode # (4294967295 (0x2 0xffffffff)) in ino rec, skipping rec
badly aligned inode rec (starting inode = 4294967295)
bad starting inode # (4294967295 (0x2 0xffffffff)) in ino rec, skipping rec
zeroing unused portion of secondary superblock 3 sector
zeroing unused portion of secondary superblock 4 sector
zeroing unused portion of secondary superblock 5 sector
zeroing unused portion of secondary superblock 6 sector
zeroing unused portion of secondary superblock 7 sector
root inode chunk not found
Phase 3 - for each AG...
        - scan and clear agi unlinked lists...
error following ag 0 unlinked list
found inodes not in the inode allocation tree
```

```
found inodes not in the inode allocation tree
found inodes not in the inode allocation tree
        - process known inodes and perform inode discovery...
        - agno = 0
        - agno = 1
        - agno = 2
        - agno = 3
        - agno = 4
        - agno = 5
        - agno = 6
        - agno = 7
        - process newly discovered inodes...
Phase 4 - check for duplicate blocks...
        - setting up duplicate extent list...
        - clear lost+found (if it exists) ...
        - check for inodes claiming duplicate blocks...
        - agno = 0
        - agno = 1
        - agno = 2
        - agno = 3
        - agno = 4
        - agno = 5
        - agno = 6
        - agno = 7
Phase 5 - rebuild AG headers and trees...
        - reset superblock...
Phase 6 - check inode connectivity...
        - resetting contents of realtime bitmap and summary inodes
        - ensuring existence of lost+found directory
        - traversing filesystem starting at / ...
        - traversal finished ...
        - traversing all unattached subtrees ...
        - traversals finished ...
        - moving disconnected inodes to lost+found ...
Phase 7 - verify and correct link counts...
Note - stripe unit (0) and width (0) fields have been reset.
Please set with mount -o sunit=<value>,swidth=<value>
done
```

NOTE

Don't worry about the amount of damage shown in this example—I damaged the filesystem manually to produce this sample output. Simply pulling the plug didn't cause any problems! Potential XFS users should be glad to hear that it was difficult to cause this sort of damage.

Third-Party Journaling Filesystems

IN THIS CHAPTER

After reading the previous chapters in this part of the book, you should have a firm understanding of the advantages of using a journaling filesystem to minimize system restart time. Chapter 9, "Logical Volume Management," explores the advantages of sophisticated data management features such as logical volume management (LVM) and RAID (Redundant Array of Inexpensive Disks) and how combining them with journaling filesystems could increase the flexibility, reliability, and performance of computer systems. This chapter discusses platform-independent journaling filesystem offerings available commercially and explores their availability for Linux. As such, this is a short chapter.

Most Unix workstation manufacturers provide LVM "solutions" (to steal a word from the marketing department) that are specific to their operating system and work with most RAID hardware. For example, Sun provides its Solstice Disk Suite for managing RAID devices and logical volumes as a product that you must pay for separately, and IBM provides its integrated logical volume management software with every RS/6000 that it ships.

Unfortunately and surprisingly, only Silicon Graphics (SGI) offers a commercial journaling filesystem for use with its operating system (IRIX) and has released the source code for its follow-on journaling filesystems as XFS. IBM originated the JFS journaling filesystems but used it as a research effort rather than a feature of its product line. In general, the absence of journaling filesystem support on commercial Unix workstations is amazing, sad, and one of the better arguments for using Linux in commercial production environments (after thorough testing, of course!). The opportunity to use state-of-the-art filesystems on relatively inexpensive hardware with a free operating system still boggles the mind.

Historical Commercial Journaling Filesystems

A journaling filesystem known as Episode is a part of a cross-platform system software development effort known as the *Distributed Computing Environment* (DCE), originally choreographed by a group known as the *Open Software Foundation*, OSF, (no relation to open-source software, and now a part of the Open Group). The OSF got the buy-in of companies, such as DEC, HP, and IBM, persuading them to join together for once to design something that ran on all their hardware and could tie it together on a network. The DCE provided a network time service, networked directory service, standard interplatform RPC (Remote Procedure Call) mechanism, a distributed filesystem, and the Episode journaling local filesystem. The DCE also eventually was available for Sun workstations through Transarc Corporation, now the IBM Pittsburgh Lab.

Unfortunately, the OSF was the same group that brought you Motif and the OSF/1 kernel, so the DCE turned into the Spruce Goose of interoperability products—a monolithic solution that interoperated by running equally slowly on all supported hardware platforms and operating systems. It was a great dream but one that was unfortunately beyond the capabilities of most hardware at the time it was developed.

The Episode local filesystem is a sophisticated journaling filesystem that is highly integrated with and thus dependent on the DCE, even providing the capability of exporting local filesystems over the network without resorting to NFS. Episode uses a separate area of the disk for maintaining its log, maximizing performance by using a sophisticated "lazy write" strategy to commit filesystem transactions to disk without adversely affecting the performance of the filesystem. Though work has been done to test the idea of removing DCE dependencies from Episode, no plans to parole Episode have ever been announced.

> **NOTE**
>
> For more information about the DCE, see `http://www.opengroup.org/dce`. You can download the DCE 1.2.2 source code and documentation from the Open Group, including a license for unlimited internal use, at `http://www.opengroup.org/dce/download`. The DCE has been ported to Linux as FreeDCE (with the goal of providing DCOM support) and is available at `http://sourceforge.net/projects /freedce`.

The VERITAS Filesystem

Veritas is the only company that offers a commercial, cross-platform journaling filesystem and has done so for years. Its filesystem product is cleverly marketed under the name VERITAS File System. Not surprisingly, Veritas also offers a commercial volume management software package with a similarly catchy name, the VERITAS Volume Manager. Small wonder that the Veritas marketing group probably earns the big bucks. These products are available for the HP-UX and Solaris operating systems.

The VERITAS File System is a journaling filesystem that minimizes system restart time, uses extent-based allocation for high performance, and has administrative utilities for backing up and administering the filesystem while it is in use. It also includes an integrated defragmentation utility and supports filesystems up to one Terabyte in size. The VERITAS Volume Manager supports mirroring, striping, and online volume moves, and includes a graphical administrative package known as VERITAS Visual Administrator that runs under the X Window System.

Caught up in the Linux boom of early 2000, Veritas announced that it would be porting its filesystem and volume manager to Linux by the end of the year 2000. As of July 2001, neither product was available for Linux. For more information about Veritas, its products, and their availability under Linux, see `http://www.veritas.com`.

Logical Volume Management

IN THIS CHAPTER

Although not specifically a journaling filesystem topic, logical volume management is interesting enough as a sophisticated storage management solution to merit discussion. After all, filesystems have to live somewhere, and simply storing them on finite-sized disk partitions is an irritating limitation. The combination of logical volume management with the journaling and distributed filesystems discussed in this book can help provide truly flexible, long-term solutions to your data storage and access requirements.

This chapter begins by providing an overview of logical volume management (LVM) as compared to simple physical disk storage, discusses general issues involved in using LVM to support journaling and distributed filesystems, explains how to perform the most common administrative procedures related to using logical volume management, and concludes with a discussion of RAID, a related hardware and software solution for flexible and reliable storage allocation.

Overview of Logical Volume Management

Logical volume management provides a mechanism for creating large collections of storage space that can be allocated to different filesystems (volumes) but managed as a whole. As discussed in Chapter 1, "Introduction to Filesystems," logical volumes provide a way around the fact that all physical storage media has a finite size. The use of logical volumes provides a level of abstraction between requests to store or retrieve data and the physical devices on which that storage actually lives. This level of abstraction, the volume management layer, then can translate requests for data from logical volumes into requests for data on any number of physical devices. To applications and users, logical volumes are identical to the traditional filesystems created on single disk partitions. To administrators and filesystem developers, they still work the same way, but are much cooler.

When managing computer systems, a classic problem is the research project or business unit gone haywire, whose storage requirements far exceed its current allocation and perhaps any amount of storage currently available on the systems that they are using. Good examples of this sort of thing are simulation and image analysis projects, or my research into backing up my entire CD collection on disk. Some filesystems support soft and hard quotas, which are ways of imposing upper bounds on disk space use by specific users or groups. When users or groups try to exceed the amount of space that they have been allocated, they receive a warning when they exceed a soft quota and cannot save any files that would cause them to exceed their hard quota.

Quotas are a relatively fascist solution to the problem of managing disk use. It certainly is true that quotas may actually be necessary in organizations with absolutely no budget for additional disk storage or in which rules are more important than productivity. The best argument for imposing quotas that I can think of is that they make users and groups aware of their disk space consumption and force them to delete files that they no longer need. I personally prefer the public humiliation method of storage management, where you send around weekly mail identifying the most conspicuous consumers of disk space and the directories in which that storage resides. You'd be amazed how quickly users with vast amounts of storage space in ~/porn will reduce their storage requirements after that sort of mail hits the bulletin boards or their manager's Inbox.

For the most part, quotas don't solve the actual problem, which is the "fixed-size" aspect of disk storage. Logical volumes solve this problem in a truly elegant fashion, by making it easy to add new disk storage to the volumes on which existing directories are located. Without logical volumes, you could still add new disk storage to those volumes by formatting new disks and partitions and mounting them at various locations in the existing filesystem, but your system would quickly become an unmanageable administrative nightmare of mountpoints and symbolic links pointing all over the place.

When using logical volume management, the pool of storage space from which specific volumes are created is known as a *volume group*. Volume groups are created by first formatting specific physical devices or partitions as physical volumes using the pvcreate command and then creating the volume group on some number of physical volumes using the vgcreate command. When the volume group is created, it divides the physical volumes of which it is composed into physical *extents*, which are the actual allocation units within a volume group. The physical extent size associated with a specific volume group can be set from 8 KB to 512 MB in powers of 2 when the volume group is created, with a default size of 4 MB.

NOTE

The basic relationships between logical volumes, volume groups, and physical volumes were explained in Chapter 1 in the section "Physical and Logical Storage."

When you create a volume group, a directory with the same name as that volume group is created in your system's /dev directory, and a character-special device file called "group" is created in that directory. As you create logical volumes in that volume group, the block-special files associated with each of them also are created in this directory.

After you've created a volume group, you can use the lvcreate command to create logical volumes from the accumulation of storage associated with that volume group. Physical extents from the volume group are allocated to logical volumes by mapping them through logical extents, which have a one-to-one correspondence to specific physical extents but provide yet another level of abstraction between physical and logical storage space. Using logical extents reduces the impact of certain administrative operations, such as moving the physical extents on a specific physical volume to another physical volume if you suspect (or, even worse, know) that the disk on which a specific physical volume is located is going bad.

> **NOTE**
>
> Using specific logical volume management commands is explained later in this chapter, in the section "Using and Administering the Logical Volume Management System."

After you create a logical volume, you can create your favorite type of filesystem on it using the mkfs command, specifying the type of filesystem by using the -t type option. You then can use Linuxconf, use some other system administration utility, or directly modify the /etc/fstab file to mount the new logical volume wherever you want, and you're in business.

Using LVM with Different Types of Filesystems

This section discusses the advantages and any potential caveats of creating different types of journaling and distributed filesystems on logical volumes. This section provides a conceptual overview of these topics, not specific performance data. Where relevant, the discussion of each filesystem in this book provides information about its performance on physical disks and on logical volumes.

Benchmarks are general comparisons and can't anticipate the specific data requirements and usage patterns on your computer systems. The information on using logical volumes in this chapter provides conceptual and hands-on guidance—determining whether the benefits of using logical volumes outweigh the administrative overhead on your computer systems is up to you. My vote is "yes." Your mileage may vary.

Finally, remember that increasing the number of levels of abstraction that separate data from the physical media that it is stored on also increases the number of points at which bugs or misfeatures can surface. It also increases the administrative overhead of managing the system and the level of knowledge that all administrators of the system must have. These are just points to be aware of, not true warnings. If people hesitated to make improvements because problems might result, I'd be writing this book on punch cards. A handy fortune cookie to remember here is "No pain, no gain."

However, although infinitely large and flexible storage is a great conceptual goal, arbitrarily making all volumes huge isn't always a no-brainer for a variety of other administrative reasons. The next few sections highlight the primary administrative, operational, and performance issues to consider when deciding whether logical volumes provide a suitable foundation for different types of filesystems.

Administrative Considerations

Aside from the straightforward administrative overhead of introducing another level of system administration, logical volume management introduces some interesting administrative issues.

Most sophisticated distributed filesystems (such as OpenAFS and Coda) use a volume management system, relying on the capabilities of any LVM system provided by the host operating system whenever possible. LVM is therefore a "fact of administration" in AFS and Coda environments.

In large-scale distributed computing environments, moving volumes from one file server to another is a relatively common administrative task. Distributed filesystems provide opportunities for load-balancing across file servers by monitoring volume access. By identifying heavily used volumes, administrators often can smooth out "hot spots" (heavily used volumes and file servers) by either moving heavily used volumes to higher performance file servers, distributing heavily used volumes across multiple file servers, or both. This procedure often is automated.

A potential side effect of using volume management to create large volumes is that this can make it impossible to move certain volumes to other file servers because they are simply too large to move while other volumes exist on the target file server. This obviously doesn't preclude the use of large logical volumes, but often makes it necessary to logically divide your file servers into administrative "clusters" in which each file server in the cluster has sufficient disk space to be a candidate for being the target of a logical move.

Doing backups of live logical volumes is a problem regardless of the type of filesystem they support because the volumes are constantly changing. To simplify making backups while a logical volume is being used, Linux LVM and distributed filesystems both provide the idea of "copy on write" volume copies. In LVM, these are known as *snapshots*, whereas these are usually referred to as *backup volumes* or *clones* in distributed filesystem speak. Functionally, these provide a read-only copy of a logical volume at the time of the snapshot or clone operation.

To minimize the amount of space required for these read-only copies, the copies are not complete copies of their parent logical volumes, but are instead copies only of the tables of currently allocated extents throughout the volume. As these extents change in the actual logical volume, the old data is copied to the snapshot or clone. For this reason, the amount of space on a file server or logical volume group required for a snapshot or clone is only the amount of data that you believe will change in the parent volume while the snapshot or clone is in use. You can allocate a much smaller amount of space for a snapshot, clone, or backup volume than would be required for a complete copy of the parent volume.

When making a snapshot, clone, or backup volume, it is best to flush all pending writes to its parent before creating the copy. This is almost impossible with journaling filesystems, but any inconsistencies in the copy usually can be repaired by replaying its log after the copy has completed.

9

LOGICAL VOLUME
MANAGEMENT

Maintaining synchronized copies of logical volumes, whether mirrored through RAID or replicated using the facilities provided by distributed filesystems, can be both computationally and financially expensive. RAID-1 mirroring of large logical volumes is expensive. Environments that use RAID to mirror large logical volumes therefore usually do so by a combination of LVM and RAID-5. Using RAID-5 reduces the media costs involved in mirroring, whereas logical volume management makes it easy to use large volumes in the first place.

Operational Considerations

Many old-time Unix sites limited volume size to simplify backups. Larger volumes took more tapes (reels, cartridges, and so on) and also took more time to be backed up. Large volumes were therefore verboten to minimize the amount of operator intervention required and also to minimize the amount of time that a system was down if it were necessary to do backups without users on the system. However, these issues aren't as relevant as they once were. Today's backup devices are faster and have exponentially more capacity than they used to.

Because Linux supports all the standard generic devices protocols (SCSI, FDDI, and so son) out of the box, using modern, high-capacity backup devices almost always is possible. If Linux support for your favorite backup device isn't available, the easiest way to help guarantee that it will be is to flame the manufacturer. Letters of the form "I would have spent a gazillion dollars on your hardware, but it didn't support Linux" are to sales organizations what sticks are to ant's nests—they usually cause a lot of activity. Another approach is to give an instance of that backup device to your local Linux User's Group or the best Linux hacker you know. You'll have any necessary drivers before you know it.

Performance Considerations

The primary goal of journaling filesystems is to improve system restart times by eliminating the need to do extensive filesystem consistency checking. Seen from this perspective, logical volumes are a natural choice for supporting journaling filesystems. Traditionally, using the fsck command to verify the consistency of a huge filesystem would take a proportionately huge amount of time. Because you rarely have to verify the consistency of journaling filesystems using a fsck-like administrative tool, it follows that journaling filesystems enable you to use larger filesystems, which naturally feeds into LVM because it enables you to use larger filesystems without the limitations imposed by the size of physical devices.

Many Unix system administrators have an ingrained resistance to using large volumes for reasons that are essentially not an issue any more. For example, standard Unix filesystems historically have had performance problems when using large directories because of the lookup time involved when searching chains of indirect blocks. It also understandably takes longer to seek for data through a huge volume than a smaller one.

These sorts of issues are the reasons why you often run across Unix shops where, for example, user directories are stored on volumes based on the first letter of the user login (one volume gets all users whose logins begin with the letters 'A' through 'G', another gets all users whose logins begin with the letters 'H' through 'R', and so on). This sort of rule is certainly an administrative pain. First, you have to make sure that you create a user's home directory on the right volume and create the appropriate symlink from /usr/foo or /home/foo to the right volume. Second, you also have to do some calculations to figure out which set of backup tapes to grab when someone accidentally deletes his resume or some project data that shouldn't have been in his home directory in the first place.

Today's journaling and distributed filesystems use much more sophisticated algorithms and internal data structures to store and retrieve files and directories, substantially improving lookup and file and directory access time. Today's disk drives are faster, often exponentially, than the drives that were in use when these types of procedures were implemented. Most of the performance limitations that fostered these sorts of procedures aren't real issues anymore.

Adding Logical Volume Management Support to Your System

This section explains how to activate LVM support in your kernel, and how to compile the version of the Linux LVM tools provided on the CD that accompanies this book. You must be root to execute any of the commands described in this section. For more information about any of the commands used in this section, including a list of error codes that you may receive if problems are encountered, see the online manual page for the appropriate command.

Building a Kernel with LVM Support

The 2.4 family of Linux kernels provides built-in support for LVM. Unfortunately, although this support is built-in, it often isn't compiled into the kernel that distributions such as Red Hat install by default.

This book isn't designed to provide a complete description of every kernel compilation option. For that sort of information, see a book such as *Red Hat Linux Unleashed*. This section provides the basic information necessary to install and compile a kernel with integrated support for the Linux LVM system. The examples in this book were compiled and tested using the Linux 2.4.9 kernel included in the kernels subdirectory of the CD that accompanies this book.

For information about installing the kernel source from the CD included with this book, building in support for the devices currently located on your system, assigning the kernel a unique name so that you don't simply overwrite your current kernel, and general kernel compilation tips, see Appendix A, "Using the CD-ROM: Installing, Updating, and Compiling Kernels."

This section explains only how to activate the Linux LVM system from the X Window System version of the kernel configurator to recompile the kernel.

To add support for LVM to the current kernel source code configuration, follow these steps:

1. Make sure that the X Window System is running and use the su command to become the root user in an xterm or other terminal window.

2. Change your working directory to the directory /usr/src/linux-2.4.9.

3. Type the command **make xconfig** and press Enter. The Tcl kernel configurator displays, as shown in Figure 9.1.

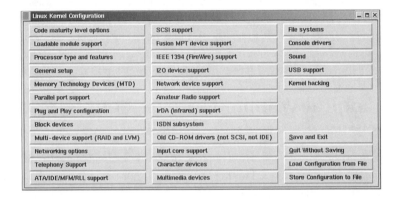

FIGURE 9.1

The Tcl Kernel Configuration dialog.

4. Click the Multi-Device Support (RAID and LVM) button. The Multi-Device Support dialog displays, as shown in Figure 9.2.

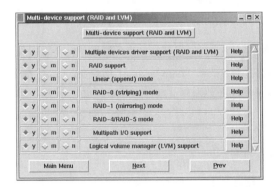

FIGURE 9.2

The Multi-Device Support Configuration dialog.

5. Click Y beside the Multiple Devices Driver Support (RAID and LVM) entry to activate the multiple device drivers.

6. Click Y beside the Logical Volume Manager (LVM) Support entry.

7. Click Main Menu to close this dialog and return to the main kernel configuration screen.

8. Click Save and Exit to save your changes and close the kernel configurator.

9. A dialog displays, confirming that your changes have been saved and reminding you that you must next execute the `make dep` command to ensure that all the dependencies used by the `make` program when compiling the kernel are set correctly. Click OK to close this dialog.

10. In the window where you executed the `make xconfig` command, type the command **make dep** and press Enter.

11. In this same window, type the command **make** and press Enter to build the new kernel.

12. After the compilation completes, type the command **make install** to install the new kernel.

13. Type the command **/sbin/lilo** and press Enter to guarantee that the boot loader knows about your new kernel. Double-check the `/etc/lilo.conf` file to make sure that the kernel you just built is the default kernel used when your system boots.

14. Reboot your machine after saving the data in all other applications. My favorite shutdown command is `shutdown -r now`.

When your system reboots, select the kernel that you want to run from the Lilo boot screen and press Enter. If you followed the conventions suggested in Appendix A, this will be a kernel with a name like "linux-LFSU" or perhaps "linux-lvm," depending on the extension you defined in the kernel's Makefile.

Compiling and Installing the LVM Tools

To install version 1.0 of the `Logical Volume Management tools` package, included on the CD that accompanies this book, do the following:

1. Mount the CD and extract the `LVM 1.0` package from the file `lvm/lvm_1_0.tar.gz` to a directory on your system using a command like the following:

```
cd <target-directory>
tar zxvf <path-to-CD>/lvm_1_0.tar.gz
```

2. Change directory to `<target-directory>`/LVM/1.0 and run the configure script to correctly configure the `LVM` Makefile for your system and Linux distribution:

```
./configure
```

This produces verbose output that's not useful to replicate here.

3. After the Makefile is correctly configured, execute the `make` command to build the new versions of the utilities in the LVM package:

```
make
```

Once again, this produces verbose, system-specific output that's not useful to replicate here.

4. After all the utilities are compiled, install them on your system using the following command:

```
make install
```

Your system now has version 1.0 of the LVM utilities and associated reference (man page) documentation installed.

Using and Administering the Logical Volume Management System

This section discusses the most common administrative operations that system administrators using LVM have to perform. You must be root to execute any of the commands described in this section. For more information about any of the commands used in this section, including a list of error codes that you may receive if problems are encountered, see the online manual page for the appropriate command.

> **NOTE**
>
> For a more complete discussion of administrative issues in LVM, see the LVM HOWTO at http://www.sistina.com/lvm_howtos/lvm_howto/.

Creating a Physical Volume

This section explains how to create a physical volume, which prepares a partition for use with logical volume management by creating the volume group descriptor areas on the partition. A physical volume must exist on any partition before a volume group can be created that uses that space or the partition can be added to an existing volume group.

9

LOGICAL VOLUME
MANAGEMENT

> **NOTE**
>
> If you are adding a new disk to your system and want to allocate all of it for logical volume management, you must use the `fdisk` command to create a single partition that spans the entire disk before you can proceed. To create a physical volume on a partition, you must also use the `fdisk` command to set the type of that partition to 8e (hexadecimal) in the disk label.

If the physical volume you are creating is the first one ever created on your system, you must first create the file `/etc/lvmtab` and the `/etc/lvmtab.d` directories used by logical volume management on Linux. You can create these by executing the `vgscan` command with no arguments, as in the following example:

```
# vgscan
vgscan -- reading all physical volumes (this may take a while...)
vgscan -- no volume groups found
vgscan -- "/etc/lvmtab" and "/etc/lvmtab.d" successfully created
```

If the `vgscan` command found volume groups on your system, its output would look something like the following example where the volume group vg1 already exists:

```
#  vgscan
vgscan -- reading all physical volumes (this may take a while...)
vgscan -- found active volume group "vg1"
vgscan -- "/etc/lvmtab" and "/etc/lvmtab.d" successfully created
vgscan -- WARNING: you may not have an actual VGDA backup of your volume group
```

To create a physical volume, execute the `pvcreate` command, supplying the name of one or more partitions on which you want to create a physical volume as an argument. If there were no errors, you will see very little output, as in the following example:

```
# pvcreate /dev/hdb5
pvcreate -- physical volume "/dev/hdb5" successfully created
```

If you're interested in seeing the steps that are actually involved in creating a physical volume, you can execute the `pvcreate` command with the `-v` (verbose) option, as in the following example:

```
# pvcreate -v /dev/hdb5
pvcreate -- locking logical volume manager
pvcreate -- checking physical volume name "/dev/hdb5"
pvcreate -- getting physical volume size
```

```
pvcreate -- checking partition type
pvcreate -- creating new physical volume
pvcreate -- setting up physical volume for /dev/hdb5 with 24113502 sectors
pvcreate -- writing physical volume data to disk "/dev/hdb5"
pvcreate -- physical volume "/dev/hdb5" successfully created
pvcreate -- unlocking logical volume manager
```

Creating a Volume Group

After you have created some number of physical volumes, you must assign them to a volume group to create logical volumes in the space that they provide. Creating a volume group is done using the vgcreate command. The basic allocation unit of any volume subsequently created in that volume group, the physical extent size, is set when you create the volume group, so you might want to consider the basic allocation unit that you want to have in any logical volumes that you create. The default physical extent size for a volume group is 4 MB, but you can set this to any value between 8 KB and 512 MB. The 2.4.2 Linux kernel limits a logical volume to containing 65536 physical extents. A smaller physical extent size therefore enables finer control over data allocation in any logical volume created in your volume group but limits the maximum size of a logical volume in that volume group.

To create a volume group, use the vgcreate command to create a volume group from the storage on physical volumes that you have already created. You must specify the name of the volume group that you want to create as the first argument to the vgcreate command, followed by the names of the physical volumes that you want to use for the volume group.

For example, using the vgcreate command to create the volume group vg1 from the storage available on the physical volumes on the partitions /dev/hda6 and /dev/hdb5 would produce output like the following:

```
# vgcreate vg1 /dev/hda6 /dev/hdb5
vgcreate -- INFO: using default physical extent size 4 MB
vgcreate -- INFO: maximum logical volume size is 255.99 Gigabyte
vgcreate -- doing automatic backup of volume group "vg1"
vgcreate -- volume group "vg1" successfully created and activated
```

After this command has completed successfully, the basic structure of the volume group will have been created in the /dev directory, as shown by the following output from the ls command:

```
# ls -al /dev/vg1
total 116
dr-xr-xr-x   2 root     root        4096 Jul 29 19:31 .
drwxr-xr-x  16 root     root      110592 Jul 29 19:31 ..
crw-r-----   1 root     disk    109,   0 Jul 29 19:31 group
```

To get a better idea of exactly what the vgcreate command is doing, you could execute the vgcreate command with the -v option, which would provide verbose documentation for every step of the creation process but could add a pound or two to this book if an example were shown here.

To create the same volume group with a different physical extent size, you would use the -s option to set the physical extent size. The following example shows creating the same volume group as in the previous example but with a physical extent size of 8 KB:

```
# vgcreate -s 8K vg1 /dev/hda6 /dev/hdb5
vgcreate -- INFO: maximum logical volume size is 511.98 Megabyte
vgcreate -- doing automatic backup of volume group "vg1"
vgcreate -- volume group "vg1" successfully created and activated
```

Because the maximum number of physical extents that can be associated with a logical volume is 65536 in the Linux 2.4.2 kernel, this command warns you that the maximum size of a logical volume that you create in this volume group is 511.98 MB.

Getting Information About a Physical Volume

After you have assigned a physical volume to a volume group, you can use the pvdisplay command to display information about any of the physical volumes in any volume group, as in the following example:

```
# pvdisplay /dev/hda6
--- Physical volume ---
PV Name                 /dev/hda6
VG Name                 vg1
PV Size                 9.77 GB / NOT usable 5.01 MB [LVM: 5 MB]
PV#                     1
PV Status               available
Allocatable             yes
Cur LV                  0
PE Size (KByte)         8
Total PE                1279535
Free PE                 1279535
Allocated PE            0
PV UUID                 LJhu0M-ZAyt-e0nR-cE5u-riRs-Tj16-R6GJpB
```

The pvdisplay command can be useful for verifying the status of a physical volume. Table 9.1 lists the fields in its output and the information they provide.

TABLE 9.1   pvdisplay Fields and their definitions

pvdisplay Field	Meaning
PV Name	The name of the device on which the physical volume is located.
VG Name	The name of the volume group to which the physical volume is allocated.
PV Size	The size of the physical volume and any space that cannot be allocated because it is used internally by the physical volume.
PV#	The physical volume number used internally by the LVM system.
PV Status	The status of the physical volume.
Allocatable	Whether space can be allocated on the physical volume.
Cur LV	The number of logical volumes currently using space on the physical volume.
PE Size (KByte)	The physical extent size, in kilobytes.
Total PE	The total number of physical extents available on the physical volume.
Free PE	The number of physical extents that are free on the physical volume.
Allocated PE	The number of physical extents that have already been allocated on the physical volume.
PV UUID	A Universal Unique IDentifier generated for the physical volume when it was created. This provides a permanent identifier that can always be used to uniquely identify a specific physical volume.

Prior to associating a physical volume with a volume group, the output of the pvdisplay command would look like the following:

```
# pvdisplay /dev/hda6
pvdisplay -- "/dev/hda6" is a new physical volume of 9.77 GB
```

Adding New Storage to a Volume Group

Adding another physical volume to a volume group is done using the vgextend command. To add an unallocated physical volume to an existing volume group, use the vgextend command to add the physical volume, specifying the name of the volume group to which you want to add the new storage, followed by the name(s) of the physical volume(s) you want to add to that volume group, as in the following example:

```
# vgextend vg1 /dev/hdb6
vgextend -- INFO: maximum logical volume size is 511.98 Megabyte
vgextend -- doing automatic backup of volume group "vg1"
vgextend -- volume group "vg1" successfully extended
```

Adding a physical volume to an existing volume group creates physical extents on the new volume of the same size as those associated with the volume group. You can verify this using the `pvdisplay` command.

Getting Information About a Volume Group

After you have created a volume group, you can use the `vgdisplay` command to display information about it, as in the following example:

```
# vgdisplay vg1
--- Volume group ---
VG Name               vg1
VG Access             read/write
VG Status             available/resizable
VG #                  0
MAX LV                256
Cur LV                0
Open LV               0
MAX LV Size           255.99 GB
Max PV                256
Cur PV                2
Act PV                2
VG Size               21.26 GB
PE Size               4 MB
Total PE              5443
Alloc PE / Size       0 / 0
Free  PE / Size       5443 / 21.26 GB
VG UUID               0L47wU-vmh7-uLpk-9ebP-zxuv-50lq-86PFs8
```

The output of this command is similar to that of the `pvdisplay` command. The `vgdisplay` command most often is used to determine the amount of unallocated space still available on a volume group (Free PE/ Size) or the maximum size of a logical volume that you can create (VG Size) on a specific volume group.

Creating a Logical Volume

Creating a logical volume is done using the `lvcreate` command. After you have created a logical volume, you can create a filesystem on it using the appropriate application for the types of filesystem that you are creating (mke2fs, mkreiserfs, and so on).

To create a logical volume within an existing volume group, use the `lvcreate` command to create a logical volume in an existing volume group. You must provide the following arguments to the `lvcreate` command:

- The size of the volume that you want to create. You can specify this in one of two ways. Because there is a one-to-one mapping between physical and logical extents, you can use the -l option to specify the number of logical extents that you want to allocate to the new logical volume. This requires a bit of math. An easier alternative is to use the -L option to specify the total size of the logical volume that you want to create. Acceptable units for the -L option are terabytes (T), gigabytes (G), megabytes (M), or kilobytes (K, if you really want to type a lot of numbers).

- The name that you want to assign to the logical volume you are creating. The logical volume name is specified by using the -n option.

- The name of the volume group in which you want to create the specified logical volume.

The following is an example of using the lvcreate command to create a 5 gigabyte volume named volume1 in the volume group vg1:

```
# lvcreate -L 5G -n volume1 vg1
lvcreate -- doing automatic backup of "vg1"
lvcreate -- logical volume "/dev/vg1/volume1" successfully created
```

You then could use the lvdisplay command to verify that the logical volume you created has the correct size and other attributes, as in the following example:

```
# lvdisplay /dev/vg1/volume1
--- Logical volume ---
LV Name                /dev/vg1/volume1
VG Name                vg1
LV Write Access        read/write
LV Status              available
LV #                   1
# open                 0
LV Size                5 GB
Current LE             1280
Allocated LE           1280
Allocation             next free
Read ahead sectors     120
Block device           58:0
```

If the underlying storage for a volume group is located on different physical devices, you can potentially improve the performance of the logical volumes that you create by creating them so that they are striped across different physical devices. This provides the opportunity for disk writes to take place to multiple devices in parallel rather than serially to a single device. To do this, use the lvcreate command's --stripes option, which takes an integer argument that is the number of physical devices across which the logical volume should be striped. The --stripes option can be abbreviated to -i to provide job security for Linux sysadmins and writers such as myself.

For example, the following output shows creating the same logical volume as in the previous example, but striped evenly across the physical devices that make up the volume group:

```
# lvcreate -L 5G -n volume1 -i 2 vg1
lvcreate -- INFO: using default stripe size 16 KB
lvcreate -- doing automatic backup of "vg1"
lvcreate -- logical volume "/dev/vg1/volume1" successfully created
```

> **TIP**
>
> When using striping, the volume size divided by the number of drives can't be larger than the smallest partition in the set because each disk in the system must be able to hold the appropriate fraction of the volume.

Using the lvdisplay command would show that the logical volume now consisted of two stripes, as in the following example:

```
# lvdisplay /dev/vg1/volume1
--- Logical volume ---
LV Name                 /dev/vg1/volume1
VG Name                 vg1
LV Write Access         read/write
LV Status               available
LV #                    1
# open                  0
LV Size                 5 GB
Current LE              1280
Allocated LE            1280
Stripes                 2
Stripe size (KByte)     16
Allocation              next free
Read ahead sectors      120
Block device            58:0
```

Increasing the Size of a Logical Volume

Use the lvextend command to increase the size of your logical volume, supplying the following arguments:

- The -l or -L options to specify the new size in units of logical extents or the standard terabytes (T), gigabytes (G), megabytes (M), or kilobytes (K). You can express the new size of the logical volume in absolute terms such as "-l 1536" or "-L 6G," or you can specify the amount by which you want to increase the size of the volume in either of those units by prefacing the numeric value with a plus (+) sign.

- The name of the logical volume that you want to enlarge.

The following is an example of using the lvextend command to enlarge the size of the 5-gigabyte logical volume /dev/vg1/volume1 to 6 gigabytes:

```
# lvextend -L 6G /dev/vg1/volume1
lvextend -- extending logical volume "/dev/vg1/volume1" to 6 GB
lvextend -- doing automatic backup of volume group "vg1"
lvextend -- logical volume "/dev/vg1/volume1" successfully extended
```

The following command would be equivalent:

```
# lvextend -L +1G /dev/vg1/volume1
```

Increasing the size of a logical volume follows its current layout. For example, if you had striped a logical volume across two physical devices, each of the stripes would be increased in size appropriately.

Reducing the Size of a Logical Volume

The lvreduce command lets you decrease the size of an existing logical volume. Its syntax is essentially identical to that of the lvextend command. However, when you reduce the size of a logical volume, you run the risk of losing data if it is stored in the portion of the logical volume that has been removed. Before using the lvreduce command on any partition that contains data, you should always first back up the entire volume.

To decrease the size of an existing logical volume, use the lvreduce command, supplying the following arguments:

- The -l or -L options to specify the new size in units of logical extents or the standard terabytes (T), gigabytes (G), megabytes (M), or kilobytes (K). You can express the new size of the logical volume in absolute terms such as "-l 1280" or "-L 5G", or you can specify the amount by which you want to decrease the size of the volume in either of those units by prefacing the numeric value with a minus (-) sign.
- The name of the logical volume that you want to reduce in size.

The following is an example of using the lvreduce command to decrease the size of the 6-gigabyte logical volume /dev/vg1/volume1 to 5 gigabytes:

```
# lvreduce -L 5G /dev/vg1/volume1
lvreduce -- WARNING: reducing active logical volume to 5 GB
lvreduce -- THIS MAY DESTROY YOUR DATA (filesystem etc.)
lvreduce -- do you really want to reduce "/dev/vg1/volume1"? [y/n]: y
lvreduce -- doing automatic backup of volume group "vg1"
lvreduce -- logical volume "/dev/vg1/volume1" successfully reduced
```

The following command would be equivalent:

```
# lvreduce -L -1G /dev/vg1/volume1
```

Removing Logical Volumes, Volume Groups, and Physical Volumes

If you are experimenting with creating logical volumes and volume groups, you can quickly remove these by using the lvremove and vgremove commands. These take the name of a logical volume and volume group as arguments, and remove those entities. The space allocated to any logical volumes that you create is automatically returned to the pool of available space in the volume group where the logical volume was located.

To remove a volume group, you must first remove any logical volumes that you have created in that volume group.

To return a physical volume for use in another volume group or for formatting as a standard filesystem partition, you must first use the vgreduce command to remove it from any volume groups with which it is associated.

Summary of LVM Commands

The previous section listed the most common LVM operations that I've found myself doing in the time that logical volume management in Linux has been robust. Not surprisingly, many more commands are available for modifying different aspects of physical volumes, volume groups, and logical volumes, and for collecting information about the LVM system itself. I'm not so desperate to increase the size of this book that I would include all the online manual pages for all the commands related to the Linux logical volume management suite. After all, you have a Linux box, and "man foo" isn't all that hard to type. On the other hand, I've always found it useful to keep a summary of the logical volume management commands, just so I know what to type instead of "foo" in the previous example. For your convenience, this section lists the available commands and provides short summaries of what they do.

NOTE

The types of commands available for logical volumes and volumes groups are fairly consistent. This makes it easier to either remember or guess the name of a particular command.

9

LOGICAL VOLUME
MANAGEMENT

TABLE 9.2   Physical Volume Commands

pvchange	Changes the attributes of a physical volume
pvcreate	Creates a physical volume
pvdata	Displays debugging information about a physical volume

TABLE 9.2   Continued

pvdisplay	Displays information about a physical volume
pvmove	Moves physical extents from one physical volume to another
pvscan	Locates and lists all physical volumes

TABLE 9.3   Logical Volume Group Commands

vgcfgbackup	Backs up the volume group descriptor area
vgcfgrestore	Restores the volume group descriptor area to disk
vgchange	Changes the attributes of a volume group
vgck	Checks the volume group descriptor area for consistency
vgcreate	Creates a volume group from physical volume(s)
vgdisplay	Displays the attributes of a volume group
vgexport	Makes volume group(s) unknown to the system
vgextend	Adds physical volume(s) to a volume group
vgimport	Makes volume group(s) known to the system
vgmerge	Merges two volume groups
vgmknodes	Creates volume group directory and special files
vgreduce	Removes physical volume(s) from a volume group
vgremove	Removes a volume group
vgrename	Renames a volume group
vgscan	Locates and lists all volume groups
vgsplit	Splits a volume group

TABLE 9.4   Logical Volume Commands

lvchange	Changes attributes of a logical volume
lvcreate	Creates a logical volume
lvdisplay	Displays the attributes of a logical volume
lvextend	Increases the size of a logical volume
lvreduce	Reduces the size of a logical volume
lvremove	Removes a logical volume
lvrename	Renames a logical volume
lvscan	Locates and lists all logical volumes, creating /etc/lvmtab and /etc/lvmtab.d/*

TABLE 9.5 Logical Volume Management System Commands

`lvmchange`	Changes attributes of the LVM system
`lvmdiskscan`	Locates and lists all available disks, multiple devices, and partitions
`lvmsadc`	Collects information about LVM activity
`lvmsar`	Reports information about LVM activity

RAID and LVM

RAID (Redundant Array of Inexpensive Disks) is a hardware and software mechanism used to improve the performance and maintainability of large amounts of disk storage through some clever mechanisms. As the name suggests, RAID makes many smaller disks (referred to as a RAID array) appear to be one or more large disks as far as the operating system is concerned. RAID implements this by providing a volume management interface, which is initially what makes discussing RAID relevant to a discussion of logical volume management. The support for RAID under Linux is known as the *multiple device (md) interface*.

In theory, any type of filesystem can be created on a RAID volume, although it's easy to see that increasing the number of levels of abstraction that separate data from the physical media that it is stored on also increases the number of points at which bugs or misfeatures can surface. If you use RAID on top of logical volume management as the underpinnings of cutting-edge filesystems, such as some of those discussed in this book, you absolutely must perform long-running, extensive, rigorous performance tests before using them in a production environment. For most system administrators, this should be a "Warning: hot coffee may be hot!" type warning. The fact that additional complexity adds potential problems shouldn't be a big surprise to anyone. Luckily, the reliability and performance improvements that can be provided by RAID make it well worth considering.

Combining an array of cheaper disks into one or more larger volumes would be interesting and useful in itself, but would only compete with standard volume management support if that was all that RAID offered the system administrator. Luckily, in addition to this sort of support, most hardware implementations of RAID use mirroring and were therefore designed to enable you to remove and replace any of the drives that make up the RAID array without shutting down your system or your users noticing any problems. Striping simply increases performance rather than provides redundancy. To support the removal and replacement of drives without anyone (but you) noticing, mirroring is the capability to support multiple volumes that are exact, realtime copies of each other. If the drive containing a mirrored volume fails or is taken offline for any other reasons, the RAID system automatically begins using that volume's mirror, and no one notices its absence except for sysadmins who hurriedly start scrounging for a replacement.

As protection against single-device failures, most RAID levels support the use of spare disks in addition to mirroring. Mirroring protects you when a single device in a RAID array fails, but at this point, you are immediately vulnerable to the failure of any other device that holds data for which no mirror is currently available. RAID's use of spare disks is designed to immediately reduce this vulnerability. In the event of a device failure, the RAID subsystem immediately allocates one of the spare disks and begins creating a new mirror there for you. When using spare disks in conjunction with mirroring, you really only have a nonmirrored disk the amount of time it takes to clone the mirror to the spare disk. As explained in the next section, the automatic use of spare disks is supported only for specific RAID levels. Also, becauee of the complexity involved, RAID cards that automatically allocate spare hardware are much more expensive than cards that only support RAID levels 0 and 1.

WARNING

RAID is not a replacement for doing backups. RAID ensures that your systems can continue functioning and that users and applications can have uninterrupted access to mirrored data. However, the simultaneous failure of multiple devices in a RAID array can still take your system down and make the data that was stored on them unavailable. Only systems doing backups can be guaranteed to come back up.

RAID arrays can be implemented in both hardware and software, but hardware level 5 RAID solutions are generally expensive. This discussion of RAID therefore focuses on software RAID as implemented in Linux and is also applicable to hardware RAID level 0 and 1 cards or on-the-motherboard hardware.

NOTE

For more detailed and complete information about software RAID support in Linux, see the Software RAID HOWTO, which can be found online at http://unthought.net/Software-RAID.HOWTO/Software-RAID.HOWTO.html. This HOWTO describes the version of software RAID that is provided in Linux 2.4 and greater kernels, and is a useful source of general and specific information about using software RAID under Linux.

Introduction to RAID Levels

The different capabilities provided by hardware and software RAID are grouped into different RAID levels, with the following capabilities per level:

- RAID-0—Often called *stripe mode*; volumes are created in parallel across all the devices that are part of the RAID array, allocating storage from each to provide as many opportunities for parallel reads and writes as possible. This RAID level does not support mirroring and therefore provides no redundancy in the event of a hardware failure. Adding RAID-0 devices to your standard backup schedule is critical (you do have a standard backup schedule, don't you?) because the fact that volumes are striped across different physical devices means that the failure of any device in a RAID-0 volume will leave you with an unrecoverable volume with more holes than baby Swiss cheese.

  To maximize performance, the devices on which you create a RAID-0 volume should be identical (best), of the same size (good), or approximately the same size (acceptable, but with some wasted space) to ensure that the stripes can be evenly distributed across the two volumes. If the devices differ significantly in size, you will lose the parallel write performance benefits provided by RAID-0 when writing to the volume when it is almost full.

- RAID-1—Usually known as "mirroring"; volumes are created on single devices and exact copies (mirrors) of those volumes are maintained to provide protection from the failure of a single disk through redundancy. For this reason, you cannot create a RAID-1 volume that is larger than the smallest device that makes up a part of the RAID array. RAID-1 is the lowest level that can use spare disks in the RAID array.

  Using RAID-1 volumes actually has a slight negative effect on day-to-day performance because the RAID system must always write to both the primary and mirror volumes. However, the protection that RAID-1 provides in the event of the failure of a single disk makes it well worth considering.

- RAID-4—A fairly uncommon RAID level that requires three or more devices in the RAID array. One of the drives is used to store parity information that can be used to reconstruct any data on a failed drive. Unfortunately, storing this parity information on a single drive exposes this drive as a potential single point of failure.

  RAID-4 provides performance improvements over RAID-1 because the parity information can be used to re-create any data located on a failed drive (except for the parity drive itself). This therefore provides the redundancy associated with RAID-1 without the need to maintain distinct mirrors and therefore write each bit of data twice. However, this makes the performance of the parity drive critical—it should always be the fastest disk available to you. The overall performance of a RAID-4 system never can be any better than the performance of the parity drive because it must be updated at the same time that a write to any of the other disks is done.

- RAID-5—The most popular RAID level, RAID-5 requires three or more devices in the RAID array and enables you to support mirroring through parity information without

9

LOGICAL VOLUME
MANAGEMENT

restricting the parity information to a single device. Parity information is distributed across all the devices in the RAID array, removing the bottleneck and potential single point of failure in RAID-4.

In addition to these RAID levels, the software RAID support provided in Linux also supports *linear mode*, which is the capability to concatenate two devices and treat them as a single large device. (This capability explains that pesky question on the kernel configuration screen that you always see when installing Red Hat.) Linear mode is convenient but provides no redundancy and is functionally identical to the same capabilities provided by logical volume management in Linux. The physical location of the files that users are accessing on a linear device potentially can provide the same sort of performance improvements that you get from LVM by enabling parallel reads when the files are located on different physical devices. Because linear mode simply concatenates devices in the RAID array, you may not be a total mess if one of the devices in a linear volume fails and you do not have up-to-date backups (like that would ever happen!). The linear volume will be missing the portion of the filesystem located on the defunct device.

Building a Kernel with Software RAID Support

The 2.4 family of Linux kernels provides built-in support for software RAID. Unfortunately, although this support is built-in, it may only be provided as a loadable module for the kernel that distributions such as Red Hat install by default.

The procedure for activating RAID support in a Linux kernel is exactly the same as that described in the section "Building a Kernel with LVM Support," earlier in this chapter except that in step 6, you should click Y beside the RAID Support entry, as well as beside any of the RAID levels that you want to use or experiment with. To use RAID in the context of this book, make sure that the Logical Volume Manager (LVM) Support option is still set to Y.

After you have activated RAID support, follow the remainder of the instructions in the "Building a Kernel with LVM Support" section earlier in this chapter to compile and install the kernel.

Creating RAID Devices

RAID devices are created by first using a command such as `fdisk` to change the type of those partitions to `fd`, then defining them in the file `/etc/raidtab`, and finally by using the `mkraid` command to actually create one or more RAID devices according the specified RAID configuration.

For example, the following `/etc/raidtab` file defines a linear RAID array composed of the physical devices `/dev/hda6` and `/dev/hdb5`:

```
raiddev /dev/md0
        raid-level              linear
        nr-raid-disks           2
        chunk-size              32k
        persistent-superblock   1
        device                  /dev/hda6
        raid-disk               0
        device                  /dev/hdb5
        raid-disk               1
```

Executing the `mkraid` command to create the device `/dev/md0` would produce output like the following:

```
# mkraid /dev/md0
handling MD device /dev/md0
analyzing super-block
disk 0: /dev/hda6, 10241406kB, raid superblock at 10241280kB
disk 1: /dev/hdb5, 12056751kB, raid superblock at 12056640kB
```

> **WARNING**
>
> The `mkraid` command is particular about its syntax, to err on the side of caution by not attempting to interpret what you mean and accidentally overwriting the wrong partition. If you get an error message when using the `mkraid` command, scrutinize the syntax of the command that you issued.

At this point, you can create your favorite type of filesystem on the device `/dev/md0` by using the `mkfs` command and specifying the type of filesystem by using the `-t type` option. You then can use Linuxconf, use some other system administration utility, or directly modify the `/etc/fstab` file to mount the new logical volume wherever you want, and you're in business.

A linear RAID array is RAID at its most primitive. The `/etc/raidtab` configuration file for a RAID-1 (mirroring) RAID array would look something like the following:

```
raiddev /dev/md0
        raid-level             1
        nr-raid-disks          2
        nr-spare-disks         0
        chunk-size             4k
        persistent-superblock 1
        device                 /dev/hda6
        raid-disk              0
        device                 /dev/hdb5
        raid-disk              1
```

9

LOGICAL VOLUME
MANAGEMENT

Other RAID levels are created by using the same configuration file but specifying other mandatory parameters, such as a third disk for RAID levels 4 and 5, and so on.

Combining RAID and LVM

Aside from its inherent coolness, the true reason why I'm discussing RAID in the chapter is the fact that RAID can be combined with Linux's logical volume management capabilities to provide some useful features. As explained earlier in this section, there are often good performance reasons why the devices that make up a RAID array should be the same size. If you are careful and understand the interactions between RAID and LVM, you can use Linux LVM support to create volumes of the same size on different physical devices and then use Linux RAID support to increase the reliability of this configuration through mirroring.

You must absolutely think through this sort of implementation before doing it. For example, using RAID-0 on top of LVM buys you nothing except the potential to hurt performance because striping across logical volumes that may be themselves located on different devices is an exercise for someone who is primarily interested in the mean time between failure for your disk drives. You gain nothing. Implementing RAID-1 on top of Linux LVM support can free you from limitations imposed by the size of your disk drives, but redundancy is useless if you accidentally have implemented your volumes so that portions of both the primary and mirror volumes can be located on the same physical disk.

Combining RAID and LVM is conceptually elegant and can help you create a robust, flexible system environment if carefully thought through before implementation. Where relevant, the discussion of each filesystem in this book provides information about its performance on physical disks as well as on various RAID and LVM combinations. As always, these sorts of benchmarks are general and cannot anticipate the data requirements and usage patterns on your computer systems. The information on RAID and LVM in this chapter provides conceptual and hands-on guidance; figuring out whether combining RAID and LVM on your computer systems is the "right thing" to do is up to you.

Comparing Journaling
Filesystem Performance

IN THIS CHAPTER

This chapter helps tie together the discussions and observations in the journaling filesystems portion of this book by providing empirical data about the performance of various journaling filesystems in different situations. This data was collected by running the benchmarks introduced in Chapter 1, "Introduction to Filesystems," using a variety of parameters.

The first section of this chapter describes the machine that I used for testing. Each subsequent section focuses on one of the benchmarks I've chosen to compare different journaling filesystems, discussing what each was intended to show, the types of numbers that each provides, and what each test actually does to produce those numbers. Each of these sections then provides a table showing the results of running that benchmark on each of the types of journaling filesystems discussed in this book, and then compares and discusses those results.

> **NOTE**
>
> Each of the tables of benchmark data also contains results of running that benchmark with the same settings on a standard Linux ext2 filesystem. This provides a baseline that makes it easy for you to compare the performance of the advanced journaling filesystems discussed in this book with that of the standard Linux filesystem that you are used to.

Evaluating Journaling Filesystems

Up to this point, the focus of the book has been on exploring the design and theory behind different filesystems, integrating them into a kernel so that you can try them out, and learning the administrative tools and tricks of the trade associated with each different journaling filesystem implementation. How easy it is to integrate a specific filesystem into your computing environment is an important issue: Is it difficult to get it into the kernel? Does it have the types of administrative utilities that you'll need to work with it on a daily basis? Are its administrative utilities powerful, usable, or perhaps nonexistent? Can it be backed up? Although understanding and comparing the designs and theoretical capabilities of different filesystems is interesting and helps set expectations correctly regarding the situations in which different filesystems are most useful, seeing how they work is perhaps more important.

Much of the discussion of different journaling filesystems in this book has been spiced up with comments such as "interesting," "clever," and "heuristics," and for good reason. The designers of modern journaling filesystems are smart people. However, the real test of the value of a filesystem is how well it works, at various times, under different loads, in different states, and for various usage patterns. For example, does a filesystem implementation work great when a specific partition is lightly used but slow to a crawl or crash as the partition fills up? Does the filesystem favor small directories and files over large ones? Does constant modifications to many small files cause the journal to overflow or repeatedly force a filesystem sync operation to flush all pending writes to disk? These are largely filesystem data structure questions. And then there are the usability questions. Does the filesystem favor sequential access over random access? Does a filesystem work great when people are just editing text files but slow down or explode when random access database-sized files are being used?

Different computing environments are inherently different. That is not the trivial tautology that it appears to be. (Well, perhaps it is, but it is actually a useful observation.) Different sites use filesystems differently. Companies that specialize in music, graphics, and multimedia tend to favor support for huge files and high throughput. Academic institutions may favor support for huge directories and many relatively small files to support the paper-writing and programming needs of their student populations. Using a filesystem in a production environment and seeing how it performs is the only real test of how well it will work for you. But it's nice to have a little more data than source code and an administrative overview to go on before making a major commitment in terms of deploying a filesystem, learning its administrative utilities, and spending the time required to develop a feel for its performance.

This chapter provides some empirical information to help you make an appropriate choice as to which journaling filesystem may be most useful for you and the computing environment in which you work. It primarily consists of cold, dry data made up of tables that make it easy to compare the results of various filesystem performance benchmarks designed to illustrate the performance of different filesystems under different circumstances. An overview of the benchmarks used in this book were introduced in Chapter 1. To compare the performance of journaling filesystems, I used all these benchmarks except for the Connectathon tests, which are primarily oriented toward distributed filesystems and which are therefore only used and discussed in Chapter 14, "Comparing Distributed Filesystem Performance."

This is also a good point at which to mention that the capability to freely experiment with multiple journaling filesystems and see which one best meets your needs is something that would have been unheard of as recently as a few years ago. As shown in Chapter 8, "Third-Party Journaling Filesystems," there are few commercial options for journaling filesystems not explicitly associated with a specific type of hardware. You can buy an SGI box running XFS, but you can't use XFS on your Sun workstation or PC—unless it's running Linux. Linux and the open-source movement enable you to reap the fruits of others' research efforts and technology investments. As illustrated by this book, if you are running Linux, you have an actual spectrum of journaling filesystems to choose from.

The tabular data in this chapter only provides a performance comparison of each filesystem instead of trying to invent some metric that would enable you to model how using a journaling filesystem would affect your computing environment. For example, I didn't try to capture operational statistics such as system restart times because these are totally dependent on the processes and other hardware in your machines. You can get a good idea of the time savings related to using a distributed filesystem in any computing environment that you support by a simple timing exercise each time you reboot one of your systems:

1. Measure the time that your system spends in verifying the consistency of your filesystems using the `fsck` program.

2. Compare that value to zero (or one second per filesystem if you want to be magnanimous), which is the amount of time that a journaling filesystem requires each system to spend to verify the consistency of any journaling filesystems that it mounts.

As you saw in the chapters of this book that provided background material about journaling filesystems or that discussed specific journaling filesystems, journaling filesystems can quickly and easily be integrated into your existing computing environment and can provide significant operational advantages. Let's meet our guests.

The Benchmarking Environment

All the tests in this section were done on a single machine, a Linux system running the Red Hat Roswell Beta, otherwise known as Red Hat 7.193. The machine has the following hardware specs:

- Single 500MZ Celeron CPU
- 256 MB P-133 memory
- 1 GB swap space
- IDE hard drive, onboard controller:
  - hdc: WDC WD153AA, ATA DISK drive; 16 heads, 63 sectors, 29826 cylinders
  - Physical partition size: 2 GB

All the journaling filesystem benchmarks were run on the same machine without any other users to effectively run the same tests under the same system load, minus the occasional system processes. As you can see from the preceding hardware list, this isn't an especially sexy machine—using one for test purposes would have distorted the results to some extent. This machine was assembled from the sort of random, inexpensive parts that you'd find at any of the computer gypsy shows held all over the country and, presumably, in most other countries as well. The idea of selecting a generic system for benchmarking purposes was to use a system much like one that any random reader might use, not some overblown, nitrous-oxide burning funny car kind of computer system.

All these tests were run using kernels compiled exactly as described in the associated chapters of this book and patched as needed for the various filesystems:

- ext3 on the Linux 2.4.9 kernel
- JFS on the Linux 2.4.7 kernel
- ReiserFS on the Linux 2.4.9 kernel
- XFS on the Linux 2.4.9 kernel

The only modifications from the Red Hat Roswell Beta release of Red Hat 7.2 were the kernel, any auxiliary software associated with specific journaling filesystems, and any Linux package upgrades associated with specific journaling filesystems.

The source code for all the benchmarks described in this section is provided in the benchmarks directory of the CD that accompanies this book. Providing copies of the source code for these benchmarks serves as a reference if you want to test specific systems at your site, or compare the performance of updated versions of any of the software described in this book. By definition, benchmarks are a snapshot of the behavior of a specific version of certain software running under a specific version of an operating system at a specific point in time. Your mileage will definitely vary if you run these benchmarks on any system other than one that you could only find if you came to my house.

The Bonnie Benchmark

The Bonnie benchmark is a well-known benchmark for testing I/O throughput on a specific file. By using a single file for benchmarking purposes, this benchmark is well suited for examining I/O performance without the overhead of filesystem operation, such as file and directory creation, lookups, deletion, and so on. Bonnie was written by Tim Bray. More information about the Bonnie benchmark can be found at
`http://www.textuality.com/bonnie/intro.html`.

Table 10.1 shows the results of running the Bonnie benchmark on ext2, ext3, JFS, ReiserFS, and XFS filesystems. To produce the data contained in this table, the Bonnie benchmark was run on each of these filesystems with the following four basic configurations:

- 1000 seeks into a 100 MB file
- 1000 seeks into a 100 MB file with an `fsync()` after each call to flush all pending writes to disk
- 1000 seeks into a 1000 MB file
- 1000 seeks into a 1000 MB file with an `fsync()` after each call to flush all pending writes to disk

The command line used to run the Bonnie benchmark with these values was the following:

```
bonnie -s file-size -S number-of-seeks
```

TABLE 10.1 Results from the Bonnie Benchmark

| | | | Sequential Output | | | | | | Sequential Input | | | | Random Seek | |
| | | | Per Char | | Block | | ReWrite | | Per Char | | Block | | | |
Filesystem	Mode	MB	K/Sec	%CPU	K/Sec	%CPU	K/Sec	%CPU	K/Sec	%CPU	K/Sec	%CPU	K/Sec	%CPU
ext2	Std	100	2574	62.8	3193	28.0	1661	14.2	1970	36.9	11063	36.2	287.3	19.8
ext3	Std	100	1943	50.2	2670	27.4	3618	46.5	2058	39.7	11316	43.1	358.1	27.2
jfs	Std	100	1611	38.1	2030	13.3	1942	17.6	5378	93.4	46698	99.9	2439.4	97.6
reiserfs	Std	100	1978	64.7	2269	36.0	1720	17.5	2723	52.9	10063	35.2	278.3	26.2
xfs	Std	100	2788	79.8	3856	52.2	1656	36.6	1943	36.0	45169	100	2251.0	94.5
ext2	Fsync	100	1848	43.1	1942	18.8	1679	13.4	3582	70.6	10414	37.3	346.8	27.7
ext3	Fsync	100	1970	55.9	1911	23.7	1730	11.8	4133	81.3	9533	42.2	133.0	18.2
jfs	Fsync	100	1565	36.0	2028	33.6	2071	48.6	5857	99.9	20268	43.7	2440.0	97.6
reiserfs	Fsync	100	1718	56.6	1841	35.5	1650	16.6	3322	69.2	9891	39.4	468.8	38.4
xfs	Fsync	100	1542	86.3	1972	83.0	2031	59.6	5535	95.7	45328	99.6	2335.6	98.1
ext2	Std	1000	1815	49.2	2183	20.3	1691	14.7	3143	61.3	10391	35.7	99.5	11.8
ext3	Std	1000	2064	56.8	2232	26.9	1763	12.4	3066	59.4	10530	42.7	87.0	13.6
jfs	Std	1000	1559	36.7	2097	13.8	1108	35.6	1635	65.4	2277	67.6	57.7	23.8
reiserfs	Std	1000	1605	62.9	1889	39.7	1630	18.0	3251	67.6	9703	37.1	89.7	13.3
xfs	Std	1000	1537	42.8	2046	73.8	1069	56.4	1591	67.1	2272	64.7	63.8	21.4
ext2	Fsync	1000	1933	52.4	1958	19.5	1685	15.4	3568	70.5	10294	36.2	101.5	12.4
ext3	Fsync	1000	2054	58.5	1998	24.8	1840	13.2	4274	78.5	11495	43.6	100.5	14.5
jfs	Fsync	1000	1547	37.1	1990	13.6	1109	35.8	1704	68.3	2263	66.5	59.8	22.0
reiserfs	Fsync	1000	1556	62.2	1833	38.2	1622	18.3	3358	69.7	9473	37.5	89.0	14.1
xfs	Fsync	1000	1495	43.3	1923	71.0	1091	58.0	1688	72.0	2248	62.7	64.4	18.0

The first three columns identify the type of filesystem being benchmarked; the write mode (standard operation or followed by a forced `sync`); and the size of the file being written, read, or examined. Next are six pairs of columns that should be read as "at an output/input/seek rate of (first column), the process used (second column) percent of the CPU." The first three pairs of columns provide information about write tests, the fourth and fifth pairs of columns provide information about read performance, and the last pair provides information about seek performance.

The three pairs of two columns that provide statistics about write performance and the amount of CPU required when writing data gathered this data by testing the following:

- Per-character writes done using the `putc()` function. This test primarily tests the cost of writes and associated allocation because the loop itself is small and fast enough so as not to require any other system overhead.

- Block writes done using the `write()` function. This test primarily tests the allocation mechanism provided by the filesystem.

- Rewrites done by reading chunks of the file in 16384-byte buffers, modifying the data, and rewriting it using `write()`. This test primarily examines the performance of the filesystem cache and associated data transfer speed.

The two pairs of two columns that provide statistics about read performance and the amount of CPU required when reading data gathered this data by testing the following:

- Per-character reads done using the `getc()` function. This basically tests the speed of sequential input because it shouldn't require any other system overhead.

- Block-oriented reads done using the `read()` function, testing sequential input performance.

The final pair of columns provide statistics and CPU consumption information for four processes, each of which performs 400 random seeks into the file and reads a buffer full of data using `read()`. Ten percent of the time, they modify the data and write it back out to the file.

Some observations: JFS and XFS both appear to consume more CPU resources than the other filesystems. Both received some impressive write rates and impressive read rates with smaller (100 MB) files, but at the cost of almost pegging the CPU. Whatever advantages they had for 100 MB files no longer seems to apply in larger (1 GB files)—their performance is generally worse than all the other filesystems with files of this size. ReiserFS racks up generally undistinguished numbers. As you would expect, executing `fsync` after every write hurts the overall performance of journaling filesystems, more so as there are more writes.

The IOzone Benchmark

Similar in theory to the Bonnie benchmark, the IOzone benchmark is a newer benchmark that tests I/O throughput on a specific file. By using a single file for benchmarking purposes, this benchmark is well suited for examining I/O performance without the overhead of filesystem operation such as file and directory creation, lookups, deletion, and so on. As you might guess from its name, one of its nicest features is that it explicitly provides tests for many different types of read and write operations including file descriptor I/O, file I/O, and file descriptor from offset. It can test asynchronous or synchronous I/O, which is handy for journaling filesystem testing.

Table 10.2 shows the results of running the IOzone benchmark with the following general configuration:

- A 100 MB file, processed in 1 MB chunks
- A 100 MB file, processed in 1 MB chunks, with synchronous writes (files opened in O_SYNC mode)
- A 1 GB file, processed in 10 MB chunks
- A 1 GB file, processed in 10 MB chunks, with synchronous writes (files opened in O_SYNC mode)

The command used to run the IOzone benchmark was the following:

```
iozone -s file-size -r record-size -i 0 -i 1 -i 6 -i 7 -o
```

The -i option specifies the IOzone tests to run (0=write/rewrite, 1=read/re-read, 6=fwrite/re-fwrite, 7=fread/re-fread). The -o option was used only in runs of the benchmarks to open and write files synchronously.

TABLE 10.2 Results from the IOzone Benchmark

Filesystem	I/O	KB	reclen	write	rewrite	read	reread	fwrite	frewrite	fread	freread
ext2	O_SYNC	100000	1000	1955	1973	7901	7877	3896	4550	7843	11414
ext3	O_SYNC	100000	1000	2081	9709	15899	15902	3896	5094	15869	14265
jfs	O_SYNC	100000	1000	1990	1981	15867	15928	2476	1902	15927	15746
reiserfs	O_SYNC	100000	1000	163	288	1490	1461	2370	2625	7667	7449
xfs	O_SYNC	100000	1000	205	397	15843	15845	3640	2785	15614	14346
ext2	Std	1000000	10000	2158	2146	7591	7790	2086	2048	7576	7809
ext3	Std	1000000	10000	2348	1997	8599	8672	2120	2081	8578	8518
jfs	Std	1000000	10000	2011	2060	2169	2152	1861	1875	2166	2154
reiserfs	Std	1000000	10000	2007	2100	7470	7229	1897	1993	7147	7399
xfs	Std	1000000	10000	2001	2069	2150	2171	1849	1935	2150	2127
ext2	O_SYNC	1000000	10000	1973	1984	7734	7517	2089	2059	7806	7567
ext3	O_SYNC	1000000	10000	2092	1998	8681	8471	2177	2061	8422	8682
jfs	O_SYNC	1000000	10000	1955	1963	2149	2166	1849	1932	2170	2157
reiserfs	O_SYNC	1000000	10000	208	379	1427	1425	2040	2189	8563	8333
xfs	O_SYNC	1000000	10000	205	388	1360	1359	1869	1917	2197	2196

10

COMPARING
JOURNALING
FILESYSTEM
PERFORMANCE

This benchmark uses larger files than the preceding Bonnie benchmark and shows a variety of results. Surprisingly, the ext3 filesystem seems to show the highest write speed of all the filesystems, regardless of whether writes are precharacter or block oriented. The ext3 filesystem outperforms ext2 in almost every case across the board. The ReiserFS provides the best character and block read rates of the journaling filesystems, which is not surprising due to its use of B+Trees for the majority of its internal organization. JFS seems to do much better at raw writes to large files than other journaling filesystems besides ext3 but loses this advantage for block-oriented writes, where it is surpassed by both ReiserFS and ext3.

The Postmark Benchmark

The Postmark benchmark is interesting. Developed by the folks at Network Appliance, makers of fine Network Attached Storage (NAS) devices, it was designed to simulate performance under the types of real-world loads that you would get in high-load system directories that you would want to share over a network, such as Internet news repositories, mail queues, Web-based commerce, and so on. Postmark has an incredible number of options and is interactive, which makes it tough to script but still relatively easy to use.

The Postmark benchmark begins by creating a specified number of files of random sizes delimited by an upper bound. It then performs a specified number of transactions on random files from the pool of available files. Each transaction consists of subtransactions that either create, delete, read from, or append to files. It then displays summary information and returns to its internal command prompt.

The Postmark benchmark can only be run interactively, so each run of the benchmark involved the following commands:

1. Execute the `postmark` command from the Linux command line.
2. At the pm> prompt, specify the number of files using the `set number` *XXXX* command, where *XXXX* represents the number of files that you want to create.
3. At the pm> prompt, specify the number of transactions using the `set transactions` *XXXX* command, where *XXXX* represents the number of transactions that you want to execute.
4. At the pm> prompt, specify the `run` command to actually run the Postmark benchmark.

Table 10.3 shows the output from a run of the Postmark benchmark where files of between 0 and 10 KB were used. Data was collected for each filesystem with 50000 transactions performed on 1000 of these files, and with 50000 transactions performed on 20000 of these files.

TABLE 10.3 Results from the Postmark Benchmark

Filesystem	Files	Transactions	Total Written	Time (MB)	TPS	Data (KB/sec)	Read	(MB)
Rate (KB/sec)		Data			Rate			
ext2	1000	50000	89	561	161.15	1750.00	168.38	1830.00
ext3	1000	50000	187	267	161.15	873.10	168.38	912.26
jfs	1000	50000	546	91	161.15	296.79	168.38	310.10
xfs	1000	50000	274	182	161.15	595.73	168.38	622.44
ext2	20000	50000	781	64	144.06	148.85	271.87	280.93
ext3	20000	50000	868	57	144.06	129.06	271.87	243.57
jfs	20000	50000	891	56	144.06	120.42	271.87	227.26
xfs	20000	50000	1182	42	144.06	105.44	271.87	199.00

The columns of this table reflect the time that it took to perform the specified number of transactions on the specified number of files, the number of transactions executed per second, the amount of data written and read in that time, and the rates at which the data was written and read.

In this type of benchmark, you are looking for the biggest possible number of transactions in the smallest amount of time, as a measurement of filesystem performance. This type of benchmark is typically used to compare different hardware running different operating systems but the same software (such as NFS, for example); however, when the hardware and the operating system become the constants, this benchmark provides a good deal of information about the speed at which different filesystems perform.

The results shown in Table 10.3 are interesting. The standard ext2 filesystem is far and away the best performer for the smaller number of files. When the number of files involved goes up, ext2 loses its lead in dramatic fashion but still gives the best results of any filesystem.

The Creation/Deletion Test Benchmark

Many filesystems behave differently as they begin to fill up, regardless of fragmentation. I wanted a trivial test to see whether there was an obvious curve for different filesystems when simply doing a different number of creates and deletes, so I wrote a small Perl script that does this. When run in "normal" mode (that is, not quiet), the script is verbose, reporting per-process CPU time and doing a `df -k` for each create and delete operation. This script doesn't attempt to measure real-life performance for anything but how the filesystem behaves as it fills up because every file it creates is the same size. However, you can get some interesting figures by using file sizes that are even divisors or multiples of the block size and then rerunning the script with some file size that is not.

The Perl script that runs this test is called `creation_deletion_test.pl`. Each of the creation_deletion_test benchmarks in this chapter was run with the following command line:

```
creation_deletion_test.pl file-system-type mount-point 2048000 900
```

Table 10.4 shows the results of my simple benchmark and provides some interesting results. All the journaling filesystems had better pure file creation and directory insertion performance than the ext2 filesystem. However, the ReiserFS showed the worst pure per-file delete speed of any of the filesystems, which was surprising from my experience.

TABLE 10.4 Results of the Creation/Deletion Test Benchmark

Filesystem	Operation	Best	Disk	%Used	Worst	Disk
%Used	Total					
ext2	creation	3.42	13	3.69	62	2868.97
ext3	creation	3.40	2	3.54	94	3120.54
jfs	creation	3.39	2	3.56	27	3096.91
reiserfs	creation	3.25	3	3.57	63	3070.12
xfs	creation	3.34	5	3.54	7	3111.39
ext2	deletion	0.00	0	0.01	82	1.93
ext3	deletion	0.00	NA	0.00	NA	1.78
jfs	deletion	0.00	NA	0.01	85	1.92
reiserfs	deletion	0.00	NA	0.02	62	2.29
xfs	deletion	0.00	NA	0.01	86	2.24

And the Winner is. . .

If you saw this heading in the table of contents and decided to cheat by simply skipping here to find out the name of the ultimate journaling filesystem, I'm sorry, but you lose. There is no ultimate filesystem. But there are indeed many different filesystems, each of which is appropriate for a particular environment and has its own fan club for a variety of reasons. For example, if you've spent most of your working existence on SGI machines and still use the ones that run Irix, XFS is probably your filesystem of choice. You know its ins and outs, and you're probably working in some industry where huge files and impressive bandwidth are important, if not critical. You might even be cranky that the real-time section isn't available in XFS for Linux yet. If you work for IBM, you might prefer JFS because of its AIX and OS/Too roots. If you're a dedicated SuSE Linux user, ReiserFS might be the right thing because you're probably already using it. If you want to add journaling capabilities to many existing Linux systems and continue to use the standard Linux `dump`/`restore` utilities for all your filesystems, ext3 is your only choice at this point.

What do I use? For my home computing needs, I use the kind of hybrid combination of things that you'd expect of the author of this book. On systems that support it, my `/boot` and `/` partitions are ext3. The partitions on which I store backups of my music collection are XFS. My Lintel laptop uses ext3 for all its filesystems. My iBook uses a combination of ext2 and ReiserFS. I use a distributed filesystem to house my truly long-term personal and business data, but you'll have to read Chapter 14 to find out which one. I think it's fair to say that I could only be considered a normal user on GeekWorld, and that's just fine with me. Your mileage may vary—and I hope so!

Overview of Distributed Filesystems

IN THIS CHAPTER

Networked filesystems are no big surprise today, now that every out-of-the-box Windows and Macintosh system has been sharing directories over a network for years. The Network File System (NFS), first introduced by Sun Microsystems and subsequently ported to every other Unix or Unix-like platform, provides the same sort of out-of-the-box experience for Unix systems because every Unix system (Linux included) comes with an implementation of NFS. NFS even provides cross-platform file sharing because there are myriad implementations of NFS for Windows and some for Macintosh systems, as well. (As a Unix system, MAC OS X comes with NFS.)

This chapter provides a basic introduction to networked filesystems, more generally known as *distributed filesystems* because shared files and directories can be provided by (distributed across) many different computers on a network. The first two sections of this chapter introduce some of the basic concepts and issues in distributed filesystems, explaining basic networked computing concepts such as client/server computing, peer-to-peer networking, and caching. The next section provides some historical background on distributed computing and outlines some of the higher-level issues in distributed filesystems beyond just keeping track of who is using what file. The chapter concludes by exploring the many operational advantages that distributed filesystems can provide for organizations of any size, and how their value increases as networks grow even larger.

Introduction to Distributed Filesystems

Distributed filesystems enable many users to access the same set of files from multiple computer systems. The core concept behind distributed filesystems is *client/server computing*, where one computer system provides a set of services that other computers can access. A computer that provides services for other computer systems is a *server*. The computers that can request or access those services are *clients*.

The simplest example of client/server computing is a computer system that provides print services for other computers. Client systems send files that they want to print to the server, which controls access to its printer through some synchronization mechanism, such as a print queue. If every client could simply send data directly to the printer at the same time, the resulting output would be a hodge-podge of intermingled print jobs or, more likely, a series of error messages about files being in different formats. One of the primary jobs of a server is to manage access to the resources and services that it provides to its clients.

An alternative to client/server computing is *peer-to-peer computing*, where each system on the network is essentially the same as any other system on the network, but some systems offer services that others do not, such as access to a printer. Peer-to-peer computing works well for small networks composed of roughly equivalent computer systems where cost is a significant factor. All the computer systems in a peer-to-peer network are typically located on people's

Overview of Distributed Filesystems

CHAPTER 11

251

11

OVERVIEW OF
DISTRIBUTED
FILESYSTEMS

desks'. The demands of the services that peers provide to other peers are relatively light, such as sharing access to printers. After a file has been sent across the network to another system, printing generally proceeds asynchronously, with the computer to which the printer is attached sending output to the printer whenever it has spare time.

Client/server computing is a better solution when the services required by multiple computer systems require a reasonable amount of processing power or work to manage. For example, printing to shared printers in a peer-to-peer environment is relatively slow if someone is actively working on the system that hosts the shared resource. As mentioned in the previous paragraph, resource sharing in peer-to-peer environments usually just uses left-over processing time on the system that provides the resource. Some peer-to-peer networks enable you to pre-define the amount of processing power that will be used to manage shared resources, with the remainder going to the user of the computer system.

Client/server environments enable different machines to specialize in the services they provide. Continuing with the example of a print server, printing in a client/server environment is generally much faster than in a peer-to-peer environment. The print server can focus on sending jobs to the printer as fast as it can, without worrying that this would prevent anyone using the machine for some other purpose from getting her work done. Providing servers that focus on specialized services enables clients to be more general and often simpler to install and support. For example, if a certain type of ultra-high resolution printer requires specialized control and page manipulation software, that software only has to be installed on the print server.

In client/server environments, client and server machines are usually fairly different types of machines. For example, print servers don't need to have fancy graphical displays if all they're doing is sending jobs to a printer. Similarly, print servers generally don't need much memory because the limiting factor when printing something is usually the speed at which the printer can accept data and physically eject printed pages. There's no need to keep much information about those print jobs in the print server's memory. Similarly, print servers don't need much disk space—they only require sufficient space to store a number of pending print jobs. (This is, of course, not true if hundreds of print jobs are being queued simultaneously to a slow printer.) The disks attached to a print server generally don't have to be very fast because the limiting factor of a print server is usually the speed of the printer.

Client/server computing enables you to use different types of machines for the purposes for which they are best. To continue with the print server example, you can either purchase inexpensive, low-powered machines for use as print servers, or turn former desktop machines into print servers after they are no longer fast or powerful enough to be used as desktop machines.

In many ways, client/server computing environments are easier to manage than peer-to-peer computing environments, or environments where every workstation is self-sufficient. Servers are usually only directly accessed by system administrators and are therefore less prone to accidental misconfiguration. In a peer-to-peer environment, anyone installing a new software package on a computer that also provides some shared service can accidentally make the shared service unavailable until the machine is correctly configured. Similarly, as mentioned earlier, using servers to centralize any special software that they require to manage the resources that they provide minimizes the number of places in which that software has to be installed, potentially saving significant licensing costs.

You might think that a client/server computing environment can be more fragile than a peer-to-peer environment because servers provide a central point of failure. To some extent, this is true—if a print server crashes and requires repair, no one can print until it's fixed or another print server can be deployed. In reality, this is no different from what would happen in a peer-to-peer computing environment when a desktop system that supports a printer goes down. Things might even be worse in a peer-to-peer environment. No one could access the shared printer, and the person on whose desktop it was located would also be out of action until his system could be repaired or replaced. After it was back in service, it would probably be inundated with print jobs from all over the network, slowing down the machine and probably further hampering the productivity of the person on whose desktop it lived.

To muddy the water somewhat, this is as good a time as any to mention that clients and servers do not necessarily have to be separate machines: a server can also be a client of the services it provides. For example, suppose that a system administrator needs to get a printout of the usage statistics for a printer. In this case, the print server sends a copy of those usage statistics to its own printer, inserting the job in the print queue much like any other client of the print service. The printing process then prints the jobs just as it would if it had come from some other machine.

As mentioned previously, one of the main jobs of a server that provides a specific service to other computers is managing access to that service. Synchronizing access to shared resources is relatively simple when the majority of the communication between clients and servers is one way. When using a print server, clients usually just send data to the print server. After the server has the file, it inserts it into the print queue where it waits its turn to be printed. The client doesn't need any additional information from the server until the print job is completed, at which point the server may notify the client that the print job has completed.

Synchronization becomes much more of an issue when the service that the server provides requires two-way communication, such as when a server provides access to files and directories. Servers that provide access to centralized data are typically known as *file servers*. When clients request data from a file server, the server delivers the data to the client but also has to keep a record of the fact that it has done so. If another client requests the same information, the server has to know that someone already has the same data because either client could modify the data and send it back to the server. For example, suppose that two people are working on the same report. Both people request the file containing the report from a file server. If one person modifies the file and sends it back to the server, the second person no longer has an accurate copy of the file. If the second person subsequently changes his copy of the file and is allowed to send it back to the file server, the first person's changes will be overwritten.

This situation isn't really all that much different than when multiple people are sharing access to a single computer. In the bad old days when computers were so expensive that most companies could afford only one or two, everyone accessed them using terminals, which were just display devices and were therefore inexpensive. If two people wanted to access the same file at the same time, the computer had to track who was accessing that file and make sure that after the file was modified by one of them, the second person was prevented from modifying the file. The same thing is true in distributed filesystem environments, except that this notification now has to take place over a network. Actually, distributed filesystems provide some advantages in this case because each client usually has its own copy of the file for efficiency's sake (more about this later in the chapter). The person who is accessing an outdated copy of the file can be prevented from updating the file on the server but can continue to access her copy of the old data for as long as she wants.

Centralized resources such as databases, in which many people are expected to be accessing the same file, generally synchronize access to that file by locking specific portions of the file when someone is modifying them. In databases, you can usually just lock specific records within the file when people are updating them. More sophisticated databases maintain locks on specific fields in a database entry when it is being updated, If you're correcting someone's first name in a database at the same time that I'm updating his account balance, there's no reason why we both can't be allowed to do our jobs at the same time. In practice, the chances of multiple people trying to update the same record at exactly the same time in terms of computer time are fairly remote, but you still need to prevent it from happening, just in case.

Preventing multiple people from updating the same record in a shared database at the same time is relatively easy compared to preventing multiple people from updating files at the same time when each client has his own copy of a file. Distributed filesystems use a variety of mechanisms to guarantee that the copies of data located on client machines are the same as the data on the file server. In the distributed filesystem biz, this is known as *consistency*.

The crudest way to guarantee consistency is to lock a file on a file server whenever any client requests it. This means that only one client can check out a file at one time but is a total waste of time if you want to edit a file, and I simply want to look at it. Only slightly less crude is to separate these into read and write locks. Any number of clients can request a copy of a file to read it, but only one client can request a copy of the file to be able to write to it. This has its own set of problems because it assumes that people know whether they're going to modify files before they look at them. How can someone anticipate retrieving a file, noticing a typographical error in it, and deciding to fix it? Forcing that person to re-retrieve the file at that point to lock it and guarantee that she has have an up-to-date copy is a waste of time if no one else is using the file. It would also potentially double the network traffic associated with any file update request.

Distributed filesystems where each client has a continuous network connection to a file server often use a mechanism called a *callback* to provide a powerful but lightweight solution to this sort of problem. A callback is essentially just a software promise made by a distributed file server to notify a client whenever changes are made to a file that the client has received from the server. If the version of the file on the server changes, the file server breaks the callback, sending a notice to the client that it must re-retrieve the file. The client doesn't need to do anything about this notice unless a user actually tries to update the outdated version of the file.

This doesn't solve every synchronization problem for every distributed filesystem environment. Some advanced distributed filesystem environments support *disconnected operation*, where client systems, such as laptop computers, can retrieve files from a file server and then disconnect from the network. After a client disconnects from the network, the callback model breaks down. Distributed filesystems that support disconnected operations provide some sophisticated and unique ways of identifying and resolving conflicts between the versions of files on file servers and on client systems when a client reconnects to a network after a period of disconnected operation.

Caching and Distributed Filesystems

The previous section's example of multiple clients accessing and potentially updating the same file touched on the idea that when multiple clients request access to the same file, they each get a copy of that file. Most distributed filesystems work this way for several reasons, but the most significant of these is that sending a copy of an entire file to a client when the client requests access to that file reduces the use of the network. Generally, people are more likely to want to see more of a file that they are currently working on than they are to request some other file. When a client requests access to a file, the file server has to locate the file, open it, register a callback for the file, open a network connection to the client system, and ship part of the file over the network to the client, so why not send it all at once if the file is small enough to make this possible?

The flip side of this coin is that when a client requests a file from a file server, it has to have somewhere to put it. The obvious choice is in the client's memory, both because the client is obviously running some application already in memory to have requested the file and because writing to memory is fast. Unfortunately, because today's client computers may be used by multiple people at the same time, each of whom may be running large processes, putting everything in memory is rarely possible. The number of open files on a client system would quickly exceed available memory in exactly the same way that all the processes running on a computer system can quickly account for all the physical memory on the machine.

When allocating memory, operating systems such as Linux use a portion of the disk known as *swap space* to hold portions of running programs that aren't currently in use but that may be needed again. In distributed filesystem environments, clients do something similar by using a portion of the disk to hold files that they have requested from file servers. This portion of a client workstation's disk(s) is known as a *cache*.

A cache is a portion of a client's local disk dedicated to storing a copy of files and directories that users of that client have requested from file servers. This reduces the memory requirements of the client, enables the server to operate more efficiently by sending an entire file at once, and usually helps reduce the use of the network. Whenever an application running on a client (for any user) requests a file located on a file server, the request first passes through the cache. If the file is already stored in the cache and the callback for that file has not been broken (as discussed in the previous section), the application gets a pointer to the data in the cache without requiring any network traffic. If the file is not already located in the cache, or if it is there but the callback to the file server has been broken, the client requests the file from the file server again, storing the new version of the file in the cache and returning a pointer to the cached file to the application that requested it.

Keeping a copy of files and directories from a file server in a cache on a client's local disk is known as *caching* that file or directory information. Caching improves the speed and efficiency of accessing files actually located on a distributed file server. If multiple applications or users repeatedly ask for data from the same file, that file is already in the cache on the local disk. It does not have to be re-retrieved from the file server. This reduces both the load on the network and the time it takes to satisfy users' requests for that file. Any time that any user modifies the cached file or directory, the client sends the file back to the server, which breaks any existing callbacks for that file held by other clients. This guarantees that they know that the file has been updated. If the callback between the client and server has already been broken, the file server re-sends the file to the client, updates the version in the cache, and then establishes a new callback.

Caching is critical for distributed filesystems that support disconnected operation, which was introduced in the previous section of this chapter. Disconnected clients have to keep a copy of any file that they are using to be able to work on that file when the client can't actively contact the file server. In addition to using callbacks while they are connected to a network, distributed filesystems that support disconnected operation usually provide mechanisms for synchronizing their cache with the contents of the file server when they are reconnected.

The use of a cache can improve performance for both software and hardware. Processors maintain a cache of recently executed instructions, assuming that you may execute those same instructions again soon. Disk and CD-ROM drives typically keep a cache of data "near" any data you've read recently, known as a *read-ahead cache*, in the hopes that the next data that you request will be data that they've cached and can therefore be delivered from the cache instead of having to be read from the disk.

Another way in which caching data from file servers can improve performance is by preserving and reusing cached information when you restart your system. After restarting a client system for any reason, it's a safe bet that the users of a client will probably resume working on the same files that they were working on before the system went down. If those files are still in the cache and haven't changed on the file server (that is, the callbacks can be re-established), then the client can reuse the contents of the cache without re-retrieving the files from the file server. This is known as a *persistent* cache, not because it's irritating, but because its contents persist and are often reusable across system reboots.

In the absolute worst case, you won't attempt to use any of the files already in the cache, and they will gradually be replaced by the new files that you request from a file server. Most caching mechanisms use a least recently used (LRU) cache—as new files are requested and cached, the oldest files in the cache are discarded. The client has nothing to lose by maintaining files in the cache but proceeds normally, retrieving and caching any new files requested by users of the client.

A disk cache provides one other potential optimization: as a temporary repository for files on a multiuser machine, having a cache provides a buffer that enables client applications to return more quickly after saving modified data actually stored on a file server. This enables client systems to continue working while files stored in the cache are saved back to the file server. Some distributed filesystems, such as Sun Microsystems' NFS, use a cache in this way, but the cache does not persist across reboots. Distributed filesystems such as AFS, CODA, and InterMezzo make heavy use of caching to improve performance when they can communicate directly with a file server. When CODA or InterMezzo is running disconnected from a file server, they depend on the data in the cache and resynchronize it with the data on the file server after they can reconnect to the file server. All three depend on persistent caching to reduce restart times and decrease network usage.

The World Wide Web provides an interesting example of a distributed filesystem without any coordination between clients and servers. This is especially obvious when searching for topics on index sites such as Google, NorthernLights, Dogpile, or any of the others. The software that these sites used to generate the index that they maintain does not have any information regarding the current contents of the Web pages that they have already indexed. How many times have you clicked on a link that was the result of a Web search and gotten a "404: Web page not found error"? More progressive sites such as Google now maintain a cache of the Web pages that they have indexed to help work around the dynamic and random state of the Web. Although some money-grubbing fanatics view using caching other sites' web pages as a copyright violation, I view it as just plain common sense.

General Principles of Distributed Filesystems

The previous sections provided an overview of many of the basic features of distributed filesystems. The discussion started with simple client/server computing and worked up to some optimizations that distributed filesystems use to improve performance when potentially critical files are not stored locally to each machine. None of these ideas sprang full-blown from the fingertips of the designers of early, wide-scale distributed filesystems. Optimizations such as caching relatively large amounts of file server data have only become possible as a result of today's larger, faster disks. Similarly, although distributed filesystems have been around since the mid-1980s, today's faster and more ubiquitous networks have steadily increased their popularity.

The history of distributed filesystems on commercial Unix and Unix-like systems began with the proprietary Domain network filesystem introduced on Apollo workstations in the early 1980s and continued through Sun Microsystems' NFS (Network File System), introduced in the mid-1980s. Today, the height of distributed filesystems lies in more sophisticated, higher-performance network-based filesystems such as IBM's AFS, CMU's CODA, and Stelias Computing's InterMezzo, each of which are discussed in subsequent chapters of this book. NFS was the first open implementation of a networked filesystem. Its specifications and protocols were publicly available, and NFS was thus quickly supported on many different types of computer systems.

IBM's AFS filesystem is a great example of a filesystem that has been used for a long time but has continuously improved, not only by design but also by taking advantage of technological improvements. As part of its commitment to Linux, IBM has released AFS to the Open Source community, where it is now known as OpenAFS. AFS was originally developed at Carnegie-Mellon University, where I worked in the mid-1980s, and where it was originally known as the Vice filesystem. I managed one of the labs where it was first deployed outside its funding center, the Information Technology Center, which was largely funded by IBM. What goes around comes around, I guess. At that time, running largely on Sun-2's (the 68020 machines, not SPARC-2s), it was dog slow and more of a theorist's pipe dream than a usable filesystem. At that time, I remember telling the operators who worked for me to "type 'ls' and then go out for pizza," but today I have it running at home and have devoted a chapter in this book to singing its praises. I still have the Sun-2's, but they are end tables and space heaters while AFS is better than ever.

Today's distributed filesystems provide several basic features:

- Transparent access to user files from different computers—Users don't know and don't need to know whether their files are local or located on a remote file server. Storing files on centralized file servers liberates users from having to access their files from specific machines. Users of any well-designed distributed filesystem can log in on any machine in their computing environment and access and update their files exactly as they would on any other machine. Executable programs are still platform-specific, but the user's view of the filesystem is workstation independent. Wherever you go, there you are. Getting the same view of a distributed filesystem from any participating workstation is often referred to as providing a unified namespace for all the files in the filesystem. Anyone at any AFS site in the world that is on the Internet sees the same view of the filesystem.

- Network-oriented authentication—If users can log in on any machine and access their files transparently from those machines, replicating authentication (password, group, and so on) information on every machine quickly becomes an administrative nightmare. For this reason, networked files systems typically go hand-in-hand with a networked authentication mechanism, which supersedes traditional sources of login information such as /etc/password and /etc/group on Linux/Unix systems. Network-oriented authentication mechanisms such as NIS, NIS+, and Kerberos are designed to provide network-oriented authentication.

- Time synchronization—Although not absolutely critical, it is useful if all the client and server machines in a distributed filesystem can agree on what time it is. It would definitely be a drag to attempt to update a file on a remote file server and have the file server tell me that the version of the file on the file server is newer than my version when I know that this is not the case. Filesystems such as AFS and CODA use modified versions of the standard NTP (Network Time Protocol) daemon to provide a unified source of time information within each administrative domain and automatically synchronize clocks between servers. If the time is off on a client workstation, AFS adjusts the time in 10-second increments, which can take a ridiculous amount of time (and generate a similarly absurd number of console messages) if you fire up a workstation with a seriously skewed clock.

- Replication—Replication is the capability of distributed filesystems to provide online copies (replicas) of existing portions of the distributed filesystem. Should a file server that exports a primary portion of the distributed filesystem become unavailable, replicas are instantly and transparently available to users without interrupting their work. Although absent in NFS, replication is almost critically important in environments where shared software is stored in a distributed filesystem to give everyone access to the same tools while simultaneously providing a single, central location where tools can be updated and released to the entire community at the same time.

Operational Advantages of Distributed Filesystems

Distributed filesystems provide significant advantages to almost everyone who uses or manages computers. Distributed filesystems enable users to access their data files in exactly the same way from different computers. If the machine on your desk fails, you can just use another—your files are still intact and safe on the centralized file server. Maximizing information sharing and availability on college campuses was the genesis of many of the projects that led to the filesystems described in this book.

Distributed filesystems that can be accessed in the same way from many different computer systems enable users to use the type of desktop machine that best suits their needs while still having access to a centralized filesystem. Macintosh users can take advantage of the graphics tools available under the Mac OS while transparently saving their files to centralized Linux servers. Windows users can have access to a robust filesystem while still being able to play Minesweeper. Distributed filesystems are especially attractive when trying to coordinate work between groups located in different cities, states, or countries.

For system administrators, storing important data on centralized file servers rather than on individual desktop systems simplifies administrative tasks such as backing up and restoring files; reduces hardware costs for desktop systems; and also centralizes standard system administration tasks such as creating/deactivating accounts, monitoring filesystem use, and so on. Using a centralized distributed filesystem in conjunction with logical volume management makes it easy to add storage to your computing environment without requiring downtime.

IS and IT managers responsible for enterprise computing services may already be using a distributed filesystem, such as NFS, or filesystem adapters, such as Samba, Netatalk, or the NCP tools, to unify their Linux and single-user microcomputer network environments. Global, cross-platform, distributed filesystems such as OpenAFS can provide complementary alternatives with better performance, enhanced security, and additional features, such as access control lists. Similarly, using a distributed filesystem makes it easier to share access to software, though you have to make sure that your software licenses enable you to install software into a distributed filesystem. Like the print servers that were part of the original motivation for client/server computing, distributed filesystems also simplify sharing access to specialized hardware by connecting to the system that hosts the hardware over the network and still being able to see all your files and data.

Finally, using a distributed filesystem as the repository for all user data means substantially faster client restart times because much of the data is no longer stored locally and therefore does not have to be checked for filesystem consistency after restarting a client. The combination of a distributed filesystem and using a journaling filesystem for all or most of the filesystems local to client workstations can provide amazing improvements in system restart times.

Today's fast networks, powerful local systems, and the availability of powerful, time-tested distributed filesystems in Open Source form makes it easier than ever before to propose using a distributed filesystem or to start a trial project to see how distributed filesystems can benefit personal, academic, and enterprise computing environments.

Summary of Available Distributed Filesystems

This section of the book describes how to install, configure, administer, and use a variety of different distributed filesystems. The distributed filesystems covered in this chapter were chosen because they are widely used and represent different approaches to distributed computing. The distributed filesystems discussed in this chapter are the following:

- AFS and OpenAFS—Originally developed at Carnegie-Mellon University, AFS (the Andrew File System) was designed to solve the computing needs of an academic community where students need access to their files regardless of which workstation they are logged in at, where sharing data is important, and where data security is important. AFS was designed as a high-security computing environment with centralized administrative capabilities, high availability to data, integrated logical volume management, and sophisticated access control for files and directories that can easily be configured by users. In 1989, Transarc Corporation obtained the rights to develop and market AFS commercially, introducing AFS into the commercial and government markets. In 1994, Transarc Corporation was acquired by IBM, which continued to market AFS. In 2000, IBM released a version of the AFS to the Open Source community, which is now known as OpenAFS. IBM continues to market and support AFS, whereas thousands of open-source advocates have taken OpenAFS to heart and are working on further increasing its power and portability. Installing, configuring, and using OpenAFS is described in Chapter 13, "The OpenAFS Distributed Filesystem."

- NFS (Network File System)—From Sun Microsystems, this is the most widely used distributed filesystem in the world. NFS is available for almost every Unix and Unix-like system ever made. Part of its success is due to the fact that the specifications for NFS and its communication protocols have been publicly available since the mid-1980s, which simplified its implementation and adoption on a huge number of different computing systems.

As mentioned previously, these distributed filesystems were selected because they are widely used, actively under development, and oriented toward solving different types of distributed computing problems. They meet the needs of different types of computer users who want access to a distributed filesystem.

Many other distributed filesystems are available for Linux. The fact that they are not discussed in any detail in this book is not a negative comment but simply due to the fact that I had to finish this book sometime. In the future, I hope to have the opportunity to discuss and explore additional distributed filesystems. In the meantime, the following is a partial list of other distributed filesystems currently available for Linux, along with URLs where you can get additional information about them and download source code and/or RPMs:

- Coda—Also developed at Carnegie-Mellon University, Coda is actually a sibling of AFS, having branched from the AFS source code base at the time of AFS version 2. Coda therefore shares many features with AFS but is specifically oriented toward solving problems related to poor or nonexistent network connectivity. Coda was the first distributed filesystem to introduce support for disconnected operation, which means that a Coda client can continue to work on cached files even when disconnected from the network. Many of the features of Coda were specifically designed to solve the needs of portable computer users. When reconnected, the client automatically synchronizes the state of its cached files with the appropriate file servers. For more information about Coda, see `http://www.coda.cs.cmu.edu`.

- GFS (Global File System)—A clustered filesystem for Linux that enables multiple servers to share access to a single filesystem maintained on shared SAN (Storage Area Network) devices. GFS's SAN orientation provides a high-performance distributed filesystem tightly integrated with the low-level drivers used to communicate with and manage its storage subsystems. GFS is actively supported by Sistina and used in a variety of locations. For more information about GFS, see `http://www.sistina.com/products_gfs.htm`.

- InterMezzo—Yet another distributed filesystem originally developed at Carnegie-Mellon University but now being developed by Stelias Computing. InterMezzo is a lightweight distributed filesystem designed to support disconnected operation and reduce the system and memory requirements placed on mobile computer users by other distributed filesystems. For more information about InterMezzo, see `http://www.inter-mezzo.org`.

- Sprite—A distributed operating system from the University of California at Berkeley that provided a single system image to a cluster of workstations. A high-performance distributed filesystem that used both client-side and server-side caching, Sprite also supported process migration to take advantage of idle processor time on client systems. Sprite is no longer actively supported or used, although you can obtain more information about it (and the source code) from `http://www.cs.berkeley.edu/projects/sprite/sprite.html`.

- xFS—Another distributed filesystem from the University of California at Berkeley, xFS is unique in that it provided a serverless distributed filesystem environment. xFS supported fast, high-bandwidth access to filesystem data by distributing the functionality traditionally provided by a file server among its client systems. I don't believe that xFS is currently supported or under development, but you can get additional information about the project from `http://now.cs.berkeley.edu/Xfs/xfs.html`.

As networks become more ubiquitous, distributed filesystems and distributed computing continue to be popular topics for research and development. Many other distributed filesystems have been developed for research and academic purposes, such as Archipelago, CFS, and FICUS, but central sites for information about these filesystems don't appear to exist anywhere. You can obtain further information about them by checking lists of presentations given at Usenix over the last few years.

The NFS Distributed Filesystem

IN THIS CHAPTER

Sun Microsystems' Network File System, better known simply as NFS, is the most common networked filesystem in use today, largely because it comes preinstalled and for free with almost every Unix and Unix-like system. NFS clients and servers are also available for almost every type of modern computer system, including DOS, Windows, and Macintosh.

This chapter provides an overview of NFS, discusses different versions of NFS and their capabilities, and discusses the various applications associated with NFS. This chapter also spends a fair amount of time discussing NIS, the Network Information System, a distributed authentication mechanism originally developed by Sun Microsystems and most commonly used in conjunction with NFS. NIS enables all the machines in a computing environment to share access to a centralized authentication database. The chapter concludes with practical, hands-on instructions for installing, configuring, starting, and using NFS and NIS on Linux systems.

Overview

NFS is a distributed filesystem that provides transparent access to files residing on remote disks. Developed at Sun Microsystems in the early 1980s, the NFS protocol has been revised and enhanced a number of times between then and now, and is available on all Unix systems and even for Windows systems from many vendors. The specifications for NFS have been publicly available since shortly after it was first released, making NFS a de facto standard for distributed filesystems.

Like the other distributed filesystems discussed in this book, NFS provides access to centralized filesystems stored on file servers that store centralized sets of files and directories that you want to export to multiple client systems. Good examples of files and directories that you may want to store in a centralized location but make simultaneously available to multiple computer systems are users' home directories, sitewide sets of software development tools, and centralized data resources such as mail queues and the directories used to store Internet news bulletin boards.

The following are some common usage scenarios for NFS:

- Suppose that the home directories for all your users are stored in the directory /export on your NFS file server. The password file for each of your systems (or a network-oriented password file, such as that provided by NIS) would list your user's home directories as /export/<user-name>. Users could then log in on any NFS client system and instantly see their home directory, which would be transparently made available to them over the network.

- Locating your user home directories in a directory managed by the NFS automount daemon. This is an alternative approach to the previous bullet. Whenever access to a directory managed by the automount daemon is requested by a client, the client's automount daemon automatically mounts that directory. Automounting simplifies the contents of your server's /etc/exports file by enabling you to simply export the parent directory of all home directories on the server and tell the automounter to manage that same directory on each client.

- A third common scenario is using NFS to share directories of system-specific binaries between all hosts of a specific system type in your computing environment. Suppose that you want to make all the GNU tools available on all the systems in your computing environment but also want to centralize them on an NFS server for ease of maintenance and updating. To ensure that configuration files are portable across all your systems, you might want to make these binaries available in the directory /usr/gnu regardless of the type of system you are using. You could simply build binaries for each type of system that you support, configuring them to expect to be found in the directory /usr/gnu but actually storing them in directories with names such as /export/gnu/redhat72, /export/gnu/solaris28, /export/gnu/hpux10.20, and so on. You would then configure each client of a specified type to mount the appropriate exported directory for that system type as /usr/gnu. For example, /export/gnu/redhat72 would be mounted as /usr/gnu on Red Hat Linux 7.2 systems, /export/gnu/solaris28 would be mounted as /usr/gnu on Solaris 2.8 systems, and so on). You could then simply put /usr/gnu/bin in your path and the legendary "right thing" would happen regardless of the type of system that you logged in on.

NFS is an easily configured distributed computing environment available on Linux and most Unix systems. NFS is unquestionably the most popular distributed filesystem around because it is ubiquitous and usually comes with your operating system. NFS provides an effective out-of-the-box distributed computing environment for sites that do not want the administrative overhead of installing, configuring, and administering a more complex but higher performance distributed filesystem.

How NFS Works

The underlying network communication method used by NFS is known as Remote Procedure Calls (RPCs), which can use either the lower level UDP (Universal Datagram Protocol) as their network transport mechanism (NFS version 2) or TCP (NFS version 3). For this reason, both UDP and TCP entries for port 2049, the port used by the NFS daemon, are present in the Linux /etc/services file. UDP minimizes transmission delays because it does not attempt to do sequencing or flow control, and does not provide delivery guarantees. It simply sends packets to a specific port on a given host, where some other process is waiting for input.

The design and implementation of RPCs make NFS platform independent, interoperable between different computer systems, and easily ported to a wide variety of computing architectures and

12

THE NFS DISTRIBUTED FILESYSTEM

operating systems. RPCs are a client/server communication method that involves issuing RPC calls with various parameters on client systems, which are actually executed on the server. The client doesn't need to know whether the procedure call is being executed locally or remotely—it receives the results of an RPC in exactly the same way that it would receive the results of a local procedure call.

The way in which RPCs are implemented is clever. RPCs work by using a technique known as *marshalling*, which essentially means packaging up all the arguments to the RPC on the client into a mutually agreed on format. This mutually agreed on format is known as XDR (eXternal Data Representation) and provides a sort of computer Esperanto that enables systems with different architectures and byte orders to safely exchange data with each other.

The client's RPC subsystem then ships the resulting, system-independent packet to the appropriate server. The server's RPC subsystem receives the packet and unmarshals it to extract the arguments to the procedure call in its native format. The RPC subsystem executes the procedure call locally, marshals the results into a return packet, and sends this packet back to the client. When this packet is received by the client, its RPC subsystem unmarshals the packet and sends the results to the program that invoked the RPC, returning this data in exactly the same fashion as any local procedure call. Marshalling and unmarshalling, plus the use of the common XDR data representation, make it possible for different types of systems to transparently communicate and execute functions on each other. Figure 12.1 shows the interaction between an NFS client and server.

The downside of using a common data representation such as XDR, of course, is that using a machine-independent data encoding mechanism ensures that every platform has to spend some amount of processor time unencoding the data, even when two machines of the same type are exchanging information. XDR uses fixed-length encoding for all data types, which means that the external data representation of many data values, such as most integers, necessitates transferring more machine-independent data than is actually required to specify the value of these types of parameters. The amount of overhead imposed by XDR on each RPC call and data exchange depends on a variety of factors, such as the data types being used, the amount of data being exchanged, the type and power of the computers involved in an RPC, and how well the XDR library performs on each system.

RPC communications are used for all NFS-related communications, including communications related to the authentication services used by NFS (NIS or NIS+), managing file locks, managing NFS mount requests, providing status information, and requests made to the NFS automount daemon. To enable applications to contact so many different services without requiring that each communicate through a specific, well-known port, NFS lets those services dynamically bind to any available port as long as they register with its central coordination service, the portmapper daemon. The portmapper always runs on port 111 of any host that supports RPC communications and serves as an electronic version of directory assistance. Servers register RPC-related service with the portmapper, identifying the port that the service is actually listening on. Clients then contact the portmapper at its well-known port to determine the port actually being used by the service they are looking for.

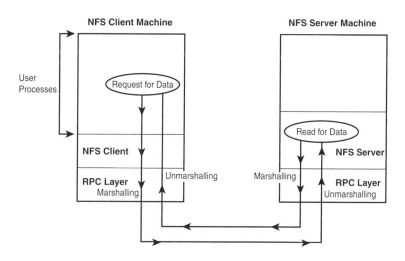

FIGURE 12.1

RPC communication between an NFS client and server.

Communication failures occur with any networked communication mechanism, and RPCs are no exception. As mentioned at the beginning of this section, UDP does not provide delivery guarantees or packet sequencing. Therefore, when the response to an RPC is not received within a specific period of time, systems will re-send RPC packets. This introduces the possibility that a remote system may execute a specific function twice, based on the same input data. Because this can happen, all NFS operations are *idempotent*, which does not indicate sexual dysfunction, but means that they can be executed any number of times and still return the same result—an NFS operation cannot change any of the data that it depends on. Even though NFS version 3 uses TCP as its network transport mechanism, the idea of idempotent requests is still part of the NFS protocol to guarantee compatibility with NFS version 2 implementations.

As another way of dealing with potential communication and system failures, NFS servers are stateless, meaning that they do not retain information about each other across system restarts. If a server crashes while a client is attempting to make an RPC to it, the client continues to retry the RPC until the server comes back up or until the number of retries exceeds its configured limit, at which time the operation aborts. Stateless operation makes the NFS protocol much simpler because it does not have to worry about maintaining consistency between client and server data. The client is always right, even after rebooting, because it does not maintain any data at that point.

Although stateless operation simplifies things, it is also noisy, inefficient, and slow. When data from a client is saved back to a server, the server must write it synchronously, not returning control to the client until all the data has been saved to the server's disk. As described in the next section, "Comparing Different Versions of NFS," newer versions of NFS do some limited write caching on clients to return control to the client applications as quickly as possible. This caching is done by the client's `rpciod` process (RPC IO Daemon), which stores pending writes to NFS servers in the hopes that it can bundle groups of them together and thus optimize the client's use of the network. In the current standard version of NFS (NFS version 3), cached client writes are still essentially dangerous because they are stored only in memory and will therefore be lost if the client crashes before the write completes.

In a totally stateless environment, a server crash would make it difficult to save data being modified on a client back to the server after it is available again. The server would have no way of knowing what file the modified data belonged to because it had no persistent information about its clients. To resolve the problem, NFS clients obtain file handles from a server whenever they open a file. *File handles* are data structures that identify both the server and the file they are associated with. If a server crashes, clients retry their write operations until the server is available again or their timeout periods are exceeded. If the server comes back up in time, it receives the modified data and the file handle from the client and can use the file handle to figure out which file the modified data should be written to.

The lack of client-side caching also has a long-term operational impact because it limits the type of dependencies that NFS clients can have on NFS servers. Because clients do not cache data from the server, they must re-retrieve any information that they need after any reboot. This can definitely slow the reboot process for any client that must execute binaries located on an NFS server as part of the reboot process. If the server is unavailable, the client cannot boot. For this reason, most NFS clients must contain a full set of system binaries and typically only share user-oriented binaries and data via NFS.

Comparing Different Versions of NFS

NFS has been around almost since the beginning of Unix workstation time, appearing on early Sun Microsystems workstations in the early 1980s. This section provides an overview of the differences between the four different versions of NFS, both for historical reasons, and to illustrate that NFS is by no means a done deal. NFS 4 resolves the biggest limitations of NFS 3, most notably adding real client-side data caching that survives reboots. Finally, something NFS-related to look forward to!

> **NOTE**
>
> NFS version 3 is the version used on most systems today and is the version discussed in this book. However, NFS 4 is right around the corner. When writing this book, I looked at NFS 4 at its project site at `http://www.citi.umich.edu/projects/nfsv4`, wondering whether I should focus on it in this book. In the end, I decided that its immaturity and some fundamental differences between it and NFS 3 were significant enough to hold off for now. The source code for a Linux kernel with NFS 4 support and related NFS 4 utilities is included on the CD that accompanies this book (in the directory `nfs/nfs4`, if you're interested in experimenting.
>
> This implementation was done by the folks at the University of Michigan's CITI project, which does top-notch work, but I was concerned that things might change significantly between this implementation and the actual release of NFS 4 for Linux. For now, I think that more people will be interested in NFS 3, which comes with all current Linux distributions.

The following list identifies the four versions of NFS and highlights the primary features of each:

- Version 1—The original NFS protocol specification was only used internally at Sun during the development of NFS, and I have never been able to find any documentation on the original specification. This would only be of historical interest.

- Version 2—NFS version 2 was the first version of the NFS protocol released for public consumption. Version 2 used UDP exclusively as its transport mechanism and defined the 18 basic RPCs that made up the original public NFS protocol. Version 2 was a 32-bit implementation of the protocol and therefore imposed a maximum file size limitation of 2 gigabytes on files in NFS and used a 32-byte file handle. NFS version 2 also limited data transfer sizes to 8 KB.

- Version 3—NFS version 3 addressed many of the shortcomings and ambiguities present in the NFS version 2 specification, and took advantage of many technological advances in the more than 10 years between the version 2 and 3 specifications. Version 3 added TCP as a network transport mechanism, making it the default if both the client and server support it, increased the maximum data transfer size between client and server to 64 KB, and was a full 64-bit implementation, thereby effectively removing file size limitations. All these were made possible by improvements in networking technology and system architecture since the NFS version 2 was released. Version 3 also added a few new RPCs to those in the original version 2 specification and removed two that had never been used (or implemented in any NFS implementation that I've ever seen). To improve performance by decreasing network traffic, version 3 introduced the notion of bundling writes from the client to the server and also automatically returned file attributes with each RPC call, instead of requiring a separate request for this information as version 2 NFS did.

- Version 4—Much of the NFS version 4 protocol is designed to position NFS for use in Internet and World Wide Web environments by increasing persistence, performance, and security. Version 4 adds persistent, client-side caching to aid in recovery from system reboots with minimal network traffic and adds support for ACLs and extended file attributes in NFS filesystems. Version 4 also adds an improved, standard API for increased security through a general RPC security mechanism known as Remote Procedure Call Security - Generic Security Services (RPCSEC_GSS). This mandates the use of the Generic Security Services Application Programming Interface (GSS-API, specified in RFC 2203) to select between available security mechanisms provided by clients and servers.

For more details on the proposed NFS Version 4 specification, see RFC 3010 at `http://www.faqs.org/rfcs/rfc3010.html`.

NFS Process Summary

On Linux systems, the NFS daemon process is known as `knfsd`, for the Kernel NFS Daemon. The NFS daemon has been integrated into the Linux kernel since revision 2.2 and, as a kernel service, is fast. The following is a list of the other daemons used by NFS and the services that they provide:

- `portmap`—As mentioned earlier in this section, the portmapper is the process that handles incoming RPC requests and identifies the port on which a specific service is actually running.

- `rpciod`—The RPC IO daemon is the client-side daemon that bundles writes to NFS servers together to reduce the use of the network by NFS.

- `rpc.lockd`—The RPC lock daemon manages file locking to ensure that multiple people do not simultaneously write the same file. The protocol used to manage locking in NFS is known as NLM, the NFS Lock Manager protocol. The lock daemon uses the lock status information provided by the `rpc.statd` status daemon to determine who holds locks. In Linux kernels 2.2 and later, the RPC lock daemon is started by the in-kernel NFS daemon.

- `rpc.mountd`—The RPC mount daemon runs on an NFS server and handles requests by clients to mount any server directories listed in the file `/etc/exports`. The `rpc.mountd` daemon reads the list of available volumes on a server from the file `/var/lib/nfs/xtab`, which is produced by the `exportfs` command from the `file /etc/exports`.

- `rpc.nfsd`—The user-level portion of the NFS daemon. If the kernel version of the NFS daemon is used, the NFS daemon shows up in a list of Linux processes as `[nfsd]`, where the square brackets indicate that it is running as a kernel process. You always see a minimum of eight NFS daemon processes running on an NFS server, because each instance of the NFS daemon can only process one client request at a time.

- `rpc.quotad`—The RPC quota daemon provides a central RPC resource that clients can call to obtain user quota information, which identifies the amount of disk space that a particular user can own in a given filesystem.

- `rpc.statd`—The RPC status monitor daemon keeps a persistent record of which NFS clients hold locks on files on directories exported by the server. Because identifying whether clients have locked specific files is critical to actually being able to manage multiple client requests, the RPC status monitor is the only NFS process that saves its state information on the server so that it can survive a server crash. State information about NFS locks is saved in the file `/var/lib/nfs/statd/sm`.

Automounting NFS Filesystems

Automounting is the process of automatically mounting NFS filesystems in response to requests for access to those filesystems. Automounting is controlled by an automount daemon that runs on the client system. In addition to automatically mounting filesystems in response to requests for access to them, the automount daemon can also automatically unmount volumes when they have not been used for a specified period of time.

Using the automount daemon prevents you from having to mount shared NFS directories that you are not actually using at the moment. Mounting all NFS directories on all clients at all times causes a reasonable amount of network traffic, much of which is extraneous if those directories are not actually being used. Using the NFS automount daemon helps keep NFS-related network traffic to a minimum.

At the moment, two different automount daemons are available for Linux. The `amd` automount daemon runs in user space on client workstations and works much like the original SunOS automounter. The `amd` automounter is configured through the file `/etc/amd.conf`. For more information about amd, see the home page for the Automount Utilities at `http://www.am-utils.org`.

The other automount daemon is called `autofs` and is implemented in Linux kernel versions 2.2 and greater. The kernel automounter starts one user-space automount process for each top-level automounted directory. The `autofs` automounter daemon is configured through the file `/etc/auto.master` or through NIS maps with the same name. Because the `autofs` daemon is part of the kernel, it seems to be the automounter of choice for many Linux distributions (such as Red Hat) even though the `amd` automounter is much more mature, flexible, and better documented.

Authentication in NFS

As with any distributed filesystem, all the NFS servers and clients in a single computing environment must use consistent user and groups IDs to ensure that files created by a user on one system are still owned by that user when he or she uses another workstation in the same computing environment. The simplest way to do this is to use the same password file on all your systems, but this quickly becomes an administrative nightmare. Each time you add a user on one of your machines, you would have to add that same user to every other password and group file on every other machine. At best, this would be a tremendous hassle and a scenario that was prone to error.

To remove the need for this sort of administrative nightmare, Sun introduced the Network Information System (NIS). NIS is a distributed authentication mechanism that provides a repository of information that can be accessed from any participating machine in the local administrative entity, which is known as an *NIS domain*.

NIS is the oldest distributed authentication mechanism still in common use today, having been introduced by Sun Microsystems in 1985. Originally known as the "Yellow Pages," this distributed authentication mechanism was quickly renamed NIS because of a name/copyright conflict with another commercial entity that I can't think of at the moment. The names of many of the NIS utilities still reflect the original name of NIS—for example, ypcat lets you cat (in the Unix sense—that is, concatenate and print) the contents of any file stored in NIS.

As with NFS, Sun was wise enough to release the basic specifications of NIS to the public, causing NIS to be made available on most Unix and Unix-like platforms then and now. Much like NFS, this has made NIS the most commonly used and popular distributed authentication mechanism today. You can't beat the price or easy availability because NIS comes free with most Unix and Unix-like operating systems.

Sun showed a great deal of foresight when creating NIS in that NIS was designed to be a central repository for much more than just authentication information. Any files and information that you want to share across multiple systems can be stored and shared in NIS, including group files, host files, mail aliases, the /etc/services file listing valid network services for your computing environment, and so on. NIS is also flexible and is not limited to being used with standard Unix system files—you can also use NIS to store and provide any site-specific files and information. NIS is also designed to be replicated, intrinsically supporting the notion of a master NIS server and replicas of that server known as *slaves*.

The capability to handle the failure of a distributed authentication mechanism is a critical aspect of any successful implementation. NIS handles this problem nicely. When you access a file on your Linux system that is actually stored in NIS, the file you see is usually the combination of a file stub located on your local system, to which the NIS information has been appended. If your NIS servers ever go down, you still have administrative access to that system because, for example, the root password for your local system is stored in the stub of the password file stored on your system. If your NIS server is dead, you were not running copies (slaves), and your NIS environment is therefore hopelessly broken, you can restore service to your users relatively quickly after logging in as root by re-creating the password file locally on critical machines.

NIS data files are known as *maps*. Each NIS map is typically provided in several different ways, each organized to optimize a specific type of access to that information, such as lookups by name or by some unique numeric component (such as being able to access a group map by group ID, a hosts map by address, and so on).

NIS+, also from Sun Microsystems, is the successor to NIS and organizes information hierarchically, much like LDAP. NIS+ was designed to handle the requirements of today's larger, more complex networks. The root of an NIS+ implementation for each NIS domain is the name of that domain followed by a dot (.) and contains two primary directory entries. These are a groups_dir. directory to hold information about groups (NIS+ administrative groups, not Unix groups) and an org_dir. directory to hold NIS+ tables, which are the equivalents of the map files used by NIS.

One big problem with NIS+ is that not all Unix and Unix-like operating system vendors who provide NFS also provide NIS+. Linux is a good example of this, which rules NIS+ out for serious use as far as I'm concerned. It's not like we're all stuck using Solaris anymore.

Getting More Information About NFS and NIS

Not surprisingly, the Web provides an excellent source of additional information about NFS and NIS. For more information, consult any of the following:

- The NFS FAQ at http://nfs.sourceforge.net.
- The NFS HOWTO at http://nfs.sourceforge.net/nfs-howto.
- The NIS HOWTO is http://www.suse.de/~kukuk/nis-howto. This document is available in English, French, Japanese, Norwegian, and Polish.
- The NFS Automount Mini-HOWTO at http://www.linux.com/howto/mini/Automount-1.html.

Support Software for NFS

Built-in support for the NFS distributed filesystem is present in every commercial Linux distribution that uses a Linux kernel greater than version 2.2. Earlier versions of Linux provided user-space NFS daemons rather than the in-kernel NFS daemon provided in Linux kernels 2.2

and greater. As a consequence, every Linux distribution that I have seen in the last few years also includes the NFS utilities package, which provides the NFS RPC daemons and other NFS utilities. For your convenience, this section discusses the utilities packages associated with NFS filesystems and the features they provide.

If you want to take advantage of various Linux kernel enhancements in a kernel that is probably newer than the one used by your Linux distribution, the CD that accompanies this book includes the source code for the Linux 2.4.9 kernel in the CD's `kernels` subdirectory. Information about installing the kernel source code and NFS-related information about configuring, building, and installing a kernel is provided later in this chapter.

If your system's kernel doesn't have NFS support turned on or you want to build the newer kernel included with this book, you may also want to build and install newer versions of NFS-related utilities. At the time of this writing, this consisted of three packages: the standard NFS utilities in the package nfs-utils-0.3.1, the `amd` automount daemon and related utilities in the package am-utils-6.0.7, and the `autofs` daemon for the kernel automounter in the package autofs-3.1.7-14. The source code for the current versions of these packages is located in the NFS subdirectory of the CD.

The am-utils-6.0.7 package contains the following daemons and utilities:

- `amd`—The user-space automount daemon. You can install both this automount daemon and the `autofs` automounter daemon, but you must activate only one of them.
- `amq`—Enables you to query the state of the `amd` automount daemon.
- `fixmount`—Enables you to delete unused or irrelevant mount entries managed by a remote NFS `mountd` daemon.
- `fsinfo`—A utility that can generate a coordinated set of `amd`, mount, and `mountd` configuration files from a system configuration file.
- `hlfsd`—A daemon that implements a filesystem containing a symbolic link to a specified subdirectory within a user's home directory, depending on the user who accesses the link. It was designed to redirect incoming mail to users' home directories so that it can read from anywhere.
- `mk-amd-map`—Creates map files used by the `amd` automount daemon.
- `pawd`—Prints the current working directory for the automounter.
- `wire-test`—Locates network interfaces and associated IP address information for use by the `amd` automount daemon and also tests the NFS port on the first two network interfaces found. (The second one will fail if your machine only has a single network interface.)

The autofs-3.1.7-14 package contains automount, the user-space daemon that interacts with the in-kernel NFS `autofs` automount daemon.

The nfs-utils-0.3.1 package contains the following daemons and utilities:

- exportfs—The utility that builds the file /var/lib/nfs/xtab from the file /etc/exports, which defines the directories to be exported by an NFS server.

- lockd—The NFS daemon that manages file locking (installed as rpc.lockd).

- mountd—The NFS daemon that manages locking requests from clients.

- nfsd—The actual NFS server daemon.

- nfsstat—Retrieves and prints NFS kernel statistics.

- nhfsstone—A benchmarking application for NFS.

- rpcdebug—A utility that enables you to set or retrieve the versions of the current RPC configuration flags.

- rpcgen—A tool that generates C code that implements an RPC protocol. The input to rpcgen is a language similar to C known as the RPC Language (Remote Procedure Call Language).This utility is also installed as part of the standard Linux glibc RPM.

- rquotad—The NFS daemon that returns user quota information.

- showmount—Queries the mount daemon on a remote NFS server for server status information.

- statd—The NFS status monitor daemon that keeps track of which NFS clients are holding locks on specific files.

> **NOTE**
>
> In addition to these packages, which are located in the nfs directory of the CD that accompanies this book, the CD also includes the kernel and utility source for an early reference implementation of NFS version 4. This source code is in the file nfsv4-01-07-16.tar.gz, which is located in the nfs/nfs4_subdirectory of the CD.

Installing NFS Support on Your System

Although almost every modern Linux distribution includes support for NFS, it is conceivable that this support may not be active in your kernel. This section explains how to activate that support, and may also be useful if you are building a kernel from scratch and want to ensure NFS support in that kernel. This section also explains how to build and install the various NFS-related utility packages.

Activating NFS Support in the Kernel

This section explains how to activate support for the NFS distributed filesystem in the source code for the Linux kernel, using the sample Linux 2.4.9 kernel provided with this book as an example. For an overview of the conceptual basics behind building a modern Linux kernel and activating support for different features and hardware in the kernel, see "Configuring Your Kernel" in Appendix A, "Using the Software on the CD-ROM."

> **NOTE**
>
> It's generally a good idea to compile in support for any filesystems that your system uses regularly. You *must* install any type of filesystem that you use for your system's root partition as part of the kernel, *not* as a module. Filesystems that you only interact with occasionally (such as AppleTalk or various network filesystems) can still be compiled as modules to keep your kernel as small as possible.

> **TIP**
>
> If you have already compiled a kernel for the computer system on which you are building a new kernel, you can use the configuration information from that kernel to save time when configuring the new kernel. Reusing existing configuration data from an existing kernel is explained in Appendix A.

This section explains the options specific to activating support for the NFS distributed filesystem in the kernel we are building. This section describes how to configure NFS options using the X Window System-based Linux kernel configurator:

1. Log in as root or use the su command to become root.

2. In a terminal window running under an X Window System window manager or desktop, change to the directory /usr/src/linux-2.4.9 and execute the make xconfig command. The commands related to compiling and loading support for the Linux X Window System kernel configurator display in the window in which you executed the make xconfig command. Eventually, the X Window System Linux kernel configurator displays, as shown in Figure 12.2.

3. Click the File Systems button in the X Window System kernel configuration dialog. A new dialog displays, as shown in Figure 12.3.

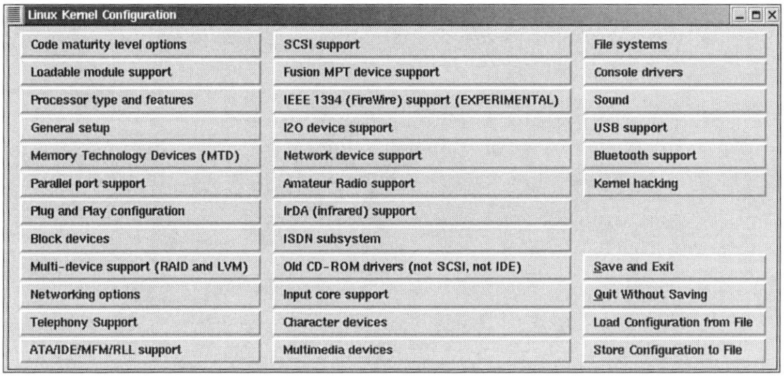

FIGURE 12.2

The X Window System-based Linux kernel configurator.

FIGURE 12.3

The File Systems dialog.

4. Click Y beside the Kernel Automounter Support entry if you want to use the in-kernel automounter for NFS version 2 and version 3 filesystems.

5. Click Y beside the Kernel Automounter Version 4 Support (also Supports v3) entry if you want to use the in-kernel automounter for NFS version 4 and version 3. NFS filesystems and are sure that you do not need to automount volumes from a version 2 NFS file server.

NOTE

You can select at most one of the two Kernel Automounter options. Optionally, you can leave both these options off and run the user-space automounter, amd, if you are not sure which versions of NFS servers you will need to contact.

6. Scroll down until you see the Network File Systems button and click it. A new dialog displays, as shown in Figure 12.4.

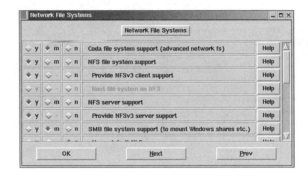

FIGURE 12.4

The Network File Systems dialog.

7. Click Y beside the NFS File System Support entry to enable your system to mount NFS volumes from remote NFS servers.

8. Click Y beside the Provide NFSv3 Client Support entry to enable your system to mount NFS volumes from remote NFS version 3 servers.

9. Click Y beside the NFS Server Support entry to enable your system to function as an NFS server. Clicking this button activates NFS version 2 support.

10. Click Y beside the Provide NFSv3 Server Support entry to enable your system to also function as an NFS version 3 server.

11. Click the Main Menu button to return to the primary make xconfig dialog.

12. After selecting any other kernel configuration options relevant to the kernel you are building (such as those specific to the hardware in your system), save your updated kernel configuration.

13. If you reused the configuration data from an existing kernel, use the Store Configuration to File button to display a dialog that enables you to explicitly save your new kernel configuration with the name .config in the main directory of the kernel that you are configuring.

14. If you configured the current kernel from scratch (that is, without reading in configuration data from another kernel), simply click the Save and Exit button.

15. Click OK to close the final dialog and return to the Linux shell prompt. You're now ready to compile the kernel!

Compiling and Installing an NFS-Aware Kernel

After configuring the Linux 2.4.9 kernel, you're ready to compile and install your new Linux kernel. All the information that you need to compile and install this kernel is provided in Appendix A. This section just provides a checklist for the steps that you should follow.

After you've installed and configured the Linux 2.4.9 kernel for NFS distributed filesystem support and to match your hardware, you must do the following to install and use that kernel:

1. Add a special extension for this kernel to its Makefile, making it easy to identify the special features in the kernel. I typically name kernels that support different filesystems along the lines of `linux-<kernel-version>-<filesystem-type>`. Using `-nfs` as the `EXTRAVERSION` entry in the Makefile is appropriate.

2. Execute the following `make` commands in this order to correctly initialize dependencies and to build and install the new kernel and any associated loadable modules:

```
make dep
make
make modules
make install
make modules_install
```

   I suggest doing these steps as discrete commands to make it easy to spot any compilation or installation failures along the way. If you're really cocky, you can reduce these commands to the following single command line, but you'd still be wise to scroll back to make sure that there were no problems:

```
make dep ; make install ; make modules ; make modules_install
```

3. Modify boot loader configuration files for the boot loader you're using on your system, as described in "Booting a New Kernel" in Appendix A and rerun `lilo` if necessary.

You're now almost ready to reboot your system and use the NFS filesystem. Before doing that, however, you must also compile and install the utilities discussed in the next section to ensure that your system can create, mount, and use JFS filesets.

Compiling and Installing the NFS Utilities

This section explains how to configure, compile, and install the various utilities that enable you to administer and use NFS filesystems on your Linux system. These utilities provide the standard user-space versions of the NFS daemons and support for the `amd` and `autofs` automounters.

12

THE NFS
DISTRIBUTED
FILESYSTEM

NOTE

I do not suggest that you compile or install these versions of these utilities unless they are not already present on your system or you absolutely must have the latest versions of the support daemons and utilities for NFS. Almost all Linux server systems come with binary versions of all these utilities preinstalled, which should be sufficient in almost all cases.

All three of the NFS-related packages are compiled and installed in exactly the same way—the only part of the instructions that differs is the name of the package. The three NFS-related packages are

- nfs-utils-0.3.1
- am-utils-6.0.7
- autofs-3.1.7-14

Depending on whether you plan to use the user-space automounter (in the package am-utils-6.0.7) or the kernel automounter (support software for which is in the package autofs-3.1.7-14), you will probably only want to install one of these.

The following is a set of generic instructions for compiling and installing any of these packages. Depending on the name of the package that you are installing, substitute the name of that package in the following instructions:

1. Mount the CD and extract the package from the file `nfs/<package>.tar.gz` to a directory on your system using a command like the following:

   ```
   cd <target-directory>
   tar zxvf <path-to-CD>/nfs/<package>.tar.gz
   ```

2. Change directory to *<target-directory>/<package>* and run the configure script to correctly configure the package's Makefile for your system and Linux distribution:

   ```
   ./configure
   ```

   This produces verbose output that's not useful to replicate here.

3. After the Makefile is correctly configured, execute the `make` command to build the new versions of the utilities in the package:

   ```
   make
   ```

   Once again, this produces verbose, system-specific output that's not useful to replicate here.

4. After all the utilities are compiled, install them on your system using the following command:

```
make install
```

Your system now has a version of the *<package>* utilities and associated reference (man page) documentation installed.

Compiling and Installing NIS

Because NFS and NIS are so interrelated, the CD that accompanies this book also includes the source code for all the NIS utilities. You should not have to compile or install these utilities unless they are not present on your system or you absolutely must have the latest versions and are not sure which are provided with your Linux distribution. The versions of the NIS utilities included on the CD that accompanies this book were the latest versions of the NIS utilities at the time that this book was written. Almost all Linux server systems come with binary versions of all these utilities preinstalled, which should be sufficient in almost all cases.

> **NOTE**
>
> If you want to check for newer versions of these utilities, see the URL
> `ftp://ftp.kernel.org/pub/linux/utils/net/NIS`.

If you decide to compile and install these packages, the procedure for compiling and installing them is the same as for any of the utilities described in the previous section. The NIS utilities are located in the CD's `nfs/nis` subdirectory and are the following:

- `ypmake-0.11.tar.gz`—A set of Perl scripts to build NIS maps; Optional
- `ypserv-2.1.tar.gz`—The NIS server
- `yp-tools-2.5.tar.gz`—The standard NIS utilities for displaying NIS files, changing your NIS password, changing the full name or shell in your NIS password file entry, and querying various aspects of an NIS server or NIS maps

Administering NFS Filesystems

This section explains how to configure, administer, and use NFS and NIS.

Configuring an NFS Server

NFS is as easy to set up and use as it is to obtain. NFS uses the user ID (UID) and group ID (GID) of each user to determine who has access to exported files and directories. This means that all your users should have the same user ID and group ID (found in their entries in the password file) on all systems to which NFS directories such as home directories are exported. This happens automatically if you are using networkwide authentication mechanisms such as NIS. Configuring and running an NIS server is explained in "Setting up NIS" later in this chapter. Configuring an NIS client is explained in "Setting Up an NIS Client," later in this chapter. If you are simply replicating password files on different machines or maintaining them in parallel, you must make sure that all your users have the same UID and GID on all your systems.

To use NFS, your machine must first be on a network, and you must do the following:

1. Create entries in the /etc/exports file for any directories on your NFS server that you want to export. Entries in the /etc/exports file have the following form:

   ```
   full-path-name-of-exported-directory   mount-options
   ```

   As you'd expect, many mount options are available. See the man page for /etc/exports (man 5 exports) for complete information. Some of the more common mount options used are

   - all_squash —Maps all NFS read or write requests to a specific user, usually "anonymous." This option is often used for public resources such as directories of Usenet news, public FTP and download areas, and so on. All files written to an NFS directory that is exported with the all_squash mount option will be assigned the UID and GID of the user anonymous or some other UID and GID specified using the anonuid and anongid mount options. The default is no_all_squash, which preserves all UIDs and GIDs.

   - insecure—Enables access to NFS directories by NFS clients running on nonstandard NFS network ports. By default, this option is off, and NFS requests must originate from ports whose port numbers are less than 1024. The insecure option may be necessary to enable access from random PC and Macintosh NFS clients. If you need to use this option, limit machines using the NFS option to a home network or secure corporate intranet. Do not use this option on any machines accessible from over the Internet because it introduces potential security problems.

   - no_root_squash—Lets root users on client workstations have the same privileges as the root user on the NFS file server. Off by default.

   - rw—Read-write. Used to export directories that you want users to be able to write to. The default is ro, which provides read-only access.

   - Specific hosts or wildcards—Specific hosts can be listed by IP address, host name, or subnet to state that only those hosts can access a specific directory exported by NFS. Entries such as 192.168.6.61 would limit access to a specific NFS directory from that host, whereas entries such as 192.168.6.* would limit access to a specific NFS directory to hosts on that subnet. By default, all hosts have access to all exported directories.

For example, you could store a copy of your Red Hat 7.2 CD-ROM in a directory and make it available to all hosts on your network using an entry like the following:

```
/home/wvh/rh72 *(ro,insecure)
```

This exports this directory in read-only mode to any NFS client, regardless of the port number from which the request originated. Similarly, you could export the Red Hat CD itself to all machines using a command like the following:

```
/mnt/cdrom *(ro,insecure)
```

Because this /etc/exports entry exports a CD-ROM via NFS, the ro keyword is somewhat redundant (but is not wrong)!

2. After you've created your /etc/exports file, you can make sure that your system is correctly configured for running NFS by issuing the following commands:

```
chkconfig nfslock on
chkconfig nfs on
```

3. Next, start the NFS lock manager, daemon, and all other server processes by executing the following commands (when logged in as root or after using the su command to become root):

```
/etc/rc.d/init.d/nfslock restart
/etc/rc.d/init.d/nfs restart
```

4. When first started, an NFS server exports any filesystems listed in the export table file /var/lib/nfs/xtab. This file has the same relationship to /etc/exports that /etc/mtab has to /etc/fstab. If you want to export other filesystems via NFS when the server is already running, you can execute the following command on your NFS file server (when logged in as root or after using su to become root):

```
/usr/sbin/exportfs -rv
```

This command rereads the /etc/exports file and synchronizes /var/lib/nfs/xtab with it. Execute this command now to make sure that your NFS server is exporting any directories that you have listed in the /etc/exports file.

NOTE

On Red Hat systems, NFS starts eight copies of the NFS daemon to service NFS requests. To improve performance when many clients are accessing NFS volumes over the network, you can up the number of copies of the NFS daemon that are started by changing the value of the RPCNFSDCOUNT variable in the startup script /etc/rc.d/init.d/nfs.

Your NFS server is now running. As a test, you can verify that your NFS server is running correctly by going to any other host on your network configured for NFS support and attempting to mount one of the directories you listed in the /etc/exports file on your NFS server. For example, if you exported your CD-ROM drive as shown in a previous example, the following command should mount the CD in the CD-ROM drive on your NFS server on the directory /cd:

```
mount -t nfs -o ro server-name:/mnt/cdrom /cd
```

After you mount the filesystem from an NFS server, you should be able to list the contents of the directory where you mounted the remote filesystem and view its contents. For more detailed information about mounting exported file servers on NFS client machines, see "Mounting Remote NFS Filesystems" later in the chapter.

When you are satisfied that your NFS server is running correctly, add symbolic links for the NFS startup scripts to the /etc/rc.d/rc3.d and /etc/rc.d/rc5.d directories, to ensure that NFS starts correctly in both your NFS server's text mode and graphical login multiuser mode.

Setting Up NIS

As mentioned earlier, NIS is the most commonly used distributed authentication mechanism today, largely because it is shipped free with almost all Unix and Unix-like systems. Another reason for the prevalence of NIS is that it's incredibly easy to set up, as shown in this section, which walks you through the process of setting up an NIS server. Setting up an NIS client is explained in the next section.

> **NOTE**
>
> This section shows how to quickly set up an NIS server for use with an NFS server. This NIS server exports the default password, group, host, and so on maps (files) found on the NIS server system. In a production environment, you would want to do substantially more customization before initiating NIS throughout your computing environment. You would also want to customize the NIS configuration files /var/yp/securenets, /etc/yp.conf, and /etc/ypserv.conf. For more complete information about setting up NIS, see the additional sources of NIS information listed in "Getting More Information About NFS and NIS" earlier in the chapter.

To set up an NIS server, log in as root, or use the su command to become root, on the system you will be configuring as an NIS server, and do the following:

1. Make sure that the NIS software is installed on your Linux system. At a minimum, you will need the /bin/domainname, /usr/sbin/ypserv, and /usr/lib/yp/ypinit programs. If these programs are not found on your system, you can either build and install

them from the source code provided on the CD that accompanies this book, as explained in "Compiling and Installing NIS" earlier in the chapter, or simply use the `rpm` command to install the ypserv and yp-tools packages from your Linux distribution CDs or after retrieving them from an RPM archive site.

2. Next, make sure that the `/etc/passwd` file has an entry for your personal account, which should also be found in the password file on the system you will be configuring as an NIS client. In the next section ("Setting Up an NIS Client"), we will use this entry to verify that NIS is running correctly.

3. Set the domain name of your new NIS domain. This should not be the same as the name of your TCP/IP domain to avoid confusing DNS and potentially compromising security in your domain. To set the NIS domain name (in this case to the domain "foo.com"), issue a command like the following:

```
/bin/domainname foo.com
```

4. Start the NIS server process using a command like the following:

```
/usr/sbin/ypserv
```

5. Initialize the NIS databases using a command like the following:

```
/usr/lib/yp/ypinit -m
```

You will see output like the following:

```
At this point, we have to construct a list of the hosts which will
run NIS servers.
  distfs.vonhagen.org is in the list of NIS server hosts.
Please continue to add the names for the other hosts, one per line.
When you are done with the list, type a <control D>.
next host to add:  distfs.vonhagen.org
next host to add:
```

The NIS hosts list uses standard host and domain names from your existing domain.

6. When prompted for the name of any other NIS servers in your domain, press Ctrl+D. You will see output like the following:

```
The current list of NIS servers looks like this:
distfs.vonhagen.org
Is this correct?  [y/n: y]
```

7. Press Enter to respond Yes. You will then see output listing the files that have been generated and added to the NIS database. This output looks like the following, where the domain name you specified will appear instead of the word *yourdomain*:

```
We need some  minutes to build the databases...
Building /var/yp/ws.com/ypservers...
Running /var/yp/Makefile...
gmake[1]: Entering directory `/var/yp/yourdomain'
```

```
Updating passwd.byname...
Updating passwd.byuid...
Updating group.byname...
Updating group.bygid...
Updating hosts.byname...
Updating hosts.byaddr...
Updating rpc.byname...
Updating rpc.bynumber...
Updating services.byname...
Updating services.byservicename...
Updating netid.byname...
Updating protocols.bynumber...
Updating protocols.byname...
Updating mail.aliases...
gmake[1]: Leaving directory `/var/yp/yourdomain'
```

That's all there is to it! Your new NIS server is up and running. You can now test that it is working correctly by following the instructions in the next section.

Setting Up an NIS Client

One of my favorite Zen sayings is "If a server is running and there are no clients to use it, is it really working?" This section explains how to set up an NIS client of the server started in the previous section, after doing some initial configuration to be able to verify that the server is actually doing "the right thing."

To do some preconfiguration to verify that NIS is actually working, log in as root, or use the su command to become root, and edit the /etc/nsswitch.conf file on the system you are using as an NIS client. Find the line that tells your system how to locate password entries and modify that line to look like the following:

```
passwd:     nis [NOTFOUND=return] files
```

This tells your system to look for password information in NIS and fail if the appropriate information isn't found.

Next, save a copy of your system's password file and then remove all user accounts from the existing password file. As the last line of the newly abbreviated password file, add the following:

```
+::::::
```

This tells NIS to append the contents of the password map (file) retrieved from the NIS server whenever password information is requested.

Notice that the entries for any individual accounts (including your own) have been removed from the abbreviated password file. This enables you to do a fairly simple test to determine whether NIS is working. If you can log in using an account that is not present in the password file on your client system but that is present in the password file on your NIS server system, then you can determine that NIS is working correctly.

To set up an NIS client, log in as root, or use the su command to become root, on the system you are using as an NIS client and do the following:

1. Make sure that the NIS client software is installed on your Linux system. At a minimum, you will need the /bin/domainname and /sbin/ypbind programs. If these programs are not found on your system, you can either build and install them from the yp-tools source code on the CD that accompanies this book, or you can retrieve the yp-tools package from your Linux distribution CD or an RPM archive site and install it.

2. Make sure that the directory /var/yp exists and create it if it does not.

3. Set the domain name of the NIS domain to which this new client will belong. This should be the same name as the domain name set in the previous section of this chapter. To set the NIS domain name (in this case to the domain "foo.com"), issue a command like the following:

```
/bin/domainname foo.com
```

4. Start the NIS client process using a command like the following:

```
/sbin/ypbind
```

5. To verify that NIS is working correctly, use telnet or shh to connect from the NIS client system back to itself and attempt to log in as yourself. Remember that your password file entry is present in the password file on the NIS server, but not in the password file on the NIS client.

You should be able to log in successfully. Congratulations! You're running NIS!

As mentioned previously, in a production NIS environment, you would do substantially more customization of the NIS configuration files. You would also add setting the NIS domain name and starting the NIS server and client to the startup procedures for any NIS client systems. You can automate starting NIS by doing the following:

1. Execute the following commands as the root user to create symbolic links that automate starting and shutting down NIS when you boot, shutdown, or change run levels on your system:

```
cd /etc/rc.d/rc3.d
ln -s ../init.d/ypbind S73ypbind
ln -s ../init.d/ypserv S74ypserv
ln -s ../init.d/yppasswdd S34yppasswdd
cd ../etc/rc.d/rc5.d
ln -s ../init.d/ypbind S73ypbind
ln -s ../init.d/ypserv S74ypserv
ln -s ../init.d/yppasswdd S34yppasswdd
```

12

THE NFS
DISTRIBUTED
FILESYSTEM

For convenience, you may want to modify the file /etc/rc.d/init.d/ypbind to explicitly set the domain name of the domain to which your computer system belongs.

> **NOTE**
>
> You should create the symbolic links for S74ypserv only on the system running your NIS server.

For more information about installing and configuring NIS clients, see "Getting More Information About NFS and NIS" earlier in the chapter.

Mounting Remote NFS Filesystems

You can manually mount an NFS volume by logging in as root or by using the su command to become root and executing a command like the following:

```
mount -t nfs -o mount-options hostname:/remote-filesystem /local-filesystem
```

> **NOTE**
>
> As discussed earlier in this chapter, NFS uses the user ID (UID) and group ID (GID) of each user to determine who has access to exported files and directories. To write data stored in NFS, you must either have the same UID and GID on all the systems that you want to share data with using NFS, you must be using NIS for authentication, or you must be the root user and have enabled root access to NFS data.

For example, to mount the remote filesystem /archive from the NFS server foobar in read/write mode, you would execute the following command:

```
mount -t nfs -o rw foobar:/archive /archive
```

When you're sure of the exported NFS directories that you want to permanently mount on your system, you should add entries to your system's /etc/fstab file for those filesystems. Entries in /etc/fstab for NFS filesystems have the following form:

```
foobar:/var/mail      /var/mail      nfs      rw,hard  0 0
foobar:/export/home   /export/home   nfs      rw,hard  0 0
```

The filesystem type is nfs, and the mount options indicate that the NFS filesystem is readable and writable (rw), whereas the hard option indicates that the system will continue trying failed file operations indefinitely.

The OpenAFS Distributed Filesystem

IN THIS CHAPTER

OpenAFS is the latest generation of a distributed filesystem that has been in constant use for more than 15 years. AFS was originally developed at Carnegie-Mellon University in the early-to-mid 1980s as a combination research project and solution for the infrastructure needs of the university. Today, AFS has grown into a commercial product with a well-established user base, storing terabytes of data. Originally marketed by Transarc Corporation in Pittsburgh, Pennsylvania, AFS became the property of IBM when it acquired Transarc in 1994.

In 2000, IBM released the then-current base source code for AFS to the Open Source community, where it is known as OpenAFS. IBM still sells and supports AFS as a commercial product, but OpenAFS has been taken to heart by the Open Source community and is flourishing in that environment.

Because AFS and OpenAFS spring from a common source code base, the basic design principles, administrative principles, and even process names are identical in the two environments. However, AFS is still a commercial product of IBM's, so I will use the term OpenAFS throughout, except where discussing some historical aspect of OpenAFS that therefore specifically refers to AFS. In places where pathnames or procedures are different between the two, I will highlight and explain these differences. This chapter will therefore be a useful guide to the principles behind both OpenAFS and AFS, and should also be useful for system administrators who need to combine AFS and OpenAFS systems into a single administrative unit.

This chapter begins with an overview of OpenAFS, explaining its design, organization, and basic principles; the various system processes necessary to support its features; and how it interacts with a variety of operating systems and environments. The next section discusses the software that makes up OpenAFS clients and servers, development projects related to OpenAFS, and IBM's AFS products. The last two sections of this chapter discuss how to build and install OpenAFS on client and server systems, and then provide detailed information about running and administering OpenAFS.

Overview

AFS is one of the most intriguing and useful distributed filesystems in the history of Unix. One of its most intriguing aspects is that it is truly cross-platform on as large a scale as any other filesystem has ever been. Now that IBM has released a version of the AFS source code as open source, free versions of OpenAFS are readily available for Linux, all other Unix and Unix-like operating systems, Mac OS X, and even Windows. Thanks to OpenAFS, you can participate in the global, Internet-wide distributed filesystem of the future for free, regardless of what type of system you are using.

OpenAFS is based on the client/server model, explained in Chapter 11, "Overview of Distributed Filesystems." *Servers* are computer systems or processes that provide specialized services to other machines or processes, which are therefore known as *clients*. The OpenAFS environment uses specialized machines, called *file servers*, to deliver files and directories to OpenAFS clients in response to requests for those files by the people using client machines. Computer systems within the OpenAFS environment are not exclusively client or server machines but are traditionally organized that way for simplicity and ease of system administration.

As discussed in Chapter 12, "The NFS Distributed Filesystem," NFS is the oldest and most widely used distributed filesystem today. NFS grew out of an existing operating and administrative environment, which was the early Unix environment supported on workstations from Sun Microsystems. The fundamental pieces of information that you need to know to support a distributed filesystem in a small networked environment are the following:

- The identity of all your users, so that you can manage access to the files and directories you are sharing

- The location of all the filesystems you are sharing, so that systems can mount and access them appropriately

NFS was originally designed to support sharing filesystems in small networked environments where it was easy to replicate user and system information across all participating systems. Over time, as networks became larger and administering participating systems in parallel became more difficult, NFS gradually evolved network-oriented administrative environments, NIS and NIS+. These environments made it possible to bind multiple computers running NFS into a single administrative entity, without replicating user information on every single machine.

AFS was originally designed to unify the computing environment of a university, made up of many different departments, each of which may have hundreds of computer systems and potentially thousands of users. This sort of scale made it impossible from the beginning to replicate authentication information across all participating systems. AFS was therefore designed from the beginning to provide a much broader authentication environment that supports wide-area information sharing while enabling participating administrative entities, such as departments, to manage their own resources.

However, even with a networked authentication mechanism, the problem of locating filesystems within a huge network environment persisted. A fundamental way in which OpenAFS and AFS differ from NFS is in how they identify the location of the servers on which distributed filesystems are stored. NFS filesystems are mounted by directly identifying the name or IP address of the server on which a specific filesystem is stored. That information is hardcoded into the /etc/fstab files of the clients that mount those filesystems.

OpenAFS provides a location-independent mechanism for finding OpenAFS filesystems, which are known as *volumes*. (Volumes are discussed in more detail in "Managing and Organizing Data in OpenAFS" later in the chapter.) OpenAFS uses a volume location database that is consulted whenever a user requests access to a file or directory. AFS identifies the volume in which that file or directory is located based on the last volume that is mounted in that file or directory path, and consults the volume location database to locate the file server where that volume is stored.

This eliminates the need for each system to know which file server houses the volume you're looking for, which is known as providing transparent access to those files. Using a volume location database also provides administrative advantages, by making it possible to move volumes from one file server to another for administrative purposes, even while clients are using files in those volumes. When a volume is moved, the volume location database is updated, and subsequent requests for the volume go to the file server on which it is currently located.

Liberating OpenAFS clients from having to hard-code the servers on which OpenAFS files and directories are located makes it possible for OpenAFS to support a global namespace for the OpenAFS filesystem. NFS clients mount separate filesystems at separate points in the local directory hierarchy on a client and do this identically on all the clients that need access to those filesystems. OpenAFS takes a fundamentally different approach by internally mounting its filesystems in a global namespace to which all systems have access, enabling each client to access that filesystem through a single, identical mountpoint. This is known as providing a uniform namespace because all clients have exactly the same view of the distributed OpenAFS filesystem, which is usually mounted as /afs, by convention. Providing a uniform namespace simplifies information sharing across wide-area networks such as the Internet because the focus and organization of the filesystem begins at a higher level than the root directory of a single machine.

Caching in OpenAFS

Because OpenAFS is a distributed filesystem designed for wide-area operation, minimizing the amount of network resources it consumes is important. This was even more critical when AFS was being developed because the networks of the time had much lower bandwidth than is available on today's networks, and the need to both optimize and minimize communications was critical, especially as more machines began to use the AFS environment. AFS developed its own communication protocol, known as RX, to communicate efficiently over the network. At the same time, AFS also introduced extensive caching to minimize redundant network communications. All these features have been inherited by OpenAFS.

As explained in Chapter 10, "Comparing Journaling Filesystem Performance" a filesystem *cache* is a portion of a system's disk or memory that temporarily houses files being used on that computer system. Suppose that a user opens a file for editing, requiring that the first few blocks of the file be fetched from the file server on which it is located. After the user edits that portion of the file, there is a fairly high chance that the user will want to edit the remainder of the file. For this reason, OpenAFS file servers tend to retrieve an entire file, whenever possible, and store it in a cache on the client machine. When the user continues to edit the file, the remainder of the file is already present in the local cache, and no additional network communication is required until it's necessary to save the file back to the server.

OpenAFS also uses a persistent cache to minimize network traffic. A *persistent cache* is one whose contents are preserved on the system even if the system is rebooted. Suppose that a client system crashes or is restarted for some administrative purpose. When the system is available to the user again, there is a high probability that she will want to continue to work with the same files that she was working on before. If the file is still present in the cache after a reboot, no network traffic is necessary to retrieve it again. If the user wants to edit another file, it would have had to be retrieved from a file server anyway, so nothing is lost by preserving the file in the local cache.

Caching is not free. Retrieving more of a file than a user needs takes more time than is absolutely necessary to get the user the data that he requires. And writing it into a cache requires more time than simply storing it in memory. However, the savings in access time and network bandwidth typically far outweigh the amount of time spent in OpenAFS caching.

> **NOTE**
>
> A cache is a feature but is not an absolute necessity. Without one, you simply lose its benefits. Even diskless workstations can access AFS and OpenAFS if they are running NFS and the NFS/AFS Translator, which you can obtain more information about from the IBM Web site. Diskless workstations aren't as popular as they once were, due to the relatively low cost of hardware today, but they still deserve an even break.

A persistent cache has another significant advantage: it helps guarantee that users will not lose their modifications to the files that they were working on in the event of a system crash or network outage. When the system comes back up or can contact the server again, the process that manages the cache (known as the *cache manager*, oddly enough) ordinarily determines that the cached file is more recent than the version on the server and delivers the version from the cache instead of fetching it from the server again. Being able to make these sorts of comparisons requires that time be closely synchronized on all clients and servers at a site running OpenAFS, which accounts for another OpenAFS-related process, a time server.

So far, we've seen that OpenAFS requires a file server process, a volume location server process, an authentication server process, and a time server process somewhere on the network. All these server processes (and more) are critical to the successful operation of OpenAFS clients, so OpenAFS also provides another server process to monitor server processes and ensure that they are always running. This overseer process periodically checks that other mandatory processes are running and starts new ones if they are not.

OpenAFS client systems run a single cache manager process that starts the other daemons required on an OpenAFS client. They must also run a client process for the network time server to synchronize their clock with the rest of the OpenAFS environment, specifically the file servers. Mounting the OpenAFS filesystem on an OpenAFS client causes the kernel to load a module that translates requests for files under the /afs directory into the specific volume location database and OpenAFS file server calls.

Managing Cache Consistency in OpenAFS

As discussed in the previous section, caching increases the speed and efficiency of file access in OpenAFS, reduces system restart times, and helps protect against data loss due to system failures. However, because OpenAFS provides the same view of its filesystem to all clients at the same time, caching also increases the chance that multiple OpenAFS clients will request and cache the same file at the same time. A crude solution to this sort of problem would be to lock files after they are requested by a client, but this is both antisocial and prohibitive. There is no real reason to prevent multiple people from viewing the same file at the same time—the only situation that must be prevented is allowing multiple users to write the same file at the same time.

Maintaining consistency between the copies of a file that may exist on multiple clients is done by using callbacks. A *callback* is essentially just a promise by a file server to a cache manager that it will notify the cache manager if any of the data that it has delivered to the cache manager changes. If a file for which a callback is established changes on the file server, the file server breaks all other callbacks for that file with any other clients.

NOTE

OpenAFS optimizes callbacks associated with files in read-only volumes. The callbacks registered with a file in a read-only volume are associated with the entire volume in which that file is located. If the client requests additional files from that same volume, no additional callbacks need to be sent. Callbacks for read-only volumes are only broken when that volume is released, because that's the only time at which the contents of the volume could actually change.

Callbacks guarantee that the cache manager can tell whether it has the latest version of a file and re-retrieves the file whenever necessary. If a user tries to write a file for which the callback has been broken, he generally receives an application-specific message informing him that the file has changed. In this case, if you've made extensive changes to a file or if the file is in some binary format (such as a word-processing file or spreadsheet), it's a good idea to save your copy under another name, reopen the original file, and attempt to merge in your changes from the copy you just saved.

Managing and Organizing Data in OpenAFS

The data on OpenAFS file servers is organized into volumes, which are conceptually similar to filesystems. *Volumes* contain discrete portions of the filesystem hierarchy of OpenAFS, can be managed as discrete units, and are mounted in OpenAFS systems just like filesystems are in standard Linux filesystems. The disk space in which volumes are created consists of physical or logical partitions (if you are using a logical volume management) that are mounted at the root of an OpenAFS file server's directory structure and have names of the form /vicep*XX*, where *XX* is one or two letters, depending on the number of physical and logical partitions that you are using with that specific file server. Typically, the first physical or logical partition on an AFS file server is mounted as /vicepa, the second as /vicepb, and on through the end of the alphabet. If you're lucky enough to have more partitions than that, the next would be /vicepaa, followed by /vicepab, and so on.

Organizing portions of the OpenAFS filesystem into volumes provides system administrators with a number of advantages over simply using standard partitions and even logical volumes:

- Volumes are independently managed entities that can be moved from one OpenAFS partition to another and even from one AFS file server to another. Volumes can easily be moved while they are mounted and actively in use. Being able to move volumes from one partition to another makes it easy to free up space to dynamically increase the size of other volumes. This also enables you to move volumes to provide load balancing or to move heavily used volumes to more powerful file servers. In AFS and OpenAFS, *load balancing* is the term used to describe more evenly distributing client requests across multiple file servers using a variety of administrative techniques.

- Volumes can be replicated to provide multiple, read-only copies of heavily used volumes, which can be distributed to multiple file servers. OpenAFS clients can be instructed to prioritize file servers differently, providing another opportunity for load balancing. The capability to replicate volumes generally increases the reliability and usability of your computing environment by reducing the likelihood that the failure of any single file server could make critical software unavailable.

- Volumes support transparent file access because they are independent of any specific file server or partition. As mentioned earlier, OpenAFS clients locate volumes by querying the Volume Location Database rather than by looking for them on a specific file server.

- Volumes provide an efficient unit for storage management because they are independent of the physical size of any given partition. Just as with standard Linux logical volume management, discussed in Chapter 9, "Logical Volume Management," OpenAFS volumes can easily be resized independently of the organization of the physical disk space on which they are located. Creating OpenAFS volumes on partitions that themselves use the logical volume management capabilities of an operating system such as Linux provides the ultimate in flexible storage management.

OpenAFS volumes are mounted on specially created mountpoints within the OpenAFS filesystem. OpenAFS volumes cannot be mounted on standard Linux directories like other filesystems because OpenAFS mountpoints provide clients with more information than a standard Unix directory. Linux and Unix systems can mount filesystems on standard directories because the system tracks mounted volumes separately, through files like /etc/fstab and /etc/mtab. This is not feasible in the OpenAFS environment, which can literally contain thousands of volumes. You can always use symbolic links to simulate the behavior of mounting an OpenAFS volume on a standard Linux directory.

OpenAFS mountpoints are actually similar in organization to standard Linux and Unix symbolic links. A symbolic link contains the name of the file that it points to. An OpenAFS mountpoint contains the name of the volume mounted at that point. This simplifies querying the Volume Location Database for the name of the file server where that volume is stored.

Using Replication in OpenAFS

One of the most interesting benefits of OpenAFS is the capability to create and maintain read-only versions of existing volumes. This process is known as replicating those volumes, and the copies are known as *replicas* or *clones* of the source volumes. Replicas do the following:

- Increase the availability of the data in the read/write volumes that they are copies of, by making multiple copies of that data available
- Help load balance file servers by distributing copies of heavily used volumes across multiple file servers

Replicas are created using the vos addsite command and are initially located on the same file server and partition as their parent volume. When first created in these locations, replicas consist only of a copy of the vnode index of the parent volume (the equivalent of a File Allocation Table for an OpenAFS volume). This is a similar mechanism to that used when creating OpenAFS backup volumes using the vos backup and vos backupsys commands and provides an efficient mechanism for maintaining a copy of a volume at a specific point in time. Because the replica is a copy of the volume's vnode index at that point in time, it already points to all the correct data blocks that represent the contents of the volume at that moment in time. No copying of data between the two is required because the copy will still point to the correct blocks even if the parent volume is updated.

Replicas only begin to consume real space when the volume that they are replicas of is released and they are moved to another partition or file server. Because pointers to data blocks within a file server partition are partition-specific, moving a replica to another partition or file server causes it to grow to the size of the parent volume at the moment that the replica is created. Read-only clones are consistent with the contents of the volumes that they are cloned from at the last time the volume was released.

Releasing a volume simply means that the current contents of a read/write volume are pushed from that volume to any clones of that volume that exist. This forces any read-only clones of that volume to be updated, regardless of the file server on which those clones are located. The release operation is done using the `vos release` command, which looks up the volume being released in the volume location database, finds any clones of it that currently exist, and updates them from a newly cloned copy of the parent volume. Updating clones of a volume is not an incremental operation because this would be too slow —replacing all existing clones of a volume with completely new clones of that volume is faster than trying to identify each difference between the two. Releasing a volume can still be time consuming, based on the number of replicas that exist of a given volume. For this reason, replication is primarily useful for volumes containing frequently used files that change infrequently.

Read-only volumes are primarily used in two ways:

- By modifying the OpenAFS server preferences file on each client so that they each prioritize a different file server from the set containing read-only replicas of a volume.

- When the server containing the read-write volume is unavailable, RPCs to that server time out, and the volume location database automatically suggests another server on which a replica of that volume is located.

Replicas provide a number of operational efficiencies for computing environments that run OpenAFS. The next section describes the use and advantages of another type of replica, a special-purpose clone of an existing read-write volume called a backup volume.

Making Backup Copies of OpenAFS Volumes

A *backup volume* is a replica located on the same partition and file server as the volume that it is a clone of. Like replicas, backup volumes start out as copies of the vnode index of their parent volume and retain pointers to deleted or modified data that has been modified in the parent volume. Backup volumes are only distinguished from other types of read-only replicas in that they typically have the extension `.backup` or `.bak` appended to their names.

There are two reasons for creating backup volumes:

- For use in the backup process. OpenAFS volumes cannot be used while they are being backed up because they work at the block level rather than the filename level. Creating backup volumes that are copies of the volumes you want to back up enables you to do backups of the backup volume while the primary volume continues to be used.

- To enable users to restore files that they accidentally deleted or overwrote, without requiring help from an operator or system administrator. This saves a tremendous amount of time—unfortunately, restoring lost files is one of the most common tasks done by operators and/or system administrators. Many OpenAFS sites automatically make a backup copy of user volumes each night, just prior to running backups. The backup of each user volume is then automatically mounted in a special, well-known location in the user's read/write volume, and users can simply change directory through that mountpoint and retrieve "lost" files from the previous day, with no problems. For example, at Transarc, the backup volume for a user's volume is always mounted at ~/OldFiles.

The OpenAFS Volume Server automatically creates a clone volume when you issue the vos backup or vos backupsys commands (to create backup volumes) or vos addsite command followed by the vos release command (read-only volumes).

> **NOTE**
>
> OpenAFS has its own backup system to support backing up and restoring OpenAFS volumes. OpenAFS volumes, files, and directories cannot be backed up or restored using the standard Linux dump and restore commands but can be archived using the Linux tar or cpio commands because these access files and directories by name rather than by inode or other filesystem data structures. Using the OpenAFS backup system involves defining dump sets that consist of scheduled sets of volumes to be backed up together, executing the vos backupsys command to create backup volumes for a number of volumes, starting backup tape coordinator (butc) processes to control the device that you are backing files up to, and then invoking the backup command to back up those volumes by coordinating with the backup server (buserver) process.
>
> OpenAFS backup and restore procedures are fully described in the OpenAFS System Administrator's Guide. Discussing them in detail here is outside the scope of this book. An alternative to using the OpenAFS backup system is integrating OpenAFS backups into a general backup management system, such as Amanda, that can use standard Linux commands such as tar to back up a number of different types of systems as a single backup set. For more information about Amanda, see Chapter 15, "Backing Up, Restoring, and Managing Linux Filesystems."

Authentication in OpenAFS

AFS was originally designed to unify the computing environment at Carnegie-Mellon University by providing a uniform namespace to all AFS client machines to simplify file sharing and access. At the same time, it's easy to see that different departments within the university would have different needs, different sets of users, and potentially different access policies for those users.

The need for enabling groups of systems and users to have their own administrative domains while still participating in the global filesystem namespace provided by AFS led to the idea of AFS cells, which are independently administered sets of file servers and client machines running

AFS, and now OpenAFS. AFS client and server machines are associated with only a single cell, which is therefore responsible for their administration and maintenance. However, users can have accounts in multiple cells.

In standard Linux and Unix authentication, users can belong to multiple groups based on the contents of the /etc/group file, but can only function as a member of a single group at any given time. The Linux and Unix newgrp command is used to change the group that a logged-in user currently belongs to. To enable AFS and OpenAFS users to simultaneously have administrative privileges in multiple cells, AFS introduced the notion of tokens, which each consist of an AFS identify and its associated privileges. By holding multiple tokens at the same time, an AFS or OpenAFS user can simultaneously hold the privileges associated with each of those tokens.

Security is critical to any computer system or filesystem and is most vulnerable in the wide-area, networked environment encouraged by AFS and OpenAFS. Anyone with root privileges on any workstation can compile and install a packet sniffer and begin watching network traffic, hoping to grab passwords or any other authentication mechanism communicated over the network. In a networked environment, authentication generally uses the "guilty until proven innocent" principle. In other words, you are disallowed access to something until you can establish your right to access it.

AFS and OpenAFS use a principle called *mutual authentication* to enable access to protected objects and privileged services. Mutual authentication requires that all parties in any transaction, such as a client and a server, prove their identities by demonstrating that they know a shared secret, most commonly an encryption key.

OpenAFS uses this sort of mutual authentication to verify the identity of a user when he logs in, using an encryption key based on the user's password.

The simplest form of mutual authentication involves two different parties, an OpenAFS client and the authentication server. When a user attempts to log in, the OpenAFS client sends a message to the server that is encrypted using the user's password as an encryption key. The authentication server can only decrypt and process the request if it too knows the same encryption key, the user's password in this case. The server then processes the request and sends back the results, encrypted with the authentication server's idea of the user's password. The client then decodes the response with its original key. None of these communications would be possible if the client and server did not both know the encryption key (password), so both the client and server can safely be assumed to be genuine.

Using key-based encryption of messages in OpenAFS provides security at several different levels by

- Enabling clients and servers to demonstrate their authenticity by using the same encryption key at both ends.

- Preventing the encryption key itself from ever being sent over the network, making it impossible to intercept a packet containing the key (the equivalent of sniffing networks for packets containing passwords).

- Encrypting all network communication in OpenAFS. The clever hacker with root privileges and a packet sniffer can examine all the packets he wants but won't be able to find and abscond with any clear-text data.

OpenAFS security is a bootstrapping process. When a user first logs in, only the client system and the authentication are parties in the authentication transaction, so only two parties need to be involved. Any subsequent OpenAFS communication uses more complex mutual authentication that involves three encryption keys and three parties. Complex mutual authentication goes like this:

1. When a client wants to communicate with a server, it first contacts a third party called a *ticket granter* (which is typically the OpenAFS authentication server). The ticket granter and the client authenticate using the simple mutual authentication procedure based on a key derived from the user's password, which only the client and the ticket granter know.

2. After authentication between the client and the ticket granter completes successfully, the ticket granter returns four pieces of information to the client:

   - A ticket to use when communicating with the server. This ticket is encrypted with the server's encryption key, which is known only to the ticket granter and the server, not to the client.

   - A session key, which is randomly generated to serve as the shared secret used in communications between the client and the server that the client wants to contact. As a further security measure, the ticket granter also embeds a copy of the session key within the ticket. A separate session key is generated for each transaction between a client and a server.

   - The name of the server for which the ticket is valid. This identifies the server that knows the encryption key used to encrypt the ticket.

   - A lifetime indicator that gives the duration of the ticket. By default, OpenAFS tickets are good for 100 hours. If the client needs to contact the server after the ticket lifetime has elapsed, the client must return to the ticket granter to get a new ticket.

   These pieces of information make up a *token*, which is the fundamental high-level unit of AFS and OpenAFS authentication. When sending all the tokens to the client, the ticket granter encrypts the token with another key known only to the ticket granter and the client, and which is usually generated from the user's password.

3. The client decrypts the information returned by the ticket granter and then contacts the server with both the ticket (which was encrypted by the server encryption key that only

the server and the ticket granter know) and the client's request, which is encrypted using the session key.

4. The server obtains the session key by decrypting the ticket using the server's encryption key and extracting the copy of the session key that the ticket granter embedded in the ticket. The server then uses the session key to decrypt the client's request.

5. After the server decrypts the client's message, it fulfills the request and sends it back to the client, encrypting it with the session key.

6. The client decrypts the return communication using the session key originally returned by the ticket granter. Voila!

At this point, assuming that all messages were decrypted correctly, everyone is happy with the identity of each other party:

- The ticket granter knows that the client is authentic because the original communication between the two was encrypted using the client's key, which both of them knew.

- The server knows that the ticket granter is genuine because the ticket granter encrypted the ticket with the server's encryption key, which both of them knew.

- The client knows that the server is genuine because the client could decrypt the return message from the server that was encrypted with the session key, which the server could only have obtained if it knew the encryption key to decrypt the ticket.

If any party in this exchange didn't share a secret with one of the other parties, some part of the transaction could not have been decrypted, and the transaction would have failed for that reason.

Using OpenAFS Access Control Lists

Proving your identity using the shared secret mechanism described in the previous section is only the first step in getting access to data. The next step is making sure that the identity you've demonstrated actually has access to the data that you requested. At the moment, standard Linux and Unix systems provide three groups of file and directory protections:

- The read, write, and execute permissions that the owner of a file has on that file or directory

- The read, write, and execute permissions that a certain group has on that file or directory

- The read, write, and execute permissions that any other person has who is not the owner of the file or directory and who is not a member of the group associated with that file or directory

These protections are fine in small networks and system clusters but are too restrictive in the context of a wide-area filesystem like OpenAFS, where there can be tens of thousands of users and an essentially unlimited number of groups. To provide the flexibility and power required in

13

such a large-scale environment, OpenAFS provides directory-level Access Control Lists (ACLs) that can be used to assign specific access privileges for a directory and its contents to up to 20 authenticated OpenAFS users or user-defined groups of OpenAFS users. These ACLs provide seven permissions rather than the three that Unix uses and are set and modified using the OpenAFS `fs setacl` command, as explained in "Setting and Modifying OpenAFS ACLs" later in the chapter.

> **NOTE**
>
> OpenAFS ACLs predate the POSIX ACL standard by more than a decade and so do not conform to that standard. Support for POSIX ACLs in standard Linux filesystems is actively under development (see `http://acl.bestbits.at` and the FAQ at `http://acl.bestbits.at/faq.html`) and is already provided by filesystems such as XFS, as explained in the section "Configuring File and Directory Access Control in XFS Filesystems" in Chapter 7, "The XFS Journaling Filesystem." When POSIX ACLs are a standard part of Linux, some effort will be required to synchronize OpenAFS ACLs with those used in local filesystems. Anyone interested in volunteering for this contentious and incredibly involved task may as well start buying clothing with a target printed on the front and back.

User-defined groups in OpenAFS can consist of any number of OpenAFS users, client machines, or IP addresses. All the groups defined by users within an AFS cell are permanently stored by the OpenAFS protection server (`ptserver`) so that they are available even when the owner of a directory is not logged in and can be reused even if the original directory that they were associated with has been deleted.

OpenAFS also defines two generic system groups that can be used in ACLs. These are the groups `system:anyuser` and `system:authuser`. Anyone who has access to an OpenAFS client is a member of `system:anyuser` even if he is not authenticated in your OpenAFS cell (hence the *any* is `system:anyuser`). Users who are authenticated to other OpenAFS cells but do not have accounts in your cell are therefore also members of `system:anyuser`. Any user authenticated to your OpenAFS cell in any fashion is a member of `system:authuser` (for authorized user) group. In addition to these generic groups, OpenAFS provides a third system group, `system:administrators`, which not too surprisingly defines all the system administrators for a cell.

An OpenAFS ACL provides the following seven permissions:

- a (administer)—Enables a user or group member to modify the ACL for a directory. Members of the `system:administrators` group always have this permission for any OpenAFS ACL. The owner of a directory always has this permission on that directory.

- d (delete)—Enables a user or group member to delete files and subdirectories within a directory, the latter only if the ACLs for the subdirectory grant the user permission to remove its contents. This permission is also required for a user or group member to move files from a directory to another location because this effectively deletes them from the current directory.

- i (insert)—Enables a user or group member to create files and directories within a directory. The capability to create files and directories within subdirectories is controlled by the ACLs for those subdirectories.

- k (lock)—Enables a user or group member to run programs that issue system calls to lock files in the directory.

- l (lookup)—Provides basic access to a directory, enabling a user or group member to list the contents of a directory or to display the ACL for that directory. The capability to examine files within a directory is still controlled by the r ACL permission. The capability to examine any subdirectory within a directory is controlled by the ACL for that subdirectory.

- r (read)—Enables a user or group member to read the contents of files in the directory.

- w (write)—Enables a user or group member to modify the contents of files in the directory and to change the Linux protections associated with those files.

When used on an OpenAFS directory, these ACL bits are represented in the order rlidwka.

NOTE

Any OpenAFS directories accessed or written to by system processes running on an OpenAFS client or server machine must have appropriate ACL settings for the system:anyuser group unless a process is running as a specific OpenAFS user.

When you create a subdirectory in OpenAFS, it initially inherits the ACL of its parent directory. Also, because ACLs apply to directories, moving a file from one directory to another causes the ACL of the new directory to apply to the file.

When accessing the files in an OpenAFS directory, OpenAFS checks the standard Linux mode bits after the rights associated with the ACL have been evaluated. (The Linux mode bits for a directory are ignored because they are superseded by the ACL.) For files in OpenAFS, the Linux mode bits have the following meanings:

- The read bit for the owner of a file (-r-------) must be set for anyone to read that file. (A user who wants to read a file must also have the 'r' and 'l' ACL permissions for the directory where the file is located.)

- The write bit for the owner of a file (- -w- - - - - - -) must be set for anyone to write the file. (A user who wants to write a file must also have the w and l ACL permissions for the directory where the file is located.)

All other Linux mode bits are ignored.

> **NOTE**
>
> In addition to these standard ACL permissions, OpenAFS ACLs also have eight other permissions that have no predefined meanings, represented by the case-sensitive letters A, B, C, D, E, F, G, and H. These ACL permissions can be accessed from within applications and assigned special, application-specific significance.

Although you will eventually become familiar with all the standard ACL permissions, OpenAFS provides special symbolic permissions that represent specific subsets of the standard ACLs. These are the following:

- all—Represents all seven standard permissions (rlidwka)
- none—Removes a specified user or group from an ACL, leaving the user with no permissions other than those available to system:anyuser or system:authuser
- read—Represents the r (read) and l (lookup) permissions
- write—Represents all permissions except a (administer)—(rlidwk)

> **NOTE**
>
> In addition to using ACLs to grant permissions to users and group members, ACLs can also be used to deny privileges to users and group members by using the fs setacl command's -negative option. Although the standard mechanism for denying access is by removing specific users and groups from an ACL, there may be cases in which you want to grant privileges to group members while denying them to a specific member of that group. See the section, "Setting and Modifying OpenAFS ACLs" later in the chapter for more information.
>
> When evaluating ACL permissions, OpenAFS first calculates the permissions granted by normal ACL settings and then subtracts rights for any users or group members who have been explicitly denied certain rights. Also, note that any permissions granted to system:anyuser takes precedence over any negative ACL settings if the user simply discards her OpenAFS tokens by using the unlog command.

OpenAFS Server Processes

As mentioned in the overview at the beginning of this chapter, OpenAFS file server machines run a number of processes. The following is a list of each server process and its function:

- Authentication server (kaserver)—Verifies user identity during login, grants Kerberos tokens, maintains the authentication database where encrypted user and server passwords are stored, and supports mutual authentication between OpenAFS clients and servers.

- Backup server—Maintains the backup database that contains a list of volumes that have been backed up and when. The backup database makes it easy to identify the sequence of backup tapes necessary for any subsequent volume restore operations.

- Basic overseer server (bosserver)—Ensures that all other server processes are running on the file server and restarts them whenever necessary. The bosserver also understands dependencies between file server processes and restarts them in the correct order. System administrators can query the bosserver for status information and can also use it to manually install, start, or stop any processes that it knows about. The bosserver also automates the process of adding or changing the server encryption keys used during authentication and manages the UserList and CellServDB files used to respectively identify privileged users and OpenAFS file server machines.

- File server process—Delivers data from the file server to a client, registers a callback, monitors the callback, and stores files that have been changed by the client. The file server process is also responsible for verifying that the client has the proper authentication to modify a file and, if not, preventing the modification and all filesystem metadata operations, such as updating access times, modification times, and other file status information.

- Network time protocol daemon (ntpd)—Manages the time within an OpenAFS cell to synchronize clients and servers, as well as to synchronize copies of the authentication, backup, protection, and volume location databases. The ntpd is not an OpenAFS-specific server process, but the time synchronization that it provides for OpenAFS clients and servers is critical to the accuracy of file and directory time stamps within an OpenAFS cell.

- Protection server (ptserver)—Supports OpenAFS access control lists (ACLs), enabling users to grant specialized permissions to individual users and user-defined groups, and maintains mappings between usernames and OpenAFS user IDs to properly use Kerberos tokens. The ptserver also maintains a protection database in which it stores any user-defined groups and enables system administrators to create ACLs based on IP addresses to provide even finer control over access to information in OpenAFS.

- runntp—An OpenAFS process that ensures that the network time protocol daemon process is running. This process is not necessary if your system already runs a standard network time protocol daemon.

- Salvager—Checks the consistency of AFS volumes whenever the file server or volume server processes fail and makes any repairs that are necessary. The salvager is not a server process but is run on file servers whenever it is necessary to verify or repair the consistency of a file server partition that contains OpenAFS volumes. The salvager is the OpenAFS equivalent of the fsck program. For more information about the salvager, see "Checking and Repairing Volume Consistency in OpenAFS" later in the chapter.

- Update server—Guarantees that all file servers are running the same set of AFS binaries by pushing them to file servers whenever necessary.

- Volume location server (vlserver)—Maintains an up-to-date list of volumes and the file servers on which they are located, providing this information to clients when queried.

- Volume server (volserver)—Enables administrators to create, delete, move, and replicate volumes.

NOTE

Most OpenAFS user and administrative commands are actually command suites, where the name of the command is followed by a specific command within that command suite, each of which has its own options and arguments. For example, the fs command suite, used to interact with a file server, has subcommands such as fs apropos, fs checkservers, fs checkvolumes, fs cleanacl, fs copyacl, fs diskfree, and many more. You can list the commands available in any OpenAFS command suite by entering the name of the command suite, followed by the help subcommand. For example, fs help would list all the available subcommands in the fs command suite.

OpenAFS Client Processes

OpenAFS client machines run many fewer OpenAFS-specific processes than AFS file servers. Aside from the cache manager, OpenAFS client machines should run an NTPD client to keep their clocks synchronized with the network time protocol daemon running within their cell.

Although it is not a specific process but is instead a loadable kernel module, the OpenAFS cache manager performs specific OpenAFS-related functions on an OpenAFS client and is treated as though it were an actual process.

The cache manager (afsd) initializes the AFS cache on a client machine; sets AFS-related memory and kernel variables; and starts a number of daemons to monitor callbacks and handle Rx remote procedure calls, manager tokens, and so on. The cache manager and the daemons it starts work in conjunction with the loadable kernel module `libafs-kernel-version.o` to translate application file requests to requests for files from appropriate file servers after consulting the volume location server and cache data on the client machine before delivering it to an application. It also manages the local cache, monitoring callbacks and requesting new copies of files as needed.

Getting More Information About OpenAFS

The home page for OpenAFS is located at `http://www.openafs.org` and provides information on OpenAFS releases, source code, and binary releases of OpenAFS for many platforms. The home page also provides HTML versions of the OpenAFS 3.6 documentation. The CD that accompanies this book includes installable versions of OpenAFS for Microsoft's Windows 95/98 and Windows NT platforms, as well as a version for Apple's Mac OS X. All these are located in the CD's `openafs` subdirectory.

You can also subscribe to any or all of three OpenAFS mailing lists from the OpenAFS Web site. Separate mailing lists are available for OpenAFS announcements (`openafs-announce`), OpenAFS developers (`openafs-devel`), and general information about OpenAFS (`openafs-info`).

A related Web site to `www.openafs.org` is `www.grandcentral.org`. This site is designed to help coordinate all the public OpenAFS cells on the Internet by providing a location from which to get AFS cell server database files (CellServDB files) that list all the public cells on the Net and their file servers.

The OpenAFS documentation set provides thorough, well-written user, administration, and reference material for all aspects of OpenAFS, though we used to joke that the AFS documentation set should be sold with casters or a dolly due to its size and weight. (Sorry about that, Tony!) You should definitely investigate the page count of any PDF document from the AFS or OpenAFS documentation set before randomly printing it.

The file `openafs-1.2.0-doc.tar.gz`, located in the `openafs` subdirectory of the CD that accompanies this book is a gzipped `tar` file of the OpenAFS 1.2.0 documentation in HTML format and also contains PDF versions of the following AFS programming and API documentation:

- AFS-3 Programmer's Reference: Architectural Overview
- AFS Programmer's Reference: Authentication Server Interface
- AFS-3 Programmer's Reference: BOS Server Interface
- AFS-3 Programmer's Reference: File Server/Cache Manager Interface
- AFS-3 Programmer's Reference: Specification for the Rx Remote Procedure Call Facility
- AFS-3 Programmer's Reference: Volume Server/Volume Location Server Interface

13

THE OPENAFS
DISTRIBUTED
FILESYSTEM

All the AFS API documentation dates from 1991 but still provides detailed information about programming the core portions of these interfaces.

Given that AFS has been in use since the mid-1980s and that OpenAFS is a direct descendant of AFS 3.6, much of the information available on AFS processes and procedures is still relevant to OpenAFS. This section lists some useful sources of AFS information.

PDF versions of the following AFS 3.6 documents, obtained from one of IBM's Web sites, are provided in the openafs subdirectory of the CD that accompanies this book:

- AFS 3.6 Release Notes
- AFS System Administrator's Guide
- AFS System Administrator's Reference
- AFS Quick Start Guide for Unix
- AFS User's Guide

The HTML documentation for AFS 3.6, the version of AFS from which the OpenAFS source code was branched, is available on the Web at http://www-124.ibm.com/developerworks/opensource/afs/docs/html. The HTML documentation for IBM's AFS 3.5 product is available at http://www.transarc.ibm.com/Library/documentation/afs/3.5/unix/index.htm.

An HTML version of the AFS Frequently Asked Questions file from Transarc Corporation (now the IBM Pittsburgh Labs) is also included on the CD.

An excellent guide and reference text for AFS, and therefore for most of OpenAFS, is Richard Campbell's *Managing AFS: The Andrew Filesystem*, ISBN 0138027293. One of the most interesting things about this book is that in it, Rick suggests that IBM might benefit the AFS community by making the source code for AFS publicly available. And here we are. . .

Support Software for OpenAFS

OpenAFS is not included as part of any commercial Linux distribution that I have used. Whether or not your favorite Linux distribution includes integrated support for the OpenAFS filesystem depends on the people who packaged your distribution. This section discusses the utilities associated with OpenAFS and the Linux packages in which they are found. If your Linux distribution does not include support for the OpenAFS filesystem, you can easily add it yourself by obtaining the following:

- Source code for your kernel. This must be present on your system and available through the directory or symbolic link /usr/src/linux to build OpenAFS.
- Source code or binary packages for OpenAFS.

If the Linux distribution and version of Linux that you are running does not include support for the OpenAFS filesystem, the CD that accompanies this book includes a sample kernel source code distribution in the CD's `kernels` subdirectory and the source code for OpenAFS 1.2.1 in the CD's `openafs` directory. Installing the kernel source code and information about building and installing OpenAFS clients and servers is provided later in this chapter.

Installing the source code for OpenAFS and configuring, compiling, and installing by following the instructions in the section "Installing an OpenAFS Client" will install the following applications on an AFS client machine:

- `afsmonitor` —Collects and displays statistics about specified file server and cache manager operations.

- `bos`—A command suite containing the commands that enable you to interact with an OpenAFS bosserver process, which runs on every file server machine to monitor the other server processes on it.

- `cmdebug`—Used to examine the status of the cache manager and cache entries on a particular AFS client machine.

- `compile_et`—Compiles a table of system error messages for your system. Designed to integrate OpenAFS messages into your system messages.

- `dlog`—Enables you to authenticate to DCE services.

- `dpass`—Enables you to change your DCE password.

- `fms`—A utility to determine a tape's capacity and set the OpenAFS filemark size on that tape to use it for backups.

- `fs`—The command suite containing the commands that enable you to interact with an OpenAFS file server process.

- `kdb`—Prints the logs from an OpenAFS authentication server.

- `klog`—A command that enables you to authenticate to OpenAFS and obtain tokens for a specified OpenAFS user.

- `klog.krb`—A command that enables you to authenticate to OpenAFS cells that use the Kerberos authentication mechanism, originally developed at MIT.

- `knfs`—Enables you to authenticate to an NFS server via the AFS/NFS translator.

- `kpasswd`—A command that enables you to change your OpenAFS password.

- `kpwvalid`—Checks the quality of a new OpenAFS password.

- `pagsh`—Creates a new command shell owned by the person who issued the command and associates a new process authentication group (PAG) with the shell and the user.

- `pagsh.krb`—Creates a new command shell owned by the person who issued the command and associates a new Kerberos process authentication group (PAG) with the shell and the user.
- `pts`—The command suite containing the commands that enable you to interact with the OpenAFS protection server.
- `rxgen`—Generates Rx client and server stubs for use when writing programs that make Rx remote procedure calls.
- `scout`—Monitors an OpenAFS file server process.
- `sys`—Returns the OpenAFS system type (`sysname`).
- `tokens`—A command that displays any OpenAFS tokens that you currently hold.
- `tokens.krb`—A command that displays any MIT Kerberos tokens that you currently hold.
- `translate_et`—Translates numbered error codes into error messages.
- `udebug`—Displays the status of a lightweight `ubik` process.
- `unlog`—Releases any tokens that you currently hold.
- `up`—Recursively copies the contents of a source directory into a destination directory, correctly setting ACLs.
- `xstat_cm_test`—Displays data collected from the cache manager.
- `xstat_fs_test`—Displays data collected from a file server.

These applications will be installed in the directory `/usr/afs/bin` if you ran the configure script with the `--enable-transarc-paths` option, and in `/usr/local/bin` without this option.

Installing the source code for OpenAFS and configuring, compiling, and installing by following the instructions given in "Installing an OpenAFS Server" will install the client applications in the previous list, as well as the following applications in `/usr/afs/bin` on an AFS server machine:

- `bos`—A command suite containing the commands that enable you to interact with an OpenAFS bosserver process, which runs on every file server machine to monitor the other server processes on it.
- `bosserver`—The OpenAFS Basic Overseer Server, which runs on every file server machine to monitor the other server processes on it.
- `buserver`—The OpenAFS backup server.
- `fileserver`—The OpenAFS file server.
- `fs`—The command suite containing the commands that enable you to interact with an OpenAFS file server process.

- `kas`—The command suite containing the commands that enable you to interact with an OpenAFS authentication server.
- `kaserver`—The OpenAFS authentication server.
- `klog`—A command that enables you to authenticate to OpenAFS and obtain tokens for a specified OpenAFS user.
- `klog.krb`—A command that enables you to authenticate to OpenAFS cells that use the Kerberos authentication mechanism, originally developed at MIT.
- `kpwvalid`—Checks the quality of a new OpenAFS password.
- `pts`—The command suite containing the commands that enable you to interact with the OpenAFS protection server.
- `ptserver`—The OpenAFS protection server.
- `pt_util`—Dumps the OpenAFS protection database into an ASCII file.
- `salvager`—The OpenAFS volume consistency checker.
- `tokens`—A command that displays any OpenAFS tokens that you currently hold.
- `tokens.krb`—A command that displays any OpenAFS Kerberos tokens that you currently hold.
- `udebug`—Displays the status of a lightweight `ubik` process.
- `upclient`—The client of the upserver process. This application installs updated server binaries on OpenAFS file servers.
- `upserver`—A server that guarantees the all file servers are running the same set or version of the OpenAFS binaries.
- `vlserver`—The OpenAFS volume location server.
- `volinfo`—Produces detailed statistics about one or more volume headers and the partition that houses those volumes.
- `volserver`—The OpenAFS volume server.
- `vos`—A suite of commands that enable you to interact with an OpenAFS volume server.

On an OpenAFS server machine, the following commands will be installed in `/usr/local/sbin`:

- `backup`—Commands in the `backup` command suite are the administrative interface to the AFS Backup System.
- `butc`—The backup tape controller process used to manage a device to which you are writing OpenAFS backups.
- `copyauth`—Copies a file server ticket from one cell to another.
- `fstrace`—The command suite that enables you to dump and manage OpenAFS file server logs.

- kadb_check—Verifies the consistency of an OpenAFS authentication database.
- kdb—Prints the logs from an OpenAFS authentication server.
- kdump-<kernel-version>—Extracts kernel symbols from a specified version of the kernel.
- kpwvalid—Checks the quality of a new OpenAFS password.
- kseal—Manually encrypts a ticket using a specified username and server key.
- prdb_check—Verifies the consistency of an OpenAFS protection database.
- read_tape—Enables you to read an OpenAFS volume dump from an OpenAFS backup tape.
- restorevol—Enables you to restore the contents of an AFS volume dump into a non-OpenAFS filesystem.
- rmtsysd—A daemon that implements system calls such as setpag and pioctl that aren't supported by operating systems on which OpenAFS is available.
- rxdebug—Performs Rx RPCs to a specified OpenAFS host and displays the results for debugging communication and system problems.
- uss—A command that enables you to create one or more OpenAFS accounts from a template.
- vldb_check—Verifies the consistency of a volume location database.
- vldb_convert—Converts older volume location databases to the current format.
- vos—Suite of commands to interact with an OpenAFS volume server.
- vsys—Performs an OpenAFS system call and displays the return code.

Installing and Configuring OpenAFS

This section provides hands-on, how-to information about building, configuring, and installing OpenAFS clients and servers.

Building OpenAFS

To install version 1.2.0 of OpenAFS, included on the CD that accompanies this book in the openafs subdirectory, do the following:

1. Mount the CD and extract the OpenAFS source code from the file openafs/openafs-1.2.0.tar.gz to a directory on your system using a command like the following:

```
cd <target-directory>
tar zxvf <path-to-CD>/openafs/openafs.1.2.0.tar.gz
```

2. Verify that the directory or symbolic link `/usr/src/linux` exists on your system and that it contains or points to the source code for your system's kernel.

3. Change directory to `<target-directory>/openafs-1.2.0` and run the configure script to correctly configure the OpenAFS Makefile for your system and Linux distribution:

   `./configure`

   This produces verbose output that's not useful to replicate here.

> **NOTE**
>
> You can configure OpenAFS so that it will be installed into two fundamentally different directory hierarchies. To compile OpenAFS using the directory hierarchy traditionally used by AFS clients and servers from Transarc (`/usr/afs/bin`, `/usr/afs/etc`), supply the `--enable-transarc-paths` option as a command-line argument to the configure script. Otherwise, AFS user commands will be installed into `/usr/local/bin` and `/usr/local/etc`.
>
> For your reference, mappings between the directories in these two locations are
>
> ```
> Transarc Mode                Default Mode and Location
> =========================    ===============================
> /usr/vice/etc                /usr/local/etc/openafs
> /usr/afs/bin (servers)       /usr/local/libexec/openafs
> /usr/afs/etc                 /usr/local/etc/openafs/server
> /usr/afs/local               /usr/local/var/openafs
> /usr/afs/db                  /usr/local/var/openafs/db
> /usr/afs/logs                /usr/local/var/openafs/logs
> ```
>
> The examples in this chapter install OpenAFS in the recommended new (default) location, as subdirectories of `/usr/local`.

4. After the Makefile is correctly configured, execute the `make` command to build the 1.2.1 version of OpenAFS:

   `make`

   Once again, this produces verbose, system-specific output that's not useful to replicate here. This also may take a fair amount of time depending on the speed of your system.

5. After OpenAFS is compiled, create the binary hierarchy that will contain the OpenAFS client and server binaries for installation purposes:

   `make dest`

Your system now has a compiled and correctly organized version of the OpenAFS daemons and related utilities.

> **NOTE**
>
> The actual name of the OpenAFS kernel module is derived from the name of the kernel running on the system where the kernel module was compiled. The name of this module is `libafs-<kernel-version>.o`, where *kernel-version* is the output of the `uname -r` command. For example, if compiled on a system where `uname -r` returns `2.4.9-afs`, the name of the OpenAFS kernel module would be `libafs-2.4.9-afs.o`. To install an OpenAFS kernel module on a system other than the one on which it was compiled, the kernel on the new system must be the same kernel as the kernel on the original system.

Installing Your First OpenAFS Server

Installing an OpenAFS server takes a fair amount of time. OpenAFS installation procedures are still under development and may have changed slightly if you install newer versions of OpenAFS. This section describes the process of installing an OpenAFS 1.2.0 server, which is the version of the OpenAFS source code included on the CD that accompanies this book.

> **NOTE**
>
> The first OpenAFS server that you install should have the lowest IP address of any OpenAFS server that you install in the cell that you are creating because it will be the first database server in the cell and thus the one that clients and other servers attempt to contact by default. If you later install an OpenAFS server with a lower IP address that is also a database server, you can manually edit the `/usr/local/etc/openafs/server/CellServDB` file to rearrange the entries for these servers.

After having compiled OpenAFS as described in the previous section, do the following to install and configure your first OpenAFS server:

1. Log in as root or use the su command to become the root user. Create the directory `/usr/local/var` using the `mkdir` command.

2. From the directory where you where you installed and built the OpenAFS source code, as described in the previous section, install the OpenAFS binaries that you just compiled using the `make install` command:

    ```
    # make install
    ```

3. Modify your path to include the directories where the OpenAFS binaries are located. You should also make this change to your `~/.bashrc` and the `/root/.bashrc` files so that you will always be able to locate the OpenAFS binaries:

```
# PATH=/usr/local/bin:/usr/local/sbin:${PATH}
```

4. After all the new binaries are installed and you have added them to your search path, change directory to the i386_linux24/dest subdirectory:

```
# cd i386_linux24/dest
```

5. Install the client and server directories and the AFS startup file on your system using the following commands:

```
# cp -rp root.client/usr /
# cp -rp root.server/usr /
# cp root.client/usr/vice/etc/afs.rc /etc/rc.d/init.d/afs
```

> **NOTE**
>
> This assumes that you will want to use the system you are building as both a client and server, which is recommended. Also, at some point, it should no longer be necessary to install the server binaries from the root.server directory because all these binaries are duplicated in the /usr/local directories when you build and install OpenAFS for use in its default location, which is in various subdirectories of /usr/local. However, at this time, the OpenAFS startup scripts expect to find the OpenAFS server binaries in the traditional server location, which is modeled under the dest directory's root.server directory.

6. Start AFS, which installs the OpenAFS loadable kernel module. At this point, OpenAFS is not completely configured, so you may see an error message about missing files, which you can safely ignore at this point:

```
# /etc/rc.d/init.d/afs start
Starting AFS services.....
afsd: some file missing or bad in /usr/local/etc/openafs
```

7. Create a directory in the root of the server's filesystem to serve as a mountpoint for each local disk partition that you will be using to store OpenAFS volumes. These directories must have names of the form /vicepXX, where XX is one or two letters. For example, the first mountpoint for a server partition should be /vicepa, the second /vicepb, and so on through /vicepZZ if you are blessed with sufficient free partitions. A single OpenAFS server can support up to 256 partitions. In this example, I am dedicating a single partition to OpenAFS:

```
# mkdir /vicepa
```

8. Format the partition you will be using to house OpenAFS volumes in ext2 format and add an entry for this partition to your /etc/fstab file, mounting it on the directory that you created in the previous step:

```
# mkfs -t ext2 /dev/hda4
```

This dedicates `/dev/hda4` to OpenAFS, so the entry in my `/etc/fstab` file would look like the following:

```
/dev/hda4        /vicepa              ext2    defaults       0 0
```

As shown by this entry, AFS partitions cannot be backed up using the standard Linux `dump` program and do not need to be checked for consistency using the `fsck` program. OpenAFS provides its own backup system (backup and associated processes) and filesystem consistency checker (salvager).

> **NOTE**
>
> Do not use any other type of filesystem for OpenAFS partitions. The OpenAFS vnode layer expects to find standard Linux inode structures, and using a journaling filesystem would also be a waste of time. If you are dedicating partitions on a RAID device to OpenAFS, only use hardware RAID. You can also use Linux logical volumes to store OpenAFS volumes, as long as they are formatted as ext2 partitions.

9. Mount the partition(s) that you just created for use by OpenAFS:

```
# mount -a
```

10. Copy the Pluggable Authentication modules for OpenAFS from the `lib` directory of the `i386_linux24/dest` directory in your OpenAFS source directory into the `/lib/security` directory and create a link to it with a basic shared library name. OpenAFS builds two PAMs, one for use with standard OpenAFS security (`pam_afs.so.1`) and a second if you are using MIT Kerberos (`pam_afs.krb.so.1`). This chapter explains installing OpenAFS with standard OpenAFS authentication, so only the standard OpenAFS PAM is installed:

```
# popd
# pushd lib
# cp pam_afs.so.1 /lib/security
# popd
# pushd /lib/security
# ln -s pam_afs.so.1 pam_afs.so
# popd
```

11. Add entries for the appropriate OpenAFS PAM to the PAM login configuration file using a text editor. When you are finished, the `/etc/pam.d/login` file should look like the following:

```
#%PAM-1.0
auth       required      /lib/security/pam_securetty.so
auth       required      /lib/security/pam_stack.so service=system-auth
```

```
auth       required     /lib/security/pam_nologin.so
auth       sufficient    /lib/security/pam_afs.so try_first_pass
ignore_root
account    required     /lib/security/pam_stack.so service=system-auth
password   required     /lib/security/pam_stack.so service=system-auth
session    required     /lib/security/pam_stack.so service=system-auth
session    optional     /lib/security/pam_console.so
session    optional     /lib/security/pam_afs.so
```

The fifth and tenth entries invoke the OpenAFS PAM during login. For more information about using PAMs and OpenAFS, see "Integrating Linux and OpenAFS Authentication" later in the chapter.

NOTE

Using PAMs as shown in this example enables you to automatically authenticate to AFS when logging in on an AFS client system. This is recommended but is actually optional; you can always forego this level of integration and use the klog command to authenticate.

12. Start the OpenAFS basic overseer server in unauthenticated mode (which can take a bit of time) and verify that it has started correctly:

```
# bosserver -noauth
# ps -ef | grep bos
root      15117    1   0 15:07 ?         00:00:00 bosserver -noauth
root      15119 15055  0 15:07 pts/4     00:00:00 grep bos
```

WARNING

When installing an OpenAFS server, you run most of the server commands in unauthenticated mode by using the -noauth option. This is extremely dangerous because it circumvents all the authentication mechanisms provided by OpenAFS. However, because OpenAFS is not yet installed and configured, it is impossible to use these services when installing a server—a classic bootstrapping problem. In normal operation of an OpenAFS server, you would rarely, if ever, run any OpenAFS command with the -noauth option.

> ### WARNING
>
> The `bos setcellname` command used in the next step must be able to look up the IP address of any host on which you will be running an OpenAFS server. Before executing the next step, make sure that your `/etc/nsswitch.conf` file correctly lists the precedence of your name service and `/etc/hosts` file. If the `/etc/nsswitch.conf` file lists the `/etc/hosts` file as a source of host information before your name service, the `bos setcellname` command may believe that your host's IP address is the loopback address (127.0.0.1), which would be totally incorrect and would prevent any AFS client from ever contacting any OpenAFS server processes running on your server because they would all be listening on the wrong interface. If you are using the `/etc/hosts` file only, you must have defined your system's actual IP address correctly in the `/etc/hosts` file.

13. Set the name of the OpenAFS cell to which this server will belong using the `bos setcellname` command, as in the following example:

    ```
    # bos setcellname dada vonhagen.org -noauth
    ```

    The arguments to this command are the name of the machine on which you are installing the OpenAFS server software (`dada`, in the preceding example), the name of the cell that the server running on this machine belongs to (`vonhagen.org`, in the preceding example), and the `-noauth` option to cause the `bos` command to run without authentication at this point.

14. Verify that the `cellname` for the machine you are using has been set correctly:

    ```
    # bos listhosts dada -noauth
    Cell name is vonhagen.org
        Host 1 is dada.vonhagen.org
    ```

15. Create entries for the OpenAFS servers in the configuration file used by the `bosserver` (`/usr/local/etc/openafs/BosConfig`) using the following commands:

    ```
    # bos create dada kaserver simple /usr/afs/bin/kaserver \
        -cell vonhagen.org -noauth
    # bos create dada buserver simple /usr/afs/bin/buserver \
        -cell vonhagen.org -noauth
    # bos create dada ptserver simple /usr/afs/bin/ptserver \
        -cell vonhagen.org -noauth
    # bos create dada vlserver simple /usr/afs/bin/vlserver \
        -cell vonhagen.org -noauth
    ```

    These commands create entries in the basic overseer server configuration file that causes the specified servers to be automatically restarted should they ever fail on this server. The

arguments to the bos create command are the name of the host on which you are
installing the OpenAFS server, an identifier for the server that you are installing (usually
the short name of the server command), the type of server that you are creating an entry
for (simply means that these servers have no dependencies on any other process), the full
pathname of the server process you are creating an entry for, the name of the cell in
which the server is running (specified using the -cell option), and the -noauth switch to
run the bos create commands without requiring authentication.

16. Create authentication server entries for the generic OpenAFS subsystem (afs) and the
OpenAFS administrator (admin) using the kas command, specifying the cell name using
the -cell option and using the -noauth switch to run kas without authentication. Enter
passwords for these entries when prompted to do so:

```
# kas -cell vonhagen.org -noauth
ka> create afs
initial_password:
Verifying, please re-enter initial_password:
ka> create admin
initial_password:
Verifying, please re-enter initial_password:
```

17. Set the administrator flag for the admin user in the authentication database to grant the
admin user administrative privileges in the OpenAFS cell that you are creating. Verify
the contents of the entry for that user, and then exit the kas program:

```
ka> setfields admin -flags admin
ka>
ka> examine admin
User data for admin (ADMIN)
  key (0) cksum is 2731756596, last cpw: Sat Sep 29 15:13:12 2001
  password will never expire.
  An unlimited number of unsuccessful authentications is permitted.
  entry never expires.  Max ticket lifetime 25.00 hours.
  last mod on Sat Sep 29 15:13:40 2001 by <none>
  permit password reuse
ka> quit
```

18. Use the bos adduser command to define the admin user as a privileged user in your
OpenAFS cell. Privileged users are listed in the bosserver's UserList file, located in the
directory /usr/local/etc/openafs/server:

```
# bos adduser dada admin -cell vonhagen.org -noauth
```

19. Use the bos addkey command to define the server's encryption key, which is stored in
the file /usr/local/etc/openafs/KeyFile:

```
# bos addkey dada -kvno 0 -cell vonhagen.org -noauth
```

The arguments to this command are the name of the server, the version number of the key, specified by the `-kvno` option, the name of your OpenAFS cell, and the `-noauth` option to execute this command without authentication. You will be prompted for a key. Enter any string of characters (and remember it!).

20. Use the `bos listkeys` command to check the server encryption key. The checksum for the key should be the same as the checksum displayed when you examined the authentication database for the admin user in a previous step:

```
# bos listkeys dada -cell vonhagen.org -noauth
key 0 has cksum 2731756596
Keys last changed on Sat Sep 29 15:15:16 2001.
All done.
```

21. Use various `pts` commands to create a parallel entry for the admin user in the OpenAFS protection database, add the admin user to the OpenAFS `system:administrators` group, and verify that the admin user was successfully added, as in the following example:

```
# pts createuser -name admin -cell vonhagen.org -noauth
User admin has id 1
# pts adduser admin system:administrators -cell vonhagen.org -noauth
# pts membership admin -cell vonhagen.org -noauth
Groups admin (id: 1) is a member of:
  system:administrators
```

22. Use the `bos restart` command to start all the OpenAFS servers that you defined in a previous step:

```
# bos restart dada -all -cell vonhagen.org -noauth
```

23. Use the `bos create` command to create an entry for the OpenAFS file server in the bosserver configuration file:

```
# bos create dada fs fs /usr/afs/bin/fileserver /usr/afs/bin/volserver \
    /usr/afs/bin/salvager -cell vonhagen.org -noauth
```

> **NOTE**
>
> The bosserver entries you defined for other OpenAFS server processes were simple entries that had no dependencies on other processes. The file server entry actually consists of three commands that should be executed in a specific sequence if the first one fails and is therefore of the special type `fs`.

24. Use the bos status command to ensure that the file server process is running correctly and has a valid configuration file entry:

```
# bos status dada fs -long -noauth
Instance fs, (type is fs) currently running normally.
    Auxiliary status is: file server running.
    Process last started at Sat Sep 29 15:19:01 2001 (2 proc starts)
    Command 1 is '/usr/local/libexec/openafs/file server'
    Command 2 is '/usr/local/libexec/openafs/volserver'
    Command 3 is '/usr/local/libexec/openafs/salvager'
```

25. Now that the file server and volume server are running, we can begin to create the basic volume necessary for an OpenAFS cell. Use the vos create command to create the root entry for your new OpenAFS cell. This volume is automatically mounted on the directory /afs whenever you start OpenAFS:

```
# vos create dada /vicepa root.afs -cell vonhagen.org -noauth
Volume 536870912 created on partition /vicepa of dada
```

The arguments to this command are the name of the file server on which you want to create the volume, the mountpoint for the partition in which you want to create that volume, the name of the volume, the name of the cell, specified by the -cell option, and the -noauth command to run this command without authentication.

26. Use the bos create command to create a bosserver configuration file entry for the OpenAFS update server, which guarantees that all the file servers in a cell are running the same binaries:

```
# bos create dada upserver simple "/usr/afs/bin/upserver \
  -crypt /usr/local/etc/openafs/server -clear /usr/afs/bin \
  /usr/local/libexec/openafs" -cell vonhagen.org -noauth
```

Arguments to the bos create command are the name of the host on which you want to create this entry, the short name of the command, the type of bosserver entry you are creating, the command to execute, and the name of the cell specified by the -cell option and the standard -noauth flag to run this command without authentication. The upserver is another "simple" server, like the authentication, backup, protection, and volume location servers, because it is a single command even though it takes arguments. Because arguments are required, the entry for the upserver command must be enclosed within double quotation marks. The arguments to the upserver command are the name of a directory whose contents must be encrypted when sent over the network, specified using the -crypt option, and a list of directories whose contents can be sent over the network in unencrypted form.

> **NOTE**
>
> For OpenAFS to work correctly, all OpenAFS clients and servers must be clients of a time synchronization service. Most Linux systems come with the most common network time protocol (NTP) daemon, ntpd, or can install it from auxiliary package files included with the distribution. See the documentation for your Linux distribution for information about configuring a time server. A popular alternative to ntpd is xntpd, a more advanced NTP daemon, or chrony, an NTP daemon better suited to OpenAFS cells that may not be constantly connected to the Internet, and therefore cannot depend on always being able to constantly synchronize their clocks from an Internet time source.

27. Now, we're ready to make the OpenAFS server an OpenAFS client. The first step is to create symbolic links for the Cell identification file and the cell database server definition file in the central AFS configuration directory:

```
# cd /usr/vice/etc
# ln -s /usr/local/etc/openafs/server/ThisCell
# ln -s /usr/local/etc/openafs/server/CellServDB
```

28. Next, create the directory on which OpenAFS will be mounted, create the OpenAFS cache directory, and create the cache configuration file that defines the parameters of the cache to the cache manager:

```
# mkdir /afs
# mkdir /usr/vice/cache
# echo "/afs:/usr/vice/cache:50000" > /usr/local/etc/openafs/cacheinfo
```

This cache configuration file entry states that the cache for the OpenAFS hierarchy mounted as /afs is located in the directory /usr/vice/cache and can grow to 50,000 KB.

29. The next step is to set the startup parameters for OpenAFS so that the system knows that it is both a client and a server. Edit the file /usr/vice/etc/afs.conf, modifying the line that says AFS_SERVER=off so that it reads AFS_SERVER=on.

30. After updating the /usr/vice/etc/afs.conf file, copy it to the system configuration directory (/etc/sysconfig) with the name afs:

```
# cp /usr/vice/etc/afs.conf /etc/sysconfig/afs
```

31. At this point, shut down the unauthenticated bosserver process and either reboot your system or simply stop and start the OpenAFS processes. I recommend stopping and starting the OpenAFS processes to simplify recovering from any authentication problems, as in the following example:

```
# bos shutdown dada -noauth -wait
# /etc/rc.d/init.d/afs stop
Stopping AFS services.....
# /etc/rc.d/init.d/afs start
Starting AFS services.....
afsd: All AFS daemons started.
```

NOTE

If you are using xinetd rather than the older inetd, you should comment out the inetd section of the OpenAFS startup file.

32. If all goes well, you should now be running an OpenAFS client and server with authentication. To verify this, use the klog command to obtain authentication tokens as the admin user, and use the tokens command to verify that you successfully obtained tokens:

```
# klog admin
Password:
# tokens
Tokens held by the Cache Manager:
User's (AFS ID 1) tokens for afs@vonhagen.org [Expires Sep 30 17:09]
    --End of list--
```

33. Add starting OpenAFS to your system's startup process by using the chkconfig command to create symbolic links for your system's multiuser run levels in the directories /etc/rc.d/rc3.d and /etc/rc.d/rc5.d:

```
# /sbin/chkconfig --add afs
```

34. Use the fs checkvolumes command to guarantee that the file server's volume location database is up-to-date (even though you only have one volume at this point):

```
# fs checkvolumes
All volumeID/name mappings checked.
```

35. At this point, it's time to create the additional volumes that make up the core of an OpenAFS cell and set ACL permissions in the /afs directory. Use the fs setacl command to give any user the ability to list the contents of the /afs directory, and then use the vos create command create the root.cell volume that will be mounted in /afs as the root of your cell:

```
# fs setacl /afs system:anyuser rl
# vos create dada /vicepa root.cell
Volume 536870915 created on partition /vicepa of dada
```

The arguments to the `fs setacl` command identify an OpenAFS directory, the user or group that you want to add to the ACLs for that directory, and the permissions that you want to set on that directory. The arguments to the `vos create` command are the name of the file server on which you want to create the volume, the partition on which you want to create the volume, and the name of the volume that you want to create.

36. Create an OpenAFS mountpoint to mount this volume under `/afs` with the name of your cell, set an ACL to enable people to list the contents of your cell, and optionally create a short name by which you can more conveniently refer to your cell:

```
# fs mkmount /afs/vonhagen.org root.cell
# fs setacl /afs/vonhagen.org system:anyuser rl
# cd /afs
# ln -s vonhagen.org vh
```

> **NOTE**
>
> If you choose to create a short name as a symbolic link, that short name will only be visible in your local OpenAFS space. If you choose to make your cell publicly available by mounting its `root.cell` volume in a shared `/afs` directory (such as the one maintained by `grandcental.org`), the symbolic link will not be available there unless it is created there.

37. You can now create a read/write mountpoint for your `root.cell` volume. Following standard AFS and OpenAFS conventions, the read/write mountpoint for your `root.cell` volume is the name of your cell, preceded by a period:

```
# fs mkmount /afs/.vonhagen.org root.cell -rw
```

The `-rw` option specifies that this is a read/write mountpoint.

38. Create replicas of your cell's `root.afs` and `root.cell` volumes, and release those volumes to create the replicas:

```
# vos addsite dada /vicepa root.afs
Added replication site dada /vicepa for volume root.afs
# vos addsite dada /vicepa root.cell
Added replication site dada /vicepa for volume root.cell
# vos release root.afs
Released volume root.afs successfully
# vos release root.cell
Released volume root.cell successfully
```

As discussed earlier, replicated volumes must be released in order to update all of the read-only replicas of that volume.

39. Almost done! Now create an OpenAFS account for your login so that you can verify that the PAMs work correctly. (The root user is excluded from the OpenAFS PAM entry you

added to /etc/pam.d/login because of the ignore_root entry.) To create an authentication account that maps to your Linux account, you will need to know your Linux user ID (UID), which you can find out by examining your entry in the /etc/passwd file. The following commands create an OpenAFS authentication account for the user wvh.

```
# grep wvh /etc/passwd
wvh:x:500:500:William von Hagen:/home/wvh:/bin/bash
# pts createuser wvh 500
User wvh has id 500
# kas create wvh -admin admin
Administrator's (admin) Password:
initial_password:
Verifying, please re-enter initial_password:
```

<table>
<tr><td>NOTE</td></tr>
</table>

When prompted to enter a password for your OpenAFS account, enter the same password that you use for your Linux account. Using the same password in both Linux and OpenAFS prevents you from having to enter two passwords.

40. Create a directory in your cell for user directories, and create an OpenAFS volume for yourself and mount it there:

```
# mkdir /afs/vonhagen.org/usr
# vos create dada /vicepa user.wvh -maxquota 50000
Volume 536870918 created on partition /vicepa of dada
# fs mkmount /afs/vonhagen.org/usr/wvh user.wvh
```

41. Give yourself all ACL permissions on the directory where the volume is mounted, change the ownership of the volume so that it is actually yours, and release the root.cell volume to propagate your changes to the root.cell volume to its replica:

```
# fs setacl /afs/vonhagen.org/usr/wvh -acl wvh all
# chown wvh /afs/vonhagen.org/usr/wvh
# vos release root.cell
Released volume root.cell successfully
```

42. As the final step, verify that you can correctly log in on your machine and simultaneously authenticate to OpenAFS. The easiest way to do this is to telnet to your machine (if you've enabled telnet under xinetd or inetd) and attempt to create a file in your OpenAFS directory, as I did in the following example:

```
# telnet dada
Trying 192.168.6.33...
Connected to dada.vonhagen.org (192.168.6.33).
Escape character is '^]'.
Red Hat Linux release 7.1.93 (Roswell)
```

```
Kernel 2.4.9-afs on an i686
login: wvh
Password:
Last login: Sat Sep 29 12:32:29 on :0
$ cd /afs/vonhagen.org/usr/wvh
$ touch foo
$ ls -al
total 4
drwxrwxrwx    2 wvh       root         2048 Sep 29 16:10 .
drwxr-xr-x    2 bin       root         2048 Sep 29 16:05 ..
-rw-rw-r--    1 wvh       wvh             0 Sep 29 16:10 foo
$ logout
```

NOTE

At this point, you may want to modify the /etc/password entry for your account so that your home directory is in OpenAFS, which in my case would be the directory /afs/vonhagen.org/usr/wvh. You can then copy the contents of your previous home directory into your OpenAFS directory and delete the version of the directory local to your machine. There's no point in wasting local disk space now that your directory is available from any OpenAFS client in your cell.

I would say "that's all there is to it," but that was an involved procedure. However, at this point, you're running the full-blown, authenticated OpenAFS distributed filesystem on a machine that is both an OpenAFS client and server. Not too shabby for 42 steps—perhaps OpenAFS is the meaning of life? This answers some great questions, indeed.

Installing an OpenAFS Client

As mentioned in "Building OpenAFS" earlier in the chapter, you cannot use an OpenAFS kernel module compiled under one kernel on a system running another kernel. When installing an OpenAFS client, you must either make sure that both systems are running the same kernel or recompile OpenAFS on that system. For safety's sake, this section assumes that you have recompiled OpenAFS on each system where you will be installing it.

NOTE

You must have installed or have access to an OpenAFS server before installing an OpenAFS client.

After compiling OpenAFS as described in "Building OpenAFS," do the following to install and configure an OpenAFS client:

1. Log in as or use the `su` command to become the root user. From the directory where you where you installed and built the OpenAFS source code, as described in the previous section, install the OpenAFS binaries that you just compiled using the `make install` command:

   ```
   # make install
   ```

2. Modify your path to include the directories where the OpenAFS binaries are located. Also make this change to your `~/.bashrc` and the `/root/.bashrc` files so that you will always be able to locate the OpenAFS binaries:

   ```
   # PATH=/usr/local/bin:/usr/local/sbin:${PATH}
   ```

3. After all the new binaries are installed and you have added them to your search path, change directory to the `i386_linux24/dest` subdirectory:

   ```
   # cd i386_linux24/dest
   ```

4. Install the client directory on your system using the following command:

   ```
   # cp -rp root.client/usr /
   ```

5. Change directory to the central OpenAFS configuration directory and copy the OpenAFS startup file to the central startup script directory using the following commands:

   ```
   # pushd /usr/vice/etc
   # cp -p afs.rc /etc/rc.d/init.d/afs
   ```

> **TIP**
>
> Using the `pushd` command to change directories will save you having to type long pathnames in the OpenAFS server configuration procedure.

6. Copy the `/usr/vice/etc/afs.conf` file to the system configuration directory (`/etc/sysconfig`) with the name `afs`:

   ```
   # cp afs.conf /etc/sysconfig/afs
   ```

7. Add starting OpenAFS to your system's startup process by using the `chkconfig` command to create symbolic links for your system's multiuser run levels in the directories `/etc/rc.d/rc3.d` and `/etc/rc.d/rc5.d`:

   ```
   # /sbin/chkconfig --add afs
   ```

8. Create the Open AFS `Cell` definition file by echoing the name of your OpenAFS cell into the `/usr/vice/etc/ThisCell` file:

   ```
   # echo "vonhagen.org" > ThisCell
   ```

9. Use the `ftp` program to transfer a copy of the `/usr/vice/etc/CellServDB` file to the `/usr/vice/etc` directory on the client, or create it using the `cat` command or a text editor. The `CellServDB` file must be exactly the same as the one on your OpenAFS server system. An example of a `CellServDB` file (from the server installed in the previous section) is the following:

```
>vonhagen.org     #Cell name
192.168.6.33      #dada.vonhagen.org
```

The first line contains a right-arrow, followed immediately by the name of the cell. The second line contains the IP address of the cell's database server. If the cell has more than one database server, this line would be followed by similar line for each database server, containing its IP address.

10. Create the directory on which OpenAFS will be mounted on the client system, create the OpenAFS client's cache directory, and create the cache configuration file that defines the parameters of the cache to the client's cache manager:

```
# mkdir /afs
# mkdir /usr/vice/cache# echo "/afs:/usr/vice/cache:50000" >
/usr/vice/etc/cacheinfo
```

> **WARNING**
>
> The filesystem in which the OpenAFS cache is located (usually the partition mounted as /) must *not* be a journaling filesystem. OpenAFS maintains its own cache, which must not be journaled by the filesystem itself.

This cache configuration file entry states that the cache for the OpenAFS hierarchy mounted as `/afs` is located in the directory `/usr/vice/cache` and can grow to 50,000 KB.

> **NOTE**
>
> You can decrease the size of the cache on systems where disk space is at a premium, but making it too small can potentially hurt performance and increase network usage as the cache manager has to retrieve files from the server more frequently.

11. Create a symbolic link to ensure that all OpenAFS utilities can find the files that they need and initialize the AFSLog file:

```
# ln -s /usr/vice/etc /usr/local/etc/openafs
# touch /usr/vice/etc/AFSLog
```

12. Start the OpenAFS cache manager on the client system:

```
# /etc/rc.d/init.d/afs start
Starting AFS services.....
afsd: All AFS daemons started.
```

> **NOTE**
>
> Loading the kernel module is part of the startup process. If this script fails for some reason, you will have to manually use the rmmod command to remove the OpenAFS kernel module or issue the /etc/rc.d/init.d/afs stop command before you can retry.

13. To automate authenticating to OpenAFS when you log in, install the OpenAFS PAM module, as explained in the next section, "Integrating Linux and OpenAFS Authentication."

Your system is now an OpenAFS client.

Installing Additional OpenAFS Servers

Installing other OpenAFS servers is similar to the process required to install the first one, except that it is simpler because the administrative or structural basics of the OpenAFS environment already exist. The primary differences are

- You do not need to create administrative accounts.
- You do not need to create specific volumes.
- Rather than using the bos command to create a BosConfig entry for an update server (updserver) on the file server, you create entries for the update client (updclient) to guarantee that the new file server binaries and configuration files are synchronized with your primary server.

For complete information on the process of adding OpenAFS servers to an existing OpenAFS environment, see the OpenAFS documentation.

Integrating Linux and OpenAFS Authentication

There are two common ways of integrating OpenAFS authentication with the Linux login process:

- Add the klog command to your .bashrc file, surrounding it with some sort of semaphore so that it is only executed once during each login session. You will then be

13

THE OPENAFS
DISTRIBUTED
FILESYSTEM

prompted for your OpenAFS password when you log in, after you have entered your Linux login and password.

- Add the OpenAFS Pluggable Authentication Module (PAM) to the authentication procedure for any process that requires authentication, such as login, Samba, su, xdm, and even the xscreensaver program.

A simple way to add the klog command to your Linux login process is the following:

1. Add the following shell commands to the end of your ~/.bashrc file:

```
if [ ! -f ~/.klogged ] ; then
    /usr/local/bin/klog wvh
    touch ~/.klogged
fi
```

2. Add the following command to the end of your ~/.bash_logout file:

```
rm -f ~/.klogged
```

If the file .klogged does not exist in your home directory, starting a shell (such as after you log in) executes the klog command, prompting you for your password. It then creates this file in your home directory. Any subsequent shell that you start on this system will detect the file and not execute the klog command. When you log out, the commands in the .bash_logout file in your home directory are executed, including the one that forces removal of the .klogged file in your home directory.

> **NOTE**
>
> This type of semaphore approach is somewhat problematic. For example, if your client system crashes or if you telnet to a system on which you are already logged in, the ~/.klogged file will already exist, and you will have to manually execute the klog command from the command line. This file may also survive when you log out through the X Window System.

A more permanent way of integrating OpenAFS authentication is by adding the OpenAFS PAM to the authentication procedure for any process that requires separate authentication.

For example, you can integrate OpenAFS authentication into the login process by doing the following:

1. Log in as root or use the su command to become the superuser.

2. Change directory to the i386_linux24/dest/lib subdirectory of the directory containing the OpenAFS source code (named openafs-1.2.0 if you are using the OpenAFS source code found on the CD that accompanies this book).

3. If you are using standard OpenAFS authentication (which is the security mechanism that you configured by following the instructions in the "Installing an OpenAFS Server" and "Installing an OpenAFS Client" sections of this book), copy the file pam_afs.so.1 to the /lib/security directory on your machine:

```
# cp pam_afs.so.1 /lib/security
```

If you are using MIT Kerberos, copy the file pam_afs.krb.so.1 to the /lib/security directory on your machine:

```
# cp pam_afs.krb.so.1 /lib/security
```

> **NOTE**
>
> MIT Kerberos is not the default authentication mechanism. You would only be using MIT Kerberos at this point if an OpenAFS cell is already running in your computing environment and that cell has been explicitly configured to use MIT Kerberos.

4. Change to the /lib/security directory and create a symbolic link to the PAM you just installed. The symbolic link should have the name of the equivalent nonversioned shared object library. Use whichever of the following symbolic link creation commands is appropriate:

```
# cd /lib/security
# ln -s pam_afs.so.1 pam_afs.so
# ln -s pam_afs.krb.so.1 pam_afs.krb.so
```

5. Change to the /etc/pam.d directory and use a text editor to modify the login file so that it looks like the following:

```
#%PAM-1.0
auth        required      /lib/security/pam_securetty.so
auth        required      /lib/security/pam_stack.so service=system-auth
auth        required      /lib/security/pam_nologin.so
auth        sufficient    /lib/security/pam_afs.so try_first_pass
ignore_root
account     required      /lib/security/pam_stack.so service=system-auth
password    required      /lib/security/pam_stack.so service=system-auth
session     required      /lib/security/pam_stack.so service=system-auth
session     optional      /lib/security/pam_console.so
session     optional      /lib/security/pam_afs.so
```

The fifth and tenth lines in this file invoke the standard OpenAFS PAM module. If you were using non-OpenAFS Kerberos authentication, these lines would refer to the PAM /lib/security/pam_afs.krb.o.

The fifth line in this example invokes the standard OpenAFS PAM. The options mean that the PAM should first try to authenticate using the password entered for previous steps. The ignore_root option means that this PAM is not used when the Linux User ID of the user who is trying to log in is 0, as is the case for the root user.

The tenth line in this example tells the OpenAFS PAM to drop your tokens when your login session ends. Otherwise, your tokens would remain in system memory and could be co-opted by a sophisticated user.

6. Save the modified file. The next time you log in, the login authentication password will automatically attempt to use your standard Linux password to authenticate to OpenAFS. If your Linux and OpenAFS passwords are the same, you will be automatically authenticated to OpenAFS. If they are different, you will be prompted for your OpenAFS password.

For more information about PAMs, the organization of a PAM configuration file, and the structure of the rules that it contains, see the online Linux reference page for PAM by executing the command man pam on your Linux system.

Aside from the try_first_pass and ignore_root options shown previously in the sample PAM definition file for the login process, there are a number of other options that you can supply as modifiers for the behavior of the OpenAFS PAM. The options that you can use with either of the OpenAFS PAMs are the following:

- dont_fork —This OpenAFS PAM option causes authentication to take place as a part of the main process associated with a PAM definition file, instead of being performed by a subprocess. This option is provided to support the requirements of the Apache Web server's mod_auth_pam modules.

- no_unlog—This OpenAFS PAM option causes tokens to be retained in memory after a session ends. This option is largely provided for backward compatibility because this was the default behavior for OpenAFS PAMs until OpenAFS 1.1.1. It is also useful for commands such as su that are executed as subprocesses of a current login session.

- ignore_root—As discussed earlier, this OpenAFS PAM option tells the OpenAFS PAM to ignore any user with UID 0 (zero). This means that the PAM will not attempt to authenticate a user with the Linux UID of 0 to OpenAFS, but will simply return a status code indicating success.

- ignore_uid uid—This OpenAFS PAM option is an extension of the ignore_root option. The additional parameter is the minimum UID that a user can have without this PAM being skipped. The PAM will not try to authenticate any users to OpenAFS whose UID is less than the specified value. This option is convenient if you want to use the OpenAFS PAM but don't want to have to create OpenAFS authentication accounts for all your system accounts. In this case, the specified UID number is usually the number of the highest system account (root, bin, daemon, adm, and so on) that you might want to log in as. Most system accounts do not need to authenticate to OpenAFS to execute the local processes that they are responsible for.

- `refresh_token`—This OpenAFS PAM option provides the same functionality as the `set_token` option, except that it only refreshes any existing tokens instead of creating a new process authentication group (PAG).

- `remainlifetime sec`—This OpenAFS PAM option causes OpenAFS tokens to remain active for the specified number of seconds, at which point they are deleted from memory. This option is provided for applications that save configuration information to OpenAFS directories after a session ends, giving writes time to complete before the tokens are deleted.

- `set_token`—This OpenAFS PAM option is used with applications that don't call the `pam_setcred()` function to establish the appropriate credentials for their session. This option causes the `pam_sm_authenticate()` function to be used instead, removing the need to call `pam_setcred()`. Do not use this option with applications that actually do call `pam_setcred()`. Using this option is an alternative if your OpenAFS PAM entry and password are correct, but the application is still failing due to insufficient authentication. If the application works correctly after you add this option, this means that session management is not correctly implemented in the application. This should be reported to the author of the program as a bug.

- `setenv_password_expires`—This OpenAFS PAM option sets the environment variable `PASSWORD_EXPIRES` to the value of the expiration date of the user's AFS password, as recorded in the authentication database.

- `try_first_pass`—As discussed earlier, this OpenAFS PAM option tells the OpenAFS PAM to first try authenticating using the password provided to a previous PAM. If your Linux and OpenAFS passwords are not the same, you will be prompted for your OpenAFS password.

- `use_klog`—This OpenAFS PAM option causes authentication to be done by calling the external program `klog`, which must be located somewhere in the root user's `PATH`. The version of `kdm` (the KDE display manager) provided with KDE versions 2.X is an example of a program for which this option is necessary.

The PAM definition file for login authentication is the most common authentication configuration file to which you will want to add the OpenAFS PAM, but you may want to add it to others as well. You may also want to add the OpenAFS PAM to the following other PAM authentication definition files:

- `/etc/pam.d/httpd`—A PAM definition file for the Apache Web server, `httpd`, would only be meaningful if the `mod_auth_pam module` was loaded in the `/etc/httpd/conf/`

13

THE OPENAFS
DISTRIBUTED
FILESYSTEM

`httpd.conf` file on Red Hat Systems, or in `/usr/local/apache/conf` or `/usr/local/apache2/conf` (depending on the version of Apache that you are running) and would look like the following:

```
auth       required    /lib/security/pam_afs.so ignore_uid 100 dont_fork
```

This entry would enable users with UIDs 100 or less to authenticate to the Apache Web server without having to have AFS authentication accounts if they could satisfy any other authentication requirements specified in subsequent lines. (These would be site-specific, and therefore are not shown here.) Users with UIDs greater than 100 who successfully authenticated to OpenAFS would also have to satisfy any other site-specific authentication requirements specified in subsequent lines.

- `/etc/pam.d/samba`—A Samba PAM definition file containing the OpenAFS PAM would look like the following:

```
auth       required        /lib/security/pam_afs.so ignore_uid 500
auth       required        /lib/security/pam_stack.so service=system-auth
try_first_pass
account required        /lib/security/pam_stack.so service=system-auth
```

The entry for the OpenAFS PAM would enable users with UIDs 500 or less to authenticate to Samba without having to have AFS authentication accounts. They would still have to be able to satisfy Samba's standard authentication requirements.

- `/etc/pam.d/su`—A PAM definition file for the `su` command that contains the OpenAFS PAM might look like the following:

```
auth       sufficient   /lib/security/pam_rootok.so
# Uncomment the following line to implicitly trust users in the "wheel"
group.
#auth       sufficient   /lib/security/pam_wheel.so trust use_uid
# Uncomment the following line to require a user to be in the "wheel"
group.
#auth       required     /lib/security/pam_wheel.so use_uid
auth       required     /lib/security/pam_stack.so service=system-auth
account    required     /lib/security/pam_stack.so service=system-auth
password   required     /lib/security/pam_stack.so service=system-auth
session    optional     /lib/security/pam_afs.so no_unlog
session    required     /lib/security/pam_stack.so service=system-auth
session    optional     /lib/security/pam_xauth.so
```

The OpenAFS PAM entry for su sessions would cause tokens to be preserved after the user exited the su session and returned to using his normal UID.

- `/etc/pam.d/xdm`—A PAM definition file for the X Window System display manager that contains the OpenAFS PAM might look like the following:

```
auth       required     /lib/security/pam_stack.so service=system-auth
auth       required     /lib/security/pam_nologin.so
```

```
account    required    /lib/security/pam_stack.so service=system-auth
password   required    /lib/security/pam_stack.so service=system-auth
session    optional    /lib/security/pam_afs.so remainlifetime 10
session    required    /lib/security/pam_stack.so service=system-auth
session    optional    /lib/security/pam_console.so
```

The OpenAFS PAM entry in this file would cause tokens to remain in memory for 10 seconds after the user's session terminated, providing time for applications to save configuration information to OpenAFS with the user's privileges.

- /etc/pam.d/xscreensaver—A PAM definition file for the X Window System screensaver program that contains the OpenAFS PAM might look like the following:

```
auth       sufficient  /lib/security/pam_afs.so ignore_uid 100
refresh_token
auth       required    /lib/security/pam_pwdb.so shadow nullok
try_first_pass
```

The entry for the OpenAFS PAM module would enable users with UIDs 100 or less to authenticate without having to have AFS authentication accounts if they could satisfy the standard xscreensaver authentication requirements. Users with UIDs greater than 100 who successfully authenticated to OpenAFS would have their existing tokens refreshed instead of being granted new tokens.

Resolving OpenAFS Problems

This section summarizes some problems I've experienced when loading and using OpenAFS on a variety of clients and servers, and explains the ways in which I've debugged and resolved them.

Instead of rebuilding OpenAFS for each server and client, it's tempting to clone the OpenAFS kernel module to multiple systems that you believe to be running the same kernel. If you receive a message such as /afs: not a directory when starting OpenAFS, or if you have general problems loading the OpenAFS kernel modules, your kernel and OpenAFS kernel module were probably not actually compiled from the same code base. To resolve this problem, make sure that the /usr/src/linux symbolic link actually points to the kernel code from which you compiled your kernel and then recompile OpenAFS while running that kernel. You can restore your OpenAFS source directory to its initial state by executing the command make distclean before rerunning the configure script.

In general, if you are having problems starting OpenAFS on your system, you may find it useful to change the first line of the /etc/rc.d/init.d to the following to put the script into verbose mode:

```
#!/bin/sh -x
```

This causes the shell to echo each line in the file as it executes the startup script, making it easy to see the substitutions that the shell is making in the scripts and to identify the line at which the error is occurring.

When running OpenAFS on some Linux systems, I've seen situations in which the kernel crashes when trying to umount OpenAFS when shutting down an OpenAFS client or scrver. This happens when the system runs the /etc/rc.d/init.d/halt script. Although not particularly elegant, a quick workaround for this problem is to insert a command that manually unmounts OpenAFS near the beginning of the halt script. A crash when the system runs this script is harmless because no users can be logged on to the system at this point, but it may prevent other filesystems from being cleanly unmounted. This results in your OpenAFS system having to run the fsck command each time it reboots.

After making this change, the first few lines in the halt script (after the initial comment block) look like the following:

```
# Set the path.
PATH=/sbin:/bin:/usr/bin:/usr/sbin

export NOLOCALE=1
. /etc/init.d/functions
umount /afs
```

Adding this line has eliminated this problem on every system I've tested OpenAFS on.

Using and Administering OpenAFS

Issues in administering and using OpenAFS are different from the issues in administering most other filesystems for a variety of reasons:

- OpenAFS provides its own authentication mechanism that uses separate accounts and protection databases to store user information. OpenAFS authentication requirements must be satisfied to provide any meaningful access to OpenAFS volumes.

- OpenAFS provides its own ACLs that provide much more sophisticated control over file access and manipulation than standard Linux permissions do.

- OpenAFS maintains its own information about volumes created in physical or logical partitions. These volumes are not visible and cannot be accessed by examining a physical or logical partition dedicated to OpenAFS.

The remaining sections of this chapter discuss the most common tasks in OpenAFS administration and in working in the OpenAFS environment. For more information about these topics than you could possibly want to know, see the OpenAFS and AFS documentation sets.

Creating and Mounting OpenAFS Volumes

OpenAFS volumes are created with the `vos create` command, which has the following full syntax:

```
vos create -server <machine name>  -partition <partition name>
           -name <volume name>  [-maxquota <initial quota (KB)>]
           [-cell <cell name>]  [-noauth]  [-localauth]  [-verbose]  [-help]
```

The required arguments for the `vos create` command are the name of the file server on which you want to create the volume, the mountpoint of the partition on that machine where you want to create the volume, and the name of the volume that you want to create. The options that specify these arguments are position-dependent, meaning that you do not have to specify those options if you supply the arguments to the `vos create` command in the correct order. For example, the following three commands are identical:

```
vos create -server dada -partition /vicepa -name user.foo
vos create dada /vicepa user.foo
vos create -partition /vicepa -name user.foo -server dada
```

The default quota associated with an OpenAFS volume is 5,000 KB. To create a volume with a larger quota, you must use the `-maxquota` option and supply the quota value in terms of kilobytes.

13

> **NOTE**
>
> OpenAFS volumes only require as much space in a partition as is necessary to store the files that they actually contain, plus some OpenAFS filesystem metadata for the volume header, any existing directories, and so on. The volume quota specifies the maximum size that the volume can grow to. For example, a volume with a quota of 500 MB that only contains one file that is 1 KB long would only require slightly more than 1 KB of space. The sum of the quotas for all the volumes on an OpenAFS partition frequently exceeds the amount of available space on that partition, in the hopes that not every volume will be filled to capacity.
>
> You must have tokens as the AFS administrator (admin) and be logged in as the Linux superuser to create volumes.

The process of creating and mounting an OpenAFS volume involves the following steps:

1. If you don't know the names of all the file servers in your cell, retrieve a prioritized list using the `fs getserverprefs` command. An example of the output of this command is the following:

```
# fs getserverprefs
dada.vonhagen.org                              5006
```

2. After selecting a file server on which to create the volume (which isn't too difficult from the output in the previous example), list the available partitions on that file server and the amount of free space that each has. You can get this information by using the `vos part-info` command and supplying the name of the server you want information about. An example of the output of this command is the following:

```
# vos partinfo dada
Free space on partition /vicepa: 17980888 K blocks out of total 17981212
```

3. Create the volume using the `vos create` command. Specify the name of the server and partition on which you want to create the volume, specify the name of the volume that you want to create, and provide a quota value if you want the volume to have a capacity other than the default 5,000 KB. An example of the output of this command is the following:

```
# vos create dada /vicepa user.foo -maxquota 500000
Volume 536870927 created on partition /vicepa of dada
```

> **NOTE**
>
> After a volume is created, it is no longer necessary to identify the server on which it is located because the OpenAFS volume location database contains and provides this information.

4. If you want to verify that the volume was created successfully, you can use the `vos examine` command to display information about the volume. An example of the output of this command is the following:

```
# vos examine user.foo
user.foo                              536870927 RW          2 K  On-line
    dada.vonhagen.org /vicepa
    RWrite  536870927 ROnly        0 Backup        0
    MaxQuota      500000 K
    Creation    Sun Sep 30 06:07:18 2001
    Last Update Sun Sep 30 06:07:18 2001
    0 accesses in the past day (i.e., vnode references)
    RWrite: 536870927
    number of sites -> 1
        server dada.vonhagen.org partition /vicepa RW Site
```

5. Create a mountpoint for the volume and mount the volume at that point using the `fs mkmount` command. An example of this command, mounting the volume `user.foo` as `/afs/.vonhagen.org/usr/foo`, is the following:

```
# fs mkmount /afs/.vonhagen.org/usr/foo user.foo
```

6. Change the user and group ownership of the volume using the standard Linux `chown` command, as in the following example:

```
# chown wvh /afs/vonhagen.org/usr/foo
# chgrp staff /afs/vonhagen.org/usr/foo
```

7. Set the ACLs on the volume so that its owner has all rights to that volume and so that any user can list the contents of the volume, as in the following example:

```
# fs setacl /afs/vonhagen.org/usr/foo -acl wvh all system:anyuser rl
```

As shown in this example, ACL entries following the `fs setacl` command's `-acl` option consist of one or more pairs of user or group names and ACL settings.

8. If the volume in which you mounted the volume you just created is replicated, use the `vos release` command to release that volume to update all the replicas, as in the following example:

```
# vos release root.cell
Released volume root.cell successfully
```

OpenAFS volumes can be deleted using the `vos remove` command. When a volume is deleted, all its contents are lost.

Replicating OpenAFS Volumes

As discussed in the section "Using Replication in OpenAFS" earlier in the chapter, replicating a volume means to create a read-only copy of that volume. Volumes are replicated to increase their availability by making replicas available on different file servers, and also to help load-balance file servers by distributing copies of heavily used volumes across different file servers. Replicas are synchronized with their parent volumes by releasing the parent volume using the `vos release` command. Until a replicated volume is released, the parent volume can be updated, but any changes made will not be visible in its replicas.

The types of volumes usually replicated are heavily used volumes that are infrequently updated, such as volumes containing software used by many people at a company.

NOTE

You must have tokens as the AFS administrator (admin) and be logged in as the Linux superuser to replicate volumes.

The process of replicating a volume involves the following steps:

1. Use the `vos addsite` command to define the server and partition on that server where you want a specified volume to be replicated, as in the following example:

```
# vos addsite futurism /vicepa  root.cell
```

This command creates a read-only replica of the `root.cell` volume on the `/vicepa` partition of the file server named `futurism`. The name of the replica is created by appending the string `.readonly` to the name of the volume. For example, the name of each read-only replica of the volume `root.cell` is `root.cell.readonly`. For this reason, you can only have one replica of a certain volume on a certain partition.

2. Use the `vos release` command to release the volume you just replicated to create the replica, as in the following example:

```
# vos release root.cell
Released volume root.cell successfully
```

3. If you replicated a volume to increase its availability, clients who need access to that volume will automatically use one of the replicas if the parent volume cannot be found or is offline.

If you replicated a volume to balance the load across different file servers, you may need to change the order in which some of your clients contact file servers to find volumes. OpenAFS clients store the order in which they access file servers in client-specific server preferences that can be queried using the `fs getserverprefs` command. For example, the `fs getserverprefs` command on a client may produce output like the following:

```
# fs getserverprefs
dada.vonhagen.org                                       5006
futurism.vonhagen.org                                   5011
```

The default rankings of various file servers are calculated based on the subnet they are located on, relative to the client. See the reference information for the `fs setserverprefs` command in the OpenAFS System Administrator's Reference for complete information about file server rankings.

When you know the current rankings of the servers, you can modify the sequence in which replicated volumes on those servers are accessed by using the `fs setserverprefs` command. Ranking values must be between 1 and 65,534. File servers with lower rankings are more likely to be used. An example of using the `fs setserverprefs` command to modify the ranking of the file server `futurism.vonhagen.org` is the following:

```
# fs setserverprefs futurism.vonhagen.org 2000
```

The `setserverprefs` command adds a random integer between 1 and 14 to the ranking value you supply to help ensure that two servers do not get identical rankings. You can use `fs getserverprefs` to display the modified file server rankings:

```
# fs getserverprefs
futurism.vonhagen.org                           2003
dada.vonhagen.org                               5006
```

Creating OpenAFS Accounts

OpenAFS accounts are different from standard Linux accounts because they can involve a number of OpenAFS-specific bits of information. I say "can involve" because there are really three different types of OpenAFS accounts:

- OpenAFS accounts that permit authentication but do not involve storage in an OpenAFS cell. These are typically known as *authentication-only accounts* and are usually created for users who already have Linux accounts and now need access to files and directories in the OpenAFS filesystem.

- OpenAFS accounts that permit authentication and where the user may own volumes and files in an OpenAFS cell, but where his or her home directory is a standard Linux directory on a specific workstation. These are generally known as *basic OpenAFS accounts*. This type of account is generally given to mobile computing users who primarily use laptops and therefore cannot depend on being able to access OpenAFS at all times. These users generally access their OpenAFS volumes through symbolic links that may or may not be available depending on whether the user's system is connected to a network and has access to the OpenAFS cell.

- OpenAFS accounts where the user's home directory is located in an OpenAFS volume and which may involve ownership of other files and directories related to system services hosted in an OpenAFS cell. These are typically known as OpenAFS *login accounts*.

This section discusses some issues to consider when creating these types of accounts and explains how to manually create OpenAFS accounts using standard OpenAFS commands. The section "Automating OpenAFS Account Creation" later in the chapter explains how to use the OpenAFS uss command suite to automate and bulletproof account creation.

> **NOTE**
>
> To create OpenAFS accounts, you must be authenticated as someone with OpenAFS administrative privileges. Some related commands, such as kas, require that your account either be listed as an administrative account in the /usr/local/etc/ope-nafs/server/UserList file on the server where you are creating the account and have the ADMIN flag set in your authentication database entry, or that you use the -adm option to identify the name of an administrative account to use when executing commands. Creating OpenAFS accounts that also require modifications to files and directories in local Linux filesystems also require that you be logged in as the Linux superuser or have used the Linux su command to temporarily assume that identity.

13

THE OPENAFS
DISTRIBUTED
FILESYSTEM

To issue uss commands successfully, you usually need all the standard AFS administrative privileges: membership in the system:administrators group, inclusion in the /usr/afs/etc/UserList file on every relevant server machine, and the ADMIN flag on your Authentication Database entry.

OpenAFS accounts consist of some or all of the following elements, depending on whether they are intended for use as authentication-only accounts or as Linux accounts housed in OpenAFS. Authentication-only accounts really only require that entries for the user be created in the OpenAFS authentication and protection databases. Most authentication-only accounts are created for existing users and therefore share the same login name and User ID as an existing Linux account. However, authentication-only accounts can also be created for users who do not have actual login accounts in an OpenAFS cell, generally for purposes of cross-cell authentication. Cross-cell authentication gives users from one OpenAFS cell the ability to authenticate to another and are generally used for file transfer purposes.

The following list describes the components of an OpenAFS account and identifies the type of OpenAFS account that the item is typically associated with:

- An authentication database entry that associates a password with an OpenAFS login name. When associated with an existing Linux account, the OpenAFS login name should be the same as the user's Linux login. An authentication database entry is necessary for any type of OpenAFS account.

- A protection database entry that defines an OpenAFS login name (the name provided when authenticating to OpenAFS), an associated OpenAFS User ID, and any groups to which the user belongs. When associated with an existing Linux account, the OpenAFS UID and login name should be the same as the user's Linux UID and login. A protection database entry is necessary for any type of OpenAFS account.

- A volume that stores the user's files and directories. A volume is not necessary for an OpenAFS authentication-only account.

- A mountpoint that makes the contents of the user's volume available in the OpenAFS namespace and may serve as the user's home directory. A mountpoint is not necessary for an OpenAFS authentication-only account.

- Full access permissions on the access control list (ACL) for the user's volume and ownership of that directory. These are irrelevant for authentication-only accounts.

- An entry in the /etc/passwd and /etc/shadow file (or their equivalents) on each OpenAFS client machine. This enables the user to log in and access OpenAFS files from any OpenAFS client workstation. These are not necessary for authentication-only accounts.

OpenAFS follows the same conventions for login names as Linux does. Usernames should be less than nine characters long to guarantee interoperability with any flavor of Unix. Like Linux, file and directory ownership is actually associated with a user's User ID rather than the user's name. This means that basic OpenAFS accounts and OpenAFS login accounts should always use the same user UID and login name for a user who must exist in both OpenAFS and local Linux password files.

NOTE

As with AFS, OpenAFS reserves one UID, 32766, for the user "anonymous". OpenAFS server processes assign this identity and UID to any user who does not possess a token for the local cell. Do not assign this UID to any other user. At the same time, this is only a convention and may change in the future. Do not hard-code this value into programs or assign file ownership to this UID because it could always change in some future release of OpenAFS.

The name of a user's OpenAFS volume cannot exceed 22 characters in length (like any OpenAFS volume) and cannot include suffixes such as `.readonly` or `.backup`, which have special meanings to OpenAFS. The standard convention for the names of user volumes is `user.`*`username`*, where *username* is the user's OpenAFS login name. Using standard conventions such as this makes it easy to identify the purpose of a volume and also makes it easy to select user volumes for backup by using a single `vos backupsys` command. Related conventions are that the mountpoint for a user volume is given the user's name, and that all user volumes are typically mounted in a single OpenAFS location. For example, the mountpoint for the `user.juser` volume would usually be named `juser` and might be created as `/afs/.vonhagen.org/home/juser` in the `vonhagen.org` cell. Mounting OpenAFS user volumes in a single OpenAFS location makes it easy to identify all your user volumes and enables you to replicate the volume in which they are mounted to maximize availability to those mountpoints.

13

THE OPENAFS DISTRIBUTED FILESYSTEM

NOTE

Minimizing the number of directory entries in a single directory is a bit of standard system administrator folklore probably invented when the second user account in the history of computing was created. This was certainly an issue at one time for older filesystems. Replicating the directory that contains the mountpoints for user volumes across multiple file servers generally eliminates this as a significant performance hit in all but the largest OpenAFS cells (which can indeed be quite large).

continues

I generally feel that the added hassle and frustration associated with looking for the home directories for different users in different locations isn't worth any slight performance gains. But then, I also believe that system administrators were created to help users get their work done by making computers as easy to use as possible. Your mileage may vary. If you must create mountpoints for user volumes in distinct directories for religious reasons, you should at least create a single, well-known directory that contains symbolic links to all users' home directories to reduce the heuristics necessary to actually locate a user's home directory.

Creating an authentication-only OpenAFS account involves two simple OpenAFS commands:

1. Use the `pts createuser` command to create an entry for the user in the OpenAFS protection database, optionally specifying a UID if the user has an existing Linux account on your system. An example of this command is the following:

```
# pts createuser wvh 500
```

This command creates a protection database entry for the user wvh with the OpenAFS UID 500, which presumably matches the UID for a related Linux account.

2. Use the `kas create` command to create an authentication database entry and associated password for the user. You will need to specify the `-admin` option and the name of an OpenAFS administrator account if you are not logged in as a user who has administrative privileges in OpenAFS. An example of this command is the following:

```
# kas create wvh -admin admin
Administrator's (admin) Password:
initial_password:
Verifying, please re-enter initial_password:
```

Manually creating a basic OpenAFS account begins by executing the same two steps as creating an authentication-only OpenAFS account but also requires that you create a volume and mountpoint, set the ACLs for the mountpoint appropriately, and change the ownership of the top-level directory for that volume so that the user can actually create files and directories there. In addition to the steps shown for manually creating an OpenAFS authentication-only account, the other steps in this process are the following:

1. Use the `vos create` command to create an OpenAFS volume for the user, typically following the standard user.*username* convention for the names of user volumes. You can optionally use the `-maxquota` option to specify a quota other than the default value of 5,000 KB, which is pretty small by today's standards. One or two Microsoft Word files in there, and you're over quota! The following is an example of a volume creation command:

```
# vos create dada /vicepa user.wvh -maxquota 50000
Volume 536870918 created on partition /vicepa of dada
```

This command creates the volume user.wvh on the /vicepa partition of the dada file server, assigning it a quota of 50,000 KB.

2. Create a mountpoint for the user's volume in the standard directory where you mount user volumes, as in the following example:

```
# fs mkmount /afs/.vonhagen.org/usr/wvh user.wvh
```

This command creates the mountpoint /afs/vonhagen.org/usr/wvh and mounts the volume user.wvh there.

3. Now that you can actually get to the volume, set the ACLs for the volume such that the user associated with that volume can actually create files and directories there, as in the following example:

```
# fs setacl /afs/vonhagen.org/usr/wvh -acl wvh all
```

This command gives the user wvh full control over the root directory of the volume mounted at /afs/vonhagen.org/usr/wvh.

4. Change the Linux ownership of the volume to the user associated with that volume, and change the group ownership of that volume to the group associated with that user's Linux account, as shown in the following example:

```
# chown wvh /afs/vonhagen.org/usr/wvh
# chgrp staff /afs/vonhagen.org/usr/wvh
```

If you are unsure of the user's group membership, you can find its numeric value by using the grep command to show the user's entry in the /etc/password file and then execute the chgrp command with a numeric argument, as in the following example:

```
# grep wvh /etc/passwd
wvh:x:500:500:William von Hagen:/home/wvh:/bin/bash
# chgrp 500 /afs/vonhagen.org/usr/wvh
```

5. Release the volume in which the mountpoint for the user's volume was created if the volume where the mountpoint was created is replicated, as in the following example:

```
# vos release root.cell
Released volume root.cell successfully
```

If you are creating an OpenAFS account for a user who does not already have a Linux account, you will also need to use the Linux useradd, linuxconf, or equivalent administrative command to either:

- Create appropriate entries for the new user in the Linux /etc/passwd and /etc/shadow files (or their equivalent maps if you are stuck using NIS or NIS+) if you are creating an OpenAFS login account.

13

THE OPENAFS DISTRIBUTED FILESYSTEM

- Create a complete corresponding Linux user account if you are creating a basic OpenAFS account for a user whose login directory is located in a local Linux filesystem.

A sample command to create a complete Linux account for the user wvh, as used in the previous examples, is the following:

```
# adduser -d /home/wvh -c "William von Hagen" -g staff -p whatever -u 500 wvh
```

This command creates a Linux home directory named /home/wvh and creates the local user wvh with the User ID 500 and default membership in the staff group. The gecos field of the Linux password file entry for this user would contain the string "William von Hagen". The password specified with the -p option should be the same as the password that you specified when you created the user's authentication database entry using the kas create command.

A sample useradd command to create Linux password and shadow file entries for an OpenAFS login account for the user wvh, as used in the previous examples, is the following:

```
# adduser -d /afs/vonhagen.org/usr/wvh -c "William von Hagen" -g staff \
    -p whatever -u 500 wvh
```

Note that the only real difference between this and the previous command is that this command defines the user's home directory to be /afs/vonhagen.org/usr/wvh, which is not created if it already exists.

TIP

You may often modify the template files in /etc/skel to contain settings for environment variables, such as PATH, which are particular to your OpenAFS environment. In OpenAFS environments that support many different system types, many user binaries (/usr/local/bin and other common, central directories) are often stored in platform-specific OpenAFS directory hierarchies that identify the platform for which they were compiled, using names such as rs_aix43, sun4x_57, i386_linux24, and so on. Paths that explicitly contain entries such as these make it challenging to create and maintain platform-independent .login, .cshrc, and .bashrc files.

The most common solution to this problem is to embed the OpenAFS sys command in the paths in your startup files. The sys command returns the OpenAFS system type for the current system. This is the same value returned by the fs sysname command. By embedding the sys command within PATH settings, you can create entries in your template startup files such as /afs/vonhagen.org/usr/`sys`/local/bin, which resolves to /afs/vonhagen.org/usr/rs_aix43/local/bin on an IBM system running AIX 4.3, but to /afs/vonhagen.org/usr/i386_linux24/local/bin on your neighborhood linux machines. If you use related naming conventions when creating and mounting volumes, invoking the sys command within your template startup files enables them to be truly system-type independent.

For complete information about using the Linux `useradd` command or an equivalent account creation command, see the online Linux documentation for that command.

Automating OpenAFS Account Creation

The examples in the previous section listed the commands necessary to create OpenAFS authentication-only, basic, and login accounts. Although none of these operations involved a tremendous number of commands, repeating all of them every time you create an OpenAFS account, especially a basic OpenAFS account or an OpenAFS login account, would be tedious. When I was back in seminary school, one of the first computer science fortune cookies that I ever learned was that "a good programmer never does the same job twice, but writes a program to do it."

Although I haven't really stuck to this philosophy, the authors of AFS realized that the number of accounts that typically exist in many AFS and OpenAFS cells could easily run into the tens of thousands, which would be a tad hard on the fingers and psyche of the unlucky administrator who drew the short straw for this task. Therefore, the authors of AFS created the `uss` command suite, which enables you to create account creation templates and use them when creating one or more similar accounts. The `uss` command even has a `bulk` subcommand that enables you to supply a text file containing information about multiple accounts that you want to create using `uss` templates. After preparing an appropriate `uss` template, you can then start the `uss bulk` command and go do your laundry while hundreds or thousands of OpenAFS accounts are being automatically created.

> **NOTE**
>
> The `uss` command and `uss` template files are completely documented in the OpenAFS System Administrator's Guide. This section explains the basics of creating and using a `uss` template to create Linux accounts, providing a sample template file that creates OpenAFS login accounts on Red Hat Linux systems. For complete, detailed documentation of the `uss` command and every conceivable form of `uss` template file, see the OpenAFS System Administrator's Guide.

Templates for `uss` commands can contain many different types of entries, each of which must appear on a separate line and represents a single `uss` command. The type of command that each line performs is identified by the first field on each line, which specifies a particular `uss` command. The following list shows the commands that can be used in a `uss` template file. Examples of the syntax of each are provided in the example template file for creating OpenAFS accounts on Red Hat Linux systems, which follows this list.

The uss commands that you can use in a uss template file are the following:

- D—Creates a directory with a specified mode, owner, and default ACL settings.
- E—Executes a single command and identifies the output file into which the output from that command should be placed. This is typically used to create per-user entries that are subsequently appended to Linux system files such as /etc/passwd and /etc/shadow by a shell script identified using the uss X command entry or a script run as a nightly cron job.
- F—Creates a file with a specified mode and owner from a template for that file.
- G—Identifies a default directory in which user accounts are to be created. If more than one G entry is present in a uss template file, the uss command will randomly select one of them to identify the directory where an account will be created.
- L—Creates a hard link to a file.
- S—Creates a symbolic link to an existing file or directory.
- V—Specifies the parameters for creating a volume and an associated mountpoint, setting the owner of the volume, and setting initial ACLs on the root directory for that volume.
- X—Executes a specified command. If the command requires arguments, the entire command must be enclosed within double quotation marks.

To make them as flexible as possible, uss templates can reference a number of internal variables based on options you specify on the uss command line or values that have been set by preceding uss commands. As the uss command is processing a uss template, it substitutes the appropriate values for any variables referenced in a uss command before executing that command. If it encounters an unknown variable or a valid variable for which no value has been provided, the uss command displays an error message and exits.

The variables that you can use in a uss template are the following:

- $AUTO—Set by a previous G instruction in the uss template. If multiple G instructions are provided in the uss template, the uss command will randomly select one of them as the basis for this substitution.
- $MTPT—Specified using the uss add command's -mount option, by the value of the mount_point field in a previous V command, or by the mount_point field of an add instruction in a uss bulk input file.
- $NAME—Can take values from two different uss add and bulk input file add instructions. If the uss add command's -realname option is specified on the command line or the realname field is present in an add instruction in a uss bulk input file, the $NAME variable will be set to the specified value. Otherwise, if the uss add command's -user option is specified on the command line or the username field is specified in a bulk input file add instruction, the $NAME variable will be set to the specified value.

- $PART—Specified using the uss add command's -partition option or by the partition field in a uss bulk input file add instruction.

- $PWEXPIRES—Specified using the uss add command's -pwexpires option or by the password_expires field in a uss bulk input file add instruction.

- $SERVER—Specified using the uss add command's -server option or by the file_server field in a uss bulk input file add instruction.

- $UID—Specified using the uss add command's -uid option or by the uid field in a uss bulk input file add instruction. If neither of these is specified, the next free UID will be automatically allocated by the pts createuser command when creating the protection database entry.

- $USER—Specified using the uss add command's -user argument or by the username field in a uss bulk input file add instruction.

- $1 through $9—Specified using the uss add command's -var option or by the var1 through var9 fields in a uss bulk input file add instruction.

The following is a sample uss template file for creating an OpenAFS login account on a Red Hat Linux system. Don't worry—an explanation of each entry follows the example!

> **NOTE**
>
> A copy of this file and the shell script that it uses are provided in the openafs subdirectory of the CD that accompanies this book. The name of the uss template on the CD is redhat_template.uss, and the shell script that it invokes is named upd_system_files. Feel free to use them as a starting point for your own uss templates and associated scripts, but please note that they will not work out of the box, because both are tailored to my OpenAFS cell. Note, too, that the printed version of this file shows lines whose ends are escaped with a backslash—this is only to make the examples fit on the page and should *not* be done in real life.

13

THE OPENAFS
DISTRIBUTED
FILESYSTEM

```
#
# Define the default directory where user accounts are mounted
#
G /afs/.vonhagen.org/usr
#
# Define the default volume creation parameters
#
V user.$USER dada.vonhagen.org /vicepa 50000 $AUTO/$USER $UID $USER \
   all system:authuser rl
#
```

```
# Create a template /etc/passwd file entry for the user
#
E /afs/.vonhagen.org/usr/common/accts/passwd_$USER 0644 root
"$USER:X:$UID:11:$NAME:/afs/vonhagen.org/usr/$USER:/bin/bash"
E /afs/.vonhagen.org/usr/common/accts/shadow_$USER 0644 \
   root "$USER:!!:11383:0:99999:7:::"
#
# Run a script to update and install the common passwd and shadow files
#
X /afs/.vonhagen.org/usr/common/upd_system_files
#
# Create directories in the user's home directory
#
D $MTPT/.kde 0755 $UID $USER all
D $MTPT/.kde/Autostart 0755 $UID $USER all
D $MTPT/Desktop 0755 $UID $USER all
#
# Create file in the user's home directory from templates
#
F $MTPT/.kde/Autostart/.directory 0644 $UID /etc/skel/.kde/Autostart/.directory
F $MTPT/.kde/Autostart/Autorun.desktop 0644 $UID \
   /etc/skel/.kde/Autostart/Autorun.desktop
F $MTPT/Desktop/.directory 0644 $UID /etc/skel/Desktop/.directory
F $MTPT/Desktop/kontrol-panel 0644 $UID /etc/skel/Desktop/kontrol-panel
F "$MTPT/Desktop/Linux Documentation" 0644 $UID \
   "/etc/skel/Desktop/Linux Documentation"
F $MTPT/.bashrc 0755 $UID /etc/skel/.bashrc
F $MTPT/.emacs 0644 $UID /etc/skel/.emacs
#
# Create a Symbolic Link in the user's home directory
#
S $MTPT/.kse/Autostart $MTPT/Desktop/Autostart
#
# run the vos release command to release the known location of user mountpoints
#
X "vos release root.cell"
```

To explain the contents of this template file:

- The first thing that you will notice in this template is that comments are legal in uss template files and consist of lines whose first character is a hash mark (#).

- The G entry defines the directory (in a read/write volume) where accounts should be created. The values supplied will be used as the value of $AUTO because this is the only G entry in the file.

- The V entry states that volume names should have the form user.$USER, which means that one of the mandatory options when executing uss using this template is the username or login. The volume name field is followed by fields defining the file server on which the volume should be created; the partition where it should be created; the default quota; the mountpoint for the volume, consisting of the values of the $AUTO and $USER variables, separated by a slash; and the user's UID (which must therefore be specified on the uss add command line). These are followed by pairs of values representing ACLs that should be set on the volume—in this case, the user ($USER) should have all ACL permissions, and any authenticated user should be able to examine the contents of the directory. The appropriate volumes will be created as part of the execution of the uss command.

- The two E entries create files named passwd_$USER and shadow_$USER, which will be written to the directory /afs/.vonhagen.org/usr/common/accts. These entries consist of template entries for the new user that can be added to /etc/passwd and /etc/shadow, respectively. Note that the template for the password file uses the $NAME variable, which must be specified on the uss add command line using the -realname option.

- The X entry runs a script called upd_system_files that (in this case) merges the files produced by the E entries into the /etc/passwd and /etc/shadow files. This script is provided in the openafs subdirectory of the CD that accompanies this book.

- The D entries create directories in the directory identified by the $MTPT variable, which takes its value from the value of the mountpoint field user in the V command ($AUTO/$USER). The name of the directory to create is followed by its Linux protection mode, the User ID that the directory's ownership should be set to ($UID, from the command line), and a pair of values that represent the default ACL setting for this directory, which in this case gives only the user full access to these directories ($USER all).

- The F entries create a number of files in the directories created in the D entries, and specify the mode of those files, the $UID that should own these files, and the name of the files to copy these files from, which in all these cases are default startup files found in subdirectories of /etc/skel, which is a template for user accounts.

- The S command creates a symbolic link to the first argument with the name of the second argument.

- The final X command executes the vos release command to release the replicated volume in which the mountpoint for the user's directory was created.

13

THE OPENAFS DISTRIBUTED FILESYSTEM

> **NOTE**
>
> You may notice that the template for the /etc/shadow entry for this user does not allow Unix logins. If you are creating OpenAFS login accounts, you may want to modify the /etc/pam.d/login file so that OpenAFS authentication is all that is sufficient to authenticate users, which allows users without Linux passwords to log in. You could do this with an /etc/pam.d/login PAM description file that looks like the following:
>
> ```
> auth       required     /lib/security/pam_securetty.so
> auth       required     /lib/security/pam_nologin.so
> auth       sufficient   /lib/security/pam_afs.so try_first_pass ignore_uid
> 499
> auth       required     /lib/security/pam_stack.so service=system-auth
> account    required     /lib/security/pam_stack.so service=system-auth
> password   required     /lib/security/pam_stack.so service=system-auth
> session    required     /lib/security/pam_stack.so service=system-auth
> session    optional     /lib/security/pam_console.so
> session    sufficient   /lib/security/pam_afs.so
> ```
>
> The entries in this file verify that the user is trying to log in on an acceptable device or network connection, make sure that user logins are enabled, and then check the user's OpenAFS password if the user's UID is greater than 499 (the arbitrary cut-off for the end of system accounts that I use on my machines). If this check succeeds, the user doesn't have to perform normal Linux login authentication.

An example of the uss add command used to create a user's account according to this template would be the following:

```
# uss add -user juser -realname "Joe User" -pass IMNEW -uid 2000 \
  -template /afs/vonhagen.org/usr/common/uss.template -admin admin
```

As you can see, the commands that can be performed in a template file can logically build on one another.

Setting and Modifying OpenAFS ACLs

Previous sections of this chapter have shown a number of examples of the fs setacl command, used to set the ACL permissions on a directory in OpenAFS. A list of the ACLs supported in OpenAFS and their meanings was provided in the section "Using OpenAFS Access Control Lists" earlier in the chapter. This section summarizes the use of the fs setacl command for your reference and then discusses how to create user-defined groups in OpenAFS, define their members, and assign ACL permissions to these groups.

The general syntax of the `fs setacl` command is the following:

```
fs setacl <directory-name> <user-or-group> <ACL-settings>
```

The `directory-name` is the full or relative name of the directory that you want to set ACL permissions on and is followed by the name of the OpenAFS user or group for whom you are setting an ACL, followed by the ACL settings for the specified OpenAFS user or group. You can provide multiple pairs of user/group names and ACL settings on a single *fs setacl* command line. For example, the first two commands in the following example could be replaced by the third command:

```
# fs setacl . wvh all
# fs setacl . system:authuser rl
# fs setacl . wvh all system:authuser rl
```

You can list the ACL settings on any OpenAFS directory that you have access to by using the `fs listacl` command. This command takes the full or relative pathname of an OpenAFS directory as an argument and displays the ACL settings for that directory, as in the following example:

```
# fs listacl /afs/vonhagen.org/usr/wvh/research
Access list for /afs/vonhagen.org/usr/wvh/research is
Normal rights:
  system:administrators rlidwka
  system:authuser rl
  wvh rlidwka
```

As mentioned previously, you can use the `fs setacl` command's `-negative` option to deny access to a user who would otherwise have access to a directory due to the user's membership in a group that has access to that directory. An example of using the `-negative` option is the following:

```
# fs setacl /afs/vonhagen.org/usr/wvh/research -negative juser rl
```

This denies read and lookup permissions to the user `juser` who would otherwise have them as a member of the group `system:authuser`.

Negative ACL settings are grouped together for readability in the output of the `fs listacl` command. For example, after executing the previous command, the output of the `fs listacl` command for this directory would look like the following:

```
# fs listacl /afs/vonhagen.org/usr/wvh/research
Access list for /afs/vonhagen.org/usr/wvh/research is
Normal rights:
  system:administrators rlidwka
  system:authuser rl
  wvh rlidwka
Negative rights:
  juser rl
```

13

THE OPENAFS
DISTRIBUTED
FILESYSTEM

Per-directory ACL permissions are powerful tools for refining the people who can have certain types of access to your files and directories. ACLs are even more powerful when used with the user-defined groups provided by OpenAFS, which enable you to define your own special-named sets of users and assign them specific access rights as a group.

For example, suppose that you are working as part of a research group consisting of yourself and the users ami8, jeffp, joe25, and kwalter, and you need your fellow group members to be able to access the report you are preparing on your top-secret research project. Rather than begging your local system administrator to create a special-purpose Linux group to control access to a directory and the files that it contains, in OpenAFS, you can set this up yourself with three simple OpenAFS commands. No system administrators required—they can continue playing networked Unreal or Diablo II without your having to interrupt them. An example of the relevant commands for the directory are the following:

```
$ pts creategroup research-group
$ pts adduser -user ami8 jeffp joe25 kwalter wvh -group research-group
$ fs setacl research research-group rliw
$ fs listacl /afs/vonhagen.org/usr/wvh/research
Access list for /afs/vonhagen.org/usr/wvh/research is
Normal rights:
  research-group rliw
  system:administrators rlidwka
  system:authuser rl
  wvh rlidwka
Negative rights:
  juser rl
```

The pts creategroup command enables any user to create a group. You can then use the pts adduser command to add any number of users to that group, as shown in the second command in the previous example.

> **NOTE**
>
> Notice that I also added myself (wvh) to the group that I created, even though I already have access to the research directory because I own it. You would want to add yourself to any groups that you create if you expect others to use that same group to protect other directories. After you create a user-defined group, any OpenAFS user can add that group to the ACL for any directory that she has administrative rights for.

The third command in this example gives members of the research-group group read, lookup, insert, and write access to that directory. No one in that group can delete any files in the directory, just in case—except for the user wvh, who has all rights to the directory. If a user appears on the ACL for a directory multiple times, ACL permissions are additive (except, of course, for negative ACLs).

You can use the `pts membership` command to list the members of any group, as in the following example:

```
$ pts membership research-group
Members of research-group (id: -206) are:
  wvh
  jeffp
  kwalter
  ami8
  joe25
```

OpenAFS also provides the `pts removeuser` command to remove a user from any OpenAFS group that you create. Suppose that the user `ami8` leaves your research project. The following example removes him from the `research-group` group and verifies that this is the case:

```
$ pts removeuser ami8 research-group
$ pts membership research-group
Members of research-group (id: -206) are:
  wvh
  jeffp
  kwalter
  joe25
```

The combination of ACLs and user-defined groups makes the protection mechanisms supported by OpenAFS both incredibly powerful and incredibly flexible. The fact that user entries are stored in a database managed by a centralized protection server makes it possible for any authenticated OpenAFS user to create, examine, and use user-defined groups from any OpenAFS client in a cell.

Checking and Repairing Volume Consistency in OpenAFS

The OpenAFS salvager is the OpenAFS equivalent of the standard Linux filesystem consistency check program, `fsck`, and is used to check and repair the consistency of OpenAFS volumes and partitions whenever necessary. This process is therefore generally known as "salvaging" volumes or partitions. The salvager is automatically invoked whenever necessary after the bosserver restarts a file server or volume server process if you created the standard `fs bosserver` configuration command, which is one of the steps in installing an OpenAFS server as explained earlier in "Installing an OpenAFS Server."

You can also execute the salvager manually to check one or more OpenAFS volumes, all volumes on a partition, and even all volumes on all partitions on a server. Some common symptoms of volumes that need to be salvaged are things like the following:

- The contents of one or more of your files are binary garbage when you try to edit them, but those same files contained your thesis yesterday.

- Attempts to access a volume fail because that volume is shown as being offline when examined using the vos examine or vos listvol commands.

- Files or directories are listed in the output of the Linux ls command but cannot be accessed.

- You deleted files on a volume to free up space in the partition that houses that volume, but the output of the partinfo command doesn't show that the additional space is now available.

The salvager is invoked using the bos salvage command because the bos command interacts with the file server and volume server processes to make volumes or partitions unavailable while they are being salvaged.

The bos salvage command has an incredible number of options, as shown in the output from the bos salvage -help command (which has been slightly reformatted to make it easier to read):

```
# bos salvage -help
bos salvage -server <machine name> [-partition <salvage partition>]
    [-volume <salvage volume number or volume name>]
➡[-file <salvage log output file>]
    [-all] [-showlog] [-parallel <# of max parallel partition salvaging>]
    [-tmpdir <directory to place tmp files>]
➡[-orphans <ignore | remove | attach>]
    [-debug] [-nowrite] [-force] [-oktozap] [-rootfiles] [-salvagedirs]
➡[-blockreads]
    [-ListResidencies] [-SalvageRemote] [-SalvageArchival] [-IgnoreCheck]
➡[-ForceOnLine]
    [-UseRootDirACL] [-TraceBadLinkCounts] [-DontAskFS]
➡[-LogLevel <(MR-AFS) log level>]
    [-rxdebug] [-cell <cell name>] [-noauth] [-localauth] [-help]
```

Of these options, the most important are the following:

- -server—Identifies the name of the file server machine on which the partitions or volumes to be salvaged are located. If only the -server option is specified on the bos salvage command line, you can supply the -all command-line option to force the salvager to check all volumes on all partitions on that server.

- -partition—Identifies the name of the partition on a specified file server that is to be salvaged. If only the -server and -partition options are specified on the bos salvage command line, the salvager will check all volumes on that partition.

- -volume—Identifies a specific volume to be salvaged. If the -server, -partition, and -volume options are all specified, only that volume will be salvaged.

If you are salvaging a partition containing read-only copies of other volumes or are salvaging a read-only volume directly, the salvager only checks the volume header to verify that a read-only volume is consistent. If it is not, the salvager simply deletes the read-only volume because repairing it could make it inconsistent with its parent volume. Similarly, if a volume that needs to be salvaged is replicated, you should delete all the replicas of that volume and re-create them by replicating and releasing the volume to guarantee that all replicas are consistent with their parent volume.

If you are salvaging all the partitions on a file server, the salvager tries to minimize the time required by salvaging up to four partitions in parallel. The salvager examines the `/etc/fstab` file to identify all OpenAFS partitions on a file server through pattern matching using the name of their mountpoints, `/vicepXX`. The salvager also notes the disks on which OpenAFS partitions are located and serializes salvage operations on partitions located on the same physical disk to minimize head movement.

The OpenAFS salvager completes the set of server processes, command-line utilities, and administrative utilities provided to support the OpenAFS distributed filesystem environment. Because of their additional security mechanisms, extensive support for ACLs, sophisticated caching strategies, and general design as unified, transparent, and networkwide filesystems, AFS and OpenAFS are examples of a distributed filesystem where the whole is truly greater than the sum of its parts.

13

THE OPENAFS
DISTRIBUTED
FILESYSTEM

Comparing Distributed
Filesystem Performance

IN THIS CHAPTER

This chapter helps tie together the distributed filesystems portion of this book by providing empirical data about the performance of these distributed filesystems in various situations. This data was collected by running the benchmarks introduced in Chapter 1, "Introduction to Filesystems," using a variety of parameters.

Testing distributed filesystem performance requires a slightly different approach than testing local filesystems (see Chapter 10, "Comparing Journaling Filesystem Performance). For example, the intense read/write tests of filesystem performance in the Bonnie and IOzone benchmarks aren't particularly relevant for distributed filesystems because the goal of a distributed filesystem is to enable transparent data access, and issues such as caching can be tweaked in too many ways to totally change the behavior of the benchmark. For this reason, I've focused on the Creation/Deletion and Postmark tests.

Distributed filesystem testing also requires a minimum of two machines, one as the file server and a second as a client. The first section of this chapter describes the hardware characteristics of the machines that I used for the client and the server. Each subsequent section focuses on one of the benchmarks I've chosen to compare different distributed filesystems, discussing what each was intended to show, the types of numbers that each provides, and what each test actually does to produce those numbers. Each of these sections then provides a table showing the results of running that benchmark on each type of distributed filesystem discussed in this book and then compares and discusses those results.

NOTE

Each table of benchmark data also contains results of running that benchmark with the same settings on a standard Linux ext2 filesystem. This provides a baseline that makes it easy for you to compare the performance of the distributed filesystems discussed in this book with that of the standard Linux filesystem that you are used to.

Evaluating Distributed Filesystems

Up to this point, the focus of this portion of the book has been on exploring the design and theory behind different filesystems. Support for the NFS distributed filesystem is integrated into the Linux kernel, and adding OpenAFS to a system doesn't require kernel modification aside from adding a loadable kernel module to the Linux startup procedure. This actually makes comparing these two distributed filesystems somewhat easier from a procedural point of view. As the chapters on NFS and OpenAFS show, using and administering NFS requires a number of specific administrative procedures, mostly related to the NIS and NIS+ authentication environments. OpenAFS has an even greater number of associated administrative utilities, due not only to its authentication environment and support for its own ACLs and groups, but also because of its underlying volume structure, global namespace and associated volume mount-points, replication capabilities, and so on.

The distinct capabilities of each makes it difficult to compare NFS and OpenAFS side-by-side. When comparing distributed filesystems, performance is a significant issue (as always), but the most important issue is the features that they provide. How well do these meet your needs? Does using a particular distributed filesystem simplify your computer system operations, or does it make it more complex? Is the gain worth the pain? Using a filesystem in a production environment and seeing how it performs is the only real test of how well it will work for you. But it's nice to have a little more data than source code and an administrative overview to go on before making a major commitment in terms of deploying a filesystem, learning its admin-istrative utilities, and spending the time required to develop a feel for its performance. This is a significant investment for a distributed filesystem such as OpenAFS and has probably been one of the major issues in its adoption.

A final issue in this comparison is that NFS 4 will be available "real soon now" and will make major changes to the basics of using NFS. The most significant of these changes is in its sup-port for client-side caching, which may provide some reduction in restart times and protection from lost data that only OpenAFS provides at the moment.

This chapter provides some empirical information to help you make an appropriate choice as to which distributed filesystem may be most useful for you and the computing environment in which you work. It primarily consists of cold, dry data made up of tables that make it easy to compare the results of various filesystem performance benchmarks designed to illustrate the performance of different filesystems under different circumstances. An overview of the bench-marks used in this book was provided in Chapter 1, and Chapter 10 provided a more complete discussion of each benchmark.

This is also a good point at which to mention that the capability to freely experiment with dif-ferent distributed filesystems and see which one best meets your needs is something that would have been unheard of as recently as a few years ago. Linux and the open-source movement enable you to reap the fruits of others' research efforts and technology investments. As illus-trated by this book, if you are running Linux, you have a choice of free, distributed filesystems to install, experiment with, and use.

The tabular data in this chapter only provides a performance comparison of each filesystem instead of trying to invent some metric that would enable you to model how using a distributed filesystem would affect your computing environment. For example, I didn't try to capture oper-ational statistics such as system restart times because these are totally dependent on the processes and other hardware in your machines, the size of the OpenAFS cache you're using, and so on. Similarly, these tests were done on a lightly loaded network, and therefore do not reflect the performance of these distributed filesystems in the presence of significant network load from other sources.

14

COMPARING
DISTRIBUTED
FILESYSTEM
PERFORMANCE

As you've seen in the NFS and OpenAFS chapters of this book, it really isn't all that difficult to install and configure either distributed filesystem, although OpenAFS obviously requires much more work to get started. The bottom line, again, is what each brings to your computing environment.

The Benchmarking Environment

All the tests in this section were done using a single client machine, a Linux system running the Red Hat Roswell Beta, otherwise known as Red Hat 7.193. The machine has the following hardware specs:

- Single 500MZ Celeron CPU
- 256 MB P-133 memory
- 1 GB swap space
- IDE hard drive, onboard controller:
  - hdc: WDC WD153AA, ATA DISK drive
  - 16 heads, 63 sectors, 29826 cylinders

I also used the same server system (though it was a separate, different machine from the client, obviously) to support both sets of tests. To compare NFS and OpenAFS more fairly, I exported the same partition for each environment, although the meaning of this is slightly different in the two cases. After doing the NFS tests, I installed OpenAFS on the system and used the partition that was exported as the basic repository for the OpenAFS file space, creating the necessary OpenAFS volumes in that partition. Therefore the same amount of disk space was available in both distributed filesystem environments, though technically not all of it was preallocated for OpenAFS volumes, whereas the entire thing was available as a single, exported NFS partition.

The characteristics of the machine used as a server for the NFS and OpenAFS tests are the following:

- Dual 500MZ Celeron CPUs
- 512 MB P-133 memory
- 1 GB swap space
- IDE hard drive, onboard controller:
  - hdc: WDC WD307AA, ATA DISK drive
  - 16 heads, 63 sectors, 56833 cylinders
- Size of exported partition: 18 GB

All these tests were run on the same two machines without any other users to effectively run the same tests under the same system load, modulo the occasional system processes. As you can see from the preceding hardware list, these weren't especially sexy machines. These machines were assembled from the sort of random, inexpensive parts that you'd find at any of the computer gypsy shows held all over the country and, presumably, in most other countries as well. The idea of using generic systems for benchmarking purposes was to use systems much like one that any random reader might be using, to provide a performance snapshot in a "real" environment as opposed to run on the x86 equivalent of a couple of Crays.

> **NOTE**
>
> Disclaimer: I have used OpenAFS in a number of production environments over the years, and therefore definitely find its complex administrative commands less alien than someone installing and using OpenAFS for the first time. However, the bottom line is the same for me as for any other Linux user: Is the hassle inherent in configuring these filesystems worth the benefits that they provide?

All these tests were run using a stock Linux 2.4.9 kernel compiled exactly as described in this book, except without the need to install patches or new filesystem code directly into the kernel.

The source code for all the benchmarks described in this section is provided in the benchmarks directory of the CD that accompanies this book. Providing copies of the source code for these benchmarks serves as a reference if you want to test specific systems at your site, or compare the performance of updated versions of any of the software described in this book. By definition, benchmarks are a snapshot of the behavior of a specific version of certain software running under a specific version of an operating system at a specific point in time. Your mileage will definitely vary if you run these benchmarks on any system other than one that you could only find if you came to my office.

The Creation/Deletion Test Benchmark

As mentioned in Chapter 10, this test was written to measure filesystem performance as a filesystem begins to fill up, which isn't especially relevant in a distributed filesystem. However, it is still interesting to compare creation and deletion performance as a bottom-line metric for filesystem performance. The small Perl script that does this produces verbose, per-process CPU time and doesn't attempt to measure real-life performance for anything but how long it takes to perform these basic filesystem operations. The script also produces df output for each step, which I have left out of the table because it isn't relevant for OpenAFS filesystems, where volumes only have quotas and an internal volume management system is used to manage actual disk space allocation.

The Perl script that runs this test is called `creation_deletion_test.pl`. Each of the creation_deletion_test benchmarks in this chapter was run with the following command line:

```
creation_deletion_test.pl file-system-type mount-point 2048000 900
```

This command line causes the script to create 900 files of 2048000 bytes apiece and then to delete them all.

Table 14.1 shows the results of my simple benchmark and provides some interesting results that require some interpretation. Both NFS and OpenAFS have higher individual results for creation times than a local filesystem, which seems surprising but really isn't if you consider that both of these use subsequent processes to actually write the data back to the file server. However, in terms of overall performance, it shouldn't be surprising that a local filesystem is a better performer than a distributed one. NFS ties or outperforms OpenAFS in every one of these tests, although in a simple sequential write operation such as the one used in these tests, the overall difference isn't especially significant.

TABLE 14.1   Results of the Creation/Deletion Test Benchmark

Filesystem	Operation	Best	Worst	Total
ext2	creation	3.42	3.69	2868.97
NFS	creation	3.38	3.59	3119.96
OpenAFS	creation	3.40	4.75	3182.69
ext2	deletion	0.00	0.01	1.93
NFS	deletion	0.00	0.01	1.81
OpenAFS	deletion	0.00	0.01	2.13

The Postmark Benchmark

The Postmark benchmark is interesting. Developed by the folks at Network Appliance, makers of fine Network Attached Storage (NAS) devices, it was designed to simulate performance under the types of real-world loads that you would get in high-load system directories that you would want to share over a network, such as Internet news repositories, mail queues, Web-based commerce, and so on. Postmark has an incredible number of options and is interactive, which makes it tough to script but still relatively easy to use.

The Postmark benchmark begins by creating a specified number of files of random sizes delimited by an upper bound. It then performs a specified number of transactions on random files from the pool of available files. Each transaction consists of subtransactions that either create, delete, read from, or append to files. It then displays summary information and returns to its internal command prompt.

The Postmark benchmark can only be run interactively, so each run of the benchmark involved the following commands:

Execute the postmark command from the Linux command line.

1. At the pm>prompt, specify the number of files using the set number *XXXX* command, where *XXXX* represents the number of files that you want to create.

2. At the pm>prompt, specify the number of transactions using the set transactions *XXXX* command, where *XXXX* represents the number of transactions that you want to execute.

3. At the pm>prompt, specify the run command to actually run the Postmark benchmark.

Table 14.2 shows the output from a run of the Postmark benchmark where files of between 0 and 10 KB were used. Data was collected for each filesystem with 50000 transactions performed on 1000 of these files, and with 50000 transactions performed on 20000 of these files.

TABLE 14.2 Results from the Postmark Benchmark

Filesystem	Files	Transactions	Total Time	TPS	Data Read (MB)	Rate (KB/sec)	Data Written (MB)	Rate (KB/sec)
ext2	1000	50000	89	561	161.15	1750.00	168.38	1830.00
NFS	1000	50000	695	73	161.15	237.43	168.38	237.43
OpenAFS	1000	50000	1112	45	161.15	148.40	168.38	155.05
ext2	20000	50000	781	64	144.06	148.85	271.87	280.93
NFS	20000	50000	1511	46	144.06	97.63	271.87	184.25
OpenAFS	20000	50000	7716	7	144.06	19.12	271.87	36.08

The columns of this table reflect the time that it took to perform the specified number of transactions on the specified number of files, the number of transactions executed per second, the amount of data written and read in that time, and the rates at which the data was written and read.

In this type of benchmark, you are looking for the highest possible number of transactions in the smallest amount of time, as a measurement of filesystem performance. This type of benchmark is typically used to compare different hardware running different operating systems but the same software (such as NFS, for example); however, when the hardware and the operating system become the constants, this benchmark provides a good deal of information about the speed at which different filesystems perform.

The result shown in Table 14.2 are interesting, and not surprising. A local filesystem is always faster at reading and writing than a distributed filesystem. The performance of OpenAFS is lower than NFS in every category, especially when manipulating many files using many transactions.

And the Winner is. . .

There is no ultimate filesystem. There are many different filesystems, each of which is appropriate for a particular environment and has its own fan club for a variety of reasons. For example, if you just want to begin sharing volumes over a network, NFS is obviously the best choice. If you want to guarantee your users higher availability by replicating volumes, want greater protection from data loss during a crash, and want a transparent, unified namespace with minimal configuration on a client system, OpenAFS is the best choice.

What do I use? Frankly, for my home computing needs, I use OpenAFS to store permanent or long-term data because I am familiar with it, and the capability to see exactly the same filesystem from every client without having to worry about local configuration is a big win for me. This also provides the capability to export my OpenAFS cell to the Internet and have people actually read and write data from that cell. This has proven convenient several times, and I see that capability as the biggest win of OpenAFS. However, if I were not using OpenAFS and simply needed to share many files locally, I would certainly use NFS—it's much faster and easier to get started using.

Backing Up, Restoring, and Managing Linux Filesystems

15

IN THIS CHAPTER

The majority of this book discusses the operational advantages of using journaling filesystems, distributed filesystems, and filesystem adapter software to create a high-performance, high-productivity computing environment. After deciding on the combination of local and networked filesystems that best suits your requirements and your user community, you'll probably start to wonder how best to integrate all these technologies into your standard MIS and IT operations.

It's easy to be wooed by futuristic technologies, but after the euphoria fades, the reality of integrating these technologies into your day-to-day operations is the real meat and potatoes of how well you can support and use those filesystems. It's hard to think of anything that so thoroughly combines the mundane and mandatory as does backing up your data. It's boring. It's time consuming. And, of course, it's critical.

This chapter begins with an overview of backup, restore, and operations theory and discusses various approaches to backing up and restoring anything from files to filesystems. The next section explores the various Linux software packages you can use to back up and restore your data, ranging from time-tested, mother-approved Linux software, to filesystem-specific software, to commercial packages. Subsequent sections discuss ways in which you can simplify backing up different types of computer systems and filesystems, and how to combine good backups and hot spares of your system disks to minimize downtime and the time when you can't access critical data. The chapter concludes with a detailed discussion of the Amanda backup system, a freely available, network-aware, client/server backup system. The source code for the Amanda software is located on the CD that accompanies this book.

Overview

When a user comes to you and says that he's lost the critical source code, report, or spreadsheet he was working on, he could care less what type of filesystem or operating system it was stored on. The user just needs it back, and pronto. This isn't an unreasonable request—as long as you're prepared.

As system administrators, systems engineers, or any similar position, our responsibility is to select, integrate, and support the best technologies possible for the benefit of the users of the computer systems we're responsible for. If you're interested in filesystems and distributed computing technologies to support a user community of one—yourself—you probably feel even more responsible.

An unfortunate side-effect of using sophisticated technologies such as journaling and distributed filesystems is that they add some complexity to daily operations. Different types of filesystems have different backup and restore programs, usually specific to the design and internals of the filesystem. Integrating all those into standard daily operations can be challenging without some guidance, as provided in this chapter.

Similarly, networked environments of personal computers that use Linux filesystem adapters to provide transparent access to Linux servers give users the illusion of a standard, homogeneous computing environment when that actually may not be the case.

Before discussing the different approaches to make life as easy for yourself, your MIS/IT staff, and your user community as possible, it's useful to review some of the basic issues and approaches to backing up any kind of computer system. Although you may already be totally familiar with these concepts and occasionally mumble backup and restore commands in your sleep, providing a clear picture of what you're trying to accomplish in doing backups and how backup systems are usually designed provides a firm foundation for the material in the rest of this chapter.

Computer system administrators and other members of an MIS/IT department do backups for several reasons, helping protect you against the following types of problems:

- Natural disasters such as fires, floods, and earthquakes that physically destroy entire computer systems
- Hardware failures in disk drives or other storage media that make it impossible to access the data that they contain
- System software problems such as filesystem corruption that might cause files and directories to be deleted during filesystem consistency checks
- Software failures, such as programs that crash and corrupt or delete the files that you're working on
- Pilot error, AKA users who accidentally delete important files and directories

In addition to protecting you and your user community against these sorts of problems accessing the data you and your users require, there are a variety of procedural and business reasons to back up the data on your computer systems, providing:

- A complete historical record of your company or organization's business and financial data.
- A source for historical information about research projects and software development.
- A way of preserving data that you do not need to make continuously available online, but which you may need to refer to someday. This includes things like the contents of the home directories of users no longer employed at your company or organization, or project directories for products that your company no longer sells or supports.
- Sadly enough, a source for information that your company or organization may someday need to defend itself or to prove its case in a lawsuit or other legal proceeding.

Backups take a significant amount of time and require a significant investment in both media and backup devices. Nowadays, even home computer systems store tens of gigabytes of information, which means that either you need to have fast, high-capacity backup devices, or you must have an army of operators loading and unloading lower-capacity tapes or other archive media, the money to pay them, and the space to store mountains of backups. It's also handy to be able to find a specific backup tape or CD when you need it, which means that you have to organize and keep track of your backup media in some reasonable way. Simply knowing where a specific tape is located on a desk or in a storage area is fine as long as the person who put it there still works with you, but what if she doesn't? The information that you use to locate a specific backup must also be understandable by someone else, just in case.

A final cost issue where backups are concerned is the need for offsite storage of all or specific sets of your backups. The story of computers in business and academia is littered with horror stories about people who did backups religiously, but stored them in their computer room. After a file or natural disaster, all they were left with were poor excuses and unemployment benefits. Offsite storage is critical to your ability to recover from a true physical catastrophe, but it also raises another issue—the need for appropriate security in the storage location you select.

Wherever you store your company's current and historical backup tapes should have a level of security comparable to any of your onsite locations. Though your local cat burglar might not actively target a storage locker full of backup tapes, any competitors you have would probably be ecstatic to be able to read and analyze the complete contents of your company's computer systems. Why not just save everybody time and mail them your source code and customer lists?

NOTE

Few backup systems encrypt the data that they write to archive tapes, and the standard Linux ones certainly do not. Most backup software uses various compression algorithms to maximize the amount of data that you can write to tape, and many modern tape drives offer hardware compression with the same goal, but encryption is totally unrelated to compression. You can certainly hack encryption into some Linux backup procedures by writing backup data to standard output, piping it through anything from rot13 to pgp to encrypt it, and then redirecting the output to your backup device, but this really isn't a good idea.

Encrypting data in this fashion makes it much more fragile and prone to unreadability. A problem with a standard backup tape that might prevent you from restoring a specific file from an archive could easily make it impossible to read any data at all past that point from an encrypted archive. I can't really think of anything more frustrating than a backup that you can't read.

Now that we've discussed why to do backups and some of the basic issues related to storing them, let's review the strategy behind actually doing backups. As mentioned previously, backups take time and have significant operational costs in terms of personnel and media, but there are a variety of ways to manage and minimize those costs.

> **NOTE**
>
> This chapter doesn't distinguish between backups of system and user data. Backups of system software are usually done less often than backups of user data because system data changes less frequently and can usually be re-created fairly easily, and user data is the most important information on almost any computer system and is usually hardest to re-create. In a production environment, you would generally back up both, although your daily operations would focus on backing up user data.

There are two basic types of backups: *archive backups*, which provide a complete snapshot of the contents of a filesystem at a given time, and *incremental backups*, which reflect the changes to the contents of a filesystem since a previous backup. Archive backups, generally referred to simply as *archives*, are the ultimate source for restoring user data because they contain a copy of every file and directory on the filesystem at the time that the backup was done. In an ideal world, it would be great to be able to do daily archive backups simply because this would guarantee that no user could ever lose more than a day's work, regardless of the type of calamity that occurred to your computer system. Unfortunately, archive backups have some drawbacks:

- They take the maximum amount of time that backups could require because they make a copy of every file and directory on every filesystem on all your computer systems.

- The volume of data that archives preserve a copy of means that they use the maximum amount of backup tape or other media that backups could require.

- Producing the largest possible volume of backup tapes or other backup media maximizes the amount of storage space required to store them and makes your record keeping as complex (and as critical) as it possibly could be.

- Archives are best done when no users are working on your computer systems. This reduces the amount of time that they take (because they're not competing with users for computer time) and also guarantees the consistency of the files and directories being copied to tape, because nothing can be changing. However, taking systems down to do an archive reduces the availability of a computer system to the company, and this is time in which you can't be using the system to earn money.

Although the advantages of archive backups as a complete record of everything are significant, these issues keep archives from being a reasonable approach to daily backups for any organization. You can certainly do them less often than daily, but reducing the frequency of your backups increases your exposure to losing a significant amount of data if your disks fail or your computers crash or are destroyed.

Enter incremental backups. As mentioned before, incremental backups contain a copy of all the files and directories that have changed on a computer system since some previous backup was done. If a problem occurs and you need to restore files and directories from backups, you can restore an accurate picture of those files and directories by first restoring the backups previous to your latest incremental backups (in other words, your archives and other incremental backups prior to the last backup you have), and then overlaying the restored files and directories with the versions of them found on the most recent incremental backups. When combined with archives, incremental backups provide the following advantages:

- They help minimize the number of tapes or other backup media required to do backups. Archives usually require many tapes or other backup media, whereas incrementals inherently require less because they aren't preserving as much data.

- They can be done more quickly because they are copying less data than an archive backup would.

- The backup media to which incremental backups are written requires less storage space than archive backups because there's less of it.

- Because they require less time to do than archives, personnel costs associated with them are reduced.

- Incremental backups are typically done without taking down the computer systems and filesystems that you are backing up, so they don't reduce the availability of your computer systems.

Another nice feature of incremental backups is that they record changes to the files and directories on your computer systems since some previous backups, which are not necessarily archives. Most large computer installations organize their backup media and associated procedures in a way something like the following:

- Archives are done infrequently, perhaps every six months or so, or just before any point at which major changes to your filesystems or computer systems are being made.

- Monthly incremental backups are made of all changes since the previous archive. If your budget and backup storage capabilities are sufficient, you usually keep the monthly incremental backups around until you do another archive backup, at which point you can reuse them.

- Weekly incremental backups are made of all changes since the previous monthly backup. These can be reused each month, after the new monthly backups are done.

- Daily backups are made of all changes since the previous weekly backup. These can be reused each week, after the new weekly backups are done. Some installations even just do dailies since a previous daily or the daily done on some previous day of the week.

No backup system can make it possible to restore any version of any file on a computer system. Even if you were lucky or compulsive enough to be doing daily archives of all your computer systems, files that exist for less than a day can't be restored, and it isn't possible to restore a version of a file that is less than a day old, worst-case. When designing a backup schedule and the relationships between archive and various incremental backups, an organization has to decide the granularity with which it might need to restore lost files. For example, the general schedule of archives, monthlies, weeklies, and dailies doesn't guarantee that you can restore a version of a file that is newer than the previous archive. For example:

- If the file was deleted one day before the first set of monthly backups was done based on the archive, it would be present on the archive and on the weekly backups for a maximum of one month. At that point, the weekly tape containing that file would be overwritten, and the newest version of the file that could be restored was the version from the archive.

- If the file was deleted one day after the first set of monthly backups was done based on the archive, it would be present on the archive and on the first monthly backup for a maximum of seven months—a new archive would be done at that point, and the monthly tape wouldn't be overwritten until one month after the new archive. At that point, the monthly tape containing that file would be overwritten, and the newest version of the file that could be restored was the version from the most recent archive.

Selecting a backup strategy is essentially a calculation of how long it will take someone to notice the absence of one or more files and request a restore, taking into account the level of service that you need to provide and the cost of various levels of service in terms of media, personnel, and storage/management overhead.

> **WARNING**
>
> Just doing backups isn't a guarantee that you're safe from problems, unless you're also sure that the backups you're making are readable and that files can easily be restored from them. Although it's less common today, there's always the chance that the heads in a tape drive may be out of alignment. This either means that you can read the tapes back in only on the same tape drive that you wrote them on, or that they can't be read at all. Always verify that you can read and restore files from backups using another device than the one on which they were made.
>
> *continues*

You don't have to check every tape every day, but random spot-checks are important for peace of mind and for job security. Similarly, tapes can just stretch or wear out from use—be prepared to replace the media used to do various types of incremental backups after some set amount of time. Nobody likes WORN backup media—write once, read never.

Backup systems generally provide automatic support for doing incremental backups since a previous incremental or archive backup. The Linux dump program, which I'll discuss in the next section, assigns different numbers to different backup "levels," and keeps track of which levels of backups have been done based on the name of the device on which the filesystem is located.

One problem inherent to backups is that every type of computer media has a shelf life of some period of time, depending on the environment in which it is stored, but its life span is never an absolute. For example, backup tapes can last for years, but they can also be unreadable after a much shorter period of time. One way to reduce both storage requirements and costs is to do your backups to long-lived devices such as write-once CD-ROMs and DVDs, magento-optical devices, or even rewritable CD-ROMs. Media such as these may only be suited for certain types of backups, depending on whether your backup software writes to the backup device as a filesystem or as a raw storage device. Also, no one yet knows exactly how long those types of media will last, but they certainly take up less room than almost any kind of tape. They have a much higher capacity than tapes, so they'll certainly take up much less space, but you should make a point to also spot check old archives every few years to make sure that they're still useful.

WARNING

Aside from the fact that backups can be subject to the vagaries of the device on which they're written, having those devices available when you need to restore backups is an important point to consider. It's a well-known nerd fact that many government and military sites have huge collections of backup data written on devices that don't exist anymore, such as super low-speed tape drives and 1-inch or seven-track tapes. Even if the devices exist, the data is often not recoverable because it's written in some ancient, twisted backup format, word size, and so on.

When you retire a computer system, deciding whether you'll ever need to restore any of its archive data is an easily overlooked issue. If you're lucky, you'll be able to read in the old archives on your new system and write them back out to some newer backup media, using some newer backup format. If you're not, you've just acquired a huge number of large, awkward paperweights shaped like different types of magnetic tapes.

Aside from cost-saving issues like using higher-density media such as CD-ROMs for archive purposes, another way to reduce the number of old backups that you have to keep around, as well as minimize the time it takes to do them, is to treat different filesystems differently when you're backing them up. For example, system software changes infrequently, so you may only want to back up the partitions holding your operating system when you do an archive. Similarly, application software changes relatively infrequently, so you may only want to back that up on a similar schedule. I can count on one hand, with one finger, the number of times that someone ever asked me to restore an old version of an application. However, keeping backups of executables and operating systems is just as important as keeping copies of user data—you'll agree if the disk goes bad on which your finely-tuned and heavily-tweaked version of an operating system is located.

A final issue to consider when doing backups and restoring files is when to do them, and what privileges are required. It's generally fastest to do backups during off-peak hours, when system usage is generally at a minimum, so that the backups can complete as quickly as possible, and when people are less likely to be modifying the files that you're backing up. Can you afford to have a graveyard shift? Also, backing up user files that may be heavily protected, or using a backup system that accesses the filesystem at the filesystem level generally requires root privileges. Many people use programs such as sudo or set s-bits on privileged binaries such as backup and restore programs so that they don't have to give the root password to their systems to the operators or part-time staff that generally do backups at off-peak hours.

The issues in this chapter often give system administrators and system managers migraines but are important to designing and implementing reasonable backup policies, schedules, and disaster recovery plans. Backups are like insurance policies—you hope that you never need to use them, but if you do, they had better be available.

Backup and Restore Software for Linux

The roots of the core set of Linux utilities lie in Unix, so it's not surprising that versions of all the classic Unix backup utilities are available with all Linux distributions. Some of them are starting to show their age, but these utilities have been used for years and guarantee the portability of your backups from any Linux system to another.

NOTE

As you either already knew or have guessed from reading this chapter, backup and tape management is a critical function for businesses and is therefore one of the areas for which a significant number of commercial Linux applications are available.

continues

Unfortunately, few of them can read Linux filesystems other than ext2, and most use proprietary archive formats that have the unfortunate side-effect of locking you into a particular package. A quick Web search for "Linux Backup Utility" will give you a list of available packages, but I'm not a big fan of any of the ones that I've looked at.

The classic Unix backup utilities provided with every Linux distribution are the following, in alphabetical order:

- cpio—The cpio utility (copy input to output) was designed for doing backups, taking a list of the files to be archived from standard input and writing the archive to standard output or to a backup device using shell redirection. The cpio utility can be used with filesystems of any type because it works at the file and directory level and therefore has no built-in understanding of filesystem data structures. The cpio utility has some unique historical advantages over tar (discussed later in this section), such as the capability to copy Unix device-special files and the capability to span tapes, floppies, and other backup media. Long ago, it used to be easy to tell whether a system was a Berkeley or AT&T Unix descendant by checking whether the cpio utility was available—if it was, it was an AT&T version of variant thereof. Probably for this reason, cpio never became as popular as tar.

- dd—The original Unix backup utility is called dd, which stands for "dump device," and does exactly that, reading data from one device and writing it to another. The dd utility doesn't know anything about filesystems, dump levels, or previous runs of the program. It's simply reading data from one source and writing to another, though you can manipulate the data in between the two to do popular party tricks like converting ASCII to EBCDIC.

  The dd utility copies the complete contents of a device, such as a disk partition, to another, such as a tape drive, for backup purposes. It wasn't really designed to do backups, though there are situations in which dd is the perfect tool: if you want to copy one partition to another when a disk is failing, make on-disk copies of the partitions on a standard boot disk for easy cloning, or when you are using an application that reads and writes directly to raw disk partitions that you can only back up and restore as all or nothing. Because dd reads directly from devices and therefore doesn't recognize the concept of a filesystem, individual file restores are impossible from a partition archive created with dd without restoring the entire partition and selecting the files that you want.

- dump/restore—The dump and restore utilities were designed as a pair of utilities for backup purposes and have existed for Unix since Version 6. Whereas cpio and tar combine the capability to write archives with the capability to extract files and directories from them, and dd can't extract anything except an entire backup, the dump program only creates backups, and the `restore` program only extracts files and directories from them. Both `dump` and `restore` work at the filesystem data structure level, and therefore can only be used under Linux (at the moment) to back up and restore ext2 and ext3 filesystems. However, the dump/restore programs can accurately back up and restore any type of file found in ext2 and ext3 filesystems, including device-special files and sparse files (without exploding their contents and removing their "sparseness").

The dump/restore utilities can only be used to back up entire filesystems, although they have built-in support for doing incremental backups, keeping a record of which filesystems have been backed up, and which level of backups has been performed for those filesystems. All this information is tracked in an easily understood text file named `/etc/dumpdates`. Archives created with the `dump` utility can automatically span multiple tapes or other media if the devices support end-of-media detection but can also span cartridge or magnetic tape media by using command-line options that tell `dump` the length or capacity of the tape—dump prompts you to change tapes when these limits are reached.

The most fascinating feature of the `restore` program is the capability to execute it in interactive mode, in which case it reads the information from the tape necessary to create a virtual directory hierarchy for the archived filesystem that it contains. You can then use standard commands such as `cd` to explore the list of the files on the tape and mark specific files and directories to be restored.

- `shar`—Although not really a backup utility, the `shar` program (Shell Archiver) creates text-format archives of files listed on the command line or supplied via standard input. `shar` archives can therefore be sent between systems via e-mail and were much more popular in the 1980s as a mechanism for distributing public domain software than they are today.

- `tar`—Probably the most widely used and well-known Unix backup utility, the `tar` command (tape archiver) takes a list of files and/or directories to be backed up and archives those files to an output device or to standard output. The GNU version of `tar`, once known as `gtar` to differentiate it from the version of `tar` that came with your Unix operating system, is yet another amazing piece of work from the Free Software Foundation. It provides capabilities far and above those of classic Unix `tar`, providing the built-in capability to read from compressed `tar` archives created with `gzip`, support for incremental backups, support for multivolume archives, and much more.

The `tar` program is filesystem independent and accesses files and directories without needing to know their low-level data structures. The `tar` program has some limitations, such as not being able to archive special files such as device nodes, but this is a minor point. `tar` is far and away the most popular free archiving utility available for Linux and is used to archive almost every free software package. The Red Hat Package Manager files (RPMs) used to package and install most Linux utilities contain `tar` files, and files with the .tgz or .tar.gz (in both cases, gzipped tar files) are used to distribute most Linux source code, such as the source code for the kernel, filesystems, and utilities provided on the CD that accompanies this book.

Unifying Backups Using Linux

Traditionally, backup systems for Unix systems, DOS and Windows systems, Novell systems, and Macintosh systems have been separate animals. Most of these are customized for the specific type of system that they were designed for, require that each type of system has its own dedicated backup device, and use their own data formats. Although this approach lets you back up multiple types of systems at the same time because each package is separate and uses distinct devices, this approach can be expensive because of issues such as the number of tape or other backup devices that you have to buy, the possibility that you'll have to purchase multiple types of backup media, the cost of hiring and training people to use several different backup systems, and the cost of the backup/restore software itself for each system.

Some commercial providers of backup/restore systems have gone to a client/server model that simplifies using a single backup package to archive files from different operating systems by running clients on each instance of each type of system, which then sends data to a central server in a common format that hides filesystem and operating system-specific differences. This is much more manageable than using different programs on different systems because operators only have to master a single backup or restore system, and also because only the server needs to have a physical backup device. All the clients write to the server across the network, and the server manages the physical backup device.

Linux provides unique opportunities for either eliminating the need for multiple, platform-specific backup applications and devices in several ways:

- Linux supports the network protocols used by all the most common personal computer operating systems. A Linux file server can therefore look like a Macintosh AppleShare server to Macintosh systems by running Netatalk, like a Windows SMB or CIFS file server to Windows systems by running Samba, and like a NetWare file server to NetWare clients using IPX/SPX as their network protocol by running the mars_nwe NetWare server emulation package. Linux servers can also provide a central repository for all Unix and Linux home directories by using OpenAFS or NFS.

  If you use a Linux server as the central location for user directories regardless of the client system, all the data that you need to back up is located on a single Linux system. You can therefore use a standard Linux backup utility such as tar to back up and restore any user files for any personal computer or workstation because they are all actually Linux files in the first place. You could even use the standard Linux dump/restore program, but unfortunately not with OpenAFS filesystems.

> **Note**
>
> If you're using this approach and ever need to restore a file for a Macintosh user whose home directory lives on a Linux system, you'll need some special information about how Macintosh files are stored on Linux systems via Netatalk. This is slightly more complex than restoring other types of files because each Macintosh file has two parts (known as the *data* and the *resource forks* of the file), which are stored separately under Linux.
>
> To restore Macintosh user files stored on a Linux file server accessed via Netatalk, you must restore both the file and the file by the same name in the .AppleDouble subdirectory of the directory in which the Macintosh file is located. The .AppleDouble directory in each Linux directory holds the resource fork data for Macintosh files. For example, restoring the Macintosh application data file "My Resume" in the ~wvh/personal directory would require restoring both the files ~wvh/personal/My Resume and ~wvh/personal/.AppleDouble/My Resume.

- Linux can directly mount the filesystems from Windows and Novell NetWare file servers. (The capability to mount Macintosh filesystems on Linux does not currently work over a network and is largely read-only at this point.) This enables you to back up your Windows or NetWare user data by mounting those filesystems on your Linux system and automatically including these filesystems in standard Linux backups done using tar. (You can't use dump/restore because it only backs up filesystems based on their device names, which don't exist for filesystems mounted over the network and also because dump/restore only works with ext2 and ext3 filesystems.) Although you can back up NetWare data this way, you may not be able to restore filesystem attributes for which equivalents aren't present in Linux, such as advanced NetWare ACLs.

- You can combine the previous two approaches. For example, the mars_nwe NetWare emulator can't provide the same level of performance when used simultaneously by more than 20 users. You could therefore use a Linux system as your primary file server for Windows and Macintosh users but mount your actual NetWare filesystems on the Linux system to do backups. You could only use tar to back up this configuration, due to limitations in the dump/restore programs.

- If your user community only uses Microsoft Windows, Mac OS X, Linux, and other versions of Unix such as AIX and Solaris, you can use a distributed filesystem such as OpenAFS to give all your systems access to the OpenAFS distributed filesystem. OpenAFS is freely available for all these types of systems. You can then either use the OpenAFS backup utility to back up and restore OpenAFS volumes, or you can use a utility such as tar to back up OpenAFS data in a more portable format. However, if you back up files

15

Backing Up, Restoring, and Managing Linux Filesystems

in OpenAFS using `tar`, you will lose the OpenAFS ACL information because `tar` can't archive that type of filesystem-specific information.

- If you only use Linux or Unix systems, you can centralize your backups in either of two ways by taking advantage of the fact that NFS is provided with all Linux and Unix systems. If users need to maintain data on local workstations, you can use NFS to export the local filesystems containing user data back to a central Linux system on which you do backups. If all user data is stored on one or more Linux NFS file servers, you can either directly back up each server separately, or use NFS to mount all file server partitions on a single system from which you do backups. In either case, you would have to use `tar` because of the fact that `dump/restore` only understands ext2 and ext3 filesystems.

> **NOTE**
>
> An advantage of exporting local filesystems via NFS to a server on which backups are done is that this makes the backups independent of the underlying type of filesystem used on the host. Although XFS provides the `xfsdump` and `xfsrestore` utilities to support backing up things like XFS ACLs and extended attributes, you can only back up ReiserFS and JFS filesystems using `tar` at the moment anyway. The time savings in centralizing your backups might be worth not retaining the XFS ACLs and extended attributes for files that have to be restored.

As you can see from this list, the wide range of networking and filesystem support provided by Linux can make it easy to unify backups of user data from several different types of operating systems. I keep stressing user data in these examples because backing up Windows, NetWare, and OpenAFS filesystems by using the `tar` utility on a Linux system is unreasonable for system files for two major reasons:

- Backing up system data using utilities that require network connectivity and specific protocols is not useful if you ever need to use the backed up information to restore the system itself. Backups of system software are always best done using utilities designed for that specific type of system, and may even be bootable.
- The `tar` command doesn't preserve any file attributes that aren't present in the Linux ext2 and ext3 filesystems, such as Windows' hidden, system, and archive bits, and the ACLs in Novell or OpenAFS. Support for ACLs in GNU `tar` is under development, as is general support for ACLs in other types of Linux filesystems. But OpenAFS and NetWare both predate the POSIX ACL specification, and therefore have nonstandard ACLs as far as POSIX is concerned, which may never be supported in the `tar` utility.

Backing up user files and directories using `tar` from a Linux system is a cost-effective approach to backups, but you have to be aware of what you're sacrificing in some cases (filesystem and operating system-specific information) for that convenience.

Using the Amanda Backup System

The previous section provided a number of approaches to centralizing backups by mounting filesystems from a variety of systems on a Linux system. You could then use a standard Linux utility such as GNU `tar` to do backups that include these filesystems as though they were part of the standard Linux filesystem. The primary drawback to this approach is that the GNU `tar` utility doesn't currently preserve filesystem-specific information such as ACLs or file attributes. This is therefore a problem in using the current version of GNU `tar` to back up data stored in XFS, Novell, Windows, and AFS filesystems from another Linux system. You can easily back up all the actual data, which is the primary responsibility of a backup application, but it's both a hassle and a shame to lose and thus have to manually reset file and directory-specific information.

As mentioned in the previous section, some vendors of commercial backup utilities have moved to the client/server model to let different types of systems run special backup software that completely understands the local filesystems. It shouldn't come as a total surprise that a similar solution is available for Linux (and Unix) in the form of a distributed backup system called AMANDA, a public domain application originally developed for Unix systems at the University of Maryland in the early 1990s.

The remainder of this chapter provides an overview of Amanda and explains how to build, install, configure, and use the Amanda backup system. The final section explains how to restore files and filesystems from Amanda backups.

Overview of Amanda

AMANDA, the Advanced Maryland Automated Network Disk Archiver, (hereafter simply referred to as Amanda) is a distributed backup system that makes it easy to back up a number of client workstations to a central backup server. This isn't unique in itself because you could easily back up multiple clients from a single server by using the standard r commands and a robust set of shell scripts. But Amanda provides a complete backup management system for Linux and Unix systems. Amanda supports multiple `dump` sets with distinct configurations, tracks, and labels tapes; verifies that a valid tape is in the drive; tracks dump levels and dates on its client systems; produces detailed reports that are automatically delivered via e-mail; and keeps extensive logs that make it easy to diagnose and correct the reason(s) behind most problems.

Communication between Amanda clients and servers is encrypted to heighten security. Amanda is designed to be run as a cron job, which almost eliminates the need for any hands-on operator involvement with Amanda backups beyond its initial configuration, reading your e-mail to see how the previous night's dumps went, and changing tapes.

> **NOTE**
>
> Amanda's home Web site is at http://www.amanda.org. Several public Amanda mailing lists are available for announcements (amanda-announce), user questions (amanda-users), and technical discussions (amanda-hackers). You can join any of these by sending mail to listname-request@amanda.org, substituting the name of the list that you want to join for listname. Archives of messages from the lists can be downloaded, and the amanda-users and amanda-hackers lists can be searched online at http://groups.yahoo.com/group/listname.

Amanda minimizes the time it takes to actually do backups by maximizing parallelism between the client systems actually doing the backups. As the server receives backup data from clients, it stores these backup images in a common "holding area" on one or more of the server's disks. As client backups are completed, a separate server process feeds the backup images to the tape drive sequentially. This provides a high probability that the write process can provide a steady stream of data because the backups of various clients are beginning and ending at different times, and a new backup image is usually available to feed to the tape drive after a previous one has been written. The capability to feed a constant stream of data to a tape drive also increases the likelihood that the tape drive will be able to operate in streaming mode, which is both faster and reduces wear and tear on the drive itself.

Another way in which Amanda takes advantage of its client/server design is that it can use different backup applications on different client systems. Because the backups done by each client are handled as a backup image by the server, it isn't necessary to use the same backup application on all clients. By default, Amanda supports GNU tar (the version of the tar command found on Linux systems) and the standard dump utility on Linux or Unix clients. Amanda can also use Samba and the smbtar script to back up Microsoft Windows systems. As I'll explain later, it's also easy to change Amanda's idea of what the standard dump utility is on a system, which therefore enables you to use customized backup applications such as xfsdump on IRIX or Linux systems where XFS is the primary filesystem.

Client/server systems can be difficult to configure and often require replicating configuration across multiple systems. This is not the case with Amanda. Client configuration, explained in "Configuring Amanda Clients" later in the chapter, is simple because the majority of the work is done by the backup server—where the majority of the configuration is also done in two text files: `amanda.conf` and a `disklist` file that identifies the systems and disks on those systems to be backed up as part of each dump set or configuration.

Amanda supports a tremendous number of backup tape drives and changers and can easily be configured to work with a new tape drive by using an application provided with Amanda that explores the capacity of the device and writes its results in the form required by Amanda. As with most Amanda configurations, tape drive parameters and changer information are also stored in the `amanda.conf` file. This enables Amanda to quickly be configured to use new, higher-capacity tape drives as they become available, without requiring special drivers.

Amanda supports both the hardware compression provided by many tape drives and provides its own built-in software compression mechanisms. The two shouldn't be used together because hardware compression is usually done by analyzing the data being written to the tape drive and applying standard compression algorithms—if the data being written to the drive is already compressed, few opportunities for compression will be available, and the time spent analyzing the data stream will largely be wasted.

Most backup systems, such as the standard Linux `dump`/`restore` utility, use different dump levels to help reduce backup time by limiting the period of time in which files must have changed to be backed up. For example, a level one dump consists of files that have changed since the previous level zero dump, a level two dump consists of files that have changed since a level one dump, and so on. Amanda departs from this backup model, by calculating appropriate dump levels internally, based on a user-defined dump cycle consisting of a certain number of days. Amanda uses information about the length of the dump cycle, estimates of the possible size of various levels of client backups, and even factors in performance information from previous dumps to automatically decide whether to do full or daily backups.

Compiling and Installing Amanda

Amanda is preinstalled as a part of many Linux distributions, such as Red Hat, so you may not want or need to configure and install your own version. However, configuring, compiling, and installing Amanda yourself can help guarantee that you have the latest version, and that it has been configured in the way best suited to your environment. If you just want to get started configuring and using Amanda, you can skip this section and go to "Configuring an Amanda Server" later in the chapter.

To install version 2.4.2, patchlevel 2, of the Amanda package, included on the CD that accompanies this book, do the following:

1. Mount the CD and extract the Amanda package from the file `utils/amanda-2.4.2p2.tar.gz` to a directory on your system using a command like the following:

```
cd <target-directory>
tar zxvf <path-to-CD>/utils/amanda-2.4.2p2.tar.gz
```

2. Change directory to `<target-directory>`/amanda-2.4.2p2 and run the configure script to correctly configure the Amanda Makefile for your system and Linux distribution:

   `./configure --with-user=amanda-user --with-group=amanda-group`

   Replace `amanda-user` with the name of a user on your system who you want the Amanda server process to run as, and who must therefore have read and write access to the directory where Amanda stores its logs and to the directory that you are defining as a holding area on your server system. Similarly, replace `amanda-group` with the name of the group on your system that you want Amanda to belong to. This group must own the tape device to which you will be writing your backups. Both the holding area and the tape device should be mode 770, allowing writes by group members.

TIP

As mentioned earlier, Amanda can invoke a client's particular dump program to produce dumps in a filesystem-specific format. By default, this is the program /sbin/dump on Linux systems. To change the version of the dump program that you want to use on an Amanda client, you can modify the file config/config.h before building Amanda.

For example, to set the Amanda client to use /sbin/xfsdump rather than /sbin/dump, edit the file config/config.h and search for the value XFSDUMP. Uncomment the line /* #undef XFSDUMP */ and replace it with the line #define XFSDUMP "/sbin/xfsdump". The client that you compile will use xfsdump rather than dump, but you will have to be careful either to use it on systems that only have XFS filesystems or to dump XFS filesystems only using that client.

---

3. After the Makefile is generated and configured, execute the `make` command to build the new versions of the utilities in the Amanda package:

   `make`

   This produces verbose, system-specific output that's not useful to replicate here.

4. After all the utilities are compiled, install them on your system using the following command:

   `make install`

Your system now has the current version of the Amanda utilities, associated reference (man page) information, and documentation installed.

Configuring an Amanda Server

If you just compiled and installed Amanda without modifying the paths that it uses, all the Amanda utilities will have been installed in subdirectories of /usr/local. If you modified the name of the destination directory in your Makefile for some reason, substitute the name of the directory that you used for /usr/local in these instructions.

> **NOTE**
>
> If you are configuring a version of Amanda included with your Linux distribution, sample configuration information is probably preinstalled in /etc/amanda. If so, you can skip to step 7 and replace /usr/local/etc/amanda with /etc/amanda in subsequent steps. If you are using Red Hat Linux, Amanda is configured to use the user "amanda" and the group "disk."

To configure a newly installed Amanda server, do the following:

1. Create the directory /usr/local/etc/amanda. This is where your configuration information will be stored.

2. Select a name for the dump configuration that you are creating and create a directory by that name under the directory /usr/local/etc/amanda. This name can be anything—the default name is DailySet1. I'd suggest using this name for your initial configuration. When you're comfortable with configuring Amanda, you can create other configurations with other names.

3. Copy the files amanda.conf and disklist from the example subdirectory of the directory containing the Amanda source code to the directory with the name of your dump configuration that you created in the previous step. As an example:

   ```
   cd example
   cp amanda.conf disklist /usr/local/etc/amanda/DailySet1
   ```

4. If a user and group do not already exist with the names that you supplied when configuring Amanda, create them now using linuxconf or the system administration utility provided with your Linux distribution.

5. Recursively change the ownership of the /usr/local/etc/amanda directory and all subdirectories to the amanda user and group, as in the following example:

   ```
   chown -R amanda:disk /usr/local/etc/amanda
   ```

   Use the user and group names you supplied when configuring the Amanda source code.

6. If necessary, change the group ownership of the tape drive that you will be using to the name of the group that you supplied when configuring Amanda, and change the mode of the tape device to be writable by owner and group, as in the following examples:

   ```
   chgrp disk /dev/nst0
   chmod 660 /dev/nst0
   ```

7. Decide which disk or directory you will use as a holding area for Amanda client back-ups. Change its group ownership to the name of the group you supplied when configuring Amanda, and change its mode to be writable by group. The holding area can be any directory or partition in which you have sufficient space to store temporary copies of backups from your clients. You can estimate the amount of space needed by determining the amount of disk space used in the largest partition that you will be backing up using Amanda. If the holding area is not large enough to hold any backup image, Amanda waits until the drive is available and then writes directly to the drive rather than trying to use the holding area.

8. Change to the directory that holds the configuration you are creating, which by default is `/usr/local/etc/amanda/DailySet1`.

9. Open the file `amanda.conf` in your favorite text editor and modify the following entries. The values listed in this section are intended to get you started using Amanda and are not the only ones that you can change:

   - Set `org` to the name of your organization for reporting purposes. For example, my domain is named `vonhagen.org`, so I use the following entry:

     `org "vonhagen.org"`

   - Set `mailto` to a space delimited series of users who you want to have receive mail about Amanda dumps. For example, I set this line to the following, which sends mail to `opr` and myself. These addresses can be any valid local or Internet e-mail address. For example, in my case, `opr` is actually a `mail2news` script that posts e-mail to an internal newsgroup to which operators are expected to subscribe. The entry in my `amanda.conf` file is the following:

     `mailto "opr vonhagen@vonhagen.org"`

   - Set `dumpuser` to the name of the user that Amanda should run as. I use the `amanda` user for this because that is the user you find on the version of Amanda preinstalled on Red Hat Linux systems. My entry for this is simply:

     `dumpuser "amanda"`

   - Uncomment the `tapedev` entry if necessary, and set it to the name of the nonrewinding tape device on your system. For example, the tape drive on my backup server is the first SCSI device, so my entry for this is

     `tapedev "/dev/nst0"`

   - Set the `tapetype` to the name of a tape device supported by Amanda. Many of these are listed later in the sample `amanda.conf` file. If yours isn't listed in this file, search the online archive site for the `amanda-users` group (`http://groups.yahoo.com/group/amanda-users`) to find an appropriate `tapetype` entry that you can add to the `amanda.conf` file. I use a Dell PowerVault 110T tape drive with hardware compression off, so my entries for this are

```
tapetype PV100T
define tapetype PV100T {
    comment "Dell PowerVault 110T"
    length 19457 mbytes
    filemark 32 kbytes
    speed 1397 kps
}
```

> **TIP**
>
> If you can't find an entry for your tape drive in the `amanda.conf` file or online, Amanda's `tapetype` utility can generate one for you. To use this utility, change directory to the `tape-src` subdirectory of the directory where you installed the Amanda source code, run the command make `tapetype to build the executable`, and then run the `./tapetype` command, supplying the one-word name that you want to use for your device's `tapetype` entry and the name of the device as arguments. For example, to create a `tapetype` entry for my Dell PowerVault 110T, I might execute:
>
>   ./tapetype -t PV100T -f /dev/nst0
>
> This can take an incredibly long time to run because it calculates tape length by writing data to the drive until it fills it to calculate how much data the drive will hold. When the program finishes, paste its output into your `amanda.conf` file and set the name of the `tapetype` entry in `amanda.conf` to the name that you used.

- Directly below the `tapetype` entry is a `labelstr` entry. This defines a standard regular expression that is used to verify tape labels—the labels for the tapes you use with Amanda must be for a specific dump configuration, which must match this regular expression, or Amanda will complain and exit. This helps prevent you from accidentally overwriting existing backup tapes or reusing them prematurely. As you can see from the default entry, the default Amanda configuration expects tape labels for the default configuration to be of the form DailySet1*NN*, where *NNN* represents at least two digits. I typically just use the standard entry for this. Labeling tapes is explained in "Labeling Tapes" later in the chapter.

- In the `holdingdisk` entry labeled `hd1`, replace the directory name with the name of the directory or partition mountpoint that you will be using as a holding area, and set use to the maximum amount of space that it can hold. If you are using a directory on an existing partition as a holding area, you can supply a negative size, which means to use all available space except for that amount. This lets Amanda share a disk with other applications without the chance that it will fill up the disk. My entry, which uses a separate partition mounted at /amanda as the holding space for my backup server and tells Amanda that it can use everything but 10 MB of the space on that partition, is the following:

```
holdingdisk hd1 {
    comment "Holding Disk"
    directory "/amanda"
    use -10 Mb
}
```

- For general performance reasons, using a separate partition as a holding area is preferred. I also prefer to use negative values that reflect the amount of space that Amanda can't use because this makes the entry more flexible if I have to replace the disk on which the /amanda partition is located. If you are using a directory on an existing partition where other processes are consuming disk space, you would probably want to set this much higher to ensure that those processes aren't starved for disk space by Amanda.

- If you have multiple holding disks, you should create holdingdisk entries for each, making sure that the name of each holdingdisk definition is unique. If you use multiple holding disks, Amanda automatically uses them in parallel to provide internal load balancing.

- Set the values of infofile, logdir, and indexdir to be /usr/local/var/amanda/config-name, where config-name is the name of the dump configuration you are creating. Comment out duplicate changerfile entries. Create the directory /usr/local/var/amanda and change its ownership to the amanda user and group, making it writable by both, and changing its mode to 770. An example of my entries for these is the following:

```
infofile "/usr/local/var/amanda/DailySet1/curinfo"
logdir   "/usr/local/var/amanda/DailySet1"
indexdir "/usr/local/var/amanda/DailySet1/index"
```

- Examine the dumptype section to see which dumptype entry you will want to use to back up each of the partitions you want to back up. The dumptype entries consist of settings for things like the application you want to use to back up a certain partition, whether you want to do software compression, and so on. When getting started with Amanda, I'd suggest simply using one of the existing ones. After you've used Amanda for a while, you can create your own if necessary. I tend to use ext2 filesystems for /boot, ext2 or ext3 filesystems for the / partitions on my systems, and different journaling filesystems for others, so I back up / and /boot using dump/restore (the comp-root) entry and /home and /usr filesystems using tar (high-tar). The basic things that dumptype entries define are

- The back up utility to use. The default is `dump/restore`, and the entry for `tar` is `program "GNUTAR"`.

- The type of software compression to do—either none, `"client best"`, `"client fast"`, `"server best"`, or `"server fast"`. The `"best"` entries tell Amanda to do maximum compression on either the client or server, and the `"fast"` entries tell Amanda to do fast compression. I tend to use `"client best"` with all my Linux systems and `"server best"` for some older, slower SPARCs that I use.

- Whether to do Kerberos encryption when sending backups from a client to a server. Though this is slightly slower, I generally turn this on by using `"kerncrypt yes"`.

- The priority of the backup. This is used when tape errors occur to mark filesystems that Amanda should prioritize backing up to the holding area even if it can't write to tape.

There are many other possible options for `dumptype` entries. These are explained as comments in the default `amanda.conf` file.

- Skip to the ethernet interface definition near the end of the file, and make sure that it is appropriate for your network. The default network type in the sample `amanda.conf` file is 10 megabit ethernet—if you are using a faster network, change the kilobytes per second value to something more appropriate. I just use the standard one.

Save this file and exit the text editor.

10. Open the `disklist` file in the same directory using your favorite text editor and create entries for the partitions that you want to back up on your systems. Each entry consists of the name of a client machine, the name of a disk or directory that you want to back up, and the name of the `dumptype` entry that defines the characteristics of the dump that you want to do. A sample section of my `disklist` file looks like the following:

```
##
## buserver - holding system
##
buserver hda1 holding-disk
buserver hda2 holding-disk
buserver /usr/local high-tar
##
## journal
##
journal hda1 comp-root
journal hda3 comp-root
journal hdc2 high-tar
```

Note that the entry for my backup server uses the holding-disk entry, which is one of Amanda's predefined entries that simply tell Amanda not to use the holding-disk but to write directly to tape.

Save this file and exit the text editor.

11. Make sure that the correct entries for the ports used by the Amanda processes are found in your system's /etc/services file, and add them if they are not. These should be the following:

```
amanda        10080/tcp
amanda        10080/udp
amandaidx     10082/tcp
amidxtape     10083/tcp
```

NOTE

If any of those hosts that you are backing up are separated by a firewall, you must make sure that these ports are allowed through the firewall.

---

12. Make sure that your system's Inet daemon knows which server to activate in response to dump requests from the server. If you are using the old inetd Inet daemon, the entry in your /etc/inetd.conf would be the following:

```
amanda dgram udp wait Amanda /usr/local/libexec/amandad amandad
```

If you are using the newer xinetd Inet daemon, edit the files /etc/xinetd.d/amanda, /etc/xinetd.d/amandaidx, and /etc/xinetd.d/amidxtape, setting the disable statement in each of these files to "no".

After you edit the appropriate file(s), restart your Inet daemon by using the appropriate command from the following:

```
/etc/rc.d/init.d/inetd restart
/etc/rc.d/init.d/xinetd restart
```

13. Finally, edit the file .amandahosts, located in the home directory for the Amanda user on your system (often a directory such as /var/lib/amanda, as it is on Red Hat Linux hosts), adding entries for any Amanda servers that will contact your server. On a server that is also being backed up, this would just be an entry for your server. On any client system, this would contain an entry for any Amanda server system backing up that client. This file has the same format as a .rhosts file, defining a system that can access your system, and the name of a user that your system can be accessed as. On my server system, this file contains the following:

```
buserver.vonhagen.org amanda
```

This completes the basic tasks required to configure a simple Amanda server. After you configured the Amanda clients that you listed in the `disklist` file, you can verify that your `amanda.conf` file is valid and that the daemons on your clients are running correctly by executing the following command as the superuser on your system:

```
su amanda -c "/usr/local/sbin/amcheck DailySet1"
```

The `amcheck` utility first verifies that the `amanda.conf` file associated with the specified backup configuration is correct and then contacts all the clients listed in the `disklist` file to make sure that the Amanda daemons are running there. Sample output from a run of the `amcheck` program on a small backup system looks something like the following:

```
Amanda Tape Server Host Check
-----------------------------
Holding disk /amanda: 16890384 KB disk space available, that's plenty
NOTE: skipping tape-writable test
Tape DailySet102 label ok
Server check took 3.527 seconds
Amanda Backup Client Hosts Check
--------------------------------
Client check: 3 hosts checked in 0.137 seconds, 0 problems found
(brought to you by Amanda 2.4.2p2)
```

Some common problems that might be reported by the `amcheck` program are the following:

```
NOTE: info dir /usr/local/vare/amanda/DailySet1/curinfo: does not exist
NOTE: it will be created on the next run
NOTE: index dir /usr/local/var/amanda/DailySet1/index/dada: does not exist
```

Files that Amanda expects to find for the hosts listed in your disklist file are not present. These will be automatically created the next time Amanda actually runs.

```
ERROR: localhost: [access as amanda not allowed
    from amanda@localhost.localdomain] amandahostsauth failed
```

This error means that you have an entry in your `disklist` file for `localhost`, but that `localhost` is not listed in the `.amandahosts` file.

```
- WARNING: journal: selfcheck request timed out.  Host down?
```

This error means that the amanda daemon is not running on the client system or that the client system is down.

Configuring Amanda Clients

Configuring an Amanda client is simple because the majority of the configuration work is done in the `amanda.conf` and `disklist` files on the server.

To activate an Amanda client system, do the following:

1. Install the Amanda software.

2. If a user and group do not already exist with the names that you supplied when configuring Amanda, create them now using `linuxconf` or the system administration utility provided with your Linux distribution.

3. Edit the file `.amandahosts`, located in the home directory for the Amanda user on your system, adding entries for any Amanda servers that will contact this client. On any client system, this would contain an entry for any Amanda server system that was backing up that client. This file has the same format as a `.rhosts` file. On my server system, this file contains the following:

   ```
   buserver.vonhagen.org amanda
   ```

4. Make sure that the correct entries for the ports used by the Amanda processes are found in your `/etc/services` file and add them if they are not. These should be the following:

   ```
   amanda      10080/tcp
   amanda      10080/udp
   amandaidx   10082/tcp
   amidxtape   10083/tcp
   ```

NOTE

If any hosts that you are backing up are separated by a firewall, you must make sure that these ports are allowed through the firewall.

5. Make sure that your system's Inet daemon knows which server to activate in response to dump requests from the server. If you are using the old `inetd` Inet daemon, the entry in your `/etc/inetd.conf` would be the following:

   ```
   amanda dgram udp wait Amanda /usr/local/libexec/amandad amandad
   ```

   If you are using the newer `xinetd` Inet daemon, edit the file `/etc/xinetd.d/amanda`, setting the disable statement in this file to `"no"`.

   After you edit the appropriate file, restart your Inet daemon by using the appropriate command from the following:

   ```
   /etc/rc.d/init.d/inetd restart
   /etc/rc.d/init.d/xinetd restart
   ```

After you add entries for this client to the `disklist` file on your server, you can use the `amcheck` program on your server to verify that the new client is working correctly, as described in "Configuring an Amanda Server" earlier in the chapter.

> **NOTE**
>
> As mentioned earlier, Amanda can invoke a client's particular dump program to pro-
> duce dumps in a filesystem-specific format. In the "Compiling and Installing Amanda"
> section earlier in the chapter, I explained how to compile an Amanda client that uses
> an alternative dump program. An equivalent but sneakier approach, if you do not
> want to rebuild Amanda and the versions that you are using does not support other
> dump programs, is to move /sbin/dump on the client to /sbin/dump.ext2 and then
> hard link /sbin/xfsdump to /sbin/dump. You have to be careful to back up only XFS
> filesystems on that client using dump and back up any other using tar, but your
> backup images will at least contain all the XFS ACL and extended file attribute
> information.

Labeling Tapes

In the electronic sense, a tape label is no adhesive bit of white paper. Instead, it is a special block of information at the beginning of a tape that usually either contains information used by the application that last wrote the tape or simply identifies that program. Tape labels help applications recognize tapes that they have written. Many backup programs use tape labels to store information about when and how a tape was written.

Amanda uses special tape labels to identify tapes that are or have been used for Amanda back-ups. This is designed to help prevent someone from accidentally overwriting a backup tape already in use, or from accidentally creating two tapes with the same label, which would really confuse the restore process. All tapes used by Amanda must be labeled before use.

Labeling an Amanda tape is done using the `amlabel` command, which takes two arguments:

- The name of the dump configuration that you are labeling the tape for use with. This enables Amanda to locate the `amanda.conf` file associated with that dump configuration and to read certain entries for that dump configuration. The entries used by the `amlabel` command are the `labelstr` entry, which defines the regular expression matching the labels for tapes in that dump configuration, and the name of the Amanda user, to make sure that you should be allowed to label tapes.

- The label that you want to use for the tape.

To label a tape for use by Amanda, execute a command like the following as the superuser:

```
# su amanda -c "amlabel DailySet1 DailySet100"
rewinding, reading label, not an amanda tape
rewinding, writing label DailySet100, checking label, done.
```

This command labeled the tape `DailySet100`, which matched the regular expression defined in the `amanda.conf` file for the `DailySet1` configuration.

Automating Amanda Backups

As mentioned earlier, Amanda is designed to be run automatically by a scheduling operation such as `cron`. On Linux systems, each user has a special `crontab` file that automatically runs processes at set times on behalf of that user.

In general, you'll want to put two entries in the `crontab` file for the Amanda user on your server system:

- The first is an entry that uses the `amcheck` program to verify that a valid tape is in the drive and that clients are responding. This entry should execute sometime during daylight hours, after you remove the previous day's backup tape and replace it with the tape for the current day's backups. Running this command from `cron` sends mail to everyone in the `mailto` list in the current dump configuration if any errors occur when verifying either of these points. Run this command sometime during working hours, and sufficiently prior to the time at which the backups themselves are scheduled to run, to give yourself or your operators the time to correct the problem(s).

    A sample version of this type of `crontab` entry, provided with Amanda, is the following:

    ```
    0 16 * * 1-5    /usr/sbin/amcheck -m DailySet1
    ```

    This entry causes the `cron` process to run this command at 16:00, Monday through Friday, and sends mail if a problem is detected.

- The second is an entry that runs the `amdump` program sometime during off-peak hours.

    A sample version of this type of `crontab` entry, provided with Amanda, is the following:

    ```
    45 0 * * 2-6    /usr/sbin/amdump DailySet1
    ```

    This entry causes the `cron` process to run the `amdump` program at 00:45, Tuesday through Saturday.

If you have never created a `crontab` entry before, it is simple to do:

1. Use the `su` command to assume the identity of the Amanda user.

2. Execute the command `crontab -e` to edit the `crontab` file for that user, using the default editor for that user.

3. Create the entries that you want to execute automatically and then save the file and exit the editor.

The combination of a validation program such as `amcheck` and the capability to schedule backups to run automatically helps ensure that your backups will never be late (or forgotten entirely) due to other crises.

Restoring Files from Amanda Backups

For a complex client/server backup system, Amanda is surprisingly easy to configure and start on both clients and servers. The restore process is even easier, though not entirely intuitive. The thing to remember when initiating an Amanda restore operation is that Amanda backup tapes contain archives of local and remote backup images. When you restore something from an Amanda backup tape, you are restoring the backup image. You then have to use an appropriate utility to restore files from that backup image. For example, if you need to restore a file from a filesystem backed up using the standard dump restore program, you will still have to use the restore program to restore the files from the backup image restored from the Amanda backup tapes.

Amanda's restore program is known as `amrestore` and requires three arguments:

- The name of the tape device on which Amanda backups are stored
- The name of the host where the backups originated
- The short name of the filesystem of which the dump was done

For example, if you wanted to restore a file from Amanda's backups of the filesystem `/dev/hda1` on a host named `dada`, the command that you would issue and the output you would see would look like the following:

```
# amrestore /dev/nst0 dada hda1
amrestore:    0: skipping start of tape: date 20011004 label DailySet103
amrestore:    1: skipping distfs._etc.20011004.1
amrestore:    2: skipping journal.hdc2.20011004.1
amrestore:    3: restoring dada.hda1.20011004.1
amrestore:    4: skipping distfs.hda9.20011004.1
amrestore:    5: reached end of tape: date 20011004
```

This `amrestore` command in the previous example would create the file `dada.hda1.20011004.1` in the working directory. You can then examine the `disklist` file for the backup configuration, determine which backup program produced that backup image, and use the appropriate program to examine its contents and extract the files you were looking for.

Compatibility Filesystems, Interoperability, and Filesystem Adapters

IN THIS CHAPTER

Since the virtual beginning of time (that is, the beginning of the computer age) choosing the "right" type of computer system on which to base a college, university, or company has been a problem for any MIS/IT group. The easiest solution to this problem is to avoid it by preventing it from happening. If your graphics department knew the Mac OS, but your office staff used Windows systems, each Picasso became an instant Windows user. If your sales group was barely Windows-literate, but you were a Unix shop, it was time to teach everybody LaTeX. However, taking everyone out of their element makes them less productive. Regardless of how you slice it, simplifying computer operations by standardizing on a single operating system is a problem for everybody except your accounting department. There is no ultimate computer system, no single ultimate hardware platform, and no one set of applications that will do everything you need to do for the rest of your life. I hate to sound like a total heretic, but the goal of any MIS/IT department should be to provide a user community with the hardware and software that it needs to get its work done with the right level of quality, as quickly and easily as possible. This requires giving people the software tools and related hardware that they need to best do their jobs. Graphics and serious page layout will probably be done on Macs forever. You'll never pry Windows systems out of the hands of a sales force who depends on Act! and doesn't realize that there are other mailers and calendaring systems besides Outlook Express. Your accounting group may depend on NetWare to keep cash coming in and bills going out.

This chapter introduces the software available on Linux to help unify a computing environment composed of heterogeneous types of computer systems. It begins by discussing general issues in unifying computing systems, discusses the primary operational and business reasons that justify supporting mixed computing environments, and introduces the interoperability packages that you'll read about in the next few chapters.

Overview and Terminology

The primary computing requirement for most users is to be able to run a specific set of software packages. If a certain group needs to be able to run graphics packages that require or simply work best on a Macintosh, that's what it should have. If another needs to be able to produce marketing literature and spreadsheets or run management software specific to a Windows box, that's what that group should use.

NOTE

This isn't a plea for MIS anarchy—groups of people who work together need to be able to run the same software packages. I'd be as cranky as anyone if I didn't get a paycheck because the accounting group was split down the middle between using Macs and Windows systems.

The challenge faced by most MIS/IT groups interested in user requirements and productivity is how to provide a computing environment that makes it easy to integrate different types of computer systems. The omnipresence of networks in academic, corporate, and even home computing has greatly simplified the process of connecting different types of systems, largely eliminating the modems, serial cables, and occasional sacrificial chicken that were traditionally required.

Unfortunately, a problem in networking different types of computer systems is that each evolved differently and independently, and now has its own set of networking protocols and procedures for file and resource sharing. As discussed in the past few chapters, Linux and Unix systems use TCP/IP (Transmission Control Protocol/Internet Protocol) and UDP (Universal Datagram Protocol) to provide access to shared file servers and other resources through distributed filesystems. Macintosh systems use AppleTalk and AFP (AppleTalk Filing Protocol) to share access to AppleShare servers and AppleTalk devices. DOS and Windows systems are schizo as usual. Microsoft networking for Windows uses protocols such as NetBEUI (NetBIOS Basic Extended User Interface), TCP/IP, CIFS (Common Internet File Services—or Sharing, depending on whom you ask), and SMB (Server Message Block) protocols to share filesystems and peripherals. DOS and Windows users who couldn't wait for Microsoft to cobble together a networking solution have used Novell NetWare and NetWare Print Services via the IPX (Internetwork Packet Exchange) and TCP/IP protocols since the beginning of time. What's a girl to do?

Luckily, the answer to this problem is printed on the cover of this book: Linux. Not only is Linux a robust, high-performance operating system in its own right, but it also supports many software packages that enable Linux systems to communicate and interoperate with pretty much any type of computer system. Communicating between one type of system and another is simple—terminal programs and one-shot file transfer applications are available for every system. Interoperability is more complex—it is the capability of one type of computer system to interact with another type of computer system in the same way that it would with a computer of the same type.

The United Nations would be the same as the biblical Tower of Babel if not for one thing—interpreters. In a modern networked computing environment, Linux systems easily fill this role. Linux systems can be used as central systems that speak all the networking protocols used by different types of computer systems and can translate between them.

The primary uses for computer networks today are the following:

- To access information and applications provided on the Internet or on centralized internal servers
- To share data between computer systems and provide access to centralized file servers
- To share access to peripherals, such as printers

The first point is trivial—every modern computer system provides one or more Web browsers with built-in capabilities for accessing Web sites over the network and downloading files from them. The whole point of the Web is interoperability—accessing common data using a common, system-independent protocol (the Hypertext Transfer Protocol, HTTP).

The next two issues are slightly more complex because they involve using the protocols specific to each computer system as mentioned earlier in the chapter. Linux uses UDP and TCP/IP—and supports every one of those other protocols. By storing files and centralizing shared resources on Linux systems and running a variety of network interoperability software packages on your Linux systems, you can quickly and easily provide a unified computing environment that lets everyone use the type of desktop system that he wants to use. No more platform wars or "MIS always liked you best" complaints—your users can simply get down to the business of doing business.

Providing access to shared data via file servers is probably the most important internal corporate use for networks. For this reason, it's often useful to think of networking interoperability packages as being filesystem adapters because they convert one set of network filesystem requests into another. You can also think of them as compatibility filesystems because they provide compatibility between one type of system and filesystem and another.

Filesystem adapters and compatibility filesystems take a slightly different approach to interoperability than that provided by the distributed and networked filesystems discussed earlier in this book. Distributed computing provides interoperability by providing a meta-filesystem that all computer systems participate in. Filesystem adapters let various types of computer systems continue to use the protocols that they have always used but provide a way for integrating Linux systems and filesystems into those environments. It's totally natural to think of the distributed filesystem discussed earlier in this book as being the Linux and Unix equivalents of AppleTalk, SMB, and Novell networking.

The basic difference between filesystem adapters or compatibility filesystems and distributed filesystems is the difference between using translators at the United Nations or simply asking everyone to speak Esperanto. In the first case, you have various adapters to bridge the gap between unique ways of communicating, whereas in the second, you require everyone to speak a common language.

The networking interoperability packages discussed in the next few chapters are the following:

- Netatalk, for integrating Macintosh systems with Linux systems
- Samba, for integrating Microsoft Windows networking with Linux systems
- The NCP (Novell Core Protocol) tools and the NWFS (NetWare File System) filesystem, for integrating systems running Novell networking with Linux systems

These interoperability packages let Linux systems interoperate with the native file sharing and common resource access mechanisms used by different personal computer systems. Using these filesystem adapters, it's even possible to attach personal computer systems to Linux distributed filesystems by using the Linux systems as a gateway between personal computer file-sharing protocols and Linux distributed filesystems.

The vision of a shared, open computing environment that I've painted so far, where users of all races, creeds, and operating system persuasions live and work harmoniously, isn't the only argument for using Linux systems. Computers and their support costs money. Luckily, as I'll discuss in the next section, there are a number of solid business and cost reasons for interoperability. Standardizing on Linux for file sharing and providing centralized access to shared resources is just plain common sense.

Business Reasons for Interoperability

As mentioned previously, standardizing on a single type of computer system simplifies the lives of your MIS/IT staff, reduces training requirements for your users, and often makes selecting corporate software packages a no-brainer. It's always easy to make one choice when you don't have another. However, this is as shortsighted as it sounds.

Different types of computer systems have their own advantages, and there are often good business reasons to mix and match platforms. For example, the creative artists in your graphics department will probably be most productive on Macintosh systems, whereas your sales force may be most productive with software only found on Windows systems. Similarly, your MIS and computing support staff probably require the power, native multiprocessing capabilities, and reliability found on Linux, Unix, or Unix-like systems.

Standardizing on a single computing platform eliminates the advantages provided by different systems and software packages. It hammers every peg into a round hole regardless of its shape, limiting creativity and productivity by forcing people to use certain software simply because it runs on the "standard" operating system.

A better question to ask yourself might be "why not interoperate"? Restricting the types of computers you use in your home or business limits what you can do, the type of people that you can hire, and, often, the services that you can provide. If you raced automobiles, would you force yourself to use four-cylinder subcompacts because it was easier and cheaper to get parts and service? Hopefully not—different tasks and workers need to use the tools that can help them do the best job possible.

Many businesses and computer system administrators shy away from mixing different types of computing systems, insisting that installing, configuring, and managing a mixed computing environment is expensive, difficult, or impossible. This simply isn't true any more. All modern computer systems of every type are network-aware, and as you'll see through the next few chapters, easy solutions exist to let one computer's network file-sharing mechanism simulate and integrate with that of another.

In a mixed computing environment, your MIS and IT personnel will need to know how to deal with different types of systems. You may need to hire more sophisticated personnel with a broader knowledge of today's computer systems. This often translates into a business advantage for you because your staff can recommend and use the best computers and software available to solve your business problems, regardless of the operating system they use or the type of system they run on. The cost of hiring broader, more experienced MIS and IT staff can quickly come back to you in terms of better solutions to your business problems.

Finally, business today is more competitive than ever, and most businesses are glad to seize anything they can that enhances productivity and differentiates them from their competitors. An easy example of this sort of advantage is the ability to use a wider, more sophisticated range of software packages and computer systems than your competitors.

Operational Advantages of Interoperability

Aside from the general advantage of being able to access files stored on Linux systems and access Linux printers from Macintosh systems, some equally important advantages provided by interoperability software packages are operational ones. As discussed throughout this book, using file servers to provide centralized file storage simplifies operational tasks such as backups. Centralized file servers on which everyone has a personal storage area minimize the number of individual systems on which personal files can be stored, and which thus need to be backed up. Using a Linux system as a central storage resource for Apple Macintosh, Novell NetWare, and Microsoft Windows environments means that, for the most part, your MIS/IT staff can back up all user files by backing up the Linux system. This relieves individual personal computer users of the responsibility for correctly maintaining, exporting, and backing up local files and directories from their systems.

A less obvious advantage of serving data to clients of different types from centralized servers is that centralizing data resources on an interoperable platform such as Linux also lets you centralize your investment in high-speed, redundant data storage (such as RAID storage, especially RAID level 5, which is expensive) and high-performance backup devices such as fast, high-capacity tape drives.

Centralized file servers also provide opportunities for centralizing software distribution. They do this by providing common, shared areas for installing and storing programs that your entire user community needs access to. This simplifies the administration of these applications, making it easy to upgrade them in a single central location whenever necessary. Users will automatically discover new or updated versions of these applications when they mount a shared directory where the programs are stored. The licensing schemes used by many software packages often mandate that the software be installed in one location only and share a pool of licenses there.

Yet another advantage of centralized file servers in a computing environment composed of many different types of machines is that users can move from one type of computer system to another and still have access to the same set of personal files and directories. This would be impossible if files were simply stored on individual personal computers or workstations.

Finally, using the interoperability packages discussed in this chapter to make Linux peripherals such as printers available to users of any type of computer system as a centralized resource has distinct advantages. First, it maximizes the availability of existing computing resources by enabling users to access peripherals from any system rather than from specific ones. Second, it reduces costs by minimizing the need to duplicate resources in different computing environments. Traditionally, Macintosh networks might have their own sets of printers, and Windows networks might have another. This was partially necessary because AppleTalk printers were traditionally connected to a Localtalk or Ethernet network rather than a specific Macintosh, whereas Windows printers were traditionally connected to a specific Windows system. Thanks to Linux, networking, and interoperability packages, Macintosh, Windows, and Linux systems can share access to a single, truly common set of printers.

A Working Example Is Worth a Thousand Words

Nothing shows the advantages of interoperability better than actually doing it. The next few chapters discuss how to use Linux to store and deliver data to Macintosh, NetWare, and Windows systems. As a unifying example, each chapter contains a section that shows how to access your Linux home directory and a Linux directory that serves as a public data repository from the type of system and networking protocol being discussed in that chapter. After reading these chapters and seeing the implementation of this example in each case, you'll see how easy it is to use the filesystem adapters and compatibility filesystems provided by Linux to get to the same Linux data from everywhere.

Even after using these technologies for a few years, I occasionally step back and marvel at how impressive it is that my free Linux system looks like an AppleTalk file server to Macintosh systems, like a NetWare file server to systems running Novell Netware, and like an SMB or CIFS file server to Windows systems. I can get to the same data from everywhere, using whatever tools I prefer or need to use. Sometimes, the legendary "right thing" does indeed happen.

Using Netatalk for Macintosh and AppleTalk Connectivity

IN THIS CHAPTER

This chapter discusses the filesystem adapters for Linux that provide connectivity between Linux systems and Apple computers running Mac OS 9.2 and earlier. Ironically, even though Mac OS X is based on FreeBSD, Mach, and other Unix-like systems, AppleTalk connectivity is not available between Linux computers and Apple computer systems running Mac OS 10.0.X. The upcoming release of Mac OS 10.1 will provide full AppleTalk support.

This section begins with an overview of Netatalk, a free software package that provides AppleTalk support on Linux systems and what exactly that means. The section then discusses how to compile, install, configure, and administer Netatalk to let Mac OS systems mount shared Linux volumes on their desktops. The final section of this chapter explains how to access printers on an AppleTalk network from Linux systems.

Overview

Just as Samba gives Windows users transparent access to files on Linux and Unix systems, two free software packages for Linux provide the same transparent access to Linux or Unix systems for Macintosh users. (Using Samba is discussed in Chapter 18, "Using Samba for Windows Interoperability." Macintosh systems traditionally use their own networking protocol, known as AppleTalk, to share files, folders, and printers. Macintosh interoperability packages such as the filesystem adapters discussed in this chapter provide an AppleTalk (and AppleTalk over IP) interface to Linux and Unix directories and printers from Macintosh systems. Using these packages, Linux and Unix directories can be selected from the Macintosh Chooser just like any other shared Macintosh resource. Linux systems also can print to AppleTalk-connected printers using the capabilities provided by these packages.

General reasons for using file servers and networked storage were discussed in detail in the Chapter 11, "Overview of Distributed Filesystems," and Chapter 16, "Compatibility Filesystems, Interoperability, and Filesystem Adapters." In a nutshell, networked file servers provide many operational benefits beyond simply maximizing the availability of computing resources by enabling users to access files stored on Linux systems and access Linux printers from Macintosh systems. From a user's perspective, the most important advantage may simply be that you can use whatever type of computer system is best suited to the job at hand and still have access to the same files and directories. This would be impossible if files were simply stored on specific personal computers or workstations.

The two Macintosh interoperability packages in common use today are the Columbia AppleTalk Package (CAP), available at http://www.cs.mu.oz.au/appletalk/cap.html, and Netatalk, available from SourceForge at the project URL http://sourceforge.net/projects/netatalk. The Columbia AppleTalk Package is much less widely used than Netatalk and (unfortunately) for good reason. Although it was a powerful and impressive package in its day, installing and compiling it now involves installing between 100 and 200 patches (at the moment). Although it's difficult not to like the patch program, it is difficult to want to tweak a set of source files a hundred or so times and assume that everything will be harmonious. Because I assume that your goal is to get Macintosh connectivity working and then move on, I'm going to focus on Netatalk. I've been using Netatalk on a variety of Linux systems since first building it for Red Hat 5.0 and have found it to be stable, easy to install and configure, and tremendously useful in a mixed computing environment that includes Apple Macintosh systems and AppleTalk printers.

Netatalk consists of several servers, their configuration files, and associated support applications. One of the most impressive aspects of Netatalk is just how little configuration it actually requires. A big part of this is its faithfulness to the AppleTalk model, where AppleTalk devices discover each other quickly and painlessly. Largely for this reason, AppleTalk has a reputation for being an incredibly chatty protocol in terms of how it uses the network. This was the case long ago when all AppleTalk communications were done over Apple Localtalk networks. The abuse of the "talk" suffix in Macintosh networking is one of the biggest problems in Macintosh networking and is still the source of much confusion unless you're a true Mac aficionado.

A Few Words About AppleTalk

AppleTalk is a protocol just like TCP/IP, UDP, and many other popular acronyms. Localtalk is a bunch of cables with weird end connectors and is yet another cabling scheme just like Ethernet. The AppleTalk protocol runs on Localtalk, Ethernet, and many other network interfaces. Until the iMac, other G3 Macs, and today's G4 systems, all Macintosh systems came with a Localtalk port, which has now been replaced by standard RJ-45 ports for connectivity to standard Ethernet networks. Localtalk was great in its day because it provided a quick, plug-and-play solution for networking Macs together that was forgiving of errors in network communications. But it is incredibly slow by today's standards, maxing out at something like 230 KB per second on a lightly used network with a heavy tailwind.

Macintosh systems that have only Localtalk connectors must communicate using AppleTalk because that is the only protocol supported on a Localtalk cable. To communicate with systems that understand only TCP/IP, Macintosh systems use software such as MacIP to encapsulate TCP/IP packets inside AppleTalk packets and then send them to an AppleTalk router, which can be as simple as a Localtalk-to-10Base-T adapter that plugs into a Localtalk or printer port on the Mac. Devices such as these unwrap the AppleTalk envelope and forward the packet as plain TCP/IP onto the Ethernet. Returning packets from the TCP/IP destination are repackaged into AppleTalk packets and sent back to the Localtalk Mac.

On today's Ethernet networks, AppleTalk can be speedy and efficient, although it is still somewhat slower than TCP/IP. The primary advantage of AppleTalk is that, like every other aspect of the Macintosh, it "just works." The AppleTalk protocol automatically handles dynamic AppleTalk address assignment and other internal communications.

Macintosh systems connected to an Ethernet use the AppleTalk protocol to communicate with printers or when communicating with an Apple file sharing server. AppleTalk is used basically used for all the functions that you can select in the Mac OS Chooser (under the Apple menu). Netatalk provides an AppleTalk implementation that runs as a server named atalkd, for AppleTalk Daemon, on Linux and Unix systems, enabling you to access those systems and associated resources from the Chooser.

Macintosh systems connected to an Ethernet also talk TCP/IP directly, which is handy because it's obviously the standard for connections to most Unix machines and to the Internet. Applications such as Eudora; most other e-mail programs; browsers such as Microsoft's Internet Exploder, Netscape, Opera, and many others; and more "Unix-oriented" applications, such as telnet, ssh, and FTP all communicate using TCP/IP.

AFP and Related Macronyms

As discussed in the previous section, AppleTalk is a protocol used to communicate with devices, such as some printers and file servers, that speak that protocol only. As a faster, more modern file-sharing protocol for communicating with file servers, Apple Computer developed the AppleTalk Filing Protocol (AFP). AFP provides commands that enable you to do all the standard things you'd want to do when contacting and exchanging data with a file server, including obtaining and modifying information about the file server and the filesystems that it exports; create, read, write, and delete files and directories (oops, I mean folders); and so on.

The AFP file server implemented on Macintosh systems is known as AppleShare. Like its support for AppleTalk, Netatalk provides an AFP server for Linux and Unix systems as a daemon, called afpd. AFP servers running on non-Macintosh systems often are referred to as providing "*AFP file services*" or "*AppleShare services*". AFP removes many of the limitations of AppleTalk file servers, such as restrictions on volume size, type, and so on. AFP also includes robust support for user authentication and an access control mechanism that lets you control access to servers, filesystems, and even directories.

You can run AFP over AppleTalk, the AppleTalk Datagram Delivery Protocol (DDP), or over TCP/IP, although AFP over TCP/IP is faster than AFP over AppleTalk. Most modern Linux kernels provide built-in support for DDP that you can compile in or load as a module. In combination with Netatalk, this gives Linux systems complete compatibility with any of the communications protocols used on Macintosh systems and AppleTalk peripherals.

Filesystem Differences in Macintosh and Linux Systems

Interacting with Macintosh systems from any non-Macintosh system is somewhat more complex than it could be due to differences in the basic structure of files and directories on

Macintosh filesystems. The Macintosh filesystem stores files and directories in two parts called the data and resource forks. Actual file data is stored in the data fork, whereas the resource fork holds information such as the creator of a file, the file type, what icon is used to represent the file, and so on. Interacting with these two parts of a file is transparent on Macintosh systems because the filesystem does all the dirty work for you. This aspect of the Macintosh filesystem has caused a number of flame wars between people who claim to know whether having two forks for each file is a klugde or an elegant solution to providing mandatory information for the GUI. The operating system and low-level applications such as the Finder use this information internally to make the Macintosh GUI possible, as opposed to simply providing yet another command-line interface. My opinion is that it's reality, and we have to deal with it.

Regardless of your stand on this particular issue, the end result of Macintosh files consisting of data and resource forks is that you can't simply copy or manipulate Macintosh files from a Unix machine or Unix files from a Mac. All the files stored on Unix systems whose filesystems are made available to Macintosh systems have to appear to have files with the same organization, or those files couldn't be accessed by Macintosh applications that expect or need both parts. Similarly, Unix systems that can access Macintosh filesystems directly need to be able to manipulate the data fork without trashing the resource fork.

To deal with files on Macintosh systems that have two parts, and to make files on Linux and Unix systems appear as though they have two parts, Netatalk does some clever things. Interacting with Macintosh files from a Unix box can all be handled inside Netatalk. Making files on the Linux and Unix systems appear to have two forks is a slightly more complex problem to which Netatalk provides an elegant solution. A special hidden subdirectory called .AppleDouble is created in each directory on a Linux or Unix system that you access from a Macintosh system. This directory contains files with the same names as those in the parent directory and which represent the resource forks of all the files in the parent directory, and also includes a special file called .Parent that provides resource information for the parent directory. Each of these files is 589 bytes in length. When you execute a Macintosh Finder command, such as "Get Info" on a specific file, Netatalk translates this into a request for information from the file in the `.AppleDouble` directory that corresponds to that file.

Netatalk also creates other special directories and files associated with the AFP file servers, such as the .AppleDesktop and Network Trash Folder directories to satisfy the expectations that Macintosh systems have of Appleshare servers.

Figure 17.1 shows a Unix directory exported via Netatalk as seen from a Macintosh system running Mac OS 8.6.

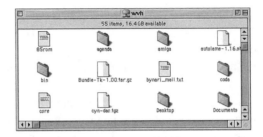

FIGURE 17.1
A Linux directory viewed from the Mac OS via Netatalk.

Getting More Information About Netatalk

Netatalk originally was developed at the University of Michigan by its Research Systems Unix Group. The University of Michigan has continued to support and extend Netatalk and still has a Web page for it at http://www.umich.edu/~rsug/netatalk. This page starts out with a pointer to the SourceForge site mentioned earlier, but still provides a great set of links to other sites at which you can find information about Netatalk, including a slightly dated Netatalk FAQ at http://www.umich.edu/~rsug/netatalk/faq.html. The University of Michigan site also provides a general links page at http://www.umich.edu/~rsug/netatalk/links.html containing links to many other Netatalk and Netatalk-related sites. Some of these are no longer available (in the grand tradition of the Web), but many still contain useful information.

NOTE

I'm only noting that the links on the University of Michigan Netatalk site are slightly dated to warn you that much of the version-specific Netatalk information there may no longer be relevant. I'm certainly not flaming—you certainly can't beat the price of Netatalk! Like most universities, the University of Michigan is in the education and research business, not the "free software support" biz. Netatalk wouldn't be where it is today, like on the CD for this book, if it wasn't for the dedication and hard work done on it at the University of Michigan.

Although the primary source for the current version of Netatalk is available at SourceForge (again, http://sourceforge.net/projects/netatalk), the documentation there is skimpy at best. The actual documentation for the SourceForge version of Netatalk, included with this book, is at http://sourceforge.net/docman/?group_id=8642. Frankly, you'll get much more information out of this chapter, the FAQs and other information at the University of Michigan, and some other links that I'll mention later than you will from SourceForge. This book helps resolve the Netatalk documentation shortage by providing a definitive explanation of installing and configuring Netatalk, as well as explaining just what all those servers actually do.

Speaking of documentation, a useful HOWTO for Netatalk on Linux is the Linux Netatalk-HOWTO by Anders Brownworth, available at `http://www.anders.com/projects/netatalk`. This is somewhat dated because it focuses on Netatalk versions other than the one on SourceForge. Luckily, most of the internals of Netatalk installation haven't changed in the last few versions, so it still provides a great deal of useful configuration information.

Support Software for AppleTalk and AFP on Linux

Unlike the packages required to support the journaling and networked filesystems discussed in this book, filesystem adapters that support network interoperability with a personal computer file-sharing mechanism are generally a single, integrated package.

To add AppleTalk and AFP support to your system, you need the following:

- A kernel that supports the AppleTalk protocol
- The Netatalk package

The latest version of this package at the time this book was written, netatalk-1.5pre7, is located in an archive file called netatalk-1.5pre7.tar.gz in the Netatalk subdirectory of the CD that accompanies this book. The Netatalk package installs many AppleTalk-related utilities in `/usr/local/bin` (by default), many of which are used internally by the Netatalk package. The Netatalk package also installs its core daemons and related applications necessary to run and use Netatalk in `/usr/local/sbin` by default. The following are the Netatalk servers and utilities that you may want to run or use directly on your system.

In `/usr/local/bin`:

- `nbplkup` — A utility that uses NBP (Name Binding Protocol) communication to find the names of AppleTalk devices on your network.
- `nbprgstr` — A utility that registers an NBP name.
- `nbpunrgstr` — A utility that unregisters an existing NBP name. This can be useful when you are installing or uninstalling printers.
- `pap` — A utility that enables you to interface with remote AppleTalk printers using the Apple PAP (Printer Access Protocol) protocol.
- `papstatus` — A utility that enables you to retrieve status from a specified printer using PAP.

In /usr/local/sbin:

- psf —A PostScript filter used to print jobs to PostScript printers using Netatalk
- papd—The PAP daemon used to send print jobs to AppleTalk printers
- atalkd—The Netatalk AppleTalk daemon
- afpd—The Netatalk Apple Filing Protocol daemon

Adding AppleTalk Support to Your System

All Linux 2.2 and better kernels have the capability to support AppleTalk at the kernel level, which may or may not be active in the kernel on your system. This section explains how to check whether AppleTalk support is already enabled; how to add that support and build a kernel that supports AppleTalk if it is not; and how to compile, install, and configure the Netatalk package.

Building a Kernel with AppleTalk Support

You can determine whether your Linux kernel already supports AppleTalk by checking for the string "Apple" in the messages displayed when your system last booted, as in the following example:

```
# grep -i apple /var/log/messages
Sep  3 02:31:23 journal kernel: NET4: AppleTalk 0.18a for Linux NET4.0
```

If your kernel displays a message like the one in the previous example and therefore already includes AppleTalk support, you can skip ahead to the section entitled "Installing Netatalk."

If you do not see a message of this form (the AppleTalk version number may be different), you will have to recompile your kernel to provide AppleTalk support, as explained in the next two sections.

Activating AppleTalk Support in the Kernel

The CD that accompanies this book includes the source code for version 2.4.9 of the Linux kernel, the most advanced version of Linux available at the time of this writing, and the one that I've therefore chosen to use to show how easy it is to add AppleTalk support to your Linux system.

> **NOTE**
>
> As mentioned in each chapter, if you have never built a kernel before, doing so is a great learning experience. Although the whole idea of prepackaged Linux installation is to protect users from the need to "roll their own" kernel and Linux utilities, compiling a kernel is an excellent way to familiarize yourself with the conceptual internals and organization of Linux. The instructions in this book for compiling kernels create kernels that have special names and will thus not overwrite the current version of the Linux kernel that you are using.

Install this kernel as described in "Installing the Kernel Source Code" in Appendix A, "Using the CD-ROM: Installing, Updating, and Compiling Kernels."

> **TIP**
>
> If you already have compiled a kernel for the computer system on which you are building a new kernel, you can use the configuration information from that kernel to save time when configuring the new kernel. Reusing existing configuration data from an existing kernel is explained in Appendix A.

After you've installed the kernel, do the following to activate AppleTalk support in the kernel:

1. Log in as root or use the su command to become root.
2. In a terminal window running under an X Window System window manager or desktop, change directory to the directory /usr/src/linux-2.4.9 and execute the make xconfig command. The commands related to compiling and loading support for the Linux X Window System kernel configurator display in the window in which you executed the make xconfig command. Eventually, the X Window System Linux kernel configurator displays, as shown in Figure 17.2.
3. Select the Networking Options command or button. The Networking Options dialog appears, as shown in Figure 17.3.
4. Scroll down and click Y beside the AppleTalk Protocol Support option.
5. Click the Main Menu button at the bottom of the dialog to close the Networking Options dialog and return to the main Linux Kernel Configuration dialog.
6. Select the Network Device Support command or button. The Network Device Support dialog appears, as shown in Figure 17.4.

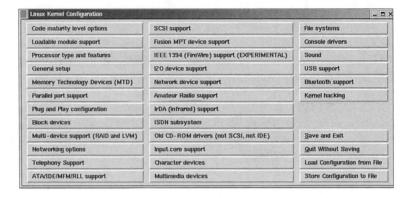

FIGURE 17.2

The X Window System-based Linux kernel configurator.

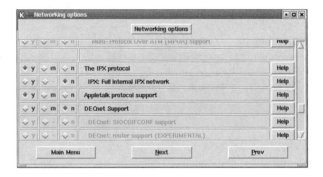

FIGURE 17.3

The Networking Options dialog.

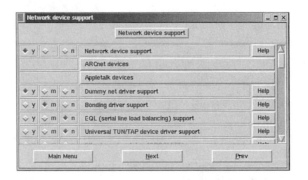

FIGURE 17.4

The Network Device Support dialog.

7. Click the AppleTalk Devices command or button. The AppleTalk Devices dialog displays, as shown in Figure 17.5.

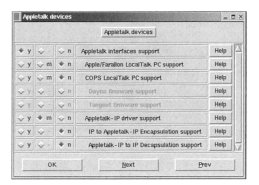

FIGURE 17.5

The AppleTalk Devices dialog.

8. Click Y beside the AppleTalk Interfaces Support entry.

9. Click M beside the AppleTalk-IP Driver Support entry. Selecting this entry is not absolutely necessary to add AppleTalk support to your kernel, but it gives you more complete support for the AppleTalk protocol in a variety of situations. This option enables IP networking in situations where you only have AppleTalk networking available. By enabling this driver, you can encapsulate IP packets inside AppleTalk if your Linux system is on an AppleTalk-only network or decapsulate, unpacking IP packets from within AppleTalk packets if you are on an AppleTalk-only network and want to use your Linux system as an Internet gateway for a network of Macintosh systems that communicate using AppleTalk.

Note that you want to add support for this option as a module, not compiled into the kernel. If you compile this into the kernel, the kernel's AppleTalk-IP support can be used only to encapsulate or decapsulate packets, but not both. If you build and install this support as a module, you will be able to do both, automatically, by loading the module twice and executing it with different options. When loading AppleTalk-IP support as a module, you should therefore also click Y beside both the IP to AppleTalk—IP Encapsulation support and IP—AppleTalk—IP Decapsulation support options.

10. Click OK button at the bottom of the dialog to close the AppleTalk Devices dialog and return to the Network Device Support dialog.

11. Click the Main Menu button to close the Network Device Support dialog and return to the primary `make xconfig` dialog.

12. Click the File Systems button in the X Window System kernel configuration dialog. The File Systems dialog appears, as shown in Figure 17.6.

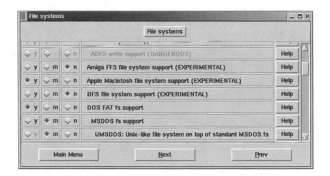

FIGURE 17.6

The File Systems Configuration dialog.

13. Scroll down until you see the Apple Macintosh File System Support (EXPERIMENTAL) option, and click M beside this entry. Selecting this option enables your Linux system to attach, mount, and access floppies and hard drives formatted with the Macintosh filesystem. Activating this option is not necessary to activate kernel support for AppleTalk, but the fact that you are interoperating with Apple Macintosh systems increases the chances that you may someday want to read an Apple floppy or attach and read a hard drive from a Macintosh system. Even if you weren't a Boy Scout in a past life, "Be Prepared" is still a good motto.

14. Click the Main Menu button to return to the primary `make xconfig` dialog.

15. After selecting any other kernel configuration options relevant to the kernel that you are building (such as those specific to the hardware in your system), save your updated kernel configuration.

16. If you reused the configuration data from an existing kernel, use the Store Configuration to File button to display a dialog that enables you to explicitly save your new kernel configuration with the name .config in the main directory of the kernel that you are configuring.

17. If you configured the current kernel from scratch (that is, without reading in configuration data from another kernel), simply click the Save and Exit button.

18. Click OK to close the final dialog and return to the Linux shell prompt. You're now ready to compile the kernel!

Compiling and Installing an AppleTalk-Aware Kernel

After configuring the Linux 2.4.9 kernel, you're ready to compile and install your new Linux kernel. All the information that you need to compile and install this kernel is provided in Appendix A. This section just provides a checklist for the steps that you should follow.

After you've installed, patched, and configured the Linux 2.4.9 kernel for AppleTalk support and to match your hardware, you must do the following to install and use that kernel:

1. Add a special extension for this kernel to its Makefile, making it easy to identify the special features in the kernel. I typically name kernels that support different filesystems along the lines of `linux-<kernel-version>-<filesystem-type>`. In this case, "atalk" might be a good suffix for the filesystem type.

2. Execute the following `make` commands in this order to correctly initialize dependencies and to build and install the new kernel and any associated loadable modules:

```
make dep
make
make modules
make install
make modules_install
```

I suggest doing these steps as discrete commands to make it easy to spot any compilation or installation failures along the way. If you're really cocky, you can reduce these commands to the following single command-line, but you'd still be wise to scroll back to make sure that there were no problems:

```
make dep ; make install ; make modules ; make modules_install
```

3. Modify boot loader configuration files for the boot loader you're using on your system, as described in "Booting a New Kernel" in Appendix A and rerun lilo or grub-install if necessary.

You're now almost ready to reboot your system, export Linux filesystems to your Macintosh systems, and access AppleTalk printers. Before doing that, however, you must also compile and install the Netatalk utility that makes the whole thing possible.

Installing Netatalk

To install version 1.5, prerelease 7 of the Netatalk package, included on the CD that accompanies this book, do the following:

1. Mount the CD and extract the Netatalk source code from the file `netatalk-1.5pre7.tar.gz` to a directory on your system using a command such as the following:

```
cd <target-directory>
tar zxvf <path-to-CD>/netatalk/netatalk-1.5pre7.tar.gz
```

17

USING NETATALK
FOR MACINTOSH
AND APPLETALK
CONNECTIVITY

2. Change directory to `<target-directory>`/netatalk-1.5pre7 and run the configure script to correctly configure the Netatalk Makefiles for your system and Linux distribution:

```
./configure
```

This produces verbose output that's not useful to replicate here.

3. After the Makefile is correctly configured, execute the `make` command to build the new versions of the utilities in the Netatalk package:

```
make
```

Once again, this produces verbose, system-specific output that's not useful to replicate here.

4. After all the utilities are compiled, install them on your system using the following command:

```
make install
```

Your system now has a version of the Netatalk utilities and associated reference (man page) documentation installed.

Before proceeding, you'll want to copy one additional file onto your system from the CD. This is the file `<path-to-CD>`/netatalk/atalk, which is an RC script that you can use to automatically start the Netatalk daemons whenever you restart your system. The basis for this script is located in the `netatalk-1.5pre7/distrib/initscripts` directory in the file `rc.atalk.redhat.tmpl`, but the one included on the CD already has been configured to reflect the default location of files in the version of Netatalk included with this book.

To configure your system to automatically start the Netatalk daemons, do the following:

1. Copy the file `<path-to-CD>`/netatalk/atalk to the directory /etc/rc.d/init.d on your system and make it executable using commands such as the following:

```
cp <path-to-CD>/netatalk/atalk /etc/rc.d/init.d
chmod 755 /etc/rc.d/init.d/atalk
```

2. Create appropriate symbolic links to start and stop this file in runlevels such as levels 3 and 5 using commands such as the following:

```
cd /etc/rc.d/rc3.d
ln -s ../init.d/atalk S91atalk
ln -s ../init.d/atalk K91atalk
cd ../rc5.d
ln -s ../init.d/atalk S91atalk
ln -s ../init.d/atalk K91atalk
```

Don't start Netatalk yet. Although mounting Linux volumes on a Macintosh system almost always works correctly as installed, you should review the configuration topics in the next section to make sure that you've configured Netatalk to make the most of its capabilities. When you're ready, you can simply reboot your system (to activate the new kernel) and automatically start Netatalk by executing the following command:

```
shutdown -r now
```

Administering Netatalk

This section discusses various topics related to optimally configuring your system for use with Netatalk.

Configuring Netatalk for Your System Environment

There are two aspects to configuring Netatalk: integrating it into your Linux system and execution environment by editing system configuration files, and then configuring the Netatalk servers themselves. Much of the integration of Netatalk into your Linux system is done when you installed it and its startup files (as explained in the previous section), but there are a few system files that you will need to edit to maximize its integration.

The first Linux file that you'll want to edit to reflect the addition of Netatalk to your system is the file /etc/services. This file lists the services available on your Linux system, the network protocols that they use, and the ports they use. The file services.atalk, located in the top level of the Netatalk source directory, lists the services provided and used by Netatalk on your Linux system. This file contains the following entries:

```
rtmp            1/ddp          # Routing Table Maintenance Protocol
nbp             2/ddp          # Name Binding Protocol
echo            4/ddp          # AppleTalk Echo Protocol
zip             6/ddp          # Zone Information Protocol
afpovertcp      548/tcp        # AFP over TCP
afpovertcp      548/udp
```

After installing Netatalk, check the /etc/services file on your Linux system to make sure that all these entries are present in that file. If any are not, add them to the file and save the updated copy.

Next, determine whether you have to modify the primary Netatalk configuration file and the configuration files used by the basic Netatalk servers. These configuration files and their default locations are the following:

- /usr/local/etc/netatalk/netatalk.conf —The primary configuration file for Netatalk, this file rarely requires modification unless you want to increase things such as the maximum number of AppleTalk clients that can connect to a Netatalk daemon, the authentication modules used by Netatalk, and so on. The default version of this file installed by Netatalk is configured for most common usage patterns and contains comments that make it easy to determine the meaning of the various entries in the file.

- /usr/local/etc/netatalk/atalkd.conf—The configuration file for the Netatalk AppleTalk daemon. This file rarely requires any modifications. Older versions of Netatalk required that you specifically identify any Ethernet interfaces in your machine using this file. The version of Netatalk included with this book automatically detects your Ethernet interfaces and begins listening on them appropriately. If you only have a single Ethernet interface in your machine or you have multiple Ethernet interfaces, but eth0 is the interface through which you want to export your Linux system, you will not have to modify this file. If you have multiple Ethernet interfaces and you want to export your Linux system to AppleTalk through an interface other than eth0, you'll want to modify the atalkd.conf configuration file. To identify the Ethernet interface that you want to use for Macintosh/Linux connectivity, add a single line to the end of this file, naming the Ethernet interface that you want to use.

- /usr/local/etc/netatalk/afpd.conf—The configuration file for the Netatalk AppleTalk Filing Protocol daemon. This file does not specifically require modification unless you want to run multiple AFP servers on different ports, with different characteristics. This file provides extensive information about the options that Netatalk provides for doing these sorts of things.

- /usr/local/etc/netatalk/papd.conf—The configuration file for the Printer Access Protocol daemon used by Netatalk to give Macintosh systems access to Linux printers. You will almost certainly want to modify this file on Linux systems to accurately reflect the printers that you are using. For more detailed information, see the section "Printer Sharing Between Macintosh and Linux Systems" later in this chapter.

In addition to these configuration files, Netatalk uses two files containing common definitions for file and volume interoperability between Linux and Macintosh systems. These are the files /usr/local/etc/netatalk/AppleVolumes.default and /usr/local/etc/netatalk/AppleVolumes.system. These files enable you to add common system mount requests and mappings between file extensions and to define Macintosh Type/Creator information that you want to use when mounting Linux directories on a Macintosh.

The file /usr/local/etc/netatalk/AppleVolumes.system is read when any user logs in (including "guest" users), and the auxiliary mappings in /usr/local/etc/netatalk/ AppleVolumes.default are read when any nonguest user logs in. For example, you may want to add an entry such as the following to the end of the file /usr/local/etc/netatalk/ AppleVolumes.system:

```
#
# volumes
#
/home/public Public
```

The last line (the only noncomment line in these entries) will automatically mount the directory /home/public on the Macintosh desktop as the volume Public whenever any user logs in. As discussed in the section in Chapter 18 entitled "A Working Example Is Worth a Thousand Words," this provides the opportunity to access files stored in a public directory on Linux from a Macintosh. Files that you might want to access from any platform are personnel, human resources, bug report, or any other companywide files that any user will need to access, regardless of the types of desktop computer that he is using.

> **NOTE**
>
> The last entry in the AppleVolumes.default file is ~ Home, which means that any user who can log in on the Linux system as a Registered User will automatically see her home directory mounted on the Macintosh desktop as a volume with her login name.

Finally, to use the Netatalk libraries and user authentication libraries provided with Netatalk, you will need to modify your system's /etc/ld.so.conf file to include the directories in which these libraries are located and then execute the Linux ldconfig command to correctly update the Linux library loader's idea of where to find the Netatalk libraries. If you installed Netatalk in the default location, you can do this by adding the following lines to your /etc/ld.so.conf file (when logged in as the root user):

```
/usr/local/lib
/usr/local/etc/netatalk/uams
```

After adding these entries, execute the command /sbin/ldconfig to update the list of libraries that the library loader knows about and their locations.

Using Netatalk User Authentication Modules

Macintosh systems use a flexible authentication mechanism for networked services called User Authentication Modules (UAMs). Conceptually, UAMs are similar to the Pluggable Authentication Modules (PAMs) used on Linux and many Unix systems to provide flexible authentication schemes that can be easily upgraded, enhanced, or modified. For example, companies such as Microsoft and Novell that provide commercial interoperability products for Macintosh systems provide UAMs that extend the authentication capabilities built into Macintosh systems by enabling Macintosh users to authenticate to those companies' standard authentication processes.

Traditionally, UAMs run on Macintosh systems for interoperability with different authentication mechanisms. Because Netatalk provides AppleTalk and AFP interfaces for communicating with Linux systems by essentially appearing to be yet another Macintosh, Netatalk must provide

UAMs that integrate Macintosh systems with Linux and Unix security mechanisms. Netatalk comes with the following UAMs, which are located in the directory `/usr/local/etc/netatalk/uams` by default:

- `uams_guest.so` —Allows guest logins, which are logins that do not require the user to have an account on the Linux system that runs Netatalk. This does not authenticate users and therefore only gives people access to shared areas, as opposed to personal directories.
- `uams_clrtxt.so`—Allows logins with passwords transmitted in the clear. This UAM invokes the UAMs `uams_pam.so` or `uams_passwd.so`, depending on whether the Linux system running Netatalk uses PAMs or the standard password file for authentication purposes.
- `uams_randnum.so`—Allows Random Number and Two-Way Random Number exchange for authentication purposes.
- `uams_dhx.so`—Allows Diffie-Hellman eXchange (DHX) for authentication purposes. This UAM invokes the UAMs `uams_dhx_pam.so` or `uams_dhx_passwd.so`, depending on whether the Linux system running Netatalk uses PAMs or the standard password file for authentication purposes.

As mentioned previously, commercial providers of Macintosh interoperability packages for networked systems such as Microsoft Windows and Novell NetWare supply UAMs with these packages that integrate Macintosh systems with their networking products. These UAMs all run on Macintosh. If you want to integrate Macintosh systems and Linux and Unix systems running other networking packages, such as AFS and OpenAFS, you will need to obtain UAMs that integrate Macintosh systems with the authentication mechanisms used by these systems.

Creating Personal Netatalk Configuration Files

After Netatalk has started successfully, but before you log in using the Chooser, you can create any personal mount and Text/Creator mapping settings in a file in your Linux home directory called .AppleVolumes. For example, assume that you added the following lines to the file `~/.AppleVolumes`:

```
#
# Custom Volume Mounts for wvh
#
/home/wvh/download Download
#
# My favorite Apps
#
.txt TEXT EMAC "Emacs Text Document"
```

These personal settings do two things:

- They cause the Linux directory `/home/wvh/download` to be mounted on my desktop as the shared volume `Download` whenever I connect to my Linux system using Netatalk. (Mac fans will realize that this volume will just be one of those offered to me in the Chooser; whether or not it is actually mounted depends on whether I select the volume for mounting.)

- They map files with the .txt extension to Macintosh file Type `TEXT`, creator `EMAC`, which is the version of the emacs text editor that I use on the Mac. (I love Macs, but emacs is the one true editor, after all!) When I log in, this overrides the default setting in the file `/usr/local/etc/netatalk/AppleVolumes.system`. (The default setting maps files with the `.txt` extension to the Macintosh SimpleText application.)

Printer Sharing Between Macintosh and Linux Systems

If you installed Netatalk in the default location, the configuration file for Netatalk printer support is `/usr/local/etc/netatalk/papd.conf`. This file provides the Netatalk PAP (Printer Access Protocol) daemon with the information necessary to enable Macintosh users to print to any Linux printers for which entries exist in the file.

The default papd.conf file installed with Netatalk describes the format of the entries in this file in great detail. The most critical entries in this file are the `pr` entry, which defines the printer or the mechanism for sending data to a specific printer; the `op` entry, which provides the name of a valid Linux user (used when queuing the print job); and the `pd` entry, which identifies a PostScript Printer Definition file that defines the characteristics of the printer. A sample entry from my `/usr/local/netatalk/etc/papd.conf` file follows:

```
journal:\
        :pr=|/usr/bin/lpr -Psilentwriter:op=wvh:\
        :pd=/usr/local/etc/netatalk/PPD/HPLJ4.PPD:
```

This defines a printer that appears in the Macintosh Chooser as being named `journal`, and "just works" on my Red Hat Linux systems.

One drawback of the Macintosh printing mechanism is the need to be able to find the PPD files for your printer. PPD files are available from Adobe, Inc., via anonymous ftp at the URL `ftp://ftp.adobe.com//pub/adobe/printerdrivers/mac/all/ppdfiles`, through a Web browser using the URL `http://download.sourceforge.net/lpr/hp-ppd-0.2.tar.gz`, or from the manufacturer of your printer. For your convenience, the CD that accompanies this book includes the PPD files for printers from Apple, Epson, Hewlett-Packard, and NEC. These all are located in the Netatalk/PPD subdirectory of the CD and were obtained from Adobe via FTP. I've included both the Macintosh archive files for these PPD files, as well as unpacked versions of them in their own directories. Trying to unpack Macintosh StuffIt and HQX archives on a Linux box can be a pain.

Correctly configuring printers can be time consuming and irritating, primarily because the `papd` daemon doesn't have a truly verbose mode that tells you what's actually happening. Also, because it is automatically started inside the `atalk` initialization script, it's easy to overlook an error until you actually print. Aside from obvious error messages that cause it to exit (`"Bad pcap entry"` and `"Bad termcap entry"` being two of my personal favorites), you don't really get much of a feel for what's causing the problem—printouts simply don't appear. Your only other source for information about what's really happening is the Linux system log, `/var/log/messages`. This at least displays messages as to whether `papd` has started correctly.

A common problem when configuring Linux printers for use by `papd` is specifying the wrong printer or related command. For example, messages such as the following indicate that `papd` can't open a lock file:

```
Sep  3 20:39:04 journal papd[24626]: lp_init: lock: No such file or directory
Sep  3 20:39:04 journal papd[24626]: lp_open failed
```

The best solution for this problem is to use a `pr` specification that doesn't force `papd` to try to open a lock file but lets the standard Linux print mechanism handle it. Instead of simply using a `pr` entry such as `pr=silentwriter` to send output to a Linux printer named silentwriter, the `pr` definition `pr=|/usr/bin/lpr -Psilentwriter:` does essentially the same thing but offloads lock creation onto the Linux printer subsystem. Voila!

When starting and restarting the Netatalk `papd` process, you may need to manually remove the lock file that it uses to prevent multiple copies from being started (`/var/lock/papd`) or manually unregister your Linux printer before attempting to restart `papd`. To see what printers are defined, you can use the `nbplkup :LaserWriter` command. To manually unregister a Netatalk printer (or any other AppleTalk device, for that matter), you can use the `nbpunrgstr` command, supplying the name of the printer or other device that you want to unregister as an argument.

While you're working on creating a valid printer entry, you can test printing to it from your Linux system by using the Linux `pap` program to print to that printer via AppleTalk rather than using the standard Linux print commands. (Remember to send PostScript files!) A sample `pap` command to do this and the output that it creates are as follows:

```
[wvh@journal netatalk]$ pap -p journal:LaserWriter foo.ps
Trying 65280.220:129 ...
status: print spooler processing job
Connected to journal:LaserWriter@*.
Connection closed.
```

In this example, `journal:LaserWriter` is the NBP name of the printer I was testing, and `foo.ps` is the file that I wanted to print.

After you've created valid entries for your Linux printers in the papd.conf file, accessing those printers from your Macintosh systems is as easy as you'd hope. Whenever you connect to a Netatalk server from a Macintosh using the Macintosh Chooser, any Linux printers exported by that server automatically are installed as available printers from your Macintosh system.

Using Samba for Windows Interoperability

IN THIS CHAPTER

Like it or not, the planet is infested with Windows machines. As you can see from statements like that, I'm probably as guilty as anyone of propagating the "us versus them" mentality when it comes to Windows versus Linux. How I personally feel about Windows and Microsoft really doesn't matter. The important thing in this chapter is to discuss the various ways in which the filesystem adapters and interoperability software available on Linux systems make it easy to integrate Linux and Windows filesystems in both directions, getting features like automatic printer sharing as freebies along the way.

You'd have to have been living in a cave for the last five or so years not to have heard of Samba, arguably one of the most popular applications ever written for Unix systems. In a nutshell (sorry, O'Reilly guys), Samba is a set of applications originally developed to provide support for Microsoft's networking protocols on Unix systems, but which has been ported to just about every other network-aware operating system.

Many books are dedicated to discussing Samba, explaining every nuance of its configuration files, installation, and use. My goal in this chapter is not to embed another one inside a book on Linux filesystems. The first section of this chapter provides an overview of Windows networking, introduces Samba, and gives an overview of the different ways in which Linux and Windows systems can interoperate. The next section explains how to activate support for Windows networking and resource sharing in the Linux kernel. The chapter concludes with a section that provides a quick start guide to help you access Linux filesystems from Windows machines and Windows filesystems from Linux machines.

> **NOTE**
>
> Although every Linux distribution that I've ever seen includes a precompiled version of Samba, the CD that accompanies this book includes source code for the latest version at the time of this writing, version 2.2.1a. Compiling and installing this version will guarantee that the examples provided in this chapter, the Samba configuration file, and the configuration instructions discussed in this chapter will work correctly on your system.

Overview

When you get right down to it, there is probably more data stored on Windows systems than on any other type of computer system. All those 10-gigabyte home and office systems add up to a tremendous number of Windows filesystems holding a staggering amount of data. Samba gives Linux users transparent access to Windows filesystems but is more commonly used to give Windows users transparent access to Linux and Unix systems. Samba does this by providing a network interface compatible with the networked file and printer sharing protocols used between Windows systems. To a Windows system, a Linux system running Samba looks exactly like a random Windows system that is sharing filesystems across the network. This enables Windows users to take advantage of the speed, power, and capacity of Linux systems without even realizing that they are accessing Linux filesystems.

> **NOTE**
>
> Most network appliances sold today run Linux and provide instant network attached storage (NAS) for Windows users by running Samba, for Apple Macintosh users by running Netatalk (as explained in Chapter 17, "Using Netatalk to Connect to Macintosh Filesystems"), and for Linux and Unix users by supporting NFS (discussed in Chapter 12, "The NFS Distributed Filesystem").

Interoperability between Linux and Windows systems is much more than just Samba. The Linux kernel provides built-in support for the protocols used to access Windows filesystems, enabling Linux users to mount Windows filesystems via entries in /etc/fstab, just like any other filesystem resource.

To understand exactly how Windows systems use a network to share resources and how Linux interoperates with Windows systems, the next section provides an overview of Windows networking to help clarify the protocols used for various levels of Windows networking.

Overview of Windows Networking

Networking and related technologies such as routing are probably responsible for more acronyms than any other aspect of the computer industry. DOS and Windows networking has contributed its share, largely due to the ubiquity of these operating systems in modern computing environments. Because of the popularity of DOS systems (yesterday) and Windows systems (today), today's Windows systems provide support for almost everyone's networking protocols.

Windows frankly does an admirable job of continuing to make forward progress while still maintaining backward compatibility with almost every ancient DOS application and networking protocol. Windows systems still support the IPX (Internet Packet Exchange) and SPX (Sequenced Packet Exchange) networking protocols used by Novell to provide the first PC file servers (discussed in Chapter 19, "NetWare Filesystem Support in Linux"). However, more relevant for our discussion here are the networking protocols and attendant acronyms developed by Microsoft and used to provide file and resource sharing over PC networks without requiring the involvement of any third parties, thank you very much.

The Basic Input and Output System used by PCs to interact with local devices is best known by its initials as the PC's BIOS. As networks began to appear, Microsoft and IBM extended the capabilities of the BIOS to support accessing and sharing information over a network, naming the related protocols the network BIOS, or as it's more popularly known, NetBIOS. Just as the BIOS provides the basic functions that support all system input and output, the NetBIOS provides the basic functions that let you use and administer network services. NetBIOS commands and functions must be exchanged between networked systems and therefore require a lower-level network transport mechanism to move network packets from one host to another. The lower-level transport protocols still in common use in PC networking today are IPX, NetBEUI (Network Basic Extended User Interface), and TCP/IP (Transmission Control Protocol/Internet Protocol). Interestingly, the "Internet" in the full names of both IPX and TCP/IP refers to inter-network communications, not the Internet as we know it today.

Samba sends its NetBIOS requests by using TCP/IP as a transport protocol. On top of the NetBIOS level, Windows networking provides a higher level interface for network services known as the SMB (Server Message Block) protocol, which is a networking protocol that can be easily used by applications. SMB is a connection-oriented protocol rather than a broadcast protocol, meaning that it depends on establishing connections to specific networked services provided by other networked hosts rather than simply broadcasting its availability. After a connection is established, SMB provides four basic types of functions:

- Session functions are responsible for negotiating and establishing networked connections between machines (often referred to as *virtual circuits*), authenticating, and verifying the access privileges that each party has with the other.
- File functions enable applications to open, close, read, and write remote files, shared directories, and so on.
- Printer functions enable applications to spool output to remote output devices.
- Message functions enable applications to send and receive control, status, and informational messages between different systems on the network.

SMB became an Open Group standard for networking interoperability in the early 1990s. Samba takes its name from SMB; the addition of two vowels makes it easily pronounced and somewhat softer than the YAA (Yet Another Acronym).

In recent developments, an enhanced version of the SMB protocol called CIFS (Common Internet File System) has been submitted to the IETF (Internet Engineering Task Force), an open association of people interested in the architecture of Internet communication and the smooth operation of the Internet. CIFS extends the capabilities of SMB by expanding its focus to sharing resources using even more open, cross-platform standards such as HTTP URLs (Hypertext Transfer Protocol Uniform Resource Locators) and DNS (the Domain Name System used to map host names to IP addresses and vice versa).

Introduction to Samba

Samba is a free and impressive interface for Linux, Unix, and other types of systems to any other networked device that can communicate using the SMB protocol, most notably Windows systems that provide networked access to files, directories, and printers. Samba enables Windows users to access Linux filesystems and resources just like any other Windows shared filesystem or networked resource. For example, with Samba running on a Linux system on your network, Windows users can mount their Linux home directories as networked Windows drives and can automatically print to Linux printers just like any other networking Windows printer. Samba was originally authored by Andrew Tridgell and is one of the most impressive pieces of interoperability software ever developed.

Figure 18.1 shows a Linux directory exported via Samba as seen from a Windows system. If there wasn't a core dump in there, you could swear that it was just yet another Windows system.

FIGURE 18.1

A Linux directory viewed from Windows via Samba.

Samba includes both client and server software—in other words, client software that enables users to communicate from Linux machines to SMB hosts on your network, and server software that provides an SMB interface for your Linux machine. The Samba server actually consists of two processes, both of which can be started from the command line or automatically by integrating them into your system's startup procedure, as described in "Configuring Samba to Start at Boot Time" later in the chapter. These processes are /usr/local/samba/bin/smbd, the Samba daemon that provides file sharing and print services to Windows clients, and /usr/local/samba/bin/nmbd, the NetBIOS name server that maps the NetBIOS names used by Windows SMB requests to the IP addresses used by Linux systems. The Samba daemon is configured by modifying its configuration file, /usr/local/samba/lib/samba/smb.conf, as described in "Quickstart—Configuring Samba" later in the chapter.

> **NOTE**
>
> The default location for the configuration files used by most preinstalled versions of Samba is the directory /etc/samba.

Examples of the clients provided with Samba are the smbclient and smbmount programs, both of which are discussed in the next section.

Summary of Windows/Linux Interaction

This section provides an overview of the basic types of file sharing and interoperability possible between Linux and Windows systems using the Samba software and other freely available software packages. This section is intended to introduce all the possibilities and to highlight the ones that are most interesting from a networked filesystems point of view.

> **NOTE**
>
> When using Samba to share files between Linux and Windows systems, make sure that all the correct Windows services packs have been installed on your Windows systems to bring them up-to-date. This is especially important for Windows 2000 systems, where, for example, Service Pack 2 is mandatory.

The simplest type of file sharing between Linux and Windows systems is one-way file transfer. Though not particularly interesting from a file sharing and interoperability perspective, transferring files is still a valid mechanism for exchanging files between Linux and Windows systems in a pinch. There are two primary tools for transferring files between Linux and Windows systems:

- ftp —Windows provides an FTP client that you can use to send or retrieve files from any Linux host on which an FTP server is installed and running. Most recent Linux distributions use the xinetd package to enable or disable an FTP server. The wu-ftpd FTP server, though notoriously insecure, is shipped with most Linux distributions. Starting the server on your Linux system will let any Windows user with a valid account on the Linux machine connect to the Linux machine using the FTP client bundled with Windows. You can then send and retrieve files from the Windows system. Windows does not provide an FTP server (except as part of the IIS server used with some less security conscious Windows 2000 installations), so all file transfers must be initiated from a Windows system.

- `smbclient` —Part of the Samba suite, the `smbclient` package enables Linux users to connect to Windows systems over a network using SMB. To connect to a remote Windows system, the Samba daemons discussed in the previous section must be running and properly configured, and DNS or `/etc/hosts` entries must provide host to IP address mappings for your Windows clients. You must also be able to authenticate on the Windows system that you are trying to connect to, which is most easily done by specifying your Windows login using the `smbclient` application's `-U` option. The syntax of an `smbclient` command is

```
smbclient //host/share -U wvh
```

In this example, `host` would be the Windows name of the Windows system exporting the shared directory that you want to connect to, represented by `share` in this example. After executing this command, you'll be prompted for the specified user's password (in this case, the password for `wvh`). If the password is correct, you will see prompt like `smb: \>`. From this prompt, you can change directories and use commands such as `put` and `get` to send and receive files. For more complete information, see the online man pages for the `smbclient` application.

The next type of file sharing possible between Linux and Windows systems is the capability to mount Linux volumes on Windows systems. This is a completely interactive file sharing mechanism that enables Windows users to drag and drop files to and from the Linux volume using SMB. To use this type of file sharing, the Samba daemons must be correctly configured and running on the Linux systems whose volumes you want to access. You must also be able to authenticate to the SMB server on the Linux machine, which is usually enabled by creating entries in the Samba password file, `/usr/local/samba/lib/smbpasswd`. Entries in this file are created using the `/usr/local/samba/bin/smbpasswd` command. Finally, you must map the Linux directory or volume to a Windows drive letter. For complete information on mounting Linux volumes on your Windows desktop, see "Accessing Linux Directories from Windows Systems" later in the chapter.

The final type of file sharing possible between Linux and Windows systems is the capability to mount shared Windows drives on Linux directories, just like any other networked filesystem. To be able to do this, you must compile SMB filesystem support into the kernel running on your Linux system, as explained in the section "Building a Kernel with SMB Filesystem Support." The Samba software must be installed on your system, although the Samba daemons don't actually have to be running because importing Windows filesystem resources into the Linux environment is handled by the kernel's SMB support, not Samba. Finally, if you want to mount a Windows share as a normal user, the `/usr/local/bin/smbmnt` program must be owned by root and must be installed with the suid bit set (mode 4755). For complete instructions on mounting Windows volumes on Linux systems, see "Accessing Windows Filesystems from Linux Systems" later in the chapter.

18

USING SAMBA
FOR WINDOWS
INTEROPERABILITY

Support Software for Windows Networking on Linux

To add support for remote SMB requests to access resources on your Linux system, and to enable your system to issue its own SMB requests to access remote SMB resources, you will need to have the following:

- A kernel that supports SMB filesystems
- The Samba package. The latest version of this package at the time this book was written, samba-2.2.1a, is located in an archive files called `samba-2.2.1a.tar.gz` in the `samba` subdirectory of the CD that accompanies this book. The Samba package installs many SMB-related utilities in `/usr/local/samba/bin` (by default), many of which are used internally by the Samba package. The following are the Samba servers and client utilities that you will want to use on your system:

  - `make_printerdef` —Creates printer definition (PPD) files
  - `make_smbcodepage`—Creates codepage (NLS) files from templates
  - `make_unicodemap`—Creates Unicode (NLS) files from templates
  - `nmbd`—The NetBIOS daemon that translates NetBIOS names to IP addresses
  - `rpcclient`—A client application to support Remote Procedure Call (RPC) pipes
  - `smbadduser`—Enables you to specify multiple users on the command line and creates an entry in the `smbpasswd` file for each of them
  - `smbcacls`—An access control list (ACL) utility for Samba
  - `smbclient`—An SMB client that provides an FTP-like interface for interactive file transfers from SMB hosts
  - `smbcontrol`—Enables you to send control messages to Samba processes
  - `smbd`—The Samba daemon, responsible for providing an SMB interface for your Linux system and servicing incoming SMB requests from remote hosts to your Linux system
  - `smbmnt`—A helper utility for the `smbmount` program, which is used to mount SMB filesystems on Linux systems
  - `smbmount`—A utility that enables you to mount SMB filesystems on your Linux desktop
  - `smbpasswd`—Creates Samba password file entries
  - `smbprint`—Sends a file to a specified SMB printer
  - `smbspool`—Sends files to an SMB printer

- `smbstatus`—Reports on currently active SMB connections
- `smbtar`—A shell script for backing up SMB/CIFS shares to Linux backup devices
- `smbumount`—Unmounts a remote SMB filesystem currently mounted on a Linux system
- `swat`—An administrative utility for configuring and controlling Samba
- `testparm`—Examines the Samba configuration file (`smb.conf`) and verifies that it is syntactically correct
- `testprns`—Tests that a given printer name can be used with Samba

Adding SMB Filesystem Support to Your System

As explained in the previous section, the SMB support available in Linux consists of both kernel enhancements and the Samba utility package. To add support for remote SMB requests to access resources on your Linux system, you will need to install Samba. To enable your system to issue its own SMB requests to access remote SMB resources, you will need to install a version of the Linux kernel that provides support for SMB filesystems.

The first part of this chapter explains how to install, configure, and build a Linux kernel with support for SMB filesystems. The second part of this chapter explains how to install the latest version of Samba that was available at the time of this writing. Most Linux distributions already come with Samba installed. If your system has Samba installed, you can skip installing the new version, but the configuration file entries discussed in the section, "Quickstart—Configuring Samba" will almost certainly be installed in different locations than those described in this book, and the discussion of the Samba configuration file in this book may not match your Samba configuration file unless you are running the latest version of Samba.

> **NOTE**
>
> If you are using a version of Samba preinstalled with your Linux distribution, you should also make sure that all the Samba commands referred to in this chapter are actually installed on your system.

Building a Kernel with SMB Filesystem Support

Linux kernels have had the capability to support SMB networking at the kernel level for a few years now. However, support for SMB filesystems may not be active in the kernel on your system. This section explains how to install the version of the 2.4.9 Linux kernel provided on the CD that accompanies this book, how to activate SMB filesystem support in that kernel, and how to compile and install your new kernel.

Activating SMB Filesystem Support in the Kernel

The 2.4.9 Linux kernel is the most advanced version of Linux available at the time of this writing, and the one that I've therefore chosen to use to show how easy it is to activate SMB support in your Linux system.

> **NOTE**
>
> As mentioned in each chapter, if you have never built a kernel before, doing so is a great learning experience. Although the whole idea of prepackaged Linux installation is to protect users from the need to "roll their own" kernel and Linux utilities, compiling a kernel is an excellent way to familiarize yourself with the conceptual internals and organization of Linux. The instructions in this book for compiling kernels create kernels that have special names and will thus not overwrite the current version of the Linux kernel that you are using.

The source for the Linux 2.4.9 kernel is located in the `kernels` subdirectory of the CD that accompanies this book. Install this kernel as described in "Installing the Kernel Source Code" in Appendix A, "Using the CD-ROM: Installing, Updating, and Compiling Kernels."

> **NOTE**
>
> If you already compiled a kernel for the computer system on which you are building a new kernel, you can use the configuration information from that kernel to save time when configuring the new kernel. Reusing existing configuration data from an existing kernel is explained in Appendix A.

After you install the kernel, do the following to activate SMB support in the kernel:

1. Log in as root or use the `su` command to become root.
2. In a terminal window running under an X Window System window manager or desktop, change to the directory `/usr/src/linux-2.4.9` and execute the `make xconfig` command. The commands related to compiling and loading support for the Linux X Window System kernel configurator display in the window in which you executed the `make xconfig` command. Eventually, the X Window System Linux kernel configurator displays, as shown in Figure 18.2.

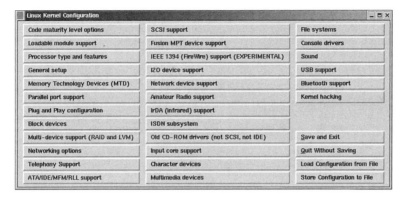

FIGURE 18.2

The X Window System-based Linux kernel configurator.

3. Click the File Systems button in the X Window System Kernel Configuration dialog. The File Systems dialog displays, as shown in Figure 18.3.

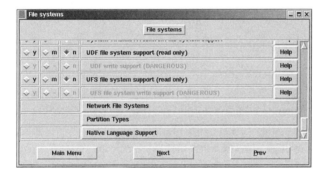

FIGURE 18.3

The File Systems dialog.

4. Scroll down until you see the Network File Systems button and click it to display the Network File Systems dialog, as shown in Figure 18.4.

5. Click Y beside the SMB File System Support label. Oddly enough, this activates SMB filesystem support in the kernel. You can optionally select M beside this entry to build SMB filesystem support as a loadable kernel module. This makes the kernel slightly smaller but requires that the kernel load an external SMB loadable kernel module each time you need to access an SMB filesystem. Unless you are really tight on disk space, select Y.

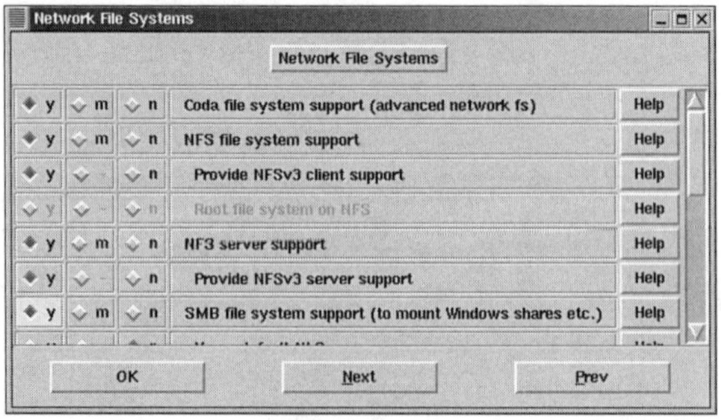

FIGURE 18.4
The Network File Systems dialog.

NOTE

When you activate the SMB File System Support option, the Use a Default NLS option is made selectable. This selection is optional but enables the kernel's SMB support modules (smbfs) to use NLS.

---

6. Click OK button at the bottom of the Network File Systems dialog to return to the File Systems dialog.

7. Click the Main Menu button to return to the primary make xconfig dialog.

8. After selecting any other kernel configuration options relevant to the kernel that you are building (such as those specific to the hardware in your system), save your updated kernel configuration.

   If you reused the configuration data from an existing kernel, use the Store Configuration to File button to display a dialog that enables you to explicitly save your new kernel configuration with the name .config in the main directory of the kernel that you are configuring.

   If you configured the current kernel from scratch (that is, without reading in configuration data from another kernel), simply click the Save and Exit button.

9. Click OK to close the final dialog and return to the Linux shell prompt. You're now ready to compile the kernel!

Compiling and Installing an SMB-Aware Kernel

After applying patches to and configuring the Linux 2.4.9 kernel, you're ready to compile and install your new Linux kernel. All the information that you need to compile and install this kernel is provided in Appendix A. This section just provides a checklist for the steps that you should follow.

After you install, patch, and configure the Linux 2.4.9 kernel for SMB support and to match your hardware, you must do the following to install and use that kernel:

1. Add a special extension for this kernel to its Makefile, making it easy to identify the special features in the kernel. I typically name kernels that support different filesystem along the lines of `linux-<kernel-version>-<filesystem-type>`. In this case, "smb" might be a good suffix for the filesystem type.

2. Execute the following `make` commands in this order to correctly initialize dependencies and to build and install the new kernel and any associated loadable modules:

   - `make dep`
   - `make`
   - `make modules`
   - `make install`
   - `make modules_install`

   I suggest doing these steps as discrete commands to make it easy to spot any compilation or installation failures along the way. If you're really cocky, you can reduce these commands to the following single command line, but you'd still be wise to scroll back to make sure that there are no problems:

   ```
   make dep ; make install ; make modules; make modules_install
   ```

3. Modify boot loader configuration files for the boot loader you're using on your system, as described in "Booting a New Kernel" in Appendix A and rerun LILO if necessary.

You're now almost ready to reboot your system and mount and access SMB file and print servers. Before doing that, however, you must also compile and install the Samba utilities that provide an SMB interface for your Linux system.

18

USING SAMBA
FOR WINDOWS
INTEROPERABILITY

Installing Samba

To install version 2.2.1a of the Samba package, included on the CD that accompanies this book, do the following:

1. Mount the CD and extract the Samba source code from the file `samba-2.2.1a.tar.gz` to a directory on your system using command like the following:

   ```
   cd <target-directory>
   tar zxvf <path-to-CD>/samba/samba-2.2.1a.tar.gz
   ```

2. Change directory to `<target-directory>/samba-2.2.1a/source` and run the configure script to correctly configure the Samba Makefiles for your system and Linux distribution:

   ```
   ./configure
   ```

   This produces verbose output that's not useful to replicate here.

3. After the Makefile is correctly configured, execute the `make` command to build the new versions of the utilities in the Samba package:

```
make
```

Once again, this produces verbose, system-specific output that's not useful to replicate here.

4. After all the utilities are compiled, install them on your system using the following command:

```
make install
```

Congratulations! Your system now has a version of the Samba utilities and associated reference (man page) documentation installed.

NOTE

By default, the latest version of Samba installs itself in subdirectories of the directory `/usr/local/samba`. If your system had a previous version of Samba installed, check the directories `/sbin`, `/bin`, and `/usr/bin` for the Samba-related utilities listed in "Support Software for Windows Networking on Linux" earlier in the chapter and delete the old versions of the files to avoid any possible confusion regarding which version of the binaries you are running.

Configuring Samba to Start at Boot Time

Linux uses files in subdirectories of the `/etc/rc.d` directory to determine what processes to start at boot time and stop when you are shutting down your system. These files are organized into subdirectories named `rc.X`, where X is the Linux run level at which you want the process to be started or the run level at which the program will be terminated if you are shutting down the system. The files used to start processes are usually referred to as *start files* because their names all begin with a capital "S." The files used to terminate processes are usually referred to as *kill files* because their names all begin with a capital "K."

When you install Samba, only process kill files are created in the directories specific to various run levels where Samba is appropriate, which are run levels 3 (multiuser mode with a standard text-based login) and 5 (multiuser mode with X Window System logins). These files, called `K35smb`, are symbolic links to the file `/etc/rc.d/init.d/smb`. To automatically activate Samba whenever your system boots, you will have to create associated start files, named `S35smb` by default, in your `/etc/rc.d/rc3.d` and `/etc/rc.d/rc5.d` directories. You can create these symbolic links using commands like the following:

```
cd /etc/rc.d/rc3.d
ln -s ../init.d/smb S35smb
cd /etc/rc.d/rc5.d
ln -s ../init.d/smb S35smb
```

NOTE

If you use the `linuxconf` utility to activate Samba, you do not have to manually create symbolic links to start Samba. In any case, always verify that there are no existing Startup links before manually creating new ones.

These links guarantee that Samba will be started at boot time when the system processes either of the multiuser run levels, 3 or 5.

NOTE

If you are running a Samba server on a Linux laptop that uses a PCMCIA Ethernet card, you will want to create the start and kill file links to `/etc/rc.d/init.d` with numbers higher than 45, where the PCMCIA drivers are initialized, because this is when your Ethernet services will actually be activated. I typically create symbolic links to `/etc/rc.d/init.d/smb` with the names `S55smb` and `K55smb` to guarantee that the network is available before starting Samba.

18

USING SAMBA
FOR WINDOWS
INTEROPERABILITY

Accessing Windows Filesystems from Linux Systems

Accessing shared Windows filesystems is easy after your Linux system is properly configured. Shared Windows directories are mounted on existing Linux directories, just like any other filesystem.

To be able to mount shared Windows directories on a Linux system, your system must be configured in the following way:

- You must have compiled SMB filesystem support into the kernel running on your Linux system, as explained in "Building a Kernel with SMB Filesystem Support."

- The Samba software must be installed on your system so that you have access to the appropriate Samba client software. The Samba daemons don't actually have to be running because importing Windows filesystem resources into the Linux environment is handled by the kernel's SMB support, not by Samba.

After these requirements are satisfied, you can mount shared Windows directories on your Linux system in one of two ways:

- As the superuser. By default, shared Windows drives are mounted as being owned by the user who mounted them. To mount a shared Windows drive as root but have the mounted filesystem be owned by a specific Linux user, you will have to supply the name of the user who you want to authenticate as and the Linux user ID and group ID of that person. A sample command for mounting a drive as the Windows user wvh, with the Linux user ID 500, and the Linux group ID 500 would look like the following:

  ```
  mount.smb //wvh/C-DRIVE /mnt/windows -o username=wvh,uid=500,gid=500
  ```

  You will be prompted for the user's password. In this example, the shared drive \\wvh\C-DRIVE would be mounted on the directory /mnt/windows, owned by the Linux user with the user ID 500 and with the group ID set to 500. (These would presumably be the user and group IDs of the Linux user who has the Windows login wvh.

NOTE

Windows systems use backslashes as system and directory separators, whereas Linux systems use forward slashes. You must use forward slashes in Windows pathnames when specifying them on the Linux command line, because the backslash has a special meaning to all Linux shells (it escapes the following character, preventing its misinterpretation. All Samba utilities automatically perform the correct translation from slashes to backslahses.

- As a normal user. To mount a shared Windows drive as a normal user, the /usr/bin/smbmnt program must be owned by root and must be installed with the suid bit set (mode 4755). (You should also change the SMB unmount program, Smbumount, to the same mode!) After these conditions are satisfied, you can mount a Windows share from any Windows system to which you can authenticate using a command like the following:

  ```
  smbmnt //wvh/C-DRIVE foo
  ```

  You will be prompted for the password. If your Windows username is different than your Linux login, you can mount the Windows share with a command like the following:

  ```
  smbmnt //wvh/C-DRIVE foo -o username=vonhagen
  ```

Administering and Using Samba

This section explains how to do the initial configuration to get Samba up and running on your Linux system as a properly configured member of your existing Windows environment. This enables authenticated Windows users to mount Linux directories on their Windows desktops, and also to print to Linux printers from their Windows systems just as they would to any other networked printer. Subsequent sections explain the basic organization of the Samba configuration file, leaving the details to the online documentation for Samba or your favorite Samba reference text. The last section explains how to actually mount the Linux directories exported by Samba on your Windows desktop, in case you are new to Windows.

Quickstart—Configuring Samba

Samba is configured by editing a single text file that provides incredibly detailed control over how your Samba daemons will be integrated into your existing Windows environment, and who can access them. Samba's configuration file is /usr/local/samba/lib/smb.conf if you installed the version of Samba included with this book or the file /etc/samba/smb.conf on most preinstalled versions of Samba. Because Samba's configuration file is a standard text file, you can edit it using your favorite text editor.

The smb.conf file has many sections, each with multiple entries. Each section in the smb.conf file is preceded by the name of that section, enclosed in square brackets. This section focuses on the minimum number of configuration commands that you will want to activate to be able to use Samba with a reasonable degree of security.

Although Samba's configuration file is relatively large, much of it is taken up by comments that help you understand the purpose of each entry in the file. Each comment line begins with a hash mark (#), which causes the smb daemon to ignore that line when reading the file.

Configuring the [global] Section

This section of the Samba configuration file contains the following entries that you should set. These entries describe setting for Windows 98 systems—you will need to set other options if you are using Samba with Windows NT systems, all of which are clearly identified in the configuration file.

> **NOTE**
>
> To comment out any entries in the Samba configuration file, begin the line on which they appear with a semicolon. Similarly, you may need to remove existing semicolons to enable some of the commands that you will need to use to correctly configure Samba.

The minimum set of Samba configuration file entries that you will need to set are the following:

- workgroup —This is the name of the Windows Workgroup or Windows NT domain that your Samba and NetBIOS Name servers should belong to. It is critical that this is the

18

USING SAMBA FOR WINDOWS INTEROPERABILITY

same as it is on any PCs that you want to connect to your Linux systems using Samba. To find out the name of your Workgroup or Domain on Windows systems, select the Start menu's Settings menu, and select Control Panel. Double-click the Network Control Panel applet and select the Identification tab. The name of your workgroup is displayed as the second entry on this panel.

- `hosts allow`—If you want to restrict access to Samba to certain IP addresses or subnets, enter those addresses or subnets here. The following example restricts access to hosts on the 192.168.6 subnet, anything on the loopback interface, and to a single host with the IP address 192.168.5.121:

```
hosts allow = 192.168.6. 127. 192.168.5.121
```

- `printcap name = /etc/printcap`—Tells Samba where to obtain information about available printers on your Linux system. This command should be followed by the command `load printers = yes` to automatically read this information and make those printers available to Windows via Samba. On your Windows system, you will still have to load appropriate printer drivers for those printers, mapping those print drivers to appropriate network printer ports such as `\\samba-server\Linux-printer-name`.

- `log file = /var/log/samba/log.%m`—This command creates a separate log file for each Windows system that tries to connect to Samba, giving it a name of the form `log.hostname` and storing these files in the directory `/var/log/samba`. Maintaining separate log files is invaluable if any of your users have problems accessing Samba. You can examine the log files for the hosts having problems connecting and will generally be able to identify the problem fairly quickly.

- `security = user`—This command sets per-user security via passwords.

- `password server = <NT-Server-Name>`—This option must be commented out unless you are using Samba on a Windows network that uses a Windows NT password server for authentication.

- `encrypt passwords = yes`—This is an important Samba option that is the cause of many problems when first setting up Samba. Early Windows 95 systems used plain text passwords, but all subsequent Windows systems use encrypted passwords for added security. Samba can use encrypted passwords but only if this option (and the `smb password file` option, discussed next) are active. An alternative to this is going to every Windows machine in your organization and hacking the registry to support plain text passwords, which is at best time consuming and irritating.

- `smb password file = /etc/smbpasswd`—This option must be active to use encrypted passwords. Entries for any Samba users who want to access your Linux system must be present in this file. This file is created using the `/usr/bin/smbpasswd` command. To initially create this file, execute a command like the following:

```
/usr/local/samba/bin/smbpasswd /etc/smbpasswd wvh
```

The file /etc/smbpasswd will be created (or emptied, if it already exists, so be careful). You will be prompted for a password, and an entry for (in this case) the user wvh will be added to this file. You can subsequently add other users, such as rjh, to this file using a command like:

```
/usr/local/samba/bin/smbpasswd -a rjh
```

NOTE

Always try to use the same password for Samba as you do for your Linux account and for your Windows network logins. Using the same password means that you'll only have to enter it once when you log in on your PC, and that you will instantly be able to remount Samba and shared PC volumes.

Configuring the [homes] Section

The [homes] section of your smb.conf file enables users to automatically mount their Linux home directories as shared Windows volumes. The entries in this section should look like the following:

```
[homes]
    comment = Home Directories
    browseable = no
    writable = yes
    valid users = %S
    create mode = 0664
    directory mode = 0775
```

Configuring the [tmp] Section

It is often useful to provide a shared Windows directory that any user can write to or read files from. This makes it easy to distribute software via Samba, by copying the files to this directory and then mounting that shared directory on each system where you want to install the software. An active [tmp] section should look like the following:

```
[tmp]
    comment = Temporary file space
    path = /tmp
    read only = no
    public = yes
```

This maps the Linux /tmp directory to a share named tmp that any user can mount, read files from, or write files to. You can also use entries such as this to export CD-ROM drives from your Linux systems to all your Samba clients.

The remainder of the default `smb.conf` file contains many sections that illustrate different ways of creating resources shared by specific users or Linux/Unix groups. However, the settings discussed in this section are the critical ones for you to start and test Samba.

Starting Samba

To start Samba manually after modifying its configuration file for the first time, log in as the superuser or execute the `su` command to become root, and execute the following command:

```
/etc/rc.d/init.d/smb start
```

To shut down Samba manually, you can execute the command

```
/etc/rc.d/init.d/smb stop
```

For information about installing Samba so that it always starts automatically when you restart your system, see "Configuring Samba to Start at Boot Time" earlier in the chapter.

Accessing Linux Directories from Windows Systems

After you start Samba on your Linux system and it reports success for both the SMB and NMB processes, you're ready to try accessing your Linux system from a Windows machine. To be able to successfully access Linux directories from a Windows system, you must also be able to authenticate to the Samba daemon (the `smbd` process) on the Linux machine. This is usually enabled by creating entries in the Samba password file, either `/etc/smbpasswd` on most preinstalled versions of Samba or `/usr/local/samba/lib/smbpasswd` if you installed the version of Samba included with this book. Entries in this file are created using the `/usr/local/samba/bin/smbpasswd` command.

Go to a Windows machine and double-click on the Network Neighborhood icon. An icon with the name of the Linux system running Samba should be displayed in the list of other SMB hosts in your workgroup. You can traverse this icon by double-clicking until you get to the icon for the volume you want to access. To map that icon to a drive letter in Windows, right-click that icon and select the Map Network Drive command. This brings up the standard drive mapping dialog and associates the selected volume with a drive letter. You can even specify Reconnect at Login if you want to automatically remount this drive each time you boot your system and it is connected to the appropriate network.

After you successfully map a Linux directory to a Windows drive letter, the Linux directory looks and behaves exactly like any other drive letter. This enables Windows users to drag and drop files to and from the Linux volume from their Windows desktops, just as if they were accessing a Windows server.

NetWare Filesystem Support in Linux

IN THIS CHAPTER

Long before personal computer networking was a glimmer in Microsoft's eye, many thousands of DOS users were already happily working in a secure, powerful, networked environment thanks to a company from Provo, Utah called Novell. Novell's NetWare product set the standard for DOS networking and was also the standard networking solution for Windows up to Windows 3.11 and Windows for Workgroups, when Microsoft noticed a market that it had yet to monopolize.

The odd thing about NetWare is that it has refused to die. Largely thanks to a huge installed base of satisfied customers, NetWare is still in use in thousands of installations all over the world. Not too surprisingly, Linux includes built-in support for the networking protocols used by NetWare. Most Linux distributions also come with a set of tools needed to access NetWare servers, mount NetWare volumes, integrate with other Novell services, and so on.

This chapter explains how to configure your system to access NetWare file servers, integrate those file servers into a Linux environment, access NetWare server volumes from Linux, and integrate a Linux system into NetWare printing mechanisms.

Overview

This chapter makes a few assumptions, primary among which is that you wouldn't be reading it if you didn't already have some involvement with NetWare. I like to hack Linux as much as anyone, but even I wouldn't install a NetWare network just so that I could subsequently migrate it to Linux. This leaves three potential classes of readers:

- Linux sysadmins who are interested in helping their company save money and streamline operations while still getting work done, by integrating Linux systems into existing operations and reducing NetWare-related expenses

- Linux sysadmins who want to obtain some experience in the NetWare environment in case a corporate need for NetWare arises.

- Novell sysadmins who are curious about Linux and want to understand how it interoperates with existing NetWare environments

The next section, "Overview of NetWare Networking," provides an overview of NetWare, its history, the features and networking services it provides, and the networking protocols it uses. This information is primarily intended for Linux sysadmins who may not know much about NetWare and need to understand where it came from, why it exists, and how it works to determine how best to integrate Linux and Novell systems. This information should also help Linux sysadmins "pass" at social gatherings composed of NetWare administrators. Aside from some historical information, I doubt that this section will provide many surprises for existing NetWare administrators other than those who want to do anything more than fact and sanity checking.

The subsequent section, "NetWare Support in Linux," is designed for both audiences. That section provides an overview of the types of NetWare support available for Linux and how that support and its requirements are intrinsically different from the scope of and rational for the Windows and Macintosh networking support provided by Linux.

Overview of NetWare Networking

Like all modern personal computer and workstation networking, the roots of NetWare lie in the networking protocols invented by Xerox Corporation at its Palo Alto Research Center (Xerox PARC). Xerox PARC was the Garden of Eden for most of the computing mechanisms, models, and even the forerunners of much of the computing hardware that we take for granted today. Although Xerox PARC provides a shining model for anyone trying to build a pure, forward-looking research institute, its inability to successfully market any of its innovations is like the before picture in a before/after comparison for anyone building a marketing organization.

Xerox invented the workstation, the bitmapped display, Ethernet, laser printers, and most of the characteristics of the modern graphical user interface (GUI), and had the client/server model of computing running in a networked environment of file servers by the mid-to-late 1970s. Would everyone who is currently using a Xerox network card or workstation please raise his or her hand? I thought not. For some reason, Xerox was unable to sell any of these things to just about anyone, leaving that to subsequent innovators and entrepreneurs who made zillions of dollars from Xerox's research efforts.

Novell was one of the companies both smart enough to recognize a good thing when it saw it and to decide to do it on its own instead of waiting for Xerox sales and marketing efforts to ramp up. Novell was originally a personal computer hardware company making CP/M machines (Control Program for Microprocessors, the one true personal computer operating system before DOS, and DOS's direct parent thanks to Seattle Computer System's "port" of CP/M to the 8086 processor family). Novell quickly saw that just about anyone could make personal computer hardware, but that few people could make a profit at it, and thus seized on a local research project, a networked environment for personal computers, as its true future.

Novell did this for all the right reasons, understanding that the ability to centralize storage on file servers provided some amazing advantages for personal computer users. You could access the same files from any personal computer, and backups and administrative procedures could be centralized. The original NetWare file servers were dedicated 68000-based machines, but NetWare itself was migrated to run natively on Intel processors when the IBM XT was introduced.

The foundations of the networking protocols originally used by NetWare lie in the Xerox Network System (XNS). Because XNS already existed and Xerox had demonstrated (internally) that it worked, most of the early networking companies, such as 3Com, Novell, and

19

NETWARE
FILESYSTEM
SUPPORT IN LINUX

Ungermann-Bass adopted and extended the basic XNS protocols. Various generations of NetWare have used the following protocols for workstation/file server communication:

- Internetwork Packet Exchange (IPX)—Based on the XNS Internet Datagram Protocol (IDP), IPX is a connectionless protocol that provides a basic logical addressing and delivery mechanism for packets on a network, without providing any guarantees about packet order or delivery.

- NetWare Core Protocol (NCP)—Riding on top of IPX and SPX, NCP supports requests for specific NetWare services, such as opening, reading, writing, and closing files, searching directories, accessing other remote resources such as printers, and so on.

- NetWare Link State Protocol (NLSP)—A replacement for the RIP and SAP protocols designed to reduce the amount of broadcast traffic on a network. NLSP was introduced with NetWare 3.

- Routing Information Protocol (RIP)—A broadcast protocol used between IPX routers on a network to exchange information about how to find various network destinations. IPX routers can either be dedicated network routers or, with NetWare 3.12 and greater, can be any NetWare server. RIP is not limited to use with NetWare but is primarily found in that context.

- Sequenced Packet Exchange (SPX)—Based on the XNS Sequenced Packet Protocol (SPP), SPX is a connection-oriented protocol that provides delivery and ordering guarantees for packets on a network. The fact that SPX is designed to establish and maintain connections between specific network objects makes it more reliable and deterministic than IPX after a connection has been established.

- Service Advertisement Protocol (SAP)—A broadcast protocol useful for informing NetWare clients about the various NetWare services (file servers and printers) available on a network. Even later versions of NetWare that use directory services to store the lists and locations of services available on the network use SAP for bootstrapping purposes (that is, advertising the location of the network directories).

- Transmission Control Protocol/Internet Protocol (TCP/IP)—Every modern computer user's favorite protocol, TCP/IP can be used by NetWare versions 5 and greater to replace IPX/SPX as its basic transport protocols.

In a nutshell, NetWare provides the following high-level services to computer users via these protocols:

- Connections to file servers, providing access to common and user-specific files, directories, and volumes.

- A security mechanism that supports basic authentication to a NetWare file server as well as fine-grained control over which users have access to any NetWare resource, such as specific files, directories, volumes, print queues, and printers. Per-resource protections are supported through Access Control Lists (ACLs) that can be associated with any NetWare resource down to the file level.

One interesting innovation of Novell's was the realization that there was no need for client systems and file servers to share the same on-disk volume formats. To maximize performance, NetWare servers therefore use their own proprietary high-performance NetWare volume formats—the original NetWare volume format and the NetWare Storage System (NSS) volume format. NSS, a full 64-bit filesystem, was introduced with NetWare 5 to support higher volume and therefore file server capacities, consisting of up to 127 volumes per server with a per-volume limit of 8 terabytes.

Over time, different versions of NetWare have provided a continuing series of enhancements to the capabilities and capacities of NetWare file and print servers. The following is a capsule summary of the capabilities and enhancements provided by different versions of NetWare:

- 2.X and earlier—16-bit operating systems that provided basic file and print services with no built-in support for TCP/IP. I still own a Novell 2.11 network that uses packet drivers to support TCP/IP and IPX/SPX networking through the same network interface cards.

- 3.X—32-bit operating systems that introduced NetWare Loadable Modules (NLMs) to enable third-party firms to integrate their software and hardware into the NetWare environment. TCP/IP support added.

- 4.X—32-bit operating systems that introduced NDS, a directory service to simplify finding and accessing NetWare objects on a network and provided a high-level logical view of an entire NetWare network as a single logical whole. NetWare 4.X provided enhanced integration with other networking protocols and more robust clients for non-DOS operating systems. It also delivered improvements in IPX routing and the capacity of NetWare volumes, as well as improved system administration and licensing capabilities. This was the first version of NetWare to come on a CD-ROM, a huge improvement for anyone who had installed previous versions from an ever-increasing stack of floppies.

- 5.X—64-bit operating systems that provided native support for TCP/IP as the transport protocol for all NetWare communications, virtual memory support, and support for the NSS volume format, which exponentially increased the potential amount of storage that a single NetWare file server could manage. As a tip of the hat to modernism, NetWare 5.0 also introduced an X Window System-based console, enabling NetWare servers to theoretically be managed from the desktops of any system running the X Window System. NetWare 5.0 also provided World Wide Web-based support and services and was the first version of NetWare to include a Java virtual Machine.

- 6.X—Still in Beta testing as I write this, NetWare 6 provides substantially greater integration with other operating systems and networking utilities, largely eliminating the

19

NETWARE
FILESYSTEM
SUPPORT IN LINUX

need to install specific NetWare client software on your desktop. NetWare 6 also includes improved print services and administration, enhanced NDS capabilities, file synchronization between servers and multiple desktops, built-in support for clustering that you can use to roll your own Storage Area Network (SAN), and (big surprise) a greater Web-orientation for both users and administrators.

As manifested by the enhancements in NetWare 6 that make NetWare servers more seamlessly available to clients, Novell realizes that the curtain is coming down on the era of proprietary networking products. Microsoft's "embrace, extend, smother, and loot" strategy initially claimed a big portion of Novell's customer base, and the subsequent availability of Linux and its inherent lack of cost has cost Novell a few profitable quarters, with no turnaround in sight. The folks at Novell are smart people and have therefore been developing other products to help plug the holes in their hull.

The most interesting and open of Novell's new products is its Network Directory Service (NDS), which was originally introduced as a more flexible mechanism for locating information about NetWare services, devices, users, and just about anything else. Major portions of NDS are freely available for Linux and other Unix and Unix-like systems, in the hopes that NDS might be adopted wholesale by the Internet community. Conceptually similar to LDAP, NDS provides a network-accessible directory where any sort of information can be stored, organized hierarchically, protected, and retrieved. NDS provides the fundamental model for all Novell security and other sorts of record-keeping.

Versions of NetWare prior to version 4 stored security and printer information in a server-specific database called the *bindery*. The bindery was a robust service but didn't provide the truly high-level view of a network that NDS provides. Because the view of a NetWare network provided by NDS includes all servers registered with that directory service, NDS eliminates the need to duplicate account and resource information across different servers. Novell introduced NDS in NetWare 4 without alienating existing customers by providing bindery emulation in NDS (now known as *bindery services*) that enabled existing NetWare clients to access authentication and location information from NDS.

NetWare Support in Linux

The support provided for Novell filesystems in Linux is a slightly different animal than that provided by the other filesystem adapters available for Linux and discussed in this book. To recap, Netatalk enables Macintosh users to access and mount Linux directories on the Macintosh desktop. Because directories serve as the mountpoints for filesystems in Linux and Unix, being able to mount Linux directories on a Macintosh desktop enables you to access entire filesystems, as long as you have the proper Linux credentials. In the way that Samba is most commonly used, it does the same thing, enabling Windows users to mount and access

Linux filesystems and directories on the Windows desktop. Linux users can also use Samba's `smbclient` application to temporarily mount a Windows shared directory with a specific process and provides an FTP-like interface for transferring files but not accessing them directly.

Linux provides two types of support for Novell NetWare. One is its emulation support, which enables Linux to run a process that looks like yet another NetWare file server to existing NetWare clients. I'll discuss these briefly later in the chapter in the section "NetWare File Servers for Linux," but although NetWare emulation is technically and conceptually interesting, this basically just perpetuates the use of NetWare in a computing environment. Why bother?

It's easy to see why filesystem adapters such as Netatalk exist because they provide an interface to Linux file servers from the Macintosh personal computing platform, which is intrinsically useful because it has millions of devotees and thousands of powerful applications that people need to use to get their work done.

It's also easy to see why Samba is useful—not so much because there are unique and useful applications for Windows, but more because people have Windows systems on their desktops and need connectivity to a robust file server and print environment that works the same way every time. Windows users need a computing backbone that they can depend on, and Linux provides just that. This is either charity or philanthropy, depending on your perspective—regardless, it would be just plain rude not to help out, because we can.

The situation with Novell connectivity and interoperability is completely different. NetWare is an add-on to existing operating systems, providing fast, secure networking. However, as an add-on to existing systems, it basically doesn't provide applications that are useful outside the scope of its own installation and administration.

This brings us to the second type of NetWare support provided by Linux—connectivity from Linux systems to existing NetWare servers. This type of support is the focus of this chapter because there are probably terabytes of data stored on NetWare filesystems in business and even some academic computing environments. You can't ignore the reality of this, or expect anyone to arbitrarily burn the hundreds of man hours required to move all this data to Linux systems. Don't get me wrong—I like NetWare. Like the vi text editor, it is a quaint survivor from a simpler, more primitive time and has many devoted users simply because everybody grew up with it and is familiar with using it. NetWare 5.0 and greater even provide built-in support for modern languages and application environments such as the Web, Java, and Java application servers such as IBM's WebSphere. However, the business reality of NetWare is that it costs money and doesn't provide anything that you can't get out of a free Linux distribution now or in the near future.

There are certainly client-system applications that provide integrated support for the sophisticated access control mechanisms provided by NetWare, most notably accounting systems. If you're locked into one of these, you may need to continue using and paying for NetWare for the immediate future. Unix security is fine but doesn't intrinsically provide the granularity that NetWare users are used to. However, built-in support for Access Control Lists and related access sophistication is just around the corner for standard Linux filesystems such as ext2 and ext3, and is already available in filesystems such as XFS.

More sophisticated ACLs than those provided by NetWare have been available for years in the AFS distributed filesystem, now available for Linux as OpenAFS. Even commercial versions of Unix had or will have Access Control Lists soon. The Apollo workstations of yesteryear provided integrated support for ACLs right up to the point that they were axe-murdered by Hewlett-Packard. The man pages for ACLs on Solaris systems have been available for years. In the case of Solaris, the access control mechanisms that these reference pages describe should work there real soon now, too.

The point of all this is that, simply put, I can't think of any reasons to add NetWare file servers to any computing environment where NetWare is not already in use. Okay, maybe if your budget is too large and you need to spend money on something before the end of the fiscal year, but that's about it. However, migrating an existing computing environment and related applications from one platform to another is expensive, primarily in terms of man hours. This simply might not be the right time for your organization to do so.

For computing environments that have an existing investment in NetWare, the combination of Linux, existing filesystem adapters for Windows and Macintosh systems, and the NCP emulation software provided for Linux provides the best of both worlds without requiring yet another emulation layer:

- As a stable file server, Web, mail, print, and everything else server, Linux itself is the perfect replacement for any new NetWare servers that you are considering adding to your computing environment.

- Existing NetWare clients who need access to Linux filesystems can access those filesystem through the native networking protocols used on their systems—Samba for Windows systems and Netatalk for Macintosh systems.

- Linux desktop users who need access to existing NetWare file servers can use the NCP (Novell Core Protocol) tools described in this section to access their existing files. Windows systems that need access to data currently stored on NetWare file servers either can access it as they always have, or the NetWare file server volumes can be migrated to Linux and accessed from the Windows desktop via Samba. Macintosh systems that access NetWare file servers either can access them as they always have, or the NetWare file server volumes can be migrated to Linux and accessed from the Macintosh desktop via Netatalk.

Any way you look at it, you can save money by using Linux—and not just the cost of NetWare itself. After your file servers are liberated from proprietary, commercial environments, such as Windows and NetWare, you can replace the relatively expensive commercial backup software used to back up and archive NetWare volumes with free backup systems. Several free and open-source backup packages are available, such as Amanda, the OpenAFS backup system (if you are using OpenAFS), or even standard local Linux filesystem backup applications such as `dump/restore` or `xfsdump/xfsrestore` (if you are using local XFS filesystems). Some commercial backup, restore, and archive software is reasonably priced, but it's always more expensive than the equivalent free software available for Linux. Even commercial backup software for Linux is generally less expensive than equivalent Windows or standard Unix backup software.

Support Software for NetWare on Linux

As mentioned in the previous section, a variety of NetWare support and interoperability software is available for Linux. As explained in the next two sections, this support ranges from emulators that enable you to run things that look like Novell NetWare servers as Linux sub-processes, to tools that enable your Linux system to interoperate with real NetWare servers.

NetWare File Servers for Linux

Two free NetWare server emulators are available for Linux. These enable you to run a Linux process that looks like a standard NetWare 3.X/4.X vintage server to NetWare clients. These aren't emulators in the sense that they enable you to run code from Novell on your Linux system—they simply provide a Linux interface that enables existing Novell clients to access Linux systems as though they were NetWare file servers. The emulator can then be configured to export standard Linux filesystems to the Novell clients much like Samba or Netatalk export Linux filesystems to Windows and Macintosh clients, respectively.

The free NetWare server emulators available for Linux are

- `mars_nwe` (Martin Stover's NetWare Emulator) is a free NetWare server emulator that supports emulation of NetWare 2.1x and 3.x file and print services. The `mars_nwe` emulator is included and preinstalled on many Linux distributions, including Red Hat. Although it is not all that actively supported, it is stable and doesn't really need to do anything new because it's emulating antique versions of NetWare in the first place. If installed on your Linux system, the binary for the `mars_nwe` emulator is usually found as `/usr/sbin/nwserv`.

  The home page for `mars_nwe` is at `http://www.compu-art.de/mars_nwe`, much of which is unfortunately (for me) in German. (The only languages that I speak other than English are computer languages, but there's always Babelfish in a true emergency situation.) A copy of the source code for the latest version of `mars_nwe` version 0.99, patch level 20 is provided in the netware subdirectory of the CD that accompanies this book. The mars_nwe emulator stores its configuration information in the file /etc/nwserv.conf and is still actively supported and patched by Martin.

- lwared (LinWare Emulator) is a NetWare file server emulation package without any support for print services. It works well with DOS and Windows 3.1 clients but has stability problems with Windows 95, Windows 98, and Windows NT clients. The IPX configuration required by lwared is also much more complex than that for mars_nwe. For these reasons, mars_nwe is probably a better bet under almost any circumstance, but both mars_nwe and many of the NCP utilities provided with Linux owe their genesis to lwared.

As mentioned in the previous section of this book, I don't see much reason to use either of these emulators today, and therefore don't provide information on installing, configuring, or using them. At best, these emulators enable a Linux system administrator to configure a Novell emulation server to export Linux filesystems to Novell clients. Because these Novell clients are probably either Windows or Macintosh systems, you can easily export Linux filesystems to those clients using Samba or Netatalk, respectively. There's really no need to run yet another emulation package to provide roundabout exporting of Linux filesystems to NetWare clients via the familiar NetWare protocols.

> **TIP**
>
> One potential use for mars_nwe is as a staging site when migrating users off NetWare. For example, you can copy the data from your NetWare server to a Linux box by using mars_nwe or even something as simple as zipping up the NetWare directories, ftp-ing them to your Linux system, and then unpacking them there. For most of your user data, you could then use Samba and/or Netatalk to serve the data to users depending on their home platform. Finally, you could then configure the mars_nwe server to behave as a clone of the NetWare server, including print services, to support existing users while continuing to phase out the NetWare services as this becomes possible.

NCP Interoperability Software for Linux

The focus of this chapter is the NetWare Core Protocol support and interoperability software provided in the Linux ncpfs package. These tools provide support for most of the common NCP command and services, and some of the uncommon ones as well. These tools are robust and have been used for years. However, for this reason, the NCP tools provided for Linux require that you have bindery emulation (bindery services) active on the NetWare file server and NDS organizational unit that you want to access from Linux.

NOTE

If you surf the Web in search of additional information about access to Novell file servers from Linux, you will eventually find references to programs called nwclient, nwlogin, and so on. These are part of a Linux package for Novell integration that was commercially available from Caldera at one point, as part of an old version of its OpenLinux product. Caldera's NetWare support package was a powerful, optimized set of NetWare clients that included direct support for more modern NetWare bells and whistles, such as the Network Directory Service (NDS), and ran on many different versions of Linux, including Red Hat.

Unfortunately, as far as I can tell, this isn't available any longer. Although I own a copy, I've never used it much, and certainly not on recent Linux distributions—the set of NCP client applications provided by the ncpfs package and the integrated kernel support for IPX provided by Linux have always been sufficient for my needs.

Though the NCP utilities for Linux are provided as part of most Linux distributions, the source code for version 2.2.0.18 of the ncpfs package is provided in the netware subdirectory of the CD that accompanies this book. If these tools aren't provided with your Linux distribution or you simply want to install and use the latest and greatest version of them, "Installing the ncpfs Tools" later in this chapter explains how to compile and install them on your system.

The ncpfs package provides the following NCP utilities for Linux:

- ipx_configure —Displays or configures the current settings for IPX interface detection on your system. This enables you to set whether your system automatically creates an IPX interface when one is requested and whether it automatically selects a primary IPX interface.

- ipx_interface—Adds, deletes, or lists the characteristics of a specified IPX interface.

- ipx_internal_net—Adds or deletes the internal network used to provide route-independent addressing for IPX packets on a specific machine. Internal networks are optional.

- ipx_route—Adds or deletes the IPX route for a specific network.

- ipxdump—A packet sniffer for IPX Ethernet packets. This utility is not compiled or installed by default as part of the ncpfs package when you build it from source, but can be compiled and installed separately by changing directory to the ipxdump subdirectory of the directory in which you installed the ncpfs package source code and running the make program.

> **NOTE**
>
> The `ipxdump` and `ipxparse` utilities are installed by default with some Linux distributions, such as Red Hat.

- `ipxparse`—A program that takes the hexadecimal output of the `ipxdump` program, parses it, and produces slightly more readable output that may be meaningful to hexadecimally challenged IPX wizards. Like its sibling application `ipxdump`, this utility is not compiled or installed by default as part of the `ncpfs` package. It can be compiled and installed separately by changing to the `ipxdump` subdirectory of the directory in which you installed the `ncpfs` package source code and running the `make` program.

- `ncopy`—Copies one or more files from one location to another on a NetWare file server using NCP functions internal to that server, as opposed to generating additional network traffic to do the file copy through a remote mountpoint.

- `ncpmount`—Mounts a NetWare file server on a specified mountpoint, as a specific user. A symbolic link to this program named `/sbin/mount.ncp` is usually provided to enable you to list NetWare volumes in the `/etc/fstab` file and mount them automatically at boot time, though this is highly insecure at boot time because it requires a username and password that must be hidden in a configuration file. Yikes!

- `ncpumount`—Unmounts a mounted NetWare volume.

- `nprint`—Prints files on any print queue provided by a NetWare server.

- `nsend`—Sends messages to the workstations of specific NetWare users and groups.

- `nwauth`—Authenticates to a NetWare server. This program is intended for use by other applications that need to verify whether the user can successfully authenticate to a NetWare file server before proceeding.

- `nwbocreate`—Creates a specified bindery object in the bindery used by a NetWare server, or in the appropriate portion of its NDS tree, assuming that bindery emulation is enabled there.

- `nwbols`—Lists the bindery objects visible to a specified user, based on their permissions on a given NetWare server.

- `nwboprops`—lists the properties of a specified bindery object on a given NetWare server.

- `nwborm`—Removes a specified bindery object from a given NetWare server.

- `nwbpadd`—Sets the value of a bindery object property on a specified NetWare server.

- `nwbpcreate`—Creates a bindery object property on a specified NetWare server.

- `nwbprm`—Removes a bindery object property on a specified NetWare server.

- nwbpset—Creates a bindery property and optionally sets its value. This utility differs from the nwbpcreate and nwbpadd utilities in that it uses a property specification from standard input and can therefore be used as part of a Linux piped command to dynamically perform actions that would otherwise require dedicated shell scripts.

- nwbpvalues—Prints a bindery object's properties and its contents. This command is often used to supply the input to the nwbpset command after that data has been manipulated by a stream editor such as sed on Linux.

- nwdir—Lists information about files and directories on a NetWare file server currently mounted on your Linux system.

- nwdpvalues—Prints the name or ID of a specified object in the NetWare directory service.

- nwfsctrl—Executes a command on a specified NetWare server. This command enables you to perform administrative functions on a NetWare server remotely. Supported commands enable you to do things like load and unload NetWare Loadable Modules (NLMs), mount and unmount volumes, set server variables, enable or disable logins, and even shut down the server.

- nwsfind—Displays the IPX routes to one or more active NetWare servers of various types. You can find the route to a specific NetWare server by specifying its name, or display the routes to all available NetWare servers by not specifying the name of a particular server.

- nwfsinfo—Displays information about a specific NetWare server. Most often used with the -i option to display usage, version, and some configuration information.

- nwfstime—Obtains and displays current time settings from a specific NetWare file server.

- nwgrant—Enables you to grant individuals trustee rights to objects in the NetWare bindery. This command enables you to modify NetWare file and directory permissions from a Linux system. You can either specify the pathname to a NetWare file or directory that has been mounted on a Linux system or specify the file or directory name in terms of its location in a NetWare volume on a specified server.

- nwrevoke—Enables you to remove the trustee rights associated with individuals from objects in the NetWare bindery. This command enables you to modify NetWare file and directory permissions from a Linux system. You can either specify the pathname to a NetWare file or directory that has been mounted on a Linux system or specify the file or directory name in terms of its location in a NetWare volume on a specified server.

- nwpasswd—Enables you to remotely change your password on a specified NetWare file server. If you have supervisor privileges on the NetWare file server, you can use this utility to change or reset any user's password.

- nwpurge—Enables you to permanently delete and erase files and directories that have been deleted on a mounted NetWare volume. This performs the same function as the NetWare PURGE utility.

- nwrights—Shows the effective rights that you have for a specified file or directory. This performs the same function as the NetWare RIGHTS utility.

- nwtrustee—Lists the trustee rights of a specific bindery object on a NetWare file server.

- nwtrustee2—Lists the trustee rights of files or directories in a currently mounted NetWare filesystem. Returns nothing if you have no trustee rights on specified files and directories.

- nwuserlist—Lists all users on a specified NetWare file server and the connections they are using.

- nwvolinfo—Displays size, file, and directory information about a volume on a specified NetWare file server.

- pqlist—Lists the print queues available on a specified NetWare server.

- pqrm—Removes a print job from a specified print queue on a given NetWare server.

- pqstat—Displays status information about a specified print queue on a given NetWare server.

- pserver—Connects to NetWare print queues and forwards print jobs in those queues to Linux printers.

- slist—Lists available NetWare servers.

Adding NetWare Support to Your System

Linux kernels have had the capability to support the IPX protocol at the kernel level since the mid 1990s. IPX support may or may not be active in the kernel on your system. This section explains how to check whether IPX support is already enabled, how to add that support and build a kernel that supports IPX if it is not, and how to compile, install, and configure the ncpfs package.

Building a Kernel with IPX Support

You can determine whether your Linux kernel already supports IPX by checking for the string IPX in the messages displayed when your system last booted, as in the following example:

```
# grep -i IPX /var/log/messages
Sep  9 08:46:41 jrnll kernel: NET4: Linux IPX 0.47 for NET4.0
Sep  9 08:46:41 jrnl kernel: IPX Portions Copyright (c) 1995 Caldera, Inc.
Sep  9 08:46:41 jrnll kernel: IPX Portions Copyright (c) 2000, 2001 Conectiva,
Inc.
```

If your kernel displays messages like the ones shown in the output from this example and therefore already includes IPX support, you can skip ahead to the section "Installing the ncpfs Tools."

If you do not see a message of this form (the IPX version number and copyright dates may be different), you will have to recompile your kernel to provide IPX and NetWare filesystem support, as explained in the next two sections.

Activating IPX and NCP Support in the Kernel

The CD that accompanies this book includes the source code for version 2.4.9 of the Linux kernel, the most advanced version of the Linux available at the time of this writing, and the one that I've therefore chosen to use to show how easy it is to activate IPX support in your Linux system.

> **NOTE**
>
> As mentioned in each chapter, if you have never built a kernel before, doing so is a great learning experience. Although the whole idea of prepackaged Linux installation is to protect users from the need to "roll their own" kernel and Linux utilities, compiling a kernel is an excellent way to familiarize yourself with the conceptual internals and organization of Linux. The instructions in this book for compiling kernels create kernels that have special names and will thus not overwrite the current version of the Linux kernel that you are using.

The source for the Linux 2.4.9 kernel is located in the kernels subdirectory of the CD that accompanies this book. Install this kernel as described in "Installing the Kernel Source Code" in Appendix A, "Using the CD-ROM: Installing, Updating, and Compiling Kernels."

> **TIP**
>
> If you have already compiled a kernel for the computer system on which you are building a new kernel, you can use the configuration information from that kernel to save time when configuring the new kernel. Reusing existing configuration data from an existing kernel is explained in Appendix A.

19

NETWARE
FILESYSTEM
SUPPORT IN LINUX

After you've installed the kernel, do the following to activate IPX support in the kernel:

1. Log in as root or use the su command to become root.

2. In a terminal window running under an X Window System window manager or desktop, change to the directory /usr/src/linux-2.4.9 and execute the make xconfig

command. The commands related to compiling and loading support for the Linux X Window System kernel configurator display in the window in which you executed the `make xconfig` command. Eventually, the X Window System Linux kernel configurator displays, as shown in Figure 19.1.

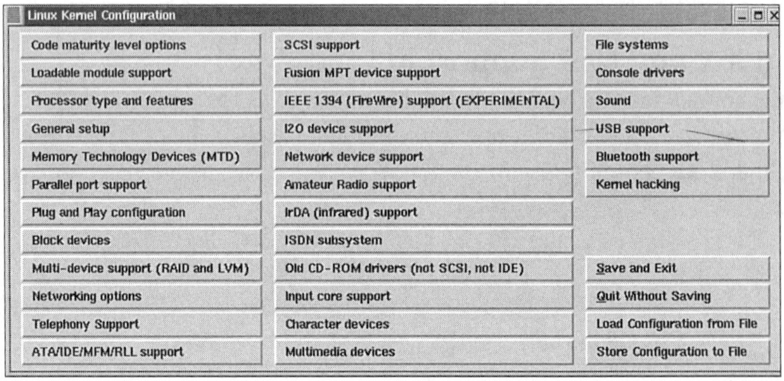

FIGURE 19.1

The X Window System-based Linux kernel configurator.

3. Select the Networking Options command or button. The Networking Options dialog displays, as shown in Figure 19.2.

FIGURE 19.2

The Linux kernel configurator's Networking Options dialog box.

4. Scroll down until you see a label for The IPX Protocol. Click Y beside this entry. This activates basic IPX support in the kernel that you will be building. You can optionally select M to compile IPX support as a kernel-loadable module if you don't expect to be accessing NetWare file or print servers frequently.

5. Click N beside the IPX Full Internal IPX Network entry unless you are familiar with IPX networking and want to access your Linux system from multiple IPX networks. You will

want to click Y if you want to be able to assign your machine an internal IPX network address that enables your system to be uniquely identified from any other IPX system that can reach it on the network. You may want to do this if you plan to use your system as a file server for multiple IPX networks. Activating full internal IPX network support disables some features that you might prefer would just work automatically, such as forwarding RIP and SAP packets to ports on a default primary network.

6. Click the Main Menu button at the bottom of the dialog to close the Networking Options dialog and return to the primary Linux kernel configurator dialog.

7. Click the File Systems button in the X Window System Linux Kernel Configuration dialog. The File Systems dialog displays, as shown in Figure 19.3.

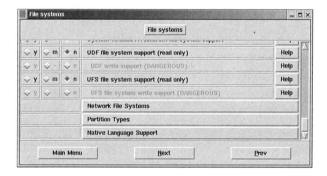

FIGURE 19.3

The File Systems dialog's Network File Systems button.

8. Scroll down until you see the Network File Systems button and click it to display the Network File Systems dialog, as shown in Figure 19.4.

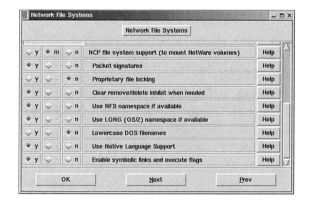

FIGURE 19.4

NCP Filesystem Entries on the Network File Systems dialog box.

9. Click Y beside the NCP File System Support (to Mount NetWare Volumes) label. This activates NCP support in the kernel. You can optionally select M beside this entry to build NCP support as a loadable kernel module. Selecting either of these options enables the other options for NCP filesystem support.

Unless you have specific IPX requirements on your network, use the following settings for the other NCP-related filesystem options:

- Click Y beside the Packet Signatures label to provide a higher level of security in IPX packets. Versions of the ncpfs utilities newer than version 2.0.12 support this option. (The version of the ncpfs utilities included on the CD that accompanies this book is 2.2.0.18.)

- Click N beside the Proprietary File Locking entry unless you have specific NetWare-based applications that can use this locking scheme. This is rare for Linux applications.

- Click Y beside the Clear Remove/Delete Inhibit When Needed entry. This option enables you to work with files and directories assigned the NetWare DELETE INHIBIT or RENAME INHIBIT attributes to prevent them from being deleted or moved. To actually manipulate these files in a NetWare volume mounted on a Linux system, you must have mounted the volume using the ncpmount command's -s option.

- Click Y beside the Use NFS Namespace if Available option if you want to enable case-sensitive filenames. You can always disable this option when mounting a NetWare volume by using the ncpmount command's -N nfs option, but you cannot activate it at that time unless it's been compiled into the kernel or loadable kernel module.

- Click Y beside the Use LONG (OS/2) Namespace if Available option if you want to be able to use case-preserving, case-insensitive filenames up to 256 characters in length on your NetWare file server. This means that filenames can be composed of uppercase and lowercase characters, but that the case of those characters will be ignored—in other words, requests for files named FOO.txt and foo.txt would resolve to the same file. You can always disable this option when mounting a NetWare volume by using the ncpmount command's -N os2 option, but you cannot activate it at that time unless it's been compiled into the kernel or loadable kernel module.

- Click N beside the Lowercase DOS Filenames option unless you want all filenames created under DOS or in the OS2/LONG namespace to automatically be displayed with lowercase filenames. This option was originally provided for backward compatibility when moving from DOS to OS2 filesystems. Given that OS/2 has been dead and buried for quite a while now, it's safe to leave this option off.

- Click Y beside the Use Native Language Support option. This option is primarily provided for Natural (sic) Language Support in filenames if you plan to access NetWare volumes and create files from operating systems that provide NLS support through code pages and I/O character sets.

- Click Y beside the Enable Symbolic Links and Execute Flags option.

10. Click OK at the bottom of the Network File Systems dialog to return to the File Systems dialog.

11. Click the Main Menu button to return to the primary `make xconfig` dialog.

12. After selecting any other kernel configuration options relevant to the kernel that you are building (such as those specific to the hardware in your system), save your updated kernel configuration.

    If you reused the configuration data from an existing kernel, use the Store Configuration to File button to display a dialog that enables you to explicitly save your new kernel configuration with the name `.config` in the main directory of the kernel that you are configuring.

    If you configured the current kernel from scratch (that is, without reading in configuration data from another kernel), simply click the Save and Exit button.

13. Click OK to close the final dialog and return to the Linux shell prompt. You're now ready to compile the kernel!

Compiling and Installing an IPX-Aware Kernel

After configuring the Linux 2.4.9 kernel, you're ready to compile and install your new Linux kernel. All the information that you need to compile and install this kernel is provided in Appendix A. This section just provides a checklist for the steps that you should follow.

After you've installed and configured the Linux 2.4.9 kernel for IPX support and to match your hardware, you must do the following to install and use that kernel:

1. Add a special extension for this kernel to its Makefile, making it easy to identify the special features in the kernel. I typically name kernels that support different filesystems along the lines of `linux-<kernel-version>-<filesystem-type>`. In this case, "ipx" might be a good suffix for the filesystem type.

2. Execute the following `make` commands in this order to correctly initialize dependencies and to build and install the new kernel and any associated loadable modules:

```
make dep
make
make modules
make install
make modules_install
```

I suggest doing these steps as discrete commands to make it easy to spot any compilation or installation failures along the way. If you're really cocky, you can reduce these commands to the following single command line, but you'd still be wise to scroll back to make sure that there were no problems:

```
make dep ; make install ; make modules; make modules_install
```

3. Modify the boot loader configuration files for the boot loader you're using on your system, as described in "Booting a New Kernel" in Appendix A and rerun LILO if necessary.

To use Linux's built-in support for NetWare, you must first correctly configure the IPX protocol on your system. This is easy to do and requires surprisingly little intervention on your part. To enable IPX support on an Ethernet interface in your system, you must tell your system to configure the IPX interface. If you are running Red Hat Linux, you can do this using Red Hat's linuxconf utility. If you are not and the graphical administrative utilities for your system do not support IPX configuration, you can manually add the IPX configuration commands to your system's startup files.

If you are using Red Hat Linux, do the following:

1. As the superuser, start the linuxconf utility and select the Network, Client Tasks, IPX Interface Setup command, shown in Figure 19.5. The dialog shown in Figure 19.6 displays.

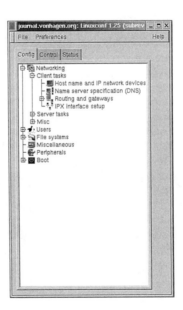

FIGURE 19.5

Locating the IPX Configuration dialog box in Red Hat's linuxconf.

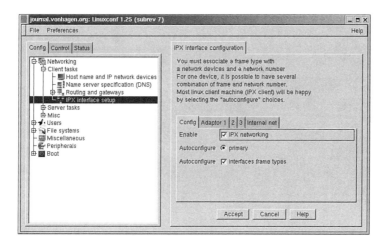

FIGURE 19.6
Linuxconf's IPX Interface Configuration dialog box.

2. Select the check box to enable IPX networking. Unless you are an IPX expert or are working in a specific, multinetwork IPX environment, select the Autoconfigure Primary radio button and the Autoconfigure Interfaces Frame Types check box.

3. If you only have one Ethernet interface in your system and you enabled the Autoconfigure options, click the Accept button to accept these configuration changes. If you are working in an IPX environment that requires manual configuration, click the tab for the network adapter that you want to configure for IPX support. Unless you have multiple Ethernet interfaces, this will be the Adapter 1 tab. The dialog shown in Figure 19.7 displays. Enter the appropriate values for your network and click the Accept button to accept the modified entries.

4. Select the Act/Changes from Linuxconf's File menu to activate the IPX configuration changes you just made. On Red Hat systems, this updates the `/etc/sysconfig/network` file that is used to set environment variables that the `/etc/rc.d/init.d/network` script depends on. Your `/etc/sysconfig/network` file will look something like the following:

```
NETWORKING=yes
HOSTNAME=journal.vonhagen.org
GATEWAY=192.168.6.61
IPX="yes"
IPXINTERNALNETNUM="0"
IPXINTERNALNODENUM="0"
IPXAUTOPRIMARY="on"
IPXAUTOFRAME="on"
```

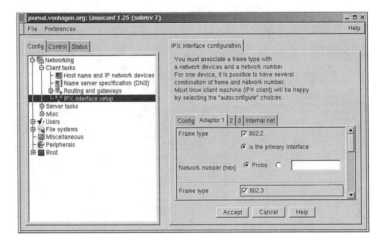

FIGURE 19.7

Manually configuring IPX frame types and addresses in Linuxconf.

> **NOTE**
>
> If you are not running Red Hat Linux and your system's graphical system administra-
> tion utility does not support IPX configuration, you can add the following command
> to your system's startup scripts to activate IPX support:
>
> ```
> ipx_configure --auto_interface=on --auto_primary=on Ethernet-interface
> ```
>
> You may first want to use the grep command to search for the ipx_configure com-
> mand in your system's startup scripts to make sure that your system does not already
> start IPX automatically.
>
> Turning on the --auto_interface option automatically creates new IPX interfaces
> when required to service additional requests, whereas the --auto_primary option
> automatically selects a primary IPX interface if none is specified. If you have multiple
> Ethernet interfaces in your system, you must enable IPX on each interface that you
> want it to be enabled on. For example, if you have multiple Ethernet interfaces in
> your system but only want to enable IPX on the interface for your private network
> (eth1), you'd use a command like the following:
>
> ```
> ipx_configure --auto_interface=on --auto_primary=on eth1
> ```
>
> If you have a single Ethernet card/interface in your system, you don't need to specify
> the Ethernet interface that you want to enable.

You're now almost ready to reboot your system and mount and access NetWare file and print
servers. Before doing that, however, you must also compile and install the ncpfs utilities that
make the whole thing possible.

Installing the `ncpfs` Tools

To install version 2.2.0.18 of the `ncpfs` package, included on the CD that accompanies this book, do the following:

1. Mount the CD and extract the `ncpfs` source code from the file `ncpfs-2.2.0.18.tar.gz` to a directory on your system using command like the following:

   ```
   cd <target-directory>
   tar zxvf <path-to-CD>/netware/ncpfs-2.2.0.18.tar.gz
   ```

2. Change directory to `<target-directory>/ncpfs-2.2.0.18` and run the configure script to correctly configure the `ncpfs` Makefiles for your system and Linux distribution:

   ```
   ./configure
   ```

   This produces verbose output that's not useful to replicate here.

3. After the Makefile is correctly configured, execute the `make` command to build the new versions of the utilities in the `ncpfs` package:

   ```
   make
   ```

   Once again, this produces verbose, system-specific output that's not useful to replicate here.

> **NOTE**
>
> If you want to use these utilities but your Linux system already came with an earlier version of these tools and you don't want to punt the versions that came with your Linux distribution, you can install them in a different directory. The default Makefile that comes with the `ncpfs` package provided on the CD that accompanies this book installs these utilities in `/usr/local/bin`, whereas most Linux distributions that include them provide them in `/usr/bin`. If you can afford the disk space, you can build them from the source that accompanies this book, install them in `/usr/local/bin`, and then run either set of utilities by using their full pathnames making sure that your path has these two directories in the "right" order to find the set that you want to run first.

4. After all the utilities are compiled, use the `su` command to become the superuser to be able to write to the system directories where you will be installing the `ncpfs` utilities. If you want to install them in `/usr/local/bin`, install them on your system using the `make install` command. If you want to install them in another directory (perhaps to overwrite any existing versions of these utilities that are already on your system), edit the `Make.rules` file, modify the value of the `prefix` entry, and then execute the `make install` command.

> **NOTE**
>
> If you installed these utilities in a directory other than /usr/bin, you should check
> that the loader configuration file /etc/ld.so.conf contains the associated lib direc-
> tory and add it and run the ldconfig utility if it does not. For example, if you
> installed these utilities in /usr/local/bin, make sure that the /etc/ld.so.conf file
> contains an entry for the directory /usr/local/lib. If it does not, add this directory
> and execute the ldconfig command.

Your system now has a version of the ncpfs utilities and associated reference (man page) documentation installed.

Using and Administering NetWare Support on Linux

This section discusses various topics related to mounting NetWare directories on your Linux
system using the ncpfs utilities and accessing NetWare files, directories, and printers from
your Linux system.

Listing Available Servers

After you've enabled IPX support in your kernel and activated an IPX interface at boot time,
you can use the slist command to list all the NetWare servers available on your network:

```
# slist
Known NetWare File Servers    Network    Node Address
- - - - - - - - - - - - - - - - - - - - - - - - - - - - - - - - - - - - - - - - - - - - - - - -
NETWARE5                      08241CEC   000000000001
```

In most cases, you'll know the names of the NetWare file servers in your environment, but this
command also provides a quick way of making sure that IPX support is working correctly on
your Linux system before you attempt to mount and access NetWare volumes from your Linux
system.

If no NetWare servers are listed or you receive an error message such as "server not found
(0x8847)" when executing this command, execute the ipx_configure command manually to
verify that your network is correctly configured for IPX support. The following command does
the right thing in most cases—for more information about using this command, see the online
reference information for ipx_configuration available through the Linux man ipx_configure
command.

```
# ipx_configure --auto_interface=on --auto_primary=on
```

If you are using Red Hat Linux and used `linuxconf` to enable your IPX interface, make sure that you selected all the frame types as being valid for IPX, and that only one is selected as a primary interface frame type. To ensure that your IPX interfaces are correctly enabled after using `linuxconf`, you should make sure that `auto_interface` and `auto_primary` are both on (by running `ipx_configure` with no arguments) and then execute the `ipx_interface delall` command to delete any existing interfaces before retrying the `slist` command.

Mounting NetWare Volumes Via NCP

You should then create a mountpoint for the NetWare filesystem that you want to mount and then use the `ncpmount` command to mount the entire NetWare file server, as in the following example:

```
# mkdir /home/wvh/netware
# ncpmount -S NETWARE5 -U wvh /home/wvh/netware -b
Logging into NETWARE5 as WVH
Password:
```

You must have sufficient Linux privileges to mount a volume on the mountpoint that you specified. You can mount any NetWare volume anywhere in the Linux filesystem as the Linux root user. You may want to do this, for example, to make specific NetWare volumes available to all Linux users by mounting them on a publicly readable mountpoint. Regular users should typically mount volumes in their home directories.

NOTE

If the NetWare server you are accessing is running Novell 4 or greater, make sure that you specify the `-b` switch to contact the file server in bindery emulation mode. Forgetting this option is the most common cause of a NetWare mount failure on Linux.

To mount specific volumes, you can use the `-V` switch (Specify volume) to mount that volume, as in the following example:

```
$ ncpmount -S NETWARE5 -U wvh -V USER /home/wvh/netware
Logging into NETWARE5 as WVH
Password:
$ ls ~/netware
HOMES  deleted.sav  typescript  vol$log.err  wvh
```

NOTE

If you are using a version of `ncpmount` that came with your Linux distribution, make sure that it has been configured to run `setuid` root (protections `-rws-r-xr-x`, and owned by root). It must be installed as setuid root for a normal user to mount a NetWare volume.

When you are finished accessing a NetWare volume, use the `ncpumount` command to unmount that volume, supplying the name of its mountpoint as an argument.

Accessing Novell Printers from Linux

NetWare has traditionally provided excellent centralized printing and spooling services for network-oriented business computing environments. On Windows systems, like NetWare's file server capabilities, NetWare's centralized printing services have largely been replaced by the free network printing capabilities now bundled with Windows 95, Windows 98, Windows 2000, and Windows NT. Still, in keeping with my computing mantra of "don't fix it if it's not broken," integrating Linux NetWare clients into existing NetWare printing services can be an easy way of quickly getting printing to work from Linux. To provide this capability, the `ncpfs` utilities package includes the `nprint` application, a NetWare print client. The `nprint` command line looks like the following:

```
nprint -S <server> -U <user> -q <queue-name> file
```

As with the `ncpmount` command, you specify the name of the server that you want to print on using the `-S` option and specify the user that you want to print as using the `-U` option. You must also specify the name of the print queue that you want to print to using the `-q` option. To list the print queues available on a specific NetWare file server, use the `pqlist` command. Depending on the version of `pqlist` that you are running, you may need to specify the name of the server on which the print queue is running, or have a default server defined in your NCP configuration file, as explained in the next section.

Creating and Protecting an NCP Configuration File

You can centralize information about various NetWare print and file servers that you want to be able to use in a file called `~/.nwclient`. This file can contain password information, and so must be mode 600 (readable/writable only by the owner) to protect its contents from prying eyes. All Linux `ncpfs` applications can use this file but will ignore it if it is not mode 600. (They will also not tell you that they're ignoring it, which can be disconcerting.)

The following is an example of a ~/.nwclient configuration file:

```
# The preferred connection. The user is prompted for a password.
#
NETWARE5/WVH
#
# A second connection, including a password.
#  Note: this is not very secure, since this file could
#  accidentally be saved with the group-readable or world-readable
#  bits turned on, depending on your Linux UMASK setting.
#
NETWARE4/WVH HELLOTHERE
#
# A password-free account on another server
#
CDSERVER/GUEST -
```

Lines beginning with a hash mark (#) are comments that are ignored when this file is read by any NCP Linux client. This sample file contains entries for three systems:

- The user WVH on the NETWARE5 NetWare server. Because this line doesn't contain a password, you'll be prompted for one. Also, because this is the first entry in the file, it will be used as the preferred connection if you don't specify a server on the command line of any ncpfs command.

- The user WVH on the NETWARE4 NetWare server. Because this line provides a password (which must be separated from the SERVER/USER tuple by whitespace, you won't be prompted for one. To specify this connection, whatever Linux NCP client you're using must at least identify the server, as in nprint -S NETWARE4 .cshrc.

- The user GUEST on the NetWare server CDSERVER. The - in the password field specifies that this user doesn't require a password.

The ~/.nwclient file can save you a lot of time (and a few brain cells) if you occasionally use connections to a number of different NetWare file and print servers. Remember that this file must be mode 600 (readable only by the owner) to be used—if it has any less-secure mode, it won't be used by the NCP clients and will enable others to see your passwords to various servers if you store your passwords in this file. For this reason, storing passwords in a file is only slightly more secure than printing them on your forehead.

Debugging IPX Network Traffic on Linux

If you are having problems accessing NetWare servers, first determine that your Linux system is configured correctly for IPX support. You can do this easily by using the ncpfs slist command to list the NetWare file servers on your network. If this command works correctly but you still can't mount volumes available on a NetWare server, you still have a few options:

- Try using the ncpmount command's -C option to preserve the case of your password when it is sent to the NetWare server. The server you are accessing may be configured to be case sensitive for security reasons.

- Try mounting a NetWare volume on any directory (/mnt/netware is my personal favorite) as the Linux superuser. If this succeeds, then the problem is probably either due to file or directory permissions on the Unix side, or you've forgotten to specify the -b option for bindery emulation when running the ncpmount command as a non-privileged user.

If both these fail, you may want to examine the traffic between your system and the Novell file server for network error messages before hunting down and consulting a local IPX wizard. First, check the end of the Linux system log file (/var/log/messages) for networking error messages. If none are present there, you may actually have to look at the network traffic yourself as a start. If you are running a mars_nwe server, you can initially verify that IPX is working correctly by connecting to it from your current machine.

The ncpfs package includes two utilities that are not compiled and installed by default when you install this package. These are the ipxdump utility, which is a packet sniffer for IPX Ethernet packets, and its attendant ipxparse utility, which takes the hexadecimal output of the ipxdump program, parses it, and produces slightly more readable output that may be meaningful to hexadecimally challenged people like myself. You can compile these utilities by changing directory to the ipxdump subdirectory of the directory in which you installed the ncpfs package source code and running the make program.

To activate the ipxdump packet sniffer and display its output in a somewhat readable form, start a separate xterm in the X Window System environment, use the su command to become the superuser (so that you can open the Ethernet interface in promiscuous mode and read all the packets that pass through it), and execute the command ipxdump | ipxparse. From another xterm window, execute the same ncpmount that failed before and watch the output in the window where the IPX packet sniffer is running. If you're lucky, you may be able to spot routing, connection, or authentication errors that you can correct before seeking help from your higher power.

The output of the ipxdump and ipxparse commands will look something like the following:

```
# ipxdump | ipxparse
000001 802.2 from 59D6D4A8:000021A78398:0452 to 59D6D4A8:FFFFFFFFFFFF:0452
 type 0x4, SAP op:0x2 General Service Response
   Name:WORDSMITHS_____MāIÌJ@@@@@D…PJ, serverType 0x278, \
     0D7422AA:000000000001:0D40 (Hops 1)
```

```
  Name:NOVELL51, serverType 0x4, 0D7422AA:000000000001:0451 (Hops 1)
  Name:WORDSMITHS_____MāIİJ@@@@D…PJ, serverType 0x26b, \
    0D7422AA:000000000001:0017 (Hops 1)
  Name:NOVELL51, serverType 0x4b, 0D7422AA:000000000001:805A (Hops 1)
  Name:BSER4.00-7.00_0D7422AA0000000000010000, serverType 0x4b, \
    0D7422AA:000000000001:8059 (Hops 1)
  Name:NOVELL51_BROKER, serverType 0x8202, 0D7422AA:000000000001:90B4 (Hops 1)
000002 802.2 from 59D6D4A8:00902762B722:4017 to 59D6D4A8:FFFFFFFFFFFF:0452
 type 0x4, SAP op:0xe Unknown
000003 802.2 from 59D6D4A8:000021A78398:0452 to 59D6D4A8:00902762B722:4017
 type 0x4, Socket 0x4017 (Other)
000004 802.2 from 59D6D4A8:00902762B722:4017 to 0D7422AA:000000000001:0451
111100FF01FF00              .......

000005 802.2 from 0D7422AA:000000000001:0451 to 59D6D4A8:00902762B722:4017
NCP respons: conn: 24    , seq: 0  , task: 1  , compl: 0  , conn_st: 0

000006 802.2 from 59D6D4A8:00902762B722:4017 to 0D7422AA:000000000001:0451
NCP request: conn: 24    , seq: 1  , task: 1  , fn: 97
Get Big Packet NCP Max Packet Size
proposed_max_size: 400
security_flag: 2
040002                       ...

000007 802.2 from 0D7422AA:000000000001:0451 to 59D6D4A8:00902762B722:4017
NCP respons: conn: 24    , seq: 1  , task: 1  , compl: 0  , conn_st: 0
accepted_max_size: 3f8
echo_socket: 4005
security_flag: 2
03F8400502                   ..@..

000008 802.2 from 59D6D4A8:00902762B722:4017 to 0D7422AA:000000000001:0451
55550218010000               UU.....

000009 802.2 from 0D7422AA:000000000001:0451 to 59D6D4A8:00902762B722:4017
NCP respons: conn: 24    , seq: 2  , task: 1  , compl: 0  , conn_st: 0

000010 802.2 from 59D6D4A8:00902762B722:4017 to 0D7422AA:000000000001:0451
111100FF02FF00              .......

000011 802.2 from 0D7422AA:000000000001:0451 to 59D6D4A8:00902762B722:4017
NCP respons: conn: 24    , seq: 0  , task: 1  , compl: 0  , conn_st: 0

000012 802.2 from 59D6D4A8:00902762B722:4017 to 0D7422AA:000000000001:0451
NCP request: conn: 24    , seq: 1  , task: 2  , fn: 97
Get Big Packet NCP Max Packet Size
```

```
proposed_max_size: 400
security_flag: 0
040000                            ...


000013 802.2 from 0D7422AA:000000000001:0451 to 59D6D4A8:00902762B722:4017
NCP respons: conn: 24    , seq: 1  , task: 1  , compl: 0  , conn_st: 0
accepted_max_size: 400
echo_socket: 4005
security_flag: 0
0400400500                        ..@..


000014 802.2 from 59D6D4A8:00902762B722:4017 to 0D7422AA:000000000001:0451
NCP request: conn: 24    , seq: 2  , task: 2  , fn: 23 , subfn: 23
Get Crypt Key


000015 802.2 from 0D7422AA:000000000001:0451 to 59D6D4A8:00902762B722:4017
NCP respons: conn: 24    , seq: 2  , task: 1  , compl: 0  , conn_st: 0
A270442D885A6301                  .pD-.Zc.


000016 802.2 from 59D6D4A8:00902762B722:4017 to 0D7422AA:000000000001:0451
NCP request: conn: 24    , seq: 3  , task: 2  , fn: 23 , subfn: 53
Get Bindery Object ID
000103575648                      ...WVH


000017 802.2 from 0D7422AA:000000000001:0451 to 59D6D4A8:00902762B722:4017
NCP respons: conn: 24    , seq: 3  , task: 1  , compl: 0  , conn_st: 0
308000000001575648000000000000000 0.....WVH.......
0000000000000000000000000000000000 ...............
0000000000000000000000000000000000 ...............
000000000000                      ......


000018 802.2 from 59D6D4A8:00902762B722:4017 to 0D7422AA:000000000001:0451
NCP request: conn: 24    , seq: 4  , task: 2  , fn: 23 , subfn: 24
Encrypted Login
8D06CF2164B10EDC000103575648      ...!d......WVH


000019 802.2 from 0D7422AA:000000000001:0451 to 59D6D4A8:00902762B722:4017
NCP respons: conn: 24    , seq: 4  , task: 1  , compl: 0  , conn_st: 0
```

Exporting Linux Directories to NetWare

Running a Novell emulator on Linux provides a convenient method of beginning to migrate users from NetWare systems to other platforms, such as Linux. Another situation in which NetWare emulation is useful is when you want to export a public folder from a Linux server, making it available to NetWare users. The mars_nwe Novell emulator is easy to configure because all its configuration is centralized in the text file, /etc/nwserv.conf.

To add a public Linux directory to the directories exported by the mars_nwe NetWare emulator, open the file /etc/nswerv.conf in a text editor and skip to the end of section 1, which defines the volumes that the emulator will export. The default entry looks like the following:

```
1       SYS             /var/mars_nwe/sys/      rk   711 600
```

After this entry, add entries like the following to share users' Linux home directories as the NetWare volume HOME, and to share the common Linux folder /usr/local/public as the volume PUBLIC. (The names of these volumes are used only as examples.):

```
1       HOME            ~                       k    -1
1       PUBLIC          /usr/local/public       rk   711 600
```

After adding these entries, skip to the end of Section 13 in the /etc/nwserv.conf file and add entries mapping NetWare usernames to Linux usernames, as in the following example:

```
13      WVH     wvh
```

This maps the NetWare user WVH in the mars_nwe emulator to the Linux user wvh.

After adding appropriate entries for any Linux directories that you want to export to NetWare users through the mars_nwe emulator, you can start the emulator by executing the command nwserv. NetWare users running IPX will then immediately be able to see and log in on the mars_nwe emulator as though it were a standard Novell server and can access their Linux directory and the contents of the /usr/local/public directory.

> **NOTE**
>
> If you have problems accessing the mars_nwe emulator from a NetWare client system, you can test it by using the ncpmount command from a Linux system to mount a test volume from that server. For information on debugging problems with IPX configuration on Linux, see the notes and tips in the "Listing Available Servers" and "Mounting NetWare Volumes Via NCP" sections, earlier in this chapter.

19

NETWARE
FILESYSTEM
SUPPORT IN LINUX

Using the CD-ROM: Installing, Updating, and Compiling Kernels

IN THIS APPENDIX

This appendix provides information about installing, configuring, compiling, and using the Linux kernels included on the CD that accompanies this book. For more information on configuring and compiling kernels, see the Linux Kernel HOWTO at `http://www.linuxdoc.org/HOWTO/Kernel-HOWTO.html`.

This appendix is not intended to provide a definitive guide to building operating system kernels and general operating system philosophies—plenty of other books and resources provide that sort of information. Instead, this section provides an overview of popular philosophies behind building operating system kernels that are both as specific to your hardware and as flexible as they need to be. Linux includes some whizzy configuration tools that simplify the precompilation configuration of your Linux kernel—selecting the features that will be built into and available to your Linux kernel. The background information in this appendix will help you understand the options available, making it easier to strike the right balance between supporting everything that you might someday need and being as efficient as possible based on your current hardware configuration.

> **NOTE**
>
> You must be logged in as root or have used the su to become the root user to execute any of the commands in this section.

As we all know, Linux is an operating system that thousands of hackers (and other flavors of programmers) have contributed to, each of which used a machine with different network cards, sound cards, motherboards, disk and CD-ROM drives, and so on. Like any operating system, the Linux kernel needs to be able to identify the hardware in any given computer system and interact with that hardware appropriately. In addition to simply being able to locate, identify, and interact with different types of hardware, the Linux kernel also provides support for many different software mechanisms for interacting with that hardware, not all of which may be necessary in the computing environment in which you plan to use the computer system for which you are building a kernel.

A good example of this is the code that the kernel uses to support networking. Not only does the Linux kernel need to be able to work with many different types of Ethernet cards, it also needs to know what networking protocols you want to use to communicate with other machines using those networking cards. Linux supports many different networking protocols, including TCP/IP, IPX, AppleTalk, DecNet, SNA, and many other protocols. Unless you're working a tremendously sexy computing environment made up of every conceivable type of machine, compiling support for all these protocols into your kernel would essentially be a waste of your time, making the kernel much larger (and therefore potentially slower) than it needs to be by including support for protocols that you're never going to use in the first place.

Linux provides two different mechanisms for dealing with different types of hardware, networking protocols, and similar internal software mechanisms that you may or may not need to use:

- The first and simplest is to build a kernel that doesn't include support for anything that you don't plan to use. When configuring a kernel build prior to actually building a kernel, you can selectively include support for only those devices physically in the system for which you are building a kernel, and the protocols and other software mechanisms that you will use to communicate with that hardware and connected systems. Although this produces kernels that are as small as possible, it is also somewhat restrictive. Small kernels tend to run faster because they require less memory and because calls to other routines within the kernel can be made more quickly, often because they may require less paging to swap in the parts of the kernel that contain them.

- The second alternative is to build in support for the devices that your system currently contains and the protocols that you will currently use and then precompile support for hardware and protocols that you may eventually want to use by building the latter as *loadable modules*. Loadable modules are kernel object code that the kernel will load when the hardware or protocols that these modules support is added, used, or required. Although the kernel will contain the hooks necessary to load these modules, it will not contain the actual object code for them until it is actually needed. Loadable modules for the kernel are stored in subdirectories of the /lib/modules directory on the root partition of your filesystem.

NOTE

When building kernels that make extensive use of loadable modules, it's important that the kernel is built with all the code that it requires to actually find and load these modules. For example, if you are building a kernel to support a specific type of filesystem and the boot partition of your machine is located on a partition of that type, support for that filesystem must actually be compiled into the kernel. You can't ask the kernel to load a module from a filesystem that it can't access until it loads that module! Similarly, always compile in support for the ext2 filesystem, or your kernel won't be able to interact with the filesystem on which it is stored, which would be (to use the technical expression) "a bad thing."

The next sections provide specific information about installing kernel source code from the CD, patching and configuring Linux kernels, and compiling and installing those kernels. The appendix concludes by explaining how to add support for multiple Linux kernels into the most common boot loaders used by Linux systems, LILO and Grub.

A

USING THE
CD-ROM

Installing Kernel Source Code

This section explains how to install the source code for the versions of the Linux kernel on which the examples in this book are based. The source code for the version of the Linux kernel used throughout this book is located in the kernel subdirectory of the CD that accompanies this book.

To install a specific version of the Linux kernel source, do the following:

1. Log in or enter the su command and the root password to become root.

2. Insert the CD into your CD drive. If the entry for your CD drive in the /etc/fstab file contains the "auto" mount option, the CD automatically is mounted on the directory specified in the /etc/fstab entry for the CD drive. If your CD entry does not specify automounting but contains the user option, you can mount the CD using a command like the following:

   ```
   mount /dev/cdrom
   ```

   This mounts the CD on the directory specified in the /etc/fstab file for your CD drive. If you do not have an entry in your /etc/fstab file for the CD drive, you can mount it on an existing directory by executing a command like the following as root:

   ```
   mount -t iso9660 /dev/cdrom /mnt/cdrom
   ```

3. Change your working directory to the /usr/src directory, the traditional location for installing and working with source code on an existing Linux system.

4. List the contents of this directory. If a kernel with the same version number as the one you want to install already exists, rename this directory to <kernel-version>.old. For example:

   ```
   mv linux-2.4.9 linux-2.4.9.old
   ```

5. Use the tar command to extract the source code for the version of the kernel that you want to install from the archive file on the CD. The different versions of the kernel source are all stored in the kernel subdirectory of the CD in archive files with names of the form linux-*<version>*.tar.gz. For example:

   ```
   tar zxvf /mnt/cdrom/kernel/linux-2.4.9.tar.gz
   ```

6. For convenience, remove any existing symbolic link with the base name of the kernel version in the /usr/src directory and create a new one to point to the specific version of that kernel that you are compiling. You can do this using commands like the following, where *<version>* is the version of the linux kernel that you want the link to point to:

   ```
   rm linux-<version>
   ln -s linux-<version> linux-<base-version>
   ```

   For example, the commands to remove an existing symbolic link and create the appropriate symbolic link for the Linux 2.4.9 kernel would be the following:

```
rm linux-2.4
ln -s linux-2.4.9 linux-2.4
```

The idea behind this symbolic link is that you can then add /usr/include/linux-
<base-version> to the path that the shell searches for include files when compiling
applications, instead of having to reference each specific kernel version. By changing the
symbolic link as you install and build the source for each new version of the kernel,
other applications that need access to kernel include files will always get the latest and
greatest versions of them.

You're now ready to apply any patches necessary to add support for new features (such as, perhaps, a specific type of filesystem?) to the generic Linux kernel that you just installed. It is not
necessary to apply kernel patches to add support for every type of filesystem discussed in this
book—some of them are natively supported in specific kernel versions. If it is necessary to
apply a patch to add support for a specific filesystem, read chapter of this book that discusses
that filesystem for instructions on installing the patch. The next section provides general information about patches, their format, and how to install them when necessary.

Applying Patches

Patches are changes to existing files that are inserted to update those files. Patch files can contain binary or text format changes to be inserted and often contain changes to multiple files
grouped into a single patch. *Patches* are text files that contain changes to existing source code
in a format thatspecifies the location in the source code where the changes should be applied.
Patches are produced by using the Linux/Unix diff program to compare old and new versions
of a specific file.

Linux kernel developers make extensive use of patches when adding support for new filesystems and other major subsystems for two main reasons:

- The people in charge of the Linux kernel (Linus Torvalds and Alan Cox) need to carefully scrutinize new features that add major changes to the kernel code. You may view
  Linux development as anarchy, but that's not possible at the kernel level. Anyone can
  make changes to his version of the Linux kernel source and offer them to Linus and
  company, but large-scale changes have to be considered carefully before being incorpo-
  rated into the definitive kernel source code. When to do this is a tough call. Linux users
  want the richest possible feature set, and they want it yesterday. On the other hand, a kernel that won't compile correctly or in which the addition of new code destabilizes existing, stable code isn't a situation that anyone can tolerate. Generally, major subsystems
  are only added to the mainline kernel code after they have been extensively tested, carefully considered, and closely examined.

A

USING THE
CD-ROM

- Patches are easier to share and circulate than an entire kernel. The whole idea behind programs such as diff and patch is that you only need to identify the things that have changed. E-mailing someone 50 KB worth of patches is much friendlier than mailing them 20 MB of compressed Linux kernel source.

Applying patches to source code is relatively simply, thanks to the patch command, which does an incredibly intelligent job of applying patch files. The patch command can even apply patches when the file you are patching is slightly different from the version of the file originally used to produce the patch. The patch command does this by examining a certain number of lines before and after the point at which each change is specified to be inserted, and inserting the modified source code correctly if matching lines are found in this region. For complete information on the patch command, see its online reference page by typing **man patch** on your Linux system.

> **NOTE**
>
> Multiple kernel patches, especially for similar experimental subsystems, are often incompatible with each other. For example, the patches to enable the ext3 filesystem may well conflict with the patches to install JFS filesystem support. This is understandable, because they may each add new sections to the same files, which would therefore make it difficult for a subsequent set of patches to identify the location where patch code should be installed. For this reason, I'd suggest that you first install and configure a basic kernel for whatever version of Linux is relevant to the chapter that discusses the filesystem that you want to use. After you have a version of that kernel that correctly supports all your hardware, you can create an archived copy of that directory using a command like the following:
>
> ```
> tar cvf - linux-2.4.9 | gzip -9 > linux247.tar.gz
> ```

You can then apply a set of patches to this kernel, give it a unique name as explained in the "Compiling a Linux Kernel" section of this appendix, and produce a kernel that supports a specific new filesystem. If you decide to experiment with another type of filesystem, you can delete your current source directory for that kernel version, reinstall a correctly configured version of that kernel from the archive file, and then patch the clean version of that kernel to produce a kernel with support for the new type of filesystem.

The general process for applying kernel patches is the following:

1. Use the su command to become root on the console, in an xterm, or another terminal window.

2. Change your working directory to the directory created when you installed the kernel source code that you want to patch:

```
cd /usr/src/linux-<version>
```

3. Use the `patch` command to apply the patch from the patch subdirectory of the CD included with this book:

```
patch -p1 < /mnt/cdrom/patches/<patch-file-name>
```

The `-p1` option tells the `patch` command how much of the filenames listed in the patch file to preen to correctly locate the files that should be patched.

The output of the `patch` command lists the name of each file being patched. After the `patch` program completes, you're ready to configure, compile, and install the patched kernel.

Configuring Your Kernel

The settings for the kernel compilation options that identify the hardware, protocols, and other software mechanisms that a kernel provides are stored in a file called .config, located in the directory that contains the source code for a specific kernel version. For example, the configuration information for a Linux 2.4.9 kernel would typically be stored in the file `/usr/src/linux-2.4.9/.config`. Linux includes two fairly whizzy mechanisms for simplifying setting the values of the compiler and preprocessor variables used to activate or deactivate different hardware and software options in the Linux kernel. Both activated through the Makefile for the Linux kernel, these are the following:

- `make xconfig` —If you are configuring and building the kernel on a system that runs the X Window System, this displays a set of X Window System-based panels that enable you to select and save kernel configuration options. Figure A.1 shows an example of the panel that displays after you execute the `make xconfig` command.

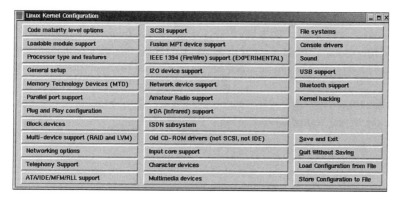

FIGURE A.1

Tcl/Tk and the X Window System simplify Linux kernel configuration.

- `make menuconfig`—If you are configuring and building the kernel using a terminal or from a console on which you are not running the X Window System, this displays a set of somewhat graphical, cursor-oriented dialogs that enable you to select and save kernel configuration options. Figure A.2 shows an example of the screen that displays after you execute the `make menuconfig` command.

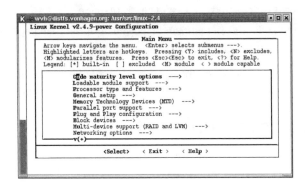

FIGURE A.2

Linux kernel configuration in a console or terminal window.

- `make config`—If you have the patience of Job and are configuring and building the kernel using a terminal or from a console on which you are not running the X Window System, `make config` displays a seemingly endless series of questions about every facet of the kernel. When necessary, using this configuration method is now simply masochism.

Compiling a Linux kernel on a running Linux system implies that you already have a working kernel. All Linux distributions ship with kernels preconfigured to support as much common hardware as possible to make it easy for you to get up and running with your Linux system as quickly as possible. Unfortunately, many Linux systems don't come complete with sample configuration files, such as the one used to build the kernels that they come with. If you are using Red Hat Linux, you can obtain some kernel configuration files to use as starting points by installing the kernel source RPM package from your Red Hat Linux distribution disks. On Red Hat systems, these are located in the configs subdirectory of the directory created when you installed the kernel source RPM package.

> **TIP**
>
> If you have already compiled a kernel on your system (and it worked correctly with all your hardware, of course), it's likely that you can reuse its configuration information for the kernel that we are building in this example.
>
> To load configuration data from a kernel that you have already compiled, click the Load Configuration from File button if you are using make xconfig or use the Page Down key to scroll down to the bottom of the screen if you are using make menuconfig and use the arrow keys to select the Load an Alternate Configuration File command. In the dialog that displays, enter the full path to the configuration file that you want to load. Press Enter to accept the filename and load the configuration data that it contains.
>
> If you reuse the configuration data from an existing kernel, you must make sure that you use the corresponding Store Configuration to File (make xconfig) or Save Configuration to an Alternate File (make menuconfig) to save the file with the name .config in the main directory of the kernel that you are configuring. You'll be depressed if you accidentally overwrite the wrong kernel configuration file.

Identifying the Hardware in Your System

If this is the first kernel you are building and you do not have access to an existing or sample kernel configuration file, don't worry that you need to be psychic or a PhD to come up with a working kernel configuration. The fact that you already have a working Linux system gives you all the information that you need. You'll have to do a bit more work, but of course you'll learn much more than you would have if someone just handed you a working kernel configuration file. If you weren't interested in learning, you probably wouldn't be reading this book in the first place.

> **NOTE**
>
> Millions of kernel options reflect both the hardware and target capabilities of your site. For a good overview of basic kernel configuration, starting from scratch, see the Linux kernel HOWTO at http://www.linuxdoc.org/HOWTO/Kernel-HOWTO.html.

A

USING THE
CD-ROM

A running Linux system provides several mechanisms for getting information about the hardware in your system and its configuration, even if you just bought it at one of the local computer gypsy shows and it's chock-full of inexpensive but bleeding-edge hardware. Equally common problems are that you built up the system over time and forgot to keep a record of the specific devices that are in it before installing a new Linux distribution, or (even more common) that it used to be a Windows box, and no one ever bothered to keep track of the hardware inside it at the board level. The next few sections highlight my favorite places to look when trying to figure out exactly what hardware is present in a Linux system and therefore what hardware and software features to activate in a Linux kernel.

Using the Kernel Boot Log to Identify Hardware

The easiest way to identify the basic configuration of your system is to check what devices the Linux kernel found and configured the last time it booted. You can do this using the /bin/dmesg command, which displays the contents of a buffer containing the most recent 16392 bytes worth of messages printed by the kernel. If this isn't sufficient, which might be the case if one of your devices is in debug mode or generating vast amounts of kernel error messages, all recent kernel messages are typically copied to the file /var/log/messages. The /var/log/messages file typically contains messages from the last few times you've booted your system, so be prepared to see some duplication.

The beginning of the output from the dmesg command should look something like the following:

```
Linux version 2.4.9-LFSU (root@journal.vonhagen.org) (gcc version 2.96 20000731
(Red Hat Linux 7.1 2.96-95)) #4
SMP Tue Aug 14 20:36:09 EDT 2001
BIOS-provided physical RAM map:
 BIOS-e820: 0000000000000000 - 000000000009fc00 (usable)
 BIOS-e820: 000000000009fc00 - 00000000000a0000 (reserved)
 BIOS-e820: 00000000000f0000 - 0000000000100000 (reserved)
 BIOS-e820: 0000000000100000 - 000000000f800000 (usable)
 BIOS-e820: 00000000ffef0000 - 00000000fff00000 (reserved)
 BIOS-e820: 00000000ffff0000 - 0000000100000000 (reserved)
Scan SMP from c0000000 for 1024 bytes.
Scan SMP from c009fc00 for 1024 bytes.
Scan SMP from c00f0000 for 65536 bytes.
Scan SMP from c009fc00 for 4096 bytes.
On node 0 totalpages: 63488
zone(0): 4096 pages.
zone(1): 59392 pages.
zone(2): 0 pages.
mapped APIC to ffffe000 (01421000)
```

```
Kernel command line: auto BOOT_IMAGE=247-ext3-lfsu ro root=305
    BOOT_FILE=/boot/vmlinuz-2.4.9-LFSU
Initializing CPU#0
Detected 501.137 MHz processor.
Console: colour VGA+ 80x25
Calibrating delay loop... 999.42 BogoMIPS
Memory: 246500k/253952k available (1738k kernel code, 7064k reserved,
    505k data, 228k init, 0k highmem)
Dentry-cache hash table entries: 32768 (order: 6, 262144 bytes)
Inode-cache hash table entries: 16384 (order: 5, 131072 bytes)
Mount-cache hash table entries: 4096 (order: 3, 32768 bytes)
Buffer-cache hash table entries: 16384 (order: 4, 65536 bytes)
Page-cache hash table entries: 65536 (order: 6, 262144 bytes)
CPU: Before vendor init, caps: 0183f9ff 00000000 00000000, vendor = 0
CPU: L1 I cache: 16K, L1 D cache: 16K
CPU: L2 cache: 128K
Intel machine check architecture supported.
Intel machine check reporting enabled on CPU#0.
CPU: After vendor init, caps: 0183f9ff 00000000 00000000 00000000
CPU:     After generic, caps: 0183f9ff 00000000 00000000 00000000
CPU:          Common caps: 0183f9ff 00000000 00000000 00000000
Enabling fast FPU save and restore... done.
Checking 'hlt' instruction... OK.
POSIX conformance testing by UNIFIX
CPU: Before vendor init, caps: 0183f9ff 00000000 00000000, vendor = 0
CPU: L1 I cache: 16K, L1 D cache: 16K
CPU: L2 cache: 128K
Intel machine check reporting enabled on CPU#0.
CPU: After vendor init, caps: 0183f9ff 00000000 00000000 00000000
CPU:     After generic, caps: 0183f9ff 00000000 00000000 00000000
CPU:          Common caps: 0183f9ff 00000000 00000000 00000000
.
.
.
```

That's all well and good, but unless you're a serious Linux kernel hacker, this output really doesn't give you much information beyond the fact that Linux kernels are in English and are only slightly more readable than line noise. To use dmesg to help identify the hardware on your system, you essentially have to know what you're looking for—not the exact things, of course, but the classes of messages that contain information that may be useful in identifying hardware. To accomplish this, I tend to use /bin/egrep, which is just a pattern-matching version of the grep command, which can be useful for looking for more complex patterns.

A

USING THE
CD-ROM

Some suggestions for egrep commands that may save you from having to search the entire output of the dmesg command for information about your hardware are the following:

- To search for information about IDE and SCSI hard drives, CD-ROM devices, and floppy drives in your system, try "dmesg | egrep "hd|sd|fd"". Some sample output from this command is

```
Kernel command line: auto BOOT_IMAGE=linux ro root=305 \
    BOOT_FILE=/boot/vmlinuz-2.4.2-2 hdc=ide-scsiide_setup: hdc=ide-scsi
ide: Assuming 33MHz system bus for PIO modes; override with idebus=xx
hda: WDC WD450AA-00BAA0, ATA DISK drive
hdb: WDC WD450AA-00BAA0, ATA DISK drive
hdc: CR-4804TE, ATAPI CD/DVD-ROM drive
ide0 at 0x1f0-0x1f7,0x3f6 on irq 14
ide1 at 0x170-0x177,0x376 on irq 15
hda: 87930864 sectors (45021 MB) w/2048KiB Cache, CHS=5473/255/63
hdb: 87930864 sectors (45021 MB) w/2048KiB Cache, CHS=5473/255/63
 hda: hda1 hda2 < hda5 hda6 hda7 hda8 hda9 >
 hdb: hdb1 hdb2 < hdb5 hdb6 >
Floppy drive(s): fd0 is 1.44M
```

Now we're getting somewhere. The system contains three IDE devices, consisting of two Western Digital hard drives and one ATAPI CD/DVD-ROM drive. It also contains a 1.44 MB floppy drive. In addition, the first line says that the CD/DVD-ROM drive is emulating a SCSI CD-ROM drive, which is often necessary if you are planning to use CD-ROM ripping or recording software. This output also gives us information about the partitioning of the hard drives, but that isn't anything that we need to know about when configuring the kernel.

In general, from this information, we know that I'd need to build a kernel with built-in support for IDE hard drives, standard floppy drives, ATAPI CD-ROM drives, and the ISO-9660 filesystem if I wanted to be able to actually access data CDs on the CD drive.

- To search for information about Ethernet devices in your system, try "dmesg | egrep eth". Some sample output from this command is

```
eth0: Intel Corp 82557 [Ethernet Pro 100], 00:90:27:62:B7:22, IRQ 3.
eth1: Davicom DM9102 at 0xdc00, 00:d0:09:14:b0:ee, IRQ 10
```

We have two Ethernet interfaces available and will need to build a kernel with built-in or module support for Ethernet and drivers for Intel Ethernet Pro and Davicom DM9102 cards.

It's easy to see that the dmesg command provides a substantial amount of low-level information about the configuration of you system, but it's also easy to see that digging that information out of dmesg requires some foreknowledge of what you want to find. The output from the dmesg command is useful in determining the combination of hardware interfaces and software protocols that your system is running, because all these produce kernel messages as they are loaded. These may be useful if you build a kernel and find, for example, that you can't connect to the Internet or other systems on your home network using commands such as telnet, ftp, and so on. If commands such as these aren't working, use a command like "dmesg | egrep -i TCP" to make sure that you've actually provided built-in or module support for TCP/IP. Output like the following indicates that TCP/IP support is active and that you may have misconfigured your Ethernet interface(s):

```
NET4: Linux TCP/IP 1.0 for NET4.0
IP Protocols: ICMP, UDP, TCP, IGMP
TCP: Hash tables configured (established 131072 bind 65536)
```

The next section explains utilities that are provided with Linux and that only provide you with information about the hardware on various interfaces in your system. Although this information isn't as useful for debugging purposes, it is probably more useful (and easier to extract) for use when initially configuring a kernel to support your hardware.

Identifying Hardware Using Linux Utilities

You may find this difficult to believe, but over the years various Linux hackers have created utilities that probe various aspects of your system and report what they find out there. These types of utilities were originally developed to help you not only identify the hardware communicating through various buses and interfaces in your system, but also perhaps more importantly provide status information that helps you determine whether that hardware is actually doing more than just saying "yes, I'm out here." The scsiprobe utility is a classic Unix utility for probing a SCSI bus and identifying the devices that it finds and has been ported to Linux, although it is not provided by default in Linux distributions such as Red Hat.

Most Linux distributions include the following utilities:

- lspci—Scans the PCI bus and lists all the devices found. Because most modern PCs are PCI-based, this utility is probably the most useful of all the scanning utilities listed in this section. Sample output from this command looks like the following:

```
00:00.0 Host bridge: VIA Tech, Inc. VT82C691 [Apollo PRO] (rev 44)
00:01.0 PCI bridge: VIA Tech, Inc. VT82C598/694x [Apollo MVP3/Pro133x AGP]
00:07.0 ISA bridge: VIA Tech, Inc. VT82C596 ISA [Mobile South] (rev 12)
00:07.1 IDE interface: VIA Technologies, Inc. Bus Master IDE (rev 06)
00:07.2 USB Controller: VIA Technologies, Inc. UHCI USB (rev 08)
00:07.3 Host bridge: VIA Tech, Inc. VT82C596 Power Management (rev 20)
00:09.0 Ethernet controller: 3Com Corporation 3c595 100BaseTX [Vortex]
00:0b.0 SCSI storage controller: Adaptec 7892A (rev 02)
00:0f.0 Multimedia audio controller: Ensoniq ES1371 [AudioPCI-97] (rev 06)
01:00.0 VGA compatible controller: ATI Technologies Inc Rage 128 RF
```

A

- scanpci—Scans the PCI bus and provides information about the cards and bridges that it finds. This utility does a good job of probing the PCI bus but a poor job of identifying the cards and bridges that it finds. Sample output from running this command is the following:

```
pci bus 0x0 cardnum 0x00 function 0x0000: vendor 0x1039 device 0x0620
 SiS  Device unknown
pci bus 0x0 cardnum 0x00 function 0x0001: vendor 0x1039 device 0x5513
 SiS  Device unknown
pci bus 0x0 cardnum 0x01 function 0x0000: vendor 0x1039 device 0x0008
 SiS  Device unknown
pci bus 0x0 cardnum 0x01 function 0x0001: vendor 0x1039 device 0x0009
 SiS  Device unknown
pci bus 0x0 cardnum 0x02 function 0x0000: vendor 0x1039 device 0x0001
 SiS SG86C201
pci bus 0x0 cardnum 0x09 function 0x0000: vendor 0x8086 device 0x1229
 Intel 82557/8/9 10/100MBit network controller
pci bus 0x0 cardnum 0x0b function 0x0000: vendor 0x1282 device 0x9102
 Device unknown
pci bus 0x0 cardnum 0x0f function 0x0000: vendor 0x13f6 device 0x0111
 Device unknown
pci bus 0x0 cardnum 0x0f function 0x0001: vendor 0x13f6 device 0x0211
 Device unknown
pci bus 0x1 cardnum 0x00 function 0x0000: vendor 0x1039 device 0x6306
 SiS 530
```

This information comes from running the scanpci command on the same system on which the lspci command was run and isn't as useful as that provided by lspci. On the other hand, running scanpci in verbose mode (by using the -v switch) provides a great deal of detailed information that can be useful in debugging or implementing drivers. For example, the following is the verbose output for the first two entries detected in the previous scanpci listing:

```
pci bus 0x0 cardnum 0x00 function 0x0000: vendor 0x1039 device 0x0620
 SiS  Device unknown
  STATUS     0x2210  COMMAND 0x0007
  CLASS      0x06 0x00 0x00   REVISION 0x02
  HEADER     0x80  LATENCY 0x20
pci bus 0x0 cardnum 0x00 function 0x0001: vendor 0x1039 device 0x5513
 SiS  Device unknown
 CardVendor 0x1039 card 0x5513 (SiS, Card unknown)
  STATUS     0x0000  COMMAND 0x0007
  CLASS      0x01 0x01 0x80   REVISION 0xd0
  BIST       0x00  HEADER 0x80  LATENCY 0x16  CACHE 0x00
  BASE0      0x000001f1  addr 0x000001f0  I/O
  BASE1      0x000003f5  addr 0x000003f4  I/O
```

```
BASE2    0x00000171  addr 0x00000170  I/O
BASE3    0x00000375  addr 0x00000374  I/O
BASE4    0x0000ffa1  addr 0x0000ffa0  I/O
MAX_LAT  0x00  MIN_GNT 0x00  INT_PIN 0x01  INT_LINE 0x00
BYTE_0   0x3030303  BYTE_1  0x00  BYTE_2  0x806c1e0  BYTE_3  0xffffffff
```

- pnpdump — Scans the ISA bus looking for plug-and-play cards. This utility is especially useful in older systems. If you don't have any plug-and-play ISA cards in your system, this utility won't do anything for you.

Getting Hardware Information from the /proc Filesystem

The Linux /proc filesystem is a filesystem that lives in virtual memory and reflects the current configuration, status, and state of your system. As an in-memory filesystem, the /proc filesystem is re-created each time you boot your Linux system and therefore always contains accurate, up-to-the-picosecond information about your Linux system. When configuring a new Linux kernel for a modern Lintel computer, several of the files in this filesystem can give you the information you need to make sure that you activate support for the necessary hardware and protocols in the kernel that you are building. The most useful files in the /proc filesystem for this purpose are the following:

- /proc/pci, which lists all the devices found when probing the system's PCI bus when the system booted. A sample section of the /proc/pci file on one of my systems looks like the following:

```
PCI devices found:
  Bus  0, device   0, function  0:
    Host bridge: Silicon Integrated Systems [SiS] 620 Host (rev 2).
      Master Capable.  Latency=32.
      Non-prefetchable 32 bit memory at 0xe8000000 [0xebffffff].
  Bus  0, device   0, function  1:
    IDE interface: Silicon Integrated Systems [SiS] 5513 [IDE] (rev 208).
      Master Capable.  Latency=22.
      I/O at 0xffa0 [0xffaf].
  Bus  0, device   1, function  0:
    ISA bridge: Silicon Integrated Systems [SiS] 85C503/5513 (rev 179).
  Bus  0, device   1, function  1:
    Class ff00: Silicon Integrated Systems [SiS] ACPI (rev 0).
  Bus  0, device   2, function  0:
    PCI bridge: Silicon Integrated Systems [SiS] 5591/5592 AGP (rev 0).
      Master Capable.  No bursts.  Min Gnt=12.
  Bus  0, device   9, function  0:
    Ethernet controller: Intel Corp 82557 [Ethernet Pro 100] (rev 8).
      IRQ 3.
      Master Capable.  Latency=64.  Min Gnt=8.Max Lat=56.
```

A

USING THE
CD-ROM

```
    Non-prefetchable 32 bit memory at 0xefffb000 [0xefffbfff].
    I/O at 0xde00 [0xde3f].
    Non-prefetchable 32 bit memory at 0xefe00000 [0xefefffff].
 Bus  0, device  11, function  0:
   Ethernet controller: Davicom Inc. Ethernet 100/10 MBit (rev 1 6).
    IRQ 10.
    Master Capable.  Latency=64.  Min Gnt=20.Max Lat=40.
    I/O at 0xdc00 [0xdc7f].
    Non-prefetchable 32 bit memory at 0xeffffaf80 [0xefffafff].
 Bus  0, device  15, function  0:
   Multimedia audio controller: C-Media Electronics Inc CM8738 (rev 16).
    IRQ 12.
    Master Capable.  Latency=64.  Min Gnt=2.Max Lat=24.
    I/O at 0xd800 [0xd8ff].
```

The first few entries in this file show that the system from which I got this information uses an SiS motherboard and describes the bridges that connect the PCI and ISA buses to the system's primary data bus, identifies the motherboard as providing a built-in IDE interface, and then begins to identify specific controllers found in the system, such as (in this excerpt), my Ethernet controllers and the multimedia controller. You need to know the specific device controllers located in your system (Ethernet, multimedia, video, communication, and so on) to make sure that the kernel that you are building contains or has access to the drivers necessary for Linux to use that hardware.

- /proc/cpuinfo, which describes the characteristics of the central processing unit(s) in a computer system. The contents of this file on one of my test systems is the following:

```
processor      : 0
vendor_id      : GenuineIntel
cpu family     : 6
model          : 6
model name     : Celeron (Mendocino)
stepping       : 5
cpu MHz        : 501.137
cache size     : 128 KB
fdiv_bug       : no
hlt_bug        : no
f00f_bug       : no
coma_bug       : no
fpu            : yes
fpu_exception  : yes
cpuid level    : 2
wp             : yes
flags          : fpu vme de pse tsc msr pae mce cx8 sep mtrr pge mca
                 cmov pat p
se36 mmx fxsr
bogomips       : 999.42
```

Although you can always compile a Linux kernel for the 386 processor family (which will therefore run on any modern x86 processor), being able to identify the specific processor in your system enables you to take advantage of optimizations and processor-specific configuration options that will help you build the fastest, most powerful kernel possible for your system.

Using the Linux Kernel Configurators

After preparing a list of the hardware and protocols that you will want to support in the kernel that you are building, you can execute either the X Window System or cursor-based Linux kernel configurations through the Makefile to select the options that you want to build into your new kernel or compile as modules.

After executing either the `make xconfig` or `make menuconfig` commands, you must select the options relevant to the hardware and software options that you want to activate in your kernel:

- If you execute the `make xconfig` command, selecting buttons on the X Window System Linux kernel configurator either activates compilation options or displays a secondary panel. To activate a kernel compilation option, click the Y radio button to compile support for the selected option into the kernel you are configuring. Click the M radio button to compile support for the selected option as a loadable module. Not all kernel compilation options can be compiled as modules. If the M radio button is not present or is grayed out, you can only compile support for the selected option into the kernel.

> **NOTE**
>
> The Help buttons to the right of each kernel configuration option often provide both an explanation of that kernel option and suggestions for when (or whether) to include that kernel option.

- You can return to the main menu for the X Window System kernel configurator at any time by clicking the Main menu button at the bottom left of any secondary kernel configurator panel.

- If you execute the `make menuconfig` command, selecting any option on the cursor-based application either activates compilation options or displays a new screen on the current console or within the current terminal window. To activate a kernel compilation option, press the space bar while the option that you want to activate is highlighted. An "M" displays to the left of the current kernel configuration option, indicating that you want to compile the selected option as a module. If you want to compile the selected option into the kernel that you are configuring, press the space bar again and an asterisk (*) displays to the left of the highlighted option. Not all kernel compilation options can be compiled

A

as modules. If an "M" does not display to the left of the highlighted kernel option, you can only compile support for that option into the kernel.

You can return to the previous menu for the cursor-based Linux kernel configurator by pressing the Esc key or by using the Tab key to select the Exit command at the bottom of the console or terminal.

After selecting any other kernel configuration options relevant to the kernel that you are building (such as those specific to the hardware in your system), save your updated kernel configuration.

If you used the make xconfig command:

- If you reused the configuration data from an existing kernel, click the Store Configuration to File button to display a dialog that enables you to explicitly save your new kernel configuration with the name .config in the main directory of the kernel that you are configuring. Figure A.3 shows this dialog.

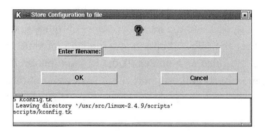

FIGURE A.3

Saving your kernel configuration to a specific file.

- If you configured the current kernel from scratch (that is, without reading in configuration data from another kernel), simply click the Save and Exit button.

- Click OK to close the final dialog and return to the Linux shell prompt.

If you used the make menuconfig command:

- If you reused the configuration data from an existing kernel, use the Save Configuration to an Alternate File command on the main menu to display a screen that enables you to save the file with the name .config in the main directory of the kernel that you are configuring. Figure A.4 shows this screen.

- If you configured the current kernel from scratch (that is, without reading in configuration data from another kernel), and used the make menuconfig command, use the Tab key to select the Exit command. If you used the make xconfig command, just click the Save and Exit button.

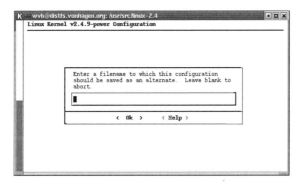

FIGURE A.4
The Save Configuration to an Alternate File screen.

- If you are using the make menuconfig command, use the Tab key to select Yes when prompted whether you want to save your new kernel configuration.

After you have configured a kernel, you must next execute the make dep command. This command recursively goes through all the directories and subdirectories of the source code for the kernel and creates dependency files that identify the relationships between the files used to build the new kernel and the executable code, libraries, and other generated files produced during the compilation process.

Compiling a Linux Kernel

Like an old Elvis record, 50,000,000 Linux fans can't be wrong. They also don't want to waste a lot of time compiling things that they don't need to recompile, so the Linux kernel comes complete with configuration and command files (known as *Makefiles*) for the Linux and Unix make command. A Makefile simplifies and automates the process of building a new Linux kernel, or any Linux program, by providing instructions that describe the relationships and dependencies between the different source code modules, libraries, and include files required to produce a functional compiled program.

The last thing that you should do before executing the make command to compile your kernel with its current configuration is to modify the Makefile in your kernel source directory so that any kernel you compile and install has a unique name. By default, kernels are installed in the /boot directory with the name of the kernel version appended to the compressed kernel name. For example, the default installed version of a kernel compiled in the /usr/src/linux-2.4.9 directory is vmlinuz-2.4.9. This isn't especially useful if you want to install several different versions of the 2.4.9 kernel, each with support for a different experimental Linux filesystem.

The easiest way to guarantee that your kernel has a unique name is to modify the Makefile in the following way:

1. Open the Makefile for the kernel in your favorite text editor.

2. Search for the line beginning with EXTRAVERSION and add a special string to the end of the line. I typically add a string that identifies the new features that the kernel contains. For example, for a kernel that I've patched to add ext3 filesystem support, I would modify the EXTRAVERSION entry to look like the following:

   EXTRAVERSION = -ext33

   When using the make install command to install the new kernel (as described in the next section), the kernel would be installed with suffix -ext3 appended to its name. For example, a Linux 2.4.9 kernel compiled with this Makefile addition would be installed as vmlinuz-2.4.9-ext3. This makes it easy to identify the purpose behind different kernels all located in the /boot directory.

After modifying the Makefile to add a meaningful extension to the kernel you are building, you can just type **make** in the kernel source directory and then go out for a coffee while the kernel builds.

After the kernel has compiled successfully, you need to compile any hardware or protocol support that you specified should be loaded as modules. To do this, execute the make modules command. Depending on the number of hardware devices and software protocols that you specified should be loaded as modules, this can take a while.

Installing a New Kernel

After successfully compiling a new kernel and associated loadable modules, you can install the kernel and reboot. Installing a new kernel actually consists of two steps:

1. Install the new kernel and any associated loadable modules.

2. Modify your system's boot loader so that you can select the kernel that you want to boot after restarting your computer.

This section explains the steps necessary to actually install the new kernel and any related file(s). The next section explains how to update your system's boot loader to know about the new kernel.

Installing a kernel creates two new files in your system's /boot directory. These files are the following:

- System.map-<version>—Contains kernel offset information about the location of various entry points required by loadable modules

- vmlinuz-<version>—The actual, bootable kernel

NOTE

Before installing a new kernel, make sure that the /boot/System.map file is actually a symbolic link to a kernel-specific System.map file. If you have a real file at /boot/System.map, rename it to /boot/System.map.<kernel-version> and then create a symbolic link named /boot/System.map that points to the kernel-specific System.map file, as in the following example from one of my systems:

```
lrwxrwxrwx    1 root      18 Aug 17 13:24 /boot/System.map -> System.map-
2.4.9
-rw-rw-r—     1 root   533015 Jul 31 00:17 /boot/System.map-2.4.2-2
-rw-rw-r—     1 root   536930 Aug 17 12:06 /boot/System.map-2.4.9
```

This example shows that I have two kernels installed on my system and that I am currently running the Linux 2.4.9 kernel.

Creating the System.map file as a symbolic link should have been done automatically during installation, but it's a good idea to verify that the "right thing" happened when you installed your system or any previous kernels. Ensuring that the System.map file is a symbolic link to a kernel-specific System.map file prevents a new installation from accidentally overwriting a Symbol.map file that another kernel may depend on for module loading information.

Installing a new kernel and new loadable modules is handled automatically by two make commands:

- The make install command verifies that your kernel compiled successfully and copies the kernel and associated files to your system's /boot directory, which is often a small, distinct partition if you follow standard Linux disk partitioning strategies.

- The make modules-install_ command first verifies that all your modules compiled correctly and then creates a directory for the modules associated with the kernel that you are installing. It then copies all the modules associated with that kernel into the correct sub-directories of this directory and builds a modules.dep file in that directory to identify the modules that it contains and any dependencies between them.

TIP

The most common error you may see when installing a new kernel is the message Warning: kernel is too big for standalone boot from floppy. This is not a problem unless you want to be able to boot your system with that kernel from a floppy disk. If you do, you will have to reconfigure the kernel to either exclude services and drivers that you don't actually need or load more services as modules rather than compiling them into the kernel.

A

After executing these two commands, you are ready to update your system's boot loader (as described in the next section) and can then reboot your system to take advantage of the capabilities of a new kernel.

Booting a New Kernel

Booting a computer system involves first reading information from a location on the boot disk that defines the operating system(s) that your system can boot. This file also defines where the boot information for each of them is located, and provides a way to select between them. The location on the boot disk from which this information is read is known as the *boot sector* or *master boot record*. In most cases, the information read in is known as the *boot loader*, which then displays any boot options that you may have. In many cases, a computer system can only boot one operating system, and you therefore aren't presented with a list of choices because this would simply delay the inevitable.

Because Linux is designed to be both powerful and flexible, all Linux boot loaders are designed to provide a great deal of control over the boot process. As you've seen in this book, there are many situations in which you may want to build and experiment with a new Linux kernel. As explained previously, the safest way to do this is to compile new kernels with different names than your original kernel and then provide a way for you to select between the different kernels available.

The next two sections explain how to configure the two types of boot loaders most commonly used on Lintel systems. LILO is the standard Linux loader, whereas GRUB is a more flexible boot loader that is fast becoming the boot loader of choice among discriminating Linux users.

> **NOTE**
>
> I apologize in advance to PPC Linux users (of which I am one), but describing the process of configuring the BootX and yaboot boot loaders is outside the scope of this appendix. Feel free to flame me. For information about BootX and yaboot, see
> `http://master.penguinppc.org/projects/bootx.shtml`.

Updating the LILO Boot Loader

LILO, the LInux LOader, is the classic Linux boot loader. LILO makes it easy for you to configure your system to select between multiple kernels at boot time. LILO uses a configuration file, `/etc/lilo.conf`, to make it easy for you to define the kernels that you want to choose between and any boot options associated with them. LILO also makes it easy for you to shoot yourself in the foot if you mistakenly believe that updating its configuration file is all that you have to do. After updating LILO's configuration file, you must run the `/sbin/lilo` command as root to actually update the contents of the master boot record. For this reason, LILO is often referred to as a *static boot loader*, because there is no direct relationship between changes to its configuration file and changes to the master boot record.

Let me repeat that, because this is the most common misconception about LILO and has probably caused a million or two meaningless reboots in the history of Linux. LILO is not dynamic. Updating the LILO configuration file means that you have updated a text file on your disk, not that you have updated your system's master boot record. To actually update the master boot record, you must run the `/sbin/lilo` command after modifying and saving the `/etc/lilo.conf` file.

LILO is an excellent boot loader that is easily configured, time-tested, and mother-approved. As long as you remember to run `/sbin/lilo` after updating the LILO configuration file, you and LILO will get along fine.

> **WARNING**
>
> Never reboot if you get errors when running `/sbin/lilo`. If there are errors or incomplete entries in `/etc/lilo.conf`, your MBR may not be updated correctly, you may not be able to boot from your hard drive, and you may need that rescue floppy after all. (You do know where it is, don't you?)

This section provides an overview of configuring and using LILO to enable you to select between multiple kernels when you boot your system(s). LILO provides many more options than those that I'll describe in this section. My goal is to get you up and running with new kernels that support different types of filesystems, not to have you create the most baroque boot loader configuration possible. For more detailed information about using LILO, see the online reference information for LILO ("man lilo"), or consult the LILO Mini-HOWTO, available on the Net at the URL `http://www.linuxdoc.org/HOWTO/mini/LILO.html`.

The following is a sample LILO configuration file from one of my systems:

```
boot=/dev/hda
map=/boot/map
install=/boot/boot.b
prompt
timeout=50
message=/boot/message
linear
default=linux
image=/boot/vmlinuz-2.4.2-2
        label=linux
        read-only
```

A

USING THE CD-ROM

```
        root=/dev/hda5
    append="hdc=ide-scsi"
image=/boot/vmlinuz-2.4.9
        label=linux-2.4.9
        read-only
        root=/dev/hda5
        append="hdc=ide-scsi"
```

A LILO configuration file consists of two types of sections: an initial section that defines global settings, followed by sections that provide specific configuration information for each kernel that you may want to boot on your system.

The basic contents of the global settings section of a LILO configuration file are the following:

- boot—Identifies the device on which LILO should search for bootable kernels.
- default—The label associated with the kernel that should be booted by default.
- install—The name of the file that contains the boot sector.
- lba32—Tells LILO to use linear block addressing, which enables the use of huge disks containing similarly huge partitions.
- linear—Tells LILO to use linear sector addresses when looking for information on the boot disk, rather than sector/head/cylinder addresses. Translating the linear sector addresses to sector/head/cylinder addresses is done when you actually boot the kernel. Linear mode is most often used on large disks, or with SCSI disks where logical partitions are actually composed of multiple physical partitions.
- map—The name of a file that contains the name and location of each bootable kernel defined in the LILO configuration file.
- message—The name of a file to be displayed after printing the LILO prompt.
- prompt—Forces the LILO prompt to be displayed. If prompt is specified and a timeout value is not, your system will not reboot automatically.
- timeout—The number of tenths of a second after which LILO will boot the kernel identified by the default keyword.

The options typically (or often) associated with each kernel-specific section are the following:

- append—(Optional) Any arguments that you want to append to the boot command for this kernel. In the example shown previously, I'm appending the hdc=ide-scsi command to tell the kernel that /dev/hdc is an IDE drive that should be handled via SCSI emulation mode (required by some CD ripping and writing software).
- image—The full pathname of the actual kernel to boot.
- label—A logical name associated with a kernel. One of these is specified in the global default command as the kernel image to boot if no other is specified.

- read-only—Specifies that the boot process should initially mount the root filesystem as read-only. Subsequent phases of the Linux boot process remount the root filesystem in read/write mode after verifying its consistency.

- root—The name of the partition on which the root filesystem is located.

As a quick example, suppose that you compiled a new kernel, installed it in the file /boot/vmlinuz-2.4.9-ext3, and wanted to make it the default kernel to boot on your system. You would need to do the following to be able to boot this kernel using LILO:

1. Add the following kernel-specific section to your /etc/lilo.conf file:

```
image=/boot/vmlinuz-2.4.9-ext3
        label=linux-2.4.9-ext3
        read-only
        root=/dev/hda5
        append="hdc=ide-scsi"
```

2. Modify the value of the default keyword to the following:

```
default=linux-2.4.9-ext3
```

3. Save the modified /etc/lilo.conf file and rerun the /sbin/lilo command. Its output should list all the labels for the kernel-specific sections of your /etc/lilo.conf file. The label of the default kernel is followed by an asterisk ("*").

Updating the GRUB Boot Loader

GRUB, the GRand Unified Boot Loader, has been under development for several years and is becoming more popular as its power and flexibility increase. GRUB was originally developed as the boot loader for the GNU HURD project, the Free Software Foundation's Unix-like operating system. Like any piece of software from the FSF, GRUB is open enough to be used with any Lintel operating system, including Linux. On Linux, GRUB is actually the up-and-coming boot loader and is an installable option for newer Linux distributions such as Red Hat 7.2.

Unlike LILO, GRUB is a dynamic loader that reads in its configuration file at boot-time, displays the appropriate menu, and can optionally start an actual shell-like interface (with command and argument completion) that enables you to modify many of your boot parameters to modify the boot environment or object. Although you can still misconfigure GRUB, its interactive nature makes it easier for you to recover from configuration errors or omissions. This has never happened to me, of course, but friends have found it useful.

The GRUB boot configuration file is /boot/grub/menu.lst (/boot/grub/grub.conf in some versions of GRUB). The following is a sample GRUB configuration file that is the equivalent of the sample LILO configuration file shown previously:

```
timeout 5
# Default Boot Entry (starting with 0)
```

A

```
#
default 0
# Entry 0:
title   Linux 2.4.2-2 Kernel
root    (hd0,0)
kernel  /vmlinuz-2.4.2-2 root=/dev/hda5 read-only
# Entry 1:
title   Linux 2.4.9 Kernel
root    (hd0,0)
kernel  /vmlinuz-2.4.9 root=/dev/hda5 read-only
```

Not only is this more compact than the equivalent LILO configuration file, it provides a slightly more verbose and friendly menu interface for booting because you can create meaningful labels for each bootable entry using GRUB's title command.

If you are moving to GRUB from LILO, the primary things you should be aware of are the following:

- Partition and disk numbering starts at 0. The /dev/hda1 partition is therefore equivalent to GRUB's (hd0,0). Keep C programming in mind, not Pascal or FORTRAN.

- Kernels are identified relative to the top level of the boot partition. Whether the partition on which a bootable kernel is located will eventually be mounted as /boot is irrelevant. The path to the kernel must be specified relative to the root of that filesystem.

- Default GRUB boot entries are numbered beginning with 0 in the GRUB menu.lst (or menu.conf) file. The first entry in this file is therefore entry 0.

As a quick example, suppose that you compiled a new kernel, installed it in the file /boot/vmlinuz-2.4.9-ext3, and wanted to make it the default kernel to boot on your system using GRUB. You would need to do the following to be able to boot this kernel using GRUB:

1. Add the following kernel-specific section to your /boot/grub/menu.lst file (or /boot/grub/grub.conf, depending on the version of grub that you are using):

   ```
   # Entry 2:
   title   Linux 2.4.9 Kernel (Updated)
   root    (hd0,0)
   kernel  /vmlinuz-2.4.9-ext3 root=/dev/hda5 read-only
   ```

2. Modify the value of the default keyword to the following:

   ```
   default 2
   ```

For more detailed information about using GRUB, see the online reference information for GRUB ("man grub"), consult the help for GRUB found in the info system ("info grub"), or consult the main GRUB HOWTOs on the Net:

- The GRUB HOWTO, available on the Net through `http://hints.linuxfrom scratch.org/index.shtml` or explicitly at `http://www.gnuchina.org/ftp/linux/ document/LFS/CVS_LFS/hints/html/GRUB-Howto.html`

- The GRUB Multiboot Mini-HOWTO, available on the Net at `http://www.linuxdoc.org/HOWTO/mini/Multiboot-with-Grub.html` (Ironically, as I write this, the Mini-HOWTO contains more information than the actual HOWTO.)

A

USING THE
CD-ROM

INDEX

What's On the CD-ROM?

On the CD-ROM you will find a variety of products, including Samba, the Coda File System, the Logical Volume Manager (LVM), benchmarking utilities, Netatalk, Linux kernels, and more.

Installation Instructions
Linux/UNIX

These installation instructions assume that you have a passing familiarity with UNIX commands and the basic setup of your machine. As UNIX has many flavors, only generic commands are used. If you have any problems with the commands, please consult the appropriate manual page or your system administrator.

Insert the disc into your CD-ROM drive.

If you have a volume manager, mounting of the CD-ROM will be automatic. If you don't have a volume manager, you can mount the CD-ROM by typing

```
mount -tiso9660 /dev/cdrom /mnt/cdrom
```

> **NOTE**
>
> /mnt/cdrom is just a mount point, but it must exist when you issue the mount command. You may also use any empty directory for a mount point if you don't want to use /mnt/cdrom. On *BSD-style operating systems, such as Slackware Linux, /cdrom is a typical mount point.
>
> Open the readme.htm or readme.txt file for descriptions and installation instructions.

You may not copy or redistribute the entire CD-ROM as a whole. Copying and redistribution of individual software programs on the CD-ROM is governed by terms set by individual copyright holders.

The installer and code from the author(s) are copyrighted by the publisher and the author(s). Individual programs and other items on the CD-ROM are copyrighted or are under an Open Source license by their various authors or other copyright holders.

This software is sold as-is without warranty of any kind, either expressed or implied, including but not limited to the implied warranties of merchantability and fitness for a particular purpose. Neither the publisher nor its dealers or distributors assumes any liability for any alleged or actual damages arising from the use of this program. (Some states do not allow for the exclusion of implied warranties, so the exclusion may not apply to you.)

NOTE

This CD-ROM uses long and mixed-case filenames requiring the use of a protected-mode CD-ROM Driver.